1,300

Critical Evaluations

of

Selected Novels and Plays

1,300
Critical Evaluations
of
Selected Novels and Plays

OFFPRINTS OF ALL THE NEW MATERIAL FROM THE
12-VOLUME REVISED EDITION OF *MASTERPLOTS*

Edited by
FRANK N. MAGILL

Volume One
A - Eno
1 - 652

SALEM PRESS
Englewood Cliffs

LIBRARY OF CONGRESS CATALOG CARD NUMBER: 78-55387

Complete Set: ISBN 0-89356-043-X
Volume 1:   ISBN 0-89356-044-8

Some of the material in this work also appears in *Masterplots*, Revised Edition (1976).

PRINTED IN THE UNITED STATES OF AMERICA

PREFACE

FOR THE SERIOUS STUDENT of literature, literary criticism can point the way to a most rewarding experience—a path taken through guidance. This approach is much better than a path not taken, where, like Frost, one never knows what was missed. As a prism refracts light to accent the brilliance of individual color bands, so the erudite literary critic may filter an author's insights to interpret nuances hidden from all but the most perceptive reader. 1,300 CRITICAL EVALUATIONS OF SELECTED NOVELS AND PLAYS offers many such opportunities.

This work is devoted to critical commentaries and evaluations of the 1,300 novels and plays that appear in MASTERPLOTS as digests. The 1,300 "Critical Evaluation" articles that appear in this four-volume set were newly written expressly for the 1976 Revised Edition of MASTERPLOTS and comprise all the *new* material published in that revision. Thus, those who have Series One, Two, Three, and Four of MASTERPLOTS and acquire this four-volume set will have all the textual material in the twelve-volume revised MASTERPLOTS of 1976.

The need for exegesis when dealing with a literary work of more than ordinary substance is well recognized. Avicenna, the brilliant eleventh century Arabic philosopher and physician, reported that he had read Aristotle's METAPHYSICS forty times and still did not understand it. An extreme example, but the young student may sometimes be equally confused when confronted with a literary work of unusual complexity and filled with allusions. Such a student might well be completely baffled by THE LOVE SONG OF J. ALFRED PRUFROCK because of Eliot's many classical and Shakespearean allusions. The same student might have little difficulty with GONE WITH THE WIND, a straightforward story whose meaning is obvious, one that races along supported by its superb, lifelike characterizations.

In a way, many of the 1,300 critical evaluations in this set serve as exegeses for students completely unfamiliar with a work under study. For example, the student facing Faulkner's THE SOUND AND THE FURY for the first time would likely be very pleased to have some help such as can be found in the Critical Evaluation beginning on page 2134 in Volume 2 of this set. And to learn on page 462 that Shakespeare relied on Holinshed and Boccaccio for key elements of the action in CYMBELINE would be enlightening to the student approaching the play without previous instruction.

Many of the works of Joseph Conrad not only require careful reading but also need some learned instruction if the student is to appreciate the great insights of this gifted writer. Perhaps the prime example of Conrad's genius is HEART OF DARKNESS, whose symbolism and psychological nuances reflect several levels of meaning. Many critics feel that this work represents the culmination of Conrad's artistic maturity. Understanding of its varied themes is virtually impossible for the unitiated reader without some guidance.

Such a seemingly simple "children's story" (it has been so labeled innumerable times) as ALICE'S ADVENTURES IN WONDERLAND can be seen as the brilliant Victorian satire it really is only if a certain amount of "exegesis" is provided for the first-time reader.

Like Conrad, Herman Melville often used the sea as a vehicle to express his vision of man; and like Conrad, his most penetrating views of the human condition are expressed through symbolism and psychological shadings. To appreciate fully Melville's two most intriguing short works—BENITO CERENO and BILLY BUDD, FORETOPMAN—the reader must understand the contrast the author provides. Writing in 1855, Melville allowed innocence to prevail over evil in the former work. But in BILLY BUDD, FORETOPMAN, written three decades later, the innocence of Billy is completely inadequate to deal with man's innate evil—represented by the enigmatic master-at-arms Claggart—and the guiltless Billy is hanged. Surely this reversal represents a darkening of the author's vision of man during the thirty years between the two statements. The student may not perceive this aspect of Melville's artistic motivation without some analytical help.

1,300 CRITICAL EVALUATIONS OF SELECTED NOVELS AND PLAYS makes available more than 700,000 words devoted to evaluation and analysis of most of the fiction and drama in MASTERPLOTS. Published separately, these evaluations can stand alone, and, hopefully, provide some guidance to better understanding of the major works of fiction and drama extant in the literary heritage of the Western World.

FRANK N. MAGILL

LIST OF TITLES IN VOLUME ONE

LIST OF TITLES

THE ABBÉ CONSTANTIN

Type of work: Novel
Author: Ludovic Halévy (1834-1908)
Type of plot: Sentimental romance
Time of plot: 1881
Locale: France
First published: 1882

The plot of The Abbé Constantin *revolves around the sale of the largest chateau in the kindly old curé's parish to a wealthy American woman. It is a happy story with little conflict; the closest character to a villain is too gentlemanly to interfere seriously in the plans of the young lovers. Because of the grace, simplicity, and melody of its style, this gentle tale has long been a favorite in French classes.*

Chiefly known in his day as a playwright, Ludovic Halévy, in collaboration with Henri Meilhac, wrote the librettos for the operettas of Offenbach and for Bizet's *Carmen.* His nondramatic works were of a high quality and included, besides stories and novels, impressions of the Franco-German War and the Parisian Commune. *The Abbé Constantin* is considered his masterpiece. He was elected to the French Academy within two years of its publication, but after that, although he was to live for another twenty-four years, he wrote virtually nothing else.

In writing *The Abbé Constantin,* Halévy above all was ruled by his conception of "taste." Nothing distasteful or excessive was allowed to invade his picture of French village life. Although the scenes are sharply observed, the settings described with color and detail, and the minor characters shrewdly drawn, the view of existence is deliberately lopsided. By eliminating the coarse and unpleasant, the author falsified his portrayal of the characters and their world. Halévy wrote as if his contemporaries, Flaubert and Maupassant, had never existed. He displays no concern for probing the realities beneath the surface, showing no sense of irony or satire. But the novel is written in a clean, graceful style that is pleasant to read. An aura of innocence seems to pervade the book, lending a charm to even the most minor incidents.

The author's observations concerning the foreign (tourist) invasion of Paris a hundred years ago are very amusing; he is particularly acute when comparing the personalities of the Americans and the French. These comments of the author are often more interesting than the story they interrupt. By far the most complex and fascinating characters in the novel are the Americans, Mrs. Scott and Miss Percival. The French characters tend to be predictable and bland. The Abbé himself, while a noble individual, does not inspire curiosity or interest in the reader.

1

ABE LINCOLN IN ILLINOIS

Type of work: Drama
Author: Robert E. Sherwood (1896-1955)
Type of plot: Historical chronicle
Time of plot: 1831-1861
Locale: New Salem and Springfield, Illinois
First presented: 1938

Sherwood's play is both allegory and history; while the action is a generally accurate recounting of events in Lincoln's life, the playwright also presents his protagonist as an embodiment of the spirit of struggling democracy.

Robert Emmet Sherwood chose to dramatize the pre-presidential career of Abraham Lincoln for three primary reasons: first, his lifelong fascination with, and admiration for, the great Civil War leader; second, his belief that Lincoln was the quintessential American, a man who embodied the basic genius of the American character, with all of its strengths, ambiguities, and contradictions; and, third, his conviction that the world in 1938 faced a crisis not unlike America's Civil War and needed, therefore, the guidance and inspiration of Lincoln's example.

Sherwood's focus is on Lincoln's humanity and the agonizing contradictions in his character: his love of life and preoccupation with death; his bearlike physicality and his gentleness; his love of people and his "misanthropy"; his need for female love and his fear of its consequences; his humor and his sadness; his sense of greatness and his feelings of mediocrity.

The play is structured as a loose chronicle covering the major crises in Lincoln's career from his beginnings as a bankrupt shopkeeper in New Salem to an elected President setting off to assume office in Washington. Except for the dramatization of one Lincoln-Douglas debate and his farewell speech, however, all of the scenes are private; that is, all show Lincoln relating to friends or associates while the pressures and tensions, external and internal, swirl about him. Two concerns are foremost: Lincoln's erratic, indecisive political career and his need for, and fears of, the love and support of a woman. And the two are intimately connected.

In Sherwood's version, Lincoln's actual decision to commit himself to a political career is a solitary one, the result of an encounter with an old friend on the Illinois prairie, but the first concrete evidence of that commitment is his return to Mary Todd. The author only suggests the complexity of their relationship in the play, but he does so brilliantly. The combination of pride and hostility that Lincoln feels toward his electoral career becomes focused on her: she glories in his success; she suffers under his resentment. The climax of their relationship fuses with the climax of his political endeavors in Lincoln's election night outburst and her hysterical response.

But perhaps the picture that remains longest in the mind is that of Lincoln the peacemaker about to lead his country into Civil War. Lincoln's resistance to his "destiny," as Sherwood presents it, was not merely a matter of personal reticence or lack of self-confidence, but was the result of his acute perception. Lincoln knew that the leader of the country in the 1860's would have the responsibility of war or peace and, given his deeply felt antagonism to violence, that was the decision he felt most unwilling and unable to make. Sherwood stated that the dramatic core of the play "was the story of a man of peace who had to face the issue of appeasement or war. He faced it."

And this, of course, was the parallel that Sherwood saw with the world situation in 1938. Given the economic issue of the Great Depression in the United States and, even more important, the specter of Naziism rising in Europe, Sherwood saw America's "neutrality" and "indecision" as potentially destroying what was left of Western civilization.

In the plays immediately preceding *Abe Lincoln in Illinois*—*The Petrified Forest* (1935), *Acropolis* (1936), and *Idiot's Delight* (1936)—Sherwood had presented a totally bleak vision of the West; the "barbarians" were getting stronger and the "civilized" men seemed too weak and vacillating to do anything about it. *Abe Lincoln in Illinois* represented a turning point in Sherwood's attitude from thorough pessimism to guarded optimism. He had come to believe that America could have the Western world by reasserting the values and strengths evident in the life and career of Abraham Lincoln.

ABRAHAM AND ISAAC

Type of work: Drama
Author: Unknown
Type of plot: Biblical story
Time of plot: Biblical antiquity
Locale: Beersheba
First presented: Fifteenth century

This fifteenth century mystery play dramatizes the Biblical story of Abraham's willingness to sacrifice his son. Verse plays such as this one were a crucial part of the tradition from which Elizabethan drama emerged.

Abraham and Isaac is a type of work that could only have been written in an age of faith. Dealing as it does with the ultimate subject of man's duty to God, it depends for its effectiveness on a set of shared assumptions between playwright and audience about the omnipotence and omnipresence of God, man's relationship to God, and God's justice. The slightest hint of skepticism or of rationalistic questioning of values that would have been taken for granted in a later age (for instance, why should God's commandment be obeyed so blindly when it appears so arbitrary and unjust?—or, how can we be sure that this *is* truly the word of God?) would be fatal. As it is, the playwright handles his subject not only with a perfect consistency of tone, but also with great clarity, dramatic power, and most important of all, with considerable insight into the human dimension, into the feelings of Abraham and Isaac and our feelings for them.

The central issue of the play is made crystal clear at the outset when God says, "I shall assay now his good will,/Whether he loveth better his child or me./All men shall take example by him my commandments how to keep." This issue never deviates thereafter. At the close of the play, the Doctor appears on stage to reinforce the moral and to make the personal application to the audience explicit. In this way, the play is an exemplum, or moralized tale.

The dramatic power of *Abraham and Isaac* derives largely from the manner in which the degrees of ignorance of father and son become knowledge. (The audience, of course, from God's first speech and also from its own intimate knowledge of the Bible, knows the significance of the events to come, making dramatic irony possible.) Abraham is at first ignorant of God's will for an appropriate sacrifice until the Angel partially (and only partially) discloses it to him. His knowledge makes him heavy with grief, and so he tries to keep Isaac ignorant of the dire event to come until it is no longer possible to conceal it. When Isaac becomes aware of God's will, he acquiesces immediately, and the plight and subsequent behavior of father and son in their state of partial knowledge become poignant in the extreme. Finally, this partial knowledge of God's purpose is revealed as true ignorance when the Angel stays Abraham's hand and informs him of God's real purpose in demanding the sacrifice of Isaac. The full knowledge thus acquired provides characters and audience with new insight not only into God's power and authority, but also into His beneficence.

If the play were merely an exemplum, it would no longer interest us except on the level of didacticism, and as an indication of medieval attitudes toward God. But this is an intensely personal work; the playwright is not simply a dramatic preacher, but a man who shares and makes his audience share the agony of Abraham and Isaac. Abraham's love for his son is one of the first dramatic facts established in this play. The loving father's anguish and near despair, as he is torn between his reverence for his God and his love for his son, is powerful even on the printed page. Isaac does even more to create audience sympathy. By turns he shows us his innocence, his filial love, his devoutness, his trustingness, his anxiety at the sight of Abraham's sword, his fear, his resignation to the will of God, his courage (even exceeding his father's), his mildness under sentence of death, his concern for his mother (in begging Abraham to tell her that he has gone to live in another land), his plea for a quick death, and finally his joy at his deliverance. He also displays his lingering fear of the knife and the hill on which he so narrowly escaped slaughter. All of these psychologically sound changes of mood, material for a play of far greater length, are handled with a dramatic skill that is economical, convincing, and intensely moving.

ABSALOM, ABSALOM!

Type of work: Novel
Author: William Faulkner (1897-1962)
Type of plot: Psychological realism
Time of plot: Nineteenth century
Locale: Mississippi
First published: 1936

Instead of his usual sustained interior monologue technique, Faulkner here uses the device of three narrators, each of whom relates the family saga of Thomas Sutpen from his or her unique point of view. This device imparts to Absalom, Absalom!, *which is a metaphor for the rich and chaotic Southern experience, a complexity, a depth of psychological insight, and an emotional intensity which might have been lost in a narrative of more traditional format.*

Faulkner's *Absalom, Absalom!* is his most comprehensive attempt to come to terms with the full implications of the Southern experience. The structure of the novel, itself an attempt by its various narrators to make some sense of the seemingly chaotic past, is indicative of the multi-faceted complexity of that experience, and the various narrators' relationship to the material suggests the difficulty that making order of the past entails. Each narrator has, to begin with, only part of the total picture—and some parts of that hearsay or conjecture—at his disposal, and each of their responses is conditioned by their individual experiences and backgrounds. Thus, Miss Rosa's idea of Sutpen depends equally upon her Calvinist background and her failure to guess why Henry Sutpen killed Charles Bon. Quentin's father responds with an ironic detachment conditioned by his insistence upon viewing the fall of the South as the result of the workings of an inevitable Fate as in Greek drama. Like Quentin, and Shreve, the reader must attempt to coördinate these partial views of the Sutpen history into a meaningful whole—with the added irony that he must also deal with Quentin's romanticism. In effect, the reader becomes yet another investigator, but one whose concern is with the entire scope of the novel rather than only with the Sutpen family.

At the very heart of the novel is Thomas Sutpen and his grand design, and our comprehension of the meaning of the work must depend upon discovery of the implications of this design. Unlike the chaos of history the narrators perceive, Sutpen's design would, by its very nature, reduce human history and experience to a mechanical and passionless process which he could control. The irony of Sutpen's failure lies in the fact that he could not achieve the design precisely because he was unable to exclude such human elements as Charles Bon's need for his father's love and recognition. But Faulkner gains more than this irony from his metaphor of design. In effect, Sutpen's design is based upon a formula of the antebellum South which reduces it to essentials. It encompasses the plantation, the slaves, the wife and family—all the external trappings of the plantation aristocracy Sutpen, as a small boy from the mountains, saw in his first encounter with this foreign world. Sutpen, who never really becomes one of the aristocracy his world tries to mirror, manages, by excluding the human element from his design, to reflect only what is worst in the South. Unmitigated by human emotion and values, the Southern society is starkly revealed to have at its heart the simple fact of possession: of the land, of the slaves, and, in Sutpen's case, even of wife and children. Thus, Faulkner demonstrates here, as he does in his great story, "The Bear," that the urge to possess is the fundamental evil from which other evils spring. Sutpen, trying to insulate himself from the pain of rejection he encountered as a child, is driven almost mad by the need to possess the semblance of the world which denies his humanity, but in his obsession he loses that humanity.

Once the idea of the design and the principle of possession in *Absalom, Absalom!* is established, Sutpen's treatment both of Charles Bon and Bon's mother is more easily understood. In Sutpen's distorted mind, that which is possessed can also be thrown away if it does not fit the design. Like certain other Faulkner characters—Benjy of *The Sound and the Fury* being the best example—Sutpen is obsessed with the need to establish a perfect order in the world into which he will fit. His first vision of tidewater Virginia after leaving the timeless anarchy of the mountains was the sight of perfectly ordered and neatly divided plantations, and, like a chick imprinted by its first contact, Sutpen spends his life trying to create a world which imitates that order, and a dynasty which will keep his spirit alive to preserve it. His rejection of Bon is essentially emotionless, mechanical, and even without rancor because Bon's black blood simply excludes him from the design. Similarly, the proposal that Rosa have his child to prove herself worthy of marriage, and the rejection of Milly when she bears a girl child are also responses dictated by the design. Thus, Sutpen, and all whose lives touch his, ultimately become victims of the mad design he has created. Nor is Sutpen its final victim: the curse of the design lives on into the present in Jim Bond, the last of Sutpen's blood.

Sutpen's rejection of Charles Bon and the consequences of that rejection are at the thematic center of *Absalom, Absalom!* In the fact that Charles is rejected for the taint of black blood, Faulkner very clearly points to the particularly Southern implication of his story. Bon must be seen, on one level, to represent the human element within Southern society which cannot be assimilated and will not be ignored. The system which so inhumanely denies the human rights and needs of some of its children, Faulkner seems to be saying, dehumanizes all it touches—master and victim alike. In asserting himself to demand the only recognition he can gain from his father—and that only at second hand through Henry—Charles Bon makes of himself an innocent sacrifice to the sin upon which the South was founded. His death also dramatizes the Biblical admonition so relevant to *Absalom, Absalom!*: a house divided against itself cannot stand.

Sutpen's history is a metaphor of the South, and his rise and fall is Southern history written in one man's experience. But the Sutpens are not the only victims in the novel. Each in his own way, the narrators too are victims and survivors of the Southern experience, and each of them seeks in Sutpen's history some clue to the meaning of their own relationship to the fall of the South. Their narratives seek to discover the designs which will impose some order on the chaos of the past.

William E. Grant

THE ABSENTEE

Type of work: Novel
Author: Maria Edgeworth (1767-1849)
Type of plot: Social criticism
Time of plot: Early nineteenth century
Locale: England and Ireland
First published: 1812

The Absentee *protests the system of landlordism under which owners of Irish estates disported themselves in fashionable London society while their tenants lived in misery and squalor, at the mercy of unscrupulous agents. Both the fresh vividness of the Irish scenes and the satirical bite of the London caricatures suggest later authors such as Surtees and Dickens.*

If the romantic plot of *The Absentee* ends happily in marriage and the restoration of the Clonbrony estates, it also delineates a tragic social phenomenon which formed a prelude to Britain's development of a modern economy. During the last half of the eighteenth century, agriculture in England and Ireland was slowly being changed into a factory system. The realization that huge plots of land under single ownership could be run more profitably than scattered farms brought about incorporation and the enclosure of commons. At the end of the century, the process was speeded by the increased demand for food during the Napoleonic Wars and the invention of numerous labor-saving devices. Incorporation and mechanization transformed rural society from a populous and self-sustaining one to one that was gradually depleted in people and controlled from London. Agriculture was being prepared as a subordinate to and supplier of the new urban, industrial complex.

Miss Edgeworth dramatizes the moral impact of this revolution on rural society and the new cosmopolitan gentry. The Clonbrony estates, left in the hands of Nicholas Garraghty, a manager whose only motive is profit, no longer provides a moral or economic stability for the countryside. The Clonbronys themselves, cut off from the land, deteriorate in a London of fortune hunting and marriage markets where wealth is no longer measured in land but in money. But Lord Colambre, their son, perceives the corruption that has set in and through a marvelous series of good fortunes is able to return his family to the land and the estates to economic and social harmony. Miss Edgeworth's conclusion, however, is a romantic dream rather than a realistic account of social developments: for better or worse Britain's future lay in Industrialism. The great agricultural past together with the eighteenth century was over.

THE ACHARNIANS

Type of work: Drama
Author: Aristophanes (c. 448-c. 385 B.C.)
Type of plot: Social satire
Time of plot: The time of the Peloponnesian War, 431-404 B.C.
Locale: Athens
First presented: 425 B.C.

The Acharnians is Aristophanes' earliest known comedy and his first prize-winner. Thematically wide-ranging, the work displays his satirical wit aimed at militarism and war, his contempt for petty politicians and informers, his delight in earthy sex play, and his spirited spoofing of Euripides.

The Acharnians won first prize for comedy when it was presented at the Lenaea in 425 B.C.—a remarkable feat for a playwright in his early twenties. Aristophanes also directed the play and acted in it, taking the part of the protagonist, a simple country man who makes a private peace with Sparta and enjoys himself while the politicians, the military, the spies, and Euripides himself are held up to public ridicule.

This comedy exhibits several of Aristophanes' stock themes: anti-war sentiment, political satire, earthy sexual gibes, parody of contemporary authors, and fantastic conceits. The playwright detested the chicanery that led to the Peloponnesian War as much as he despised the war. The son of a landowner, Aristophanes was conservative and aristocratic in attitude. He used his powerful wit and exuberant invention to ridicule the degeneration of Athens. However, the play transcends its topical subjects by showing the stupidity of all war.

The viewpoint Aristophanes takes is that of common sense. War breeds famine, corrupt politics, suspicion, a debased morality, gloomy writers, injury, and death. Peace brings plenty, success, cheerfulness. Since peace is infinitely preferable to war, and because demagogues and militarists will not permit peace, it is better to settle the thing privately, as Dicaeopolis does.

Yet the humor of *The Acharnians* lies in the fertile, wildly bizarre devices that Aristophanes uses to make his points, and in the verve of the work. The idea of borrowing one of Euripides' costumes, the heap of rags, to give a public oration is a wonderful way of poking fun at Euripides' pessimism and at the necessity of appealing to mob sympathy. Or the notion of a man selling his daughters as pigs points up the famine, the decline in morality, and the ugliness of the daughters. This might have been distasteful, but in Aristophanes' hands the episode is a brilliant vignette. It is precisely in this mixture of common sense and soaring inventiveness, coupled with a genius for lyric poetry, that the greatness of Aristophanes' comedy rests.

ADAM BEDE

Type of work: Novel
Author: George Eliot (Mary Ann Evans, 1819-1880)
Type of plot: Domestic romance
Time of plot: 1799
Locale: England
First published: 1859

This novel reflects powerfully Eliot's belief in the interrelatedness of all aspects of human life. Her conviction that there is a cause and effect relationship in human behavior led her to create in her fiction a moral universe inhabited by men and women who are responsible for the consequences of even their smallest actions, and Adam Bede *probes with particular power and insight the motivations and complex interdependencies of its characters.*

In *Adam Bede,* George Eliot makes three important contributions to the development of the modern novel in her use of narrative technique and in her handling of both physical realism and psychological realism.

In her overall narrative, Eliot uses the third-person, omniscient-author voice; but she frequently sets aside this basic form to address the reader directly. Eliot uses these first-person comments to establish an intimacy with the reader —such as in the first paragraph of the novel—or to heighten the verisimilitude of the plot. In addition, she experiments quite successfully with stream-of-consciousness narration in chapters fifteen and sixteen. A few critics have faulted Eliot for what they see is inconsistency and choppiness resulting from shifts in narrative voice, but the only genuine disruption of narrative continuity occurs in chapter seventeen, where Eliot digresses from the story to explain her theory of art. Aside from this digression, most critics praise her ingenuity and her willingness to experiment with what were then avant-garde narrative techniques.

Physical realism deals with outward appearance; it attempts to represent scene, atmosphere, and characters exactly as they are observed in real life. Eliot is more successful with scene and atmosphere than with characters. Certainly she presents some vivid portraits, such as her description of the physical contrast between Adam and Seth, or her memorable introduction of Dinah Morris. Other character descriptions, however, are not as effective. Hetty, for example, is repeatedly compared to a kitten, and is so frequently described with words such as "dimpled," "round," "soft," "pink," and "white," that the effect is monotonous. By contrast, Eliot's treatment of scene and atmosphere is guided by a landscapist's eye for detail and a peasant's intuitive understanding of the relationship between weather and crops, producing what has been called the most natural setting in any English novel.

Psychological realism, focusing on the inner being of a character, derives

from details about the thoughts and the emotions of characters: their personalities, their motives, their feelings about themselves, each other, and their
surroundings. In this regard, Eliot's work is superb. She carefully plots the
actions and motivations of her characters, never over-simplifying. Her forte is
the "soul struggle" to which both Adam and Arthur Donnithorne fall victim
—in which a character is torn in conscience between something he knows is
morally and ethically right, and something that is tempting and attractive.
Eliot's penetrating insights into Hetty's motives are another example of her
grasp of psychological realism. In fact, Eliot has been hailed as one of the
first psychological novelists, while *Adam Bede* is recognized as one of the
earliest novels in the psychological tradition.

THE ADMIRABLE CRICHTON

Type of work: Drama
Author: James M. Barrie (1860-1937)
Type of plot: Humorous satire
Time of plot: Early twentieth century
Locale: Loam House, Mayfair; a desert island
First presented: 1903

In this play, Barrie uses the old device of stranding his characters on a desert island to accentuate the follies of their former social habits, which they attempt to transplant in the new environment. Particularly, Barrie satirizes the hypocrisy of pseudoliberal aristocrats like Lord Loam, who preach the rights of man while clinging to their vested interests.

James Matthew Barrie's family was moderately well-to-do. He received a good early education and was graduated from Edinburgh University in 1882 with the M.A. degree. He began his literary career as a journalist, but by 1887 had published his first book, *Better Dead,* the first of a series of novels he was to write about Scottish life. Among these are *A Window in Thrums, Sentimental Tommy,* and *The Little Minister.* In 1895 he moved to London where he became acquainted with many prominent literary personages of the day. Among his friends he numbered such diverse figures as Thomas Hardy and George Bernard Shaw. Possibly because of Shaw's influence, Barrie became interested in the theater. He began by adapting selected earlier novels for the stage. One of his earliest dramatic works is *The Little Minister,* drawn from the novel of the same name. The success of *The Little Minister* encouraged Barrie to persevere as a dramatist. His subsequent works have remained mainstays of the theater and of popular literature, for his published plays are as delightful to read as they are to see performed. Among his best-known works are *Peter Pan, Dear Brutus, Quality Street, What Every Woman Knows,* and *The Admirable Crichton.*

The last-mentioned work is a social satire in which Barrie's wit has a field day with the British caste system, castigating the social structure as well as the stereotype figures upon which the caste system is based.

In certain other of Barrie's plays—for example, *What Every Woman Knows*—he shows an ability to characterize with great realism and fidelity to nature. His portrayal of women can be particularly sensitive. However, in *The Admirable Crichton* Barrie chooses to paint his characters originally in only one dimension. He makes stereotypes of them, and in doing so is able to exaggerate and emphasize certain traits, both personal and social. In this way he assures us that his characters are typical: Lord Loam is a typically stuffy aristocrat, suffering from various delusions about social equality. And in much the same way Barrie gives his reader Crichton, a typically British butler (who knows his place). Lady Mary can be described as a typically

British lady, and Ernest, Loam's nephew, is a typically British rotter.

Once he establishes the fact that his characters are satiric stereotypes, Barrie proceeds to twist the knife a bit. Lord Loam advocates the political theories popular with England's working class, while Crichton swears by that old standby of the elitist, the theory which says men assume through their inborn abilities that place in society which nature has suited them for, and they should therefore have no need to change their station or seek to better themselves, remaining instead content with the role which they have been allotted. Barrie is preparing for the juxtaposition of roles in Act II, making Crichton out as the conservative.

Having established this basic attitudinal inversion while maintaining the stereotypes, Barrie is able to complete the juxtaposition on the island. There the roles are reversed and a great deal of caustic comment is made upon the caste system through this device.

Barrie's wit is evident throughout the play but nowhere more obviously than in the second act where he is free to satirize these Victorian theories of social organization with contrasting theories which he manages to inject with an interesting and devastatingly accurate (if somewhat exaggerated) portrait of Victorian behavior.

ADOLPHE

Type of work: Novel
Author: Benjamin Constant (1767-1830)
Type of plot: Psychological romance
Time of plot: Late eighteenth and early nineteenth centuries
Locale: Germany and Poland
First published: 1815

This unique work might be described as a seventeenth century tragedy written in lucid eighteenth century prose about a nineteenth century situation by a twentieth century analytical consciousness. To modern readers, Adolphe *is strangely familiar in its remorseless survey of that interior wasteland whose most marked characteristic is gradual emotional atrophy.*

Benjamin Constant pretended that both the story and the characters of *Adolphe* were fictional, but in reality he drew upon two of his own love affairs; the *I* of *Adolphe* is at least partially Constant himself, as a young man. *Adolphe,* through the self-revelation of its guilt-obsessed narrator, anticipates the modern psychological novel, but its style and manner of development belong to an earlier time. As a troubled confession it reveals in depth only one character, Adolphe. Ellénore is seen mainly through Adolphe's mind. Most of her conversation is repeated indirectly by her lover, and until he nears the account of her death, he gives only now and then a few of her actual words. Naturally, since the account is completely Adolphe's, the reader is not taken into Ellénore's mind. Thus, though she stirs the reader's pity and compassion, particularly toward the end of the story, she remains a woman largely written *about* rather than one truly revealed.

As for Adolphe, although Constant in his "Letter to the Publisher" calls him the "hero" of the novel, he strikes the reader as anything but heroic. In fact, in parading his weaknesses—his inability to make up his mind, his hypocrisy, deceit, and resentment of the happiness of the woman who loves him—Adolphe does not seem to see himself as a hero at all; he is merely conceited about his intelligence and his many abilities which, he complains, are being wasted because he cannot break Ellénore's hold upon him. He is, however, a convincingly realistic and unforgettable forerunner of many of the antiheroes of twentieth century fiction.

The fascinating characteristic of Constant's protagonist is that while he shows himself both weak and pitiable, he asks for no pity. Unlike most fictional heroes of the time, he makes no pretense at nobility. This lack of pretense marked a turning point in fiction. It is highly probable that Julien Sorel would not have existed in precisely the way he came to be if Adolphe had not existed first. The universality of Adolphe's intensely human nature remains the greatness of Constant's achievement. Adolphe is a symbol of the little weaknesses in all of us, our lack of constancy, our lack of resolution, our pettiness and pride. Above all, like all of us, Adolphe attempts to rationalize away his weaknesses. Adolphe wanted to be the classic hero, but knew too well that he was not. At the same time, *Adolphe* may be the first example of that popular twentieth century literary device, the unreliable narrator. The reader is never certain how much of the protagonist's narrative is strictly true. This sophisticated technique, deliberately confusing, probably helped to account for the book's lack of popularity when it first appeared, but it gives the novel a resonance and fascination which have placed it high in world literature.

THE AENEID

Type of work: Poem
Author: Publius Vergilius Maro (70-19 B.C.)
Type of plot: Heroic epic
Time of plot: The period immediately following the Trojan War
Locale: The Mediterranean region
First transcribed: Augustan manuscript

Written at the emperor's request as an endorsement of the newly established principate, this epic Latin poem celebrates the glory and heroism of the Roman race. In twelve books it traces the legendary founding of Rome, from the time of the Trojan War down to the establishment of the reign of Augustus Caesar.

Publius Vergilius Maro, better known as Vergil, was the greatest poet Rome produced. His finest work, the *Aeneid*, became the national epic and, when Rome collapsed, it survived to become the most influential book Rome contributed to Western culture. Dante drew direct inspiration from Book VI for *The Divine Comedy*, allowing the spirit of Vergil to guide him through the Inferno and up the heights of Purgatory. The work has been the cornerstone of liberal education from the Christian Middle Ages to the late nineteenth century. Even today it is still studied in universities and read for pleasure by a literate public.

Vergil himself was a modest, retiring man who preferred the seclusion of his country estate to life in the bustling metropolis of Rome. However, he was much liked and esteemed by important people, including the poet Horace and the Emperor Augustus. He won the patronage of the great, secured the wealth and leisure necessary to write, composed three supreme poems—the *Georgics,* the *Eclogues,* and the *Aeneid*—and died revered and honored. In his lifetime he saw the closing years of the Civil War that destroyed the Roman Republic, and the establishment of the Roman Empire under Augustus. To celebrate the *Pax Romana* and the leadership of Augustus, Vergil wrote the *Aeneid,* his patriotic epic dealing with the mythical Roman past.

According to legend, the Trojan hero Aeneas came to Italy after escaping the fall of Troy and became the ancestor of the Romans through his descendant, Romulus. Vergil took this material and, borrowing his structure from Homer, fashioned an epic of it. The first part of the poem, dealing with Aeneas' wanderings, resembles the *Odyssey* in form and content; while the second half, which treats Aeneas' war in Latium and its surroundings, imitates in some ways the *Iliad*. Certain poetic devices, such as the repeated epithet, are taken from Homer, as well as the way the gods interfere on behalf of their favorites. And yet the *Aeneid* is wholly original in concept, possessing a unique unity of its own.

The originality lies in its presentation of Aeneas, a hero who struggles and

fights, not for booty, personal fame, or any existing country, but for a civilization that will exist in the distant future, that of Rome and Augustus. Time and
again he sacrifices his personal comforts, leaving home after home because of
the prodding of his inner sense of destiny. He knows that he is to be the
founder of a new nation, but the details are revealed to him gradually in the
course of his journeying. Chronologically, the pattern is one of revelation and
sacrifice, and each new revelation about his destiny imposes a greater burden
of responsibility on him. The final revelation—when Aeneas descends with the
Sibyl into the Cavern of Death and is shown the coming glory of Rome by
his father, Anchises—prepares him spiritually and physically for the greatest
fight of his life. And, finally, he is something greater than a man. In fulfilling
his grand Fate he becomes a monument, an unstoppable force, an instrument
of the gods, like the Roman Empire itself as Vergil visualized it.

When the poem opens and Aeneas and his men are shipwrecked at Carthage, the hero already knows two things: that he has an important mission to
accomplish and that his future home lies on the western coast of Italy. This
knowledge insures, on his part, a limited commitment to Dido, whereas she
falls completely in love with him, giving herself freely even though it ruins her
as a woman and a queen when Aeneas is ordered by Jupiter to sail on to Italy.
In the coldness of his parting the founder of Rome draws upon himself all
the wrath of Dido, the founder of Carthage, which points forward to the Punic
Wars between those cities.

However, Aeneas is not hardhearted. He feels pity for those who are
crushed in trying to prevent him from accomplishing his aim—Dido, Lausus
the son of Mezentius, and even Turnus. The entire epic is weighted with the
sadness of mortality. Aeneas' sense of destiny gives him courage, fortitude,
patience, determination, and strength; yet it also makes him humorless, overbearing, and relentless. Still, without that inner conviction in the future destiny
of his line and of his fellow Trojans, he would be nothing. Pity is the most
that a person who knows he is doing right can feel for those who oppose him.
Aeneas has a noble character, though somewhat inhuman, and he seems to
embody the best traits of the Roman people.

The crux of the *Aeneid* comes, as Dante rightly perceived, in Book VI,
where Aeneas enters the realm of Death to gain enlightenment about his future.
From the fall of Troy, where the ghost of Hector warns Aeneas, to this point,
the dead are associated with revelation. And here Aeneas must purify himself
ritually, enter the Cavern of Death, brave all the terrors of Hell, meet dead
comrades, and finally, with a rite, enter the realms of the Blest to learn the
truth about himself and his fate. Like Dante's Hell, Vergil's has various places
assigned for various acts, sins, and crimes, but punishment there purges the
soul to prepare it for the Elysium Fields, from which it may reincarnate.

In this section Vergil delineates his view of the meaning of life and death.
There is a Great Soul that gave birth to all living spirits, which incarnated

themselves in flesh as assorted creatures, including man. The desires of these spirits hindered them from living up to their true purpose in bodily form, so that they must be cleansed after death, only to take on flesh again until they learn their rightful end and achieve it. Thus, death purifies and life tests one on the long road to perfection. This is the occult view, and in Vergil's case a mixture of Pythagorean reincarnation, Stoic pantheism, and Platonic mysticism. But that view gives credence to everything Anchises shows Aeneas about his illustrious descendants and the rising power of Rome. Aeneas sees the souls of the future waiting their turn and he knows how much responsibility he really bears. Anchises' judgment of Aeneas is a fitting comment on Rome itself:

> "But yours, my Roman, is the gift of government,
> That is your bent—to impose upon the nations
> The code of peace; to be clement to conquered,
> But utterly to crush the intransigent!"

In those lines Vergil summed up the particular genius of Rome, together with its greatness and its terrors.

James Weigel, Jr.

AGAINST THE GRAIN

Type of work: Novel
Author: Joris Karl Huysmans (Charles Marie Georges Huysmans, 1848-1907)
Type of plot: Exotic romance
Time of plot: Nineteenth century
Locale: Paris
First published: 1884

This novel, one of the outstanding prose works of the Decadent Movement, reflects the profound influence of Baudelaire and Mallarmé on its author. While weak in plot, the work reflects the aesthete's concern with polished, erudite style and detailed, sensuous description.

It seems incongruous that while Huysmans was writing his "breviary of Decadence," as a contemporary of his called *Against the Grain,* he was holding a regular job as a bureaucrat in the Ministry of the Interior. Such an occupation seems pale for such a vivid writer, but indeed he was. The author of what Oscar Wilde's Dorian Gray called "the strangest book that [he] had ever read" spent thirty-two years as a minor civil servant in the French government. During that time he wrote a dozen books, mostly novels, and a collection of prose poems.

Huysmans undertook *Against the Grain* as an experiment to expand the novel genre from a storytelling or basically narrative form to a frame for art, science, and history. A follower of the Goncourts, Zola, and Flaubert and a member of the naturalist school, he was surprised at the immediate popularity of the novel upon publication. Before he completed it, the novel had developed into something other than a specimen of the naturalist school. Its colorful style would be opposed by its members. The novel became a compendium of knowledge of modern times; Huysmans reportedly researched each chapter before writing it.

Des Esseintes, with his enemas, unnatural loves, and midnight lunches, represents Huysmans' view of modern man: his is a picture of disillusionment with the natural world. Des Esseintes detests modern life; the theme of the book might be summed up as escapism from unhappiness. An underlying, related theme is the sense of hopelessness and despair that accompanies Des Esseintes' lack of faith.

Huysmans' last novel, *L'Oblat,* moves away from escapism by pointing up its futility. This novel seems to be saying that an individual must accept the obligation of suffering, for himself and for others. Such a statement is far removed from Des Esseintes' sighful, unwilling return to society at the end of *Against the Grain.*

THE AGE OF INNOCENCE

Type of work: Novel
Author: Edith Wharton (1862-1937)
Type of plot: Social criticism
Time of plot: Late nineteenth century
Locale: New York City
First published: 1920

The Age of Innocence *is a subtle yet unmistakable indictment of stratified New York high society in 1920. Wharton is reminiscent of Henry James both in her psychological probing of characters' emotions and motivations and in her degree of craftsmanship. However, she maintains a style less obscure and less involved than that of James.*

Edith Wharton's *The Age of Innocence* is probably one of her most successful books because it offers an inside look at a subject the author knew very well, that is, New York society during the 1870's. That was her milieu, and her pen captures the atmosphere of aristocratic New York as its inhabitants move about in their world of subtleties, innuendoes, and strict adherence to the dictates of fashionable society. Edith Wharton describes those years for herself as "safe, guarded, and monotonous." Her only deviation as a young adult consisted in frequent journeys abroad and summers in Newport. Her marriage to Edward Wharton, a prominent Bostonian, assumed the same character as her own early life until it became apparent that he suffered from mental illness and would have to be hospitalized. During World War I, Edith Wharton worked for the allies and received the French Cross of the Legion of Honor for her work with the Red Cross in Paris. Most critics agree that her best years as a novelist were from 1911 to 1921, during which time she produced *Ethan Frome,* a grim New England study, and *The Age of Innocence,* for which she was awarded the Pulitzer Prize.

Edith Wharton's most successful theme (like that of her friend Henry James) was the plight of the young and innocent in a world which was more complicated than they were prepared for. Newland Archer and Ellen Olenska found the society of New York intricate and demanding and, as such, an impediment to their personal searches for happiness and some degree of freedom. *The Age of Innocence* is a careful blending of a nostalgia for the 1870's with a subtle, but nonetheless inescapable, criticism of its genteel timidities and clever evasions.

With respect to Wharton's style it can be generalized that she was not a particularly daring writer, nor an experimenter in form. Rather, she wrote in a comfortable, fixed, formal style which was closely designed. In some instances, her narrative becomes heavy and the intricate play and counterplay of the characters' motives can lose all but the most diligent reader. The author's presence is never forgotten and the reader feels her control throughout the story, as the narrative view is quickly established from the beginning. Wharton's characters are portrayed through their actions, and the clear lines of the plot are visible. Since *The Age of Innocence* so carefully fits a historical niche, its scope is limited and its direction narrow. That is not to say that drama is limited or lacking. On the contrary, in detailing such a small world, the drama is intense even if it is found beneath a sophisticated, polished surface.

Three figures are projected against the historical background of New York society. First, May Welland, the beautiful betrothed of Newland Archer. May was born and bred in traditions and she is completely a product of the system she seeks to perpetuate. Newland observes, after their marriage, that May and her mother are so much alike that he sees himself being treated and placated just as Mr. Welland is by his wife and daughter. There is no doubt that May will never surprise Newland "by a new idea, a weakness, a cruelty or an emotion."

Ellen Olenska, on the other hand, has freed herself from the restraints of society by her experiences abroad and through her subsequent separation from her husband, the Polish Count. Madame Olenska is not only more cosmopolitan; she is also a character of more depth and perception than the other women in the novel. She suggests by her presence as well as by her past experiences a tragic and emotionally involved element in the story. Ellen definitely does not conform to the rules of accepted behavior, yet she moves in a cloud of mystery which makes her an intriguing personality to those who observe her, if even only to criticize. As soon as she and Archer are aware of their feelings for each other, Archer tries to convince Ellen, in a halfhearted way, that one cannot purchase freedom at the expense of another. He has given her an idea by which to live and, in so doing, has unknowingly destroyed his one opportunity to find a new freedom for himself.

Newland Archer is, in many ways, a typical Wharton masculine figure. He is a man set apart from the people he knows by education, intellect, and feeling, but lacking the initiative and courage to separate himself physically from the securities of the known. The movement of the plot in *The Age of Innocence* is established by the transition from one position to another taken by Archer in his relations with either May or Ellen. Archer's failure to break the barriers of clan convention lead him to an ironic abnegation, for in the last pages of the novel we see Newland retreating from the opportunity to meet with Ellen—an opportunity his eager son Dallas is quick to arrange. Dallas is anxious to meet Ellen, for he heard from his mother shortly before she died that Archer had given up the thing he had most wanted (namely, Ellen) for her. It is sad to see that Archer, the object of two loves, has never been able to satisfy or be satisfied by either. The tragedy in the novel rests with May, for it is she who appeared to be the most innocent and naïve;

yet in the end, she is, perhaps, the most aware of them all. She has suffered quietly through the years, knowing that her husband's true desires and passions were elsewhere. Dallas' generation observes the whole situation out of context as "prehistoric." He dismisses the affair rather casually, for his contemporaries have lost that blind adherence to social custom that the Archers, Wellands, and the rest knew so well.

The Age of Innocence is a novel of manners which delineates a very small world, yet under the surface we see a world of suffering, denial, and patient resignation—a situation which deserves more attention and reflection than one might give at first reading.

Constance A. Cutler

AGNES GREY

Type of work: Novel
Author: Anne Brontë (1820-1849)
Type of plot: Sentimental romance
Time of plot: Mid-nineteenth century
Locale: England
First published: 1847

Agnes Grey is a typical nineteenth century sentimental romance in which piety and goodness triumph over arrogance and frivolity. Agnes' pious sentimentality, however, is lightened unexpectedly throughout the story by her cutting observations on contemporary life and by a certain gently but penetrating sarcasm which steals through in remarks about her employers.

The youngest child of the Reverend Patrick Brontë, Anne Brontë, is the most shadowy figure among the Brontës. Gentle and timid, she stands behind her more famous sisters and notorious brother, yet her two novels have an interest of their own, on their own merits. Although *Agnes Grey* does not possess the vigorous writing of *The Tenant of Wildfell Hall* or the depth of characterization, in its quiet way it is a more solid novel and presents a fuller picture of the life that Anne Brontë knew so well. *Agnes Grey* is a minor book by a minor writer, but it will continue to be read for its gentle humor and the integrity of its realism.

Anne was twice a governess in private houses, so she was all too familiar with the humiliations and difficulties inherent in such a position. The story of Agnes, the governess, is told in the first person, in short, straightforward chapters. The ending of the novel is sentimental, but the narrative along the way is at times sharp and always well-observed. When Agnes and Rosalie discuss the engagement of a sister to a neighboring vicar, Rosalie wonders if he is rich or handsome or young, but Agnes replies, " . . . only middling." Every aspect of the life facing Agnes and the other characters is only middling; the author does not glamorize her heroine's existence. The characters, for the most part, are described without romanticism, sometimes almost mercilessly; their lives are dragged out day by day, duty by duty. Perhaps Agnes is saved at the end by her clergyman husband, but only in a very limited sense. After her difficulties, Agnes is content with a very modest existence; in fact, from the beginning, she is a young woman of slight expectations and no pretensions. Rather like its heroine, this novel is modest and without pretensions, but is pleasantly satisfying.

AJAX

Type of work: Drama
Author: Sophocles (495?-406 B.C.)
Type of plot: Classical tragedy
Time of plot: The Trojan War
Locale: Phrygia, before Troy
First presented: c. 440 B.C.

Ajax *masterfully dramatizes the age-old problem of individual versus group prerogative. Certain aspects of Ajax's personality elicit the reader's sympathy and admiration, so that when his ungovernable pride ultimately precipitates his dissolution into unbearable humiliation and shame, the scene is one of deep pathos, and has a particularly disturbing impact.*

Ajax is considered the earliest of Sophocles' plays that have survived, first produced somewhere around 442 B.C. But the playwright was in his middle fifties at that time and had already had a successful dramatic career of twenty-five years or so. Thus *Ajax* was the work of a fully mature writer, and one who had considered life deeply. Whatever problem the play may present structurally, its felicities are remarkable.

Sophocles was the most accomplished poet among the three great Athenian dramatists. His style is marked by smoothness, simplicity, and clarity. It is at once beautiful and lofty; and it has an august dignity that Aeschylus and Euripides could not equal. With Sophocles even the most intense passions are revealed in a stately, logical, well-polished manner that can be surprisingly moving. For all the formality of his poetry, it never impresses one as being artificial. He actually created the classical style of writing, and he remains unsurpassed in it.

An accomplished athlete, an honored public dignitary, and the most successful tragedian of the Periclean Age, Sophocles had an extremely fortunate life. He lived to be ninety with his full creative and intellectual vigor intact. However, his good luck did not blind him to the suffering of others. His extant plays explore the problem of human misery with a rare honesty and thoroughness. He saw Athens reach her finest moment in the Persian Wars and then devolve into a ruthless imperial power embarking on a suicidal war. He knew very well the instability of life, and how greatness can be the source of calamity.

Ajax is a case in point. Next to Achilles, Ajax was the most formidable fighter in the Greek army at Troy. A huge, headstrong bull of a man, his pride was bitterly offended when the Greeks voted to give Achilles' immortal armor to Odysseus. To avenge himself he tries to massacre the Greeks, but madly butchers their livestock instead in a god-induced frenzy. Thus, in one night he turns from a hero into an outcast and a laughing-stock. The humiliation is too much for him, and he commits suicide. This is the heart of the story, but what is interesting is the way Sophocles develops it.

The key to Sophocles' treatment of the legend is balance. The action moves by antithesis, by the juxtaposition of opposites, in the revelation of Ajax's character and heroism. At the end of the play we have arrived at a complete assessment of this tragically flawed man, and the impersonal verdict is that he is to be buried as a hero rather than left to rot like a renegade. The decision is close, for Sophocles has shown us Ajax at his very worst, in a total degradation.

At the beginning, when Athena calls Ajax from the tent to reveal his shame to Odysseus, Ajax is insane. He is vindictively slaughtering and tormenting helpless animals in his delusion. Odysseus is appalled and touched by pity. Athena is merciless, however, because Ajax in his own mind is savagely murdering the Greeks. Ajax himself is pitiless in his wounded pride.

When his sanity returns his pain is excruciating because he failed to kill his enemies and because he made a fool of himself. He thinks of himself as a hero, and public disgrace is unbearable. As he talks to his soldiers, or to Tecmessa and Eurysaces, he shows himself to be self-centered, hard, concerned only with his damaged honor. Yet this portrait is relieved by the pity and the love these dependent people feel for him. An ignoble man could not command such loyalty.

We are further softened to his plight when he seems piously resolved to live with his shame out of concern for Tecmessa and his son. Then we realize he has simply been putting on an act to avoid a scene. He is still intent on suicide. Beyond that, we learn at this point the reason for Athena's hostility to Ajax. He deliberately affronted her in his arrogant pride by twice refusing her assistance, desiring all the glory for himself. Athena, then, operates by the same vengeful morality that Ajax does. But she merely supervises Ajax's destruction—it is actually his own pride that forces him to commit suicide. And he is proud to the last, calling upon Zeus to ruin his enemies and arrange a means of burial.

Sophocles goes further and points up the desolation caused by Ajax's stubborn vanity and death. Tecmessa, Teucer, and the Salaminian warriors are utterly bereft of comfort; friendless, unprotected, subject to ridicule, and exiled from home. Ajax has betrayed them all in his inhuman pride.

This situation makes the debate over Ajax's right to burial doubly forceful, because Teucer is defending a man who has violated every human trust, a man who has cut him off from his own father. Menelaus' argument that Ajax put himself before the good of the community has special validity in this context. Ajax even put himself before the gods. But Teucer's assertion that Ajax prevented a complete defeat of the Greek army is also true. He was a hero no matter how monstrous he became. But neither the Atridae nor Teucer are allowed to make the final judgment. The Atridae want Ajax unburied out of vindictiveness, while Teucer wants him buried out of brotherly loyalty.

Neither is impartial. It is Ajax's enemy, Odysseus, who decides that Ajax is to have a decent burial. Odysseus, who was capable of pity when Ajax was mad, is also capable of forgiving him in death. So Ajax receives his burial by sheer grace.

Sophocles demonstrates in this play the hairbreadth line between criminality and heroism. The very pride that motivates the hero to surpass everyone else can also degrade him into the vilest bestiality. Heroes do not feel the demands of others; they live by some imperious demand within their own breast. A hero can call forth extraordinary loyalty from his followers—a loyalty that persists after he betrays them—but he can also conjure up terrible hatred in his pride. And at the last it is grace alone that pronounces the verdict. *Ajax* is a profound and moving study of the nature of the hero.

James Weigel, Jr.

ALCESTIS

Type of work: Drama
Author: Euripides (480-406 B.C.)
Type of plot: Classical tragedy
Time of plot: Remote antiquity
Locale: Pherae, in ancient Greece
First presented: 438 B.C.

Alcestis *is the only surviving example of a dramatic form which combines characteristics of both tragedy and the satyr play. The comedy is mostly achieved by the drunken figure of Heracles, who also provides the* deus ex machina *conclusion when he rescues Alcestis from Hades.*

Alcestis is the earliest extant tragedy by Euripides, written when the dramatist was in his forties. It is therefore the work of a fully matured man. First staged in 438 B.C., the play is in part a product of Athens' Age of Pericles, that period between the end of the Persian Wars and the onset of the Peloponnesian War. This play shares some of the piety and optimistic confidence of that golden era in which Athens reached its greatest power and achieved its finest cultural successes. The great tragedians flourished then— Aeschylus, Sophocles, and Euripides.

In *Alcestis* Euripides reworked an old legend that had already been dramatized by the tragic poet Phrynichus. This play bears Euripides' inimitable stamp in the keen psychological portraiture, in the rare mixture of comic and tragic elements, and in the seeming *deus ex machina* ending. Presented as the fourth drama in a tetralogy, which was traditionally a satyr play, *Alcestis* is best described as a tragi-comedy. The closest example of this type would be Shakespeare's play, *The Winter's Tale,* which bears a striking resemblance to *Alcestis* in plot and theme.

The opening confrontation between Apollo and Thanatos, or Death, sets forth the central opposition that gives this play its meaning. Apollo is a radiant god, the representative of light, health, and life, while Thanatos is a dark, dismal underworld divinity with an awesome power over all living creatures. Both deities have a claim on Admetus and Alcestis, but since each belongs to a different supernatural sphere, a compromise between them is impossible. However, Apollo, with his prophetic gift, foresees a resolution in the arrival of Heracles, who will rescue Alcestis from Death.

From that point on we see the action of the play in purely human terms. The characters are recognizable as persons in their own right, with private attitudes, emotions, and choices. Euripides shows us how it feels to be Alcestis, a woman who freely sacrifices her life so that her husband may live; how it feels to be Admetus, who can ask for and accept such a sacrifice; how it feels to be the child of such a marriage; how it feels to be Admetus' old father, Pheres, reviled by his only son for refusing to lay down his life;

and how it feels to be Heracles, who accepts hospitality from the grieving Admetus, drunkenly amuses himself, and then must wrest Alcestis from Death to redeem his honor. These are not mere puppets of Fate, but men and women acting of their own volition. Yet they are torn between life and death, Apollo and Thanatos, by the choices they make.

Alcestis chooses the heroic role in laying down her life for Admetus. She knows very well what she will leave behind: the joy of her marriage bed, her small children, and the pleasures of living. She is also aware of the terrors of death, which makes her sacrifice all the greater. She loves her husband, but Alcestis is thinking of her children as well, and what would happen to them if the kingdom passed to a stranger. Her final restoration dramatically suggests the Biblical paradox that whoever loses his life for love's sake will gain new life.

Admetus suggests the complementary paradox, that whoever seeks to save his life will lose it. He has turned weak in the face of death and lets another die for him. His remorse while his wife remains alive is sheer sentimentality, for at heart he is an egoistic coward. But when she is dead he must confront his ignoble shame and live a deathlike existence of perpetual mourning.

His moment of self-recognition occurs in the bitter meeting with his father, Pheres. Admetus blames Pheres for Alcestis' death, because the old man chose to live when he might have died for his son. In Pheres we see the same cowardice that afflicts Admetus, but there is truth in Pheres' condemnation of Admetus, for no person should ask another to die in his place. Yet Pheres in clutching life has lost the only thing that mattered to him—the respect of his son—and so his life has become a curse.

If Admetus has damned his father, he has also damned his children to a motherless desolation, and damned himself as well. However, he performs one generous act by admitting Heracles as a guest and disguising the cause of his mourning. It is dramatically necessary that Heracles be ignorant of Alcestis' death so that he makes a drunken fool of himself. Oddly, the sober mood of the play is retained, for Heracles in his intoxicated solemnity discourses on death's inevitability. This leads to Heracles' discovery of the truth and of his own shame. Every man in this play must face personal shame. And with the hero Heracles shame serves to redeem the situation, for he saves the dead Alcestis by bringing her back to life. The plot is airtight; and if the final scene, where Heracles restores Alcestis to Admetus, seems contrived, it is still perfectly integrated with the pattern of the whole play, and the themes of sacrifice, loss, and redemption.

The view of life behind this drama is very coherent psychologically. It shows the heroic nature of a total sacrifice, the base nature of asking and accepting such a gift, and the path of salvation through a full realization of one's degradation and through acts of free generosity. Heracles, in entering Admetus' home, becomes involved in the same degradation and must save himself by this same path. Baseness is a form of death, Euripides seems to say, but redemption is life, true life. In *Alcestis* Euripides gave an old myth a rebirth that probed the basis of human experience.

James Weigel, Jr.

THE ALCHEMIST

Type of work: Drama
Author: Ben Jonson (1573?-1637)
Type of plot: Comedy of manners
Time of plot: Early seventeenth century
Locale: London
First presented: 1610

A masterpiece of plot construction, The Alchemist *marked the peak of Jonson's career. A delightful, entertaining satire on human greed, this play is free of the sermonizing that characterizes the dramatist's other work.*

For anyone interested in learning how to take in the gullible, Ben Jonson's *The Alchemist* is a fundamental text. "Cony-catching" was a popular practice in Elizabethan England, and Jonson, an intimate of London's jails, taverns, theaters, and places of even less repute, here reveals the technique on several of the most amusing and lucrative ploys. And his protagonist, it should be noted, gets off scot-free.

The complex and incongruous tone of life in London during that period of the first part of the Renaissance known as the Elizabethan Era helped account for the widespread faith in astrology and alchemy and helped make them leading gimmicks. Commerce thrived, but people were not far from believing in the dragons slain by King Arthur's knights. Many believed also that the dawning age of science would discover a "Philosopher's Stone" which would transmute dross into gold. Jonson's London, the London of *The Alchemist,* was growing and glittering and slightly hysterical, and cozening was easy, widespread, and immensely successful.

The critical response to the play has been intriguing. Coleridge, presumably impressed by the play's adherence to the classical unities, praised it as having one of the most perfect plots in literature. Several modern commentators have contended that while *The Alchemist* does cleave to the classical ideals, it is not a proper comedy, it has no plot at all, and it consists merely of a series of linked incidents. Romantic and Victorian critics particularly, understandably enchanted by Jonson's contemporary and diametric opposite, William Shakespeare, were put off by Jonson's classical forms, his satiric manner, and his coarseness. They also disliked his unemotional tone, controlled plots, and intellectual detachment. While *The Alchemist* lacks none of these features, they do not necessarily render it deficient.

The classical ideals are so well met in *The Alchemist* that the play is in its own way a small classical masterpiece. Jonson observes unity of time in that the dramatic situation is enacted in the same amount of time that it would take in real life. Unity of place is maintained in that the scene, Lovewit's house in the Friars, is specific and limited. The discreet beginning, middle, and inevitable conclusion of the play provide for unity of action. The characters are "types" who behave consistently, doing nothing unexpected, and thus the ideal of decorum, the paramount classical precept, is met; Jonson's prostitute is bawdy, his churchmen sanctimonious.

Faithfulness to classical concepts, however, is not the only virtue of *The Alchemist*. A talented actor as well as a writer of poetry, masques, criticism, and tragic and comic plays, Jonson was a masterful manipulator of theatrical effects. The opening argument of *The Alchemist,* presented in antic verse, catapults the play headlong into a rollicking, boisterous, bawdy life of its own. The simple yet ingenious plot provides for the multiplicity of incident dear to the Renaissance heart; costume, disguise, and transmutation of identity are similarly exploited.

The internal development is more complex than some critics suggest. The characters are introduced in approximate order of both their social status and rapacity. As these advance, so does the degree of cozening inflicted by Face and Subtle, and this progression reinforces the cohesiveness of the play. Although the fates of the characters are not contingent, since all are frauds or dupes, they interact in complex and amusing ways. These interactions, which become so dense that eventually Face and Subtle have their victims cozening each other, engender organic unity and dramatic tension simultaneously. As the play advances, the number of characters on stage increases, the pace quickens, and the scenes grow shorter. The climax is predictable but impressive, the denouement tidy, and the entire proceeding animated by a genuine and hearty spirit.

Despite its qualifications as a well-wrought, clever, and entertaining play in the classical mode, *The Alchemist* owes much of its literary interest and charm to Jonson's rhetorical flourishes. The underworld slang and alchemical jargon used by the protagonists lend color and authenticity. Double and single entendres, and simultaneous dialogue, which originated with Jonson, add to the effect. But most impressive, perhaps, is the way Subtle and Face use a debased eloquence in perpetrating their frauds. One of Subtle's elegant, highly rhetorical, pseudo-rational arguments, for example, seems unequivocally to establish the propensity of all metals to turn into gold. Surly's calm and earnest reasoning with Dame Pliant, on the other hand, seems but a pale counterfeit of Subtle's spirited equivocation.

The Alchemist dramatizes what might happen when moral order is suspended by plague in London. Lovewit, representing responsible society, jettisons civic responsibility and flees the city, leaving behind only knaves and fools. Although the reader is reminded early that order will eventually be restored, society in the hands of the unscrupulous degenerates into chaos. The servant supplants the master, science is overthrown by alchemy, reason is toppled by rhetoric, nature's secrets are transcended, and moral order is subverted as Churchmen become swindlers.

Jonson's vehicle, satire, was quite popular in Elizabethan England, and in

The Alchemist its effect is intensified by the plague in the background. Jonson intended to be instructive, even if it meant instructing by ridicule. And the classicist in him wanted to restore to England some of the glory of Augustan Rome. To this end Jonson adopted Cicero's famous definition of tragedy: "a copy of life, a mirror of custom, a representation of truth." Accordingly, he anchors his play in contemporary London and reflects the speech, behavior, and attitudes of its citizens. The Renaissance saw a shift in emphasis from the world of the Church to the world of experience, but while Jonson set an extremely worldly stage, his morality was severe and almost medieval. His moral values, clear from the first scene on, are constantly reiterated as *The Alchemist* indicts vain and wishful thinking and directs the mind to the contemplation of virtue. It is a sign of Ben Jonson's genius that he does it unequivocally and entertainingly.

Michael Levine

ALECK MAURY, SPORTSMAN

Type of work: Novel
Author: Caroline Gordon (1895-   )
Type of plot: Fictional biography
Time of plot: Late nineteenth, early twentieth centuries
Locale: Virginia, Tennessee, Mississippi, Missouri
First published: 1934

Characterized by its slow, evenly paced plot and uniformly plain style, Aleck Maury, Sportsman *is an unassuming portrait of a quiet man whose dedication to his sports gives both pleasure and pattern to his life.*

Significantly, *Aleck Maury, Sportsman* is dedicated to Ford Madox Ford, one of the most influential literary critics and greatest prose stylists of the twentieth century. Caroline Gordon's narrative is low-keyed and detailed, deliberately avoiding excesses either of syntax or event. An almost obsessive commitment to perfection of tone rules the book; not a word is allowed to stand out more vibrant or significant than any other. Above all else, the novel is a masterpiece of *writing*.

From boyhood Aleck Maury was dedicated to Latin, Greek, and sport, especially hunting and fishing. Life seems to flow almost effortlessly for Aleck, as effortlessly as Caroline Gordon's prose. He is possessed by no powerful passions or erratic impulses. A dedicated, constant love of sport rules his life, taking the place of ambition for wealth or glory or power. His wife even wonders if sportsmanship is more important to him than his family. But his love for hunting and fishing is not violent; rather, it is deep and quiet and steady, a part of his being. She cannot be jealous of it any more than she can be jealous of his arms or legs.

As Aleck Maury tells of his life, he frequently pauses to ponder a scene, to examine meticulously a place or moment. "There are times," he says, "in a man's life when every moment seems charged with meaning." This novel is composd primarily of such moments. They are held in suspension while the narrator and reader wait, interested and thoughtful, for the subsequent events to form themselves. Nothing in the book, not marriage or death, not career or raising of children, happens hurriedly. Always, an even pace is observed, as Aleck moves from stream to stream, and tramps from hunt to hunt. Some people might find his life just a little boring, despite the skill with which it is described.

ALICE ADAMS

Type of work: Novel
Author: Booth Tarkington (1869-1946)
Type of plot: Social criticism
Time of plot: Early twentieth century
Locale: A small Midwestern town
First published: 1921

Tarkington's modest style creates a quiet atmosphere and tolerant, sympathetic stance from which the author can make observations that are often sharply critical of small-town manners and morals.

Alice Adams and Booth Tarkington's other masterpiece of Americana, *The Magnificent Ambersons,* together present a surprisingly broad and perceptive picture of small town life in the first decades of the twentieth century. Because he was writing of people and places he knew intimately, the author brought an unusual understanding and insight to his portrayals. Tarkington's style, deceptively simple, actually is the perfect vehicle for his stories; his prose is clean and supple and does not distract from the vivid characterizations or well-thought-out plots. He was a superior craftsman, and *Alice Adams* is an excellent example of his sensitivity and skill.

The novel hinges on the personality of Alice. Tarkington sees into this young girl with amazing insight; her little dreams, her self-delusions, her battles with reality, all are portrayed with a touching honesty and affection. The scene in which Alice, dressed in simple but good taste attends a party full of pushy, overdressed small town "society belles" is a pointed commentary on American taste and social standards.

The reader cares deeply about Alice's little humiliations and attempts to rise beyond the limitations of her station. Her efforts to make her modest home nice and to provide a fine dinner when the young man comes to visit are painfully futile, however well-intentioned. Her little tragedies are the tragedies of everyday life for millions of people, and are captured with a deft hand. Many readers will pause and think, "Yes, that's true, that's the way it is." For many of the efforts and emotions described in the novel are so true to human nature that they do not date any more than those of the Bennett sisters in Jane Austen's *Pride and Prejudice.*

Alice Adams won the Pulitzer Prize for fiction in 1921, but Tarkington's novels have suffered a temporary eclipse. There is no doubt, however, that *Alice Adams* will endure as an honest and touching picture of real people in genuine struggles with their world.

ALICE'S ADVENTURES IN WONDERLAND

Type of work: Imaginative tale
Author: Lewis Carroll (Charles Lutwidge Dodgson, 1832-1898)
Type of plot: Fantasy
Time of plot: Victorian England
Locale: The dream world of an imaginative child
First published: 1865

Carroll's classic fantasy can be read on many levels and appreciated by diverse audiences: it is at once a biting social and political satire sufficiently complex to satisfy the most sophisticated adult, and a delightfully whimsical fairy tale to capture the fancy of the imaginative child.

One summer afternoon in 1862, the Rev. Charles Lutwidge Dodgson, an Oxford friend, and three little girls set out on a boat trip. Somewhere along the way *Alice's Adventures in Wonderland* was born. It was not the first story that Dodgson had told the girls, children of Henry George Liddell, dean of Christ Church, Oxford. But it was one which immediately captured Alice Liddell, the prototype for the fictional seven-year-old heroine. And her later requests for Dodgson to "write it down" were to turn him into one of the world's favorite authors, with his work translated into 47 languages and part of the heritage of most literate people.

Dodgson, who transposed his first two names into the pen name Lewis Carroll, was on the surface a shy but seemingly conventional Oxford mathematician. But today his outwardly harmless affinity for little girls is viewed as the sign of a serious neurosis, an inability to grow up, which also revealed itself in his writings. Alice was only one of many young girls who would provide Carroll with the only love—innocent and sexless as it seemed—to which he could respond. As she matured, each child was replaced in Carroll's affections by another young lady who shared the secret world of childhood in which he spent much of his adult life.

Expressing itself in many ways, this attraction to fantasy gave rise to Carroll's love of whimsical letters, gadgets, theatricals, toys, and, of course, to the Alice stories. First prepared in a handwritten manuscript book for Alice Liddell (then called *Alice's Adventures Under Ground*), the book was published in its present form in 1865 and was almost immediately popular. Adding to its originality were the famous illustrations by Sir John Tenniel who did not use the real Alice for his model. She, unlike the pictured child, had short dark hair and bangs.

Followed in 1871 by the even more brilliant sequel, *Through the Looking-Glass and What Alice Found There,* the book has always been enjoyed on several levels. Initially, of course, it is a very special children's story, but it is also a book teeming with fascination for certain specialists—mathematicians, linguists, logicians, Freudians, and even those who envision the book as an example of a drug trip. Yet perhaps its philosophical suggestions give the work most of its never-ending appeal for adults.

If we examine the book as children's literature, we see that it offered its young readers a charming new outlook dispensing with the moralistic viewpoint then prevalent in almost all tales for youngsters. Alice is neither continuously nice nor thoroughly naughty, for she is simply a curious child whose queries lead her into strange situations, and in the end she is neither punished nor rewarded. A moral proposing that she do this or that is absent. Departing even further from the saccharine stories praising standard virtues, Carroll pokes fun at many of the ideas with which Alice, a well-bred English child, has been imbued. The Mock Turtle, for instance, chides the sacred subject of learning by terming the branches of arithmetic Ambition, Distraction, Uglification, and Derision. And children who read the book are permitted to see adults quite unlike the perfect beings usually portrayed. It is the story's adults rather than Alice who are rude, demanding, and ridiculous.

As a work for the specialist, *Alice's Adventures in Wonderland* touches on many puzzles more thoroughly presented in *Through the Looking-Glass and What Alice Found There.* Its playfulness with language, for example, involves puns, parodies, and clever phrasing, but it does not deal as fully with the basic nature of language as does its sequel. Yet even in *Alice's Adventures in Wonderland,* Carroll's casual amusement with words often has deeper meaning. When he parodies the well-known poems and songs of his day, he is again questioning their supercilious platitudes. When he makes a pun (the Gryphon tells us that boots and shoes under the sea are "done" with whiting rather than blacking and are, of course, made of soles and eels), Carroll is asserting the total logic of illogic. And when he designs a Cheshire cat, he is taking a common but unclear phrase of his time ("Grin like a Cheshire cat" referred either to inn signs in the county of Cheshire depicting a grinning lion or to Cheshire cheeses modeled in the shape of a smiling cat) and turning it into a concrete reality. Logicians also find a multitude of tidbits. The Cheshire cat "proves" it is not mad by adopting the premise that if a dog is not mad, anyone who reacts in ways opposite to a dog must be. The March Hare offers a nice exercise in logic and language with his discussion of taking "more" versus taking "less" and his challenge as to whether "I mean what I say" is the same as "I say what I mean."

For mathematicians Carroll presents the Mad Hatter's watch which tells the day of the month rather than the hour. That watch does not bother with the hour since from the center of the earth the sun would always look the same whereas the moon's phases would be visible. For the Freudians, the book is also a mass of complicated mysteries. Freudians see significance in most of the characters and incidents, but the fall down the rabbit hole, the changes in size, the interest in eating and drinking, the obnoxious mature females, and Alice's continual anxiety are some of the most revealing topics suggesting Carroll's neuroses about women and sex.

The larger philosophical questions raised by Alice center on the order of life as we know it. Set in the context of the dream vision, a journey different from a conscious quest, the book asks whether there is indeed any pattern or meaning to life. Alice is the curious innocent who compares so favorably with the jaded and even wicked grown-ups. Always sensible and open to experience, she would seem the ideal messenger to bring us a true concept. Yet her adventures hint that all we may know is the ridiculousness of logic and what we imagine to be reality and the logic of nonsense. We see that Wonderland is no more incomprehensible than Victorian England, that the Mad Duchess lives next door, that as the Cheshire cat says, "We're all mad here."

To Wonderland Alice brings a strong belief in order and certain concepts, and she must continually refuse to accept the chaos which she finds there. When Wonderland turns her views askew, she can withstand the strain for only so long. Then she must rebel. The trial, which in our world is the last refuge of justice, is the key factor in Alice's rejection of Wonderland. For it is a trial of Wonderland itself, with many of the earlier encountered creatures reassembled to assert forcefully once more that expectations and rules are meaningless. Like the child of our world that she is, Alice (and Carroll) must deny the truth that there is no truth. She must shout "Nonsense" to it all. As one critic has pointed out, she rejects "mad sanity in favor of the sane madness of the ordinary existence." Facing the same confusion and frightened by what it hints, the reader also rebels. He laughs and turns to more "serious" considerations.

Judith Bolch

ALL FOOLS

Type of work: Drama
Author: George Chapman (c. 1559-1634)
Type of plot: Romantic comedy
Time of plot: Sixteenth century
Locale: Italy
First presented: c. 1604

Adapted from two comedies by the Roman playwright Terence, All Fools *sports delightful comic scenes arising from Chapman's deft handling of complicated intrigue. The play's effectiveness is further enhanced by the author's use of individualized and skillfully motivated characters in place of the one-dimensional stereotypes often found in early romantic comedies.*

George Chapman was a notable writer in various categories during the Elizabethan and Jacobean periods. He was some five years older than Shakespeare and Marlowe, and a dozen years older than Ben Jonson. He was a university man, and was widely read in the classics. Possibly he is most famed now for his multivolume translation of Homer, 1598-1616. Chapman's earliest published works were poems in 1594. In 1598 he wrote a completion for Marlowe's *Hero and Leander.* By 1596 he had begun writing plays, and continued for years to write them—comedies, tragedies, and masques.

Jonson was long a friend and rival playwright. Chapman, like Jonson, was a substantial scholar and made much dramatic use of his learning. His use of "humours" in dramatic writing preceded that of Ben Jonson, or may coincide with Jonson's earliest. Chapman's comedy *All Fools,* about 1604, is based upon two Latin comedies by the great Roman playwright Terence, of the second century B.C.

All Fools uses Italian settings and names, and the Terentian complicated rapid action of involved love plots among young persons. Schemes of deception and deceptions-within-deception are devised to fool and upset parents and others. On the stage the deceptions and confusions are less difficult to understand than they are for a reader. Clever acting and shrewd costuming help the audience concentrate and so keep abreast of the deceptions that are being perpetrated. English audiences in the sixteenth and seventeenth centuries enjoyed watching painful practical pokes; and they enjoyed the mental challenge of the entanglement of multiple plot action.

In this play almost all of the major characters are fools or are made fools of, especially the two fathers Gostanzo and Marc Antonio, and the jealous husband Cornelio. Even the master trickster Rinaldo is tricked.

Although much of the action and characterization in this play is drawn from older works, Chapman gives the type-characters a new vitality through individualizing them. He provides, furthermore, improved motivations for the action.

ALL FOR LOVE

Type of work: Drama
Author: John Dryden (1631-1700)
Type of plot: Romantic tragedy
Time of plot: First century B.C.
Locale: Alexandria, Egypt
First presented: 1677

Although he deeply admired Shakespeare, Dryden felt that the Elizabethan playwrights paid too little attention to the classical unities of time, place, and action. In strict adherence to these traditional concepts of drama, therefore, he retold the story of Antony and Cleopatra's tragic end. Excellent in its own right, All for Love *nevertheless lacks the emotional vibrancy of Shakespeare's version of the tale; Dryden concentrates less on the lovers than on the conflict between Cleopatra and Antony's wife, his general, and his best friend.*

John Dryden, the premier poet of his age, is honored primarily as a satirist and controversialist in the political and religious skirmishes of the Restoration. Yet, it was in the drama that he honed the fine poetic skills of his later poems. Between 1667 and 1678, he wrote a series of comedies and tragedies which provided him with the opportunity to develop the authority and control which distinguish his major poetry. Dryden was never a truly successful comic dramatist, perhaps because the prospect of foolish or flawed man's getting better than he deserved was at odds with his essentially satiric sensibility. He did, however, create a series of tragedies, including *The Conquest of Granada, Aureng-Zebe, Tyrranick Love,* and *All for Love,* which set the norm for heroic drama in the period.

The Restoration was an exciting period in the history of the drama with the reopening of the theaters and the introduction of women playing female roles. The heroic drama, the dominant serious form, was an exaggerated and stylized presentation of themes of epic proportions. Large heroes and heroines confronted dastardly villains with a great deal of bombastic rhetoric, usually in heroic couplets. Through his tragedies, Dryden had been building towards a greater control of the excesses of the genre and, in *All for Love,* he abandoned the couplet for blank verse and managed his highly romantic subject matter with distance and restraint.

All for Love is a retelling of the story of Antony and Cleopatra but, despite Dryden's great admiration for Shakespeare, it is in no sense an adaptation of Shakespeare's version. Dryden's play lacks the panoramic sweep of Shakespeare's *Antony and Cleopatra,* which ranges broadly over the civilized world. As a devotee of a more rational kind of theater based on a strict interpretation of Aristotle, Dryden was much more concerned about the unities of time, place, and action. The whole drama unfolds in Alexandria and is narrowly limited to the period after the defeat of Antony at the battle of

Actium.

The play does not have a climax in the usual sense of the term. The climax of a drama is ordinarily a focal point towards which the conflicts and complications build. It is true that in some Shakespearean plays the climax is early, as in *Macbeth* where the murder of Duncan is accomplished in the second act so that we may concentrate on the consequences of Macbeth's crime. Dryden went a step further. If *All for Love* has a climax at all, it occurs before the beginning of the action on stage. The play traces the complex chain of results of the battle of Actium, which changed the course of history, sealed the fate of Antony, and doomed Egyptian civilization.

Such a context is the natural element of Restoration heroic drama: a hero larger than life, worthy of the grandest exploits, is thrust into a moribund civilization. As R. J. Kaufmann has noted, heroic drama is fashioned by a sort of terminal poetic. The overreacher, the hero who monumentally represents all that is best in us and who tests the justice and the restraining limits of the universe, is gone. Instead, we have heroes, noble beyond reproach, who are cast into a twilight world. Even Dryden's images of sunsets and twilight reinforce the impression of finality.

The optimism of Renaissance drama has been replaced, if not by despair, at least by resignation to a world in decline. Antony had challenged the world, but that time is now past. He is left to examine his passions in a series of *ex post facto* confrontations. New attitudes about what is efficacious social behavior had emerged from the Restoration's predilection for order and stability. The heroic drama is a transposition of the daring hero into a more subdued context. As Kaufmann puts it, "This incapacity to believe in the continuing social utility of heroic energy is what makes Dryden's plays less than high tragedy." But at the same time, Dryden establishes a new kind of tragedy which recognizes this impotence and searches out what is beyond.

Unlike Shakespeare, Dryden does not use setting (e.g., Alexandria) as a premise for characterization. Dryden takes pains to remove his characters from the particularities of any specific time or place, to isolate them in a sterile world free of extraneous distractions. In this context Antony, his great exploits over, is free to confront himself. It is probably a limitation of the dramatic form that these complications seem to be thrust externally upon Antony, but the fact remains that he must face a series of trials, each of which is designed to challenge another facet of his sorely burdened moral identity. As Antony faces his troubles, he is no more a passionate sot than he is any longer the potent hero. He is not a weak man. The conflict is no longer a simple dichotomy of passion and responsibility—although that is there. Rather it is a matter of Antony, through the blandishments of Ventidius and Cleopatra, trying to decide who he is by discovering where his true loyalties lie.

It is typical of this oddly muted tragic world that its passions are manipulated and stage-managed by the eunuch Alexas. Octavius, the hero in the ascendant, never appears on stage, for if he did, he would inevitably over-whelm the afterlight in which the declining heroism of Antony is bathed. Indeed, it is this very descent from godhead to humanity that is the source of the special tragedy of *All for Love*. Antony's experience brings him to a self-perception and an understanding of passion, loyalty, and power which are beyond the hero at the height of his success. Heroic perception of this diminished sort is the appropriate insight for an age which reduced man back to his own image. If it is less exciting in its aspirations, it is more demanding of the individual human being. Tamburlanes and Lears no longer fight the battles for mankind; Antonys must face up to themselves and the limitations of their heroism.

Edward E. Foster

ALL MEN ARE BROTHERS

Type of work: Novel
Author: Shih Nai-an (fl. fourteenth century)
Type of plot: Picaresque romance
Time of plot: Thirteenth century or earlier
Locale: China
First transcribed: Possibly the fourteenth or fifteenth century

A panoramic saga of Chinese life, this "novel" follows the exploits of a band of 108 robbers who have joined together after having been forced to flee government persecution.

Pearl Buck has said that the reader must simply let the narrative of this vast fictional tale flow over him, like a river or sea, and she is correct. This huge book is like a force of nature, tumultuous, ever-changing, beyond instant comprehension, yet colorful and filled with life and interest. Although not strictly speaking a novel in the modern sense, *All Men Are Brothers* is filled with fascinating and memorable characters. Of the thousands of faces which appear in these pages the reader will be able to remember only a few, but they all possess independent lives and amazing vitality. Their psychology is not probed, but their actions are often as subtle as they are frequently violent. Some of the characters, such as Lu Ta, the warrior who rescues Jade Lotus and her old father from the Pig Butcher (and later becomes the Priest Lu Chi Shen) are both complicated and child-like, possessing a primitive innocence combined with an age-old subtlety inherited from generations past. This union of the primitive and violent, plus the old and subtle gives the people and the tale a unique fascination for the Western reader.

When Pearl Buck translated this book in 1933, she said that it still represented the people of China, although it dated back to the fourteenth century. Much has happened in China since then, and there seems to be little similarity between the renegades who fill these pages and modern China. Yet perhaps it still bears relation to the Chinese of today in the way that Chaucer relates to the modern English; one feels in *All Men Are Brothers* the tremendous vitality of a vast people, of an ancient civilization, and of values that refuse to die. The lustiness, humor, and violence are all part of human life, and they endure, for better or for worse.

The class structure is very strong in the period of the novel, and serves both to protect and oppress the people. Often the characters express vast frustration and anger, and are unable to find an outlet for it. A common expression is "Ah, bitterness, bitterness," which is usually followed by uneasy resignation. The book has been considered revolutionary; certainly, the freedom of movement of the renegades was unusual for the time. Only outlaws possessed any true liberty in thirteenth century China, and, necessarily, it was precarious. Yet the book does not seem to make a plea for revolution, except in that it describes the lusty joys of even the briefest freedom. Perhaps that was enough to worry the rulers of the past who occasionally banished it.

ALL QUIET ON THE WESTERN FRONT

Type of work: Novel
Author: Erich Maria Remarque (1898-1970)
Type of plot: Social criticism
Time of plot: World War I
Locale: Germany and France
First published: 1929

Reflecting the bitter disillusionment of anti-war sentiment in the 1920's, Remarque's simple yet powerful novel dramatizes the horror and futility of war.

All Quiet on the Western Front, while regarded somewhat patronizingly by scholars, was a greatly successful popular novel in Germany, where it sold over a million copies. Today it is known as well through the popular film version. It was written a decade after the war's end and appeared at a time when pacifism was widespread in Germany; it became the voice of those who regarded war as meaningless slaughter, a waste of the nation's youth.

Remarque belongs to the Post-Expressionist generation of writers who were striving for a return to objectivity and a matter-of-fact presentation of events. He says in a foreword that the novel is to be neither an accusation nor a confession, but a report. The facts, simply presented and minutely observed, are to speak for themselves, and understatement is one of the marks of his style. There is an economy in the novel that sharpens its impact; it is a short 258 pages.

The pathos which develops is not sentimentalized, although Remarque has justly been accused of oversimplifying the issues, and of stereotyping his figures, especially the officers and the older generation, so as to develop the virtues and appeal of his young soldiers. It is true that he centers his novel not on the average man but on an especially sensitive type, capable of reflection and introspection; but it is also true that this portrait of the dehumanization of war, and of the unrelenting horror which an entire generation of young men was forced to endure, builds to a powerful statement, clear to all, which is at once a confession and an accusation. Though the novel was widely read, it is the ultimate tragedy that its message went unheard.

ALL THE KING'S MEN

Type of work: Novel
Author: Robert Penn Warren (1905-   )
Type of plot: Social criticism
Time of plot: Late 1920's and early 1930's
Locale: Southern U.S.A.
First published: 1946

Ostensibly the story of political boss Willie Stark's rise to power, the real issue in the novel lies in the character of the caustic, talented journalist Jack Burden. Having smothered the ideals of his youth in a pervasive cynicism and amoral philosophical outlook, the personal entanglements of his past life and his present career finally converge to force Jack to key moral realizations.

One of the richest and most powerful of modern American novels is Robert Penn Warren's *All the King's Men.* In its pages the reader can trace a multitude of fascinating subjects ranging from politics to religion, from sociology to philosophy. He can discover an equally wide scope of thematic questions. Arousing as it does various responses to its complexities, responses which, for example, praise it as Christian or revile it as nihilistic on exactly the same grounds, the book is generally regarded as the masterpiece of a novelist (*The Cave, World Enough and Time, Band of Angels*) who is also a respected poet, critic, and professor. Warren, a Kentucky native, has a special affinity for the South, and much of his work suggests the traditions and problems of this region. *All the King's Men,* while exploring issues universal as well as regional, also has an unmistakable Southern flavor in areas more vital than mere setting.

An immediate query regarding this Pulitzer Prize-winning book usually touches on the relationship of Willie Stark and Huey Long. Governor of Louisiana from 1928 to 1931, Long led a career parallel to what Warren designs for Stark and presented a similar powerful and paradoxical personality. The product of a poor background, Long nevertheless became a lawyer at twenty-one after completing the three-year Tulane University course in eight months. Aggressive and determined, at twenty-four he sought and won the one state office open at his age—a seat on the Railroad Commission. An unorthodox champion of the little man, Long in his 1924 race for governor was unsuccessful when he tried to remain moderate on the Ku Klux Klan issue. But his 1928 try for the office was a triumph, and at thirty-five the outspoken country boy was a governor who almost singlehandedly ruled the state. Using patronage as his lever, Long talked the legislature into a thirty-million-dollar bond issue to finance farm roads, hospitals, free school books, and other programs popular with the poor folk but infuriating to his opponents. Like Stark, Long soon found himself impeached, charged with bribery, plotting the murder of a senator, misusing state funds, and various other crimes, some of which this strange mixture of demagogue and selfless public servant no doubt committed. But his promises and threats kept Long in office when enough senators signed a round robin promising not to convict him no matter what the evidence.

Long's career, which included the unprecedented move of becoming a United States senator while still serving in effect as governor, as well as plans to seek the Presidency, was halted by assassination. In a 1935 scene almost recreated in *All the King's Men,* a man stepped from behind a pillar at the Capitol and shot once, hitting Long. Felled by 61 bullets from Long's bodyguards, the man, Dr. Carl A. Weiss, died within seconds. Thirty hours later, Long, the "Kingfish," was also dead. Weiss's motivations were obscure; speculation said that he was angered when Long's maneuvering cost his father a judgeship.

Despite the overwhelming similarities between Long and Stark, Warren denies that he attempted merely to create a fictional counterpart of a political figure. But, he says, the "line of thinking and feeling" in the book does evolve from the atmosphere of Louisiana he encountered while he was a teacher at Louisiana State University, an atmosphere dominated and directed by Long's tenure as governor.

Central to the book is the primary theme of man's search for knowledge; all other facets are subordinate to and supportive of this theme. Knowledge includes both objective and subjective comprehensions, with the end goal being self-knowledge. "Life is Motion toward Knowledge," we read in *All the King's Men.* Elsewhere Warren asserts that the right to knowledge is man's "right to exist, to be himself, to be a man." Man defines himself through knowledge, and the book's pivotal incident demands accumulation of knowledge. Jack, assigned to "dig something up" on the Judge, does indeed uncover the Judge's dishonor, but the information precipitates a far more meaningful understanding.

For each of the characters it is a lack of knowledge or an incomplete knowledge which constitutes his chief problem, and those who eventually blunder forward do so only when they see what has previously been hidden from them. As the narrator, for example, Jack Burden is allegedly telling Willie Stark's story. Yet we sense that as he relates the events, Jack is clarifying their meaning mostly for his own benefit. The product of an aristocratic background, Jack in essence eschews knowledge throughout most of the story, for he exists in a vacuum, refusing to be touched or to feel. At moments of crisis, he seeks oblivion in The Great Sleep or by adhering to a belief in The Great Twitch: "Nobody has any responsibility for anything." He is a man of reflection only until those reflections become troublesome.

Seemingly Willie is the book's most knowing character. Yet his knowledge is questioned, at first only occasionally, then fully. Unlike Jack, who drops his idealism for inertia, Stark is always a man of action, action based sometimes on only partial knowledge. His innocence, lost by the "knowledge" that he has been betrayed, is replaced by a willingness to use evil if it is necessary for his purposes. He can justify blackmail or protection of a crook on this basis. For a time, Willie maintains and understands the balance between good and evil, but "obsessed with the evil in human nature and with his power to manipulate it," he is drawn completely onto the side of this dark force.

Jack ignores both ideals and the world, Willie the ideals. The third important character is Adam Stanton, who ignores the world. Make good out of evil, says Willie, for the bad is all you have to work with. Horrified by such a philosophy, Adam denies that honor, purity, and justice can commingle with blackness. When his preconceptions of the state of the universe prove false, he repudiates not his ideas but the universe. He is the man of idea untainted by fact or action; thus his knowledge is also faulty and weak, a situation which leads him to tragedy.

Through his investigation of the Judge, Jack inadvertently stumbles on the greater truth for himself and for the novel. He learns who he is in that he discovers his true father, but more importantly, he learns what he is as a man: an imperfect being who must accept imperfection in himself and others and lovingly make what he may out of that state. He, like Cass Mastern, learns that men cannot be separated from other men, that no action or idea exists alone, that past, present, and future are entangled in the web. He realizes what Willie initially knew, yet forgot, but reclaimed at the end of the novel. When he tells Jack that all might have been different, Willie implies that his fate might have been different had he remembered that although both good and evil exist and influence each other they are not the same.

Closely aligned with the knowledge theme is the Humpty Dumpty motif. The title hints at multiple meanings, for on one level Willie is the King (the Boss), and the characters "all the king's men." Yet perhaps greater significance arises if we see Willie as Humpty, for both fall to their doom and cannot be repaired. In this view the King is God, and the King's men are all of us. The fall becomes The Fall because Willie ruins himself by his knowledge of evil unbalanced by a corresponding ability to overcome its effects. We may also view Jack as another Humpty, one whose breakage is not irrevocable because his understanding and knowledge of evil ultimately correspond to an appropriate conception of the nature of good.

Judith Bolch

ALL'S WELL THAT ENDS WELL

Type of work: Drama
Author: William Shakespeare (1564-1616)
Type of plot: Romantic comedy
Time of plot: Sixteenth century
Locale: France and Italy
First presented: c. 1602

Uneven in tone, All's Well That Ends Well *ranges from scenes of farce to moments of serious insight. Helena's character, of rather dubious virtue in terms of her tactics with Bertram, sheds interesting ambiguity on the play's general theme of the blindness of prejudice and unreason.*

There are many heroines in Shakespeare's plays who manipulate their lovers. Rosalind in *As You Like It* leads Orlando out of his naïve and overly romantic love into greater maturity, counseling him while she is disguised as a man. *All's Well That Ends Well* parodies this pattern. In the end, Helena seems indeed to have taught Bertram the virtues of honor in love, and duty to wife and king. Her striving is inspired by her high idealism; he is a "bright particular star." It is not surprising that Shakespeare should write a parody of what was, to some extent, a popular theme. The theme of male passivity before a woman implies a high probability of ambivalence—whatever gratification gained being offset by possible social censure. The two views of women, as charming or as domineering, are extended in this play to the point of contradiction.

Helena's positive traits are those normally reserved for "good" characters. She inspires the goodwill of other "good" characters: the king, the countess, and Diana; there is no reason to believe she has tricked them. They, like the author, seem to ignore Helena's rather obvious negative side. This is shown in the fact that she forces, humiliates, and tricks Bertram into being her husband. To trick him, she exploits his bad character: his presumed seduction of Diana. Helena's tactics would seem absurdly heavy-handed but for the fact that Bertram in falsely denouncing Diana had proved himself capable of the exact cowardice of a Parolles, who had betrayed Bertram to the "enemy." The parody devalues the "good" woman of the pattern, but offers no real standard of virtue or evil. This blur of moral vision is typical of the "dark" comedies.

ALMAYER'S FOLLY

Type of work: Novel
Author: Joseph Conrad (Józef Teodor Konrad Korzeniowski, 1857-1924)
Type of plot: Romantic realism
Time of plot: Late nineteenth century
Locale: Dutch East Indies
First published: 1895

Set in the Far East and played out against the backdrop of inscrutable nature, this tale dramatizes the Western European's inability to comprehend the civilizations they have come to dominate forcibly, and the futility of their attempts to impose their values and systems on the Eastern mind.

Almayer's new house stands as the palpable symbol of "the undying folly of his heart"; Conrad calls it "that new ruin," meaning both the house, built in unrealistic expectation of commercial prosperity, and the edifice of his imagination, that castle of air reared up out of his invincible and seemingly willful misunderstanding of the motives of everyone about him. His is the folly of Europeans who, taking for granted a natural superiority in respect of civilization, and inferring from it the right of command in native affairs, ignore the very nature of the people they expect to control. This is a favorite theme of Conrad, this despairing bafflement in the face of the unyielding complexity of native life; such meddling leads eventually to paralysis of the spirit.

Almayer's feverish preparations for the gold-seeking expedition, after years of virtual immobility, are the last gasp of his will. When that hope is shattered, he sinks into mortal fixity, accusing Nina in his heart. But it is not Nina who has betrayed him; it is rather his own reliance on people who despise him, a blind belief in what is due him as a European. Captain Lingard's role rings another change on this motif, for his assumption of power over the life of a Malay orphan whom he does not at all understand, fires Almayer's at once exalted and trivial ambitions to wealth and social standing.

In addition, the novel is profoundly misogynist, linking the immobilizing moil of sexuality to the enormous, indifferent, and soul-battering wilderness where "the very air seemed dead . . . poisoned with the corruption of countless ages." Mrs. Almayer's passionate hatred and contempt for her husband that cause her to cuckold him with Lakamba; Nina's love for Dain so intimately mixed with policy; Taminah's passion that instigates the most craven revenge—all find their judgment in Dain's words: " 'The sea, O Nina, is like a woman's heart.' "

AMADÍS DE GAUL

Type of work: Novel
Author: Vasco de Lobeira (c. 1360-c. 1403)
Type of plot: Chivalric romance
Time of plot: First century
Locale: France, England, and the rest of Europe
First published: 1508

"The best of all books of this kind and unique in its art," as Cervantes had Don Quixote describe it, Amadis de Gaul *was the finest of dozens of sixteenth century Spanish chivalric romances. Although scholars dispute the authorship of Vasco de Lobeira, the work is known to have been rewritten in its effulgent Renaissance prose and expanded with a fourth book by Garci Ordóñez (or Rodriguez de Montalvo), the Mayor of Medina del Campo.*

Amadís de Gaul had much to do with creating the splendid "Golden Century" of Spain and Portugal. Romances of chivalry, especially *Amadís de Gaul,* appealed so strongly to both aristocratic and popular tastes that they helped mold, especially psychologically, the redoubtable breed of men and women who made Spain and Portugal great in every field of sixteenth century endeavor. They helped develop an entire culture, and were one reason why Spain's *tercios* were invincible on European battlefields for more than a century.

Obviously, *Amadís de Gaul* also influenced the masterwork of Spanish literature, Cervantes' *Don Quixote de la Mancha.* The latter work was not merely an attack on romances of chivalry, as is so often stated, but an attempt at modernizing them. It was also a defense of the spiritual against the material, as was *Amadís de Gaul. The Lusiads,* Portugal's literary masterwork, was also influenced by *Amadís de Gaul,* and in Camoëns' epic the seamen on Vasco da Gama's flagship were listening to tales from a romance of chivalry on the night before the discovery of India in 1498. Thus, *Amadís de Gaul* helped to shape the two great epics of the Iberian Peninsula's Golden Age, which in turn served as the spiritual-literary fount of the colonial literatures of Spanish-America and Brazil.

The literary and spiritual virtues of *Amadís de Gaul* are much greater than is usually supposed. The book vaunts moral, rather than physical, superiority, for only God gives victory and the knight is God's agent. The knight must be brave without being haughty and must pity the vanquished enemy. Arrogance and greed are condemned; grace is shown to be superior to sin and the angelic superior to the beastly. For such reasons, Ignatius de Loyola, founder of the Jesuits, considered the order of knighthood as being almost supernatural. *Amadís de Gaul* has also been likened by Félix Olmedo to a great narrative poem because this prose "flows in purity, freshness, and transparency, with the movement of life itself. . . ." Olmedo and other scholars have praised the novel's depiction of laughter, flowers, flights of birds, heavenly stars, clouds, and crags. A novel of war, love, and courtesy, *Amadís de Gaul* has been praised by John J. O'Connor as being "as close to the hearts of its sixteenth century readers as it is distant from ours."

THE AMBASSADORS

Type of work: Novel
Author: Henry James (1843-1916)
Type of plot: Psychological realism
Time of plot: About 1900
Locale: Paris, France
First published: 1903

The Ambassadors *marks a turning point in James's attitude toward his American characters. This novel contains none of the embarrassment found in many of the earlier works, which portray the author's fellow Americans as slightly barbaric in their inability to appreciate the fineness and subtlety of European culture.*

In Henry James's *The Ambassadors* plot is minimal; the storyline consists simply in Mrs. Newsome sending Lambert Strether to Europe to bring home her son, Chad. The important action is psychological rather than physical; the crucial activities are thought and conversation. The pace of the novel is slow. Events unfold as they do in life: in their own good time.

Because of these qualities, James's work demands certain responses from the reader. He must not expect boisterous action, shocking or violent occurrences, sensational coincidences, quickly mounting suspense, or breathtaking climaxes: these devices have no place in a Henry James novel. Rather, the reader must bring to the work a sensitivity to problems of conscience, an appreciation of the meaning beneath manners, and an awareness of the intricacies of human relationships. Finally, and of the utmost importance, the reader must be patient; the power of a novel like *The Ambassadors* is only revealed quietly and without haste. This is why, perhaps more than any other modern author, James requires rereading—not merely because of the complexity of his style, but because the richly layered texture of his prose contains a multiplicity of meanings, a wealth of subtle shadings.

In *The Ambassadors,* which James considered his masterpiece, this subtlety and complexity is due partially to his perfection of his technique for handling point of view. Departing from traditional eighteenth and nineteenth century use of the omniscient narrator, James experimented extensively with the limited point of view, exploring the device to discover what advantages it might have over the older method. He found that what was lost in panoramic scope and comprehensiveness, the limited viewpoint more than compensated for in focus, concentration, and intensity. It was the technique perfectly suited to an author whose primary concern was with presenting the thoughts, emotions, and motivations of an intelligent character, with understanding the psychological makeup of a sensitive mind and charting its growth.

The sensitive and intelligent character through whose mind all events in the novel are filtered is Lambert Strether. The reader sees and hears only what

Strether sees and hears; all experiences, preceptions, and judgments are his.
Strictly adhered to, this device proved too restricted for James's purpose;
therefore, he utilized other characters—called confidants—who enabled him to
expand the scope of his narrative without sacrificing advantages inherent in the
limited point of view. The basic function of these "listening characters" is to
expand and enrich Strether's experience. Miss Gostrey, Little Bilham, Way-
marsh, and Miss Barrace—all share with him attitudes and insights arising
from their widely diverse backgrounds; they provide him with a wider range of
knowledge than he could ever gain from firsthand experience. Maria Gostrey,
who is Strether's primary confidante, illustrates the fact that James's listening
characters are deep and memorable personalities in their own right. Miss Gostrey not only listens to Strether but she also becomes an important figure in
the plot, and as she gradually falls in love with Strether, engages the reader's
sympathy as well.

Lambert Strether interacts with and learns from the environment of Paris as
well as from the people he meets there; thus, the setting is far more than a
mere backdrop against which events in the plot occur. To understand the significance of Paris as the setting, the reader must appreciate the meaning which
the author, throughout his fiction, attached to certain places. James was
fascinated by what he saw as the underlying differences in the cultures of
America and Europe, and in particular in the opposing values of a booming
American factory town like Woollett and an ancient European capital such as
Paris. In these two places, very different qualities are held in esteem. In Woollett, Mrs. Newsome admires practicality, individuality, and enterprise, while in
Paris, her son appreciates good food and expensive wine, conversation with a
close circle of friends, and leisure time quietly spent. Woollett pursues com-
mercialism, higher social status, and rigid moral codes with untiring vigor;
Paris values the beauty of nature, the pleasure of companionship, and an
appreciation of the arts with studied simplicity. Thus, the implications of a
native of Woollett, like Lambert Strether, going to Paris at the end of his life
are manifold; and it is through his journey that the theme of the novel is
played out.

The theme consists of a question of conscience: Should Strether, in his
capacity as Mrs. Newsome's ambassador, be faithful to his mission of bringing
Chad home, once he no longer believes in that mission? That he ceases to
believe is the result of his conversion during his stay in Paris. He is exposed
to a side of life that he had not known previously; furthermore, he finds it to be
good. As a man of noble nature and sensitive conscience, he cannot ignore or
deny, as Sarah Newsome later does, that life in Paris has vastly improved Chad.
Ultimately, therefore, he must oppose rather than promote the young man's
return. The honesty of this action not only destroys his chance for financial
security in marriage to Chad's mother, but also prevents him from returning
the love of Maria Gostrey. Although Strether's discovery of a different set of

values comes too late in life for his own benefit, he at least can save Chad. The lesson he learns is the one he passionately seeks to impart to Little Bilham: "Live all you can; it's a mistake not to. It doesn't so much matter what you do in particular, so long as you have your life. . . . Don't, at any rate, miss things out of stupidity. . . . Live!"

If in reading *The Ambassadors* the reader's expectations are for keenness of observation, insight into motivations, comprehension of mental processes, and powerful characterizations, he will not be disappointed. If Henry James demands the effort, concentration, and commitment of his reader, he also— with his depth and breadth of vision and the sheer beauty of his craftsmanship —repays him a hundredfold.

Nancy G. Ballard

AMELIA

Type of work: Novel
Author: Henry Fielding (1707-1754)
Type of plot: Domestic realism
Time of plot: 1740's
Locale: England
First published: 1751

Although Amelia *lacks the extravagant humor of Fielding's earlier novels, it develops several memorably true-to-life characterizations. Also noteworthy are the realistic pictures of English courts and prison life, worked into the narrative by the author, for many years a magistrate, for the purpose of interesting readers in penal and legal reform.*

Amelia was intended to appeal to a psychological and social awareness, rather than to an intellectual consciousness. Between the publication of *Tom Jones* and *Amelia,* the nature of Fielding's moral feelings deepened and with it the means and techniques by which he expressed his thoughts concerning his intensified ethical purposes. Impressed by the social problems he daily encountered in the world around him, he adopted a reformist spirit and felt an immediate necessity to promote virtue and to expose the evils which infected England. He abandoned his satirical comic mode and all of its traits such as impartiality, restraint, mockery, irony, and aesthetic distance. He adopted a serious and sentimental tone that is almost consciously middle class.

The characters in *Amelia* give strong indications of Fielding's intensified moral purposes. They are more fiery, vehement, and immediate embodiments of his beliefs and concern than the figures of his earlier works. Abandoning the aesthetic distance between himself and his characters, he seems, in *Amelia,* to live and act directly in them. This results in a new kind of immediacy and closeness between the novel's characters and the writer's psychological concerns. The cost of this immediacy is the rejection of almost all formal conventions of characterization. The description of the heroine is typical. On a number of occasions she is described by the emotions which are reflected in her face or by her physical reactions to situations which bring pain or joy; but in contrast to Fielding's elaborate descriptions of the beauty of the heroines of his earlier works, the beauty of Amelia is never delineated. Amelia's beauty in Fielding's eyes and in those of the reader is embodied in the qualities she represents. The same might be said for the other characters in the novel. Fielding is more concerned with the moral make-up of each one than in their physical appearance.

In *Amelia,* the author does not segregate the reader and the characters. Each character reveals himself to the reader through his own words and deeds. This technique causes the characters to appear as individuals rather than types.

The central theme of Fielding's portrait of a marriage concerns not so much the issue of adultery as it does the tragic irony of the marital distrust that accompanies it. Although Booth's infidelity with Miss Matthews strains the marriage and seems disgusting when contrasted with Amelia's steadfast loyalty, that is not what almost wrecks the marriage. Amelia, of course, knew about it before Booth made his confession and had forgiven him for it. The marriage is almost undone because Booth, throughout most of the novel, cannot bring himself, because of fear and pride, to confess his adultery. He does not trust in his wife's understanding and love for him. Amelia, who is beset, almost from the beginning of her marriage, by amorous advances, fails to confide to her husband the real motive behind James's pretense of friendship because she fears Booth will lose his temper and attack James. Thus man and wife, because they will not trust in each other totally, work unconsciously to the detriment of their marriage.

In *Amelia,* the reader cares more about the heroine but the action turns on Booth. It is on the adequacy or inadequacy of Booth that the novel succeeds or fails for the reader. Amelia is the stable character. Booth constantly poses the problems of marriage while she endures and solves them.

Booth's ordeal reflects Fielding's own increasing despair with social conditions. The grim social picture of this novel is Fielding's solemn warning that society may destroy itself on the larger plane, as it very nearly destroys the Booths on the smaller plane. The placement of a woman of Amelia's moral character within a society which preys upon her, effectively points up the evils of that society in relation to the constant moral Christianity of the heroine. It is Fielding's most emphatic statement of Christian morality through the treatment of the subject within marriage. The loss of faith in individual morality portrayed in this novel through the assaults on Amelia's virtue and the setbacks suffered by Booth are easily transferred from the plane of individuals to reflect criticism of society as a whole.

Amelia was published to much rancor and ridicule on the part of the majority of the critics. This book unfortunately lent itself to ridicule more readily than any other Fielding wrote. The characters were reviled as being low and the situations as being too sordid. Enemies gleefully pounced on Fielding's oversight in failing to mend his heroine's broken nose. Earlier victims of Fielding's satire, notably Samuel Richardson, author of *Pamela,* were gleeful over the adverse reception of this novel and joined in denouncing it.

In spite of the early critical reaction, the success of the novel with the modern reader depends on a willingness to take it for what it is, a serious denunciation, as Fielding himself said, "of glaring evils of the age."

Patricia Ann King

THE AMERICAN

Type of work: Novel
Author: Henry James (1843-1916)
Type of plot: Psychological realism
Time of plot: Mid-nineteenth century
Locale: Paris, France
First published: 1877

In this novel James juxtaposes the pragmatic and materialistic values of American democratic society, as exhibited in Christopher Newman, with the traditional complex aristocratic French culture in which he becomes involved.

Christopher Newman of *The American* represents new world culture in conflict with the rigid traditions of the European aristocracy. Newman, a natural aristocrat in his own right, epitomizes the democratic spirit and pragmatic values of a culture in which accomplishment is alone the measure of individual worth. Though Newman suffers from a naïveté which blinds him to the complications of the complex society he encounters in France, he is an essentially moral person whose values ultimately prove superior to those of his detractors.

True to his materialistic background, Newman comes to Paris determined to acquire the best that European culture has to offer. He quickly reveals that he has little instinct for the best in art, and his judgment of people will prove equally inept. His choice of Claire de Cintré is based equally upon his vision of her as his ideal woman and as the ultimate possession to crown his success. His failure to achieve her depends upon his failure to recognize her subordination to the family will and the Bellegarde family's determination not to surrender the aristocratic tradition which is all that remains of their nobility.

Expecting that the Bellegardes will finally sacrifice family tradition to their material interests, Newman enters into a game with rules he never fully understands. His own democratic spirit makes it impossible that he should ever comprehend the almost religious idolatry of family which characterizes the Bellegardes. As the Bellegardes show their true colors, including criminal responsibility for the death of Claire's father, their "nobility" is shown to be based entirely upon tradition—it has no moral and human equivalent. Newman, on the other hand, rises in our estimation as a natural aristocrat whose moral superiority makes him the real measure of the best in the human condition.

AN AMERICAN TRAGEDY

Type of work: Novel
Author: Theodore Dreiser (1871-1945)
Type of plot: Social criticism
Time of plot: Early twentieth century
Locale: Kansas City, Chicago, and Lycurgus, New York
First published: 1925

Considered by most to be Dreiser's best novel, An American Tragedy *is a naturalist's indictment of the American economic system, which instills the craving and expectation for material prosperity in all its citizens, while allowing only a few to attain the dream of luxury and privilege with which it bedazzles the masses. The novel follows the career of Clyde Griffiths, a weak-willed man whose greed and false values lead him to attempt murder, and end finally in his own destruction.*

Few readers claim to "like" the works of Theodore Dreiser, for his novels are not ones which charm or delight. Nor are they clever stories which we explore for their plot. Even his characters are mostly obnoxious beings who fail to appeal in any usual sense. Why then is Dreiser considered by some a genius? Why do we read his books at all? The answer lies in a strange paradox: Dreiser's very faults are what attract us again and again. His stumbling, awkward style, his convoluted philosophies, and his pitiable personages combine to present us with a world view which, perhaps more successfully than that of any other American writer, conveys the naturalistic atmosphere. Dreiser's books, like the universe he seeks to describe, impress and repel us by their very disorder, their mystery, their powerful demands on our comfortable assumptions.

All of Dreiser's characteristics are most clearly reflected in *An American Tragedy,* the masterpiece of an author who had earlier published three important novels, *Sister Carrie, Jennie Gerhardt* and *The Financier.* In this book Dreiser the naturalist asserts the doctrine that man is struggling endlessly to survive in an uncaring world where he is a victim of heredity, environment, and chance which leave him small room for free choice or action. Dreiser's theory of life is basically mechanistic, and for *An American Tragedy* he invented the term "chemism" to explain the chemical forces which he believed propelled man to act in a certain way. Man, Dreiser said, is a "mechanism, undevised and uncreated and a badly and carelessly driven one at that." Such a poor creature is Clyde Griffiths, the central character of *An American Tragedy.* The book, which is full of scientific imagery, shows us how Clyde is driven to his final destruction.

Dreiser chooses to concentrate on man's struggle against one particular force: society and its institutions. Clyde in each of the novel's three sections strives not against a malign God nor a malevolent fate but against the unyielding structure of his culture. In other times men have defined themselves by other touchstones (religion, honor, war), but Clyde can answer his craving for meaning in only one way. For to matter in America means, in the book's terms, to be masterful, to have material goods and status. His America tempts him with its powerful businesses, its glittering social affairs, and its promises that anyone who is deserving can share in these riches. That is, of course, a false promise, for the American tragedy is the gap between the country's ideals and its reality.

Doomed to failure in his quest, Clyde, whose story has been called a "parable of our national experience," cannot be blamed for desiring what he sees all about him. Nor can he be criticized for the weaknesses and handicaps which assure his end. Immature and shallow, offering a "Gee" on all occasions, uneducated and poor, Clyde is willing to compromise in any necessary fashion in order to become materially successful. Yet his very lack of moral or intellectual distinction, when coupled with the intensity of his desires, makes him the ideal and innocent representative of a culture where achievement is gauged by such measurements. In the novel, inspired by a 1906 murder case involving a Chester Gillette who killed an inconveniently pregnant girl friend for reasons much like those in the book, Clyde's attorney calls him a "mental as well as a moral coward—no more and no less," but later adds that Clyde cannot help this state. "('After all, you didn't make yourself, did you?')"

What did "make" Clyde includes poor parents just as inept as he. Impractical and ineffectual, the Griffiths offer him only their God who, as he can plainly see, has brought them none of the things he (or they) want. Religion is one obstacle Clyde can and does remove when he ignores their protests and responds instead to his environment and inner urgings. His adaptability is exploited in the Arabian Nights atmosphere of the hotels in which he works, places where luxury alone is vital and kindness and honesty mere trifles. When in the second part of the novel Clyde finds himself in Lycurgus, he once again gravitates helplessly toward the surrounding values. Named after the Spartan who initiated that society's rigid rules, Lycurgus is just as tantalizing as the hotels. It is a "walled city" which, as one of the novel's major symbols, allows outsiders to peek at its glories but rarely permits them to enter its gates. Clyde, fascinated and overwhelmed, abandons the simple pleasures he has found with Roberta and attempts to climb its walls.

Whenever Clyde struggles free of his environmental influences, he is frustrated by the accidents and coincidences which haunt him. He unwillingly leaves Kansas City because of the car accident, and he leaves Chicago because of a seemingly happy encounter with his uncle. His chance meeting with Sondra and the mistaken identity developed their relationship, just as Roberta's unplanned pregnancy so rudely obstructs his dreams. Even his murder scheme is derived from a chance newspaper article, and the murder itself is in a sense self-initiated, for Clyde *allows* rather than *forces* Roberta's drowning.

Other characters in the novel are equally victims of the roles in which they find themselves. While many of them are compellingly presented, their main importance is to provide background and stimuli for Clyde. Since he rarely sees them as people but rather as impediments (his family, Roberta) or as exciting objects (Sondra), we too are interested in them mostly in this respect, and the book belongs almost entirely to Clyde.

In *An American Tragedy,* Dreiser, a former newspaperman and editor of women's publications, watches his world and its foibles and is moved by men's shared helplessness. He shows us how useless moral judgment is in solving such dilemmas and insists, as he does in all his works, that all we may expect of one another is compassion for our common plights. Although he offers us little encouragement, Dreiser does hint that perhaps the human condition may improve. The final scene—"Dusk, of a summer night"—closely resembles the opening. A small boy once again troops reluctantly with a group of street missionaries. Yet Mrs. Griffiths responds to the frustrations of Esta's child as she had never done to Clyde's and gives him money for an ice-cream cone. This child, she promises herself, will be different.

Judith Bolch

AMPHITRYON

Type of work: Drama
Author: Titus Maccius Plautus (c. 254-184 B.C.)
Type of plot: Farce
Time of plot: The Heroic Age
Locale: Thebes
First presented: c. 185 B.C.

This comedy of mistaken identity has been the basis for numerous translations, adaptations, and imitations; such great dramatists as Dryden, Molière, and Shakespeare have borrowed from its plot, structure, and theme. Plautus' play has been adapted successfully as recently as 1929, when Jean Giraudoux produced his version under the title Amphitryon 38.

One of Plautus' finest extant comedies, *Amphitryon* is both exuberant and well-constructed, a funny dramatization of a practical joke. Presumably this Roman farce was adapted from a work of the Greek New Comedy, which was usually the case with Roman comedies. However, since almost nothing of the hundreds of the Greek originals survived, it is impossible to pinpoint Plautus' models with any certainty. Judging purely by titles, *The Long Night* by the comic Plato or *The Night* by Philemon may have provided the plot and characters for *Amphitryon,* but this is conjecture. When the Roman writers adapted Greek comedies, they eliminated the chorus completely, thereby making the action continuous. They also made song and dance an integral part of the play, much like our musical comedies. An analogous situation is the way Lerner and Lowe transformed Shaw's *Pygmalion* into *My Fair Lady.*

Tradition says that Plautus learned stagecraft early in life, put his earnings into trade, went bankrupt, had to work in a flour mill, and there began writing his comedies, of which over a hundred were attributed to him. Twenty have come down to us, and from these we can see that Plautus was indeed very experienced in stage technique. He knew the value of timing, of comic repetition, of puns, double entendre, idiomatic speech, of varying his poetic meters. His humor was suggestive rather than lewd. And he was a past master at being funny. In reading his plays it is essential to visualize the action as taking place on the stage in front of a backdrop of a house or two. Imagination is necessary to recreate the humor of Plautus. Otherwise, his jokes are as stale as the ones on bar napkins, particularly in translation.

His plays were performed outdoors at public festivals in a carnival atmosphere, and they had to compete with other entertainments. The audiences were restive, unsophisticated, and tended to be straitlaced in that period of Roman history. Under such conditions a dramatist has to be continuously interesting, and a comic dramatist must be amusing at all costs. Plautus knew his audience thoroughly. He took the threadbare formulas of Greek New Comedy and inspirited them with his own vivacity.

Amphitryon is the only extant Roman comedy to treat Greek mythology. The story derives from a myth in which Zeus (Jupiter) lengthened a night into seventy-two hours and, disguised as Amphitryon, made love to Amphitryon's wife Alcmena. The supreme god did this in order to engender the great hero Heracles (Hercules). In this play, however, Jupiter is simply having a long, free night of dalliance with Alcmena just before she gives birth to Hercules and Iphicles. The effect is to make Jupiter appear as an insatiably lecherous and trouble-making bully who would do anything to satisfy his whims. He and Mercury are rogues playing a rather nasty practical joke on three decent people. It is a joke that gets out of hand and threatens to become tragic when Amphitryon intends to divorce Alcmena for adultery. Yet Jupiter unravels the mystery, restoring an equilibrium, when he has had enough amusement at their expense. Thus the play blends two of Plautus' favorite plots— the comedy of mistaken identity and the comedy of deliberate deception. The result is more than mere farce; it is tragi-comedy presented in a farcical manner.

The structure is surprisingly well done for Plautus, who usually took few pains to construct a sound plot. He makes excellent use of dramatic irony in the confusions of the human characters balanced against the knowledge of the divine characters, which the audience shares. We are given an Olympian viewpoint from which we witness the befuddlement of human beings as they encounter their exact duplicates and are bested at every turn. Much of the humor lies in the way Plautus exposes the discrepancy between perplexed humans and clear-sighted, interfering immortals. It is very funny when Sosia comes to doubt his own identity, having been displaced in his household by another Sosia who is identical in every respect. He thinks he has somehow twinned himself. The joke is still good later when Amphitryon and Jupiter ask Blepharo the pilot to decide who is the real Amphitryon. The theme of twins, the *döppelganger,* is carried through right to the end, when Alcmena gives birth to twins, one of human and the other of divine origin.

Yet the play becomes serious where Alcmena is accused of adultery because she found no difference between Amphitryon and Jupiter playing Amphitryon. Her husband comes to seem like an utter lunatic vacillating wildly between tenderness and incomprehensible jealousy. She genuinely loves Amphitryon and is deeply hurt by his accusations. Plautus gives a sympathetic portrayal of her as the duped wife. Amphitryon, although he loves Alcmena, seems like a proud, hot-tempered stuffed shirt who deserves, in part, his humiliation at Jupiter's hands. Plautus lifts both of these characters above the farcical level to reveal two people tricked and thwarted by the gods. But their love endures these buffetings.

Of later treatments of the Amphitryon story, which range from Molière and Dryden to Giraudoux' *Amphitryon 38,* not one approaches Plautus for sheer verve and the humanity of his characterization.

James Weigel, Jr.

AND QUIET FLOWS THE DON

Type of work: Novel
Author: Mikhail Sholokhov (1905-   )
Type of plot: Historical chronicle
Time of plot: 1913-1918
Locale: Tatarsk, Russia
First published: 1928

And Quiet Flows the Don *is successful both as historical fiction and as an intensely interesting story of people's lives during a tumultuous period in Russian history. Through the eyes of a young Cossack, Gregor Melekhov, Sholokhov presents the violence, confusion, and bewildering lack of meaning endured by soldiers and civilians alike during the upheaval.*

Gregor Melekhov, the central figure in Mikhail Sholokhov's work *And Quiet Flows the Don,* is born into the third generation of Melekhov Cossacks, veterans of the Turkish Wars, the Japanese-Russian War, the German-Russian War, and the Civil War. War permeates the work, lapsing only long enough for Gregor to entangle himself in a scandalous love affair with his neighbor Aksinia while her husband Stepan is serving in the military, and to be "married off" to Natalia.

The moral and spiritual decay of the soldiers and citizens affected by the war is painfully evident as the struggle against unintelligible forces rages endlessly. The Cossacks react against the government during the German-Russian War. They have been a minority easily manipulated by the Whites, but they are won over by the arguments of the Socialist Democrats, who support the peasants and successfully divide the people of the Don region by class. Peasants of Russia become disenchanted with fighting their German counterparts.

The issue is not an easily polarized class conflict, however, as the struggle internalizes within Russia. The philosophies of the Reds, the Whites, and the Separatists collide and become muddled. Soldiers take sides, desert, and change sides again; but the fighting continues.

Gregor shares in the confusion over the wider meaning of the historical events. He is first a pro-government loyalist whose Cross of St. George, though venerated by the people of Tatarsk, is devoid of meaning for him. He encounters the revolutionary teachings of Bunchuk, inclines to the Reds, and is consequently rejected by his people. Gregor is appalled at the killing by both Reds and Whites. The once-united Cossacks bear the excruciating pain of a fratricidal civil war. This graphic novel reveals many important aspects of the decisive period of history from which the modern Soviet Union emerged.

ANDERSEN'S FAIRY TALES
(SELECTIONS)

Type of work: Tales
Author: Hans Christian Andersen (1805-1875)
Type of plots: Folk tradition
Time of plots: Indeterminate
Locale: Denmark
First published: At intervals, 1835-1872

These tales, whether traditional or original, all reflect the incredibly fertile and diverse imagination of a writer steeped in his country's colorful legends, superstitions, and folk customs. Although Andersen's thematic concerns are all firmly rooted in his strong sense of right and wrong, the moods of different tales range from gaily whimsical to bleak and frightening.

The 168 tales written by Hans Christian Andersen may be classified in two general groups. The first group comprises the traditional European folk tales retold by Andersen and includes selections like "Little Claus and Big Claus" (based on the traditional "Hudden and Dudden"), "The Wild Swans" (a retelling of Grimms' "The Six Swans"), and "The Three Little Pigs." These are excellent versions in which the spirit of the source is maintained while the tale is enhanced by the author's gift for storytelling. But the majority of the tales belong to the second group, composed of Andersen's original stories; among these one finds a great variety, ranging from stories imitative of the folk tale style, to moral allegories, to stories which seem to foreshadow modern fantasy tales. Despite their diversity, however, all of Andersen's tales are marked by common features in both their content and their style.

To a greater or lesser degree, almost all the tales directly reflect the author's real experiences. Perhaps the most striking example of this is "The Ugly Duckling," which may be read both as a literal and a spiritual autobiography. Similarly, Karen in "The Red Shoes" directly parallels the young Hans, who at his confirmation was more thrilled with his leather shoes, so new that they squeaked, than with the religious ceremony. In addition to occasional fictionalized accounts of the author's past, we find a multitude of tales which are more subtly sprinkled with the author's childhood experiences and with the rich lore and colorful traditions of Odense, the provincial town in Denmark where he grew up. The appearance of benevolent grandmothers in so many of the stories, for example, is owing to Anderson's own kindly grandmother, who not only gave the boy sympathy and support, but also fed his imagination with peasant tales and reports of the eerie happenings in the insane alylum near which she worked. The many portraits of witches in the fairy tales owe their vividness to the author's terrifying memories of the local 'witches" for whom his mother sent when he was ill; towns like Odense in the early nineteenth century were still steeped in medieval beliefs, and mothers of peasant background like Andersen's might still trust in a witch's potion rather than a doctor's prescription to cure their children. Still other tales in the collection are built around recollected daydreams rather than the actual physical experiences of the author. Such is the beautiful story "The Nightingale," inspired by Andersen's fanciful habit as a boy of singing in the evening to the emperor of China, reputed by the peasants to reside directly under the Odense River.

Perhaps the single most important feature of Andersen's tales is the meaning or significance with which they are charged; a tale is rarely told solely for the sake of a catchy or entertaining plot. This certainly is not to say that the plots are dull—they are never that—or that the stories are heavily didactic, but rather that all of Andersen's work is illuminated (unobtrusively, for the most part) by a moral outlook on life. Sometimes this outlook takes the form of sharp social criticism, as in "The Emperor's New Clothes," which satirizes the pompousness and vanity of court life through its portrait of the unscrupulous weavers, the ridiculous emperor, and the hypocritical courtiers. Similarly, "The Swineherd" attacks the artificial and materialistic values which blind people to the true worth of things. Occasionally, a tale will be particularly frightening in its harsh presentation of a moral lesson; "The Red Shoes," in which a girl's amputated feet go dancing off, leaving her a cripple in punishment for her vanity over a new pair of shoes, is an especially grim and severe illustration. This type of story is the exception rather than the rule, however; for the most part, Andersen's humor is gentle rather than scathing, and his moral viewpoint characterized by its subtlety and sensitivity, its kindliness and concern for others.

One distinctive device which Andersen developed as a highly effective way of presenting his ideas was the transformation of inanimate objects into creatures with personalities. Perhaps most memorable is the steadfast tin soldier whose struggles to remain fearless through all his trials for the sake of his beloved paper ballerina exemplify the spirit of true devotion. In "The Old Streetlamp," Andersen uses a worthy (and very human) old lamppost to weave a symbolic tale about how fear of death robs the soul of its tranquility, and about the hope that leads to inner peace. Interspersed with these tales peopled by tin soldiers and lampposts, drops of water and darning needles, candles and inkstands, are others containing the more traditional talking animals and trees, which are also used to convey various themes. "The Three Little Pigs" illustrates the superiority of brains over physical strength; while in "The Buckwheat," a wise old oak tree weeps over a proud stalk of wheat that is destroyed because he refuses to take advice from his neighbors.

Andersen's ability to create such vivid and sympathetic characters, be they humans, animals, or objects, is due to his exceptional handling of dialogue. His interest in dialogue began early in his childhood, when, with the aid of a polyglot dictionary, he wrote whimsical stories in which each character spoke a different language. By the time he came to write the fairy tales, his characters all spoke the same language, but he had mastered the secret of revealing their personalities and motives through their speech. Rather than describing what a character is like, Andersen lets the characters expose themselves. Thus, in "The Shepherdess and the Sweep," the Shepherdess shows both her frivolity and petulance—"I'll never be happy until we are out in the big, wide world"—and her flightiness and shallowness: "I followed you faithfully out into the world, and if you love me the least bit you'll take me right home." And the chimney sweep's speech shows him to be sensible yet devoted: "Have you thought how big [the wide world] is, and that we can never come back here?"

Andersen saves his descriptive passages for presenting scenery and landscape, and at this, too, he is masterful. He reproduces with loving detail the inside of a humble cottage kitchen, or brings a towering mountain range before the reader's eyes with equal skill. In this excerpt from "The Ice Maiden," one of the longer tales, the author's descriptive power is at its best:

> Often the clouds hang around the towering peaks like thick curtains of smoke, while down in the valley dotted with brown wooden houses, a ray of the sun may be shining brightly, throwing into sharp relief a brilliant patch of green, until it seems transparent.

Toward the end of his life, Andersen made the statement, "I have imagined so much and had so little." He was referring in part to his frequent romantic attachments to women who ended up marrying other men, and to his long life spent as a bachelor. Still, coming from a man, beloved by all his countrymen, whose friendship was valued by Dumas, Hugo, Balzac, and Dickens, and whose society was sought after by nearly all the courts of Europe, the words "so little" seem incongruous. With the "so much," however, no one who has read Andersen's tales will quarrel, except to call the phrase an understatement.

Nancy G. Ballard

68

ANDRIA

Type of work: Drama
Author: Terence (Publius Terentius Afer, c. 190-159 B.C.)
Type of plot: Comedy
Time of plot: Second century B.C.
Locale: Athens
First presented: 166 B.C.

This first of Terence's plays reveals those same characteristics for which the dramatist was noted throughout his career: a closely knit plot, comedy with a serious rather than slapstick turn, and a natural style of language. Many modern authors have adapted or borrowed from Andria, *including Sir Richard Steele in* The Conscious Lovers *and Thornton Wilder in* The Woman of Andros.

As Terence's first play, produced in 166 B.C. when the author was twenty-one, *Andria* shows the direction and concerns of the playwright's later work. Like each of Terence's dramas, this was adapted from the Greek New Comedy, and Menander in particular. He frankly acknowledged in the Prologue to *Andria* that he borrowed from Menander's *The Girl from Andros* and *The Girl from Perinthos*. Among critics there is wide variance of opinion as to just how much of Terentian comedy was due to the original sources, and since these have been lost there is no way of settling the dispute. It seems likely, however, that the tone and the use of the double plot are distinctly Terence's.

If we compare him to his only predecessor whose plays have survived, Plautus, there is striking dissimilarity in these two comic playwrights, even though both adapted from Menander and his contemporaries. Plautus is preëminently a man of the stage; ebullient, funny, always ready to sacrifice plot construction for the sake of humor and interest. Terence is more the writer than the playwright; a careful craftsman, he is concerned with polished style, character delineation, a smooth and elegant plot. If he lacks Plautus' vivacity, he is always agreeably humane.

Terence's career itself was remarkable. Born in North Africa, he was brought to Rome as a slave while still a child. His master, Terentius Lucanus, educated him and eventually freed him, which allowed Terence to develop his interest in drama. He was admitted into the aristocratic circle of the Scipios, which was interested in disseminating Greek culture in Rome. As a youthful member, he achieved early success with his plays and encountered the envious spite of the elderly dramatist Luscius Lanuvinus, whom he took pains to answer in his Prologues. His career, though, was cut short at about the age of twenty-eight when he mysteriously disappeared on a trip to Greece. Tradition says that he was lost at sea.

The dramas of Terence, then, are the work of a young man, and they reflect the interests and assumptions of youth. The two primary subjects with which he deals are romance and the relations of sons and fathers, both of these being related in his plots. Generally, his stories center on a double love affair, each of which is thwarted or clandestine usually because of fatherly opposition, and each tends to be resolved satisfactorily for both youths. Often there is a clever slave who complicates matters by his deceptions, acting on behalf of one of the young men and against the will of the father.

In *Andria* we see Terence's initial development of this subject matter. While later works would handle the double plot with greater virtuosity, this play is fresher, livelier, and shows considerable maturity. In it we find his penchant for natural, idiomatic dialogue, for the neat maxim, for appealing, if misguided, characters, and for a plot that depends on intrigue and revelation. In fact, *Andria* is the first romantic comedy to come down to us from antiquity and is a precursor of Shakespearean comedy. One thinks of all the double romances in Shakespeare's work from *Two Gentlemen of Verona* to *Twelfth Night* and one is struck by the similarities to Terence.

The basic problem in *Andria* is that of getting Simo to consent to Pamphilus' marriage to Glycerium, when Simo has become intent on having his son marry Chremes' daughter, Philumena. The difficulty is that Simo, a forceful old man, believes what he wishes to believe, and he interprets what he sees in terms of his self-delusion. Thus, he pretends a forthcoming marriage between Pamphilus and Philumena to test his son's feelings, but also because he wants it to occur in actuality, since Philumena has birth, wealth, and status, whereas Glycerium has none of these. By threatening the slave Davus he gets Davus to support his mistake, which results in an actual marriage-to-be. This is a calamity for both Pamphilus, who loves Glycerium, and Charinus, who loves Philumena. Having lied successfully, Davus is now forced to tell the truth to extricate Pamphilus; and no matter what he does Simo refuses to believe him, insisting on the marriage at all costs. The trouble becomes grave when Simo disowns his son for visiting Glycerium. Everything is settled, however, by a *deus ex machina* ending in which Glycerium's parentage, citizenship, status, and wealth are established. In this plot Simo is the center of the action. His character determines the fates of Davus, Pamphilus, Charinus, and Glycerium. And, finally, it is his wish to have his son marry well that must be appeased by the arbitrary ending.

The other characters, while peripheral to Simo, are clearly delineated. Chremes is a sensible old man who wants his daughter to marry happily, in contrast to the deluded Simo, who wants his son to marry unhappily. Pamphilus has a passionate nature like his father, and he ardently cares for Glycerium. Charinus, on the other hand, is theatrical, and one has the impression that his love is make-believe, founded on a desire to marry into status and money. Davus at first secures his own safety by lying and getting Pamphilus to pretend compliance to Simo, but when that backfires, he risks and receives punishment in order to reveal the truth. None of these characters, not even the stubborn ones, is unsympathetic.

In *Andria* it is age that must be respected. no matter how mistaken a father may be. But as Terence continued to write, it increasingly becomes youth that must be served, although Terence felt some restraints must be exercised on the whims of young men. *Andria* has influenced playwrights such as Baron and Steele and the novelist Thornton Wilder, who directly adapted it in his novel, *The Woman from Andros*. A great borrower himself, Terence would have felt honored.

James Weigel, Jr.

ANDROMACHE

Type of work: Drama
Author: Euripides (c. 485-c. 406 B.C.)
Type of plot: Tragedy of intrigue
Time of plot: About a decade after the Trojan War
Locale: The temple of Thetis in Thessaly
First presented: c. 426 B.C.

One of Euripides' most poorly constructed plays, Andromache *seems to be strongly motivated by the author's intense hatred of Spartan character traits, as dramatized in the arrogance of Hermione, the treachery of Orestes, and the criminal brutality of Menelaus.*

When D. W. Lucas, writing of Euripides' *Andromache,* complained that the play "falls feebly and mysteriously to pieces," he was referring to the structural weakness of the plot. The most disconcerting problem is Andromache's complete disappearance from the story midway through the play. The action falls basically into three stages which are only slenderly connected. In the first stage, Andromache provides the focus, as her life and the life of her small son are imperiled by Hermione's jealous hatred; in the second, Hermione, beside herself with fear after her plot fails, is finally rescued by her old lover, Orestes. In the last stage, Neoptolemus is brutally murdered by Orestes, leaving his aged grandfather Peleus to mourn his death until his divine mate, Thetis, appears to comfort him.

For the most part, critics have reacted negatively to this discontinuous plot structure; not all have been as strong in their criticism as Lucas, however, and some have proposed that the play's episodic plot is compensated for by a unity of theme or characterization. It has been suggested, for example, that *Andromache* is a bitter attack on the Spartan national character, particularly on its qualities of arrogance, treachery, and ruthlessness. This theory is certainly supported in the first two parts of the play; Andromache, generalizing from the individual wrongs committed against her, denounces all Spartans as liars and cheats, while Hermione's vengefulness and Menelaus' cowardly, bullying, bragging nature seem to confirm her judgment. The interpretation is much less convincing, however, when applied to the last portion of the play, since it is never made clear that Orestes is meant to represent Spartan villainy. Other readings have seen the play variously as a denunciation of slavery; a dramatization of the political failure of Greek alliances; or a warning against forced or inadvisable marriages.

Perhaps more convincing than these views, as well as more consistent with Euripides' values as expressed throughout his other dramas, is the interpretation of *Andromache* as a portrayal of the tragedy of war. The theme of war —its trivial causes, its horrible course, its disastrous aftermath—is everywhere present; although the Trojan War has been over for ten years, it continues to dominate the lives of the characters, rather directly or indirectly. Andromache combines within herself all the tragic ills suffered by victims of war: she is not only widowed and orphaned, but enslaved in the enemy's land. Menelaus, who represents the victors, is shown as totally worthless and self-serving; after leaving the fighting and dying to men like Achilles, he returns to strut about and reap a hero's reward. Even Orestes, who was not personally involved in the war, is presented as someone whose character has been warped by the influence of all the evil circumstances surrounding the conflict.

ANDROMACHE

Type of work: Drama
Author: Jean Baptiste Racine (1639-1699)
Type of plot: Neo-classical tragedy
Time of plot: Shortly after the close of the Trojan War
Locale: Epirus
First presented: 1667

A seminal event in the history of French theater, the staging of Andromache *also marked the beginning of the greatest period in Racine's career. Of the four main characters, three are destroyed or driven mad by their obsessive emotions, while only Andromache, the sole person capable of unselfish grief, is left.*

Andromache, with its interplay of human passions, its frenzied picture of love turning to fierce jealousy and then to hatred and finally to madness and crime, began the main cycle of Racinian drama. Although his earlier plays, *La Thébaïde* (1664) and *Alexandre Le Grand* (1665) established Racine's reputation as a dramatist, *Andromache* is clearly a more sophisticated and mature work. The French theater of the seventeenth century accepted, on what it thought was the authority of Aristotle, the three unities of time, place, and action. Racine's predecessor, Corneille, deliberately accepted the principle that the action of the play must take place in a single day, that it must be concerned with a single situation in one circumscribed locality. Corneille found it difficult to confine himself to these limitations, but Racine's plays, concentrating on the moment more than the story, fit into this mold more easily and with great dramatic force. *Andromache* showed what could be done within these conventions.

Racinean tragedy is of a different type from Shakespearean; there is not the rich variety, the comedy mingled with tragedy, the breathless sweeping from scene to scene, the mad beauty of language thrown out almost recklessly. Instead, in the meticulously worded tragedies of *Andromache* and *Phèdre* there burns a peculiar, if rather decorous, beauty. The action is concentrated, and is less important than the mental reactions of the characters. In *Andromache,* the room in the Palace of Pyrrhus mentioned in the stage directions is, in a sense, any room anywhere, a place where tortured souls display their agony, their inner conflict, and their ultimate strength. The narrowness of the scene actually helps to concentrate the attention of the audience upon Racine's psychological analysis. The characters are not only Homeric Greeks, but *man and woman* in the most universal sense. The neoclassic tragedy of *Andromache* moves with a feverish intensity, exposing as seldom done on the stage the moment of passion and its consequences.

Racine theorized less about the neoclassic rules than Corneille, but he followed them more closely. He was a disciple of reason, as was Corneille, his teacher and later rival, but he saw reason more as a guide for the author than the character. To Racine this meant that his plays must be free from fantastic or irrational characterizations, that he must avoid complicated and impossible plots or climaxes that had nothing to do with what had gone before in the plays. He sought, within his conventions, a naturalness in drama. *Andromache* is probably the play in which Racine most perfectly achieved the combination of passionate concentration and reasonable naturalness.

Andromache launched Racine into his greatest period. It was the time of Molière's masterpieces *Tartuffe, Don Juan, The Misanthrope,* and Corneille's greatest plays were already behind him. Racine struck out for himself in *Andromache,* attempting a realistic portrayal of human passion. Hermione is shown as a jealous and neglected woman seeking revenge. In a sense, the problem of the play is the *crime passionnel* always so popular in French newspapers. Even in Racine's day, such cases were well known. French literature was filled with such women, but this was the first time that the psychology of such a character had been put upon the stage.

Racine took these men and women from the Homeric tales and transformed them into Frenchmen and Frenchwomen. Andromache, in spite of her intense fidelity to Hector's memory, understood the power of her sex over King Pyrrhus. Racine interpreted the drama more as a battle between the sexes than ever had been attempted before. The universality of the playwright's vision brought the characters from the dignity of history to the fire of human passion, thus creating modern men and women.

Pyrrhus, King of Epirus, is one of the most interesting characters in the play, and in all of Racine. A fierce barbarian of a man, the son of Achilles, he is yet curiously at home within the walls of his palace, ever analyzing emotions and mental conditions. This dual nature almost strikes us today as contradictory, perhaps even unlikely. But in 1667 Racine had to defend his complex portrait of Pyrrhus from the charge of brutality. Such a virile, dominant man, with the warrior's blunt nature, never before had appeared so nakedly on the stage. Racine covered new ground in this play with his male characters as well as with the now more famous female characters.

The plot of *Andromache* depends more upon inner action expressed in words than upon external action such as the romantic Shakespearean drama often represents. Racine was the great psychological poet and analyzer of character, the beginning of a long line of such writers in French literature, leading up to Maupassant, Colette, and finally, in the twentieth century, Gide. Racine's men and women might step out of their period costumes and don the clothes of any other age. The plot of the play, which these men and women subtly maneuver through, develops logically and precisely, to its inevitable and tragic conclusion. The audience's reaction to *Andromache* must be more mental than emotional, more one of admiration than sympathy.

The world Racine shows us in *Andromache* is a world in which honor is still a way of life. In this realm men and women are responsible for their own conduct. Nothing, not love or even life, is as important as honor. Today this seems a strange and old-fashioned code, but it is fundamental to the tragic point of view, and the heart of all of Racine's dramas. The character of Andromache alone emerges from the play with her honor—in the broadest conception of the word—intact. The others have compromised their honor and have paid the price. Modern audiences, accustomed to a world in which everybody denies responsibility for everything, may find it difficult to understand this code by which the characters of *Andromache* must live and die, yet they cannot help but find it impressive and possibly inspiring. The morality upon which the conduct of these men and women is based is universal, reaching back to classical antiquity and forward to our own time.

Bruce D. Reeves

ÁNGEL GUERRA

Type of work: Novel
Author: Benito Pérez Galdós (1843-1920)
Type of plot: Political and religious tragedy
Time of plot: Late nineteenth century
Locale: Madrid and Toledo
First published: 1890-1891

Local color artist Pérez Galdós was author of thirty novels in addition to the forty-six in his National Episodes series: Ángel Guerra *belongs to a group of about eight that present a picture of religious faith and the results of fanaticism on Spanish life. This novel presents a philosophy of religion that resulted from the influence of a deeply religious atmosphere on an essentially realistic and modern writer. The author depicts violence and crime as curing idealism and shows the working of fate on his characters.*

Ángel Guerra is a pathological case study. It is the second-longest of Pérez Galdós' novels, and its subject matter has been compared to William James's *The Varieties of Religious Experience* (published some ten years after *Ángel Guerra*). Some critics describe *Ángel Guerra* as the last of Pérez Galdós' works that can be read with enjoyment, for it was the fruit of a spiritual crisis that had gradually been enveloping Pérez Galdós ever since he had written his masterpiece, *Fortunata and Jacinta,* in 1886-1887. *Ángel Guerra* was also written when Pérez Galdós was nearing his fiftieth birthday, he having written forty works in the preceding twenty-three years. At the time he wrote *Ángel Guerra,* Pérez Galdós feared that something was ailing Europe's middle class, and he became convinced that politics was the key to the solution of social problems, while his anticlerical sentiments of younger years surged back, along with a propensity for Christian socialism.

Ángel Guerra gives a pleasant view of pure charity, and a close-up view of one person, Ángel Guerra. The latter was seized with a vision of a better world, but died when he came face to face with the iron reality of life and the world. Angel is an agnostic at the novel's start, but then, imbued with the "holy fire" of Christian charity, he decides to invest his resources in a Brotherhood of Mercy, whose male branch he is to head, and whose female branch Leré is to head. Ángel feels that man can triumph only through love and implementation of the Sermon on the Mount—a conviction recently acquired by Pérez Galdós himself. A tolerance for human frailties, a deep spiritual charity, and Christian love are also expressed through the personality of Ángel Guerra. Having read Hegel, Schopenhauer, and many other German philosophers, Pérez Galdós had himself become convinced that poverty was man's healthiest state, a conviction also mirrored in *Ángel Guerra.*

Ángel's abnormality and frustrated dreams are thus best understood against the backdrop of Pérez Galdós' sudden spiritual evolution. Ángel's unhappy youth also supplies a vehicle for understanding his development, while Leré is so pathological that her eyes are like those of a mechanical doll. *Ángel Guerra* is often criticized for lack of humor and imagination, and for being riddled with too many neurotic types among its secondary characters. General morbidity is also supposed to be one of the novel's faults, and it has been negatively compared to Dostoevski's better works; however, the novel does leave the reader with hope even in spite of its neurotic flavor.

ANNA CHRISTIE

Type of work: Drama
Author: Eugene O'Neill (1888-1953)
Type of plot: Social realism
Time of plot: Early twentieth century
Locale: Johnny the Priest's saloon, New York City, and Provincetown harbor
First presented: 1921

Winner of the Pulitzer Prize in 1922, Anna Christie *dramatizes O'Neill's belief that man's character is his fate; Anna's destiny is controlled less by the forces of the naturalist's mechanistic universe than by her own personality and behavior.*

Although earlier critical opinion mainly interpreted *Anna Christie* in symbolic and philosophical terms, contemporary readers will inevitably seize on the play's feminist implications. In doing so, however, they will be struck by the radical inconsistency of the final act.

Throughout the first three acts, O'Neill engages in what appears to be a relentless attack on male irresponsibility and the sexual double standard. Chris's eagerness to abandon Marthy is an early indication of his essentially escapist life style. He is willing to care for Anna only to assuage his paternal guilt-feelings and to acquire the prestige which goes along with protecting a "virtuous" lady. Chris does not perceive Anna's suffering or its source. He cheerfully plans her life for her and stops his ears when she tries to tell him the truth about her past. His only redeeming quality is his consciousness of his faults, but that he continues to the end blaming "dat ole davil sea" shows his inability to change.

Mat Burke's simple charm and vitality account for Anna's attraction to him. But his domineering, egotistic nature makes him completely insensitive to her despair. Oblivious to the suffering he has caused innumerable prostitutes, he cannot see that Anna's misanthropy implicates him. His obsession with virginity is not less intense than Chris's, and both men assume they have the right to command Anna. But Mat goes much further in believing that he would be justified in killing her. The play's true climax thus comes in Act III, when Anna warns that "nobody owns me, see?—'cepting myself."

Her ultimate submission to Mat is difficult to explain, especially because it is preceded both by his threatening her life and a series of humiliating oath-takings. Since both Chris and Mat are about to abandon her, the bargain seems doubly loathsome, and Mat's promise that Anna will have a child to ease her loneliness seals the impression of his irresponsibility. We do not believe her when she says, "as for me being alone, that runs in the family, and I'll get used to it." Unfortunately, this may have been O'Neill's own way of resolving the problem.

ANNA KARÉNINA

Type of work: Novel
Author: Count Leo Tolstoy (1828-1910)
Type of plot: Social criticism
Time of plot: Nineteenth century
Locale: Russia
First published: 1875-1877

The first of the dual plots in this novel relates the tragic story of Anna Karénina, who falls in love with a handsome young officer; when he leaves her, she commits suicide by throwing herself under a train. The second plot, which centers around the happy marriage of Konstantine Levin and his young wife Kitty, is Tolstoy's vehicle for dramatizing a search for the meaning of life and a philosophy and manner of living similar to his own.

The time from when Leo Tolstoy first conceived *Anna Karénina* to the time when he finished the novel covered a span of seven years, the last four of which were spent in the actual task of writing. According to his wife Sonia's diary, the idea of writing a novel about adultery first occurred to Tolstoy in 1870. But it was not until three years later, as Tolstoy remarked in a letter to a friend, that impetus to begin work on the book was provided by Tolstoy's rereading of a fragment in Alexander Pushkin's *Tales of Belkin*. Tolstoy attributed the inspiration to a line which conjured in his imagination the scene of a reception in fashionable society—the scene manifests itself as Princess Betsy Tvershaya's party (II:7-8). However, Pushkin's influence was perhaps greater than Tolstoy realized, for in some aspects of character and appearance Anna Karénina resembles Pushkin's protagonist Zinaida Volsky. Still, Tolstoy's work on the novel proceeded at an agonizingly slow pace, leaving the writer endlessly frustrated by what he described as a "block" which hampered his progress. Thus, although the opening chapters appeared in 1875—the novel was first published in installments—the last chapters did not find their way into print until 1877. Tolstoy's perfectionism was such that he would allow nothing less than his best writing to be published, regardless of the personal anguish which the constant rewriting caused him.

The epigraph to *Anna Karénina*—a quotation from Romans 12:19: " 'Vengeance is mine: I will repay,' saith the Lord"—is suggestive of its theme, for Tolstoy, like his contemporary Fyodor Dostoevski, was deeply concerned with sin (or crime), guilt, punishment, and atonement. Moreover, the epigraph implies, along with its express prohibition of human retribution, that judgment, too, is a divine prerogative. It thus furnishes a key to Tolstoy's treatment of characters in the novel. He does not, for example, explicitly praise or condemn Anna, since such a value judgment would usurp a godly privilege. So also with other characters: Tolstoy does not evaluate; he describes. Yet it is difficult to avoid drawing some conclusions because the plot resolves around adultery, an offense with both social and theological ramifications. Still, Tolstoy maintained that his intent was to show that all of the adverse consequences of evil ultimately originated with God. In this context, then, Anna's ostracism from polite society, for instance, would have to be understood as a manifestation of God's will—an interpretation consonant with Tolstoy's mystical religious beliefs. There is no doubt that Anna has sinned, and society's punishment of her appears to confirm God's guilty verdict. Thus, no matter how extenuating the circumstances, Tolstoy seems to say, God's punishment of sinners is inexorable.

In developing this theme in *Anna Karénina,* Tolstoy minimizes the purely secular interest which society has in suppressing adultery as an act disruptive of the social order, although this aspect of the problem has been dealt with by other novelists writing about adultery. Two examples will suffice here. In *The Scarlet Letter* (1850), Nathaniel Hawthorne depicts Hester Prynne's adultery as both a crime against society and a sin against God. But while Hester admits she is a sinner, she will not concede that she is a criminal. And the spiritual strength which she derives from her admission of sinful guilt enables her to cope with her social isolation and ultimately to survive. Yet Hawthorne, despite portraying Hester in a sympathetic light, does not clearly exonerate her, for he sees value in society's standards, too. In effect, he declines to choose between the two. However, in *Madame Bovary* (1857), Gustave Flaubert presents Emma's adulteries strictly as transgressions against society; theological considerations are virtually nonexistent. Obsessed with romantic fantasies, Emma has no conception of the real-life strictures of society. Her multiple infidelities carry her deep into debt: gifts for her lovers; clothing, perfumes, and cosmetics for herself. When she is at last forced to accept the reality that she cannot pay her creditor, she is overwhelmed with guilt, remorse, despair, and the fear of discovery. She then takes arsenic and dies quickly but painfully, unable to face the punishment society is certain to exact. Flaubert thus underscores both the power and the primacy of society's norms.

These three well-known novels about adultery—*The Scarlet Letter, Madame Bovary,* and *Anna Karénina*—differ in their emphases, but their treatment of adultery is essentially similar. On the one hand, the emphasis in *The Scarlet Letter* is on the tension between Establishment values (religious and social) and individual values; in *Madame Bovary,* on the transcendence of society's values; in *Anna Karénina,* on the immanence of spiritual values and God's will. On the other hand, all three novels disapprove of adultery, although their reasons vary according to their biases as revealed through their respective emphases.

In *Anna Karénina,* Tolstoy wrote a moving story of human emotional needs conflicting with the dominant social mores of the time. And given Tolstoy's religious mysticism combined with his incipient Socialism, this elemental conflict could be resolved in no other way. For the crucial factor in the equation revolves around what is usually characterized, euphemistically, as "the Russian soul," a quality lacking in Hawthorne and Flaubert. This nearly ineffable quality amalgamates religious mysticism and nationalism into almost divine chauvinism, the pressures of which eventually drive Anna to suicide, since her sense of betrayal of moral imperatives is nonetheless acute for her having betrayed them. She is thus uniquely representative of what is called "the Russian soul." And as such, she symbolizes Tolstoy's genuinely Russian insistence upon the marrying of eternal verities with modern conditions. Thus, for this reason, many critics believe that *Anna Karénina* stands not second to but equal with *War and Peace* in Tolstoy's corpus as a profound insight into the relationship between an individual and the surrounding society.

Joanne G. Kashdan

ANNA OF THE FIVE TOWNS

Type of work: Novel
Author: Arnold Bennett (1867-1931)
Type of plot: Domestic realism
Time of plot: Late nineteenth century
Locale: Rural England
First published: 1902

This first of Bennett's novels dealing with the pottery region of the Five Towns is a novel of character rather than action. Anna's character, however, develops very little, since she is unable to alter her original nature; this is her tragedy and the book's flaw. The novel also presents Bennett's most detailed study of the repressive effects of Wesleyanism.

The story of Anna Tellwright is different from the novels dealing with the Five Towns following it. *The Old Wives' Tale* and *The Clayhanger Trilogy* are epic in nature, panoramic studies of life crammed with social and natural detail. It became Bennett's forte to continue in the vein of Trollope and provide the plenitude of the real English world. He advanced on Trollope's easygoing realism by introducing his own brand of naturalism. Life was brought into sharp focus by the "scientific eye."

Anna's pliability and deference to her miser-father are treated with compassion rather than detached judgment. In Bennett's later work his compassion for his characters tends to give way to the often belittling revelations of the "scientific eye." But even at her weakest moment, Anna is ennobled by the tragic dimension of her situation; although she realizes that she loves Willie Price, she remains true to her promise to marry Mynors. Always a child of duty, Anna cannot suddenly become a reckless and passionate girl. She cannot run away with Willie and remain herself. Hers is a tested identity fired in the realization that renunciation is her truth.

Bennett gets us to believe in the moral strength of Anna by balancing her innocence and humility with powerful examples of her honesty and courage. Despite her commitment to Mynors and her loyalty to her father, she cannot deny her deepest convictions and is unable to accept public salvation at the Methodist revival. Her tenderest feelings for Willie and his father give her the fortitude to stand up to her enraged father in the matter of the forged note. Anna, finally, is *of* the Five Towns, but she is not with them in soul.

ANNALS OF THE PARISH

Type of work: Novel
Author: John Galt (1779-1839)
Type of plot: Social chronicle
Time of plot: 1760-1810
Locale: Scotland
First published: 1821

Unfortunately overshadowed by the immense popularity of the romances of Sir Walter Scott, the fiction of John Galt was neglected both by its original readers and by later generations. In contrast to Scott's work, Galt's novel is marked by modesty and quiet simplicity, and lovingly describes humble scenes of Scottish life while it chronicles the fifty-year period which saw the onset of the Industrial Revolution.

In the tradition of Daniel Defoe's *Moll Flanders,* John Galt's *Annals of the Parish* is a fictional "autobiography," chronological in form. It is successful in conveying a diarist's immediate experience of the kind of daily living that has a way of becoming social and cultural history. Some will think it blasphemous to juxtapose Defoe's story of a thief and bawd with Galt's account of a pious clergyman, but both works share a common psychological impulse: the need of the central protagonist to combine factual objectivity, confessional in spirit, with self-justification.

Galt himself noted that his desire to write *Annals of the Parish* was sparked by Goldsmith's *The Vicar of Wakefield.* He wanted to do for Scotland what that book had done for England: to record the life of a rural. In the early planning stages of his book, Galt almost switched from minister to schoolmaster because the latter promised to be a better vehicle for transmitting rural values. But Galt finally stuck to his original concept and began writing in the summer of 1813. However, publishers discouraged him from continuing with the project, and he did not actually finish the book until 1820 when there was renewed interest in Scottish themes.

With the appearance of Micah Balwhidder, the English literary public finally had the Scottish answer to Dr. Primrose—not to mention Pastor Balwhidder's similarity to other memorable English fictional characters like Parson Adams, Uncle Toby, and Sir Roger de Coverley. Like them, Micah Balwhidder combined naïveté, ingenuousness, and occasional absurdity with common sense, tact, and kindness.

In addition to the memorable creation of Balwhidder, Galt's book is known as a rich repository of Scottish historical data: agricultural reform, industrialization, domestic economy, rural education, church affairs, and theological fashions. Modern critics find it a fault that Galt filters all the data through Balwhidder's limited intellect in such a way that we are not always sure how reliable the information is.

ANTHONY ADVERSE

Type of work: Novel
Author: Hervey Allen (1889-1949)
Type of plot: Picaresque romance
Time of plot: Late eighteenth and early nineteenth centuries
Locale: Western Europe, Africa, North America
First published: 1933

Set in Europe during the Napoleonic era, the novel follows the ramblings and rousing adventures of a soldier of fortune, Anthony Adverse. In the colorful tradition of picaresque entertainment, the story contains a wealth of incident and enjoys a multitude of settings.

A massive novel of intrigue and romance, heavily spiced with history and action, *Anthony Adverse* was immensely popular when it was first published. The characters all are larger than life, ruled by jealousies, enormous greed, and overwhelming cravings for vengeance, yet thanks to the vitality of the narrative, they never seem merely absurd. Few novels of such size move with such an unrelenting pace. As coaches and horses ceaselessly rush from one part of Europe to another, so the story catapults from one subplot to another. The author is in no hurry to tell his story, but he never risks boring the reader. Although the characters are not analyzed in depth, their motives are always clear. If the book has a flaw, perhaps it is that there is little mystery to the characters, although they are involved *in* mysteries. The obscure corners of the human personality are never explored, but the characters do not suffer from this lack; they are filled with life, and are both amusing and memorable. Don Luis, Faith, and Mr. Bonnyfeather are old-fashioned, Dickensian characters, carefully formed of "characteristics" rather than allowed to develop according to the psychological insights of the author.

Nearly one hundred pages pass before the hero of this picaresque novel makes his appearance as a baby, but the scene is set for the intrigues which follow. The novel is intricately constructed, with characters reappearing and long-hidden secrets suddenly changing the course of the action. This attempt to create a modern *Tom Jones* is not entirely unsuccessful. The difficulty is that this book does not speak for its time as Fielding's book did for its time. Ultimately, *Anthony Adverse* is no more than a superior entertainment, well-crafted and enjoyable, but making no statement and a part of no literary tradition.

The precocious and lusty personality of Anthony is the finest part of the book. His spirit of adventure, his determination and cleverness win the reader's admiration, and his vitality holds the reader's interest. As with *Tom Jones,* the hero's destiny is a secret which can be discovered only by unraveling certain clues; and as with Fielding's protagonist, Anthony does not let himself be inhibited by his lack of definite origins. If the book as a whole is less than the sum of its parts, it is not Anthony's fault; he comes close to being a major literary figure. Angela is perhaps the most intriguing character in the book, and one can easily imagine her rising to become Napoleon's mistress. More of her inner life and emotions are revealed than those of any other character.

ANTIGONE

Type of work: Drama
Author: Sophocles (495?-406 B.C.)
Type of plot: Classical tragedy
Time of plot: Remote antiquity
Locale: The city of Thebes
First presented: 441 B.C.

This play was so successful with its original Athenian audience that they rewarded the playwright with a generalship in the war against Samos. The tragedy in the play arises from the age-old conflict between individual moral responsibility (the necessity of proper burial) and the demands of the State (the obedience owed to Creon as the legitimate ruler).

Antigone is one of the finest, most moving tragedies ever written. It was very successful when it was first produced in 441 B.C., and tradition says that Sophocles was made an Athenian general in the war against Samos because of it. Modern audiences, too, find this play meaningful, particularly in the conflict between individual conscience and the State policy. But the fundamental issue of the play goes deeper than that conflict. It probes the nature of suffering, and finds in it a universal condition, one that exists at the very heart of the human experience.

Sophocles did not share Aeschylus' view that man learns by pain, or the Christian idea that we are purified by agony. Both opinions are ultimately optimistic because they are based on hope in some future vindication of our misery. But Sophocles faced the problem of pain without hope, as an essential fact of life that no one could escape. With this outlook he was keenly attuned to both the sadness and the tragedy inherent in living.

Ironically, Sophocles himself enjoyed the most fortunate life possible to a Greek. His life was crowned with honors from early manhood on to the age of ninety, when he died. He was a skilled athlete, he achieved public position. But most important, he had an extremely creative and successful dramatic career, writing more than one hundred and twenty plays, ninety-six of which were awarded first place in the Athenian drama competitions. He was the foremost tragedian in an age of magnificent literary, artistic, and political genius—Periclean Athens. Moreover, he won a lasting reputation as one of the supreme playwrights of all time. *Antigone,* written when Sophocles was in his fifties, affords a penetrating look at his dramatic prowess.

The meaning of this play is to be found in the antithesis between Antigone and her uncle Creon. The issue of burying Polynices depends on a grasp of Greek ideas about death. An unburied body meant a soul condemned to torment. It was the profound obligation of the family, therefore, to see that a body was properly inhumed. This was more than a matter of family loyalty, it was an act of piety demanded by the gods. Antigone undertakes that obligation even though it means treason to the State, the rejection of her only sister Ismene, the renunciation of her fiancé, and her own death. She is absolutely uncompromising about it, knowing all the consequences beforehand. As it turns out, she is justified. But we do not know this until Tiresias appears and then it is too late to matter, for she has hanged herself.

Creon also has a valid stand. The traitor Polynices should be punished in death. A conscientious ruler, he is concerned about loyalty to the State. But in his position as king he confuses his own will with the good of Thebes. In pursuing his edict, which says that anyone who buries Polynices will be put to death, he changes from a good king into a tyrant. His vanity is involved: he will not be put in the wrong by a young woman or his son in front of the chorus of Theban elders. His flaw lies in his stubborn, self-righteous inflexibility when the tide of evidence turns against him. He angrily maintains his stand in the face of Antigone's martyrdom, his son's pleading, the sympathy of the townspeople with Antigone, and Tiresias' warnings. He only relents because of the fear he feels after Tiresias has prophesied doom for his family and for the city. But, again, his penitence comes too late to save himself.

However, it is wrong to see Antigone as a perfect heroine or Creon as a willing malefactor. The same passion that goes into Antigone's heroic treason in burying her brother makes her unjustly cruel to her gentle sister Ismene; and she has no thought whatever for Haemon, her fiancé. She is right, but she is also unbearably self-righteous. The only time we feel sympathy for her is when she laments that she will never have a husband or a child, but she made that choice freely and passionately. As far as character goes, there is no difference whatever between Antigone's self-righteousness and Creon's. Both are hard and unyielding.

The difference between the two lies in the principle by which they live. Antigone chooses to serve the gods, or divine law, while Creon makes the State his top priority. Both serve their principle with all the force of their being. But because Creon has chosen the lesser law, and because the State as he conceives it is indistinguishable from his own ego, he must bow in the end to the gods, and they crush him. Ironically, he faces the same suffering he meted out to Antigone. Just as he deprived her of the chance to have a husband and child, so he is bereft of his wife and son.

Creon's fate is sad because he blundered into it unwittingly, through stubbornly upholding a limited idea. The man lacked wisdom. Yet Antigone's death is tragic because she voluntarily accepted it as the consequence of her heroism. For all her hardness, there is something truly grand and edifying in her fate. When suffering is a part of every man's condition, there is a vast difference in how one takes it. A man can fumble into it through ignorance and flaws of character, as Creon does, which makes him merely pathetic. This is the normal human lot. Or a person can freely choose suffering with open eyes by taking on a divine obligation in spite of all obstacles. This way is intense and tragic, but in the end it is the only path that can enlarge our humanity. The greatness of *Antigone* lies in the clarity, the poignance, and the integrity with which Sophocles presented these two possibilities.

James Weigel, Jr.

THE ANTIQUARY

Type of work: Novel
Author: Sir Walter Scott (1771-1832)
Type of plot: Domestic romance
Time of plot: Late eighteenth century
Locale: Scotland
First published: 1816

A member of the Waverley group, this novel has the setting most nearly contemporary to the author's own time. A novel of manners as well as a romance, Scott admitted that when necessary, he sacrificed plot to the portrayal of customs and manners; perhaps this explains why The Antiquary *is not one of the most popular novels in the Scott canon.*

This, the third novel in the Waverley series, published in 1816, met with unprecedented sales. Scott himself remarked that "it has been more fortunate than any of them . . . for six thousand went off in the first six days. . . ." It reached a fifth edition in 1818 and was translated during ensuing years into at least seven languages.

In spite of its being a potpourri of Gothic, supernatural escapades among abbey ruins at night, scheming tricks of a charlatan magician, romantic rescue up sheer cliffs from a wild and sudden high tide, the usual genteel and static hero and heroine falling at the end into marriage as well as vast inherited wealth, the novel succeeded for other, more significant reasons.

Its true value is based upon the scenes of village life, the real lower-class people of Scotland and their colorful dialogue. These embody the wit and pathos of the novel, a sane balance to unreal elements in which the upper-class characters are involved. The links between the two levels of the tale are the Antiquary, Jonathan Oldbuck of Monkbarns (who has much of Scott's interests and learning), and the wandering beggar Edie Ochiltree. The two move from fishing village and country people back and forth to the nobility and their estates, keeping the book from splitting literally into two different novels.

Scott drew the background of *The Antiquary* from recent history: religious opposition of Catholics and Covenanters and political conflict between England and France. However, these issues form only a backdrop and do not enter seriously into the suspense and tension of the novel.

Lively scenes like that in the Fairport post office when the village gossips speculate about the newly arrived mail, or truly pathetic ones such as the Mucklebackit family's gathering in their cottage after their son Steenie's drowning, are remarkable because of their vividness. These scenes are the core of the novel: its color and poetry. Perhaps these lower-class characters in their milieu are more alive because Scott apparently drew them from individuals he had known from boyhood and sketched the topography from areas with which he had long been familiar.

The humor of *The Antiquary* ranges from sardonic comment to open slapstick. Although they aid the suspense, even the highly improbable events taking place among the lackluster protagonists cannot dim the prevailing comic atmosphere. In this penetrating and good-humored study of manners, Scott is at his best; he handles the Scots dialogue with accuracy and spice. His common characters come alive and express themselves simply but with moving emotion.

One can ignore the usual contrived plot; action and meaning belong to old Elspeth crooning her eerie ballads, Edie Ochiltree maintaining his pride and religious feeling though merely an "auld" beggar, Maggie haggling with Monkbarns over the price of fish, and Mucklebackit senior trying to cope with his grief. This is a novel of lower-class manners as Scott declared it to be; as such it succeeds.

ANTONY AND CLEOPATRA

Type of work: Drama
Author: William Shakespeare (1564-1616)
Type of plot: Romantic tragedy
Time of plot: About 30 B.C.
Locale: Egypt and various parts of the Roman Empire
First presented: 1606-1607

Antony and Cleopatra *is the tragedy of a man destined to rule the world who instead brings himself to ruin through capitulation to desires of the flesh; deserted by friends and subjects, he is forced to seek the escape of ignoble suicide. Shakespeare's source for the play was Sir Thomas North's translation of Plutarch's* Lives. *It is interesting to note that for many years Dryden's version of the story,* All for Love, *was the more frequently performed of the two plays.*

In *Antony and Cleopatra* Shakespeare has not bound himself with the Aristotelian unities. He moves swiftly across the whole of the civilized world with a panorama of scenes and characters; he creates a majestic expanse suitable to the broad significance of the tragedy. The play is Shakespeare's longest and is broken up into small units, which intensify the impression of rapid movement. Written immediately after the four great tragedies, it rivals them in tragic effect even though it has no plot which Aristotle would recognize. The story is taken from North's translation of Plutarch, but is refashioned into a complex rendering of a corruption which ennobles as it destroys. It may lack the poignantly representative character of the great tragedies, but it extends its significance by taking the whole world for its canvas.

As a standard tragic figure, Antony leaves much to be desired. His actions are little more than a series of vacillations between commitment to a set of responsibilities, which are his by virtue of his person and his office, and submission to the overpowering passion which repeatedly draws him back to the fatal influence of Cleopatra. His nobility is of an odd sort. He commands respect and admiration as one of the two omnipotent rulers of the world, but we are told of his greatness; we do not see it represented in his actions. Antony travels, but he does not really do anything until his suicide—and he does not even do that very efficiently. His nobility, attested to by his past deeds and his association with the glories of Rome, is a pre-condition of which we are frequently reminded, but it is not something earned within the play.

Antony has another impediment to tragic stature: he is somewhat too intelligent and aware of what he is doing. Although it is true that he behaves irresponsibly, the fact remains, as Mark Van Doren has noted, that he lives "in the full light of accepted illusion." There is no duping of the hero: Cleopatra is not Antony's Iago. Nor is there any self-deception; Antony does not cheer himself up by pretending that their love is anything more than it is.

Yet, what their love is is sufficiently great to endow Antony with whatever nobility he salvages in the play. It is not simply that he is a hero brought to disgrace by lust, although that much is true. Viewed from another angle, he is a hero set free from the limits of heroism by a love which frees him from a commitment to honor for a commitment to life. Of course, his liberation is also his humiliation and destruction because he is a Roman hero of great power and historical significance. Both noble and depraved, both consequential and trivial, Antony finds new greatness in the intense passion which simultaneously lays him low.

Cleopatra is an equally complex character, but her complexity is less the result of paradox than of infinite variation. Throughout the first four acts she lies, poses, cajoles, and entices, ringing manifold changes on her powers to attract. Yet, she is not a coarse temptress, not a personification of evil loosed upon a helpless victim. As her behavior in the last act reminds us, she is also an empress, whose dignity should be recalled throughout her machinations. For Cleopatra too is swept along by overwhelming passion. She is not only a proud queen and conniving seducer, but a sincere and passionate lover. Despite her tarnished past, her plottings in *Antony and Cleopatra* are given the dignity of underlying love. Like Antony, she is not the sort of character who challenges the universe and transcends personal destruction. Rather, her dignity lies somewhere beyond, or outside of, traditional heroism.

The complexity of Cleopatra is most apparent in the motivation for her suicide. Certainly one motive is the desire to avoid the humiliation of being led in a triumph through Rome by the victorious Octavius Caesar. But if that were all, then she would be nothing more than an egoistic conniver. However, she is also motivated by her sincere unwillingness to survive Antony. The two motives become intertwined since the humiliation of slavery would also extend to Antony and taint his reputation because his failures left her vulnerable. This mixture of motives is a model of the way in which the two lovers are simultaneously the undoing and the salvation of each other. Their mutual destruction springs from the same love that provides both with their anti-heroic greatness. Love is lower than honor in the Roman world, but it can generate an intensity which makes heroism irrelevant. Antony is too intelligent, Cleopatra is too witty, and their love is too intricate for ordinary tragedy.

The structure of the plot also departs from the tragic norm. There is almost none of the complication and unraveling which we expect in tragedy. Rather, the action moves in fits and starts through the forty-two scenes of the play. These brief segments appear to be a series of unequal waves, which sweep over the characters and finally carry them to destruction. The plethora of scenes and the rapid shifting of locations create a jerky dramatic movement. Although the action of the play must extend over a long period of time, the quick succession of scenes suggests an unsteady hurtling towards a conclusion.

The helter-skelter quality is reinforced by the language of the play. Few speeches are long and there are many abrupt exchanges. There are many quick, wide-ranging allusions. Finally, Shakespeare uses feminine endings and spills the sense over the ends of lines in a metrical reflection of the nervous vitality of the play. Thus, plot and language spread the drama over the whole world and hasten its conclusion in order to maximize the tensions of a heroic "world well lost" for love.

Edward E. Foster

THE APOSTLE

Type of work: Novel
Author: Sholem Asch (1880-1957)
Type of plot: Religious chronicle
Time of plot: Shortly after the Crucifixion
Locale: The Roman Empire
First published: 1943

A chronicle of the lives of the two great apostles, Peter and Paul, this novel adheres faithfully to the history of the period; a sympathetic account, the novel offers vivid pictures of the struggles of Christians in the difficult time following the Crucifixion.

The Apostle is the story of Saul of Tarshish, the man who heard a voice while traveling the road to Damascus, and whose whole life was changed as a result. He gave up former ideals, following instead the new religion of the Messiah, and suffering shipwreck, hunger, scourging, imprisonment, and finally death as a result of his faith. The novel is the story of one man's search for the meaning of life, told against the larger backdrop of the story of all the early Christians in their struggles after the crucifixion. As a Jew steeped in the writings of the Old Testament from his youth, Sholem Asch was well qualified to write this powerful and beautiful story. He clearly and vividly traces the Jewish heritage of the Christian faith and shows how the fulfillment of the law of Moses links the Christian and the Jew inextricably.

The characterizations in the novel, especially those of Peter and Paul, are clearly and movingly drawn. Peter—gentle, humble, and devoted—is in sharp contrast to Paul—intense, proud, and overbearing; yet the two men are brothers in their faith in Jesus and their desire to spread His word in all parts of the Roman empire. Paul is a difficult personality to identify with— he is fanatical and abrasive by nature; but in the years following his conversion he becomes more loving and compassionate, as he relinquishes all claim to the pleasures of this life in order to preach the redemptive spirit of love to the outcast gentiles. Beyond telling the stories of individuals like Peter and Paul, however, Asch chronicles the historic struggle for dominance between the Pharisees, who believed in the resurrection of the soul and a life after death, and the High Priests, or Saducees, who believed only in this life.

In addition to his true-to-life characterizations and his faithful yet vivid rendering into fiction of historical information, Asch is more than competent as a descriptive writer; he creates settings which bring the story alive for the reader. One example is the memorable scene of Paul's landing in Antioch, an idyllic place where oleanders nod gently in the breeze, cypress and laurel trees perfume the air, and meadows thick with poppies, violets, jasmine, and lilies glow triumphantly in the sun. Yet it is a tainted Eden, as Paul discovers when he encounters scenes such as the procession of madly dancing naked priests who slash their own wrists with their teeth to show their devotion to Apolens, the fish-goddess. All this Asch renders with great skill and descriptive power.

No one can read *The Apostle* without learning a great deal about the Judeo-Christian heritage of Western civilization; no reader will finish the novel untouched by the devotion and zealous energy which one man called forth in the hearts of so many people.

THE APPLE OF THE EYE

Type of work: Novel
Author: Glenway Wescott (1901-   )
Type of plot: Regional romance
Time of plot: Twentieth century
Locale: Rural Wisconsin
First published: 1924

In this novel of a youth and his newly forming relationships, Wescott questions the traditional religious values concerning sex and marriage by contrasting them to the natural spontaneity and goodness of Hannah Madoc's behavior.

The Apple of the Eye is a novel concerned with sexuality and the impact of sexuality on human relationships and religious values. It is a novel written by a young man—filled with lyrical passages and obsessed with the emergence and demands of sex.

The novel is organized in three interrelated sections. The first, devoted to Hannah Madoc, is by far the most successful. The later sections, more philosophical and autobiographical, filled with long, abstract conversations, are less impressive.

The central question posed by the novel is whether a satisfactory and happy life can be achieved within the boundaries of conventional relationships. The story of Hannah Madoc demonstrates that there are a variety of fulfilling lives. She is a woman who violates the conventions and has the courage to defend herself; but at the same time she pays a rather stiff penalty for her passion.

The story of Rosalia and Mike elaborates this idea. Although Dan is initially taken completely by Mike's hedonism, Rosalia's death proves that living for the body alone is dangerous, even fatal. Wescott stresses this point in his description of Rosalia's decomposed body. Its ugliness has a tremendous moral impact on Dan. Through Dan's evaluation of his own feelings, Wescott suggests that Mike's hedonism and Mrs. Strane's puritanism are each one-sided. Neither offers, by itself, a system of values which is ultimately workable.

The Apple of the Eye does not, finally, offer a system of its own to replace these alternatives. But, like other American novels of the 1920's, it asks significant questions. In an era when old values were being seriously questioned, writers such as Wescott attempted to explore the implications of different systems of values. It was an effort to search for standards by which people could conduct themselves, and which would enable Americans to lead fulfilling lives. This effort, in the case of The Apple of the Eye, is certainly worthwhile.

APPOINTMENT IN SAMARRA

Type of work: Novel
Author: John O'Hara (1905-1970)
Type of plot: Naturalism
Time of plot: 1930
Locale: Pennsylvania
First published: 1934

Dealing with prohibition, bootlegging, and easy morals, this novel recalls the style of Fitzgerald and the character analysis of Sinclair Lewis. Its sensationalism is only in subject matter, however; Appointment in Samarra *is a moral tale in which people's lives, as the title implies, often lead to no moral or meaningful end.*

John O'Hara was supreme in the art and craft of the short story. Perhaps because of his newspaper background, he was able to condense a tale to its fundamentals and produce a tightly crafted and powerful short fiction. With his ear for speech and eye for effect, he was able to bring to life in two or three sentences a character from nearly any walk of life. This gift also gave his novels the primary value that they possess, and perhaps this is especially true of his first novel, *Appointment in Samarra*.

One of O'Hara's shortest and best-structured novels, *Appointment in Samarra* is the story of *hubris* in a modern setting. It takes place in 1930, after the crash of 1929 but before people understood just how bad the Depression was to become. The hero of the novel, Julian English, has status but destroys himself by not living up to it. Julian has two problems: people and alcohol, but both are revealed to be part of his own inner problems which ultimately ruin him. There is much discussion in the book of who "belongs" and who does not, of which clubs count in Gibbsville, and what prep schools and colleges matter, and where one should be seen, or not be seen. The laborer, mobster, and society man all think constantly about how they fit into the social ladder. Julian English thinks about it too much.

There is presented in the novel an accurate picture of a broad cross section of Gibbsville society. With the observations of the different kinds of people, from the secretary in the automobile agency to the ex-convict working for the gangland boss to the society matron, O'Hara achieved a new kind of fictional reporting, in the best sense of the term. The humor and fast pace of the novel and the clean, sure style give it a surface slickness which is almost misleading, for it is not a superficial novel. There is depth behind the meretricious glitter and hard-boiled sensual flavor. The book's racy language and sexual candor continued the pathbreaking trend begun only a short time before by Hemingway. The characters are concerned with superficialities, but that does not make them superficial characters. O'Hara is able to capture, especially in his dialogue, the nuances of tone which reveal the hidden depths of his many characters.

Julian English, the central figure of the novel, is also the most complex and interesting of the characters. Some individuals seem to burn with a compulsion to self-destruction; Julian English is one of these people. Yet, however drunk he gets, part of his mind warns him when he is about to do something dangerous. Like many intelligent people, he observes himself as he moves through life. But he recklessly plunges ahead, throwing the drink in Harry Reilly's face, dancing and going out to the car with Helene Holman at the roadhouse, getting deliberately drunk so that he won't care what happens. (By the time he quarrels with Froggy Ogden at the club and fights with the lawyers in the dining room, he has given up all hope—he is as contemptuous of himself as he is of them. Rational action has ceased to have any meaning for him.) Julian English is a direct forerunner of the existential heroes of Sartre and Camus a decade later—who were influenced by O'Hara and Hemingway and other writers of the American "hard-boiled" school of writing—as he toys with his fate with an almost objective curiosity. "If I do this," he seems to think, "will I get away with it?" Of course, he knows somewhere deep inside of him that he will not "get away" with it, that nobody ever gets away with anything. He is filled with "tremendous excitement" when he realizes that "he is in for it." Perhaps, as he contemplates his "unknown, well-deserved punishment" he is even slightly masochistic in his longing for pain and destruction.

Julian English's fatalism, and the fatalism that permeates the novel (and gives it its title), seems to be influenced in part by the novels and stories of Hemingway and Fitzgerald, but O'Hara, while lacking the poetic vision and poetic style of Fitzgerald also avoids the hard-boiled pose of Hemingway, and adds a poignant ruthlessness of his own. With economy and artistry, O'Hara draws the painful and engrossing portrait of a complex and fascinating and doomed individual.

An inevitable progression, gaining in momentum like a ball rolling down a steep hill, takes over Julian English's fate, until it would take a miracle to halt the inevitable doom that waits for him at the end. And, as Julian knows, miracles do not happen for people such as he. His death is early foreshadowed by the suicide of his grandfather. His own father frequently expresses fears that Julian's character is as weak as that of his grandfather; Julian, himself, comes to believe in his defective character, and that he is doomed by it. This belief numbs him and renders him helpless before the onrush of events.

This novel rises above O'Hara's other long works of fiction because it makes more of an attempt to deal with significant ideas and values. Often, his technique of recording action with the detachment of a photographer fails to establish a moral frame of reference. The reader does not know what the author's attitude toward the characters and events is. But the character of Julian English lifts *Appointment in Samarra* above the author's other novels.

O'Hara always surrounds his dramatic action with great pieces of historical exposition and discussion and long descriptions of styles of the period, the fashions, the horses and clubs, the automobiles and other transitory items that date a moment in history. In *Appointment in Samarra* the precise documentation of social strata lends vividness and realism to the story. O'Hara's accuracy with labels and styles had not yet become the excessive mannerism which weighted down his later novels.

O'Hara was born in 1905 in Pottsville, Pennsylvania, the prototype of the Gibbsville of many of his novels and stories. He had a varied career in journalism, as a reporter, critic, and social commentator; later, after his first success as a writer, he became a screenwriter, and used much of his Hollywood experience in his fiction. His late work added little to his stature, but his early novels and his stories have shown a remarkable durability.

Bruce D. Reeves

THE ARABIAN NIGHTS' ENTERTAINMENTS
(SELECTIONS)

Type of work: Tales
Author: Unknown
Type of plots: Adventure romances
Time of plots: The legendary past
Locale: India, China, Persia, Arabia
First transcribed: Fifteenth century

This group of tales, more properly called The Thousand and One Nights, *was passed down by word of mouth in many lands throughout the East and was eventually formalized and standardized by bazaar storytellers. Most scholars believe that the collection took its present form in Cairo in the fifteenth century; it was introduced to the West in Antoine Gallad's 1704 translation published in Paris. The stories often have striking parallels to Biblical tales and incidents from the* Iliad *and the* Odyssey.

These selected tales are from a collection of Arabic stories sometimes referred to by the original title, *The Book of the Thousand Nights and One Night*. The older title refers to the implied dramatic situation in which Scheherazade tells a story (or part of one) to Shahriar every night for the famous number of nights in order to forestall her death on the following morning. The tales are embedded in a frame-story, in the tradition of Boccaccio's *Decameron* and Chaucer's *Canterbury Tales*. Like the *Canterbury Tales,* the *Arabian Nights* includes some tales which are enriched by the situation of their framework.

If we keep in mind Shahriar's repeated vow to kill his wife in the morning, there is much more of a point to one of Scheherazade's first tales to her new husband and king. "The History of the Fisherman and the Genie" involves another powerful character, the genie, who has similarly vowed to kill. In both cases, the vow would involve the killing of one who has performed an act of charity or of love toward the avowed killer: in the fisherman's case, freeing the genie, and in Scheherazade's case marrying the king. When the fisherman chastises the rebottled genie, predicting Allah's certain vengeance upon him for killing, the humble man is in fact a mask through which Scheherazade is speaking to Shahriar.

In "The History of the Young King of the Black Isles," other details of the framework are alluded to. It will be remembered that Shahriar's reason for his vow is rooted in his painful experience with his unfaithful wife, whom he discovered to be engaged in adultery with a black slave. The fact that his brother's case paralleled his would indicate that the societies in which this book took form were preoccupied with a sense of inadequacy when placed in sexual competition with blacks.

This racial, psycho-sexual problem amounts to the thematic focus of the story. The Young King has likewise discovered his wife's infidelity and is greatly disturbed at her fiercely expressed preference for her black lover. Throughout the story, black and white are pointedly juxtaposed. The king is himself described as extremely pale with only the smallest touch of black, a mole. His palace is black, perhaps an omen of his catastrophe. On the first two occasions of the spoiled fish (they are blackened), a fair lady comes out of the wall to upset the pan; on the third occasion it is a black giant who performs the same act. The Young King's being turned to stone below the waist is part of the allegory signifying his impotence upon having his male ego destroyed by his wife's preference for the slave. The sympathy and vengeance provided by the Sultan are obviously designed to soothe Shahriar even further.

With "The History of Sindbad the Sailor," a smaller frame-story within the larger, we come to the end of selections which contain pointed allusions to Shahriar's life and problems. All that can be said of the remaining selections' relationship to the framework is that they contain within their allegorical forms a wisdom about the ways of the world which at one and the same time accords with Scheherazade's great learning, and would no doubt impress Shahriar so much as to purge him of his unfortunate vision of all women as faithless and blind in their lust.

Sindbad, a wealthy man, tells his seven tales to a poor porter of the same name. The purpose of telling the tales is to justify the wealth of the rich Sindbad to the envious poor Sindbad. In each story, the wealth is justified by a different example of perils endured by the storyteller. Each of the seven stories follows a narrative pattern in which Sindbad (1) sets out to sea to make money, (2) loses everything in a catastrophe, (3) undergoes a frightening experience (usually underground), (4) escapes by means of his wits (5) with far greater riches than would ever have been possible by ordinary trading. The most frightening part of each episode is invariably a close brush with death for Sindbad, and is recognizably a descent into the mythic world of the dead. Sindbad returns from each descent with treasures commensurate with the risks he has taken.

In "The History of Prince Ahmed," we meet with the now-familiar motif of trials undergone for the hand of a princess. In this case, however, there are two princesses, one mortal and one faerie. Ahmed and his brothers vie for the mortal princess, unaware of the faerie princess' love for Ahmed and of her having planned every detail of their adventures. The allegory involves Ahmed's being led unwittingly (and unwillingly) past the mortal princess and inexorably to the faerie princess (who is more beautiful and wise in the extreme). The story points to the superiority of spiritual riches over material wealth. The Sultan is depicted as foolish (and so deserving of his ultimate overthrow) when he ignores the superiority of Ahmed's magic apple, when he disqualifies Ahmed's archery for his arrow's being unrecoverable by ordinary mortal means, and when he demands material wealth of Ahmed.

"The History of Ali Baba and the Forty Thieves" depicts Ali Baba as a man who prospers through his lack of greed. He is contrasted with his brother Cassim in this; Cassim apparently married for money, while Ali Baba married a poor woman and was a woodcutter. When Ali Baba learns the magic formula for opening the door to wealth, he takes only as much as would not be missed. Cassim's greed, by contrast, causes him to become so excited by the wealth that he forgets the magic word and is killed. It is significant that Cassim, when he is trapped in the cave, has the entire treasure and, having it, has death along with it. When the threat of death for Ali Baba is resolved with the death of the thieves, the hero draws so temperately upon his secret cache that it supports his family for many generations. (The fact that Ali Baba's life and fortunes are preserved by a clever woman, Morgiana, would not be lost on Shahriar.)

This story is another example of riches obtained by a successful descent into the underworld, as is the next, "The History of Aladdin, or the Wonderful Lamp." Aladdin is another *naif,* not suspecting the great material value of the gold and silver trays, considering the food they had carried to be of the utmost importance. This sort of naïveté is of course the stuff of which wisdom is made, making him truly worthy of the Sultan's daughter and of the powerful lamp.

It is helpful in understanding and enjoying *The Arabian Nights' Entertainments* to keep in mind the parallel symbolism of wealth, power, and beautiful women: all are symbolic of spiritual fulfillment. The omnipresence of the three in this book is one clear indication of the work's purpose: to teach a moral lesson as well as to entertain. It is a storehouse of wisdom couched in the terms all cultures know best, the terms of sight, smell, and touch, and of the delightful forms those sensations take in the imagination.

John J. Brugaletta

THE ARBITRATION

Type of work: Drama
Author: Menander (342-291 B.C.)
Type of plot: Comedy of manners
Time of plot: Fourth century B.C.
Locale: A suburb of Athens
First presented: c. 310 B.C.

Whereas Greek comedy in the age of Aristophanes utilized the formal chorus and usually contained scenes of intervention by the gods, the New Comedy—of which Menander's works were the most numerous and representative—was characterized by a less formal structure which dispensed with both chorus and gods and dealt instead with the domestic problems of ordinary mortals. Arbitration contains such familiar stock types, for example, as the harsh father, the knavish slave, and the servant girl with a heart of gold.

If Aristophanes was the greatest writer of the Old Comedy in fifth century Athens, Menander was certainly the finest practitioner of the New Comedy that flourished there a century later. The difference between those two kinds of theater is vast. The bawdiness and the fearless political and personal satire had given way, in the face of Macedonian military might, to the more timid and bourgeois comedy of manners, in which the characters are stock types repeated over and over. The poetic meters are simpler, and the language more colloquial. The chorus has been cut to a bare minimum, usually appearing as a band of revelers bearing no relation to the plot, and whose songs are generally omitted from the manuscripts. New Comedy found its subject matter in domestic life and the complications of romance. It exploited sentiment, was given to moralizing, and used complex and improbable plots. Basically it lacked the exuberant vigor that marked the Old Comedy.

This whole development may be due, at least in part, to the fact that New Comedy was churned out at a prodigious rate. Menander himself was credited with writing more than a hundred plays, although he was not much older than fifty when he died. Dramatists vied with one another to give their plots ingenious twists as they reworked the same subject matter and the same stereotyped characters. Menander managed to individualize his characters more than his contemporaries, and he gained an international reputation in his lifetime. The Roman playwrights Plautus and Terence adapted Menander's comedies to suit Latin audiences. Through them Menander became the precursor of later Western drama and a direct ancestor of Shakespeare and Molière.

Menander's own predecessor was Euripides, the tragedian. Euripides dealt with the theme of the foundling in *Ion* and possibly other plays, a theme which would form a substantial part of the New Comedy. Euripides also handled romantic material that New Comedy writers adapted to their purpose.

And he treated commonplace people in a way that suggested new developments in the theater. Further, Euripides developed a near-colloquial diction that anticipated the later comedy. However, the later dramatists eliminated the divine interventions that Euripides had staged, to concentrate on the element of coincidence in the resolution of human problems. It seems altogether fitting that Menander was buried beside Euripides.

The Arbitration is one of two plays by Menander to have survived nearly intact. Of the rest we have merely fragments and snippets. And we would have lacked most of this if papyrus manuscripts had not been found late in the nineteenth century in Egypt. Fortunately we know the names of eighty of his plays and can judge the extent to which the Roman dramatists borrowed from him.

In this play Menander blends two common themes of New Comedy writing, those of the frustrated romance and of the foundling. He makes skillful use of dramatic irony by manipulating the plot so that the audience is fully aware of a situation to which the characters must grope, bit by bit, in understanding. It is only when the characters grasp what we already know that the solution to the problem occurs. So the suspense lies in the author's bag of tricks to delay the solution, to prolong it as tautly as possible. We are logically led into a maze where the end is what was stated in the Prologue, and where a lot of cleverness has been spent in making the maze as complex as possible. In *The Arbitration* we know that Charisius is the sole cause of the misery through which he and his wife Pamphila are going. We do not have the end of the play, but it is certain that Charisius must recognize his guilt and beg Pamphila's forgiveness before the comedy can end.

If the plot is more or less a pat formula, the characters are something more than pure types. Of course they conform to stage patterns—Smicrines (Small) being the tight-fisted father; Habrotonon (Pretty Thing) being the mistress with the heart of gold; Onesimus being the rascally servant; Pamphila (Wholly Lovable) being the forgiving wife; and so on. But they transcend their patterns in the natural way they react to their circumstances. Habrotonon's greatest desire is to gain her liberty, for which she resorts to deception, but when the welfare of a helpless infant is at stake, she is willing to expose her deception and sacrifice her liberty. This sacrfice is not made with any great theatrical flourish, but rather as an intrinsic part of her character. Menander even takes pains to individualize Davus the goatherd and Syriscus the charcoal-burner in the arbitration scene, where Smicrines unwittingly judges the fate of his own grandson.

With this play we are in a world in which commoners are drawn with dignity, in which slavery is altogether undesirable, and in which the most unlikely people might turn out to have respectable backgrounds. This is a sharp change from the aristocratic outlook of earlier Greek drama. The theme of the foundling, here developed in Pamphila's infant and in Habrotonon, mirrors a democratic view of society, not so much in politics but in morality. It stresses that everyone, regardless of their social position, has a right to be treated with consideration. Even though Menander had privileges of birth, wealth, and fame he subscribed to this outlook wholeheartedly, and *The Arbitration* is illuminated by it.

James Weigel, Jr.

ARCADIA

Type of work: Novel
Author: Sir Philip Sidney (1554-1586)
Type of plot: Pastoral romance
Time of plot: Classical antiquity
Locale: Arcadia, in Greece
First published: 1590

Significant in the development of the English novel, this light pastoral tale served as a bridge between the delicately written Italian romances and the more sturdy prose of the Elizabethans. The four eclogues and occasional passages of poetry are carry-overs from earlier continental romances; but the relatively skillful plot and the philosophical asides of the author pointed the way toward a more serious and complex genre to follow.

The study of Sidney's *Arcadia* leads to the consideration of a number of important biographical, literary, historical, and critical issues. A difficult work—in all its variants—for the contemporary reader, it nevertheless raises important psychological and moral questions.

A serious man who thought deeply about serious matters, Sidney led a short, complicated life. He was godson of a king, nephew to four earls, brother of an earl, uncle to three earls, grandson of a duke, and a special favorite of the queen and other powerful figures. He was endowed with a pleasing personality and a fine intellect. He received schooling at Oxford and on the Continent, and was tutored by the remarkable scholar Hubert Languet. But he died in his early thirties with much promise unfulfilled, and was mourned by the most influential men and women of his day.

The connection between Sidney's life and his work, as between the life and work of any important artist, must remain speculative to a degree. But some important links can be discerned. Sidney's connections and status allowed him the freedom to develop his talents. He was influenced by the medieval courtly love tradition and this led him to consider, while in the enviable environment of the court itself, the morality of human emotions, especially that of love, as a prime human concern. At the same time, his education permitted him access to the romances of later Greek civilization. Consequently, he was neither too burdened with official duties to take up the pen, nor so absorbed in the life of the court as to lose himself in its endless, petty intrigues. In short, the depth of his interests, the breadth of his literary background, the range of his activities as poet, soldier, and statesman, and the vigor of his expression mark him as a sort of exemplary figure of the English literary Renaissance.

Sidney became involved in two literary circles. One that included Edmund Spenser and Edward Dyer, met at Leicester House in London during 1579 and 1580. The other group gathered at the home of his sister Mary, the

Countess of Pembroke. If the Leicester group were more inclined to the romantic, that which collected at his sister's country estate was neoclassic in orientation, more concerned with the rules of literature than its reach, and more taken with the laws governing its dimensions than with love scenes in faraway lands. But it was at his sister's house (where he retreated after losing favor with the court) and in a climate rather uncongenial for literary romance that Sidney composed *Arcadia*. He wrote it, he said, for the entertainment of his sister. Arcadia, however, is more than mere entertainment.

But before evaluating the worth of *Arcadia,* there is a choice of texts to be made. Much scholarly debate, over many years, has centered on the textual problems of *Arcadia*. But the discussion can be organized around two points: the establishment of the various texts and the value that can be attributed to each.

There are actually three versions of *Arcadia*: the original, called "old" *Arcadia,* probably written in 1580; the "new" *Arcadia* which is Sidney's incomplete revision of the "old" *Arcadia;* and finally the last three books of the original "old" *Arcadia* combined with the revised, "new" *Arcadia*. The old *Arcadia,* which Sidney says he intended mainly for his sister and close friends, originally circulated in numerous manuscript copies. One of these copies of the old *Arcadia* was obtained by a London bookseller who wanted to print it. Fulke Greville, later Lord Brooke, Sidney's friend from school days and his biographer, objected to this printing. Greville stated that he had a revised edition—which he did have; but the revision only covered half of *Arcadia,* or two and one half of the five books. So another printer, Ponsanby, published the new *Arcadia* and, a few years later, this new *Arcadia* was joined to the old *Arcadia* and published to form the composite. This composite, which is the best known version of Sidney's *Arcadia,* is the one that was read by Shakespeare, Milton, and Lamb.

It was not until the twentieth century that the old *Arcadia* (known as *The Countess of Pembroke's Arcadia*) emerged from manuscript form to publication. Since then, however, there has been considerable controversy about which is more "authentic," which reflects more clearly Sidney's "real" intent. Generally speaking, the old *Arcadia* is a relatively simple and straightforward story of prophecy, turmoil, love, disguise, reversal, and ingenious resolution. The five books of the old *Arcadia* correspond to five acts. There is rising action, complication, and seeming resolution by the end of Book III. Book IV contains the reversal of fortunes and Book V resolves these final, and potentially deadly, problems to yield a happy ending.

In many ways, the new *Arcadia* (and the composite) are different and more complex versions of the same double-stranded love story. At the same time, however, Book III has been altered and enlarged almost beyond recognition: new characters have been introduced, characters who play a new and decisive role in the action; new speeches, arguments, debates, and incidents have been carefully inserted into the narrative, so that their effect, and the cumulative effect of all the changes, is more a transformation of the old *Arcadia* than an expansion of it.

There is a great variety of sources, in Greek, Roman, Italian, and English literature from which Sidney drew his scenes, plot, ideas, and style. He has woven together two traditions, the pastoral and the romantic/chivalric. The latter, derived partly from adventures related in later Greek literature, full of intrigues, disguises, and mysteries, appealed greatly to writers of the English Renaissance. Scenes and incidents were taken directly from *Ethiopica* by Heliodorus. There are also characters and incidents from Malory's *Le Morte d'Arthur,* a work filled with tales of chivalrous knights, that no doubt suggested scenes and actions for *Arcadia.*

The contribution of earlier pastoral romances seems to have been largely, though not entirely, structural and organizational. The shape of the romance, its direction and main divisions, were determined by pastoral conventions.

The world of *Arcadia,* and the world of the pastoral, is based on the creation of an artificial, rural setting populated by shepherds and shepherdesses. In this setting, it is possible for men and women to establish relationships and to discuss questions that would be impossible in the turmoil of the world as it is. The post-classical pastoral writers were especially interested in having characters pursue the topic of love and having them establish more harmonious relations with the other sex and with nature, thus allowing them to move closer to God.

Sidney's *Arcadia* elaborates this pastoral convention and uses that elaboration to discuss ethics, politics, and theology. First, there is the tumultuous world outside Arcadia proper. This external world, including Asia Minor, and the homes of Pyrocles and Musidorus, stands in contrast to Arcadia itself.

The second world, contained within the first, is the setting in which the two heroes fall in love. It is a transition between the outside chaos and the retreat within Arcadia that Basilius has chosen. This last and "purest" setting enables the process of love, and its development toward perfection, to occur.

But Sidney's intention, though modeled on an elaboration of the pastoral structure, goes beyond the pastoral. First, there is a great variety of incidents, scenes, imagery, and concrete description ordinarily absent from the pastoral (these images provide the basis for more extensive discussions than are usually found in pastoral works). Second, although the thematic content of *Arcadia* is centered in the Neoplatonic searching for love and the purification of romantic feelings, there are many political, ethical, and philosophical questions considered that are outside the customary range of the pastoral.

Thus, while Sidney describes his work as mere entertainment, it clearly has rather large ambitions. As Greville wrote in *The Life of the Renowned Sir Philip Sidney,* the goal of *Arcadia* "was not vanishing pleasure alone, but morall Images and Examples, (as directing threds) to guide every man through the confused *Labyrinth* of his own desires, and life."

Howard Lee Hertz

ARGENIS

Type of work: Prose romance
Author: John Barclay (1582-1621)
Type of plot: Pseudo-classical heroic allegory
Time of plot: The Hellenistic era
Locale: Sicily and the Western Mediterranean
First published: 1621

Argenis *owed its original popularity to the satire disguised in its allegorical form: the love story of Poliarchus and Argenis represents the wars and intrigues in France before the Concordant under Henry IV, and the whole work is designed to attack the opponents of monarchy. Although long praised for its grandeur of style, noble theme, and heroic characterizations, the work holds only historical interest for the modern reader.*

A literary curiosity, *Argenis* is not truly a novel; Thomas Deloney in *Jack of Newberry* and other works contributed more to the development of prose fiction as a popular art form. Where Deloney looked forward, Barclay looked backward, even to the point of composing his work in the "universal language" —Latin. The 1629 translation by Sir Robert le Grys is graceful and accurate, but very difficult to come by, nowadays. Written in long, carefully constructed sentences, *Argenis* produces an effect of grandeur and majesty seldom, if ever, encountered in modern literature. The story, despite all of the embroidery, is at times exciting, filled with violent action and passions.

Argenis is probably the Scottish satirist's most famous work, although he was known in his day for his *Satyricon,* a severe satire on the Jesuits and modeled on Petronius. The reader of *Argenis* and Barclay's other writings should not look for realistic characterization or plot development. The characters are impetuous and the action often implausible; both are used freely by Barclay to help make his satirical point. The characters dance around one another in elaborate patterns, suggesting at times a baroque opera rather than a piece of "realistic" fiction. When the tale is romantic it is *very* romantic; and when it is violent, the violence is extreme. The reader can almost visualize the story as a stage spectacle, the sets, costumes, and elaborate machinery all by Inigo Jones. But this very extravagance makes the work surprisingly enjoyable, providing the reader possesses the patience to persevere with the obscure allusions, and the now forgotten political and social satire.

The work is crowded with incident, including storms and shipwrecks, violent battles, and pirate treasure; but the motivation of the characters is not always clear. Fierce anger, friendship, and several varieties of passion all play a part in the complicated, fairy tale-like plot. Extravagant and amazing, *Argenis* is almost unique in British literature, interesting but possessing only the charm of a museum piece.

DER ARME HEINRICH

Type of work: Poem
Author: Hartmann von Aue (c. 1170–between 1210 and 1220)
Type of plot: Didactic romance
Time of plot: Late twelfth century
Locale: Germany
First transcribed: Between 1192 and 1202

The fusion of religious and secular elements in this poem mirrors the basic conflict in Hartmann von Aue's life: the struggle of a knight who had been educated in monastery schools to choose between a life of writing and a career of soldiering. Today Hartmann is regarded as the founder of the German court epic. This poem reflects the influence of popular martyr legends in the inspired speech and actions of the peasant girl, and it displays the author's gift for vividly portraying medieval life and thought.

German scholars characterize *Der arme Heinrich* as a courtly legend: courtly because of the setting and the central position of the worldly values of honor and public position, and a legend in the medieval sense of the word —a story embodying religious values, such as a saint's life, and suitable for reading in a religious setting. In his prologue to the work, Hartmann, proud of his learning, tells how he examined many books to find a tale that would both delight his readers and help lighten their hours while also serving God's honor. Giving his name, he asks that the listener, or reader, pray for him. Clearly the poem is intended to be a pious work.

The work is built around the tension between the need for God's grace and the quest for worldly honor, and the problem of how to live in the world so that neither is lost. In a series of works—*Erec, Iwein, Gregorius,* and *Der arme Heinrich*—Hartmann explores various aspects of the problem which was a central one for many writers of the period. In the present work, Heinrich, who has enjoyed great prosperity and high position, falls victim to leprosy, a disease which excludes him from human society, especially the world of courtly honor. It is a negation of his very existence. He sees this illness as a punishment for his pride and unwillingness to acknowledge dependence on God, but it is also the vehicle of his salvation. It leads Heinrich on a path to insight and to penance culminating in the demonstration of his spiritual growth in his voluntary renunciation of the peasant girl's sacrifice. At this point, the spiritual cause of the leprosy being removed, Heinrich is cured, and restored to his position in the world. Thus the demands of worldly honor and God's grace achieve harmony and coexistence in the purified and restored figure of Heinrich.

ARNE

Type of work: Novel
Author: Björnstjerne Björnson (1832-1910)
Type of plot: Pastoral romance
Time of plot: Early nineteenth century
Locale: Norway
First published: 1858

Before turning to playwrighting, in which field he became a friend and rival of Henrik Ibsen, Björnson wrote a series of "peasant novels." Arne belongs to this group and reflects the author's deep interest in the Norwegian people, their customs, and their legends.

The legends and folktales of the Norwegian country people are woven into this story of Arne and his songs. The novel is a strange mixture of realism and fancy, of accurate description of peasant life and of symbolism and poetry. The reader becomes immersed in the sense of magic which pervaded the life of the simple Norwegian country folk of a century and more ago. The prose is graceful and poetic, but never pretentious or false. The symbols arise naturally from the story, such as the black dress of the grandmother which becomes a shirt for the sober young Arne after she dies, and her spectacles which are crushed beneath Arne's heel the day she is buried.

Although he dies early, Nils is in some ways the most interesting character in the book. He is a complex man who nurses a grudge because of frustrated ambitions. He is a deeply flawed individual, with a bad temper and a weak character, but he is ultimately a sympathetic person. His wife, Margit, Arne's mother, is a long-suffering woman, meant to be sympathetic, yet she comes perilously close to becoming a stereotype.

From childhood, Arne finds it difficult to express or act upon his emotions. His early life was one that taught him to suppress outward signs of his feelings. Young Arne's fluctuating attitudes toward his parents are portrayed with subtlety and compassion. As he matures, he wrestles with both his own nature and the world in which he finds himself confined. Always, his songs give him comfort. These songs are a major part of the narrative, both revealing the young man's feelings and thoughts and lending a poetic and magical quality to the tale. As he finds his way into adulthood, Arne is haunted by the one time he raised his hand to his father, the moment when Nils died. The guilt festers inside Arne, until he fears for his sanity. And when he falls in love, it is with the daughter of his father's enemy. It seems to him that he never can escape his past, with its one act of wrath.

Björnson sought in his fiction and dramas to liberate Norwegian literature from the dominance of Denmark. For years, Norway had been subservient to Danish ideas, both politically and artistically. By turning to the legends of his own northern land, Björnson helped to establish a distinctive Norwegian literature. *Arne* was one of the first of his novels of peasant life; it had a great influence on other writers, and was acclaimed around the world. It is an unusual work, but one which still can be enjoyed for its poetic qualities and for its sympathetic portrayals of human weakness and desire.

ARROWSMITH

Type of work: Novel
Author: Sinclair Lewis (1885-1951)
Type of plot: Social criticism
Time of plot: Early twentieth century
Locale: United States and West Indies
First published: 1925

Just as Babbitt *exposed the false values of the middle-class American business-man, so* Arrowsmith *is an indictment of American medical practices. Lewis has tried to show that the progressive doctor is not appreciated in private practice; that the public health system is politically corrupt; that fashionable clinics are often commercial enterprises; and that research institutes are primarily interested in publicity.*

In the 1920's, Sinclair Lewis hit his full stride as a novelist—during that time, he wrote *Main Street* (1920), *Babbitt* (1922), *Arrowsmith* (1925), and *Dodsworth* (1929), among other novels—and enjoyed both popular and critical acclaim. His considerable achievement in that decade earned for Lewis the Nobel Prize for literature in 1930, the first American author to be thus distinguished. Even earlier, *Arrowsmith* was selected for the 1926 Pulitzer Prize for the novel. Lewis, however, objected to one of the criteria for award-ing the prize, finding it incompatible with intellectual freedom; he therefore declined to accept. Such political bickering notwithstanding, *Arrowsmith* as a work of art is typical of Lewis' work at the peak of his literary productivity. It contains the fundamental elements of realism and satire that characterize Lewis' style at its best.

In *Arrowsmith,* as in other novels of this period, Lewis' realism is most obviously demonstrated in the generous use of detail. Almost in the fashion of a television documentary, Lewis embellishes the verisimilitude and credibility of his story with fact piled upon fact.

As for satire, the ethical dilemmas of the medical profession still abound: the issues may change, but the controversy endures. Martin Arrowsmith, emotionally wracked by the deaths from bubonic plague of his colleague, Gustave Sondelius, and his wife, Leora, is no less obsessed and no less caught in ethical conflicts than today's practitioner dealing with a victim of cancer. The satiric view emerges from this double vision of life: pursue pure science or save whatever lives can be saved. To a certain extent, the dichotomy is artificial, for such "either-or" simplicity is not characteristic of medical deci-sions or any other decisions. But in practical terms, it is very real: a choice between short-term and long-term benefits. Martin Arrowsmith chooses short-term benefits. He provides anti-toxin for all, destroying the scientific validity of the tests which were to be conducted. The satiric flavor thus emerges as Martin's obligatory choice between two impossible alternatives.

Still, Martin himself is a somewhat ambiguous character. Are we to admire him or despise him? Part of the answer will revolve around personal commitments to abstract "good" or immediate practical benefits. But we may nonetheless view Dr. Arrowsmith as somewhat profoundly influenced by his mentors and professional colleagues; he does indeed strive for the best his fellows represent. If he falls short, Lewis would have us believe that Arrowsmith's intentions are nevertheless worthy of respect.

But a legitimate question remains: does Professor Max Gottlieb (significantly, translated as "Love of God") appear as a secret protagonist in the novel? Does Gottlieb represent the guiding force behind Martin Arrowsmith's actions?

The answer is by no means definitive, but it is evident that Lewis himself was not at all clear on the issue of whether Arrowsmith or Gottlieb should triumph. By presenting a dilemma, rather than trying to solve it, Lewis established himself as a realist and a satirist, for he depicted an unvarnished human condition and portrayed the hazards of moral choice. His satire of medicine—like his satire of middle-class attitudes (*Babbitt*), of religious evangelism (*Elmer Gantry*), and of middle-class business (*Dodsworth*)—rang, and still rings, true.

ARTAMÈNE

Type of work: Novel
Author: Madeleine de Scudéry (1607-1701)
Type of plot: Sentimental romance
Time of plot: 500 B.C.
Locale: Asia Minor
First published: 1646-1653

This sentimental romance, in spite of its ten-volume length, has a remarkable unity of interest. The author indulges in lengthy stories-within-the-story; however, because these successive stories are ingeniously knitted together by means of casually introduced characters who reappear in later sequences, it is difficult to understand any separate story once it is removed from the context of the overall plot.

Madeleine de Scudéry, known to her contemporaries as the "illustrious Sappho," founded the most important salon in the Paris of the 1640's. She belonged to the *précieux,* women who consciously tried to reestablish the courtly manners and language of the Italian Renaissance. Her novels—better characterized as "heroic romances"—helped to spread this tradition by means of both plot and language. Writing anonymously or with a pseudonym, Mlle. de Scudéry became enormously successful both because of her own popularity and because her works were *romans à clef,* which included thinly-disguised portrayals of her readers.

Though hardly read today, the incredibly prolix *Artamène* (which runs to some 12,000 pages) is a landmark work in terms of the development of the novel. The heroic romance represents an important development over earlier stages of prose fiction, the pastoral romance and the historical chronicle. In *Artamène* plot is made central, even in so long a work. In the "Address to the Reader," Mlle. de Scudéry makes clear that she understands the uniqueness of her method, for she says she chooses incidents from her various classical sources not for their historical accuracy but for the purpose of interest. The plot has a central idea, even though interspersed with every possible type of digression—subplots, stories within stories, *récits,* elaborate explanation, long description, introduction of minor characters, dramatic "business," *ad infinitum.*

One can note how far behind drama was fiction in the creation of character. There still are no real characters in *Artamène* such as one later finds in fiction, but the people do have "qualities"; still, the personages are more "types" than characters. One does find hints of character in two maids, Martésie and Doralise. There is almost no real dialogue, but only, in George Saintsbury's words, "harangue, narrative, soliloquy, and passing of compliments." Both French and British fiction were greatly influenced by this work: Mme. Marie de La Fayette's *The Princess of Clèves* (1678) owes much to *Artamène,* as does Samuel Richardson's *Clarissa* (1747-1748).

After the French Revolution women lost many rights—the Napoleonic code decreed that women were economically and legally dependent on men —but ever since Scudéry's time, women novelists have been producing the most popular "period" or "historical" fiction.

THE ARTAMONOV BUSINESS

Type of work: Novel
Author: Maxim Gorky (Aleksei Maksimovich Peshkov, 1868-1936)
Type of plot: Family chronicle
Time of plot: c. 1862-1918
Locale: Russia
First published: 1925

A supporter of the Bolshevik revolution and a popular novelist under the new Communist regime, Gorky was unable to eliminate elements of romanticism from his works, despite his predominantly political orientation. In The Artamonov Business, *Gorky is still far away from a purely socialistic novel; his pre-Revolution characters reflect his romantic tendencies, and he makes no attempt to discard the powerful influence of Christianity on his heroes.*

The Artamonov Business is a brilliant portrayal of the birth, evolution, and disintegration of capitalism in Russia in the period before 1917. Gorky shows this movement through the characters of the Artamonov family, owners and developers of a factory, a family business.

Ilia Artamonov, the founder of the factory, is a lively, energetic, imaginative man who works alongside his employees and who revolutionizes economic and social relations in a stagnant, backwater town. Gorky portrays him as "inevitable" and unstoppable. He scandalizes and then dominates the town. Most of all, he is energetic and creative—and represents the opening or the progressive phase of capitalism.

But his three sons are unable to carry on this work as a group. One of them, Nikita, retreats to a monastery. Nikita possesses his father's intensity, but this intensity is channeled into moral and religious outlets rather than business.

Alexey, on the other hand, is characterized as an intellectual. He is "apart"; he collects antiques, adopts aristocratic mannerisms, and marries a "liberated" woman. From Ilia's standpoint, both these sons represent perversions of or, at best, diversions from the on-going capitalist movement.

Only Peter, the founder's oldest son, is able to run the factory and even expand it. The bulk of the novel is devoted to Peter and to Peter's view of events. Gorky uses Peter to show the middle stage of capitalist development, a stage in which the work force expands and the enterprise becomes more profitable but the workers become alienated and disaffected.

A minor thread running through the book is Peter's relations with Tikhon Vialov, a worker in the factory. Although Vialov was close to his father, Peter finds him incomprehensible and irritating (especially after Peter murders a worker's child who is influencing one of his own children.) Vialov knows too much and, at the same time, refuses to submit completely to Peter's authority.

The third phase of capitalist development is embodied in Yakov and Ilia, Peter's children. Ilia joins a communist political group dedicated to overthrowing capitalists like his father. Yakov, who carries on his father's (later) weakness for women, but not his earlier strength, is incapable of working with his employees.

Discontent spreads through the factory and he must resort to spies. In other words, the economic authority he represents has degenerated; and his alliance with Uliana Baimakov is only the political corollary of this economic weakening.

The novel is particularly interesting in its attempt to portray the social, economic, intellectual, and political impulses of prerevolutionary Russia through the specific lives of men and women. It contains no long speeches or polemics, but it is highly political and didactic. Finally, given its scope and the richness of its characterizations, both individual and social, it is nearly epic in ambition.

AS I LAY DYING

Type of work: Novel
Author: William Faulkner (1897-1962)
Type of plot: Psychological realism
Time of plot: Early twentieth century
Locale: Mississippi
First published: 1930

Centering around the effect of Addie Bundren's death and burial on members of her family, this novel has a powerful unity not always found in Faulkner's longer works. Although his method of shifting between the multiple points of view of the different family members binds Faulkner's characters into a homogeneous unit through their common suffering, individual personalities with their special emotions and abnormalities nevertheless emerge.

Considered by many contemporary critics the greatest American fiction writer, Faulkner was awarded the Nobel Prize for Literature in 1949, after a prolific career that included nineteen novels and two volumes of poetry. Although his formal education was limited, Faulkner read prodigiously in the Greek and Roman classics, the Bible, Shakespeare, the English Romantics, Conrad, Joyce, and Eliot. After relatively undistinguished early attempts in poetry and prose, Faulkner was advised by Sherwood Anderson to concentrate on his "own postage stamp of native soil." This led to the saga of Yoknapatawpha County, its partly true regional history (based on Oxford, Mississippi) merging imperceptibly into a coherent myth, that began to unravel with *Sartoris* (1929), and was continued in *The Sound and the Fury* (1929) and *As I Lay Dying* (1930.)

In the Yoknapatawpha novels Faulkner placed himself in the forefront of the avant-garde with his intricate plot organization, his bold experiments in the dislocation of narrative time, and his use of the stream-of-consciousness technique. His stylistic view of time was affected by his sense that past events continue into the present. As he once said, "There is no such thing as *was*; if *was* existed, there would be no grief or sorrow." These stylistic characteristics were undergirded by the development of a complex social structure that enabled Faulkner to explore the inherited guilt of the Southern past, the incapacity of the white aristocracy to cope with modern life, the relations between classes, and the relations between black and white.

Starkly realistic, poignantly symbolic, grotesquely comic and immensely complicated as an experiment in points of view, *As I Lay Dying* ranks with Faulkner's greatest novels: *The Sound and the Fury, Sanctuary* (1931), *Light in August* (1932) and *Absalom, Absalom!* (1936). The relative simplicity of its style, characterized by staccato-like sentences and repetitive dialogue, enhances the tragicomic effect. At the same time the prosaic quality of the narrative often renders into poetry—as when Dewey Dell becomes the symbol of heedless motherhood by wiping everything on her dress, when Darl sees stars first in the bucket then in his dipper, when Jewel's horse appears "enclosed by a glittering maze of hooves as by an illusion of wings," when the buzzards accompanying Addie's coffin are juxtaposed suddenly with the sparks that make the stars flow backward for Vardaman, or when Darl, in his visionary fashion, speculates: "It is as though the space between us were time: an irrevocable quality. It is as though time, no longer running straight before us in a diminishing line, now runs parallel between us like a looping string, the distance between the doubling accretion of the thread and not the interval between."

The novel's theme, in the very widest terms, is man's absurdly comic distinction between being and not-being. Peabody describes death as "merely a function of the mind—and that of the ones who suffer the bereavement." But the theme is stated most clearly in the single chapter narrated from Addie's viewpoint: "I could just remember how my father used to say that the reason for living was to get ready to stay dead a long time." Addie has long since considered Anse dead, because she realizes that he, like most humans, cannot distinguish between the "thin line" of words that float upward into nothingness and the terrible reality of "doing [that] goes along the earth, clinging to it." Her attitude is expressed tersely and succinctly when she comments, after allusively revealing her affair with Whitfield: "Then I found that I had Jewel. When I waked to remember to discover it, he was two months gone."

Nineteen of the fifty-nine chapters are narrated from Darl's viewpoint, making him the primary *persona* of the novel. His reference to his family's conglomerate madness sets the tone: "In sunset we fall into furious attitudes, dead gestures of dolls." The novel proceeds in a jerky, doll-like movement, as the narration passes through the viewpoints of fifteen different characters, not without occasional retrogression and hiatus. Although Darl might be called the primary narrator, whose voice is most representative of the author's own, he is not the only interesting one. Vardaman, with ten chapters, displays a mentality reminiscent of Benjy's in *The Sound and the Fury,* showing us the crazy events connected with the burial through the eyes of a confused and simple-minded child. The third chapter from his viewpoint consists of a single sentence: "My mother is a fish." Only three chapters present Anse's viewpoint; but that is enough to show that he is a bizarre combination of his sons' characteristics: Darl's imagination, Vardaman's insanity, Cash's stubborn practicality, and Dewey Dell's earthiness (which also sets her in contrast with the bitterness of Addie's outlook toward sex and motherhood).

As he does in *The Sound and the Fury,* with Jason's chapter, Faulkner achieves his greatest artistic success with the least intrinsically interesting character, Cash. The first chapter (of five) from Cash's viewpoint is an artistic *coup.* Until this point we have heard, through many different viewpoints, the steady buzzing of Cash's saw preparing his mother's coffin—a sound that provides the thread of continuity through the first half of the novel. Even through the rain and through the night, Cash will not cease his labor: "Yet the motion of the saw has not faltered, as though it and the arm functioned in a tranquil conviction that rain was an illusion of the mind." Finally we hear his own voice, in Chapter 18: "I made it on the bevel." After this statement, Cash proceeds to explain what he means as Faulkner presents the carpenter's methodological mind in a straightforward list: "1. There is more surface for the nails to grip," ending with, "13. It makes a neater job." Cash's second chapter is a nine-line warning to his impatient father and brothers that the coffin "wasn't on a balance" in the wagon. When the tragedy in the river results from their ignoring his warning, Faulkner present's Cash's third chapter in three lines, beginning with, "It wasn't on a balance," and not even mentioning the fact that Cash's leg has been broken. Cash's single-minded craftsmanship and superhuman patience become a reflection of the author's own technique. The final chapter is Cash's.

Kenneth John Atchity

AS YOU LIKE IT

Type of work: Drama
Author: William Shakespeare (1564-1616)
Type of plot: Pastoral romance
Time of plot: The Middle Ages
Locale: The Forest of Arden in medieval France
First presented: 1598-1600

A pastoral romantic comedy set in the Middle Ages, As You Like It *takes its plot from Thomas Lodge's popular romance,* Rosalyde *(1590). Involving the eventual union of four very different pairs of lovers who represent the diverse faces of love, the story is marked by its mood of kindliness, fellowship, and good humor.*

As You Like It is a splendid comedy on love and alternate life styles that more than fulfills the promise of its title. Its characters are, for the most part, wonderfully enamored of love, one another, and themselves. The play has the feeling of freshness and vitality, and although adapted from an older story full of artifice, suggests a world of spontaneity and life.

To understand *As You Like It,* one must understand the conventions it uses. *As You Like It* is often called a pastoral comedy because it engages the conventions of pastoral literature. Pastoral literature, beginning in the third century B.C. and popular in the late sixteenth century, enabled poets, novelists, and dramatists to contrast the everyday world's fears, anxieties, disloyalties, uncertainties, and tensions with the imagined, mythical world of a previous age when peace, longevity, contentment, and fulfillment reigned in men's lives. Each age develops its own manner of describing lost happiness, far removed from the normal toil of human existence. The pastoral was the dominant such vision in the late sixteenth century.

In the pastoral, the mythic, lost, "golden" world is set in a simple, rural environment, which then becomes the image of all things desirable to honest men. *As You Like It* is typical of this convention and it contains two contrasting worlds: the world of the court and the rural world—in this case the Forest of Arden. The court is inhabited by corrupt men; namely, Duke Frederick and Oliver. It is not significant that the gentle Duke, Orlando, Rosalind, and Celia once resided there. Rather, as the play develops, the court is the natural home of the wicked and ambitious. Yet, we do not witness the degeneration of Duke Frederick and Oliver; they are naturally wicked, and the court is their proper milieu.

The elder Duke, Orlando, Rosalind, and Celia, on the other hand, are naturally good, and the forest is their natural milieu. If the court represents elaborate artifice, ambition, avarice, cruelty, and deception, the forest represents openness, tolerance, simplicity, and freedom. In the pastoral, rather than develop immensely complex characters such as Hamlet, who like most humans has good and bad characteristics, good and bad traits are apportioned to separate characters. This allocation then imposes a necessary artifice upon the play, which colors all actions, from falling in love to hating or helping a brother. In a play such as *As You Like It,* one does not expect naturalistic behavior. On the other hand, by using the conventions and artifice adroitly, Shakespeare achieved a remarkable exploration of love and its attendant values.

In the opening scene, Orlando, who has been denied an education and kept like an animal by his brother, is seen to be naturally good and decent. Talking to his brother Oliver, Orlando says, "You have train'd me like a peasant, obscuring and hiding from me all gentleman-like qualities. The spirit of my father grows strong in me, and I will no longer endure it: therefore allow me such exercises as may become a gentleman . . ." (I.i.71-76). Oliver, on the other hand, is just as naturally wicked as Orlando is decent. He says, "for my soul—yet I know not why—hates nothing more than he" (I.i.171-172). Logic has no necessary place in this world. Love, however, does.

Love is a natural part of the pastoral world. Practically at first glance, Rosalind and Orlando are in love. Shakespeare's magic in *As You Like It* is to take the contrived love that is the expected part of the pastoral convention, and make of it a deeply felt experience that the audience can understand and to which it can react. Shakespeare manages this not only through the extraordinary beauty of his language but also through the structure of his play.

As You Like It is full of parallel actions. Orlando and Rosalind meet and immediately fall in love. Silvius and Phebe are in love. Touchstone meets Audrey in the forest, and they fall in love. At the end of the play Celia meets the reformed Oliver, and they fall in love just as quickly as Rosalind and Orlando had at the beginning of the play. The love match at the play's end nicely sets off the love match at the beginning.

Each love pairing serves a particular purpose. The focus of the play is primarily upon the Rosalind-Orlando match. Rosalind is the more interesting of the pair, for while she recognizes the silliness of the lover's ardor, she is as much victim as those she scorns. In Act IV, while in boy's disguise, she pretends to Orlando that his Rosalind will not have him. He says, "Then . . . I die" (IV.i.93). Her response pokes fun at the expiring love: "No, faith, die by attorney. The poor world is almost six thousand years old, and in all this time there was not any man died in his own person, *videlicet,* in a love-cause. . . . Men have died from time to time and worms have eaten them, but not for love" (IV.i.93-108). She can toy with Orlando in her disguise as Ganymede, yet she is completely dominated by her love passion. Strong passion is a part of the love experience, but Rosalind's and Orlando's passion is highly refined; the passion others know is more earthly.

Touchstone, in his quest for Audrey, exemplifies this side of love. He at first wants to marry her out of church so when he tires of her, he can claim their marriage was invalid. The kind of love he represents is physical passion.

The Phebe-Silvius pairing shows yet another face of love. Silvius exemplifies the typical pastoral lover, hopelessly in love with a fickle mistress. He sighs on his pillow and breaks off from company, forlornly calling out his mistress' name. Touchstone's and Silvius' brands of love are extreme versions of qualities in Rosalind's love. In the comedies Shakespeare often used this device of apportioning diverse characteristics to multiple characters rather than building one complete character. Without Touchstone, love in the play may be too sentimental to take seriously. Without Silvius, it may be too crude. With both, love as exemplified by Rosalind and Orlando becomes a precious balance of substance and nonsense, spirituality and silliness.

Curious things happen in *As You Like It*. Good men leave the honorable forest to return to the wicked court. Wicked men who enter the forest are instantly converted in their ways. At the end of the play Oliver, who came to the Forest of Arden to hunt down his brother Orlando, gives his estate to Orlando and marries Celia, vowing to remain in the forest and live and die a shepherd. Duke Frederick also came to the Forest of Arden in order to kill his brother. Meeting "an old religious man" in the forest, Duke Frederick "was converted/Both from his enterprise and from the world." He too gives up his estate, and his crown, to his brother. The forest, the pastoral world, has the power to convert.

Why, then, do the elder Duke, Orlando, and Rosalind elect to return to the court, home of wickedness? They do so because in the end *As You Like It* is not a fairy tale, but an expression of humanly felt experiences. The forest ultimately is to be used as a cleansing and regenerative experience, a place to which one may retire in order to renew simplicity, honesty, and virtue. It is not, however, to be a permanent retreat. Good men stained by labor and trouble in their everyday world in the end must still participate in that world. They can retreat to the pastoral world in order to renew and reinvigorate themselves, but finally they must return, refreshed and fortified, to the community of men, to take on the responsibilities all must face.

Brian L. Mark

ASHES

Type of work: Novel
Author: Stefan Żeromski (1864-1925)
Type of plot: Historical romance
Time of plot: 1796-1812
Locale: Poland and Spain
First published: 1904

In its detailed descriptions of nature and long sections of philosophical contemplation, Ashes *owes much to the German romantic tradition. In its presentation of historical scenes, however, such as those depicting the Napoleonic campaigns, Żeromski achieves that precision and realism essential to fine historical fiction.*

The idealistic hero of this novel, Raphael Olbromski, questions the meaning of existence; and certainly, in the course of his life he has had reason to doubt the purpose of human suffering. Yet he has an idealism which centers in his love for Helen and in his patriotism.

The plot of *Ashes* is romantic and fanciful, although often embellished in a realistic covering of details and description. At times, it suggests the picaresque tales of Fielding and other eighteenth century novelists, but with a lushness and romanticism more German than English. Raphael is essentially passive, letting others work on him; his actions are unpremeditated and often foolish. His father, the Prince, the brigands, and others, send him hither and thither, changing the course of his existence; and, having no particular ambitions, he obeys or yields to these forces which are stronger than he. He is led to join the Masons, but through no convictions of his own; impressionable, he mistakenly feels that this may signal a change in his life. Impetuous and naïve, Raphael often gets into trouble (for example, when he and Christopher return to school naked, when he runs away, when he kisses Elizabeth after rescuing her, and when he and Helen flee together). More than once, his character comes close to straining the reader's credulity.

Żeromski possesses a gift for describing action. The novel is filled with excellently realized scenes, such as the hunting scene which opens the book, the scene of the sleighs rushing between estates in the *kulig* holiday festivities, the scene of Raphael and Baska chased by wolves, and the scene of riding through snow on Baska to Helen's house. The characterization is often fine; Żeromski can in a single detail encompass a whole personality, as in his description of the superior half-smile always on the faces of Prince Gintult and his sister, Elizabeth.

Raphael is torn between the shallow society of the cities and the life of the country. He is educated, but not dedicated to books, preferring hunting and roaming about in the woods and fields. For a long time, he exists on the fringes of the great world, barely aware of the momentous happenings occurring elsewhere. Then he is caught up in the wheel of history. When his fortunes become so low that they cannot sink any lower, his old friend Christopher Cedro appears as a *deus ex machina* to save him. Raphael, appropriately, tries to build up his uncle's old estate, but again history and Christopher carry him away; once more, Raphael's fate is determined by forces outside himself. Perhaps Żeromski is suggesting through the life of his protagonist that it is futile for men to struggle against the forces of destiny and history.

AT THE SIGN OF THE REINE PÉDAUQUE

Type of work: Novel
Author: Anatole France (Jacques Anatole Thibault, 1844-1924)
Type of plot: Humorous satire
Time of plot: Eighteenth century
Locale: France
First published: 1893

The first of his works to exhibit his peculiar talents, this tale displays France's vast erudition in philosophy and ancient history as well as his unique brand of subtle but wicked humor. Most memorable of the characterizations is that of Abbé Jérôme, the fluent scoundrel of a cleric who wins the reader's affection despite his rascally nature.

This novel with its discreet mocking of the occult and its refined and occasionally lusty intelligence, appeals more to the brain than the senses. Anatole France's careful artistry and pure style are the perfect vehicle for his peculiar combination of sensitivity and irony. He disliked Romanticism and condemned the crudity of the realistic school of fiction, and, indeed, there is little of either the romantic or the realistic in this or his other novels. He scorned prose that claimed profundity in obscurity, stating that a good style is complex but does not appear so. Clarity and purity were fundamental qualities of his art, and nowhere do these virtues stand out more admirably than in *At the Sign of the Reine Pédauque.*

The narrative and dialogue are both crowded with epigrams and witticisms, sometimes to the point of almost paralyzing what little action there is in the book. Jacques tells his own story with a strangely sophisticated innocence. Every aspect of life is intellectualized, from eating to lovemaking to battling the world for survival. Many of the monologues are short essays, and the dialogues between characters are more philosophical than dramatic. Whole discourses are presented on subjects such as the influence of food upon civilized history. Much of the talk that fills the book is humorous, and most of it makes its point sharply and bitingly. France was never a great inventor of incident in his fiction, and the value of this novel, as of so many of his, lies in the reflections and comments which fill its pages.

Influenced by the irony of Renan, the bitter wit of Voltaire, and the use of the eighteenth century setting of Diderot, France attempted to interweave his tale of the adventures of the Rabelaisian, philosophical monk and his faithful follower, Jacques, with satire of quasi-magic and astrology; the story is filled with the irreverence which came to be its author's trademark. France was steeped in borrowed thought and language, and his weak narrative construction reduces his plot in places to a kind of loping commentary, yet his grace and wit raise *At the Sign of the Reine Pédauque* to the level of high art.

ATALA

Type of work: Novel
Author: François René de Chateaubriand (1768-1848)
Type of plot: Philosophical romance
Time of plot: Early eighteenth century
Locale: Louisiana
First published: 1801

A tale of passionate but pure love, Atala *is another of the "Noble Savage" stories which found such favor in European romantic circles in the nineteenth century. Against a background of the primitive American wilderness, the two lovers and a gentle priest wage a successful battle against sin and paganism.*

Atala is one of the significant literary expressions of the Romantic Movement which developed essentially in France, Germany, and England in the latter part of the eighteenth century and constituted a revolution in man's thinking about virtually every phase of life. The aspects of the movement which are given literary expression in *Atala* include an awareness of the distinction between the true nature of the individual and the apparent or superficial nature which society imposes on him or which he adopts because of the expectations of those around him. The "true self" of Atala is that of a young woman with a natural warmth, compassion for the sufferings of others, and a readiness to love and be loved. A vow which had societal but not natural force was imposed upon her by her mother; this and a misunderstanding of true religion make it impossible for her to be her natural self.

A second aspect of Romanticism—the "blue flower" concept expressed by Novalis in his *Heinrich von Ofterdingen*—is a recognition that sensitive people may catch glimpses of an ideal (often an ideal love), but that the full ideal is never completely attainable except through intuition or imagination. Love, then, may remain in a pure or ideal state only if it cannot become actual marriage. Chactas' love for Atala remains pure throughout his long life colored by a tint of sadness for "what might have been" even while it remains more beautiful than it could have been in the realities of marriage, work, home, and children.

It is somewhat in this vein that the "noble savage" is idealized; he *can* be idealized by Europeans, because his life is known to them almost exclusively through their imaginations.

With nature it is not the same. European civilization had "tamed" nature; the ultimate in controlled natural beauty was—and is—the gardens of the palace at Versailles. The romanticist (Wordsworth and Chateaubriand are prime examples) discovered and deeply felt the beauties of uncontrolled nature, and *Atala* gives excellent testimony to the harmony of the receptive human spirit with that love of unspoiled nature, even with the hardships it may impose.

Chateaubriand does not represent the full range of romantic thought; perhaps no single author incorporates all aspects of any literary period. But he is France's best prose representative of European Romanticism.

ATALANTA IN CALYDON

Type of work: Poem
Author: Algernon Charles Swinburne (1837-1909)
Type of plot: Classical tragedy
Time of plot: Remote antiquity
Locale: Ancient Greece
First published: 1865

Atalanta in Calydon, *typical of the Victorian treatment of Greek tragedy, first attracted critical notice to Swinburne's works. Although criticized for using excessive intensity and too violent colors in his poetry, Swinburne needed these elements to describe successfully the passionate and soul-searching nature of his characters' fateful existence. As in the case of his other poetic dramas,* Atalanta in Calydon *was intended for reading rather than stage presentation.*

Swinburne adhered so closely to the principles of Greek drama in *Atalanta in Calydon* that what he achieved must be likened to a reproduction Greek statue clothed in English. His model was most likely Ovid's version of the Atalanta myth in *Metamorphoses,* elaborated and embellished within conventions of form, theme, and meter in the Greek drama. Nevertheless, the degree to which Swinburne succeeded in his imitation Greek drama is almost without parallel, as his first critics pointed out.

Atalanta and Meleager, gears in the machinations of Artemis' revenge upon Œneus, enact a drama of love and death which fulfills the Fates's prophecy to Althæa. Swinburne's characters embody and exemplify themes— love, fate, revenge, and death—but without conveying effect, because Swinburne's poem is pessimistic, sentimental, and didactic, rather than tragic. It is only in the choruses that Swinburne conveys effect, notably when the Chorus sings "We have seen thee, O love, thou art fair." Here, love is seen accompanied by a bridal couple, Fate and Death: Swinburne defines the rose by showing the thorn.

The success of *Atalanta in Calydon* as imitation is also the poem's limitation. It does not transcend imitation, remaining a distinctly literary play in a literary context; but that was Swinburne's interpretation of "art for art's sake," a doctrine which flourished in the Victorian literary circles of Rossetti and the Pre-Raphaelites.

T. S. Eliot, in his essay "Swinburne as Poet," described Swinburne's aesthetics as diffuse and uprooted: using words in a way which mixed image, sound, and idea for rhetorical purposes only—words *as* words and not related to objects in the world. This quality in Swinburne's poetry may be seen particularly in the chorus "Before the beginning of years," which follows Althæa's speech on the Fates's prophecy.

Atalanta in Calydon represents a high point of artifice in the pre-Raphaelite movement. Rather than an imitation of life, as Aristotle defined the drama in *The Poetics,* Swinburne's *Atalanta in Calydon* is an imitation of art.

AUCASSIN AND NICOLETTE

Type of work: Tale
Author: Unknown
Type of plot: Chivalric romance
Time of plot: Twelfth century
Locale: Provence, in France
First transcribed: Fourteenth-century manuscript

Aucassin and Nicolette *is considered by many scholars to be the masterpiece among romances of chivalry. Written in the style of what is called the* chante-fable, *or song-story—a prose tale containing verse passages which are sung by a minstrel—this work contains a wealth of folklore and many interesting Oriental elements.*

Star-crossed lovers, Aucassin and Nicolette brave all the obstacles of war, family objection, and cruel separation. Finally, unlike Romeo and Juliet, they are reunited and enjoy all the nobility and power that kept them apart. The ending of this ancient chante-fable, unique in its combination of prose and verse, is significant for the way it sanctions their union: the Saracen slave girl, turned Carthaginian princess, is betrothed to the French Count de Beaucaire. The formal bifurcation of the tale (prose and poetry) echoes the cultural marginality of its hero and heroine. They transcend the political and cultural distinctions of their world—so great is their love. Their union symbolizes the cosmopolitan vision underlying so much of medieval romance and epic: it can be seen in the noble respect between Saracen and Christian knights in the *Song of Roland*. It is a social dream going back to Alexander's feast of Susa, where the Greek and Persian nobles were joined in a great communal marriage.

In addition to setting a social and diplomatic model, their great love is a miraculous force that can cure physical wounds: Nicolette's "surgery" on Aucassin's shoulder. Love also reunites them simply through the power of its aura: the coincidences that govern their reunion in the forest and later in the Court of Beaucaire seem uncontrived because we come to believe in the undeniable power of their love. It weathers all that time or circumstance can do.

The loyalty these lovers extend to each other is in the highest tradition of "fin amor" or courtly love. Nicolette's beauty is Aucassin's sole inspiration; she motivates his noblest actions, in war and love, and his reward is her total acceptance of his worship—so total that the conventional pattern of the knight scaling the lady's tower is reversed and Nicolette comes to Aucassin.

THE AUTOBIOGRAPHY OF BENVENUTO CELLINI

Type of work: Autobiography
Author: Benvenuto Cellini (1500-1571)
Type of plot: Chronicle of adventure and art
Time of plot: 1500-1562
Locale: Italy and France
First published: Sixteenth-century manuscript

This autobiography, written between 1558 and 1562 and circulated in manuscript form until it was printed in 1730, is probably the finest document from the period of the Italian Renaissance to come down to us. Through the eyes of a sensitive, artistic, and adventurous individual, we view intimately the lives of great artists and sculptors, and of ordinary men and women as well as dukes, princes, and popes.

The Florentine Benvenuto Cellini—contemporary of Michelangelo, Titian, Tintoretto, and Sansovino—was a completely natural man of his time. Utterly unself-conscious and uncritical, he presented himself through his *Autobiography* in the context of the Italian Renaissance, totally involved in its art, its politics, its religion, its entire culture. His was the life *engagée*. And by examining this *Autobiography,* we learn what Italian Renaissance life was really like.

Characteristically, Cellini's temper and temperament were, by modern standards, a mixture of extremes. He loved and he hated; he concentrated intensely and he wasted time. In his lifetime, he killed several men, yet he was at the same time tender, compassionate, and concerned about both men and women who, he was convinced, were in need of succor. His love affairs were equally extravagant. He loved many women, produced at least six offspring out of wedlock (some of whom were legitimated), but married only once, from which union issued two legitimate children. He frequently offended— as often as he pleased—powerful men in high position. As a consequence, he spent some time in prison and at other times was banished or exiled from his home, wherever it happened to be. At still other times, he was richly rewarded. He was obsessed with vengeance and honor. He killed his brother's murderer and similarly revenged other outrages. He insisted upon maintaining his honor, regardless of how onerous the circumstances might be. In fact, honor and revenge were the key concepts in his life and, in turn, keys to the Renaissance mind.

This Renaissance fusion of apparent contradictions also delineates the versatility of the period. Cellini was indeed versatile. As a man of letters, he wrote his *Autobiography* (most of it dictated to a scribe), valuable treatises on goldsmithing and sculpture, and other discourses on art. Some of his letters and his petitions are extant. He also produced some poetry, which has been largely ignored. But he wrote in the lusty Tuscan dialect, more vital than other conventional modes of communication. He was best known, deservedly, as goldsmith and sculptor, but he was also an adept swordsman and a diligent soldier. And his engineering skills—particularly in the martial sphere—should not be underrated. This amazing versatility was typical of cultured men of Cellini's time.

Despite his talents, Cellini was dependent upon patronage, relying for his livelihood upon commissions for artistic works from wealthy patrons. Hence, he executed vases and other vessels and plates as well as a variety of medals and jewelry for popes and prelates, royalty and nobles; busts and statuary for the Medici and for King Francis I of France; a crucifix for the Medici; and a famous salt cellar for Francis I, among other works. But his irascible temper constantly brought him into conflict with his patrons. Nevertheless, Cellini was honored, respected, and rewarded in his own time.

It was not necessary that an artist sycophantically cater to the tastes of his patron. Cellini thus conceived his ideas first and then convinced his patron that the ideas were worthy of support for their execution. Likewise, artists were not required to live morally or legally exemplary lives. They lived their boisterous, disorderly lives in bohemian quarters wherever and whenever they congregated in urban centers. Their idiosyncrasies and eccentricities were tolerated by their patrons and by the general public because of their over-riding contribution to culture at large. Rebellious religious and political activities were severely punished, however, as Cellini learned from his many imprisonments and exiles. But private immorality and public peculation were more leniently viewed.

It was under such circumstances as these that Cellini produced his master-works of art. Categorization is difficult. The sculptures have about them certain qualities of realism, even naturalism, yet they, like the goldsmithery, are more often placed by art critics in the Mannerist School. In fact, such facile classification does injustice to precisely that quality which distinguishes Cellini's artistry, for Cellini was above all *the* Renaissance man. His very versatility defies conventional classification. It is therefore more appropriate to say what he did and how he did it than to apply labels.

Among the goldsmithing works, the jewelry, always with gold settings which Cellini himself cast, was often enameled, encrusted with precious and semi-precious gems, and occasionally embellished with exquisitely intricate filigree work, which Cellini also used to decorate a variety of vessels and small casks. Other works—rings, medals, clasps, breviary covers, buckles, crucifixes—were done in gold leaf delicately beaten to form high- or low-relief designs or figures. Among the most famous of such works is the elegant salt cellar created for Francis I, a large vessel, nearly twelve inches high, featuring the figures of Neptune and Mother Earth set on an elaborately embossed base. Cellini also cast seals for the bulls of cardinals and for official documents of state, made dies for the stamping of coins, and struck medals. In addition, he designed plates for engraving and etching. And he produced larger metal works, both hammered and cast, such as ornate vases and chalices as well as life-size cast figures.

As for sculpture, Cellini was adept in several media. He chiseled, for example, from white Carrara marble a life-size Christ crucified and set the figure upon a cross of black Carrara marble to create a tremendous sculpture, a study in contrasts between stark white and stark black. (This crucifix now hangs in the Church of San Lorenzo in the Escorial.) And for the gateway to Francis I's palace at Fontainebleau, he cast in bronze a reclining nymph— now known as the Nymph of Fontainebleau—more than ten feet long, sur- rounded by animals and flanked by two figures symbolizing Victory. But for sheer elegance, the Nymph is outshone by Cellini's silver Jupiter, also executed for Francis I, a gorgeous statue set upon a gilded pedestal which conceals hard wooden ball bearings, allowing the statue to be moved with hardly more than a touch of the hand. However, a "colossus"—a sixty-foot statue of Mars—planned for Francis I's fountain at Fontainebleau was never brought to fruition. Yet, it is the slightly larger than life-size cast bronze Perseus with the Head of Medusa—made for Cosimo de' Medici and still standing in the Loggia de' Lanzia—for which Cellini is best known and most admired. Using methods similar to those employed in creating the Nymph of Fontaine- bleau, he cast the figure of Perseus all in one piece, an amazing achievement of both art and craft. For this reason, Cellini's description of the process forms one of the high points in his *Autobiography,* which otherwise shows him to be a truly versatile Renaissance man as well.

Joanne G. Kashdan

THE AWAKENING OF SPRING

Type of work: Drama
Author: Frank Wedekind (1864-1918)
Type of plot: Psychological realism
Time of plot: Nineteenth century
Locale: Germany
First presented: 1891

The plot of The Awakening of Spring *is a harshly naturalistic account of the clash between awakening sexuality in the young and the hypocritical and unexplained strictures against sex put forth by an adult society. The play depends for its dramatic intensity upon swift modulations between satire and tragedy, caricature and lyrical statement, and the commonplace and the horrific.*

Wedekind's "children's tragedy," *The Awakening of Spring,* was his first major work, and the play which made him famous—and infamous. The work was generally regarded as pornographic. Riots broke out at performances and it was subjected to repeated censorship. Yet the work clearly avoids the explicit and obscene, and later generations have come to see it as a powerful creation, shaped out of Wedekind's inner experience, revealing the world as seen through the eyes of his protagonists and rendering it with all the distortion of subjective vision.

The world of anxiety in which his students live and suffer was familiar to him from his own school years. Even the suicides are drawn from reality. Yet he shapes the work not as a documentary, but as a bizarre fantasy, charged with irony. The adults, especially the teachers and the pastor, are grotesque parodies. Even their names translate as the sort of mocking epithets students might invent. The scenes of Melchior's interrogation by the faculty, or of Moritz' funeral are bitter parodies of the cruelty and inanity of the adults as perceived by the children. Indeed, Wedekind places all the lyricism and humanity in the play in the world of the young, perhaps for the first time on the German stage giving expression to the unique experience of this age group.

Using the techniques of the Naturalists, he accurately captured the speech patterns and behavior of these young people, while yet lifting them beyond the level of mere naturalism. The play is clearly allied more to the Symbolist mode, as is evident from the fantasy of the final scenes, the temptation of Melchior by Moritz, and his rescue by the "muffled gentleman." Wedekind dedicated the play to this mysterious figure, who clearly represents the life force, perhaps within Melchior himself, which enables him to reject death and return to the world of the living, grotesque though it may be, to experience the fullness of life, of which Moritz, by his suicide, has robbed himself.

THE AXE

Type of work: Novel
Author: Sigrid Undset (1882-1949)
Type of plot: Historical chronicle
Time of plot: Late thirteenth century
Locale: Norway
First published: 1925

The Axe *is the first volume of a tetralogy entitled* The Master of Hestviken, *which also includes* The Snake Pit, In the Wilderness, *and* The Son Avenger. *In this story of thirteenth century Norway, Undset presents a world poised between paganism and Christianity and peopled with characters whose conflicts are timeless and universal.*

This first novel of *The Master of Hestviken* tetralogy sets the stage for the conflict of those antagonistic principles which characterize Undset's larger works: the struggle of the individual against the mass will of society, of man's will with God's will, and of Christian ethic against pagan imperative. It also shows the origin of the bond between Olav and Ingunn, and how it prefigures their future struggles. We see how the psychological truth of their situation binds Olav and Ingunn together, while the physical circumstances—demands of honor and social rectitude—with which that truth must be made to agree, work to force them apart. Their first sexual encounter, for instance, takes them unawares and bears them away on a tide of unreason; afterwards, the social and religious ramifications exert a pressure which both skews the original act and changes Olav's feelings both for Ingunn and for Arnvid, his only friend. Indeed, the need to square his thoughtless act with his own conscience leads Olav into the habit of rationalization and self-delusion which is to plague him in later life.

In striking down Einar Kolbeinsson and later Teit, the Icelander, he succumbs to the urgings of the pagan past. In each case, his blood rejoices even as his soul quails. Indeed, these two actions are paradigmatic, for to the end of his life he is to be restrained from doing what God requires by his duty to his dependents, and from doing what is lawful with regard to Eirik by his attachment to Ingunn. Without hope at last, he will take pride in that stoic endurance which is the other face of the pagan virtue, defiance. It is no coincidence that the dancing of the Kraaka-maal, the ancient lay of Ragnar in the snake pit, immediately precedes Ingunn's first night of love with Olav, and later her infidelity with Teit; for she, being "of little wit," obeys the urgings of the blood, which are pre-Christian and even prepagan. And the consequences of her acts are to make of her married life a snake pit indeed.

BABBITT

Type of work: Novel
Author: Sinclair Lewis (1885-1951)
Type of plot: Social satire
Time of plot: The 1920's
Locale: Zenith, fictional Midwestern town
First published: 1922

Babbitt *is a pungent satire about a man who typifies complacent mediocrity. Middle-class businessman George F. Babbitt revels in his popularity, his automobile, and his ability to make money. He drinks bootleg whiskey, bullies his wife, and ogles his manicurist. Because he is firmly grounded in realism,* Babbitt *is one of American fiction's most memorable characters; his very name has entered the language as a synonym for the widespread phenomenon he represents.*

Zenith, "the Zip City—Zeal, Zest, and Zowie," is Sinclair Lewis' satirical composite picture of the typical progressive American "business city" of the 1920's, and middle-aged, middle-class Midwesterner George F. Babbitt is its average prosperous citizen. Everything about Zenith is modern. A few old buildings, ramshackle witnesses of the city's nineteenth century origins, are embarrassing, discordant notes amid the harmony of newness produced by shining skyscrapers, factories, and railroads. One by one the old buildings are surrounded and bulldozed. The thrust of all energies in the city is toward growth: one of Zenith's most booming businesses is real estate; one of its favorite occupations is the religious tallying and charting of population increase.

As Lewis presents his characters, however, the reader discovers that the prosperity and growth of Zenith has been inversely proportional to the intellectual bankruptcy and spiritual stagnation of its inhabitants. Because they subscribe to the values of Zenith's culture, which are all based on the "Dollar Ethic," Lewis' characters think in terms of production and consumption, judge people on the grounds of their purchasing power, and seek happiness in the earning and spending of money. This creed of prosperity permeates every aspect of society. It is evident not only in political and economic beliefs (discussion between Babbitt and his friends about government affairs is limited to the monotonous refrain, "What this country needs is a good, sound business administration"), but in moral and religious attitudes as well. Thus, Dr. Drew attracts followers to his "Salvation and Five Percent" church with a combined cross-and-dollar-sign approach. Even more sinister is the facility with which the upright Babbitt carries through crooked deals in his real estate business. In one maneuver, he plots with a speculator to force a struggling grocer to buy the store building (which he has been renting for years) at a scalper's price. The money ethic is so elemental to Babbitt's conscience that he honestly feels nothing but delight and pride when the deal is completed; his only regret is that the speculator carries off nine thousand dollars while Babbitt receives a mere four hundred and fifty dollar commission. At the same time, Babbitt—with no inkling of his hypocrisy—discourses on his virtue to his friend Paul Riesling, touting his own integrity while denigrating the morality of his competitors.

The value placed on money also determines Zenith's aesthetic standards. There is no frivolity about the city's architecture; the most important structures are the strictly functional business buildings. Other structures, such as the Athletic Club—where the businessmen go to "relax" and discuss weighty matters of finance—are gaudy, unabashed copies of past styles; the Club's motley conglomeration includes everything from Roman to Gothic to Chinese. The culmination of literary talent in Zenith is the work of Chum Frink, whose daily newspaper lyrics are indistinguishable from his Zeeco car ads. He comes to Babbitt's dinner party fresh from having written a lyric in praise of drinking water instead of poison booze; with bootleg cocktail in hand, he identifies the American genius as the fellow who can run a successful business or the man who writes the Prince Albert Tobacco ads.

But most important of all, the prosperity ethic is at the heart of social norms in Zenith; it is the basis upon which each citizen judges his individual worth. Lewis' novel includes caricatures of men in every major field of endeavor: Howard Littlefield is the scholar; T. Cholmondeley Frink, the poet; Mike Monday, the popular preacher; Jake Offut, the politician; Vergil Gunch, the industrialist. Yet despite their various professions, these men are identical in their values; they are united in their complacent pride at their own success, and in their scorn for those who haven't "made it." A man is measured by his income and his possesions. Thus, Babbitt's car is far more than his means of transportation, and his acquisition of gimmicks like the nickle-plated cigar cutter more than mere whim; both car and cigar cutter are affirmations of competence and virility. But the more Babbitt and his peers strive to distinguish themselves through ownership, the more alike they seem. Thus, the men of Zenith, since they are saturated day after day with the demands of the business life and its values, are even more alike than the women, who are not as immersed in the "rat race" as their husbands.

Mercilessly revealing and minutely detailed as the portrait of Zenith is, however, *Babbitt* would not be the excellent novel it is if Lewis had stopped at that. But in addition to being an exposé of shallowness, the novel is the chronicle of one man's feeble and half-conscious attempt to break out of a meaningless and sterile existence. In the first half of the book, George Babbitt is the Zenithite *par excellence*; but in the realtor's sporadic bursts of discontent, Lewis plants seeds of the rebellion to come. Babbitt's complacency is occasionally punctured by disturbing questions: Might his wife be right that he bullied Zilla only to strut and show off his strength and virtue? Are his friends really interesting people? Does he really love his wife and enjoy his career? These nagging questions and the pressures in his life finally build sufficient tension to push Babbitt to the unprecedented step of taking a week's vacation in Maine without his wife and children. The trip relieves his tension and dissolves the questions, and he returns to another year in Zenith with renewed vigor and enthusiasm for Boosters, baseball, dinner parties, and real estate.

It takes the personal tragedy of his friend Paul Riesling to really shock Babbitt out of his routine way of life; Paul's shooting of his wife and consequent imprisonment, which occur approximately midway in the novel, shake Babbitt to his foundations. The Babbitt of the first half of the story is a parody; the Babbitt of the second half, a weak and struggling human being. After Paul goes to prison, Babbitt, to all appearances, throws over his whole previous life style: he drinks, smokes, and curses; he frequents wild parties, befriends the city's "bohemian set," adopts radical opinions, and has a love affair. All these things are part of his rebellion against stifling circumstances and his attempt to escape into individuality. The attempt fails because he lacks the inner strength to be independent, and his revolt is ultimately little more than a teapot tempest. Whether preaching the philosophy of the Elks or rebelliously praising the radical politics of Seneca Doane, whether giving a dinner party with his wife or sneaking out to see Mrs. Judique, Babbitt never truly acts on his own.

Thus, by the end of the novel, Babbitt has "returned to the fold," joining the Good Citizen's League and redoubling his zeal in behalf of Zenith Booster activities. But even though Babbitt lacks the strength to break out of his mold, Lewis does not imply that he is unchanged by his experience. On the contrary, Babbitt rediscovers his love for his wife, and learns something about himself. The Babbitt at the close of the novel has grown in awareness, even if he has proven himself incapable of essentially changing his life. If he has lost his own individuality, he is still able to hope for better things for his son Ted, of whose elopement he secretly approves.

Nancy G. Ballard

THE BACCHAE

Type of work: Drama
Author: Euripides (480-406 B.C.)
Type of plot: Classical tragedy
Time of plot: Remote antiquity
Locale: Thebes, in Boeotia
First presented: c. 405 B.C.

This complex and disturbing drama has been the subject of interpretations so diverse as to be sometimes diametrically opposed. It has been treated, for example, on the one hand as a condemnation of religious excess, and on the other as the playwright's late acceptance of the Dionysian rites.

The Bacchae, written in Macedonia after the author's voluntary exile from Athens and produced posthumously, is one of Euripides' most poetically beautiful as well as thematically difficult dramas. The play abounds in passages of nature description unsurpassed in any of the playwright's other works; the lyrics of the chorus in praise of Dionysus and his gifts of wine and sensuality are particularly exquisite. The vivid landscapes and hymns to bacchanalian pleasure in the first part of the play are so intriguing, in fact, that Pentheus seems a combined brute and prude for opposing the spread of the Dionysian cult in Thebes. In the second half of the play, Euripides' descriptive talent turns to a different purpose with equal effectiveness, as he presents the grisly scene of Pentheus' slaughter by the revelers, terrifying in their mindless, maddened frenzy.

The fact that *The Bacchae* has been alternately interpreted as Euripides' approval of the Dionysian nature-worship cult and as his condemnation of religious excess, attests to the play's thematic complexity. Critics of the first persuasion can cite several undeniable facts as evidence. Perhaps the first thing one notices upon beginning the play is that the Chorus, which traditionally functions as the upholder of moral values and mouthpiece of social standards, in *The Bacchae* aligns itself with Dionysus and fully supports his attempt to introduce his cult into Thebes. Also a follower of the god-man is Tiresias, the familiar blind prophet of Greek tragedy, who vehemently exhorts Pentheus to accept the new cult and accompany him—along with Pentheus' grandfather, Cadmus—to the worship rites. But perhaps the strongest evidence that can be used to support this interpretation is that the doom foretold by the Chorus for Pentheus, if he persists in opposing what they view as the unquestionable right of the gods to demand worship, comes true; the king of Thebes is killed by his own mother in a most savage and gruesome manner. And yet critics who feel that the play is Euripides' condemnation of excessive emotionalism and religious fanaticism can turn this same event of Pentheus' cruel death around: is the author not portraying the king as a victim of an unnecessary, unreasoning frenzy? This reading can also be supported by pointing out that Pentheus is not an evil character by any means, but a king who has a duty to protect his city from disruptive social influences. Furthermore, this second interpretation would explain Agave's sentence of lifelong exile at the close of the play.

In view of Euripides' rational and humanistic stance throughout all his dramas, however, it would seem most likely that each interpretation contains some amount of truth, but that both are greatly oversimplified. It is true, for example, that Pentheus is not an evil king, but on the other hand he is unwise in his rejection of advice from his elders and total reliance on his own reason. His insistence that the cult be destroyed is a denial of one powerful aspect of man's nature; Dionysus represents a force—man's animal nature which must be reckoned with. It is also true that Agave is banished. But she is banished, one must not forget, by Dionysus himself, against whom she has sinned; and her sin certainly is not in worshiping him, but in perverting her worship by carrying it to such excessive lengths that she kills her own son. Thus it would seem that in *The Bacchae,* as elsewhere, Euripides is arguing for moderation in all things: pure reason which denies the animal element in man leads to destruction just as surely as pure sensuality unleashed without reasonable control.

BAMBI

Type of work: Novel
Author: Felix Salten (1869-1945)
Type of plot: Pastoral allegory
Time of plot: Indefinite
Locale: The woods
First published: 1923

Bambi is one of the few successful attempts to humanize animals in fiction. Salten's novel, which can be read both as a child's fairy tale and as an adult allegory, tells the story of a deer who learns that he must travel alone if he is to be strong and wise.

The first widely acclaimed work by the Austrian novelist Felix Salten (born Salzmann), *Bambi* has not only remained a classic of children's literature, but has also earned the discriminating approval of writers like John Chamberlain, Alfred Werner, and John Galsworthy. It has been reprinted often, even before Walt Disney's sentimentalized movie version extended its popularity, and has been translated into most modern languages, including Hebrew and Chinese. Yet unlike many other children's favorites adapted by Disney, *Bambi* is neither a story of comfortable sentimentality nor whimsical humor. Instead, it is a touching, lyrical, sometimes gently melancholy romance of growth and developing awareness.

Possibly the melancholy of the novel springs in part from the writer's own childhood experiences. Salten suffered early in life from rootlessness and poverty. Until a relative discovered him destitute, friendless and nearly famished, and offered him employment, he despaired ever of surviving in a world of cruel indifference. To repay his benefactor, Salten, whose formal education was meager, began to write sketches at first, then longer pieces influenced by Guy de Maupassant and Gottfried Keller. The success of *Bambi* established for Salten a demand for more children's nature books that were to include, among his best, *Fifteen Rabbits* (1930) and *Perri* (1938). In addition to juvenile fiction, Salten wrote excellent criticism and travel literature, mostly revealing his appreciation for the United States (his adopted home after 1939) and Israel.

To the child's imagination, *Bambi* treats human experiences in the form of an animal fable. Young readers learn from the book the lessons of growing up, attaining independence, enduring the sorrows of loss, and meeting the challenges of change, especially the change from youth to maturity. Although many children's fairy tales resolve conflicts in the plot through wonderful interference, in *Bambi* life experiences are treated as natural, without the interference of magic or chance. On the contrary, the book deals honestly with the most terrible emotional crises for a child: the estrangement of a father, the death of a mother. Bambi learns to become self-reliant, to earn from other forest creatures the respect owing to the powerful and fully matured. At the same time, Bambi comes to understand the weaknesses of his eternal enemy (Man); he masters his sexual rivals (Karus and Ronno), wins his mate Faline, and sires her young; and above all, he comes to terms with the Old Prince—the father-figure that has always protected and, from a distance, sustained him. From the Old Prince Bambi learns the great lesson of resolute independence. Whereas Gobo had tried to live with Man and died from his trusting mistake, the old stag has lived alone, true to the challenge he once gave Bambi: "Can't you stay by yourself?" Bambi learns to stay free, indifferent to comfort, even to friendship. He protects himself from dangers, yet is sensible to the need of protecting the weak who cannot defend themselves. Thus he provides for children—and perhaps for their parents also—Salten's message of survival in a hostile world.

BARABBAS

Type of work: Novel
Author: Pär Lagerkvist (1891-1974)
Type of plot: Realistic symbolism
Time of plot: First century
Locale: Palestine, the Near East, Rome
First published: 1949

On the surface a historical novel, Barabbas *is actually a symbolic fable of a primitive man's unwitting search for God. Lagerkvist's portrait of the criminal's emerging conscience parallels the emergence of Christian doctrine from the bewildered superstition which, the author implies, was the populace's first reaction to the Crucifixion.*

The transformation of a soul is the subject of *Barabbas*. Lagerkvist has written the novel in the tone and manner of an ancient, oft-told story, recounted simply but with feeling. The tale is told with an austerity that renders it all the more moving for being pared down to essentials. The poetic prose is precise and vivid, despite its leanness; at the end of the book, the reader realizes with amazement how clearly the author has pictured by means of a word here and a phrase there the ancient, Biblical world. *Barabbas* is a superbly-written, enigmatic novel, open to many possible interpretations. If it possesses any fault, it is only that occasionally the prose is almost self-consciously understated, that the sophistication of the author which underlies the simplicity of the narration seems to peek through; but this is a minor flaw and in no way detracts from the power of the book.

The question raised by *Barabbas* is that which haunts all of mankind, the question of what lies beyond each mortal man. Barabbas is compelled by his fate to question the universe in a manner that he does not understand or desire. Ordinarily such an uneducated thief would not have concerned himself with philosophical and moral issues, but the fact that he was acquitted and Jesus was crucified in his stead turned his world upside down. And so the book traces his wandering, both physically and spiritually, until his own end, also upon a cross. It is not the solution which is important in this novel, but the struggle. Lagerkvist deliberately leaves the ending ambiguous when he states that Barabbas's words were "as though" spoken to the darkness. The stages of this struggle are poignantly portrayed, from the initial confusion and wonderment through the denial to the final reassessment. Barabbas *wants* to believe, as so many human beings hunger for belief, but he cannot deceive himself; his belief must be hard-won, or it is meaningless and false.

The novel is rich with symbols, but symbols which never intrude; rather, they enrich the tale and serve to give it an added resonance. Most of the men and women who pass through the story are scarred, including Barabbas himself, who was at an early age scarred by his own father (whom he later unknowingly kills). These marked and deformed human beings seem to represent all of humanity, the battered multitudes who stare into the darkness, as does Barabbas, and wonder what is out there waiting for them. Love is the answer, Barabbas is told, but he finds it hard to believe; yet, the fat woman and the girl with the harelip both find momentary happiness because he has seemed briefly to love them. The slave's badge that he wears around his neck becomes a double symbol, representing both the bondage of mankind to the earth and its powers and, after it is engraved with the name of the Savior, possibilities of freedom and happiness. Of course, the Christian symbols are woven into the narrative, but they seem to arise naturally from the gradually developing Christian religion, to appear as they are needed, to help the followers keep faith. Although the short novel seems simple, it is amazingly complex and intricate, probing as it does both the human mind and the human spirit. As with so much of the best literature, *Barabbas* can be read and appreciated on several different levels, and reread from time to time with pleasure and profit.

THE BARBER OF SEVILLE

Type of work: Drama
Author: Pierre Augustin Caron de Beaumarchais (1732-1799)
Type of plot: Romantic comedy
Time of plot: Eighteenth century
Locale: Seville, Spain
First presented: 1775

Although the plot of this play has been used numerous times by dramatists and composers, Beaumarchais' approach is fresh and entertaining; it inspired Rossini's famous opera, while its sequel, The Marriage of Figaro, *became the basis of Mozart's opera of the same title.* The Barber of Seville *contains all the necessary ingredients for a romantic comedy: intrigue, wit, satire, and a brisk, fast-moving plot.*

Modern readers may be put off by the stereotypic characterization and blatant implausibility of the action of *The Barber of Seville,* but they are more than compensated by other elements of the play. Wit, humor and gaiety; sprightly movement; structural ingenuity—the sheer fun of the piece—are qualities that assure its immortality, just as they do Rossini's opera *The Barber of Seville* and Mozart's *Marriage of Figaro,* based on the sequel to that play.

To be sure, probability and depth of character are sacrificed to the plot. But this superbly constructed plot is well worth the sacrifice. It is a masterpiece of ingenuity and invention. Antagonist (Bartholo) and protagonists (Rosine, the count, Figaro) are expert chess players attempting to outwit one another. Or, given the physical vitality of the play, we might more aptly compare them to highly charged contestants in a tennis match.

In the best tradition of farce, particularly French farce, the action never seems to flag or hesitate. Even the catching songs that seemingly interrupt the action are, in fact, organic parts of it. Beginning somewhat slowly in the first act, much of which is necessary exposition, the action quickly gathers momentum, twists and turns, moves from climax to higher climax, and ends abruptly in a quick denouement. The characters are confronted with one obstacle after another, accompanied by the traditional "high" and "low" points in their fortunes; there is withheld information revealed at telling points in the play; and, finally, there is the "big scene," or *scène à faire.*

Equally entertaining is the play's humor, which ranges from broad burlesque and farce to sophisticated comedy of manners. Slapstick is punctuated with brilliant wit and trenchant observations about man and society. Yet Beaumarchais' touch is always light. Though Bartholo is ridiculed as the stock jealous cuckold pursuing a lady young enough to be his daughter, the satire stops short of bitterness or vituperation. His only punishment is that he loses Rosine, whom he never possessed in the first place. Seriousness and heavy handed moralizing is also averted. There is, of course, a moral: youthful lovers can always outwit a foolish old man. But the moral gets lost in, is absorbed by, the rollicking dialogue and madcap antics of Figaro and the count. Here the "conquest" of innocence is less offensive or cynical than in earlier neoclassical plays dealing with the same theme (Wycherley's *Country Wife* immediately comes to mind); Count Almaviva does not seduce Rosine but marries her. Not only love, but good will and lighthearted humor triumph.

BARCHESTER TOWERS

Type of work: Novel
Author: Anthony Trollope (1815-1882)
Type of plot: Social satire
Time of plot: Mid-nineteenth century
Locale: "Barchester," an English cathedral town
First published: 1857

This sequel to The Warden *is probably the best-known of the novels in the Barsetshire series.* Barchester Towers *is a story of clerical intrigue centering on the power struggle between an obnoxious and imperious bishop's wife and her scheming, sneaking chaplain. Trollope's fine irony of tone, and his delightful characterizations create a light and purely entertaining novel unburdened by social comment or philosophical questioning.*

As a young man, Anthony Trollope, son of a ne'er-do-well barrister of good family, seemed destined to further the decline of the family. An undistinguished student in two distinguished public schools, he had no hopes for university or career. His mother persuaded a family friend to find work for him in the London Post Office where his performance as a clerk was to be rated as "worthless." Indeed, the burdens of the family fell upon his indefatigable mother, who had converted a family business failure in Cincinnati, Ohio, into a literary career with her satiric study *Domestic Manners of Americans* (1832). Like his mother, the son found his way after a change of scenery. When the Post Office sent him to the south of Ireland to assist in a postal survey, his career in the postal service began to advance, he married happily, and he began to write.

Success as a novelist came when the Post Office sent Trollope to survey southwest England. A midsummer visit to the beautiful cathedral town of Salisbury produced the idea for *The Warden* (1855) and, more importantly, furnished the outlines for a fictional county, Barsetshire, which is as impressive as Hardy's Wessex or Faulkner's Yoknapatawpha. When he returned in *Barchester Towers* to the milieu of *The Warden,* which had been a modest success, he achieved resounding success. Afterwards he was to write four more novels in the series known as the Barsetshire Novels, set in the chiefly agricultural county with its seat of Barchester, a quiet town in the West of England, noted for its beautiful cathedral and fine monuments, but hardly for its commercial prosperity. Thus at middle age began the career of one of the most prolific of the Victorians and, until his last years, one of the most popular.

In his own day Trollope was admired as a realist. He himself was delighted with Hawthorne's appraisal that his novels were "just as real as if some giant had hewn a great lump out of the earth and put it under a glass case, with all its inhabitants going about their daily business, and not suspecting that they were being made a show of." Today Trollope's novels are generally viewed as comic works. Instead of merely being people going about their daily affairs, Trollope's characters are in the grip of a firmly controlled irony.

The irony which Trollope perceives in the affairs of the men of Barchester arises from discrepancies between the ideals they uphold and the means by which they uphold their ideals. A layman with no special knowledge of the Church of England, Trollope vividly depicts the internecine war which breaks out between the party of the new Bishop of Barchester and that of the former Bishop's son, Archdeacon Grantly. Both parties intend to preserve the integrity of the Church. However, the Church is vested in buildings, furnishings, livings; and these clergymen fight for power over the appurtenances, the worldly forms of the Church spiritual.

Barchester Towers consists of a number of subplots, all of which are related to the ecclesiastical power struggle. Since buildings, furnishings, and livings are occupied by human beings, the clerics who guard the Church must also dispose of the lives of men. The subplots involve characters who become mere objects in a dispute over power—for example, Mr. Harding and the Quiverfuls in the competition for wardenship of Hiram's Hospital, or Eleanor Bold in the rivalry of two clergymen for her hand in marriage. Episodes not directly related to the ecclesiastical battles serve to underscore them: as in the parallel between the rivalry of Mrs. Lookaloft and Mrs. Greenacre and the absurd ploys of the higher orders that abound in the novel.

The main conflicts of the novel are those which engage the high and the mighty of Barchester. The strength of Trollope's satire lies in his refusal to oversimplify the motives of these worldlings of the Church or to deny them sincerity in their defense of the Church. Even as Slope genuinely believes Grantly and his type to be the enemies of religion, so also does the Archdeacon honestly believe that Slope is the kind who could well ruin the Church of England.

One of Trollope's devices for deflating these militant clerics is to treat their wars in the mock heroic vein. After the first meeting between the Archdeacon and the Proudies, the author declares, "And now, had I the pen of a mighty poet, would I sing in epic verse the noble wrath of the Archdeacon." In time, Mrs. Proudie is ironically likened unto Juno, Medea, even Achilles, while the Archdeacon's extravagance in celebrating Eleanor Bold's marriage to his champion, Arabin, is suggestive of the glorious warrior returning from the fields with his spoils.

The reduction of martial glory is furthered by a recurrent analogy with games, underscoring the truth that Barchester's leadership is really concerned with social rather than spiritual or moral issues. Slope's major defeats arise from his indecorous behavior with Madeline Neroni, who is alert to every possible move. Worse, he underestimates his other opponent, Mrs. Proudie, and at the end he discovers that "Mrs. Proudie had checkmated him."

Human strife is incongruous with the idealized setting of peaceful Barchester, its venerable church and close, its rural villages round about, all endowed with a loveliness suggestive of the age-old pastoral tradition. The cathedral itself seems to judge the folly of its worldly champions. As the battles commence, Archdeacon Grantly looks up to the cathedral towers as if evoking a blessing for his efforts. However genial the comedy played out beneath the Barchester towers, the outcome is not without serious significance. For the ultimate result is the further separation of man from his ideals. In the end, the Bishop's wife finds that her "sphere is more extended, more noble, and more suited to her ambition than that of a cathedral city," while the Bishop himself "had learnt that his proper sphere of action lay in close contiguity with Mrs. Proudie's wardrobe." As Mr. Slope makes his ignominious final departure from the city, "he gave no longing lingering look after the cathedral towers." As for the Archdeacon, it is sufficient for him to "walk down the High Street of Barchester without feeling that those who see him are comparing his claims with those of Mr. Slope."

Despite the futility of its human strivings, *Barchester Towers* is a cheerful novel, not merely because the satire provokes laughter, but also because occasionally, briefly, the real and the ideal meet. Mr. Harding, for example, is too peaceable, too naïve, too reticent to be effective in the world. Nonetheless, when he is prompted by his dedication to simple justice to introduce Mr. Quiverful personally to his own former charges at Hiram Hospital, an action representing the union of his profession and practice, the consequence is greater than the act would suggest for it caused the Barchester world to treat Mr. Quiverful with more respect as he assumes his duties.

Quite appropriately, then, Trollope brings the novel to its close with pastoral serenity by offering a word of Mr. Harding, who functions not as a hero and not as a perfect divine, but as a good, humble man without guile.

Catherine E. Moore

BARNABY RUDGE

Type of work: Novel
Author: Charles Dickens (1812-1870)
Type of plot: Historical romance
Time of plot: 1775-1780
Locale: England
First published: 1841

Barnaby Rudge *was Dickens' first venture into the field of historical fiction. A novel filled with violence and melodrama, it treats with particular vividness the historic Gordon riots and the burning of Newgate prison. Although Dickens attempted to create suspense and sustain interest through the nightmarish plot, which combines the dual themes of private crime and public disorder, it is for its unforgettable minor characters that readers still continue to appreciate the work.*

Written when the author was already famous and financially successful, *Barnaby Rudge* heralds the period of his great socially conscious novels culminating with *Dombey and Son* (1846) and *David Copperfield* (1849). *Barnaby Rudge* treats the same theme of the evil effects of social institutions on children dealt with in *Oliver Twist* and *Nicholas Nickleby,* but expands it considerably, concentrating on society's atrocities against the poor and implying that this phenomenon makes crime virtually inevitable. The madness spreading across all levels of society in this novel is reminiscent of Sir Walter Scott's depiction of the Porteous riots in *The Heart of Midlothian.*

The binding force of the novel, both thematically and structurally, is crime. Dickens' own unfortunate experiences from his youth emerge in themes repeated in most of his works: Barnaby's unhappy childhood; an irresponsible father; prisons in need of reform; a child improperly nurtured. For Barnaby is not a half-wit by chance; rather, he merely pays the consequences of both his father's and society's malign neglect. These notions are combined with Barnaby's contribution to the riots in which he innocently participates solely for the pleasure of carrying a flag and wearing a bow. Romantic and Gothic views of society are structurally interwoven also by crime.

Many of Dickens' novels, including *Barnaby Rudge,* have been criticized for their melodrama. As Dickens' later attraction to theatrics suggests, melodrama was not a careless result of his plots. Rather, because he was a satirist Dickens sought to involve his audience emotionally with his characters as a surer way of convincingly exposing social ills. As an example of this satirical technique, *Barnaby Rudge* is both pathetic and successful.

BARON MÜNCHAUSEN'S NARRATIVE

Type of work: Mock-heroic chronicle
Author (in part): Rudolph Erich Raspe (1737-1794)
Type of plot: Picaresque romance
Time of plot: Eighteenth century
Locale: Various countries and the moon
First published: 1785

This collection of tales was begun by Raspe, but went through so many subsequent editions, each of which included newly added tales, that by the time of the seventh edition, the stories began to lose their original distinctive flavor. In their freewheeling fancy and outrageous, good-humored boasting, these stories of the Baron's feats foreshadow the exploits of the American folk hero, Paul Bunyan.

Creative literature, like all products of a society, explains in its own fashion the values and aspirations of the culture from which it springs. *Baron Münchausen's Narrative* is no exception to this rule.

Rudolph Raspe, the creator of Münchausen, led his main character on a raucous tour of many eighteenth century European countries as well as through outer space and earth's inner space. The tour also covered several traditional literary genres, including the Rabelaisian adventure, the European travel journal, and broad-based satire. It is as a work of satire, however, that *Baron Münchausen's Narrative* is best understood.

Raspe intended Münchausen as a spoof on the pretentions of the French Enlightenment's intellectual heritage. By 1785, when Münchausen appeared in print, the rational, skeptical intellectual influences then coming to the forefront of French intellectual life had begun to attract a sympathetic public in similar German circles. Like their French cousins, the German *philosophes* embraced the notion that man was a rational, perfectable creature, capable of understanding and controlling himself and his environment with the aid of science. The enlightened German thinker had little regard for those who persisted in explaining social or natural events as the working of change, fate, or luck. Man controlled, or had the potential to control, his own destiny. He did not need chance; he had his own wits.

Münchausen's adventures and his explanation of them do not conform to the rationalist view of the world. In his peregrinations, Münchausen constantly finds himself ensnared in one implausible, unanticipated, and precarious misadventure after another. No less amazing is his ability to extricate himself from his predicaments through no rational or calculated action on his own part. Chance, not human reason, is the harpie which grants Münchausen a plentitude of reprieves. Luck, not man's cognitive powers, is the mysterious measure of all things. In ridiculing the Enlightenment tradition, Raspe helped to implement the developing intellectual structure which would soon prove to be the most incisive critique of Enlightenment thought: Romanticism.

BARREN GROUND

Type of work: Novel
Author: Ellen Glasgow (1874-1945)
Type of plot: Social criticism
Time of plot: Late nineteenth and early twentieth centuries
Locale: Rural Virginia
First published: 1925

In this realistic novel of the South, Glasgow portrays the struggle of an aristocratic class to maintain high living standards in the face of humiliating economic facts. Dorinda, the heroine, is contrasted in her strength and vitality to her weak-willed lover Jason.

Barren Ground is a disturbing novel because it represents the ways life can be lived under the most harrowing of circumstances. Glasgow writes about farmers who are faced with the difficulties of making an unwilling earth— a waste land in fact—yield. A few triumph against the odds; some do their best and barely survive; others give up and die early. All except those in the last category work exceedingly hard. Glasgow believes, as she says in the 1933 Preface to *Barren Ground,* that "the novel is experience illumined by imagination." In this novel, she is faithful to her own experience in her native Virginia, but, as in much of her work, she colors that experience with a dark imagination, an imagination that views human life as a constant struggle in which even the strong do not always survive. And those who do survive must adjust their idealism to fit reality.

The main theme of the novel is stated by its main character, Dorinda Oakley, who thinks that for the majority life is "barren ground where they have to struggle to make anything grow." Dorinda has more than the soil of rural Virginia to make her feel this way. At the age of twenty she has the seed of love planted in her heart only to have it uprooted by her lover's weakness: he marries Geneva Ellgood under the duress of her brothers. Henceforward her heart is indeed barren ground where passion is concerned. And, Glasgow seems to suggest, Dorinda's life is also barren ground as far as happiness is concerned. To women, Glasgow writes, "love and happiness [are] interchangeable terms." After Jason jilts her, Dorinda spends a lifetime distrusting men and building up emotional, mental, physical, and financial walls in order to protect herself from them. She permits herself to marry Nathan Pedlar only because she fears loneliness and because he is submissive to her and is willing to live without any physical intimacy with her. Dorinda becomes a cynic about love and marriage, believing that they seldom, if ever, go together; and even when they do the love does not endure.

Dorinda, like the characters of Thomas Hardy, is driven by forces beyond her control, by the "eternal purpose." She feels that the trivial incidents in life are the crucial ones. One of these trivial incidents was Nathan's train trip, which resulted in his heroic death. That incident

> was apparently as trivial as her meeting with Jason in the road, as the
> failure of her aim when the gun had gone off, as the particular place and
> moment when she had fallen down in Fifth Avenue. These accidents had
> changed the course of her life. Yet none of them could she have foreseen
> and prevented; and only once, she felt, in that hospital in New York, had
> the accident or the device of fortune been in her favour.

Much like Dreiser's Carrie Meeber or Hurstwood, Dorinda is "a straw in the
wind, a leaf on a stream."

But Glasgow, as she says in her Preface, believes that "character is fate," so
that the individual destinies of her characters are partly determined by the
nature they inherit, by, that is, their blood: destiny is in the genes. The "vein
of iron" that keeps Dorinda struggling (and that helps her to succeed) is a
product of the "sense" of her great-grandfather, a member of the Southern
upper class, and the physical strength of her father, a member of the "poor
white" class. Jason fails, like his father had, because of "bad blood." Even
though unforeseen events control our destinies, our characters determine
what we do under the unasked-for circumstances.

Archetypally, Dorinda is at first Medea, who falls in love with a Jason
who will forsake her for another. But she becomes an Artemis or an Atalanta,
the devouring female who remains estranged physically and psychologically,
from the male. (In the last analysis, Glasgow shows that each individual
is always isolated from his fellow creatures.) She is also, paradoxically, an
Earth Mother, who causes the soil to be productive and who keeps the best
cows in the state. Her maternal instinct is satisfied by this bond with the soil
as well as by her adoption through marriage of Nathan's children, John
Abner in particular.

Though she is never a whole person psychologically, Dorinda does the best
she can, given her character and experience. She achieves a wholeness that
most never achieve. Though a woman, she farms better than most of the men
in her rural community. Her black hair symbolizes her relationship with the
earth and combines with its opposite, the sky, in her blue eyes. Her experiences are much like her mother's (an early separation from a lover, a loveless
marriage), but she manages to combine her mother's hard-work habits with
a contentment—if not a happiness—that her morally repressed mother never
had. Jason goes away to New York and comes back to a dying father just
as Dorinda is to do. But Jason allows the interminable broomsedge to conquer him. Dorinda does not.

BARRY LYNDON

Type of work: Novel
Author: William Makepeace Thackeray (1811-1863)
Type of plot: Picaresque romance
Time of plot: Eighteenth century
Locale: England, Ireland, and Europe
First published: 1843

From the first boastful paragraph to the last petulant complaint against his wife's deceit, Redmond Barry in his narrative constantly exposes himself as a man of the basest tendencies. Given to murder, adept at winning at cards, a skillful and deceitful wooer, he is a thoroughly corrupt scoundrel in the pattern of Fielding's Jonathan Wild.

Published three years before *Vanity Fair, The Luck of Barry Lyndon: A Romance of the Last Century,* as it was titled in serial presentation, is a minor masterpiece of classic comedy, embodying many of the same concerns with sham, materialistic values, and egoism found in Thackeray's later major novel. The twentieth century reader will recognize the anti-hero type as many of Thackeray's contemporaries did not. For Barry, the appealing rogue, is true to his own code and values, reprehensible as they might seem. His autobiography, cast in the vehicle of adult remembrance of some forty years of his life, shows Thackeray's skillful handling of time and imaginative creation of picaresque episodes so that Barry may ingenuously, naïvely, and yet arrogantly, reveal his own vices and ambiguous virtues.

Readers who admit to an ambivalent delight in *Vanity Fair's* picara, Becky Sharp, will recognize the psychology of Barry, a man whose vigor, daring, and self-concern vividly emerge far beyond mere revelations of eighteenth century life. Thackeray is much more than a social historian. The three-part arrangement of the novel permits the reader to view Barry in adolescence and first love in Ireland, then abroad in English and Prussian military service, gambling in Europe, and the return to England in a marital conquest after his martial and monetary luck. In the tradition of Defoe, Smollett, and Fielding, Thackeray provides a picaro who can reveal the tawdriness of empire and gaming as well as reflect on the kinds of truths by which all people deceive themselves. Readers of Hardy's *Tess of the d'Urbervilles* recognize Barry's longing for place and position—for his rightful aristocratic heritage—distorted though such longing may be, along with his ruthless manipulation of others, especially women, to gain his goal.

In *Barry Lyndon,* Thackeray provides a deftly compressed, imaginative re-creation of a past age. But ultimately what gives the "romance" far more substance than that offered by the usual historical novel is the skillfully sustained self-revelation of a man true to false values.

BARTHOLOMEW FAIR

Type of work: Drama
Author: Ben Jonson (1573?-1637)
Type of plot: Satirical comedy
Time of plot: Early seventeenth century
Locale: Smithfield, London
First presented: 1614

The slender plotline of this comedy is similar to the Arabian Night's *tale of Harun-al-Rashid, as Adam Overdo, in disguise, metes out justice to various people. The play teems with life and is unsurpassed for its delineation of English low types of the early Jacobean period.*

Two years after the first performance of *Bartholomew Fair,* Jonson published his accumulated plays in a folio volume entitled *Works.* Such an act was as unprecedented as it was audacious because it implied both that Jonson considered himself worthy of serious attention as a writer and that drama should be considered an important part of literature. *Bartholomew Fair* comes from Jonson's greatest period as a comic dramatist. Like *Volpone, Epicœne,* and *The Alchemist,* Jonson's *Bartholomew Fair* is characterized by a remarkable unity provided by a particular event or location. Plot and character are thus focused around a prevailing mania or social evil resident in that place. Jonson, in all these plays, makes an incisive analysis of the social scene and shows his opposition to man's acquisitive tendencies. *Bartholomew Fair* is one of Jonson's most direct defenses of drama (and art in general), a form which, though "illusory" in nature, is a means to the truth. The play is, as well, a clear portrayal of the reality of the world's evil and a plea for a sober appreciation of the depth of that evil.

The play is framed by an "induction" given by the stage keeper and the bookholder in which the illusory character of drama as reality is raised for our consideration. The "induction" includes an agreement between the audience and the author about what the audience can and cannot expect in the forthcoming drama, with a reminder that the audience should not look for real persons in the characters on stage, nor should it expect to see the Smithfield fair presented there. This disclaimer is of course ironic, for Jonson intends that his audience see itself in his characters. At the end of the play, the audience is invited to participate in the final celebration at Overdo's house, thus bringing the convention of life-as-drama full circle by drawing the audience into the world of the fair.

The puppet play which occurs in Act V is the center of Jonson's statement about drama and art. The puppet play is referred to in each act, since Littlewit has written the script and several characters look forward to attending the production. It is the climax of *Bartholomew Fair,* as there the various characters' delusions are torn away. The range of possible aesthetic reactions to the illusion of drama is nicely detailed by the play-within-a-play. There is Cokes' naïve belief, Busy's Puritan denunciation of the theater, and Leatherhead's manipulation (as puppet master) of the audience's sensibilities. We also see Grace, Winwife, Knockem, and others in the audience who not only watch the puppet show but comment on Cokes' and Busy's comments. Jonson's audience or his reader is, of course, observing those observers. Cokes worries about the injury one of the puppets may have received with a blow on the head and naïvely repeats all the puppets' lines as truth. Busy carries on the traditional Puritan argument against theater with the puppet Dionysius, charging that actors are unnatural since males dress up as females. The puppet answers that puppets are neither male nor female and lifts his garment to prove it. Busy, so gullible as to believe he was seriously arguing with a person, accepts the puppet's refutation.

The puppet show itself reduces the two greatest myths of Renaissance literature—the Hero and Leander ideal of love and the Damon and Pythias ideal of friendship—to the story of Hero the whore and the ale house roisterers Damon and Pythias. The obscenities and scatological references in the puppet play are appropriate when humanity is reduced to that most elemental level where even sexual differences disappear, as in the puppets themselves.

The real protagonist of the play is the fair itself, and Bartholomew Fair becomes a metaphor for the world. The two sets of characters—the "respectable" fair-goers and the disreputable fair employees—are seen to be essentially alike. They come together in the common acts of buying, drinking, and eating. Finally, there is no difference between them. What is there to choose between Edgeworth the cutpurse and a drunken Waspe? Or between the madman Trouble-All and Quarlous, disguised as a madman? Or between Knockem and Busy? The madness of the fair is the madness of the world. Certain words recur as motifs in the play, and the action comes to reflect these words: "vapours," meaning a game of arguing or irrational whims; "mad" and "madness"; "enormity"; and "warrant," meaning license. For Jonson, the whole world is regarded as *mad,* governed by follies and *vapours,* committing *enormities* of one sort or another, entirely governed by irrationalities, and seeking *warrants* of various kinds to justify its behavior.

Different characters refuse to accept the fair for what it is or to acknowledge the reality of the world's madness. Overdo disguises himself in order to catch troublemakers and mete out justice; instead, he is always too late and is mistaken for a criminal himself. Cokes is blinded by his innocent country origins and duped over and over again. Busy deceives himself by equating the fair not with the world but with sin. He reduces himself to an animal by closing his eyes to keep out the corruption of the fair and sniffing his way to Ursula's tent for roast pig. Dame Purecraft goes to the opposite extreme by embracing madness; falling in love with Trouble-All is a way out of the madness of the world. As she says, "Mad do they call him! the world is mad in error, but he is mad in truth." Ursula is the only one who accepts her role without illusion or inhibition. She is a caricature of the *Urmutter,* fat and gross, but honest.

Each of these characters, with the exception of Ursula, makes elaborate attempts to disguise from himself the true nature of mankind; that animal nature is fully expressed at the fair. Justice Adam Overdo is gently chastened at the end of the play by Quarlous with a line that can stand for Jonson's reminder to his audience: "Remember you are but Adam, flesh and blood." In *Bartholomew Fair* Jonson is no longer trying to change the world; instead he is urging acceptance, without illusion, of the corruption of the world.

Margaret McFadden-Gerber

THE BEACH OF FALESÁ

Type of work: Novella
Author: Robert Louis Stevenson (1850-1894)
Type of plot: Adventure romance
Time of plot: Nineteenth century
Locale: An island in the South Seas
First published: 1892

A suspenseful tale of intrigue in the South Seas, this novella is distinguished from Stevenson's other works of fiction by its realism. It pictures unregenerate human nature—the natives with their superstition and gullibility; the traders with their crudeness, treachery and degradation, and the missionaries with their misguided zeal.

The first person narrative of *The Beach of Falesá,* apparently casual, is written in the flawless, graceful prose of which Stevenson was a master. The colloqualisms that Wiltshire uses are just enough to suggest his character and degree of education (or lack of education), but the descriptions and action are the artful work of one of the finest prose craftsmen in the English language.

The story presents the hypocrisy of Europeans opposed to the simplicity and honesty of the islanders. From the tale's beginning, with the fake "marriages," Stevenson establishes this conflict. At the same time, the question of morality and religion (in the person of the missionaries) is raised. The story is compact, but dense and rich, suggesting much more than appears on the surface.

Wiltshire's reaction to Uma's story dramatically illustrates the kind of man he is; perhaps even he does not realize how extraordinary a gesture he is making when he destroys the fake marriage certificate and has the traveling missionary perform a legitimate ceremony. Although uncertain about the significance of the situation and the eventual outcome, the reader understands now that Wiltshire is a man of genuine—if rough and ready—integrity.

One of Stevenson's last completed long stories, *The Beach of Falesá* suggests that he was moving into a new realm of serious and symbolic fiction before he died. Not much longer than *Dr. Jekyll and Mr. Hyde,* the tale penetrates more directly and perhaps more accurately the depths of the human personality. The scenes of the discovery and destruction of the fake devils are both terrifying and rich with meaning. As Wiltshire implies, all of us nurse these irrational fears within us, a carry-over possibly from childhood, and if we are to be free, we must destroy these devils. *The Beach of Falesá* is far more than an adventure yarn of the South Seas; it suggests some of the same concerns that Conrad was to investigate in such stories as *Heart of Darkness.*

BEAUCHAMP'S CAREER

Type of work: Novel
Author: George Meredith (1828-1909)
Type of plot: Political romance
Time of plot: Nineteenth century
Locale: England
First published: 1874-1875

Since Beauchamp's Career *appeared only a short time before Meredith published his famous* Essay on Comedy, *the novel bears the stamp of Meredith's theorizing. The comedy is characteristically subtle, and is used as a complex device for social criticism; the plot is simple and the dialogue less discursive than is most Meredith novels.*

George Meredith's novels have never attracted as wide an audience as the fiction of his contemporaries, Dickens, Thackeray, and George Eliot; critics in his own day generally ignored Meredith's work. Not until the publication of *The Egoist* in 1879 did the author gain much critical attention or public popularity. Meredith's lack of popularity among the general public has been partially due to his difficult prose style, and partially to the inaccessibility of his abstract and philosophical comic vision. His style is an odd mixture of the intellectual and emotional, the analytical and lyrical; his famous epigrams, for example, are often so compact and riddle-like as to elude easy understanding, while his descriptive passages and love scenes are frequently laden with rich images and inspired with great sensitivity. Meredith was primarily a philosopher who pleaded for the classical ideal of the golden mean; his witty comedy was aimed at restoring sanity and balance, at bringing men to their senses by making them laugh at the spectacle of their follies.

In *Beauchamp's Career,* Meredith brings his rational comic vision to bear in his examination of politics; this novel is political both on the surface and on the deeper thematic level. On the surface, the plot concerns the political career of Nevil Beauchamp, and follows first his experiences in the Crimean War, and later, his campaign as candidate for Bevisham (based on the campaign of the author's friend, F. A. Maxse, in an election at Southampton). On a deeper level, however, *Beauchamp's Career* traces the hero's growth to political awareness through the events in his personal life; Meredith brilliantly dramatizes the inseparable nature of the political and personal in real life.

Nevil begins as a foolish young man, infatuated with hazy romantic notions, who rushes forth to defend English honor against French insolence, and then goes to fight in the Crimea. His first love affair, with the French aristocrat Renée, results from his naïve and idealistic romanticism, which retains its hold on him for some time afterwards, as seen in his chivalric answer to his old lover's summons during the height of his campaign in Bevisham. In his second love relationship—with rich, beautiful, Tory Cecelia Halkett—Nevil becomes much more complexly and realistically involved; both he and Cecelia are forced to deal with the problem of their conflicting ideologies and backgrounds. His last involvement is with Jenny Denham, Dr. Shrapnel's niece. Although Meredith himself was a Radical, he uses the rather absurd figure of the doctor to illustrate the follies to which such a stance, untempered by good sense, can descend. But Dr. Shrapnel's niece is both sensitive and sensible, an intellectual woman who, unlike her uncle, blends emotional depth with rational intelligence. Ironically, it is Jenny—who is not an active person politically—who at last becomes Nevil's permanent partner; and, also ironically, it is shortly after their union and the birth of their child that Nevil dies as a result of an act of humanity, an act at once apolitical and the most intensely political of his career.

THE BEAUX' STRATAGEM

Type of work: Drama
Author: George Farquhar (1678-1707)
Type of plot: Comedy of manners
Time of plot: Early eighteenth century
Locale: Lichfield, England
First presented: 1707

Instead of the standard Restoration setting of London or Bath, this comedy takes place in the English town of Lichfield and sports lively tavern scenes and warm pictures of small-town life. Particularly interesting is the author's stance, generally unheard of except for Milton's tracts sixty years earlier, in favor of divorce.

Restoration Comedy has been condemned as immoral and superficial, but neither the moral indignation of its critics in centuries past nor the cool contempt of modern commentators has diminished its perennial appeal. Despite its carefree attitude toward moral conventions and its willingness to indulge in trivial humor, the comedy written at the end of the seventeenth and in the very early eighteenth centuries continues to enjoy a theatrical and literary life.

George Farquhar's plays were written at a time when the early exuberance and rakish irreverence of Restoration Comedy was beginning to give way to a more sentimental and moralized comedy. Farquhar's heart was with his Restoration masters, particularly Etherege, whose comedies written some thirty years earlier reveled in cynicism, wit, and the ridicule of pretentious dandified behavior. But Farquhar knew his audiences wanted more to "feel" than to "think" so he curbed his natural bent toward wit and tried to develop a sentimental side. His Dorinda is compassionate enough, but one has the impression Farquhar would have preferred to make her more like Etherege's Harriet in *The Man of Mode* (1676)—a woman possessing no less charm and far more wit and worldly wisdom.

If Farquhar had to soften his satire, he managed to direct some of the energy that his precursors would have used for purposes of ridicule toward criticism of social injustice. It is one of the ironies of literary and dramatic history that a dramatist less comfortable with sentiment and feeling than with contempt and ridicule should have launched what we have come to know as the theater of social protest; ironic, because ordinarily we do not associate contempt with caring.

The cause that Farquhar championed was divorce. Here too there is delicious irony. The prevailing theme of Restoration Comedy was seduction; its favorite butt, the cuckold. Infidelity was the fuel on which the cavalier "engines" ran. Happiness in marriage was as rare in fact as it was naïve in principle. For the famous Restoration rakes of Etherege and Wycherley marriage was a trap to be avoided at all cost; its greatest danger was that it exposed the husband to the risk of cuckoldry. (Sullen, at one point, even tells his wife "if you can contrive any way of being a whore without making me a cuckold, do it and welcome.) That is one danger a bachelor escaped. So for Farquhar to make such an eloquent case for Mrs. Sullen's liberation from marriage is in one sense only to free her and her husband from the dangers of social embarrassment. Divorced, Mrs. Sullen is free to love Archer without cuckolding her husband.

Nevertheless, Farquhar's bid for divorce involves more than the oddity of Restoration manners. It is obvious that he has drifted far enough from Restoration cynicism to believe in the unnaturalness of an unhappy marriage. Although he admired Restoration sophistication and the stylish cultivation of a studied and brilliant artificiality, Farquhar was enough of a child of the dawning Age of Sentiment to sympathize with the cry for nature, the plea for true sentiment. At the end of Act III, Mrs. Sullen is eloquent in her desperate assertions to Dorinda regarding the emotional suffering attendant on an unhappy marriage: Who can prove "the unaccountable disaffections of wedlock? Can a jury sum up the endless aversions that are rooted in our souls, or can a bench give judgment upon antipathies?" Such speeches open the flood gates to truly serious feeling; they open the play's action to problems wit alone cannot solve. There is no clever answer, nor did Farquhar intend that there should be, to Mrs. Sullen's question, "Can radical hatreds ever be reconciled?" And when she closes the act with the famous exclamation, "No, no sister, nature is the first lawgiver," we know that Farquhar has left the ranks of Restoration dramatists. That exclamation is followed by a rhymed epilogue (that closes the act) which contrasts the harmony of the earth's elements to the agonizing disharmony of a bad marriage. Mrs. Sullen becomes reminiscent of Ulysses in Shakespeare's *Troilus and Cressida*; when the perspicacious Greek hero analyzes the disunity of the Greeks, he makes similar allusions to the harmony of the spheres. There can be no victory for the Greeks unless each man and faction take their proper place in the ranks of the Greek host. Mrs. Sullen sounds no less noble when she insists that without harmony and understanding between a husband and wife the marriage can have no center— nor tolerate a master: "Omnipotence is just, were man but wise."

The divorce theme is treated seriously, but Farquhar will not follow through on the sublime note of Mrs. Sullen's epilogue. Her husband finally agrees to a separation, but if Archer had not secured the papers from the robbers and placed them in Sir Charles Freeman's hands, Sullen would never have agreed to a divorce. He is tricked, then, in the spirit of Restoration foolery into agreeing to the divorce on which Mrs. Sullen lavished so much sincere emotion. However, the charm of their brisk repartee at parting redeems the tone of Restoration theater itself and leaves the audience stunned with the brilliance of Farquhar's benevolent satire as the two adversaries shower barbs of polite insult in taking leave of each other.

Farquhar's closing tone reminds us again that he has been writing a

Restoration Comedy, not a sentimental domestic problem play. The happiness of the separated couple is as great as that of the united lovers, Dorinda and Aimwell. The Restoration rake-heroes, Archer and Aimwell, have out-thieved the thieves and stolen their way into the hearts—and fortunes—of their ladies. Mrs. Sullen is freed by Archer's trickery, and we are assured that she has freed herself from a brute only to fall into the hands of a fortune hunter—a charming one, to be sure, and not at all "sullen." The wry note on which the play ends reestablishes the "way of the world" as Restoration Comedy had conceived it. Farquhar may have tipped his hat to sentimental values, but the buttons of his costumes are firmly snapped by the same tailors who fashioned the theater of Etherege and Wycherley, Vanbrugh and Congreve. The divorce theme lingers in the mind, but the antics of Archer and Aimwell, the disguises, the "catechisms" of love (Archer and Cherry, the Landlord's daughter), and the farcical confrontation of Count Bellair and Sullen all distinguish Farquhar as the last of the Restoration comic dramatists.

Peter A. Brier

THE BEAVER COAT

Type of work: Drama
Author: Gerhart Hauptmann (1862-1946)
Type of plot: Satiric comedy
Time of plot: Nineteenth century
Locale: Prussia, on the outskirts of Berlin
First presented: 1893

In this folk comedy, the author of The Weavers—*a starkly realistic proletarian drama—displays another side of his genius. His theme of mistaken identity centers around a person universally praised, though cunning and depraved; and the portrait of the stupid magistrate and his inefficient court is a satirical masterpiece.*

Gerhart Hauptmann's career spans an enormous variety of themes and styles, and includes masterpieces in each genre. *The Beaver Coat* is one of the few great comedies of the German stage, turning the usually tragic world view of the naturalists to a comic variation, though tinged with satire that bites as well as amuses. Set among the common people of the Berlin that Hauptmann knew firsthand, it captures not only individuals but a whole social organism, growing and changing. Each of the characters has a past which helps to explain his present life, and the future directions, not only of the individual lives, but of the suburb itself, are evident. Indeed, a decade later Hauptmann turned once again to the world of *The Beaver Coat* and wrote a sequel, *The Red Rooster,* though in the later work the comedy was darkened with tragic overtones.

The themes and characters of the work may owe their intense life to their closeness to Hauptmann's own experience. Many of the sources for the work may be found in Hauptmann's autobiography—his own landlord, for example, served as a model for Krüger. His experience with Prussian bureaucrats, who had attempted to censor his works, gave the tone for the character of Von Wehrhahn, a type which Hauptmann detested. It is ironic that just such a benighted official was assigned to censor this very play; he passed it because he was sure it was totally harmless and bound to fail. Hauptmann's depiction of this character, whose arrogance actually prevents the discovery of a crime, harkens back to Kleist's *The Broken Jug.* But whereas Kleist's dishonest judge is discovered and disgraced, Hauptmann's work ends with irony, not justice. In this, he is true to his Naturalist conceptions of drama, but also demonstrates the inevitable collapse of the Prussian system, hopelessly ineffective in trying to stop the forces of life and change, whether it be Dr. Fleischer's liberalism or Frau Wolff's dream of prosperity.

THE BEGGARS' BUSH

Type of work: Drama
Authors: John Fletcher (1579-1625) and Philip Massinger (1583-1640)
Type of plot: Romantic comedy
Time of plot: The Renaissance
Locale: The Netherlands
First presented: c. 1622

The Beggar's Bush *displays the staples of Elizabethan romantic comedy: nobility in disguise, a villainous usurper, and the repeated contrasting of the falsehood and sterility of the court to the truth and beauty of the country. The pastoral element is central to the play, for it is in the forest that lovers are united, villains confounded, and men of noble heart vindicated.*

In *Table Talk* for February 17, 1833, Coleridge wrote that he enjoyed *The Beggars' Bush* so heartily that he could read the play "from morning to night." He exclaimed: "How sylvan and sunshiny it is!" Certainly, for its idealized scenes of sylvan escapism and rustic good fellowship the play may be compared to *As You Like It.* Gerrard, like the banished Duke in Shakespeare's comedy, makes the best of his lot as king of the beggars, surrounds himself with jovial outcasts, and eventually triumphs over the courtiers who have usurped his rightful place. Yet the audience comes to understand that Gerrard's return to civilization—to the intrigues of court—is a cause for some sentimental regret: the simpler life of the beggars was, after all, free and joyous. For another Shakespearean parallel, Florez, Gerrard's son and the true Earl of Flanders, resembles Antonio in *The Merchant of Venice.* The character of the resolute, "spruce" merchant of Bruges must have pleased the middle-class shopkeepers in the audience as much as the low-comedy beggars delighted the groundlings in the pit.

The Beggars' Bush is also interesting because it anticipates, in many ways, John Gay's *The Beggar's Opera,* which was produced about a hundred years later. Both plays deal with people outside the law; both are light and bawdy; both have simple, vigorous diction. Unlike the Fletcher-Massinger play, however, *The Beggar's Opera* is a musical piece with social and literary satire. Nevertheless, there is a lyrical quality (including several songs) in the earlier play, and Fletcher and Massinger point some lines of social comment: for a society to function as a unit, the proper hierarchy must be maintained. Even the beggars, who do not abide by the law, have their own hierarchy which parallels that of society at large. And compared to Peachum and his gang, the beggars' crimes are small indeed, especially when we consider the genuine good humor, warmth, and even generosity they display.

The same qualities are to be found in the main character, Florez. From the first to the final act we see him as a selfless, understanding person, one who saves a pirate's life because "want / Of what he could not live without compell'd him / To that he did . . . ." Florez also finds it in his heart to spare Wolfort, whom Vandunke would have hanged, although Florez does banish the usurper from his kingdom. In the end, both the societal and the individual means are restored, and the beggars prepare to establish a new "Bush" in England, where they hope to continue their idyllic life.

THE BEGGAR'S OPERA

Type of work: Comic opera
Author: John Gay (1685-1732)
Type of plot: Social satire
Time of plot: Early eighteenth century
Locale: London
First presented: 1728

In the satiric tradition of Swift and Pope, Gay ridicules the corrupt politics of his day and the follies of polite society. Highwaymen and thieves represent the lords and public officials of Georgian England, and crime and vice thrive in all strata of society.

The Beggar's Opera, one of the finest plays written in English in the early eighteenth century, has remained popular ever since, both in Gay's original form (the music for which has been rewritten by such men as Benjamin Britten and Arthur Bliss) and in Bertolt Brecht's adaptation (with music by Kurt Weill) of the original, *The Threepenny Opera*. Another example of the play's continued popularity is the fine British film version, made in 1953, which stars Laurence Olivier, Dorothy Tustin, and Stanley Holloway. But the "test of time" is not the only measure of the success of Gay's play. It is a masterpiece for many reasons. *The Beggar's Opera* stands at the forefront of the history of the musical. It was written as a satire of the government of King George II (in the play represented by Macheath) and the Whig Prime Minister, Robert Walpole (represented by Peachum). Gay's play also is both a satire of the contrived, but popular Italian operas and a more simple, though elegant, English alternative to them. Gay employs well-known English and Scottish ballads and airs to which he adds his own lyrics, which are appropriate to the context of the play.

Colley Cibber, whom Pope satirizes in the *Dunciad* and who managed the Drury Lane Theatre when Gay wrote his play in 1727, unwisely declined to produce *The Beggar's Opera* when Gay submitted it to him. At length a reluctant John Rich, of the Theatre Royal, agreed to produce the play. His fears of failure proved unwarranted, however, when the play became a great financial success. People were fond of remarking that *The Beggar's Opera* had made Gay rich while at the same time it had made Rich gay.

Gay's achievement and the reason for the play's continued success is that *The Beggar's Opera* can be enjoyed on a surface level, without a knowledge of the contemporary political and theatrical milieu that it satirizes. The tone throughout is jocular and bawdy, and it never lapses into bitterness or mere vulgarity. The diction is simple, the satire sharp but not overly subjective or acidic. The play may itself be considered as one long song, for it has that lyrical, bell-like quality of its finest airs. The plot, unlike the comedies of manners, the burlesques, and the farces popular at the time, is extremely simple, with no complicated and intertwining subplots to divert attention.

Like a song or ballad, *The Beggar's Opera* has several refrains. One of these is the familiar cynical view of love and marriage, a favorite theme of the comedy of manners. Note, for example, Mrs. Peachum's speech in Act I, scene 5:

> Never was a man more out of the way in an argument than my husband! Why must our Polly, forsooth, differ from her sex, and love only her husband? And why must Polly's marriage, contrary to all observation, make her the less followed by other men? All men are thieves in love, and like a woman the better for being another's property.

There is, too, the typical anti-feminism (" 'Tis woman that seduces all mankind," sings Filch, Act I, scene 2). But Gay realizes that neither sex is faultless when it comes to romance. "Love," says Lucy Lockit, "is so very whimsical in both sexes, that it is impossible to be lasting" (Act III, scene 8). But that Macheath and Polly will, by the end of the play, at least attempt a lasting relationship is suggested by this song he sings to Polly in Act I, scene 13:

> My heart was so free,
> It rov'd like the bee,
> 'Till Polly my passion requited;
> I sipt each flower,
> I chang'd ev'ry hour,
> But here ev'ry flower is united.

Not the least aspect of this song's effectiveness lies in its sexual imagery, which is typical of the play.

Two other refrains are the plays Gay makes on the words "duty" and "honor." Polly, say her parents, must have her husband "peach'd" (impeached, given to the authorities for reward money) because it is her "duty" thus to obey her parents—a subversion of the Biblical commandment to honor one's parents. Mrs. Peachum admonishes Polly: "But your duty to your parents, hussy, obliges you to hang him [Macheath]" (Act I, scene 10). Further, it is the "duty" of the thieves to rob, of the whores to "love," and of Polly to stand by her husband, who is anything but faithful.

Another refrain, the pun on the word "honour," effectively criticizes the manners of the court. Thus the honor of the Peachums (that is, the Walpoles) is in question if Polly makes an unsuccessful marriage, one, in other words, which is not remunerative. Polly, however, insists: "I did not marry him (as 'tis the fashion) cooly and deliberately for honour or money. But, I love him" (Act I, scene 8). The gang of thieves are "men of honour" only in name, just as are the courtiers. And Lockit, with heavy irony, declares to his fellow mob-ster, Peachum: "He that attacks my honour, attacks my livelyhood [sic]" (Act II, scene 10).

A song Lockit had just sung advises: "When you censure the age, / Be cautious and sage. . . ." As subtle and sophisticated as his censure of the Court and Walpole's government was, the Prime Minister saw through it and refused to allow the production of *Polly* (1729), Gay's sequel to *The Beggar's Opera*. By 1737 the Licensing Act was in effect and the theaters were closed, thereby ending dramatic criticism of the government. (*The Beggar's Opera*, as well as the plays of Henry Fielding, are largely credited with bring-ing on the 1737 Act.) But Gay's masterpiece, as a poetic lyric of delightful comedy, has not only survived; it has thrived.

Clifton M. Snider

BEL-AMI

Type of work: Novel
Author: Guy de Maupassant (1850-1893)
Type of plot: Naturalism
Time of plot: About 1885
Locale: Paris and Cannes
First published: 1885

Bel-Ami, *subtitled* The History of a Scoundrel, *relates the story of an intriguer who climbs to a position of wealth and power by publishing the story of his first wife's disgrace and later cheating her of part of her fortune. The unscrupulous parvenu and the women he dupes are excellent examples of characterizations admired by adherents of French realism.*

In *Bel-Ami,* Georges Duroy, who might be considered the male counterpart of Thackeray's Becky Sharp, represents the restlessness of a certain class as the once-frozen class strata begins slowly to thaw. He illustrates the morally debilitating nature of poverty. Although Maupassant scrupulously avoids comment, he seems to be suggesting that while it is easy enough to be moral with enough money in one's pocket, society should hesitate to condemn those who must use their wits to survive (and are not too particular about how they do it). Duroy automatically looks for prey (as he did when stationed in Africa) to help him get ahead, and if confronted would ask, what else could a man in his position do?

Duroy's essential laziness prevents him from taking advantage of all the opportunities that open before him, but a natural shrewdness and ruthlessness carry him along far enough to be within sight of his tantalizing goal. He is a man who never can be satisfied. Neither his background nor his instincts have given him a moral base on which to conduct his life; to him "honor" is a catchword, not a code which touches him to the core. Nothing touches him deeply. Pleasure, for him, equals happiness.

Ambition and death alternate as themes in the novel, the latter showing the ultimate futility of the former. The long and painful death of Charles Forestier provides Duroy with a greater opportunity for getting on in the world with the aid of Madeleine Forestier, but it also foreshadows the end which awaits Duroy and everyone else. A sense of terror crushes Duroy when he sits by the body of Forestier, and he wonders what is the difference between flies who live a few hours and men who live a few years. He has no ideals, no purpose to his life other than temporary physical sensations, and he can even see how without meaning they are. But he is not a profound enough thinker to pursue this train of thought. Soon, he is back at his usual scheming and plotting. Maupassant, with superb understatement, says at this point: "Duroy returned to all his old habits."

The young Maupassant considered himself a disciple of Flaubert. Certainly the supple prose and carefully selected details, as well as the understated irony of the novel, are true to Flaubert's literary teachings. Maupassant also belonged to the circle of realists which included Zola and Turgenev. He presents his characters in *Bel-Ami* with strict objectivity, noting always the word or gesture that betrays the essential personality of each one. Conciseness and a rigorous economy of words and images underlie the art of the novel. He gives in *Bel-Ami* a true picture of the society of his time. Every detail is precise and factual; yet the view of mankind implied is one of powerful universality.

A BELL FOR ADANO

Type of work: Novel
Author: John Hersey (1914-)
Type of plot: Social criticism
Time of plot: 1943
Locale: Adano, Italy
First published: 1944

Hersey won a Pulitzer Prize for this story of an American officer's attempts to acquire a new church bell for an Italian village after the old bell had been removed by the Fascists. The enthusiasm which greeted the book's 1944 publication—it was hailed as the greatest novel to come out of World War II—has diminished with the perspective of time, but A Bell for Adano *remains a sympathetic portrait of the American invasion army, with excellent characterizations of townspeople and common soldiers.*

John Hersey's *A Bell for Adano* was popularly regarded as the finest novel to come out of World War II when it first appeared in 1944. The passing of time has removed it from this position, but along with *Mr. Roberts* and *Catch-22,* it shows that the war was far better represented in humor than melodrama. The early appeal of the book was found in the light-hearted episodes of life in a post-liberation Sicilian village, Adano, and in the appeal of the character of the protagonist, Major Joppolo.

To the American public of the postwar period, Joppolo was the embodiment of the "father-husband-brother" figure who was fighting for democracy in a strife-torn world. He was what Americans thought they were: young, sensitive, and good. General Marvin, on the other hand, was the embodiment of a pompous autocrat, thus creating much of the novel's sense of conflict.

Hersey, a war correspondent, was at his best, however, when portraying the common soldier or farmer—ordinary men who were caught up in the circumstances of war and were neither all good nor all bad. Early reviewers of the book admitted that they enjoyed reading the book, but its lack of critical character analysis and unity has caused it more and more to be regarded as second rate literature. Most saw it as a dramatized attempt at nonfiction rather than a novel. Some critics also made mention of the rather "off-color" language of the soldiers in the book. Though rather mild by later standards, some of the words in the book were harsh for the reading public of the middle 1940's. Critics aside, however, it was the American people who made *A Bell for Adano* a best seller, a hit play on Broadway, and later a popular motion picture.

BEN-HUR: A TALE OF THE CHRIST

Type of work: Novel
Author: Lewis (Lew) Wallace (1827-1905)
Type of plot: Historical romance
Time of plot: At the time of Christ
Locale: Antioch and Jerusalem
First published: 1880

Ben-Hur *is an odd mixture of melodramic adventure and scholarly research. The novel's strength lies in Wallace's comfortable familiarity with Roman and Jewish history and social customs; its weakness is in the characterizations, which never quite come alive.*

Lewis Wallace was a man of many vocations: in addition to writing several novels, he was, at one time or another during his life, a soldier, a lawyer, territorial governor of New Mexico, and minister to Turkey. His knowledge of and experience in the military, the law, government, and diplomacy developed in him an appreciation for history which enhanced the historical verisimilitude of his novels. And it is that quality of evoking the spirit of the times which, in large part, accounts for the popular success of Wallace's two best novels, *The Fair God* (1873) and *Ben-Hur*. In fact, *Ben-Hur* is one of the all-time best-selling novels in English, having sold more than two million copies. The book has also been widely translated into several foreign languages.

Like Wallace's other books, *Ben-Hur* is a historical novel in the mainstream of that venerable tradition. Basic elements in the genre include a background of genuine historical events, which Wallace provides in his depictions of Roman decadence counterpointed against the birth of Christianity. Also included are genuine historical figures in minor roles in the narrative, just as Wallace uses King Herod, Balthasar, Pontius Pilate, Nero, and Jesus in cameo parts. The third element is a fictional protagonist whose deeds are not part of the historical record and whose actions and emotions can thus be manipulated at will by the novelist to suit the needs of his tale. Judah Ben-Hur is just such a protagonist. Finally, the central focus of the plot is on events related to the personal and individual concerns of the protagonist, with historical matters relegated to the periphery of the action in the novel or used to highlight—sometimes ironically—the protagonist's role (usually a minor one) in the major affairs of his time. Thus, Wallace devotes most of his attention to the tribulations of the Jewish protagonist Ben-Hur and the perfidies of the Roman antagonist Messala, with historical events forming parentheses, as it were, around the beginning and the end of this central narrative.

It is interesting, moreover, that the final historical note in *Ben-Hur* depicts the protagonist—by then a convert to the Christian cause—as building the Roman catacombs for the sheltering and the protection of persecuted

Christians: interesting because *Hur* is the Hebrew word for cave or cavern (*ben* is a Hebrew prefix signifying *son of*). Surely, given Wallace's penchant for accurate details, his choice of a name for his protagonist was neither accidental nor coincidental. The entire novel bears out this view, for in *Ben-Hur* Wallace has produced a novel which vividly demonstrates the classic elements of the historical romance.

BENITO CERENO

Type of work: Short story
Author: Herman Melville (1819-1891)
Type of plot: Adventure romance
Time of plot: 1799
Locale: The harbor of St. Maria, off the coast of Chile; Lima, Peru
First published: 1856

Superficially, this is a story of slavery and mutiny on the high seas, but beneath the adventure-charged plot lies Melville's examination of that subject which so fascinated him: the confrontation of extreme forces of good and evil in the universe. The irony of the tale is that goodhearted, naïve Delano is only victorious in rescuing the victimized Benito because he is too innocent to comprehend the horror and depravity into which he wanders.

Originally serialized in *Putnam's Monthly* in 1855, *Benito Cereno* first appeared, slightly revised, in book form as the first story in Melville's *Piazza Tales* in 1856. It was not reprinted until 1924, when interest was being revived in Melville's writings. Since then it has often been praised as not only one of Melville's best fictional works but also one of the finest short novels in American literature. In 1964 Robert Lowell adapted *Benito Cereno* into verse-drama as the third act of his play *The Old Glory*.

Benito Cereno is Herman Melville's version of a true story he had read in Amasa Delano's *Narrative of Voyages and Travels in the Northern and Southern Hemispheres* (1817). Melville freely adapts Delano's account to his own fictional purposes. The court depositions which make up a considerable part of the latter half of *Benito Cereno* have been shown to be close to those in Delano's account, though Melville omitted some of the court material. In contrast, the creation of atmosphere, the building of suspense, the development of the three main characters—Delano, Cereno, and Babo—and the extended use of symbolism are among Melville's chief contributions to the original story. Also, the thematically important conversation between Delano and Cereno at the end of *Benito Cereno* was added by Melville.

The remarkable third paragraph of the story illustrates Melville's careful combining of atmospheric detail, color symbolism, and both dramatic and thematic foreshadowing.

> The morning was one peculiar to that coast. Everything was mute and calm; everything grey. The sea, though undulated into long roods of swells, seemed fixed, and was sleeked at the surface like waved lead that has cooled and set in the smelter's mould. The sky seemed a grey surtout. Flights of troubled grey vapours among which they were mixed, skimmed low and fitfully over the waters, as swallows over meadows before storms. Shadows present, foreshadowing deeper shadows to come.

The description, with its repeated use of *grey* and *seemed*, is important in setting the scene for a story the action of which will be, as seen through Delano's eyes, ambiguous and deceptive until the light of truth suddenly blazes upon the American captain's mind. Until that time, he will be seeing both action and character through a mist. The *grey* is symbolically significant also because Delano's clouded vision will cause him to misjudge both the whites and blacks aboard the *San Dominick*. In the light of the final revelations of the story, the *grey* has a moral symbolism too, perhaps for Melville and surely for the modern reader, since Cereno and Delano are not morally pure white or good, nor is Babo all black or bad. The Spaniard is a slaver and the American appears to condone the trade though he is not a part of it; the slave is certainly justified in seeking an escape from captivity for himself and his fellow blacks, though one cannot justify some of the atrocities consciously committed by Babo and his followers. The closing sentence of this mist-shrouded paragraph—"Shadows present, foreshadowing deeper shadows to come"—not only looks forward to the mystery which so long remains veiled; it also anticipates the final words of the two captains, words which partly suggest the great difference in their characters. Delano says, "You are saved: what has cast such a shadow upon you?" Cereno replies, "The negro."

In reading *Benito Cereno* one is caught up in the same mystery which Captain Delano cannot penetrate, and one longs for a final release of the suspense, a solution to the strange puzzle. Melville's hold upon the reader until the flash of illumination in the climax is maintained by his use of Delano's consciousness as the lens through which are viewed scene, character, and action. The revelation is so long delayed because of Delano's being the kind of man he is: " . . . a person of a singularly undistrustful good nature, not liable, except on extraordinary and repeated incentives, and hardly then, to indulge in personal alarms, any way involving the imputation of malign evil in man." His heart is benevolent but his mind is slow to perceive through the dragging hours from his boarding the *San Dominick* until he is finally shocked into recognition of the truth when Babo prepares to stab Don Benito with the dagger he had concealed in his hair. Delano is alternately repelled by Don Benito's manner or suspicious of his intentions and then inclined to acquit Cereno of seeming rudeness because of his frail health or condemn himself for his suspicions with the excuse that "the poor invalid scarcely knew what he was about."

As Melville may have intended to portray Delano as representing a type of American—good-hearted, friendly, and helpful but rather slow-witted and naïve—so he may have delineated Don Benito as emblematic of eighteenth century Spanish aristocracy—proud, enfeebled, and, finally, troubled in conscience over such moral crimes as slave-trading. To Delano he first appears as "a gentlemanly, reserved-looking, and rather young man . . . dressed with singular richness, but bearing plain traces of recent sleepless cares and disquietudes." Later, Don Benito's manner "conveyed a sort of sour and gloomy disdain [which] the American in charity ascribed to the harassing effects of sickness." Further observation leads Delano to conclude that Don Benito's "singular alternations of courtesy and ill-breeding" are the result of either "innocent lunacy, or wicked imposture." He is finally undeceived and apologizes for having suspected villainy in Don Benito toward the end of the danger-filled encounter with the slaves. Delano is lighthearted and eager to dismiss the affair when the danger is over and his suspicions have been erased. But Don Benito's mind is of a different cast. He broods on the results in human experience of the confusing of appearance and reality. " . . . you were with me all day," he says to Delano; "stood with me, sat with me, looked at me, ate with me, drank with me, and yet, your last act was to clutch for a monster, not only an innocent man, but the most pitiable of all men. To such degree may malign machinations and deceptions impose. So far may ever the best man err, in judging the conduct of one with the recesses of whose condition he is not acquainted."

The horrors resulting from the slave mutiny and the tensions and terror that followed Delano's kind offer to aid a ship in apparent distress, leave an already ill man a dejected and broken one. The shadow of "the negro" has been cast forever upon him. He retires to the monastery on the symbolically named Mount Agonia and three months later is released from his sufferings.

Babo, the third major character in *Benito Cereno,* is unforgettable, one of the first important black characters in American fiction (Mrs. Stowe's Uncle Tom had preceded him by only four years). He is one of the most striking of Melville's "masked" men who appear in his work from beginning to end, hiding their true selves behind the semblance they present to the world. Captain Delano is completely deceived in his first sight of Babo with Don Benito: "By his side stood a black of small stature, in whose rude face, as occasionally, like a shepherd's dog, he mutely turned it up into the Spaniard's, sorrow and affection were equally blended." His attentiveness makes him seem "less a servant than a devoted companion" to Don Benito. Though he speaks little, his few brief speeches suggest the intelligence which enables him to lead the revolt on the *San Dominick.* He is capable of irony when Benito explains that it is to Babo he owes his preservation and that Babo pacified "his more ignorant brethren, when at intervals tempted to murmurings." "Ah, master," he sighs, " . . . what Babo has done was but duty." The remark is as masked as Babo's bowed face, and the American is so completely taken in that, "As master and man stood before him, the black upholding the white, Captain Delano could not but bethink him of the beauty of that relationship which could present such a spectacle of fidelity on the one hand and confidence on the other."

With its many ironies—an aristocratic Spanish slaver captured by his slaves, a murderous black posing as a faithful servant, a naïve American protected from violent death through his own innocence and uncovering villainy by accident—*Benito Cereno* may be read as a magnificently contrived parable of limited, rational, well-ordered man struggling against evil in the social and natural universe and achieving at least a partial victory.

Henderson Kincheloe

Type of work: Poem
Author: Unknown
Type of plot: Heroic epic
Time of plot: c. Sixth century
Locale: Denmark, southern Sweden (land of the Geats)
First transcribed: c. 1000

In 3,200 lines of alliterative verse, this Anglo-Saxon epic is a pagan story overlaid with a veneer of Christian theology. Its content originated in a fusion of Norse legend and Danish historical events, which were passed on by oral tradition. When Danish invaders carried the tale to England, it gradually absorbed Christian influences, and was finally transcribed in Old English by a single, unknown poet.

Beowulf is the earliest extant heroic poem in any modern European language. The poem has come down to us in a single manuscript, which was damaged and almost destroyed in the 1731 fire in the Cotton Library. Although the manuscript dates from the tenth century, the poem was probably composed in the eighth century and deals with sixth century events, before the migration of the Germanic tribes to Britain.

The poem was composed and performed orally. Old English bards, or *scops*, most likely began by piecing together traditional short songs, called heroic lays; they then gradually added to that base until the poem grew to its present size. The verse form is the standard Old English isochronic: each line contains four stresses; there is a strong caesura in the middle of the lines and the resultant half lines are bound together by alliteration. Although little Old English poetry survives, *Beowulf's* polished verse and reflective, allusive development suggest that it is part of a rich poetic tradition.

Besides having unusual literary merit, *Beowulf* also provides information about and insight into the social, political, and ethical systems of Anglo-Saxon culture. There is a strong emphasis on courage in battle, fidelity to one's word, and loyalty to kinsmen. This is a violent but highly principled society in which struggle is everywhere and honor is everything. The hero, bound by family ties, by his own word, and by a strict code of revenge, is surrounded by his *comitatus*, his band of devoted comrades in arms. Christianity enters into the poem, and the society, but more an Old Testament variety, stressing justice rather than love. There is controversy about whether the Christian elements are intrinsic or are interpolations by a tenth century monastic scribe. In any case, the Christianity does not much resemble that of the High Middle Ages or of the modern world. Frequently the poem seems a reflection on the traditional pagan value system from the moral point of view of the new, incompletely assimilated Christianity.

Despite the fact that the heroic poem centers on valorous exploits, *Beowulf* contains curiously little action. The plot is embedded in a mass of other materials which some critics have seen as irrelevant or peripheral. However, the poem is basically reflective and ruminative and the digressive materials provide the context in which the action of the poem is to be seen and interpreted. Consequently, *Beowulf* contains historical information, ceremonial descriptions, lengthy genealogies, elaborate speeches, and interspersed heroic songs which reveal much about the world in which *Beowulf* acts. For example, it is important that the action is entwined in a historical sequence of events, because complex loyalties and responsibilities are thereby implied: Beowulf helps Hrothgar because of the past links between their families and much later, when Beowulf succumbs to the dragon, it is clear that the future of his whole people is in jeopardy. In addition, the songs of the *scop* at Hrothgar's court indicate the value of poetry as a means of recording the past and honoring the brave. In like manner, the genealogies dignify characters by uniting them with revered ancestors, and the ceremonies underscore the importance of present deeds and past worth. Through these apparently extrinsic materials, the poet builds a continuity between past and present and extends the significance of his poem and characters to the whole of society.

In this context Beowulf meets a series of challenges embodied in the poem's three monsters. That Beowulf battles imposing monsters rather than human adversaries suggests that his actions bear larger meanings. The hero arrives at the court of Hrothgar at the height of his youthful abilities. Not a neophyte, he has already fought bravely and demonstrated his preternatural power and charisma. He has no doubts or hesitancies as he prepares to fight. Grendel, a descendant of the line of Cain, is hateful to God, a lonely and vicious outcast, who hates light and joy and exacts bloody vengeance on man. All the more fearful because of his vague but imposing physique, Grendel is a representative of the physical evil which was so present in the lives and imaginations of the Anglo-Saxons, as witnessed in poems such as *The Wanderer* and *The Seafarer*. Beowulf confronts that physical evil and, bolstered by lineage and loyalty, routs the inimical force with which all men must contend.

However, Grendel, mortally wounded, escapes to his undersea lair, a submerged area devoid of light and appropriate to his joyless evil. Beowulf must, as a result, trace evil to its source if he is to be truly victorious. He ultimately returns with Grendel's head as a sign of victory, but to do that he must descend to the depths and exterminate the source of evil figured in Grendel's mother. This battle is more difficult and ominous: Beowulf doubts his capacities and his men almost give up on him. Naturally this battle is more arduous, because he is facing the intellectual or moral evil which is at the root of the physical evil that threatens human life and joy. The poem is not a moral allegory in which Beowulf roots evil out of the world, but an exemplum of how each man must face adversity.

One greater challenge remains for Beowulf and it is significant that it is separated, by space and years, from these youthful encounters. As a young warrior, Beowulf faced evil in vigorous foreign exploits; as an old king in his own country, he faces the dragon, the ultimate test of his courage. The dragon is at once less horrible (he is not a humanoid) and more fearsome. Beowulf, as the representative of his society, must enter the battle in which he knows he will die. The nonhuman dragon is a figure of the metaphysical evil which is woven into the fabric of the universe. Physical and moral evil can be challenged and overcome, but the ultimate evil (perhaps, at its extremity, age and death) cannot be avoided. Beowulf slays his antagonist and transcends his own death. By dying as he lived, he is a model for triumph in the last struggle every man must face.

Edward E. Foster

Type of work: Drama
Author: Jean Baptiste Racine (1639-1699)
Type of plot: Tragedy
Time of plot: First century
Locale: Rome
First presented: 1670

Racine presents in Titus his concept of the ideal sovereign, a dedicated man of the highest principles, a man who, as both guardian and victim of Roman law, must sacrifice love to duty. Bérénice *contains some of Racine's most beautiful love verses.*

The action of *Bérénice* is the least complicated of Racine's tragedies. It is, as he remarks in his preface, "extremely simple." There is only Bérénice being told of Titus' decision, an action already taken, which constitutes the plot.

There are two major lines of interpretation available for this play. The more traditional takes the choice between Duty and Love at face value, but a more recent reading views Titus' decision as only "falsely Cornelian." The second seems more convincing. In this approach the appeal to Duty becomes an "excuse" in the service of Titus' simple, although unconscious, wish to rid himself of Bérénice, whom he does not really love.

What, then, *is* the conflict in Titus? His hypocrisy stems from his lack of self-understanding and his fear. His conflict is that having assumed his father's position, he becomes all the more subjected to his authority. Vespian left Titus to love whomever he chose, even Bérénice. She had saved him from debauchery, had been "everything" for him—a mother figure as well as a mistress. Titus is happy to assume the place of emperor; he perhaps even killed his father ("I even wished my father's place,") but he cannot, finally, go so far as to marry the forbidden woman. His "official" reasons, that Roman tradition forbids the union, are weak, vague arguments a Racinean hero would not normally let stand between himself and his love.

The other side of the conflict, which renders it almost comic with regard to Titus, is that he cannot openly renounce his attachment to Bérénice. He is rather afraid of her, too. He is afraid of a servile fidelity made of guilt from their long bond. Their "love" would be humiliating to him because it would be dominated by her, filling the vacuum of his actual indifference. Thus, in another way, he would be like Antiochus: fidelity that cannot ever assert its own eros, thereby remaining humiliated.

THE BETROTHED

Type of work: Novel
Author: Alessandro Manzoni (1785-1873)
Type of plot: Historical romance
Time of plot: Seventeenth century
Locale: Milan, Italy
First published: 1825-1826

It was the work of Manzoni, particularly The Betrothed, *which did most to raise the low reputation of Italian writing during the nineteenth century to a respectable position in European fiction. This novel is a multi-faceted portrait of the life and culture of Milan during the 1620's, a time of Spanish domination; its pages teem with various types, from villainous noblemen and humble peasants, to bravos and citizens, nuns and churchmen, petty officials and leaders in high office.*

The complex and involuted history of Manzoni's revisions of his work and the drama of his artistic self-consciousness in their elaboration are as romantic, in essence, as the story itself. *The Betrothed* underwent its first massive revision from 1823, the date of the completion of the autograph, until its eventual publication in 1827 as *Fermo e Lucia,* a revision overseen by the author's friend and adviser, Flauriel. The revision witnessed changes in the names and roles of most of the major characters, the modification of their motivation and psychology, and the excision of numerous digressions such as the story of Gertrude, as well as endless linguistic and stylistic changes. Nevertheless, a second major revision of the novel took place between its publication as *Fermo e Lucia* and its definitive form as *The Betrothed (I Promessi Sposi)* which reflected not only Manzoni's concern about such issues as the work's commitment to doctrinal and historical truth, but also his scrupulousness toward the language of the novel down to its very orthography, typography, and punctuation. As Michele Barbi has shown, the work underwent changes not only from edition to edition, but even from copy to copy within the edition as whole pages were removed and reinserted. It would seem that the arbitrariness of time more than artistic inevitability governed the novel's final form. There is, finally, no personal emended copy that has come down to us.

Manzoni's Milan was alive with new ideas largely imported from France, but lacked commanding figures to propound them. Milanese culture was undergoing a tumultuous change from the ideals of the Enlightenment to those of Romanticism, as the last waves of the French Revolution and the Napoleonic era ebbed, yielding to the Austrian Restoration. The Restoration was in turn accompanied by an increasingly painful awareness on the part of the Italians of their disunity, which found its most potent symbol in the absence of a national language. The creation of this national language became one of Manzoni's goals in writing *The Betrothed,*and both literary and ethical concerns would converge in it. The novel demanded a language that would be current, literary, and rich enough to express the profoundest values and ideas of the seventeenth century Italy it would portray while remaining accessible to the simple folk for whom it was intended. Manzoni found this language in Florentine during his 1827 sojourn in Florence, and he began the linguistic revision which would eliminate from his novel the archaisms, stilted literary language, and regionalisms that impeded his goals.

Many of Manzoni's revisions illustrate his personal rejection of the Enlightenment literary tradition and his espousal of Romanticism. The first version of *The Betrothed* yoked much of the picaresque violence of Voltaire with the rustic idyls popular at the time; they were fated for early excision. Scott's *Ivanhoe* replaced the influence of Voltaire's *Candide* in the later versions by offering Manzoni its conception of the use of poetic invention for a better understanding of history. To this end, Manzoni's fancy was served by such works as Ripamonti's *Storia di Milano* and Gioia's *Economia e Statistica* which contained the historical material which his imagination would fuse into the episodes of the famine and the henchmen. Yet where such history in Scott is essentially the picturesque background for tales of adventure, in Manzoni it becomes the means to an essentially moral end: understanding the limits of human freedom in the struggle between good and evil, and the particular nature of that struggle in a given age. Manzoni made the historical novel a Pascalian *traité de l'homme* that illuminated the nature of being in the world by concerning itself with individual men and women in particular, minutely studied historical situations. If, as Salvatorelli observes, Manzoni appears often obtuse about the larger historical and political implications of a major event, such as, for example, the siege of Casale, it is largely because of this concern with the individual and his struggle.

Both Manzoni's Romanticism and his Catholicism dictated the democratic ends and themes of the work; it would both concern itself with and be written for the humble folk of the world—its artisans, peasants, and laborers. Such an audience conditioned both the choice of spoken Florentine as the language of the novel as well as the characterization of the protagonists which bestowed upon them their spontaneity, naturalness, thirst for justice, and sincere religiosity. By making the poor the heroes of moral struggle, Manzoni showed that they need not merely suffer history, but, by realizing the Christian message, create it. The social and ethical struggle of the work is accordingly the central struggle of Christianity itself: the struggle between pride and humility. In Christianity, Adam fell in pride and, in so doing, damned all mankind, which had to await its redemption in the humble Christ. In *The Betrothed,* pride is that of wealth and power represented by Don Rodrigo and the Governor of Milan whose lives are circumscribed by an irrationality which their high positions seem to impose on them. This is typified by their code of honor which leads them to seek Lorenzo's destruction. Humility is virtually personified by Lorenzo, Lucia, and Fra Cristoforo who realize in their lives their values of gentleness, charity, and brotherhood. On the macrocosmic level, the struggle betwen pride and humility translated itself ultimately for Manzoni into the struggle between the oppressive Austrians and the subjugated Italians.

Since Croce, criticism of *The Betrothed* has centered about the degree to which the novel can be said to create new values and meanings which are not reducible to the banalities of Christian teaching. Croce regarded the work as mere Christian apologetics inferior to the lyrics, the victim of a violent imposition of a pre-existent moral system. But if Croce would damn the novel, Momigliano, the great Crocean, would redeem it as the epic of providence. Historicist critics have supported this view while undermining its intent by claiming the influence of Bossuet's *Discours sur l'Histoire Universelle* which would make every human action dependent upon the action of providence. An event such as the conversion of the Un-Named would then display the violence of the miraculous on the development of plot and character. Others have argued that it is the extraordinary coherence of character that is at issue, since the Un-Named's fear of death and damnation conform perfectly to his previous behavior and virtually assure his conversion. It is Manzoni's choice of weak characters such as Don Abbondio and ultimately perhaps the Un-Named himself that sets into relief his concern with the loneliness of moral choice. That is, the certainty of the authorial voice that tells the story and is aware of its outcome is unavailable to the character who must make his choice in anxiey. Moreover, Manzoni's literary technique itself guarantees the freedom of his characters, for by refusing prolonged psychological studies, he avoided what the critic De Lollis would call the "deterministic penchant." Although every description of nature or surroundings ultimately enhances either plot or characterization, such overarching harmony only serves as a counterpoint to the situation of the moral agent. Manzoni's Christianity may indeed moralize reality and offer itself as the ultimate key to the understanding of human nature, but it does so only in the end when the outcome is clear to all. Manzoni's treatment of choice, however, remains true to its Pascalian influences.

James Thomas Chiampi

BETWEEN THE ACTS

Type of work: Novel
Author: Virginia Woolf (1882-1941)
Type of plot: Symbolic allegory
Time of plot: June, 1939
Locale: England
First published: 1941

A work filled with cryptic and portentious symbols, Between the Acts *was written during the early years of World War II. A mood of threat and impending doom pervades the novel, reinforced by the planes droning overhead during the pageant. But the true drama lies neither in the destructiveness of war nor in the stark human history played out for the villagers, but, rather, in the lives of the trivial, selfish, frustrated, idealistic people who must face one another between the acts.*

Between the Acts was completed without final revision before Virginia Woolf's suicide in 1941; in it she returns to the tightly controlled structure, the classical unities of time and place, used before in *Mrs. Dalloway. Between the Acts* takes place all in a single day, the day of the annual village pageant, and in the house or on the grounds of Pointz Hall.

The title suggests the book's three levels of meaning. *Between the Acts* refers first of all to events, relationships, and conversation taking place between the acts of the village pageant. Second, it refers to that precarious time between the two world wars. Third, the story occurs between the times when Giles and Isa truly communicate. Significantly, the novel's last lines are: "Then the curtain rose. They spoke."

Miss La Trobe, director of the pageant and probably a lesbian, is the one character who has contact with all others; she, with her pageant of English history, provides another unity to the work. She is, as well, a representative of Virginia Woolf's ideal of the androgynous artist, a creator who is "woman-manly."

The impending war, although seldom directly spoken of, is always in the background in the novel, referred to briefly in spectators' conversation and more directly in the sound of airplanes at the end. British civilization, celebrated in the pageant, is what may be lost in the coming battles. The last war had fragmented mankind both socially and psychologically; now the spectators see themselves in the mirrors held by the actors as somewhat fragmented. For a moment, however, Miss La Trobe creates a unity in the audience by means of music; a state of harmony is reached wherein male and female, the one and the many, the silent and the speaking are joined. Such a unity Woolf is always searching for in her art, a way to reconcile opposites.

BEVIS OF HAMPTON

Type of work: Poem
Author: Unknown
Type of plot: Chivalric romance
Time of plot: c. Tenth century
Locale: England, the Holy Land, Western Europe
First transcribed: c. 1200-1250

This Middle English romance, which also exists in many versions from France, Scandanavia, and Italy, contains a wealth of incident parallel to that found in native romances of France. The special importance of Bevis of Hampton *is that it also contains typically English elements, thus serving as a fine example of the transition from the rude Anglo-Saxon tales to the more refined French romances which prevailed after 1066.*

Bevis of Hampton is often spoken of and linked together with Guy of Warwick: both English heroes upholding the Christian faith in Saracen lands, valiant youths from a very early age. They are both Crusades knights, although the romance of *Bevis of Hampton* is far more Christian in theme and characterization.

The story of Bevis probably originated in France; there are three different versions in verse and one in prose. The poem was translated into Italian, Scandinavian prose, Dutch verse, Celtic versions, and several English redactions. Its popularity is further attested by the numerous references in other medieval works, among them the *Speculum Vitae* and Chaucer's "Sir Thopas" of *The Canterbury Tales.*

From studies of the dialect, it appears that the work was composed in the south of England, probably near Southampton, where Bevis is supposed to have been born. Like *Guy of Warwick,* it is written in two different rhyme schemes. Chaucer seems to have borrowed the meter of the first half for most of "Sir Thopas."

The narrative itself encompasses a longer period of time than many medieval romances; it begins when Bevis was sold into slavery at the age of seven, continues through the time when his grown sons fight alongside him, to the moment when both he and his faithful wife die within a few minutes of each other, presumably at a mature age.

Although there is little character differentiation, there are realistic touches such as detailed description of hand-to-hand combats, of weapons and military engines. The author also shows his knowledge of London in the passages where Bevis and his sons resist the inhabitants aroused by the king's evil steward.

The author uses an entire arsenal of stereotyped materials: typical expressions of grief, pious benedictions, greetings, oaths, similes, transitional phrases, promises, character traits, methods of wounding and slaying enemies.

Much of this repetition is necessitated by demands of the rhyme scheme of metrical romance. *Bevis of Hampton* even begins with the oral formula of the typical metrical romance, probably used by traveling minstrels to gather crowds in a market place: "Lordinges, herkneth to me tale!"

Still it moves rapidly, has a Christian theme carefully adhered to, and, not unlike other such romances, has comic touches in several scenes. It is not so robust nor so natively English as *Havelok the Dane,* since it has been refined through French adaptation. Nevertheless, it celebrates one of England's earliest and most stalwart heroes.

BEYOND HUMAN POWER, II

Type of work: Drama
Author: Björnstjerne Björnson (1832-1910)
Type of plot: Social criticism
Time of plot: Late nineteenth century
Locale: Norway
First presented: 1895

In this second and more powerful half of a dual social protest play, Björnson probes the inability of labor and management to understand each other. His solution is propounded by Pastor Falk, who preaches patience and forbearance, and by Rachel Sang, a moderate liberal who attempts to spread social enlightenment. The play is an effective social protest despite its rather disconcerting mixture of naturalistic and expressionistic elements.

Playwright, novelist, poet, orator, politician, and national symbol, Björnstjerne Björnson was one of the greatest "Renaissance Men" of the nineteenth century and a dominating figure both in the politics and the arts of his native Norway. As an orator and public figure he was for half a century the driving force in the quest for Norwegian national identity, parliamentary democracy, and social justice. As a novelist and playwright he was Norway's most popular serious writer and a literary artist of world stature. The best of his intense dramatizations of contemporary problems equals that of his more illustrious compatriot Henrik Ibsen in immediate theatrical impact, if not in depth and profundity. Moreover, without Björnson's earlier theatrical forays into realism it is doubtful that Ibsen could have found an audience for his stark, disturbing dramas.

In *Beyond Human Power, II (Over Ævne II)*, written twelve years after Part One, Björnson extends the thematic statement made about religion in the first play to politics, economics, and social reform. In the earlier play Björnson demonstrates the damage that results from a fanatical reliance on supernatural intervention. In *Beyond Human Power, II* Björnson points out the pain and violence that is unleashed when that same kind of fanatical idealism attempts to impose Utopian solutions—whether "Capitalistic" or "Revolutionary"—on the human problems of labor strife and social justice. All such idealistic solutions are "beyond human power," suggests Björnson; the solutions to man's problems can come only from a series of practical, moderate, imperfect compromises.

Critics have differed greatly in their opinions of the relative merits of the two plays. *Beyond Human Power, I* is certainly the more unified, controlled, and direct in both its rhetorical message and its emotional impact. *Beyond Human Power, II,* on the other hand, is the more extravagant, uneven, and ambitious. Its mixture of styles and frequent lack of focus denies it the clarity of its predecessor and diffuses its emotional impact, but the same things contribute to its greater daring, imagination, and, in some ways, theatricality.

The play has all of the ingredients of the classic labor confrontation play: a long strike, desperate workers and recalcitrant owners, demagogues on both sides (Bratt the ex-pastor for the workers; Holger, the industrialist, for the owners), and an impending sense of violence. The issues are crystalized by two events, the suicide of Maren Haug, a worker's wife, and the owners' decision to meet and form a company union to suppress the workers.

But the primary characters do not conform to the usual stereotypes. The industrialist, Holger, is implacable in his opposition to negotiations with the workmen; he has seemingly no compassion for their plight, nor does he see any justice whatsoever in their demands; and he is willing to spill blood to keep them in place. And yet, he is generous in his personal relationships. He turns his home over to Rachel Sang for a hospital and lavishly supplies her with equipment. He actually wants his workers to have the good life—but he believes that only he can provide it for them. Society, he insists, must be dominated by "big personalities who dare and can proclaim their own selves. When we get away from ant-heap ideas and centipedal dreams back to big men with genius and will."

Bratt's "communistic" vision is initially opposed to Holger's hyper-individualism, but the union leader is soon pushed aside by Elias Sang's passionate extremism. Anguished by the conditions of the workers, despondent over the probable failure of the strike, obsessed by a vision of the revolution and a future worker's paradise, he decides that a "great act" is needed to bring all the forces together and, for himself, he accepts a "religion of martyrdom." Thus, he becomes the driving force behind the plot to dynamite the castle and kill all of the meeting industrialists.

It is in this bizarre "castle" scene, where the capitalists are destroyed en masse, that the play reaches its "expressionistic" peak. What began as a matter-of-fact economic conflict becomes a surrealistic, Kafka-like vision of frenzy, insanity, and destruction. But such a nightmare is inevitable, Björnson insists, when men, violating "unwritten" laws, "overreach" and attempt to go "beyond human power" to resolve their problems. Instead of achieving Utopia, such extremes only unleash the daemonic side of man or what Björnson calls his "racial pessimism."

Beyond Human Power, II may not be a great play, but it is a fascinating one. A final irony of the play—one of which Björnson himself probably was aware—is that, while thematically the play demonstrates the folly of man's tendency to "overreach" his capacities, *Beyond Human Power, II* is a classic example of the play that "overreaches." Too many characters, ideas, and techniques are crowded into the single dramatic effort. But what the play loses in clarity it gains in excitement. These two powerful plays represent the pinnacle of Björnson's dramatic career and entitle him to a place beside his great Scandinavian contemporaries, Henrik Ibsen and August Strindberg.

THE BIG SKY

Type of work: Novel
Author: A. B. Guthrie, Jr. (1901-   )
Type of plot: Adventure romance
Time of plot: 1830-1843
Locale: Western United States
First published: 1947

The Big Sky *is outstanding both for its constant and varied action and for its philosophical passages about the spirit of the Western hunter and trapper which occur between episodes. The author's skillful use of frontier dialect, and his talent for communicating elemental emotions and the feel of open spaces make this novel a notable contribution to regional and historical fiction.*

In the tradition of James Fenimore Cooper's "Leatherstocking" romances, *The Big Sky* is distinguished among other fine historical novels for its realism and sharp insight into the psychology of the American Western pioneer. Like Cooper's land-adventure fiction, A. B. Guthrie's book treats the clash between two cultures—that of the retreating Indian tribes and of the advancing Yankee frontiersman. As the frontier expands westward, the Indians are forced to surrender their lands, their freedom, and their spiritual heritage. In the unequal struggle, the white pioneer, too, loses a portion of his heritage: a sense of idealism.

The "big sky" of Guthrie's title is the vast open land of the frontier, once teeming with wildlife, but slowly—even within the chronology of the novel, 1830-1843—changing, with the slaughter of buffalo, beaver, and other creatures of the forests and plains. In his descriptions of the land, its vegetation, and animals as well as of the rough frontiersmen, Guthrie has the eye of a naturalist: the smallest detail does not escape his attention. From *The Big Sky* one learns how a trapped beaver expires, its eyes bulging in terror; how deer, elk, and mountain goats survive in the wilderness; how rivermen operate a keelboat; how fur-hunters kill and strip game; how mountain men endure the bitter Northern winters. Unlike many other adventure stories treating the western movement, Guthrie's novel is without sentimentality. For the hunters, traders, and marginal farmers of the outlying territories, life is hard, often brutal. In his realism Guthrie does not gloss over the harsh truths of the time. Trapped in a winter storm without food, Beauchamp becomes a cannibal and devours his dead companion, Zenon. Boone Caudill murders his best friend, Jim Deakins, whom he wrongly suspects of fathering his half-Indian son. The child himself is born blind, an innocent victim of the white man's syphilis. Guthrie's treatment of the Indians is similarly unsentimental. The squaws who mate with the white hunters are described, for the most part, as dirty, complaisant whores; whole tribes, like the Piegans, are wiped out by smallpox; others are reduced to the condition of drunken sops; Poordevil, the Blackfoot who accompanies Boone, Jim, Dick Summers, and the other trappers, is a driveling alcoholic. Thus, to Guthrie, the clash between the two cultures brutalizes both the whites and the native Indians.

In his analysis of the characters' motivation, the author is also a tough-minded realist. His protagonist, Boone, is a violent, headstrong, mostly insensitive man whose redeeming virtue is his loyalty. Throughout most of his adventures he trusts, with good reason, his longtime friend Jim. Yet at the last, he kills Jim when he fears, mistakenly, that his friend has betrayed him. In a similar vengeful action, he abandons his beloved Indian wife, Teal Eye, when he suspects her of adultery. From these impulsive actions he brings about the ruin of his dreams. Guthrie once wrote that the theme of *The Big Sky* (paraphrasing Oscar Wilde) is that each man destroys the thing he loves best. Nevertheless, Boone's destructive impulse results as much from his early experiences as from his conscious will. Abused by his fathers, robbed by the clever rascal Jonathan Bedwell, cheated by the law—he has come to regard men warily, as objects of his revenge. His passions, too elemental to be curbed by reason, run their course, as in Greek tragedy. But in a larger sense, his personal defeat is insignificant judged by the greater tragedy of the dwindling American frontier. Although Boone and his fellow frontiersmen love the land, they are at least partly responsible for ravaging it. By 1843, the year when the novel ends, much of the frontier still remains—Oregon, for example; but the pattern for its destruction has already been established. The "big sky," like the mountain-men's idealistic ambitions, must henceforth be diminished.

BILLY BUDD, FORETOPMAN

Type of work: Novel
Author: Herman Melville (1819-1891)
Type of plot: Symbolic tragedy
Time of plot: 1797
Locale: Aboard a British man-of-war
First published: 1924

In this last of Melville's works, published posthumously, the author dramatized the clash between natural goodness and innocence as personified by Billy Budd, and unprovoked evil as embodied in Claggart. Captain Vere, as his name suggests, is the upholder of truth and right in the story. When Billy inadvertently kills his antagonizer in a fight, Vere is caught between his love for Billy and his duty to uphold the law and maintain order; he opts for justice over mercy, and decides that he must hang the boy.

According to Harrison Hayford and Merton M. Sealts, the editors of *Billy Budd, Sailor,* Melville began the novel in 1886, developed and revised it through several stages, and then left it unpublished when he died in 1891. The Hayford-Sealts text, published in 1962, differs considerably from earlier ones published in 1924 and 1948. Among the noteworthy differences is the change of name for the ship on which the action occurs from *Indomitable* to *Bellipotent.* The symbolism of the latter name relates it to the emphasis which Melville places in the novel on war, man's involvement in it, and the effects of war on the individual.

That Melville did not wish his readers to mistake the nature or the general intent of his novel is clear in his early warning that Billy "is not presented as a conventional hero" and "that the story in which he is the main figure is no romance." The story itself is extremely simple. A young sailor on a British merchant ship is impressed for service on a British warship. He offers no resistance but accepts his new assignment with good will and attempts to be an ideal sailor. The ship's master-at-arms takes an immediate and unwarranted dislike to the sailor, plots to cause him trouble, and then accuses him to the captain of having plotted mutiny. The captain summons the sailor, asks him to defend himself, and sees him strike and accidentally kill his accuser. The captain imprisons him, convenes a court-martial, condemns him to death, and has him hanged. This plot is the vehicle for Melville's extended use of moral symbolism throughout the novel.

Billy Budd, Claggart, and Captain Vere are all clearly symbolic characters, and Melville brings out the symbolism through information supplied about their backgrounds, language used to describe them, and authorial comment of moral, theological, and philosophical import.

Melville employs a double symbolism for Billy: he is both a Christ-figure and a representation of innocent or Adamic man. Before Billy is removed from the merchant ship, the captain explains to the lieutenant from the warship that Billy has been most useful in quieting the "rat-pit of quarrels" that formerly infested his forecastle. "Not that he preached to them or said or did anything in particular; but a virtue went out of him, sugaring the sour ones." The captain's words echo Luke, 6:19: "And the whole multitude sought to touch him: for there went virtue out of him, and healed them all." When the lieutenant is adamant about Billy's impressment, the captain's last words to him are: " . . . you are going to take away my peacemaker." Again, there is no mistaking the reference to the Prince of Peace. In describing Billy as he appears to the men and officers on the warship, Melville mentions "something in the mobile expression, and every chance attitude and movement, something suggestive of a mother eminently favored by Love and the Graces." An officer asks, "Who was your father?" and Billy answers, "God knows, sir." Though Billy explains that he was told he was a foundling, the hint has already been given of a divine paternity. Melville drops the Christ symbolism of Billy until the confrontation with Claggart when Billy, unable to reply to Captain Vere's request that he defend himself, shows in his face "an expression which was as a crucifixion to behold." At the hanging, Billy's last words are, "God bless Captain Vere!" and the reader recalls Christ's words on the Cross, "Father, forgive them; for they know not what they do." The symbolism continues with the hanging itself. Captain Vere gives a silent signal and "At the same moment it chanced that the vapory fleece hanging low in the East was shot through with a soft glory as of the fleece of the Lamb of God seen in mystical vision, and simultaneously therewith, watched by the wedged mass of upturned faces, Billy ascended; and, ascending, took the full rose of the dawn." In the final chapter, Melville adds that "The spar from which the foretopman was suspended was for some few years kept trace of by the bluejackets. . . . To them a chip from it was as a piece of the Cross. . . . They recalled a fresh young image of the Handsome Sailor, that face never deformed by a sneer or subtler vile freak of the heart within. This impression of him was doubtless deepened by the fact that he was gone, and in a measure mysteriously gone." Even in the verses which close the novel, with Billy's words, "They'll give me a nibble—bit o' biscuit ere I go./ Sure a messmate will reach me the last parting cup," one cannot miss the Last Supper reference.

Yet, though Billy is Christlike, he belongs to the race of man, and Melville repeatedly employs him as an archetype. His complete innocence is first suggested in Melville's comment that " . . . Billy in many respects was little more than a sort of upright barbarian, much such perhaps as Adam presumably might have been ere the urbane Serpent wriggled himself into his company." Later, Captain Vere thinks of the handsome sailor as one "who in the nude might have posed for a statue of young Adam before the Fall." But innocence will not protect Billy. As Adam's human imperfection led to his fall, so an imperfection in Billy leads to his destruction. In times of stress Billy stutters or is even speechless and, says Melville, "In this particular Billy was a striking instance that the arch interferer, the envious marplot of Eden, still has more or less to do with every human consignment to this planet of Earth."

The innocence that is his "blinder" causes Billy (or "Baby" as he is called) to fail to see and be on guard against the evil in Claggart, and his "vocal defect" deprives him of speech when he faces his false accuser. He strikes out as instinctively as a cornered animal, and his enemy dies. Billy did not intend to commit murder but, as Captain Vere tells his officers, "The prisoner's deed —with that alone we have to do." Billy does not live in an animal's instinctive world of nature. His life is bound by social law and particularly by naval law in a time of war. As Captain Vere explains, innocent Billy will be acquitted by God at "the last Assizes," but "We proceed under the law of the Mutiny Act." That act demands death for Billy's deed, and he dies in order that discipline may be maintained in the great navy which must protect Britain against her enemies.

As Billy symbolizes innocent man, Claggart represents the spirit of evil, the foe of innocence. There is a mystery in Claggart's enmity toward harmless Billy. For, says Melville, "what can more partake of the mysterious than an antipathy spontaneous and profound such as is evoked in certain exceptional mortals by the mere aspect of some other mortal, however harmless he may be, if not called forth by this very harmlessness itself?" Claggart's evil nature was not acquired, "not engendered by vicious training or corrupting books or licentious living, but born with him and innate. . . ." He can recognize the good but is "powerless to be it." His energies are self-destructive; his nature is doomed to "act out to the end the part allotted to it." Though he destroys an innocent man, he must himself be destroyed as well.

As Billy at one extreme is Christlike and childishly innocent and Claggart at the other is Satanic, Captain Vere represents the kind of officer needed to preserve such an institution as the navy he serves. He is a man of balance, "mindful of the welfare of his men, but never tolerating an infraction of discipline; thoroughly versed in the science of his profession, and intrepid to the verge of temerity, though never injudiciously so." His reading tastes incline toward "books treating of actual men and events . . . history, biography, and unconventional writers like Montaigne, who, free from cant and convention, honestly and in the spirit of common sense philosophize upon realities." More intellectual than his fellow officers, he seems somewhat "pedantic" to them, and Melville hints that, in reporting Vere's long speech to his junior officers of the drumhead court, he has simplified the phrasing of the argument. Yet elsewhere Captain Vere's speech is simple, brief, and direct.

Though Captain Vere is a thoughtful, reserved man, he is not without feeling. Quickly recognizing Billy's inability to speak when he has been ordered to defend himself, he soothingly says, "There is no hurry, my boy. Take your time, take your time." He is even capable of momentary vehemence as when he surprises the surgeon with the outburst, "Struck dead by an angel of God! Yet the angel must hang!" But he quickly regains control. Melville does not report what Captain Vere says to Billy when he informs him privately of the death sentence, though he suggests that Vere may have shown compassion by catching Billy "to his heart, even as Abraham may have caught young Isaac on the brink of resolutely offering him up. . . . " Vere is seemingly overcome after Billy's last words, "God bless Captain Vere!" and the echo from the crew, since "either through stoic self-control or a sort of momentary paralysis induced by emotional shock," he stands "rigidly erect as a musket. . . . " The final view of a man whose heart balanced his mind is given in the report of Captain Vere's dying words, "Billy Budd, Billy Budd," spoken not in "the accents of remorse." Though capable of fatherly feeling toward an unfortunate young man, he had caused to be carried out a sentence he believed was needed if the strength of order was to be maintained in the turmoil of a war.

Though *Billy Budd* has occasionally been read as a veiled attack on the unjust treatment of a hapless man by an impersonal, authoritarian state, a close reading of the novel makes it seem more likely that Melville's intent was to show, especially through Captain Vere, that the protection of a state during a time of war must inevitably involve on occasion the sacrifice of an individual. Melville does include scattered satiric comments on the imperfections of both men and organizations, but his overwhelmingly favorable portrait of Captain Vere as a high-principled and dedicated representative of the state, leaves the reader with the final impression that Melville had at last become sadly resigned to the fact that imperfect man living in an imperfect world has no guarantee against suffering an unjust fate. That Billy uncomplainingly accepts his end, even asking God's blessing upon the man who is sending him to death, suggests that Melville too had become reconciled to the eternal coexistence of good and evil in the world.

Henderson Kincheloe

THE BIRDS

Type of work: Drama
Author: Aristophanes (c. 448-385 B.C.)
Type of plot: Social satire
Time of plot: Second Peloponnesian War
Locale: Athens and Nephelo-Coccygia, the city of the birds
First presented: 414 B.C.

On a political level, this comedy ridicules the disastrous Greek expedition to Sicily in 413 B.C. More generally, The Birds *is a rollicking commentary on man's eternal dissatisfaction with his lot; his habit of ignoring the divinities which shape his ends; his crowded, evil-breeding cities; and his tendency to disturb the equilibrium of the universe. Pisthetaerus, with his irresistible rhetoric, surely is a forebear of the men who sell salvation or the world's goods with equal glibness and ease.*

First shown at the City Dionysia festival in 414 B.C., *The Birds* is commonly regarded today as Aristophanes' finest work, although it only won second prize at the festival. Richly imaginative, full of scintillating wit and lovely lyrical songs, *The Birds* is unquestionably a comic masterpiece. In fact, it is unique in that it takes a fantastic and amusing idea and quite literally soars off into infinity with it. The entire play is a sustained and wonderful joke that carries one rollicking into heaven. And if that heaven is completely unconventional, what else could one expect from a genius such as Aristophanes'?

Some critics have felt that this play satirizes the airy hopes of conquest that gripped Athens while the comedy was being written. In 415 B.C. a huge military expedition had sailed to subdue Sicily and establish an empire in the west. Two years later the expedition proved a fiasco, but in the meantime Athens was rife with grand rumors and expectations. *The Birds* does present a grand, crazy scheme of bringing both men and gods to heel, and it seems to convey some of the ebullience of the time. But more likely, it uses fantasy as a means of delivering several well-aimed kicks at contemporary figures, at Athens, and at men and gods in general. A modern reader or audience can appreciate this comedy simply for its escapism and its beautiful lyrics, with no knowledge of its topical allusions. The important facts are contained within the play itself.

Here Aristophanes adapts an idea that appears in *The Clouds,* where Socrates explores the starry heavens in a basket, and makes it the basis of this comedy. Debt-ridden, plagued by lawsuits in Athens, and seeking a restful retirement community, the hero, Pisthetærus, has a brainstorm. Why not found a kingdom in the sky with the help of the birds? By organizing the birds effectively he could subdue the gods through starving them, since the birds could intercept the sacred offerings. And he could bring men to their knees by using the birds to control harvests and livestock. Elderly, quick-witted, confident, Pisthetærus is likeable as well, a kind of supersalesman. He convinces the birds and, by this through-the-looking-glass logic, he gains absolute mastery of the cosmos, winning a goddess for a bride in addition.

Yet his true glory rests in the kingdom to which he gives birth—Nephelo-coccygia, or Cloudcuckooland. It is the equivalent of the Big Rock Candy Mountain, a place where all one's dreams come true. This Utopia is in harmony with nature, as represented by the birds. But it attracts idlers, para-sites, nuisances. Bad poets, a false prophet, a father-beater, a magistrate, a process-server, an informer, a surveyor, and a sycophant flock to Cloud-cuckooland, which gives Pisthetærus the chance to either reform them or repel them. Even the gods are not really welcome. Pisthetærus' own companion, Euelpides, leaves of his own accord, sick of being ordered around. Thus the hero exercises his power mainly to exclude undesirables. When he finishes, his only comrades are the birds.

This rejection of human pests allows Aristophanes' satirical gift free play. These parasites are the usual types that the dramatist lampooned: the legal profession, fake seers, awful poets, toadies, cowards, pederasts, scientists, informers. Aristophanes seems to say that without these types a community could be a paradise.

But he goes further than this. The birds, and particularly the chorus, sing some very beautiful songs that astonish one with their lyrical virtuosity. These songs are vastly superior to anything the poets in the play invent. Again, almost all of the birds have beautiful plummage, but the humans by contrast are shabbily dressed. And whereas the birds are friendly once Pisthetærus wins them over, the men are typically rapacious or looking for a hand-out. In short, the birds are altogether more desirable as companions than men. Even the gods come off poorly by comparison. They are merely immortal versions of the human species, full of greed and anxious to take advantage of their position.

The Birds is not completely misanthropic, for it pays ample tribute to man's eternal desire to achieve birdlike freedom and beauty, and to soar through the skies unimpeded by reality. It suggests that a man can best gain a Utopia by his own wits, and in friendly communion with nature. The stage is singu-larly bleak, with a single bare tree and a rock, yet it is precisely here that Pisthetærus founds his fabulous empire. It is a realm of sheer imagination, where any man can erect castles in the air, fashioned of daydreams and free of life's demands. This is the place where a person can find peace with friends of his own choosing, the kingdom where he can win out over the gods and his human foes alike. Imagination is the single area where a man can enthrone himself as ruler of the universe. And in a sense, *The Birds* is a dramatic hymn to schizophrenia. All the shackles of reality and of human limitation are in abeyance, while the play sails straight up into the wild blue yonder. It is escapist of course, but a daring, witty, songful, exhilarating kind of escape.

James Weigel, Jr.

THE BLACK ARROW

Type of work: Novel
Author: Robert Louis Stevenson (1850-1894)
Type of plot: Historical romance
Time of plot: Fifteenth century
Locale: England
First published: 1888

This historical romance intended for young readers is mediocre by comparison to Stevenson's other masterpieces of children's literature, Treasure Island *and* Kidnapped. *Set during a minor battle of the Wars of the Roses, the most interesting scenes deal with Dick Shelton's adventures in outwitting his scheming guardian, Sir Daniel.*

It is reported that Stevenson never liked *The Black Arrow* and for that reason would never read it. Certainly it is a passable adventure yarn with enough action and vivid characterization to satisfy most readers, but Stevenson's dislike of it is in many ways understandable. The incidents cohere poorly at times; often they seem to be selected gratuitously. None of the characters except Richard Shelton is sustained long enough in the novel to be very interesting, and even Richard is not a fully satisfying fictional character. The narrative reads aimlessly for chapters at a stretch, then seems to thrash out a conclusion rather than arrive at it naturally. In addition—and this is critical—the novel promises adventures and characterizations that it never fulfills. For example, the fellowship of The Black Arrow (it is the book's title, after all) has a Robin Hood appeal which strangely goes begging in the tale.

Where the novel succeeds best is in contrasting a youthful Richard Shelton with a cunning, sin-worn world. Beset on every side by duplicity and selfishness, he maintains at least an elementary sense of forthright honesty. His errors, then, result from youthful indiscretion, not calculated hypocrisy. He loves well, fights well, and succeeds well in a world where love, battle, and success are as whimsical as the daily change from Lancaster to York.

The Black Arrow is not without other redeeming features. Richard, Duke of Gloucester, is a character who seems to have pleased Stevenson. Admittedly, he enters the novel almost at the last moment and is a rather one-dimensionally cruel figure, but his diabolical energy, akin to that of James Durie, Master of Ballantrae, makes for interesting reading. Lawless, whose very name suggests manifold possibilities, gets misplaced by the author during the book but flourishes throughout his brief stay. Alicia Risingham, companion to Joanna Sedley, is by far the more engaging female character with her bold, risqué manner. Finally, there are a few exciting episodes to spice up the action—one, the foundering of a rescue ship; another, the fierce battle of Shoreby.

Still, *The Black Arrow* is not a successful novel. It lies somewhere between *Treasure Island* and *Kidnapped* on the one hand—both much better tales—and *The Master of Ballantrae* on the other, more artful study of man's dark, ambivalent nature. As a result it is neither a child's tale nor an adult's novel but an odd mixture of both.

BLACK LAMB AND GREY FALCON

Type of work: Record of travel
Author: Rebecca West (Cecily Fairfield Andrews, 1892-)
Type of plot: Travel sketches
Time of plot: 1937
Locale: Yugoslavia
First published: 1941

More than a mere narrative of her journey through Yugoslavia, West's book— which was several years in writing—reflects the author's long-term study of her subject. Research combined with firsthand impressions produce interesting digressions on anthropology, architecture, cultural history, literature, politics, philosophy, and Yugoslavian psychology.

Black Lamb and Grey Falcon is a travelogue of epic sweep through Yugoslavia and her many cultural regions: Croatia, Dalmatia, Herzegovina, Bosnia, Serbia, Macedonia, Old Serbia, and Montenegro. Rebecca West recreated the experience of her journey through culture and history, intertwining the near and distant past, in a narrative which possesses something of the flavor of the great works of Proust. Her guide, the poet Constantine, speaks as the poetic imagination of the Yugoslavian people in this cultural dialogue between Eastern and Western Europe.

The book's focus is on the folk culture of Yugoslavia and the reactions and impressions of the narrator. The black lamb in the title refers to an incident in the book in which a lamb is sacrificed as part of an ancient religious custom; the grey falcon alludes to an old and popular Slavic folk song. Set in the years just prior to World War II, *Black Lamb and Grey Falcon* evokes the political attitudes of the period, somewhat sentimental expressions of the Marxist leanings of Constantine and the humanism of West and her husband, ironically counterposed by history, with Naziism and Fascism nascent in the background. The philosophical digressions on love and jealousy, for instance, are interesting though less than profound. The tone of the book throughout is polite, almost to a fault, for it disguises a patronizing and sentimental stance toward the "picturesque" life of the peasants.

Rebecca West's style is elegant, witty, and rhetorically grand. Her first-person narrative permits frequent and delightful digressions into entertaining personal vignettes. The book is a compendium of intellectual and historical reactions to a personal experience, relayed through the highly literate consciousness of West. It is literature of the literate experience, a highly elaborate curio, which despite its condescension does not fail to entertain.

BLACK VALLEY

Type of work: Novel
Author: Hugo Wast (Gustavo Martínez Zuviría, 1883-1962)
Type of plot: Regional romance
Time of plot: Early twentieth century
Locale: Córdoba and the hill country of northern Argentina
First published: 1918

A romantic story of elemental emotions and a primitive way of life, Black Valley *shows to excellent advantage Wast's talent for painting landscapes of wild natural beauty. The plot, episodic yet well-ordered, follows with increasing emotional and dramatic interest the dual stories of Flavia and Don Pablo's ill-fated love and Gracián and Mirra's relationship.*

Black Valley is a fertile work. It embodies Hugo Wast's basic writing techniques—the use of a clear style, sustained suspense, melodrama, deep interest, and spontaneous sprouting of the story. Wast used Argentine geography in all of his backgrounds, and spent most of his life in Santa Fe Province, in Argentina's Far West. *Black Valley* is thus laced with local color, life style, and personality. Even the title reflects the novel's tone, for this wind-whipped, isolated valley has weird beauty such as hidden caves, wild beasts, wild flowers, and a misty, Nordic beauty. The latter flavor perhaps reflects Wast's political bent, since, after becoming Argentina's Minister of Education just before World War II, he was accused of pro-German and anti-Semitic views. In any event, Wast's earlier and prolonged popularity with Argentine readers might have stemmed not only from his nationalism, but from his knack of jerking urban readers out of their stifling settings and, through sublimation, establishing them in rustic beauty and peace.

Black Valley was sneeringly dismissed in a local contest as being beneath consideration, but promptly became a best-seller and won a gold medal from the prestigious Spanish Academy, which paid Wast the added honor of including his Argentine idiomatic expressions in its dictionary. Written with slight touches of Alexandre Dumas, *Black Valley* is readable and entertaining. Its characters are not too numerous, nor do they enter and leave the story like shooting stars, but steadily grow as a function of the plot. *Black Valley* also reflects Wast's tastes for blending romantic idealism in his imaginative elements with *costumbrista* realism in his observed elements. He almost attains a Biblical flavor when describing individual misfortunes. Manias, foolishness, odd notions, and other human failings are lampooned.

Wast was educated by Jesuits just before the end of the nineteenth century. He felt that women were morally superior to men, and he excoriated cruelty, selfishness, and the flint-hearted rich. Atheism and communism were attacked in his oceanic literary output, but he also criticized clergymen who lacked spartan qualities. In his novels, large cathedrals are considered inferior to

small and humble churches that serve as oases of peace for individuals suffering affliction.

BLEAK HOUSE

Type of work: Novel
Author: Charles Dickens (1812-1870)
Type of plot: Social criticism
Time of plot: Mid-nineteenth century
Locale: London, Lincolnshire, and Hertfordshire, England
First published: 1852-1853

Bleak House, *a satire on the methods of an English equity court, is based upon an actual case in Chancery, while several of the minor characters are caricatures of well-known literary figures of the day. Although the complicated Lady Dedlock plot which gave* Bleak House *its contemporary popularity is rather thin, the novel as a whole stands up remarkably well.*

Bleak House, after publication as a serial, first appeared in book form in 1853 at the height of Dickens' career. Preceded by *Martin Chuzzlewit* and followed by *Hard Times,* it comes early in the group of Dickens' great novels of social analysis and protest. A major critical anatomy of mid-nineteenth century England, the novel nevertheless shows some unfortunate signs of serial publication and of the author's concessions to his audience. Pathos, melodrama, and a somewhat strident moralism all reflect weaknesses in the public taste, yet Dickens manages to weave out of these a controlled assessment of the corruption at the heart of his society.

At the center of its intricate plot is the lawsuit of Jarndyce and Jarndyce. To this meager frame Dickens piles sub-plot upon sub-plot, all ultimately interrelated. In one sense, the plot is a series of thin detective stories woven together in such a way as to involve all strata of society. As character after fascinating character appears, each episode is interesting in its own right and, in the masterly resolution, no action or detail remains extraneous.

The third-person narrator of most of *Bleak House* is a sharply ironic commentator on the political, social, and moral evils which abound in the book. There is never any question of the narrator's attitude towards the selfishness and irresponsibility he recounts, but he is not quite so sardonic or homiletic as the narrator of *Hard Times.* The stern attitude of this narrator is both relieved and reinforced by the introduction of a second, first-person narrator, Esther Summerson. Many critics have seen the dual narration as an aesthetic flaw, but each narrator does contribute a different perspective. Although Esther is a bit simpering and saccharine, she does represent a sympathetic and morally responsible attitude which is rare in the world of *Bleak House.* She is a compassionate insider who adds both a perspective and a model which, if sometimes sentimental, are a corrective to her foul environment.

As the lawsuit of Jarndyce and Jarndyce lumbers to a close after years of litigation, a gallery of characters emerges and each reveals how the moral contagion has spread to his sector. With his talent for caricature, Dickens has created memorable minor characters to flesh out the corrupt world. There is Mr. Chadband, the preacher enamored of his own voice; Mrs. Pardiggle, who would feed the poor Puseyite tracts rather than bacon; Mr. Turveydrop, who is the Model of Deportment and little else; Mrs. Jellyby, who supports noble "causes" while neglecting her own children; Mr. Skimpole, the model of unproductivity. So many of these betray the varieties of egoism and irresponsibility which have left society stagnant and infected. Perhaps the most striking is Krook, the law stationer and small-scale surrogate of the Lord Chancellor, who dies of "spontaneous combustion." Krook is a microcosm of the self-destructive tendency of a diseased society.

However, despite Dickens' talent for plot and character, *Bleak House* is primarily a novel of image and symbol. The first chapter insistently sets the moral tone as it repeats its images of fog and mud which surround the court of Chancery and, by extension, all of English life. As the fog, which surrounds all in a miasma from which there seems no escape, is a symbol of Chancery, the court itself, with its inert, irresponsible, and self-destructive wranglings, is a symbol of the calcified social and economic system strangling English life. The case of Jarndyce and Jarndyce is the perfect model of the social canker. Characters sacrifice their lives to its endless wrangling and forfeit the opportunity to accept individual responsibility and make something of themselves because of the illusory hope of instant riches. When the suit is finally settled, the fortune has been eaten up in court costs—an ironic commentary on the futility of such vain hopes.

People and places, too, in *Bleak House* so consistently have symbolic value that the novel occasionally verges on allegory. The cloudiness and rain which surround Chesney Wold symbolize the hopelessness of the nobility. Even the name of its inhabitants, Dedlock, is a sign of the moral deadlock and immobility of the ruling class. At the other end of the social spectrum, Tom-all-alone's, dirty and disease-ridden, is a symbol of the vulnerability and victimhood of the lowest classes. In gloom of one sort or another, many characters act as detectives searching out the guilty secrets and hypocrisies which permeate this world.

On the more positive side is Bleak House itself where the kindly John Jarndyce, aloof from involvement in the lawsuit, presides over a more orderly and benevolent demesne. But the contagion cannot even be kept from there. Occasionally even the admirable John Jarndyce suffers when the East Wind, a symbol of the agony and frustration outside, blows across the estate. More strikingly, Ada and Richard Carstone bring into their uncle's house the effects of the lawsuit as Richard destroys himself and injures those around him in his obsession with the Chancery case. Richard is another victim of the anachronistic system which destroys those who participate in it, a system which is a symbol of the inertia, complacency, and hypocrisy of the whole society. Finally, that Esther, the housekeeper, contracts smallpox from Jo is a symbol of the interrelatedness of all levels of society. Jo is at the bottom, but his misfortune becomes the misfortune of many as his contagion spreads through the social organism. The implication is that an unfeeling society can create Jo and Tom-all-alone's but it cannot protect itself from its victims.

Dickens offers no programmatic, revolutionary solution. If there is a solution, it is to be found in people like John Jarndyce, Esther Summerson, and Allan Woodcourt. Jarndyce is a figure of the selflessness which is necessary if injustice is to be rectified. Esther Summerson, as her name implies, is a bright antidote to the fog and rain. Her keys, which she shakes regularly, are a sign of her commitment to her domestic duties, an acceptance of responsibility. Dr. Woodcourt is the kind of active man society needs. The marriage of Esther and Woodcourt is a vindication of what they have to offer, as is Jarndyce's generous acceptance of their love. The new Bleak House in which they live is ironically full of the joy and goodness which can reform society. The novel does not offer the easy optimism of radical political solutions, because it is only this revolution in the heart of man which Dickens believes can cure society.

Edward E. Foster

THE BLITHEDALE ROMANCE

Type of work: Novel
Author: Nathaniel Hawthorne (1804-1864)
Type of plot: Psychological romance
Time of plot: Mid-nineteenth century
Locale: Massachusetts
First published: 1852

*Although Blithedale is modeled after the Transcendentalists' utopian commu-
nity of Brook Farm, the setting in the novel is incidental to plot and characterization. As in his greater works, Hawthorne probes the darker psychological side of
man's nature as he explores the effects upon people of living in close proximity. The
coldly inquisitive narrator Miles Coverdale; dark, queenly Zenobia; innocent and
pale Priscilla; and the proud reformer Hollingsworth are typical Hawthorne
characters.*

Hawthorne is well known as an explorer of the darker side of human consciousness. Henry James admired his powers of psychological and moral
analysis and maintained that his works gave "glimpses of a great field, of the
whole deep mystery of man's soul and conscience." It is true that readers,
imagining what lies behind the minister's black veil (in the story so titled) or
looking into Ethan Brand's fiery kiln, encounter visions of hellish torment.
In *The Blithedale Romance* there is a noticeable distancing from such visions.
Evil is in the book, but largely because of calculated effects in plotting and
point of view (Miles Coverdale's narration), it seems somewhat removed.
The form of the work, romance, provides a filter which softens the impact of
the psychological stresses the story records.

Brook Farm itself is ingenuously naïve in the earnestness with which it
pursues social and moral welfare; just as the Pilgrims' isolation and religious
fanaticism could not save them from the truth of the human heart—a theme
Hawthorne sounded most eloquently in *The Scarlet Letter*—so this idyllically
isolated settlement provides no haven from the passions animating men and
women. The Hollingsworth-Zenobia-Priscilla triangle comes to a drastic
head precisely because of the proximity of all the principals. Instead of a
social haven, Brook Farm is finally an arena for a tragedy of love.

Miles Coverdale is perhaps the most severely judged character in the novel.
His detachment and fear of accepting the consequences of his passions mark
his life as wasted. He says as much about himself in the confession which ends
the novel. The only thing that saves Miles Coverdale from the fate of a
Roger Chillingworth is that *The Blithedale Romance* is primarily a romance
and *The Scarlet Letter* categorically a tragedy.

BLOOD WEDDING

Type of work: Drama
Author: Federico García Lorca (1899-1936)
Type of plot: Romantic tragedy
Time of plot: Probably early 1900's
Locale: Spain
First presented: 1933

Blood Wedding *tells the story of a young bride who runs away with an old lover, who is then tracked down and murdered by the husband. Like his poetry and his paintings, Garcia Lorca's drama is rich in passion and symbolism and shows* avant-garde *influences. Responsible for initiating a movement to popularize Spanish drama for the masses through a system of touring theater companies during the early years of the Spanish Republic, the author was slain during the Civil War and his works proscribed by the Franco regime.*

In the three "folk tragedies"—*Blood Wedding, Yerma* (1934), and *The House of Bernarda Alba* (1936)—which culminated his poetic and dramatic career, Federico García Lorca succeeded brilliantly where a host of modern poet-dramatists had failed; he created a true poetry not in, "but *of* the theatre." The twentieth century is dotted with bad attempts at "poetic drama" by playwrights who lacked the requisite verbal facility (Eugene O'Neill, Maxwell Anderson) or versifiers whose theatrical efforts are largely unactable (Thomas Hardy, e. e. cummings). Even relatively successful verse dramatists such as T. S. Eliot, Christopher Fry, and Archibald MacLeish offer self-consciously "poetic" and "literary" efforts that lack the impact or even the "poetry," of the best prose dramas of the period. But García Lorca, who was both a great lyric poet and a practical man of the theater, fused all of the elements of the stage—language, movement, ritual, color, lighting, spectacle, and music—into a single dramatic presentation.

Much of the power of these folk plays comes from the way García Lorca combines a complex, sophisticated theatrical style with extremely simple dramatic situations. Although the original impulse for *Blood Wedding* came from a real incident, the basic plot—a bride stolen from her wedding by a lover—is a perennial one. Leonardo Felíx and The Bride are victims of their own uncontrollable emotions. He has a wife and child; she fervently desires the social and financial stability the marriage to The Bridegroom will bring. Since the entire society favors that match, they know that their passionate act will have fatal consequences. But these logical and moral considerations are irrelevant in the face of their powerful, passionate feelings.

García Lorca develops and expands the meanings of this folk tragedy with a dynamic synthesis of realistic, poetic, and symbolic theatrical devices. On the realistic level, he presents vivid, intense characterizations. The Bridegroom's Mother is an impressive, anguished woman who, having lost both husband and son, expects tragedy, but resolutely pursues the family destiny all the same. The Bridegroom is likable, sensitive, but hesitant, perhaps frightened by his pending marriage to a woman who is more strong-willed and passionate than he. The Bride's passion for Leonardo and clear disappointment at having lost him is evident from her first scene; her fervent desire for security and social respectability are doomed from the start and her troubled attempt to keep her emotions under control excites fear and pity in the audience. Leonardo—the only character in the play individualized by a name—is vital, volatile, frustrated, and overtly sexual; the intensity of his passion and the power of his attraction suggest energies and drives that are more than human. The Bride refers to him as "a dark river, choked with brush, that brought near me the undertone of its rushes and its whispered song."

All of this realistic characterization and conflict is then reinforced and extended by García Lorca's use of color, light, music, poetry, and symbolism. Even in the most realistic scenes there are patterns of imagery, both verbal and visual, that underscore the play's action. The Bridegroom's Mother broods over knives; Leonardo's mother-in-law sings a lullaby with images of "frozen horses" and "blood flowing like water"; The Bride wears black; Leonardo identifies himself with his horse—a traditional symbol of sexual passion—and The Bridegroom is likened to "a dove / with his breast a firebrand."

But it is in the masterful third act that García Lorca's "stage poetry" is fully realized. The relative realism of the first two acts gives way to a stylized forest landscape, and symbolic figures replace "real" ones. The final violence is previewed by a "debate" between the Moon—a sexually ambiguous young man—and the Beggar Woman, an image of death. The Moon stands for the primal emotion that has driven the fated couple together; the Beggar Woman represents the inevitable consequence of that passion. The scene culminates with the last meeting between Leonardo and The Bride as the realistic and the symbolic fuse into a powerful acknowledgment of unbridled love, desperate loss, and heroic defiance. The play's finale, when the bodies of Leonardo and The Bridegroom are brought in to be mourned by a stage full of bereaved women, leaves the audience completely drained of emotion—a tragic catharsis reminiscent of the greatest classical dramas.

A BLOT IN THE 'SCUTCHEON

Type of work: Drama
Author: Robert Browning (1812-1889)
Type of plot: Romantic tragedy
Time of plot: Eighteenth century
Locale: Rural England
First presented: 1843

Written at the request of the English actor and producer Macready, this drama has never been popular on the stage. While the play is Browning's invention, it nevertheless calls Shakespeare's Romeo *and* Juliet *immediately to mind; the quarrel between two great houses, the love affair between a young man and a very young girl, the duel, and the multiple deaths of the principals at the end are all paralleled in the two plays.*

Robert Browning did not write outstanding tragedies, primarily because the techniques which he used so well in his sophisticated poetry obscured the action. His love of soliloquy, for example, renders his plays somewhat slow moving and tedious. His command of the language certainly enabled him to explore the most intense emotions, yet that very strength tended to hinder the dramatic movement. In no way an exception, *A Blot in the 'Scutcheon,* although containing some effective scenes and a considerable amount of romantic action, including a duel, a suicide, and the tragic death of the heroine, is best viewed as an investigation of character and motive.

Thorold, Earl Tresham, represents the Victorian aristocrat, who in his dedication to the family honor is prepared to sacrifice the feelings of his sister, Mildred. Mildred herself, tyrannized by the idea of respectability, also helps bring about the tragedy by refusing to pretend to virginity by appearing at the altar in a white wedding gown with Henry, Earl Mertoun. Henry invites his own death by refusing to defend his life because he has been caught in a compromising situation. The three separate ideas of honor, conceived to venerate outmoded social mores, all combine to lead to the senseless tragedy.

Ironically, *A Blot in the 'Scutcheon* details a situation not unlike one in which Browning was to discover himself two years later with Elizabeth Barrett. Forbidden to marry by her domineering father, he and Elizabeth were forced to wed secretly and live in Italian exile. Mr. Barrett died twelve years later, only four years before Elizabeth herself died, never having been forgiven for her own "blot" in the 'scutcheon. From this incident it becomes clear that the Victorian themes of domestic tyranny and the power of respectability were not confined to literature, but dominated the entire mentality of bourgeois society.

THE BOHEMIANS OF THE LATIN QUARTER

Type of work: Novel
Author: Henri Murger (1822-1861)
Type of plot: Sentimental romance
Time of plot: Early nineteenth century
Locale: Paris
First published: 1848

Its events derived exclusively from Murger's own experiences, this novel was originally written for a periodical, The Corsair, *and later rewritten as a play which was a tremendous popular success; later, Puccini used the play as the basis of the perennially successful opera,* La Bohème. *Together, the novel, the play, and the opera have created the familiar picture of the Parisian Latin Quarter.*

The son of a tailor, Murger rebelled against his stolid, conservative father, and decided to become a poet. Entering the poor but gay life of the bohemian section of Paris, the young Murger nearly starved, and his health declined so much that he spent much time in the hospital. But he found success when he described in these essentially plotless and episodic chapters the life of the Latin Quarter. He wrote of himself in the character of Rodolphe, but Mimi was a composite picture of many girls that he knew. The book is filled with good-natured, if somewhat coy, humor and with youthful high spirits. The tales must be viewed in a historical context, for they no longer seem new or shocking, or even very daring, but when they first were published they caused a delighted scandal.

There is little of the sentimentality of the opera later derived from the book; the novel possesses much more vitality and humor than *La Bohème,* and is crowded with many more characters. In fact, if the book possesses any one dominant characteristic, it is the feeling for the crowded, jostling streets and alleys and cafes of the poverty-stricken but madcap artists' quarter. Faces seem to emerge from the shadows and to glow by lamplight, laughing and singing and making jokes. The lovemaking is casual and without regret; the characters' main concern is with their next meal and the cash to put off the landlord.

The novel is less a work of imaginative fiction than a piece of reportage. But the author possesses a sharp eye for detail and a certain wit and skill in creating his setting. Certain characters appear more frequently than others, but no man or woman dominates the book. The freshness and merriment, the romantic nonsense of youth still give the story an undying vitality and charm. The novel is not great literature, but it is a delightful picture of a moment in social and artistic history.

THE BONDMAN

Type of work: Drama
Author: Philip Massinger (1583-1640)
Type of plot: Tragi-comedy
Time of plot: Fourth century B.C.
Locale: Syracuse
First presented: c. 1623

This play expresses Massinger's conviction that man may be as enslaved by his own jealousy, lust, and greed as by physical bondage. While the play benefits from its swift, gripping action, it suffers in its characterizations, which are often so poorly motivated as to come dangerously close to the absurd.

The background of this play, which deals with an uprising of slaves who are overthrown not by weaponry but a display of whips, could have come from a number of sources—Justin, Giles Fletcher's *Russ Commonwealth,* Herodotus, or Diodorus, who places the event in Sicily as Massinger does. Another bit of Sicilian history is added with the appearance of Timoleon, who was the subject of one of Plutarch's *Lives* and is the Corinthian general who aids the Sicilians in the defeat of the Carthaginians. Placement of the setting in Sicily was likely Massinger's attempt to have the audience draw parallels with their own island-state: Corinth came to Siciliy's aid against Carthage as Holland hoped Britain would ally with her against Spain. With only this parallel as a beginning, it is a wonder that Sir Henry Herbert, Master of Revels, licensed the play on December 3, 1623 for a performance by the Lady Elizabeth's Men.

Indeed, throughout *The Bondman,* Massinger maintains his reputation for paralleling contemporary political events with his dramatic writing, and offering outspoken observations on the first two Stuart kings and their government —honestly criticizing what he saw and condemning that of which he disapproved. His view of politics, however, was really more moralistic than partisan. For example, many of the allusions made in *The Bondman* are directed toward the vain and dissolute favorite of Charles I—the Duke of Buckingham, George Villiers.

Several characters in *The Bondman* promote Massinger's view of political liberty, a subject dealt with more in this play than in any others of the Massinger canon. To Massinger, political liberty was synonymous with the liberty of the human soul, which could only be obtained when reason and respectable conduct ruled over baser passions, and when the social bond of the subject to ruler or state did not interfere. In Act I of *The Bondman* through the character of Timoleon, Massinger points out that freedom is deserved only by the virtuous. In the same act and scene, Cleora places the liberty of one's soul at a value worthy of the surrender of all one's worldly goods and riches. All this talk of liberty perhaps seems ironic when Massinger, being a supporter of political stability and an opposer of revolution, has the slaves in the play defeated. The resolve Massinger chooses is weak when juxtaposed with the eloquent speeches on freedom and liberty.

Another characteristic of Massinger's plays evident in *The Bondman* is his interest in the marriage or betrothal relationship. No other sixteenth or seventeenth century playwright, with the exception of Thomas Heywood, makes the relationship a central part of his drama. Massinger felt that betrothed or wed, couples had an obligation of mutual respect and trust and that infidelity or jealousy was highly disruptive in love. That Leosthenes in *The Bondman* loses Cleora because of the raging jealousy he displays, and that Marullo (Pisander) instead, becomes the captor of Cleora's heart with his unfailing trust, is moral justice in the true Massinger sense.

Perhaps it is well, then, that the Master of Revels licensed *The Bondman* for production, despite its political overtones. Without this play, we would know less about Philip Massinger, the man, and his time.

THE BONDS OF INTEREST

Type of work: Drama
Author: Jacinto Benavente y Martínez (1866-1954)
Type of plot: Comic romance
Time of plot: Early seventeenth century
Locale: Italy
First presented: 1907

This satirical comedy portrays the duality of man's complex nature, in which goodness and generosity mingle freely with the sordid and base. Benavente also makes clear in The Bonds of Interest *that every person must be made aware of the practical implications of his or her conduct.*

Benavente is a piquant realist at heart, but also a master of fantasy and always a proponent for the good, the beautiful, and the true. As is evident from *The Bonds of Interest,* he is most concerned with devising ingenious plots, like his Spanish predecessors, or illustrating the need for some reform, like the Northern writers in the theater of social criticism. Beneath the surface of the world as it is, he perceives an underlying reality, often opposed to the phenomenal world. In *The Bonds of Interest,* the best of Benavente's plays in a lighter vein, the playwright makes a moral use of the old Italian comedy of masks, but does so with a poetic delicacy intermixed with picaresque spice.

What interests Benavente in this work is the contrast between body and soul so often set forth in Spanish literature and in the works of the French romanticists. Crispin is that within us which contrives and seeks gain. Leander, redeemed by his love for Silvia, disputes Crispin's statement that "the ties of love are as nothing to the bonds of interest." As for Silvia, she affirms the existence of some divine element in our lives which will live on after the physical death of the body. This affirmation poses a dilemma to some critics who regard Benavente as a pessimist and see a dark shadow in the irony of the play. But although the author is a master of irony, he is surely not a pessimist. He is rather a keen observer commenting upon life agreeably and wisely, and with faith in the possibility of making it finer by educating the public; he writes in the hope that his dramas will affect meaningful changes in the attitudes of his audience.

The Bonds of Interest is an airy piece with a moral. Charming as it is in its fantasy, the comedy lacks the dramatic quality of some of Benavente's other works, but it is a favorite on many stages. Its morality is cheerful, sound, and sensible and requires no ardent revolt against established institutions, but is content to flick with a satiric whip those ancient butts of comedy —hypocrisy and vanity—so far as they affect the individual, rather than society as a whole.

BORIS GODUNOV

Type of work: Dramatic poem
Author: Alexander Pushkin (1799-1837)
Type of plot: Romantic tragedy
Time of plot: 1598-1605
Locale: Russia
First published: 1831

Pushkin hoped that this work, today often remembered chiefly because it furnished the libretto for Moussorgsky's opera, would bring some of the excitement and boldness of Shakespearian and Renaissance drama to the Russian stage. In this hope he was disappointed: Boris Godunov, *a perspective study of personal ambition, is excellent as a poem, but static as a play.*

Pushkin's *Boris Godunov,* following upon his masterpiece, *Eugene Onegin,* represents his turning away from Byron as a literary model, and the new appreciation of Shakespeare. Russian drama had long been dominated by the canons of French classicism, and even by the 1820's had not yet reacted to the new styles which had been developing in Germany since the discovery of Shakespeare by writers of the Storm and Stress Movement of the 1770's. Thus *Boris Godunov* was quite revolutionary in many respects. Pushkin did not divide the play into acts, but composed twenty-three scenes, totally abandoning the classical unities of time and place. He imitated Shakespeare in the use of crowd scenes, and in the mingling of comic and tragic episodes. He also adopted both the blank verse of Shakespeare and his use of prose, including the coarse language of the common people.

Unfortunately, Romantic notions of Shakespearean style emphasized looseness of structure and profusion of characters and events, often resulting in episodic works that lacked unity and focus. This is true of *Boris Godunov:* the central tragic figure appears in only six scenes, and his nemesis, Dimitry, is not really a direct opponent, but merely a political opportunist. Thus there is no clash of ideas or wills, such as defines the political struggles in Shakespeare's histories. Therefore, though the situation bears resemblances to Shakespeare's *Richard the Third* or *Macbeth,* there are major differences: Boris' crime takes place before the play begins, and he appears inactive, reacting to the shifting tides of political events while burdened with guilt. His tragedy is that of the quest for power, which succeeds only to fail, first as peace of mind disappears, and then as a sense of guilt turns a change of political fortune into a kind of retribution which destroys Boris and his family. Yet this tragedy plays against a panorama so broad that Soviet critics may well be justified in saying that the center of the play is really the Russian people itself, suffering and enduring under the shifting fortunes of ambitious despots.

THE BOURGEOIS GENTLEMAN

Type of work: Drama
Author: Molière (Jean Baptiste Poquelin, 1622-1673)
Type of plot: Comedy of manners
Time of plot: Seventeenth century
Locale: Paris, France
First presented: 1670

In this comedy, Monsieur Jourdain, a tradesman, aspires to become a gentleman by engaging various tutors to teach him such gentlemanly arts as dancing, fencing, and philosophy. Once again Molière turns his keen wit against sham and hypocrisy, although the satire is gentler and less biting than in many of his plays.

The Bourgeois Gentleman was first presented at court in 1670 in the Grand Gallery of Chambord, a royal castle on the Loire, and, like all the royal residences, large and luxurious. The play, by command of Louis XIV, was to be a "turquerie." In 1699 an ambassador from Turkey had visited the king, and enthusiasm was still high for the exotic. Giovanni Battista Lulli wrote the music and Molière added his comedy to it. The expenditures indicate that the initial production was elaborate. It was a great success, and the play has remained one of Molière's most popular.

Modern productions of the play often cut the ballet scenes. It has been pointed out that this type of "spectacle" has been rendered very old-fashioned by later extravaganzas, particularly by television and motion picture musicals of recent times. However, one should not forget nor ignore the fact that the play is actually a combination of comedy and ballet. The ballet is an integral, if *à la rigueur,* separable part. It has a "literary" or symbolic function as the extension of Monsieur Jourdain's obsession with display. And the more preposterous the ballet, the better he seems to like it.

But if it is in some way simply light entertainment, this has not impeded *The Bourgeois Gentleman* from becoming one of the best known of French plays. And Monsieur Jourdain has become one of Molière's most celebrated characters. He is something of an archetype in French tradition of the bourgeois who tries to conform to aristocratic manners and circles.

The translation of the play's title is somewhat misleading, as *gentilhomme* means "nobleman." The juxtaposition of *"Le Bourgeois"* and *Gentilhomme* should be understood as a contradiction. It is an idea, according to Molière and the court for which he wrote, worthy only of ridicule. The satire, however, is relatively mild; Monsieur Jourdain is more a buffoon, and the comedy is essentially farce, rather than a profound critique of vicious social traits.

Of the inner circle Monsier Jourdain is trying to attain, we never see more than the Marchioness, Dorimène, and Dorante. The Marchioness has a minor role, and is not only the object of Monsieur Jourdain's absurd affection, but remains relatively untainted by his foolish intrigues. Dorante is noble, too, but if he associates more or less intimately with the bourgeois, it is clearly to exploit the latter's gullible ambitions and to get the Marchioness for himself. His duplicity is charming, however, and he can not be accused of much more than shallowness, since Monsieur Jourdain appears sufficiently wealthy, and remains blissfully undeceived to the end. All of the other characters within the family circle are notable for their relatively good sense. In large measure, this good sense means knowing where one out to be (and stay), on the social hierarchy.

The principal counterpoint, or foil, for Monsieur Jourdain is Madame Jourdain. Her loyalty to her class and her proud insistence that both her and Monsieur Jourdain's fathers had been merchants, is presented as solid, if contentious, good sense. When she argues that their daughter Lucile would do better to marry a man proper to herself, a bourgeois honest, nice-looking, and rich, the absurd response of Monsieur Jourdain is that he is rich enough himself for her, and that he needs for her only "honor," so he can make her a marchioness. When she interrupts the banquet Monsieur Jourdain and Dorante are having for Dorimène, Madame Jourdain is told by Dorante that she needs better eyeglasses. The irony here is that she needs them not at all, and that of the others present, only Dorante has an inkling of what is going on, for it is his private scheme to gull Monsieur Jourdain by courting Dorimène with Jourdain's money and lavish gifts. The deceptions and self-deceptions of the play, chiefly of Monsieur Jourdain, are the main source of the humor. Self-deception is very common matter for comedy. Of comic themes it seems to lend itself to a play like *The Bourgeois Gentleman* particularly well.

From the series of educational vignettes at the opening, to the finale, Monsieur Jourdain is a victim of "stage irony." The audience is aware of something a character is unaware of, as, for example, his self-deception is quite evident, as well as the various tricks played on him. A critic has theorized that comic characters are essential types more or less constantly in a process of being *revealed,* as opposed to the self-discovery of tragedy; and the wealth of Monsieur Jourdain permits him the freedom to reveal himself very liberally. He pursues every foolish symbol that the parvenu *par excellence* feels he must have. What he constantly reveals is that the symbols, worn by him, are empty of meaning. The main action of the play displays that Monsieur Jourdain cannot see beyond display (and thus is easily duped).

An extreme example of his obsession with external symbols of status, as well as his foolish single-mindedness in their pursuit, is when the tailor's boy addresses him by titles of honor. The boy gets a larger tip for each higher title. If he had gone so far as to say "your highness," Jourdain was going to give him the whole purse. However, if the "symbol of status" is more profound than the boy's obvious flattery, as when the philosophy teacher instructs him on moderating the passions, Monsieur Jourdain is unimpressed and completely uninterested.

James Marc Hovde

BOUVARD AND PÉCUCHET

Type of work: Novel
Author: Gustave Flaubert (1821-1880)
Type of plot: Psychological realism
Time of plot: Nineteenth century
Locale: France
First published: 1881

This novel, unfinished at the author's death, concerns two bachelor friends who decide to leave their dull jobs as clerks and buy a farm together when one of them inherits a considerable sum of money. Flaubert uses this situation to satirize the habits, thought patterns, and aspirations of the two clerks. Despite the author's passionately pessimistic attitude toward the middle class they represent, however, some sympathy for his characters still comes through.

Although Flaubert intended this novel to be a satire on the middle classes and on the pretensions, both intellectual and social, of the protagonists, he was too much of a genius for his actual work to remain so limited. The reader of *Bouvard and Pécuchet* soon realizes that the author felt a genuine and deep affection for the pair of friends who bumble through the pages of this book. The charm of their unaffected enthusiasm captivates the reader as it apparently captivated their creator. In their innocence, Bouvard and Pécuchet risk foolishness; in this, they bear a kinship with Don Quixote. The heroes might also be compared to Voltaire's hero, Candide, who sought solutions to great questions, for they are committed to ideas, seek them out, confront them, and try to make use of them. Like Candide, they retain their innocence through all turmoil and trouble. Their vision is not small, even if their actual intellectual capabilities are limited.

Bouvard and Pécuchet has also been compared to Swift's *Gulliver's Travels,* but the satire is much less savage. Like Swift, Flaubert looked with horror upon the pettiness and corruption in the world. He scorned the littleness of the people around him, and feared for the quality of life as the bourgeoisie gained power. But, as a great artist, he was compelled to look deeper into every question and to penetrate to the souls of the human beings he created in his books. Because of this, *Bouvard and Pécuchet* is an uneven satire, although a masterpiece of fictional writing. The most appropriate comparison is actually to Cervantes, for he, too, saw beyond the foolishness of his hero to his heart. Bouvard and Pécuchet want to learn too quickly; they have no patience with the true scholarly approach. They are like Sterne's characters, with their "hobby horse" that warps their personalities. Yet, they are intensely likeable, and the reader becomes fond of them. They suffer the consequences of their limitations, and acquire a kind of pathos in the eyes of the reader. There is a pessimism in this book, but the greater spirit and vision of the author transcends it.

THE BRACKNELS

Type of work: Novel
Author: Forrest Reid (1876-1946)
Type of plot: Domestic chronicle
Time of plot: Early twentieth century
Locale: Ireland
First published: 1911

Like his friend Walter de la Mare, Forrest Reid had a conception of reality which was inseparable from the supernatural and imaginary; like his hero Denis, he lived in a pagan dream world of his own designing. Reid's strong interest in abnormal psychology and his poetic, mystical qualities are all easily discernible in The Bracknels, *especially in the characterization of Denis, who retreats from the evil of the world, which he finds unbearable.*

Originally a lyrical tale titled *The Moon Story, The Bracknels* was expanded and reworked into a realistic novel, keeping the moon story as a subsidiary theme but treating the overall work as a family chronicle. To counteract a tendency to the fantastic and bizarre, Forrest Reid rooted his stories in solid realistic surroundings; the setting of this novel, the valley and river, the houses and woods, were all founded on Reid's own childhood world, and are described with poetic intensity.

The Bracknels was the real start of Reid's career as a writer; it was the first book in which he presented his personal vision of life. It is the story of the development of an unusually sensitive boy, but it is also the story of a family. The complicated plot, greater action, and broader canvas mark it as an important advance over its predecessors. Perhaps the book hovers between fantasy and realism without completely achieving either; later Reid mastered the difficult task of handling the commonplace and the marvelous successfully in a single narrative. But the first experiment produced an unusual and interesting book.

Denis Bracknel stands out as the sensitive son of a self-made man—an unscrupulous Belfast merchant—and a pathetic and weak mother. Alfred, Denis' brother, is a coarse philistine, and his sisters are foolish and flirtatious. Denis' new tutor, Rusk, becomes the most important person in his life, the only one with a sense of the boy's secret inner life. Perhaps the central scene in the novel is the one in which Rusk sees Denis dancing naked in the moonlight, as if performing some sacred rite. The relationship between the two is ambiguous and in a less innocent time might have been questioned. A nightmare quality reminiscent of James's *The Turn of the Screw* pervades the book, until its natural ending in Denis' death. Reid's publisher insisted on a tacked-on ending in which Rusk returned to Ireland on a farewell visit before setting out for Australia, but in the revised version published in 1947 this scene was omitted.

THE BRAGGART SOLDIER

Type of work: Drama
Author: Titus Maccius Plautus (c. 255-184 B.C.)
Type of plot: Comedy of intrigue
Time of plot: Third century B.C.
Locale: Ephesus, in Asia Minor
First presented: c. 206 B.C.

In this comedy about a vainglorious, cowardly soldier, Plautus provided the prototype for many similar characters in later dramas, including Shakespeare's Falstaff. While the action is ingeniously contrived, the character development tends to be jerky and not fully integrated with the plot.

The Braggart Soldier *(Miles Gloriosus)* is one of Plautus' most successful and rollicking comedies. He adapted the play from a Greek original entitled *The Braggart (Alazon),* and possibly he combined two different sources. This is probably an early work by Plautus, judging by the lack of variety in the meter and by the reference to Naevius, the poet and dramatist. The comedy was most likely very popular when it was first presented, because repeat performances were given.

In staging it must have resembled the American musical comedy, with song and dance used to enliven the dramatic action. Masks and Greek costumes may have been employed. The backdrop consisted of two adjoining houses, one belonging to Pyrgopolinices and the other to Periplecomenus. The play itself is rich in buffoonery, parody, punning, comic names, and verbal ingenuity. The action is lively, and the characters—all stock types of farce— exhibit great energy in playing out their predestined roles. There is a unity of time as well as of place, since the action occurs in less than a day. Moreover, despite what many critics say, there is a unity of dramatic movement, not to mention suspense, in the way the play is constructed. The overall effect is one of exuberance carried to its utmost limits.

When Plautus wrote his plays during the early Roman Republic, Roman morality was still quite strict, and his audiences must have been titillated by the spectacle of lecherous generals, courtesans, rascally servants, and indolent lovers, all of whom were Greek. The Romans would never have allowed such characters to appear as Romans at that period, but the fact that they were Greeks must have added largely to their enjoyment. The theater, and particularly the comic theater, has often served as a liberating force, a kind of psychic safety valve, by exposing private daydreams on the stage.

The Braggart Soldier is a comedy of deception with a highly intricate plot. Superficially it has two distinct sections, the duping of Sceledrus into thinking Philocomasium is two different girls, and the duping of Pyrgopolinices into voluntarily releasing Philocomasium and Palaestrio. Both schemes are closely related, and the one follows from the other.

The opening scene, in which the vain, supremely boastful, and lewd Captain Pyrgopolinices appears with his toady, makes it clear that Pyrgopolinices is going to be the butt of the intrigue. Then the slave Palaestrio, in his prologue, explains he is going to play a trick on the slave Sceledrus in order to make Philocomasium's meetings with Pleusicles safer. But since Sceledrus has already seen the lovers together and intends to sell Pyrgopolinices, the scheme becomes a matter of necessity. It takes a lot of elaborate guile to prove to the stupid, pigheaded Sceledrus that Philocomasium is two people. And even though he is intimidated by Palaestrio and Periplecomenus, he is never truly convinced of it. He says he is leaving until the trouble blows over, but in fact he sticks around and gets drunk, which poses a threat to the later scheme to trick Pyrgopolinices.

Having subdued Sceledrus into temporary silence, Palaestrio has to invent a plan for freeing himself and Philocomasium from the intolerable Pyrgopolinices. If his first deception had failed any new one would be impossible. The connection between the two schemes is further strengthened when Palaestrio incorporates the idea for the first (Philocomasium being twins) into the second. Yet the crux of the new plan occurs to him in a supposedly irrelevant scene where old Periplecomenus pontificates on the joys of bachelorhood: why not give Periplecomenus a fake wife infatuated with Pyrgopolinices?

The characters involved talk over this plan extensively, but we do not know how it will work until Philocomasium and Palaestrio are almost freed, which maintains suspense. Suspense is also maintained tactically, when we learn that Sceledrus is getting drunk, when Palaestrio and Milphidippa nearly burst out laughing in Pyrgopolinices' face, when Philocomasium and Pleusicles almost begin making love before Pyrgopolinices' eyes, and when Palaestrio dangerously delays his escape in saying goodbye to Pyrgopolinices. All these things give excitement to the intrigue, making us forget how improbable it really is.

However, it is not enough to swindle Pyrgopolinices of his courtesan and his slave girl—he must be put in a position where retaliation becomes impossible. And to do that he must be completely humiliated and deflated. Hence, the sub-scheme by which he is enticed into Periplecomenus' house to ravish the phoney wife makes it possible for Periplecomenus to drag him in his underwear out into the street to be beaten and threatened with castration, the punishment for adultery. The threat is enough to get the desired result from the lascivious Pyrgopolinices, securing the safety of Palaestrio and Philocomasium. At the end Pyrgopolinices is left standing on the stage in his underwear, vanity collapsed, asking the audience to applaud. This conclusion is unique among comedies of deception in the way merry practical joking has led up to such a brutal, shaming finish.

This whole complex story revolves around a few simple elements of charac-

ter—the colossal vanity and lust of Pyrgopolinices, the desire of Philocomasium to be free and reunited with her lover, and Palaestrio's ingenuity in
securing their mutual freedom. In keeping with the martial nature of Pyrgopolinices' profession, the strategy against him is spoken of in military terms.
Pyrgopolinices, of course, is one of a long line of cowardly, conceited,
boastful, lecherous soldiers in the theater, not the least of which is Shakespeare's Falstaff. And Palaestrio, the wily slave, is the forerunner of the artful
servant from Renaissance theater to the present day.

James Weigel, Jr.

BRAND

Type of work: Drama
Author: Henrik Ibsen (1828-1906)
Type of plot: Social criticism
Time of plot: Nineteenth century
Locale: West coast of Norway
First published: 1866

Brand, *Ibsen's first major play to gain wide European acclaim, was written during the author's voluntary exile in Italy to protest Norway's failure to join Denmark in its war against invading Prussia. A verse drama, it tells the symbolic story of a priest who sacrifices his wife and child to his unshakable sense of duty to his parish. Although addressed to his fellow Norwegians, the drama has universal appeal in its depiction of the soul's struggle to seek uncompromising truth.*

Brand, although not his first successful play, brought Henrik Ibsen to prominent stature as a dramatist. This verse drama—a play in poetry—was written in the first phase of Ibsen's career when his plays dealt mainly with historical themes, folklore, and romantic pageantry, before the playwright turned to prose and social issues in the second phase of his career. *Brand* was, however, the first of Ibsen's masterpieces, foreshadowing his best-known plays of social criticism. In addition, the play did more than enhance Ibsen's personal reputation. It vitalized the Norwegian theater, which had been languishing under the shadow of the Danish theater in Copenhagen even after Norway's separation from Denmark in 1814. *Brand* thus has historical significance as well as artistic importance.

The play combines poetry and moral passion in a grim Norwegian landscape of jagged mountains, deep-fissured valleys, and cruelly cold temperatures. The setting is an apt complement to the solemn, tragic mood of the play and to the dour cynicism of many of Brand's parishioners and fellow villagers. Indeed, gloom pervades the play, affecting characters like some malign virus. At the beginning of the play, for example, Einar and Agnes were symbols of light heartedness to Brand—a light heartedness which, not incidentally, the priest deplored as evil. Later Agnes broke off her engagement to Einar in order to marry the stern Brand and live a life of great sacrifice, terminating in early death. Likewise, Einar subsequently foresook his lighthearted ways and became a religious fanatic. It is the image of Brand, however, that dominates the play, most vividly reflecting the atmosphere and mood of the drama.

Brand is, after all, the tragedy of a supreme idealist misled by an image of holiness. The protagonist's uncompromising attitude in his dealings with others—even with his wife and in matters relating to the survival of their son —reveals his conviction that the path to holiness is too narrow for concessions or backsliding. Every ideal must be maintained unblemished, for there is no or backsliding. Every ideal must be maintained unblemished, for there is no bargaining with God. Brand was so convinced of his rightness that even his mountain-climbing injuries appeared as vindicating stigmata just before he caught sight of the Ice-church. Yet, Brand's epiphany was ironically shattered by the rifle shot of Gerd, his one remaining follower and a social outcast (she was half gipsy) like the now-repudiated priest. Then, only seconds before the roaring avalanche would engulf Brand and Gerd, a desembodied voice, echoing the reassurance given to Goethe's Faust, proclaimed to Brand that message of forgiveness from a God of love. This manifestation of the transcendant mercy of God, however, is not a validation of Brand's beliefs. Rather, it is Ibsen's way of showing that even the most pious and dedicated priest can do wrong or be wrong, and thus stand in need of the divine solace he earlier exhorted his sinful parishioners to seek. *Brand* depicts the humbling of a proud man whose ideals and idealism blinded him to his own pride. Quite rightly is this powerful drama considered among Ibsen's masterpieces.

BRAVE NEW WORLD

Type of work: Novel
Author: Aldous Huxley (1894-1963)
Type of plot: Social satire
Time of plot: 632 years After Ford
Locale: London and New Mexico
First published: 1932

In this grim satirical novel, Huxley paints a horrifying picture of future society based upon his vision of where present social and scientific trends could lead in six hundred year's time. In the year 632 AF (After Ford), the Bokanovsky Process for growing embryos in bottles has been perfected. Each individual is conditioned, both before and after birth, into one of the predestined classes, which range from Epsilon Minus Morons to Alpha Plus Intellectuals depending upon what function the person will be programmed to perform for society.

The best utopian—or anti-utopian—fiction is not really about the future; it is an indirect view of the present. The authors of such works begin with aspects of their own society that they like, dislike, desire, or fear, and, by extrapolating them into a possible future, demonstrate the likely consequences of such tendencies or pressures developed to their extremes. If the reader does not see his own society reflected in an exaggerated, distinctive, but recognizable form, it is unlikely that the projected world will offer more than amused distraction. *Brave New World* has endured as a classic of the genre because Aldous Huxley's vision was not only frighteningly believable when first presented, but has become more immediate since its initial appearance. Indeed, in *Brave New World Revisited* (1958), an extended expository gloss on the original, Huxley suggested that his only important prophetic error was the assumption that it would take six centuries to implement fully the brave new world; a scant twenty-six years after the novel's publication Huxley revised his estimate of the time needed to less than a century.

The most disturbing aspect of *Brave New World* is the suspicion that many, perhaps most, people would like to live in such a society. After examining the modern Western world in general, and America in the 1920's in particular, with its assembly-line techniques, its consumerism, its hedonistic tendencies, its emphasis on social conformity, and its worship of childhood and youth, Huxley projected his observations to their logical conclusions and then asked himself how a "sane" man would react to such an environment: the result was *Brave New World*.

Given modern industrial and scientific "progress," Huxley saw that the time would soon arrive when mankind would possess the knowledge and equipment to "solve" all of its material and social problems and achieve universal "happiness," but at a very high price—the sacrifice of freedom, individuality, truth, beauty, a sense of purpose, and the concept of God. The central question is this: how many would really miss these things? Do they constitute enough of an intellectual, emotional, and moral force to alter the direction of modern society and do they possess the requisite will, conviction, and energy to do so?

Compared to such earlier efforts as *Antic Hay* (1923), *Those Barren Leaves* (1925), and especially *Point Counter Point* (1928), *Brave New World* is a model of structural simplicity. The dynamics of brave new world are presented in a long introductory tour of Huxley's futuristic society that takes up almost the first half of the book. Then a catalytic character, John the Savage, is introduced, who directly challenges the social system that has been described. This conflict leads directly to a confrontation between John, the representative of "sanity," and Mustapha Mond, who speaks for brave new world. Their extended debate serves as the novel's ideological climax. The book ends as the Savage experiences the inevitable personal consequences of that debate.

The long opening sequence begins at the beginning with assembly-line bottle births, in which the individual's potential is carefully regulated by a combination of genetic selection and chemical treatments, and then follows the life cycle to show how all tastes, attitudes, and behavior patterns are adroitly controlled by incessant conditioning. The net result of the conditioning is a society that is totally and deliberately infantile. All activities are transitory, trivial, and mindless—promiscuity replacing passion, immediate sensory stimulation replacing art ("feelies"), hallucinatory escape replacing personal growth ("Soma").

At this point John, the Savage, enters the narrative. Reared among primitives by a mother who loved him in spite of her conditioning, John has known the beauty of great art, because of his reading of Shakespeare, and the pain of loneliness, having been ostracized by the natives because of his light skin and his mother's loose morals. Primed by Linda's nostalgic memories of her former life, the Savage is ready for contact with the outside world when Bernard Marx discovers him on the Reservation and connives to use him in a revenge scheme against the Director of the Hatcheries (John's natural father). At first John is feted as an interesting freak, but, given his "primitive" moralism, a clash is inevitable. Reacting emotionally to the events surrounding Linda's death, John provokes a violent social disruption—the most serious crime in the brave new world—which leads to the discussion with Mustapha Mond, a World Controller.

This extended debate between John and Mond, which, in a bitterly funny way resembles the Grand Inquisitor scene in Fyodor Dostoevski's *The Brothers Karamazov* (1879-1880), is the rhetorical center of the book. Like Dostoevski's Inquisitor, Mond justifies his social vision as the only one compatible with human happiness and, like his literary predecessor, he indicates that he, along with the other World Controllers, have taken the pain of life's ambiguities and indecisions upon their own shoulders in order to spare those less capable from having to endure such emotional and psychological pressures. The major difference between the Inquisitor's society and the brave new world is that Dostoevski's hero-villain had only a vision, but, with the aid of modern science and industry, the World Controllers have succeeded in making the vision a permanent reality—providing all distractions such as beauty, truth, art, purpose, God, and, ironically, science itself, are suppressed. Savage rejects Mond's world out of hand, for he demands the right to be unhappy, among other things.

But, unfortunately, the brave new world cannot allow him that right, nor, if it would, is he fully capable of exercising it. His designation as "savage" is both ironical and true. He is civilized compared to the dehumanized infantilism of most brave new worlders, but he is also still the primitive, as Huxley himself admitted. Shakespeare alone is not enough to equip him for the complexities of life. His upbringing among the precivilized natives, who practice a religion that is a form of fertility cult has left him without the real emotional and religious resources needed to face a brave new world on his own. Denied a chance to escape, the Savage tries to separate himself from its influence, but it follows him and exploits him as a quaint curiosity. Frustrated and guilt-ridden, he scourges himself and is horrified to discover that the brave new worlders can incorporate even his self-abasement into their system. Caught between the "insanity" of Utopia and the "lunacy" of the primitive village, John reacts violently, first outwardly, to assault Lenina, then inwardly, to kill himself.

Thus, it remains for the other "rebellious" characters in the book to establish alternatives to the brave new world and here, perhaps, is where the book is artistically inferior to Huxley's previous works. One of the most impressive qualities in the novels that immediately preceded *Brave New World* is the way in which the author pursued and developed the qualities that he had given to his major characters. Unfortunately, in *Brave New World* he does not fully develop the possibilities latent in his primary figures.

One of the sharpest ironies in *Brave New World* lies in the way Huxley carefully demonstrates that, in spite of mechanistic reproduction and incessant conditioning, individualistic traits and inclinations persist in the brave new world. As a result of alcohol in his pre-natal blood surrogate, Bernard Marx shows elements of nonconformity. Because of an over-developed I.Q., Helmholtz Watson is dissatisfied with his situation and longs to write a book—although he cannot imagine what he wants to say. Even Lenina Crowne has dangerous tendencies toward emotional involvement. But Huxley largely fails to develop the potential of these deviations. After repeatedly showing Marx's erratic attempts to "conform" to a society that he feels essentially alienated from, Huxley abandons him once the Savage enters the narrative. On the other hand, Helmholtz Watson's character is hardly explored at all. And, after her failure to seduce John, Lenina is almost completely forgotten, except for her fleeting reappearance at the book's conclusion. Unlike the Savage, Marx and Watson are allowed a chance to travel to an isolated community and experiment with individualism, but the reader never sees the results of their austere freedom.

However, if the "positive" side of *Brave New World* is never developed and all of the artistic possibilities are not fully exploited, the novel remains a powerful, perceptive, bitterly funny vision of modern society. But let us fervently hope, along with the author, that the final importance of *Brave New World* does not come from its prophetic accuracy.

Keith Neilson

BREAD AND WINE

Type of work: Novel
Author: Ignazio Silone (1900-   )
Type of plot: Social criticism
Time of plot: 1930's
Locale: Italy
First published: 1937

Set in the late 1930's, this novel depicts the widespread compromising of ideals which took place on all levels of Italian society during Mussolini's rule. By means of his study of honest and courageous individuals who resist injustices and remain faithful to their ideals, Silone proposes that there will always be good men who continue to fight regardless of the odds.

Ignazio Silone, Italy's chief novelist of the 1930's and 1940's, was attracted to communism in the 1920's but by 1930 he had become disillusioned with the party's hypocrisy and tyranny. *Bread and Wine,* his best novel, is in part a study in political disillusionment. The novel reveals that political reaction to social injustice is at the root of Silone's impulse to write fiction. He has said, "for me writing has not been, and never could be except in a few favored moments of peace, a serene aesthetic enjoyment, but rather the painful continuation of a struggle."

The central question in *Bread and Wine* is whether one can satisfy the demands of the soul and of social betterment at the same time. At the beginning of the novel Pietro Spina is a full-fledged political propagandist and organizer for the Communists. He is against the private ownership of land and he seems to believe that the world's wealth will eventually be shared equally. Forced to hide and rest in an out-of-the-way village in the garb of a priest he begins to change his views. He asks himself whether he hasn't lost his sincerity in his wholehearted pursuit of party ideology. He asks whether he hasn't fled "the opportunism of a decadent church to fall into the Machiavellianism of a sect?" In his self-examination the question of good faith is paramount. Political action in Silone demands as much honesty and composure of soul as does a true religious vocation.

Two factors in particular contribute to Spina's change. The first is his assumption of the role of Don Paolo. As a priest people come to him in trust and his own instinctive love of truth and justice is rekindled. The second has to do with the peasants he encounters and the region they live in. The Abruzzi region is central in Silone's fiction. It is somewhat bleak and poverty-stricken but its peasants are tough and basic. They and their land bring Spina back to the basic problems governing man's relationships with his fellows.

Spina's problem can be put another way: as he becomes more and more influenced by his role as Don Paolo he must not lose sight of Pietro Spina.

He must keep Don Paolo and Spina together and integrated. His old school teacher Don Benedetto helps him here. Don Benedetto has moral authority and candor. His advice to Spina confirms him in his way. His death is a further sign to Spina that he must not back away from social problems. In his dialogues with Cristina Colamartini, Spina is also confirmed in his spiritual change. She too is sacrificed at the end of the novel. For Silone such sacrifices are necessary to the pursuit of political justice and spiritual wholeness.

Two scenes in particular reveal Pietro's independence and help to define his rejection of party politics. In the first scene, Pietro refuses to follow the party line enunciated by a character named Battipaglia. He points out that if he conforms to an edict in which he does not believe, he will be committing the same sin of which the Communists accuse the Fascists. The second scene follows directly after the first and is really a continuation of the argument begun in the first. Uliva, an old friend of Pietro, says he foresees already the corruption of their movement into orthodoxy and tyranny. The enthusiastic ideas they had as students have hardened into official doctrine. The Party cannot stand any deviation, even if it leads to the truth. Uliva's disillusionment is great: "Against this pseudolife, weighed down by pitiless laws," he cries out, "the only weapon left to man's free will is antilife, the destruction of life itself." Later he is killed in his apartment by a bomb that police evidence showed he meant for high government officials gathered in a church. This was his physical end but he had really been destroyed by the dialectical process. Between Battipaglia's cynical rigidity and Uliva's honest but misguided nihilism, Spina must find a way to perpetuate the cause. He succeeds because his faith cannot dry up, and because he is able to pass on his belief to two or three others. The process of simple communion replaces the idea of the Communist state and the revolutionary spirit is saved. Silone's communism is the primitive communism of the earliest Christianity. Poverty is its badge of honesty, and its heroes are men who travel in disguise from place to place looking for kindred souls. They like to listen to peasants and simple men rather than to the learned.

In a scene which is repeated throughout Silone's work, Spina meets one such man and says he wants to talk with him. The man proves to be a deaf mute but that does not prevent Spina from communicating with him. Indeed, it is the wordless nature of their communication which is important, for words can neither confuse nor betray them. Their spiritual communion is the most solid base on which to build a relationship. It is, Silone seems to be saying, the one thing absolutely necessary for successful political action, the only thing which should never be betrayed.

The humanistic basis of Silone's politics is stated most fully by Spina when he says to Uliva, "man doesn't really exist unless he's fighting against his own limits." At the end of *Bread and Wine,* the spirit of clandestine rebellion is abroad in the land. As in early Christian times, the history of martyrdoms and miracles has begun.

Benjamin Nyce

THE BRIDE OF LAMMERMOOR

Type of work: Novel
Author: Sir Walter Scott (1771-1832)
Type of plot: Historical romance
Time of plot: Late seventeenth century
Locale: Scotland
First published: 1819

Based on a historical incident, this novel relates the story of Edgar Ravenswood, rightful heir to an enormous estate which has been captured by the unscrupulous Lord Ashton through legal trickery. His love for Ashton's daughter Lucy—the bride of the title—ends in a tragedy made colorful by all the elements of melodrama, including murder, insanity, ghostly apparitions, and a diabolical villainess.

This novel of seventeenth century Scotland has a driving psychological as well as political, religious and social determinism. The conflict between Presbyterian (Lord Ashton and family) and Episcopalian (Master of Ravenswood) is influential in motivating plot. So, to a lesser degree, is the politico-social turmoil which involves disintegration of old order Tory values before the energetic ambitions of the Whigs. And upon the inevitable confusion, disorder, and decay resulting from these changes, popular superstition thrives. This power of the supernatural—manifest in omens, dreams, hidden fears, prophecy, visions, spectres, and other such phenomena—directs the thoughts and actions of both major and minor characters.

Such superstitious paraphernalia, however, Scott does not impose upon the story; he employs them more subtly so that they seem the result of psychological conflict within character. The Master of Ravenswood, deprived of his castle and hereditary rights, can only by submerging his proud loyalty, ally himself with the Ashtons, who have usurped all he holds significant in life. His sudden, almost unconscious love for Lucy Ashton, although a solace and partial fulfillment of loss, still in his own eyes demeans him. He knows he cannot betray the values of the past, yet he has within him youth and ardor which force him into an engagement with Lucy. All characters in the novel, and the reader as well, know that such an alliance will lead to doom. Old Alice tells him this; Caleb Balderstone, his faithful, ingenious manservant, warns him against the marriage. The apparition at Mermaiden's Well confirms Ravenswood's fears, even Lucy's passive affection and terror of her mother all underline the Master's own perception. But he remains psychologically divided, unable to free himself emotionally from what he realizes intellectually is a disastrous union.

The schism within Young Ravenswood, a truly Byronic hero, finds its dark expression in the ugly prophecies of the village hags, the superstitious talk of the sexton, the mutterings of the peasants, and Henry Ashton's shooting of the raven near the betrothed couple at the Well. But step by step

Ravenswood almost seeks his fate, driven relentlessly by factors deep within his personality.

Lucy is equally torn. She loves Ravenswood but is paralyzed before the dominating force of her mother. She submits to marriage with Bucklaw, but her divisive emotions drive her to murder, insanity, and death. Lord Ashton, too, has commendable motives in spite of his political chicanery, but he, like Lucy, is rendered ineffective by his wife's mastery.

The comic relief provided by Balderstone in his bizarre methods of replenishing the bare tables of Wolf's Crag, and the rallying of all in the village to provide adequately for the Marquis during his visit, furnish enough humor to keep the novel from sinking into grotesque morbidity and Gothic excess. Scott's sense of timing and ability to tie supernatural elements to psychological divisions within personality manage to hold the novel together and make of it a controlled and well-structured work.

BRIDESHEAD REVISITED

Type of work: Novel
Author: Evelyn Waugh (1903-1966)
Type of plot: Social criticism
Time of plot: Twentieth century
Locale: England
First published: 1945

Beneath its surface buffoonery, this satire is inspired by a serious dedication to faith. One by one, the various members of the Marchmain family are reluctantly drawn back to the enduring values of the Church. Waugh presents a morbidly comic world through which man cannot find his way without faith; even the droll, mocking hero is finally converted.

Brideshead Revisited, Waugh's most "Catholic" novel, has received the least approbation from his critics. Disappointed by the absence of the acerbic wit that characterized his earlier novels, unconvinced by Lord Marchmain's deathbed conversion, and discomfited by the author's stubborn Tory politics and the condemnation of human love unsanctified by the Church, readers have relegated the novel to a minor position in his canon.

Waugh, of course, was never an easy novelist for his audience to accommodate. Even in his works predating those in which he advances a conservative theology, he called into question the sanguine social assumptions of the twentieth century. Unconvinced by facile progressivism and humanitarianism, he brutally satirized a culture without a sense of history, limit, and sin. Beginning with *Brideshead Revisited* and continuing with his greatest work, the war trilogy, including *Men at Arms, Officers and Gentlemen* and *The End of the Battle,* he dramatized the spiritual vacuity of secular man.

Charles Ryder is just that man, and, therefore, even though he is obsessed by the Marchmains, they remain a continuing enigma to him. He sees his values and happiness solely in terms of the world, whereas the Brideshead family, even the old reprobate, Lord Marchmain, finally conceives of existence as having a supernatural dimension, a complexity beyond Ryder's imagination. Therefore Sebastian's entrance into a monastery and Julia's refusal to marry him—both choices of God over the world—confound and dismay Ryder.

The very structure of the novel succinctly undercuts the validity of Ryder's moral stance. Told as a flashback, the story takes place between the end of one war and the beginning of another—both worldwide conflagrations. The civilization that Ryder holds to so tenaciously is clearly dying. Like the Brideshead house itself, then, the novel has a late medieval atmosphere, an ascetic medievalism that is half in love with death.

THE BRIDGE OF SAN LUIS REY

Type of work: Novel
Author: Thornton Wilder (1897-1975)
Type of plot: Philosophical romance
Time of plot: Early eighteenth century
Locale: Peru
First published: 1927

Set in Peru during its golden days as a Spanish colony, the plot of this novel is built around an investigation into the lives of five people who are killed when a bridge collapses. The investigation is made by a friar who witnesses the tragedy, and asks himself the philosophical question, "Was the event a random accident, or part of God's plan?" Always popular and widely read for its excellent character sketches, The Bridge of San Luis Rey *won the Pulitzer Prize in 1927.*

The Bridge of San Luis Rey marked the beginning of a key stage in Wilder's development and also revealed the essential dimensions of the artistic program he would follow. His first novel, *The Cabala* (1926), had viewed the decadent aristocracy of contemporary Rome through the eyes of a young American student. In the tradition of Henry James and Edith Wharton, the highly autobiographical work suffered by comparison and was not praised by the critics. But *The Bridge of San Luis Rey,* which vividly evoked a forgotten era and a type of society utterly foreign to Wilder's experience, sold three hundred thousand copies in its first year and made its author a celebrity. The description of early eighteenth century Peru was, in Edmund Wilson's estimation, "solid, incandescent, distinct." This success confirmed Wilder's intention to make abundant use of historical materials, and he set his next novel, *The Woman of Andros* (1930), in post-classical Greece. *The Bridge of San Luis Rey* also served notice that a major philosophical and theological writer had entered the literary scene. The engaging simplicity of the book drew its readers towards problems no less recondite than those of the justice of God, the possibility of disinterested love, and the role of memory in human relationships. That Wilder's subsequent works consistently returned to these themes was a surprise to no one, so powerfully had this novel stated them.

The Christianity which inspires and informs *The Bridge of San Luis Rey* is existential and pessimistic. "Only one reader in a thousand notices that I have asserted a denial of the survival of identity after death," Wilder once remarked of the book. He also denies the value of the apologetic task which Brother Juniper undertakes. For even if human reason could "scientifically demonstrate" God's providence—a proposition Wilder rejects —man would inevitably employ this knowledge in a self-aggrandizing manner. The inherent mystery of the divine intention is a check to human pride.

And pride is Wilder's overriding concern, especially that pride which cloaks itself in the guise of "unselfish love." If there is providence, Wilder suggests, it most clearly operates as something which exposes the egoistic taint in all love and reveals to the lover his need to be forgiven both by the one he loves and the social community.

Despite the ostensible importance of Brother Juniper, Uncle Pio, and Esteban, only Wilder's female characters develop sufficiently to gain awareness of the meaning of the novel's action. The marquesa undergoes the clearest transformation. The maternal love which she cultivates so assiduously is neither spontaneous nor generous. Rather, the marquesa craves her daughter's affection as an antidote to her own insecurity. Her imagination first magnifies the daughter's virtues and prestige; then, to assuage a deep self-loathing, she demands from this "great lady" a meticulous and servile devotion. Aware of her manipulative impulses, the marquesa is nevertheless powerless to conquer them. And she is not aware of how her distorted passion causes misery to those around her. The revelation of Pepita's agonized loneliness shames and humiliates her. But she thereby gains the strength to eliminate the element of tyranny in the love she bears for her daughter.

Because La Périchole (Camila) appears in each of the three tales, she is the novel's most real character. Her satirical attack on the marquesa becomes ironic when, later on, her own ugliness and avarice also make her the object of gossip and scorn. And like the marquesa, she does not believe herself to be intrinsically valuable. But Uncle Pio, who first treated Camila as something to dominate and take aesthetic delight in, now loves her unconditionally. Her willingness to accept this fact and express her love causes him to suffer and isolates her unnaturally from society. Such a painful yet liberating acceptance is made possible both by Pio's persistence and her love for Jaime. Her grief, and the possibility of disinterested love which it implies, moves her at last to present her disfigured self to society.

Even though her moral insight makes the abbess the standard against which all in the novel is measured, she too must suffer and grow. Unlike the abstract and detached Brother Juniper, she makes herself vulnerable to the pains which love and service involve. Unlike the marquesa, she does not demand instant expressions of servile devotion from those who love her. But she does yearn to have her work remembered, to gain that (in Wilder's view illusory) immortality which comes to those who labor for great causes. Consequently, she manipulates Pepita much as Uncle Pio manipulates Camila. That Pepita died lonely and forsaken reveals to the abbess the results of her misguided passion. Her faith undergoes a purification when she confronts the fact that "Even memory is not necessary for love."

The episode of Esteban and Manuel does not fit neatly into the pattern Wilder generally establishes. Some critics have suggested that Wilder here meant to deal with homosexual love. This view is partially refuted by the heterosexual activity of both youths and by Esteban's evident unwillingness to stand between Manuel and Camila. But does Esteban unconsciously attempt to retain possession of his brother, communicating his feelings through the uncanny channels of sympathy which bind these twins? Even if this were so, there remains the fact that Manuel also is unable to conceive of a separation. The tale thus seems to constitute a digression, one which serves to underscore the enormous mystery and intensity of all relationships of love. It is linked to the central thematic pattern by Esteban's deep feelings for the abbess, which enables him to reach out to another human being despite his tragic sorrow.

For Wilder, it is almost impossible for human beings to live serenely and faithfully knowing that their personalities will neither be remembered by society nor allowed to survive death in a hereafter. This prospect creates an anxiety which pervades all their efforts to love. They persistently use the beloved to prove themselves worthy and immortal. Then to love are added additional, degrading elements. Men never realize, in the abbess' words, that "the love will have been enough." Wilder's views could have led him to enormous sentimentality but in truth, *The Bridge of San Luis Rey* is extraordinarily stark. It is sustained only by the single hope that "all those impulses of love return to the love that made them."

Leslie E. Gerber

BRITANNICUS

Type of work: Drama
Author: Jean Baptiste Racine (1639-1699)
Type of plot: Neo-classical tragedy
Time of plot: A.D. 55
Locale: Rome, the palace of Néron
First presented: 1669

Intended to rival or even surpass Corneille's neoclassical dramas, Racine's Roman political tragedy deals with Emperor Néron's first crime, which sets the evil pattern for the rest of his reign. The conflict in the play arises from the struggle between two tutors to dominate in their influence upon the young emperor. Burrhus fights to keep the virtuous instincts in Néron's character uppermost, while the opportunistic Narcisse works to bring out the baser elements.

Jean Racine is generally remembered in connection with his predecessor, Corneille, in whose footsteps he followed. Racine was born in the provinces, therefore little can with certainty be said about his education, though the themes of his plays indicate that his understanding of history, the Scriptures, and classical Greek was thorough and perceptive. His early years were spent in company with the Jansenists at Port Royal. By the mid-seventeenth century the Jansenist influence had done much to revitalize certain aspects of Church life; it had, however, also contributed to the poor state of the arts in connection with the Church at that time. It is interesting to note that Racine, who contributed so much to French theater, spent his early years among that very group of people who advocated the excommunication of all stage actors on the premise that their actions on stage could and did stimulate the passions of the audience. It is known that he eventually quarreled with the Jansenists and went to Paris. Once there he was quickly taken into the fashionable society of that city and numbered Molière among his friends.

Britannicus cannot be ranked with Racine's best work, such as *Phèdre*. The story of Phèdre is one with universal appeal, while that of Britannicus is a more limited play, both in scope of emotion and in range of thought. In *Phèdre* the heroine places herself in a position which defies the laws of society, and, by implication, society itself. The climax of the tragedy is her death, which provides a universal conflict and a powerful sense of tragedy. *Britannicus* displays a much more limited point of view, and highly specialized conflicts.

Well illustrated in this play are the French neoclassical tendencies to isolate and elevate their tragic figures. They are excluded from reality, and their isolation is made palpable through the exclusion of all references to life outside their given tragic situation. The French attended more strictly than did the Greeks themselves to the concept of the kingly tragic figure, and tended to involve themselves with his figure directly, cutting away even the court attendants. This exclusivity usually serves to heighten the sense of tragedy, as it does here.

BROAD AND ALIEN IS THE WORLD

Type of work: Novel
Author: Ciro Alegría (1909-1967)
Type of plot: Social chronicle
Time of plot: 1912-1926
Locale: Peru
First published: 1941

Often referred to as a South American version of Steinbeck's The Grapes of
Wrath, *this work is Alegria's plea for justice for the Peruvian Indians, a group
forever exploited by racial, social, and political self-seekers. In addition, the novel
offers a storehouse of Peruvian lore as it portrays the Indian community with its
dignity, traditions, and tragic history.*

Ciro Alegría's panoramic novel mirrors life in the Peruvian Andes early in
the twentieth century. Its many themes include defense of the downtrodden,
justice against injustice, the tragedy of human life, dishonest lawyers and
courts, litigation over land boundaries, suffering, villainy and heroism, and
racism.

The novel's power lies in its defense of the abused Indian populace of
Rumi. The reader lives with Rumi's people throughout the story and identifies
with them. Unforgettable is the noble old leader of Rumi, Rosendo Maquis,
and his efforts, ideals, character, misfortunes, and death. Grave and good
like the community of Rumi itself, Rosendo incarnates his people, who are
idealized by Alegría. The dark night and demise of Rumi itself is another
Wagnerian touch ably painted by Alegría, giving the novel an epic reach.
Besides its many regionalist qualities, moreover, *Broad and Alien Is the World*
has a well-developed plot and generally convincing characterization that rank
it as one of the better contributions to the literature of *Indianismo,* which
defends the Indian peoples of Latin America. The plot reaches a final
crescendo with the destruction of Rumi and all that the recently murdered
Rosendo stood for; but the noble Rosendo, his wife the pathetic Pascuala,
black-clad Fiero Vásquez, and Benito Castro still live and stand out in the
reader's memory.

Alegría's style has its virtues. His language is poetic, lively, and colorful.
He uses standard Spanish laced with occasional regionalisms, including
Quechua words, to good effect. Dialogue is authentic. The reader's interest
is captured from the opening sentence, which is "Danger!" The novel is
nevertheless unwieldly, structurally chaotic, and betrays a lack of careful
planning owing to its hasty composition (it was completed in a matter of
months).

Geography is always a silent presence in the novel. At times it is almost a
dominant character, reflecting the fact of the importance of geography in Peru's
culture. One thus sees the lofty Andean sierra with its crisp, thin air, its gaunt

landscapes, sparse vegetation, and rocky soil, and pastel Rumi with its cobbled, windswept streets and huddled houses. Rumi's people grow potatoes and tend their llamas, but they chew coca to cope with hunger and the cold and their chests are like those of pouter pigeons since the air has so little oxygen.

Alegría was born and reared on a *hacienda* in the same region that he set his novel. Although his parents were his first teachers, he later credited the whole Peruvian people with having molded him and caused him to understand their grief. An Indian wet nurse cradled him in her arms and taught him to walk; he played as a child with Indian children, and later "saw things that he couldn't forget." In *Broad and Alien Is the World,* thus, Alegría penetrates the Indian mind, revealing the native's feeling for the soil, his poverty, stoicism, dignity, superstition, and occasional lapsing into alcoholism or sexual license. Unfortunately, Alegría ladled out some crude propaganda by lambasting safely unpopular types such as white men, priests, and landowners. These stock, one-dimensional figures are reminiscent of Diego Rivera's murals with their pasty-faced, evil whites, bloated priests, cruel-faced landowners, and clean-cut Indians. Thus, neither Don Amenabar, Bismarck Ruiz, nor the poltroonish priest are convincingly drawn. Alegría reveals unconscious prejudice in this respect, even though his own family owned land and was Nordic-Caucasian in appearance. Thus, as is so often the case in Spanish-American literature, a talented writer produces an inspired and sincerely motivated work but simultaneously betrays the fact that he himself belongs to a privileged social class and has not been as truly a member of the working classes as, say, John Steinbeck, Jack London, or José Villareal.

Nevertheless, one of Alegría's great contributions is his pictorial depiction of rural Peruvian society. One thus sees many social types and their folkways, traditions, mentality, society, and sorrows. In Rumi we see the kaleidoscopic results of four centuries of blending between Inca and Spaniard. One of the finest examples is the colorful sketch of Rumi's village meeting, with its touches of imagery wherein bronzed Indian faces mingle with lighter mestizos and an occasional white face, against a background of Inca and Spanish dress, manners, postures, and gestures. The novel is thus a storehouse of all that has happened to Peru, from the days of the mysterious Inca Empire, through the dramatic conquest by the Renaissance men of Spain, and the four ensuing centuries of racial and cultural blending. It is said that all of Alegría's works demonstrate a determination to create an original literature that not only interprets the Peruvian reality but which expresses contemporary Peru's peculiarities. He therefore draws the mestizo, whose heart is rooted to the Peruvian soil and in whose soul exists a harmonious mixture. A mestizo is the central personality in all of Alegría's novels with the possible exception of *Broad and Alien Is the World,* and even in that work the mestizo Benito Castro inherits Rosendo Maquis' role and develops into the most significant personality of the latter part of the novel.

Broad and Alien Is the World is essentially a novel of the high sierra as other Spanish American novels are novels of the pampa, llanos, desert, jungle, or city. It nevertheless broadens the social and human conflict beyond the boundaries of the community of Rumi to Peru's coast and jungle—nowhere under the Peruvian flag is there a place that is not hostile to the Indian. Benito Castro is regarded as an extremist agitator in Lima; one of Rosendo's sons is blinded by the explosion of a rubber ball in the eastern jungles; Calixto Páucar dies in a mine shaft; other emigrants from Rumi meet misfortune in many parts of the Peruvian Republic, for "broad and alien is the world." Alegría's great achievement, thus, is that his masterpiece has undoubtedly helped to implement reform in favor of the mountain-dwelling Indians and mestizos of Central Peru, for their lot has slowly but surely improved since the day when, while writing a scene for another novel concerning the expulsion of some Indians from their community, Alegría was struck with such force "by an intense gust of ideas and memories" that the inspiration for his masterpiece was born.

William Freitas

THE BROKEN JUG

Type of work: Drama
Author: Heinrich von Kleist (1777-1811)
Type of plot: Farce
Time of plot: Late eighteenth century
Locale: A village in the Netherlands
First presented: 1808

Written in jest as a result of a wager between three friends, The Broken Jug *is a highly successful farce reminiscent of Molière's comedies. In addition, it is a robust and delightfully humorous attack on the questionable procedures used in German courts.*

Kleist's *The Broken Jug* is his only comedy, and one of the few successful comedies of the German stage. Though it is now recognized as a masterpiece, it was ridiculed when first performed in Weimar, and Goethe complained that it lacked action and life. In fact, its comic effect derives from its peculiar structure, that of an analytic drama, similar to Sophocles' *Oedipus Rex.* In both plays, the entire action has taken place before the curtain rises, and in both plays, the stage action consists of the unraveling of what has already taken place. In both cases, the protagonist serves as judge or investigator and, in both cases, the culprit being sought is actually the judge himself. Thus, the trial becomes identical with the action of the play and the gradual disclosure of the facts provides the dramatic tension.

The difference between Sophocles' tragedy and the comedy of Kleist is that whereas Oedipus is ignorant of his own guilt and is horrified at the revelations, Judge Adam knows he is guilty, and does everything in his power to prevent the truth from being discovered. He would probably have been successful, were it not for the presence of Counselor Walter, the inspector, who provides the second comic impulse: not only must Adam prevent the truth from being discovered, he must do so while being rigorously observed by a higher power. His predicament is a comic version of the existential plight of many of Kleist's tragic figures, and the audience sympathizes with, rather than condemns, Adam, whose name seems symbolic for man and his state of original sin.

Kleist was fascinated by the psychological problem of man caught in an irreconcilable conflict. If the law is seen here as corrupt, it is only a reflection of the corruption of the moral law to which all are subject. By good grace, in this instance, the truth is brought out and the lovers are reunited; but the jug remains broken and the mother's only recourse is to appeal to a higher court.

THE BROTHERS

Type of work: Drama
Author: Terence (Publius Terentius Afer, c. 190-159 B.C.)
Type of plot: Social comedy
Time of plot: Second century B.C.
Locale: Athens
First presented: 160 B.C.

Revolving around the question of which approach—tolerance or discipline—is preferable in rearing children, The Brothers *is one of the first "problem plays" in European literature. The play is unusually subtle for a comedy in that it never settles the problem unambiguously, and that the action is resolved by elements in the characters rather than by the usual farcical tricks and unlikely coincidences.*

The Brothers, adapted by Terence from a play by Menander of the same title, is, to the modern reader, the most appealing of his six extant dramas largely because of the two opposed theories of education which give the play its tension. Demea's principle of rearing a boy through fear, restraint, and hard work has produced the timid and hypocritical Ctesipho. Outwardly a model son, Ctesipho is inwardly corrupt in allowing his brother to take the blame for his own lecherous attachment to the slave girl. He conforms to his father's expectations merely because he is intimidated, and he indulges himself on the sly.

Micio's theory of permissiveness, however, results in the opposite extreme —a son who goes out of his way to defy morality but who is very conventional at heart. Thus Aeschinus delights in posturing as a rake until he is threatened with losing the only woman he cares about, and then he is only too happy to settle down. Love complications serve to reveal the basic character of the two brothers, and Aeschinus comes out as the more attractive of the two.

If Terence seems to lean towards lenience, however, he does so with many qualifications. Demea, the harsh father, is capable of changing when he learns the results of his method. Micio, the apostle of lenience, is well-meaning but flawed by laziness and too much tolerance, supporting his adopted son when a reprimand might be more appropriate. In the end it is Demea who is allowed to impose penalties on the lax Micio. Terence seems to imply that when fathers are faulty one should not expect their sons to be perfect. No theory of education can correct the defects of those who apply it.

THE BROTHERS ASHKENAZI

Type of work: Novel
Author: Israel Joshua Singer (1893-1944)
Type of plot: Social chronicle
Time of plot: Late nineteenth and early twentieth centuries
Locale: Poland
First published: 1936

In its two parallel stories, this novel chronicles the cyclical history of prosperity and oppression of the Jews of Lodz during the rise of industrialization, and follows the careers of the twin brothers, Jacob and Simcha. Jacob is upright and outgoing; but Simcha, the introverted schemer, outlasts his brother because he can turn any negative situation to his own advantage.

The Brothers Ashkenazi is an epic chronicle which combines the stories of the economic development of Polish industry, the evolution of the Jewish religion, the psychological and sexual lives of two brothers, and the growth of socialism, Polish nationalism and anti-Semitism. In short, *The Brothers Ashkenazi* is a huge novel that tries to give a picture of all of Eastern European society in the late nineteenth and early twentieth centuries. It succeeds remarkably well.

The novel is centered in the struggle for economic survival. Beginning with a handicraft textile industry, Lodz gradually develops into a major industrial center. The growth of this industrialization is accompanied by the decline in the old religious values of the Jewish community; and the break between small-scale commercial activity and large-scale factory production is accompanied by the break between Abraham, the father, and Simcha, his oldest son.

Simcha, who is used to characterize not only the secularization of Eastern European Jewry, but the growth of amoral, acquisitive capitalism, bears the dramatic weight of the novel. He is not a likable figure, but he is an interesting one. His schemes, his ambition, his desperation, and his complete commitment to the development of capital and capitalized industry offer a glimpse not only into an individual but into the archetypal entrepreneur. Simcha embodies, in his personal striving, all the possibilities and limitations of an economic system and historical period.

Simcha's brother, who finally saves him, is not as interesting. It may be that Singer is attempting to show another, more "human" side of this development; but the attempt is not altogether successful. Beside Simcha he is flat and a little dull.

A continuing thread in the narrative is the struggle between the workers and the owners. Although Singer portrays several characters in the leadership of the revolutionary movement, these characters never come to life as does Simcha. Even, for example, when we sympathize with Nissan and the strikers, we are never as interested in them as in Simcha.

Nevertheless, Singer has a clear grasp of the impact of these class conflicts on Simcha, Jacob, and the whole of Polish and Russian society.
Especially insightful is the connection between these economic conflicts and
the anti-Semitic campaigns which grew out of them. Singer shows how
pogroms were used to divert economic grievances into racial violence.

The social realism of *The Brothers Ashkenazi* is conveyed in a straightforward, realistic style. There is little lyricism and little exaggeration. There
is much attention paid to social, geographic, and especially economic detail.
This attenion to detail lends a depth and richness to the work as a whole.

THE BROTHERS KARAMAZOV

Type of work: Novel
Author: Fyodor Mikhailovich Dostoevski (1821-1881)
Type of plot: Impressionistic realism
Time of plot: Nineteenth century
Locale: Russia
First published: 1880

The anguish caused by man's dual nature reverberates throughout this powerful novel, which tells the story of the effects of greed, passion, and depravity on a father and his sons. Considered to be the author's best work, The Brothers Karamazov *is filled with brilliant characterizations which in turn are underpinned by the ethical and psychological probings for which Dostoevski is famous.*

Fyodor Dostoevski's budding literary career was interrupted in 1849 by a nine-year exile in Siberia and Asian Russia for political subversion, a charge never fully substantiated. When he resumed his career, at the age of 38, he began to work at a frenetic pace—as novelist, journalist, and editor—a pace that he maintained until his death, just one year after the publication of *The Brothers Karamazov.* Dostoevski was an inveterate gambler, frequently indulging gambling binges of up to two weeks in duration; when his gambling debts mounted and his other creditors became insistent, he wrote, in a furiously intense burst of energy, to pay his bills. In addition, other catastrophes punctuated his hectic life. His first wife died; he began to have epileptic seizures; he got into further trouble with the government; he found it impossible to resist beautiful women. And woven through all of this were the epiphanic flights of imagination which culminated in his superb novels and the agonized soul-searching of a man deeply concerned with truth, peace of mind, and religious faith. Indeed, the turbulence of Dostoevski's life never really subsided, although he did enjoy a relative calm of sorts during the last few years of his life under the careful ministrations of his second wife. And that turbulence is reflected in Dostoevski's novels, particularly *The Brothers Karamazov,* his last novel and presumably the most mature expression of his style and his thought.

Like the other novels, *The Brothers Karamazov* is a psychological novel: less emphasis is placed on plot, action, and setting (although Dostoevski was a master craftsman at all three) than on emotions and thoughts. In fact, Dostoevski's psychological insights are so sharp that Freud selected *The Brothers Karamazov* as one of the three greatest works in world literature. (The other two were *Oedipus Rex* and *Hamlet.* All three involve the death of a father and a love triangle.) Moreover, Freud's essay on *The Brothers Karamazov,* "Dostoevsky and Parricide [sic]," is considered a classic in both psychology and literary criticism. For in it, Freud gives a thorough explanation of the strong Oedipal theme in the novel, echoing, according to Freud,

Dostoevski's own unresolved Oedipal conflicts. And in this Freudian age, it is most difficult to cast Dmitri's hostility toward Fyodor in any other light. Ivan also resents his father as does Alyosha, each in his own fashion and for his own reasons. But all three legitimate sons bear no greater grudge against Fyodor than his illegitimate son, Smerdyakov. Hence, all four sons have some justification—stemming largely from greed or vengeance—for wanting Fyodor dead.

It is evident, then, that the story proceeds from something more profound than plot: the characters are not simply tied up at the end and dropped; a sequel could have followed. But the loose structure of the novel is offset by its intensity. It is frequently lurid, but Dostoevski never avoids a difficult question; he amalgamates thinking and feeling in a carefully planned interplay between the two. One of the consequences of this technique is an early foreshadowing of events that later come to pass—the creation of an atmosphere of premonition, as it were. There is, for example, frequent and early mention of patricide, especially in the scenes between Ivan and Smerdyakov, revealing a pathological obsession which besets both father and sons. Furthermore, the selection of details and their accretion contribute not only to the novel's verisimilitude but also to its psychological depth and profundity. Even so seemingly trivial a matter as numerous references to time sequence—all of them accurate—indicates Dostoevski's meticulous orchestration of his characters' emotions. But these techniques serve only to enhance a novel whose impact ultimately derives from its head-on confrontation with the larger issues which have concerned man since the dawn of recorded time.

In *The Brothers Karamazov,* Dostoevski's search for truth leads him to the question, "What is the nature of man?" The answer takes shape in the characterization of three of the brothers. Dmitri is dominated by sensuality; Ivan prizes the intellectual; Alyosha represents spirituality, although his asceticism sometimes clashes with his incipient sensuality. Together, the three personalities are symbolic of man. But another question: "Is there a God?" is less easily answered because neither "The Grand Inquisitor" legend (V:5) nor "The Devil: Ivan's Nightmare" (XI:9) definitively resolves the matter. Likewise, the question of man's relationship to God remains nebulous for the same reasons, Father Zossima notwithstanding. But the questions about man's relationship to man and man's relationship to society are more concretely dealt with: hostility, fear, and resentment, commingled with morbid curiosity, characterize the relationship of man to man, appearing to mirror the same qualities in the relationship of man to society. Thus, when Dostoevski poses the question "Does man have free will?" the tentative answer is that free will, if it exists at all, is very limited. Man can hardly see his destiny, much less exert substantial control over it, as Dmitri, among others, so tragically learns. And finally, Dostoevski wonders whether or not man's intellect is capable of development or change; but since the entire novel is an exposition of the predestined Karamazov family, the answer here is a foregone conclusion. These deep philosophical considerations permeate the book without dwarfing its characters. Indeed, what could diminish the operatic rages and the petty buffoonery of Fyodor Karamazov; the screaming frustrations of Dmitri; the barely repressed seething indignation of Ivan; the incredible shock of Alyoosha's raped spiritual innocence? Thus, philosophy and psychology go hand-in-hand in *The Brothers Karamazov* to shape a tale of immense emotional range and profound philosophical depth, for all its flaws judged by many to be Dostoevski's masterpiece.

Joanne G. Kashdan

THE BRUSHWOOD BOY

Type of work: Novelette
Author: Rudyard Kipling (1865-1936)
Type of plot: Fantasy
Time of plot: Nineteenth century
Locale: England and India
First published: 1895

One of Kipling's lesser known works, "The Brushwood Boy," from The Day's Work, *follows the career of a boy haunted by the same dream of a lovely girl companion who grows with him from infancy until his years in the army. A brief, fantastic romance, this novel differs sharply from Kipling's more popular works in theme and treatment.*

This novelette, so suggestive in its theme, appears to be at variance with other works by Kipling. Kipling, in his celebration of the troops and administrative staff of the British Empire, and in his adventure stories, seems at first glance an unlikely candidate for the authorship of *The Brushwood Boy.*

The tale does, however, contain some of Kipling's special interests: the qualities of military leadership, the adventures of youth, and the commitment to the British way of life during the days of the Empire.

Essentially, *The Brushwood Boy* is an intense, childlike fantasy based on the ambiguous device of a shared dream. It is never clear whether the children had shared experiences and fantasies in their young lives, or only imagined they had. (This ambiguity at the end preserves Kipling from the merely supernatural.) But Kipling's device is less interesting as "story" than as psychological examination.

In recent years, Kipling has come to be viewed as more important as a thinker, or rather as the literary representative of a certain type of thought, than as a serious writer of fiction or verse. Although he wrote some memorable lines and phrases and created new rhythms in his poetry, and although some of his books are still of great interest to children, Kipling's heavy-handed treatments and moralizing have reduced his popularity.

The Brushwood Boy is interesting, then, more for the psychological portrait of a military leader it offers, perhaps unintentionally, than for its plot or characterization. Georgie is an ideal leader of men, the type most admired by Kipling. A young man of the highest moral character, yet able to relate to the most hard-bitten of his subordinates, he quickly rises in the military apparatus established by the British in India. He is loved and respected by his family, his commanders, and most of all, by his men.

What forms the central interest of *The Brushwood Boy,* however, is Georgie's continuing fantasies. These fantasies center around a pile of brushwood, which is a sort of imaginary touchstone; they consist of adventurous travels beyond the bounds of the known world and beyond the bounds of rules and regulations, into a world of danger and irresponsible, malignant authority. (One of the recurring aspects of the dreams is a confrontation with an unfriendly policeman.) All these dream experiences contrast sharply with the external demeanor of such an exemplary soldier. In fact, *The Brushwood Boy* appears to offer a sort of underground vision of the British imperial mentality, or the mentality of its administrative stalwarts. Beneath the "stiff upper lip" there is a residual, childlike world of wishes existing independently of the honor of Empire.

Kipling's manner of narration, simple and full of wonder, is entirely appropriate for his subject. Though *The Brushwood Boy* is not one of his better known works, its psychological insight into the functioning of a British "hero" of a bygone era remains interesting.

BUDDENBROOKS

Type of work: Novel
Author: Thomas Mann (1875–1955)
Type of plot: Social chronicle
Time of plot: Nineteenth century
Locale: Germany
First published: 1901

An exposé of decadence in a materialistic society, this chronicle of a nineteenth century German industrial family follows its members from their peak of wealth and power into gradual decay and eventual ruin. Originally an exemplary family imbued with honesty, loyalty, and strong traditions, they succumb slowly but surely to decadence. Mann sees in a frail Hanno, the last of the Buddenbrook line, the culmination of a symbolic clash between the antithetical forces of art and life.

Buddenbrooks was Thomas Mann's first novel, and it was a great success. It is still one of his most popular works, and has enjoyed international fame. Though not as complex or problematic as his later novels, it develops most of the major themes that came to occupy him throughout his career. The work had originally been planned as a novella about the boy, Hanno Buddenbrook, but in assembling the material, Mann found himself compelled to trace the story back four generations. Thus the novel became a family chronicle with a broad social milieu, a type of novel rare in German literature, which has tended to concentrate on the *Bildüngsroman,* or novel of development, a form that traces the growth of a single character. *Buddenbrooks* further departs from the tradition in that it reverses the emphasis on growth and development to concentrate on decay and decadence. In this, it represents a typical aspect of Mann's work, the fascination with the conflict between the life force and the death wish, especially as it appears in the artist type. Mann's artist figures are the product of robust bourgeois stock, families whose drive for work and achievement has led to prosperity and comfort. But as the family attains to greater refinement and sensitivity, the life force slackens. At this stage the artist figure appears, estranged from the bourgeois world and its values, and curiously drawn toward disease and death. It is no accident that several of Mann's works take place in sanatoriums, or that typhus, syphilis, and tuberculosis figure prominently in his work.

The importance of this theme is perhaps best explained by the fact that it is essentially autobiographical and *Buddenbrooks* is the most thoroughly autobiographical of his novels. Every character in it can be traced to an actual prototype; the people of Lübeck were quite shocked when the novel appeared, and protested what amounted to an invasion of privacy. The streets and houses, the seashore and the countryside were all identifiable as actual places, and the Buddenbrooks are, in fact, the Mann family. Yet Mann is obviously not Hanno, though parallels may be drawn—Thomas Mann was an artist, working in words rather than in music, and he rejected his family, a middle-class career, and the expectations of his community. He had left Lübeck for Italy, where, in fact, he began to write the Buddenbrooks chronicle. Thus the stuff of the novel was intensely personal to him. Yet in spite of the autobiographical aspect, Mann has carefully structured the work so that the process of family decay proceeds in a clear and almost inevitable movement, by stages through the four generations, gathering momentum and expressing itself simultaneously in the business fortunes, physical characteristics, mannerisms, and psychological makeup of the four eldest sons, Johann, Jean, Thomas and Hanno.

At each stage there is both a descent and an ascent. Vitality and physical vigor decline, and the business skill likewise is lost, as is evidenced by the steadily declining capital. But this external decline, reflected even in such details as increasing susceptibility to tooth decay, is counterbalanced by an increase in sensitivity, an inclincation toward art and metaphysics, and an increasingly active interior life. Johann may indeed play the flute—a necessary social grace for the eighteenth century gentleman—but he is not given to introspection. He lives to a ripe old age, and while an honest man, he has no scruples about the propriety of business and profit and he has a sure sense of investment. His son Jean is far more concerned with moral principles, and business is no longer for him a natural drive, but a responsibility. His health is diminished, and his life shorter, but his capacity for artistic enjoyment and religious emotion is greater. A tension between inner and outer begins to manifest itself, which becomes evident in Thomas. In him, refinement becomes elegance, and an inclination for the exotic manifests itself in his choice of a wife. Yet the strain of preserving his exterior form—a new house, high social position, and the fortunes of the business—show in his weakened physical constitution and in his attraction, late in his short (forty-eight years) life, to the philosophy of Schopenhauer, in which he sees the possibility of the dissolution of his embattled individuality into an eternal impersonal spiritual existence. Hanno, the last of the Buddenbrooks, dies still a boy, his life filled with pain, but rich in its inner creativity, expressed in his Wagnerian flights of musical composition. Wagner was for Mann always linked with decadence and the death wish.

Many of the elements of this sequence recur in Mann's other works, especially his early works; the family is instantly recognizable. And it is clear that Mann is absorbed by the psychological development of his figures. The novel dwells more and more intensely on the inner states of the later characters. Hanno, who was the starting point of Mann's conception, retains a disproportionately large share of the novel's pages and remains one of Mann's most engaging and memorable creations. Yet it is also clear that Mann, for all his understanding and sympathy toward the artistically inclined temperaments of the declining Buddenbrook family, drew a clear line between that sympathy and his own allegiance. Not only does he dwell on the increasingly difficult lives and demeaning deaths of the later characters—the eloquent and self-possessed Thomas collapsing and dying in a pool of filth on the street, Hanno's dying suddenly of typhus—but in the case of Hanno he unequivocally attributes the death to a failure of the will to live. In one of the most remarkable chapters of the book, the narrator, who has generally retained his objectivity in chronicling the fortunes of the family, describes the course of a typical case of typhus, raising it to a mythical encounter between life and death: at the crisis, the victim may either exert his will to live, and return, or proceed onward on the path to self-dissolution in death. Hanno, whose music has expressed this longing for release from the demands of life to which he is not equal, takes the latter course and dies. Here any similarity between Mann and his characters ends. Although Mann as an artist felt himself estranged from the social world of the bourgeois, for him, unlike Hanno, art becomes itself the means by which he can retain his focus on life. *Buddenbrooks* may describe a family's loss of the will to live, but in so doing it affirms the writer's most profound love of life.

Steven C. Schaber

THE BULWARK

Type of work: Novel
Author: Theodore Dreiser (1871-1945)
Type of plot: Social realism
Time of plot: 1890 to the mid-1920's
Locale: Dukla, Pennsylvania, Philadelphia, New York City, Atlantic City
First published: 1946

The Bulwark *deals with three generations of the Barnes family and the impact of American social changes upon their Quaker way of life. Less crowded and repetitious than some of Dreiser's earlier works, this novel dramatizes man's struggle to channel his experience into a meaningful pattern in the face of inexorable forces of the outside world and of his own personality, which substantially thwart him.*

As the foremost twentieth century American exponent of naturalism, Theodore Dreiser dramatized in his fiction a view of life which saw man as the victim of a variety of internal and external forces that prevented him from exercising free choice and controlling his destiny. Dreiser believed that all of a person's actions were predetermined by the essential qualities of his temperament, which was itself molded by forces of environment, both natural and social, and by circumstance. He saw nearly all man's problems as arising from the conflict between his natural animal instincts, which were usually suppressed, and the restrictions imposed by artificial social and moral conventions. In particular, in novels such as *The Financier* and *The "Genius,"* he was concerned with the problems posed by life in an industrial, commercial world where natural human desires were all but stifled beneath materialistic ambition and the pursuit of social status. In most of Dreiser's works, including novels such as *Sister Carrie, Jennie Gerhardt,* and *An American Tragedy,* this naturalistic vision is conveyed through an atmosphere of angry, bitter, or fatalistic feelings; but in such a late work as *The Bulwark* (published posthumously), the tone is much more mellow. The naturalistic underpinnings are there, but their manifestations are markedly softened in comparison to the earlier novels.

In addition to its quieter tone, *The Bulwark* is marked by its relatively small amount of economic and social background and stronger emphasis on individual character motivations; it is an excellent piece of sensitive demography without the statistical accoutrements. The novel tells the story of three generations of the Barnes family, and traces the increasing struggle of its members to reconcile the Quaker ideal of a pious, unselfish life with the demands made by a modern materialistic world. Dreiser depicts all the stages of the change that gradually occurs, from the staunch Quaker patriarch Rufus and his wife Hannah, with their unshakable convictions and their disapproval of dancing, singing, art, literature, and undue wealth, to their young grand-children, who marry for money and social position, engage in loveless extra-marital affairs, pursue business ambitions, and amass wealth.

By the time Solon's youngest son Stewart commits suicide in his prison cell, it has become clear to the father that somewhere in the course of his life he has lost that "Inner Light" which was the essence of his Quaker faith. Solon dies soon after this realization, but Dreiser ends on a more optimistic note than usual: Solon's sensitive daughter Etta, long detached from her family and living with a Greenwich Village artist, returns home to be reconciled with her father; after his death she rediscovers her own identity and the true spirit of Quakerism, which she embraces in place of the values of the contemporary commercial world.

BUSSY D'AMBOIS

Type of work: Drama
Author: George Chapman (1559?-1634)
Type of plot: Tragedy of blood
Time of plot: Sixteenth century
Locale: Paris
First presented: c. 1604

Based on the actual career of Louis de Clermont, this drama follows the fortunes of a soldier who gains favor in the corrupt court of Henry III by sheer ruthlessness and ambition. Bussy's offensive manners and unwise choice of partners in illicit love affairs lead to many duels and eventually to his death in a trap laid by an irate husband.

It is ironic that despite his long life and large output, George Chapman is best known not for his own work, but from the title of John Keats' famous sonnet, *On First Looking into Chapman's Homer*. Chapman, an acquaintance of Christopher Marlowe and Ben Jonson, was a jack-of-all-trades among Elizabethan writers, turning out poetry and translations as well as plays. His reputation was first established as a poet with his *The Shadow of Night* (1594) and Ovid's *Banquet of Sense* (1595), but his only poem much read today was begun by another man: when Marlowe's *Hero and Leander* was left unfinished at his death, Chapman completed the poem by adding the final four books.

By about 1595 Chapman had begun writing for the theater, supplying plays to Philip Henslowe's company of actors, the Lord Admiral's Men. Although a contemporary source cites Chapman as a tragic author, whatever works led to that opinion have been lost; some comedies, written both alone and in collaboration with John Marston and Ben Jonson, are all that survive of his early dramas. In 1599 he left the Lord Admiral's company, but continued to write for the stage until 1614. His translations of Homer's *Iliad* and *Odyssey* were published in 1616. He may have had financial troubles in his later years; he died in 1634.

Chapman wrote *Bussy d'Ambois* about 1604 and, surprisingly (given the play's subject), it was probably first acted by Paul's Boys, a children's company. Paul's Boys was one of the then popular groups of child actors, in this case an outgrowth of the choir school at St. Paul's Cathedral. The play exists in two printed versions, one produced in 1607, and a later one, printed in 1641, which is noticeably different. Most critics believe the 1641 version to derive from a revision of the play made by Chapman himself. The play was extremely successful on stage: it continued to be performed until the closing of the theaters in 1642. After the Restoration of Charles II, the play was revived, and its last performance is recorded in 1691.

The source of *Bussy d'Ambois* is the life of a historical figure of that name, a minor courtier during the reign of Henry III of France. Although he was widely known in his time, the historical Bussy seems to have been every bit the swaggering bravo who appears in Chapman's play. Known for his dueling, his poetry, and his love affairs, Bussy was murdered by a jealous husband when he was about thirty years old. It might be wondered whether meaningful tragedy could be made from such unpromising material, but Bussy d'Ambois' life furnished Chapman with a scarecrow on which to drape his philosophy.

In Chapman's play, Bussy embodies the Renaissance ideal of the man who, by virtue of his physical, mental, and moral powers, is a law unto himself. In this sense, Bussy is a relative of the superheroes we find in Marlowe's *Tamburlaine* and *Doctor Faustus*. Although not bent on evil, Bussy resembles Shakespeare's Richard III, in that neither recognizes any moral force higher than himself, nor submits to anything but his own will. Just exactly what virtues Bussy possesses is not always clear to the modern reader; indeed, what he calls his honor leads him to kill in a duel three men who have insulted him by snickering at the wrong time. But that same honor does not prevent him from speaking bawdily to strange women at court, or committing adultery when the opportunity presents itself. Yet Bussy is steadfast in his belief that he owes obedience to no one, not even to the king, as he states to the king's face in the scene in which he is pardoned for dueling.

Chapman often seems to sacrifice the plausibility of the plot to show his hero flouting society: Bussy's lover succumbs to an overwhelming passion for him at first sight. This in itself is not so hard to believe, but that Bussy should conceive the same desire for her is harder, since he had ignored her a few scenes earlier at court. In the play's least convincing moment, this adulterous passion is approved by a friar, who then consents to act as their go-between. Clearly, who characters are, and the reasons for what they do, are not of as much interest to Chapman as are the illustrations of Bussy's independence of customary morality.

The style of the play is rhetorical in the extreme, with long passages of obscure philosophizing that often bring the action of the play to a halt. (Chapman's contemporaries accused him of obscurity, and he defended himself by claiming that the language was appropriate to the gravity and nobility of the subject.) In some cases, the grammar of the speeches breaks down entirely, leaving the reader wondering just what is being said. In view of these and similar difficulties, the taste of the audiences that made the play so popular for so long a time might be questioned.

But the play retains more than enough elements of the Elizabethan tragedy of blood to satisfy those who desire action, and plenty of it. Duels and murder fill the stage; the betrayed husband tortures his wife; the friar drops dead (providing the requisite ghost at the end of the play); and, in a scene hearkening back to the Miracle plays of the fifteenth century, a bona fide devil is raised by Bussy in an attempt to discover his enemies' plots. The final scene shows Bussy and the ghost holding off a pack of paid killers, when one of the assassins with more sense than superstition draws a pistol and shoots Bussy down. With action like this, a good part of the audience must have simply endured the moralizing in the sure knowledge that something grisly would soon happen.

Bussy d'Ambois today seems alternately dull and ludicrous, but if it is possible to judge an age by looking at its heroes, the play provides us with an insight into the temper and taste of the early seventeenth century.

Walter E. Meyers

THE CABALA

Type of work: Novel
Author: Thornton Wilder (1897-1975)
Type of plot: Fantasy
Time of plot: About 1920
Locale: Rome
First published: 1926

This "novel" is actually a series of sketches held together by their locale and a group of people who have something in common. The Cabala *is a fantastic tale of pagan gods grown old and weak, whom Christianity and modern society often drive to despair, madness, and death; nevertheless, they manage to survive into each new age.*

Like *The Woman of Andros,* the sister work to *The Cabala,* this novel explores the haunting connections between pagan and Christian states of mind. Wilder was fascinated by the interpenetration in the modern mind of these radically different world views. Ever since the Church fathers "Christianized" the Greek philosophers, and Renaissance artists reinterpreted Christian ideas in pagan forms, Western civilization has been torn by the opposing forces within it. Wilder's fantasy records the inevitably self-destructive effect of trying to live in totally opposite worlds. The soul is literally torn asunder in its impossible yearning for immanence in an alienated world. Marcantanio and Alix are sacrificed to their hedonistic instincts; as "lost" gods they cannot find worshipers, only tormentors and judges. Like Milton's pagan deities in "On the Morning of Christ's Nativity" they flee the conquering Christ—who is ironically represented in the Puritan Americans, Samuele and James, apostles of modern Christianity.

In *The Woman of Andros* Wilder directs his pagan heroine toward Christian piety and feeling; that novel records a rite of passage and is full of wonder and awe at the evolution of religious consciousness from pagan to Christian values. But *The Cabala* concentrates on the incompleted passage, the unaccommodated pagan consciousness which survives despite the nominal victory of Christianity. Although the bulk of the novel records the pain of the pagan gods in the modern world, the closing speech of Virgil closes on an elegiac and even heroic note. Can we ever stop loving Rome? Can we confront the modern city without the ancient one in our hearts?

THE CABIN

Type of work: Novel
Author: Vicente Blasco Ibáñez (1867-1928)
Type of plot: Regional realism
Time of plot: Nineteenth century
Locale: The country near Valencia, Spain
First published: 1898

The Cabin *presents a vivid, realistic picture of life in a Spanish village. It is the story of a family's efforts to overcome the stigma attached to the farm they buy, and their eventual defeat at the hands of blind, undying hatred.*

As is obvious in *The Cabin,* Blasco Ibáñez had both superficial and deep qualities as a novelist. His superficial qualities can be seen in *The Cabin*'s occasionally slovenly style, its spotty characterization, and attendant minor defects. The novel's virtues are numerous, however, and stem from Blasco Ibáñez's innate storytelling skill, his sheer descriptive ability, and knack for selecting topics that are perennially fresh and timely. Still magnetic today are the novel's basic themes of the land, human malice, and the heroic tenacity of Batiste, who never surrendered. Even *The Cabin*'s handling of the key rural problem of water rights represents one of the infrequent treatments of this topic in world literature, even though water rights have been historically and are today a crucial factor for ranchers throughout the world, including in the American West.

The Cabin (La Barraca) has a firm structure. Artistically brilliant, its clear plot is not cluttered with secondary plots, and it gives one of the best pictures of peasant life in any language. Some of the characterizations live with the reader (for example, Batiste) and the peasant is portrayed as a product of the land. In keeping with Blasco Ibáñez's belief that the novelist should observe things closely and clearly, both the pathos and the harsher emotions of the Valencian peasant are drawn, especially his stubbornness and durability. We also see the whitewashed houses, green fields, and blue coastline of the area so clearly that the author's use of color and sheen has been compared to the canvases of Sorolla y Bastida (1863-1923), the noted Valencian painter and friend of Blasco Ibáñez.

Shortly before his death, Blasco Ibáñez advised those youths who were excessively impatient for literary glory to reflect on the history of *The Cabin* and its almost accidental publication. He also commented that despite his apparent haste in writing, he composed novels in his mind slowly, over a long period of time, before writing them down at a furious pace. All novels, he added, are actually something seen through an individual temperament, or comparable to a mirror passing down a road. The best critic of the true literary worth of a novel, he insisted, is the public, not other novelists or literati.

CADMUS

Type of work: Classical legend
Source: Unknown
Type of plot: Heroic adventure
Time of plot: Remote antiquity
Locale: Ancient Greece
First transcribed: Unknown

In this myth, Cadmus is sent from Phenicia to seek his abducted sister, Europa. Following the advice of the Delphic oracle, Cadmus stopped on the Plain of Panope at a spot to which a cow with a moon-shaped mark had guided him. There he founded Thebes. The city was established when Cadmus killed a dragon sacred to Ares and sowed its teeth. From each tooth sprang an armed soldier; these warriors slew one another, except for five who became the hero's allies and helped him build the new city.

Although the origins of the Cadmus legend are lost in the primeval mists, the tale has both enduring literary value and enduring historical value as a repository of archetypal themes which suggest an East-West interchange that modern readers may find somewhat unique. *Cadmus* combines elements of Greek and Roman mythology as well as Hindu legend and Far Eastern folklore.

Among the distinctly Greek analogs in the Cadmus legend is the archetypal theme of Cadmus' seeking of advice from Apollo's oracle at Delphi in much the same manner as Oedipus did. Likewise, Cadmus' pause to give thanks to the gods and offer a sacrifice to them echoes the sacrifice demanded of Agamemnon about to embark on the Trojan War in the *Iliad*. So, too, does Cadmus' confrontation with the dragon suggest similar encounters with monsters with which Ulysses had to cope in the *Odyssey*. Most particularly, Cadmus' ill fortune—the death of his children, alienation from his spouse, and general disquietude—reminds one of comparable curses of the gods visited upon Oedipus.

Both Greek and Roman myth recounts the theme of the search or the journey in the *Odyssey,* the legend of *The Golden Fleece,* and the *Aeneid,* much after the fashion of Cadmus' assigned task of finding his abducted sister. And in all cases, the search or journey culminated in the founding or the restoration of a kingdom. In addition, the metamorphosis theme—Ulysses' men turned into swine, Ovid's *Metamorphoses*—emerges in Cadmus' transformation, and later his wife's, into a serpent.

On a somewhat wider cultural scale, the divinely sanctioned marriage of Cadmus and Harmonia finds counterparts in Helen's marriage to Menelaus (the *Iliad*) and Sakuntala's marriage to Dushyanta (in the Hindu legend from the *Mahabharata*), just as the uxorious devotion of Harmonia is mirrored in the fidelity of Penelope (the *Odyssey*) and the loyalty of Sakuntala. But even more ubiquitous are the implications of Cadmus' sowing of the dragon's teeth. Throughout Western culture we find the symbolism of sowing the seeds of evil, while in both the Near East and the Far East the dragon was associated with malign influences. So, too, as Cadmus' antagonistic "harvest" ultimately separated into wheat and chaff, with the latter destroyed and the former engaged in productive pursuits, Far Eastern legend also vindicates the evil dragon by making it not only a force of evil but also a guardian of good as the patron of higher science.

All in all, *Cadmus* is a curiosity of literature, an unusual composite of many cross-cultural features; however, it is still an interesting tale, full of adventure and excitement, and intrinsically valuable as a work of art even aside from its anthropological interests.

CAESAR OR NOTHING

Type of work: Novel
Author: Pío Baroja (1872-1956)
Type of plot: Political satire
Time of plot: Early twentieth century
Locale: Spain, Italy, France
First published: 1919

The satire in this novel is directed against those elements of Spanish life which Baroja considered antithetical to the improvement of the condition of the common man: the aristocracy and the Catholic Church.

Caesar or Nothing is, in several ways, Baroja's flirtation with the Nietzschean superman; his hero exemplifies the sort of will-to-power that is easily associated with Nietzsche. Caesar's views on morality are little more than a restatement of the German philosopher's doctrine: all that is good comes from power, and all that is bad comes from weakness. The cornerstones of his approach to life are energy, action, and courage.

In his book *Youth and Egolatry* Baroja readily admits that Nietzsche's work influenced him. The portrait of Caesar is an exercise in the ethic of the superman. His interest in the Borgias is the result of a natural affinity for their conviction that might is right. He adopts Cesare Borgia's motto for his own, seeing in it the perfect expression of his own ambition. Like Nietzsche's superman he breaks with Christian morality, having no feelings of guilt or sin. He is opposed to Christianity for several reasons, one of which is its tendency to renounce this life: he is unable to accept such otherworldliness. In fact, he goes so far as to say that Christianity is a retrogression compared to paganism. He does not believe in a personal God.

Caesar's objection to Christianity is based not only on metaphysical and ethical grounds, but also on social, political, and economic ones. He sees injustice in Spain and concludes that the Church is largely responsible, because of its opposition to reform and its defense of the few against the masses. He cannot accept its insistence on tradition in the midst of people dying of hunger.

In the final analysis, it is Caesar's pessimism which prevents him from attaining the stature of a fully developed Nietzschean superman. He ultimately lacks the will to struggle against apparently insuperable obstacles, to overcome the forces of reaction that impede social progress. It is not so much Caesar's weakness, however, but the strength of the establishment in Spain that ensures his defeat.

CAIN

Type of work: Drama
Author: George Gordon, Lord Byron (1788-1824)
Type of plot: Romantic tragedy
Time of plot: The period of Genesis
Locale: Outside Eden
First published: 1821

Byron, religiously unorthodox and bitterly critical of his society's mores, managed to adapt this Biblical tale to an expression of his own temperament. Cain's motivation in murdering his brother lies deep within his tortured soul, which lusts for a truth that is constantly denied. Byron's Cain is the eternal romantic rebel.

Byron suffered from excessive guilt over a sin he never clearly identified in any of his works or letters. But biographers are almost in universal agreement that the sin was incest with his half sister, Augusta. Whether this sin, or the many others he indulged in as a student and continental traveler, is the shaping force in his poetry is largely a matter of conjecture. Nevertheless, from his early melodramatic verse tales such as *The Giaour* (1813) to his later dramatic poems, *Manfred* (1817) and *Cain,* the protagonist is always haunted by a sense of his corruption and at the same time sustained by strong feelings of individual power, uniqueness, and worth.

In *Manfred,* for example, the hero dies refusing to acknowledge the power of Death over his soul. Although suffering from remorse, Manfred cannot accept any jurisdiction over his soul other than the judgment of his own mind. *Cain* begins by establishing the protagonist's anger, his indignation at the injustice of his fate. Why should his mother Eve's eating of the forbidden fruit have cost him his immortality? Cain's complaint has the same urgency and authority that animated the political and social revolutions of Byron's time. Why should the forms of the past dictate the possibilities of the future? What distinguishes *Cain* from Byron's other works on the remorseful hero is that whereas in the others the hero's individual sense of power compensates him for the self-loathing of his guilt, in *Cain* the protagonist discovers his uniqueness through the help of Lucifer and then plunges into the action—the killing of his brother—which stamps him with everlasting guilt.

Byron could not separate man's genius from his propensity toward evil. Like Blake, Byron understood the misplaced energy in so much of man's misguided actions. To adapt a phrase of Blake, Byron "was of the devil's party *with* knowing it." But he lacked a mystical vision like Blake's to explain the paradox of his own sensibility. It was Byron's fate, like Cain's, to live a life of exile, literally and spiritually.

CAKES AND ALE

Type of work: Novel
Author: W. Somerset Maugham (1874-1965)
Type of plot: Literary satire
Time of plot: Early twentieth century
Locale: London and Kent
First published: 1930

Written with a lightness that defies description, Cakes and Ale *is a pungent satire on literary life and manners in England. By contrasting a popular novelist's inflated opinion of the Victorian author Edward Driffield with Driffield as the narrator knew him, Maugham exposes the sham of the world of letters as he gradually deepens our insight into Driffield's character.*

Somerset Maugham is one of the master craftsmen of the English novel. Although his talents have been underrated by some critics who scoff at the apparent simplicity of his novels, others more astutely point out Maugham's considerable storytelling skills. Through his fiction, Maugham sought the general truth in all things. His expression was direct, plain, and concise, easily capturing the rhythms and colloquialisms of informal conversation. His themes were usually not explicit since he preferred to let his characters form the bases of philosophies. Evidence suggests, however, that Maugham was intensely interested in religion, ethics, and the psychology of artistic creativity. He rarely dealt with political history because, to him, people were more important than world events. The result was a large output of novels which have enjoyed great popular success.

Maugham's emphasis on the human element is reflected in his technique of characterization: most often, characters are paired in a thesis-antithesis relationship. In *Cakes and Ale,* Ashenden, the narrator, is depicted as the writer with integrity and Kear as the venal hack; Kemp is recalled as the dashing lover and Driffield as the rather indifferent husband; Rosie is portrayed as a kind, loving person and Amy, the second Mrs. Driffield, as a hypocritical prude. These pairings should not, however, be construed as over-simplifications of characterization, because the complexities of each character are gradually revealed over the course of the entire novel. Consequently, Kear, Driffield, and Amy are not irredeemably bad any more than Ashenden, Kemp, and Rosie are flawlessly good. Rather, all of them are human beings with strengths and weaknesses which Maugham skillfully discloses through his thesis-antithesis technique of characterization.

When *Cakes and Ale* was first published, it was a *succès de scandale,* since the character of Driffield was widely believed to be a caricature of the English novelist Thomas Hardy. Maugham denied any connection between his novel and Hardy's biography, and when the furor subsided, readers were left with an incisive satire of the English literary world, including such well-known types as the celebrity, the neophyte, the genuine artist, and the commercial scribbler. The barbed parodies of pretentious drawing-room conversations about literature echo—even in the novel's title—Proust's "tea and cakes"; similarly, they call to mind T. S. Eliot's stinging rebukes of pseudo-sophisticated discussions about art in "The Love Song of J. Alfred Prufrock." Maugham once admitted that he preferred *Cakes and Ale* over his two more popular novels, *Of Human Bondage* and *The Moon and Sixpence*. To read *Cakes and Ale* is to know why.

CALEB WILLIAMS

Type of work: Novel
Author: William Godwin (1756-1836)
Type of plot: Mystery romance
Time of plot: Eighteenth century
Locale: England
First published: 1794

The unity of Caleb Williams *suffers somewhat from the divided interest of being both social criticism and adventure story. Godwin, a social reformer, arranged his plot so that all of Caleb's miseries are caused by unjust English laws, which permitted wealthy landowners to hold power over the poor, who comprised a majority of the citizens.*

Historians of the novel have always encountered great difficulty in categorizing William Godwin's *Caleb Williams*. It has been called a great "tragic" novel, the first "pursuit" novel, a "crime" or "mystery" novel, a "chase-and-capture" adventure, a political thesis fiction, a Gothic Romance, a "terror" or "sensation" novel, even a "sentimental" tale. To some extent it is all of these —and none of them. The novel has, like most enduring works of art, taken on many shapes and meanings as new readers interpret the narrative in terms of their own personal, cultural, and historical experiences.

Godwin himself had no doubts about the book's meaning or about the effect he hoped to achieve with it: "I will write a tale that shall constitute an epoch in the mind of the reader, that no one, after he has read it, shall ever be exactly the same man that he was before." Having achieved fame in 1793 with his powerful, influential, and controversial political treatise *Enquiry Concerning the Principles of Political Justice,* he sought a form in which to dramatize his ideas. Thus, *Caleb Williams* can be seen at the most obvious level as a fictional gloss on Godwin's previous political masterpiece.

But *Caleb Williams* is no simple political tract. Godwin knew that he must first of all develop a narrative, in his words, "distinguished by a very powerful interest," if he expected readers to absorb and seriously consider his philosophical and social ideas. So he took the most exciting situation he could conceive, creating, as he said, "a series of adventures of flight and pursuit; the fugitive in perpetual apprehension of being overwhelmed with the worst calamities, and the pursuer, by his ingenuity and resources, keeping his victim in a state of the most fearful alarm." And thus, having first decided on the outcome of his adventure, Godwin worked backwards, like a modern mystery story writer, to develop a sequence of events leading up to his climax. The result is a well-constructed narrative in which each of the three volumes are tightly connected, both structurally and thematically, the action developing logically and directly with ever-mounting tension to a powerful, even tragic, dénouement.

logically and directly with ever-mounting tension to a powerful, even tragic, dénouement.

Ferdinando Falkland has the ability to, in Godwin's words, "alarm and harass his victim with an inextinguishable resolution never to allow him the least interval of peace and security," because of an unjust and fundamentally corrupt society. The worst villain is a legal system that gives absolute power to the rich and victimizes the poor, all in the name of "justice." Falkland fears Caleb's knowledge because Falkland has committed the only crime that an aristocrat can commit in eighteenth century England—a crime against a social equal. Had Tyrrel been poor, the issue would never have been raised. Caleb's alleged crime—stealing from his master and accusing the master of conspiracy against him—arouses such extreme repugnance because it challenges the social hierarchy and the assumptions that support it.

But the problem is not one of simple, conscious tyranny. Both rich and poor are unaware of the injustice and cruelty that their social institutions foster. They have been conditioned by their environment to accept the system as necessary, proper, and even benevolent. It is not the willful malevolence of a few, but "society" itself that distorts and dissipates the best qualities in men, regardless of their social class, although the poor suffer the most obvious physical oppressions. Falkland is not an example of deliberate evil; he is a good man who has, because of his social role, accepted a body of attitudes and moral values which are destructive. His passion to conceal his crime and his persecution of Caleb are the result not of any fear of legal punishment, but of his obsessive concern for his aristocratic "honor." "Though I be the blackest of villains," he tells Caleb, "I will leave behind me a spotless and illustrious name. There is no crime so malignant, no scene of blood so horrible in which that object cannot engage me."

Thus, there are no human villains in this novel; social institutions are Godwin's targets. This explains the novel's strange ending which seems to reverse all of the book's previous assumptions. Having finally succeeded in turning the law against his tormentor, Caleb realizes, as he faces a broken Falkland, that he, Caleb, is the real enemy. Falkland, for his part, admits his guilt and embraces Caleb. But, to Godwin, neither man is guilty. Both have been caught up in a series of causal circumstances created by their environment and resulting in their inevitable mutual destruction. Only when the environment can be altered to allow men's natural capacities to emerge, undistorted and unfettered by artificial, malevolent environmental conditioning, can such self-destruction be avoided and human potential realized.

THE CALL OF THE WILD

Type of work: Novel
Author: Jack London (1876-1916)
Type of plot: Adventure romance
Time of plot: 1897
Locale: Alaska
First published: 1903

London's most popular novel, The Call of the Wild *tells the story of Buck, who is stolen and taken to Alaska to be trained as a sled dog. In his new environment he must learn the elements of survival, from cunning and ruthlessness to courage and loyalty.*

On its simplest, most superficial and insensitive level, *The Call of the Wild* is just another of Jack London's "dog stories," which also include *White Fang* (1906) and *Jerry of the Islands* (1917). But so cavalier a dismissal of *The Call of the Wild*—usually accompanied by contemptuous allegations that the novel is nothing more than a potboiler—is quite unwarranted. Buck's story has far broader implications than the first, hasty reading may reveal. Admittedly, the book's popular success stems largely from its romantic-adventure qualities, yet there is much more to the novel than mere entertainment.

Jack London led a checkered life and had a checkered career; his experiences and knowledge are reflected in his novels and short stories, particularly his sociopolitical and economic views. At best, London's position could be described as eclectic; at worst, vacillating. He admired Herbert Spencer, Charles Darwin, Karl Marx, and Friedrich Nietzsche simultaneously and without much recognition of the contradictions among them. He embraced socialist causes while espousing Nietzschean "superman" theories. It is thus that Buck—under the presumably civilizing influence of John Thornton—becomes a good socialist; that is, Buck works for the common good rather than for his individual advancement. But, bereft of Thornton's guidance when his mentor dies, Buck reverts to the Darwinian survival of the fittest and the Nietzschean superman principles for his own protection.

To be sure, the novel has been faulted for Buck's so-called reversion to the wild. Even the most venerable of critics have praised *White Fang* and *Jerry of the Islands* for depicting savagery under civilized control, while disparaging *The Call of the Wild* as a clarion call to brute force. Yet, however such critics deplore the Darwinian-Nietzschean point of view, they seem to ignore the realities of the Marxian position: peasants and poor people—like Buck—can work with their kind for mutual benefit; but without a spirit of cooperation and without leadership or guidance, they must fend for themselves, or they will not endure. The cruelties of life are severe for both man and dog. And here the dog Buck is virtually an allegory for Everyman, in the pristine medieval sense, symbolizing the plight of the oppressed and the downtrodden everywhere in their struggle to maintain life. Whatever his intentions or his convictions, and no matter how skewed, London has portrayed, in *The Call of the Wild,* a vivid picture of the dilemma of the disadvantaged, even though he did so by using a dog as his protagonist.

CAMILLE

Type of work: Drama
Author: Alexandre Dumas, fils (1824-1895)
Type of plot: Sentimental romance
Time of plot: Nineteenth century
Locale: France
First presented: 1852

First published as a novel in 1848, Camille *is better known in its dramatic version; its story is possibly most familiar to modern readers through Verdi's opera* La Traviata. *Although the plot is sentimental and the characters unreal, when first presented on the French stage* Camille *marked a new treatment of social and moral problems.*

The extraordinary success of *Camille,* as novel and stage play, is primarily due to two intrinsic merits in Dumas' story: the humanity of the central figure, Camille Gautier, and the authenticity of the picture of contemporary Parisian life. The reader feels that Dumas must have drawn from his own experience to have created such a convincing portrait. The subject of the rehabilitated courtesan might have been hackneyed even in 1848, but it was in a modern setting and was drawn from actual life, as Dumas' public soon realized. *Camille* is not spoiled by the moralizing and preaching which has prevented Dumas' other works from surviving beyond his own time.

Dumas *fils,* was a different type of artist from his father, the author of so many famous romantic adventure novels. The son was at his best when his subject was close to him and inspired by intimate knowledge. The actual woman upon whom the heroine of *Camille* was based, Marie Plessis, was probably Dumas' own mistress; she died at twenty-three, but seems to have created in a few short years an enduring legend based both on her beauty and courage. However, the symbol which came to represent her fictional counterpart, the ever-present camellia, was invented by the author. Dumas created the notion, which captured the imagination of so many readers and audiences, that in her extreme sensitivity, his heroine could not endure the odor of flowers and therefore selected the lush but scentless camellia to be her sole ornament.

The sharpness and brightness of the detail in the work, the vividness of the characterizations, and the delicate concepts of a romantic period in literature have given *Camille* a unique place in both fictional and dramatic history. The combination of realism and romance seldom has been so effectively executed.

CAMPASPE

Type of work: Drama
Author: John Lyly (c. 1554-1606)
Type of plot: Historical-romantic comedy
Time of plot: c. 325 B.C.
Locale: Athens
First presented: 1584

Lyly's primary ambition in his writings was to refine the rude speech of the Elizabethan age. Consequently, Campaspe, *while it lacks character development, careful plotting, and a dramatic climax, is graceful and elegant in its diction, and is further enhanced by the periodic inclusion of charming lyrics.*

John Lyly is remembered primarily for the prose style of his "Euphues" novels, in which the balanced construction, rhetorical questions, and multiple similes which had previously been added to English prose style were combined and intensified. This style, known as euphuistic, is used throughout *Campaspe,* as, for example, when Hephestion asks Alexander, "Will you handle the spindle with Hercules, when you should shake the spear with Achilles?"

The plot of this play is a slender one, consisting almost wholly of two events: Alexander falls in love, and Alexander resists love. It is not for stage action that one turns to *Campaspe,* but rather for lively and thoughtful dialogue, quick thrusts of cynical retorts and artfully designed orations in defense of one opinion or another.

Diogenes is the master of the curt reply, as in this example: Alexander: "How should one learn to be content?" Diogenes: "Unlearn to covet." Hephestion, Alexander, Apelles, and Diogenes all deliver set speeches against love, for love, on Campaspe's beauty, and on the moral ills of the Athenians.

But the spine of the play is the point of its debate. The central question is: should men live *in* the world or *above* it? Living in the world would include the food which Diogenes denies himself and his slave, as well as the woman whom Alexander covets. Living above the world, according to Lyly, would seem not only to include Diogenes' life style, but also Alexander's life as a full-time conqueror, and Apelles' life as an artist.

Lyly's taste for balanced antithesis is as evident in his contrast of Alexander and Apelles as it is in his prose style: as Alexander moves away from his recent attraction to the life of the flesh, Apelles moves toward it. Most Elizabethans would have regarded Alexander's final decision as the best one for all concerned.

CANDIDE

Type of work: Novel
Author: François Marie Arouet de Voltaire (1694-1778)
Type of plot: Social satire
Time of plot: Eighteenth century
Locale: Europe and South America
First published: 1759

This most popular of Voltaire's works is a masterful satire on the follies and vices of men, particularly of the belief embodied by Pangloss that "All is for the best in this best of all possible worlds." The author, through the outrageous misadventures of his hero, disproves this theory utterly, taking to task all of man's most prized institutions: science, philosophy, religion, government, and romance.

Candide, Voltaire's tour de force, goes beyond most other famous satires. Like Pope's *Rape of the Lock,* it castigates the pretentiousness of the upper classes; like Orwell's *Animal Farm,* it undercuts political systems; like Swift's ambitious *Gulliver's Travels,* it sheds sharp light on man's grossness, his cupidity, and his stupidity, as well as on his crude and frequently cruel institutions. But it goes beyond man and his society to examine the entire world in which man finds himself. Its thesis is contrived in explicit response to Leibnitzian optimism that this is "the best of all possible worlds."

The problem of the existence of evil in the world has bothered man ever since he dared speculate about the nature of things. It is treated in the literature of the West at least as early as the book of Genesis, which attributes evil to man's disobedient nature. St. Augustine and, later, John Milton enlarged on this theory, claiming that God limited his own interference in the world when he created man "sufficient to stand though free to fall." The book of Job in the Bible centers more specifically on the problem of suffering. Its answer is essentially no answer except for God's overwhelming (some have said obscene) demonstration of power which humbles Job into acceptance. A third century Persian philosopher, Mani, devised the theory that earth is a field of dispute between two nearly matched powers—one of light, one of darkness—with man caught in the middle.

Most later explanations appear to be variations on these three. The seventeenth century Frenchman Blaise Pascal believed, like the author of Job, that man's vision cannot perceive the justice in God's overall plan. Gottfried Wilhelm von Leibnitz developed this explanation further. In his *Théodicée,* published in 1710, he described a harmonious universe in which all events are linked into a chain of cause-and-effect, and in which apparent evil is compensated by some greater good which may not be evident in the short run to the limited human mind. The English poet Alexander Pope expressed similar views in rhymed couplets:

> All Nature is but art, unknown to thee;
> All chance, direction, which thou canst not see;
> All discord, harmony not understood;
> All partial evil, universal good:
> And, in spite of pride, in erring reason's spite,
> One truth is clear: Whatever IS, IS RIGHT.

In his early life, Voltaire had been generally optimistic. Beginning in 1752, however, his writings evidence growing pessimism. On November 1, 1755, an earthquake in Lisbon, Portugal, killed thirty to forty thousand people. This catastrophe provided Voltaire with a perfect springboard for his skepticism about the basic goodness of this world. "If Pope had been at Lisbon," he wrote, "would he have dared to say *All is well?*" His fellow Frenchman Jean Jacques Rousseau responded that man, not God, is to blame for evil, including earthquakes: that man brings misfortune upon himself by congregating in cities instead of living naturally in the country.

Voltaire continued the debate by composing *Candide.* He created a young, impressionable protagonist and set him upon an incredible string of adventures, many of which are drawn from real life: for example, the Lisbon earthquake and subsequent auto-da-fé; the political chaos of Morocco; and the execution of an admiral (Voltaire had tried to intercede in just such a situation). Like such other wandering heroes as Gulliver and Huckleberry Finn, Candide is naïve. For a time, like a schoolboy, he reacts to such events as torture, war, and catastrophe by recalling the favorite principles of his tutor, Pangloss: "Every effect has a cause"; and "All is for the best in this best of all possible worlds." But as horror piles on horror, his doubts increase. Pangloss reappears periodically to soothe his pupil with the most illogical logic imaginable, but hard experience takes its toll.

Candide's visit to Eldorado, the famed lost city of the New World, is a high-water mark. Here all is placid and serene. People live in absolute harmony. Suffering and poverty are unknown. There is no greed; the natives smile at Candide's interest in the gold and jewels which lie on the ground as "clay and pebbles." Eldorado is Utopia—as J. G. Weightman has put it, "a sunny interlude between two series of disasters to show us how happy and pious we might have been had God not given us our ungovernable natures and put us into a world containing inexplicable evil." In his desire to regain his lost love, Cunegonde, Candide leaves Eldorado; but having seen a truly harmonious world, he can no longer accept cruelty, catastrophe, and suffering as necessary ingredients for a universal good.

In the final chapter, Candide and his little band, including his former tutor, Pangloss; his more recent friend, the pessimistic Martin; and Cunegonde, now grown old and ugly, settle on a small farm "till the company should meet with a more favorable destiny." There they become almost as distressed by boredom as they previously were by disaster. Two neighbors, however, bring to them enlightenment. A dervish, questioned about the existence of evil, responds, "What signifies it whether there be evil or good? When his highness sends a ship to Egypt does he trouble his head whether the rats in the vessel are at their ease or not?" This echo of a metaphor Voltaire had contrived as early as 1736 briefly asserts the notion that the world may in the view of the "divine architect" be excellent indeed—but it is not designed for man, the "mouse" in the hold, any more than noses were designed for spectacles.

The second neighbor, a contented old farmer, advises Candide's group of the worthwhileness of labor, which "keeps off from us three great evils— idleness, vice, and want." For once, those philosophical opposites, Pangloss and Martin, agree; the little community settles down to work in earnest, each member doing his part with a good will and deriving satisfaction therefrom.

Candide, then, while an attack on philosophical optimism, is not a pessimistic work: its ending, with the hero remarking that "we must cultivate our garden," reminds one of the words of another realistic, but hopeful, man, Anton Chekhov, who was to observe more than a century later, "If everyone in the world did all he was capable of on his own plot of land, what a beautiful world it would be!"

Sally Buckner

THE CANTERBURY TALES
(SELECTIONS)

Type of work: Poem
Author: Geoffrey Chaucer (1340?-1400)
Types of plots: Chivalric romance, folk tradition, and saint's legend
Times of plots: Remote antiquity to fourteenth century
Locale: England
First transcribed: 1380-1390

In this great Middle English classic, Chaucer uses an imaginative "frame story" format to present twenty-four tales: a group of pilgrims meet at a tavern on their way to the shrine of Becket at Canterbury, and agree to pass the long hours of their journey in a storytelling contest to be judged by the innkeeper. The stories range from bawdy burlesques to tales of chivalry, from local folk legends to sermons. Chaucer's genius is such that the tales reveal the personalities of their tellers; in addition, the pilgrims grow as distinct personalities as they converse and argue between stories.

Geoffrey Chaucer, the first great poet in English literature, left behind him a work of perennial attraction and enjoyment. Not only was *The Canterbury Tales* popular from the time of its composition; it has been read ever since, edited, reprinted endlessly, taught in schools, adapted in part for the stage, and used for political parody.

Why should a work written in Middle English six centuries ago have such a hold upon subsequent generations? What does its author contribute in his collection of stories that appeals so to all classes of individuals down the years? Why is *The Canterbury Tales* considered one of the outstanding works of English literature?

Answers to these questions are not difficult when one reads the tales either in their original language or in modern translation. Immediately one finds an author who had a tremendous feeling for life, understood human motivation, and could tell a story with great gusto.

The collection of pilgrims making their way to the shrine of Canterbury is a fair cross section of people from various walks of life and professions. Chaucer draws them with detailed individual characteristics but still with universal qualities that allow them to come alive in any generation. And he has taken consummate care to match these stories to their tellers.

No one, for example, can forget the brief portrait in the Prologue of the Wife of Bath, a florid woman, gaudy and bold in appearance. She is a lower middle-class weaver from beside the town of Bath and has had five husbands; Chaucer slyly adds "not to speak of other company in her youth." Yet the story she tells is an Arthurian romance stressing the virtues of courtesy and gentilesse. It has been termed a wish-fulfillment tale in which the ugly old woman wins sovereignty over her unwilling youthful husband and then turns young and beautiful. Careful study of this tale with the Wife's Prologue portrait, her conversation with other pilgrims, her lusty confessional prologue reveals another side of this apparently crude and brash woman. She is more complex than one at first realizes, but Chaucer handles this point subtly without stating the fact.

Another pilgrim who fascinates readers is the Pardoner, a thorough charlatan, admittedly evil, who brags of his scandalous treatment of those he should serve. It is again important that Chaucer never says the Pardoner is a rogue; as with all the characters, he is allowed to state so himself, or to reveal his character through quarrels with other pilgrims or by the type of story he relates.

The purposeful ambiguity in the portrait of the Nun, who concentrates on social concerns—feeding delicate morsels to her pet dogs and watching her table manners—instead of showing more Christian traits, makes a comment, though again indirect. Her tale reveals little human sympathy but is a typical miracle story she might have learned by rote.

Throughout *The Canterbury Tales,* Chaucer, who places himself along with other pilgrims as a naïve, unobservant traveling companion, uses this *persona* to effect satire and irony in the portraits.

But seldom is the work didactic; Chaucer does not condemn clerics, tradespeople, or any other group. Instead, he allows them to reveal their own faults or makes clever asides to the reader to suggest a viewpoint. We see the pilgrims as they are with all their virtues and vices, and we can readily identify with their humanness.

Another reason for this great work's popularity lies in the variety of tales. Chaucer handles with equal facility different genres of medieval literature from the courtly romance told by the Knight down to the bawdy tales of the Miller and Reeve. In the collection of twenty-four stories, there is something for everyone. If the reader does not care for one, Chaucer advises "turn over the leaf and choose another tale." If anyone is offended by a tale of lechery, he can select a saint's legend or something in between.

Chaucer also handles with dexterity different levels of language: courtly speech, bawdy expressions, elegant prayers—language of the church, street and tavern. He can also use a clipped reporting style and turn out a parody of the excesses in metrical romance. He has at command a whole bag of rhetorical tricks.

Critics and readers have attempted over the centuries to find an encompassing theme in *The Canterbury Tales.* Are these a mere collection of unrelated stories or do they in one way or another deal with a single topic such as love (human or divine), or the question of who should have the upper hand in marriage? Attempts at making the tales conform to a selected theme have mainly been unsuccessful; one can always find certain tales which do not fit a chosen category or treat of similar themes. It seems more likely that the Canterbury collection represents a panorama of representative humanity—a *comédie humaine,* not only of the fourteenth century but of all ages.

One other reason for the lasting quality of this first great work in English literature is that, like Shakespeare's drama, it opens innumerable possibilities to the reader. It poses questions about human motivation, aspirations. It probes into established attitudes, questions existing institutions. *The Canterbury Tales* reveals the tensions of the time, the alternatives for man in a changing world, where many long-cherished customs and opinions were disintegrating.

Chaucer's pilgrims with their tales reveal the hopes and uncertainties of life, the heights to which man can climb as well as the depths to which he can descend. Perhaps all these reasons make *The Canterbury Tales* timeless.

Muriel B. Ingham

CAPTAIN HORATIO HORNBLOWER

Type of work: Novel
Author: C. S. Forester (1899-1966)
Type of plot: Historical romance
Time of plot: Early nineteenth century
Locale: The Pacific Ocean, South America, the Mediterranean, Spain, France, England
  and the Atlantic Ocean
First published: 1937, 1938, 1939

In addition to creating a personality of wide general appeal, Forester weaves his technical knowledge of war at sea into the novel with such skill that the reader unconsciously learns the seamen's language, the parts of a fighting ship, and the details of naval gunnery.

Composed of three short novels—*Beat to Quarters, A Ship of the Line,* and *Flying Colours—Captain Horatio Hornblower* is the middle section of a series that begins with the intrepid officer's sea apprenticeship (the *Young Hornblower* trilogy) and concludes with *Commodore Hornblower, Lord Hornblower,* and *Admiral Hornblower in the West Indies.* For its broad scope and sustained vigor, the whole series has appropriately been described as a modern saga. Although Forester's Hornblower romances do not quite belong among the highest rank of sea fiction—that by Joseph Conrad, Richard Henry Dana, or Herman Melville—because they lack a philosophical and moral dimension, they certainly are the equal of sea-adventure novels by Captain Frederick Marryat or James Fenimore Cooper. Forester's novels combine meticulous historical reconstruction with a flair for storytelling. In 1932, the author began writing screenplays for Hollywood. Unlike many other distinguished novelists who were either failures or were only moderately successful in adapting their skills to this medium, Forester excelled as a scriptwriter and, in turn, learned how to use certain cinematic techniques in his fiction. Lively, fast-paced, with each scene building to a climax, his Hornblower stories are easy to visualize. At the same time, they are packed with authentic historical pieces of information. Not only are his celebrated battle scenes bristling with sharp, concrete details that capture the excitement of the moment, but in his description of English manners, customs, and topical interests during the early nineteenth century, the robust age comes alive.

As a realist, Forester does not gloss over the unpleasant truths about warfare at sea or the rigors of nautical life. Early in *Captain Horatio Hornblower* we learn that Hankey, the previous surgeon attached to H. M. S. *Lydia,* has died of the complications of drink and syphilis. Hornblower himself must perform several grisly operations on his wounded men. After one battle in *Beat to Quarters,* he cuts out a great splinter of wood lodged in a seaman's chest. Using no anesthetic (except whiskey), he performs the operation crudely, and Forester does not spare his readers the terrible details. In *Flying Colours,* similarly, Hornblower must relieve the gangrenous pressure on the stump of his friend Bush's amputated leg. Applying cold vinegar to the stump to reduce the inflammation, he opens, cleans, and then sews up the victim's wound. Other scenes of grim realism impart to the romance a sense of truth. In *Beat to Quarters* Hornblower sees a man horribly tortured by the cruel El Supremo for no reason at all, simply because the man has been judged "one of the unenlightened." Hornblower also witnesses the aftermath of battle: "dirty bodies with blood and pus and vomit." Not only in the stark scenes of battle, but also in the smallest details Forester creates realistic touches. He describes how ships are loaded with provisions, how the officers and crew function in a hierarchy of responsibilities, and how the ships operate in calm or storm. At one point Hornblower's friend Gailbraith describes a poem that he admires, "The Lay of the Last Minstrel," whose author, he says, is "an Edinburgh lawyer." Instead of identifying the author as Sir Walter Scott, Forester thus creates a sense of historical realism; for at the time of the action, Scott, not yet famous, might have been known only as a lawyer who dabbled in poetry.

Moreover, in his characterization of Horatio Hornblower, Forester provides sharp, realistic details that make his hero seem human. Although he is certainly high-minded, courageous, and capable, Hornblower is not without frailties. He is vain, sometimes squeamish, and—strange to say—naturally indolent. Near the beginning of *Beat to Quarters* Hornblower views himself critically in a mirror, noting all his physical liabilities as well as strengths. He does not like his "rounded belly" and fears that he is growing bald. Several times in the book he reflects unhappily upon his receding hair line. For a hero, he has a weak stomach for scenes of squalor or bloodshed. He must be shamed by Lady Barbara Wellesley before he allows her to dress the wounds of the injured. Furthermore he is, by his own admission, lazy. After a battle involving the *Lydia,* Hornblower retires to his hammock to sleep. Although he feels "a prick of shame" that the other officers and men have to clean up the bodies and wreckage, he confesses to his physical limitations. Again, in *Flying Colours,* he wishes "to be idle and lazy." When his gentle wife Maria dies, he is plunged into grief; when he holds his child in his arms, he feels paternal elation; and when he courts Lady Barbara, he is an ardent yet awkward lover. Thus, Forester humanizes Hornblower, making him a man as well as a hero. Such a hero is worthy of his victories.

CAPTAIN SINGLETON

Type of work: Novel
Author: Daniel Defoe (1660-1731)
Type of plot: Adventure romance
Time of plot: Eighteenth century
Locale: The navigable world
First published: 1720

This tale of adventure and piracy, while clearly inferior to Robinson Crusoe, *still contains those elements of realism and the commonsense point of view that made Defoe a crucial early developer of the English novel. Although character is subordinate to plot in* Captain Singleton, *the portraits of the egocentric, courageous captain and the shrewd pacifist, William, provide interesting contrast.*

Fascinated as they were by tales about remote nations of the world, Defoe's readers thrilled to such fictions as *Robinson Crusoe* (1719), *Colonel Jack* (1722), and *Captain Singleton.* Nor, of course, was Defoe the only writer of such literature. One thinks immediately of *Gulliver's Travels* (1726), which, if it is not altogether typical of the genre, clearly attests to its popularity.

Captain Singleton not only fulfills the requirements for travel literature of the period but does so to a fault. The emphasis of the novel is on action—at the expense of character—and colorful, incidental detail. Nearly the entire first half of the book treats Singleton's wearisome trek from the east coast of Madagascar to the west coast of Africa; the second half, something of a *non sequitur,* embarks on quite a different course—Singleton's adventures as a pirate. Thus, the novel betrays Defoe's tendency to indulge a tasteless reading public. It is diffuse, void of effective characterization, overly reportorial, and disconnected in its two major movements. Where it succeeds best is in its fertile inventiveness and easy style. Only Defoe could build a lengthy episode around the idea of laying siege to a tree, or cultivate such stylistic touches as this: "to think of Death, is to dye; and to be always thinking of it, is to be all one's Life-long a dying."

This is a novel which also embraces much Puritan theology, as one would expect from the author of *Robinson Crusoe.* Singleton is "homeless" in two distinct senses of the word: he has neither a physical nor a spiritual domicile since he has been stolen away both from his earthly parents and his divine Father. Therefore he is tractable, and indifferent to the decisions that others make for him; after all, he has no "Pilot" to direct his life. Like Crusoe, he eschews a safe, comfortable life in order to indulge his wanderlust (in *Robinson Crusoe* an evident sin against the "Father") with the result that God tries him with many perils. This theological undertow in the novel is not nearly so pronounced as it is in other Defoe novels (*Captain Singleton* is scarcely an allegory), but it is nonetheless present. In the end, Bob Singleton repents of his roguish life, but, predictably, keeps his ill-gotten gains in order to do good with them.

There are a number of minor points in the novel that are of interest, among them Defoe's intense dislike of the Portuguese (this occurs in his other works) and his familiarity with eighteenth century geography. Readers today will also appreciate his attitudes toward slavery and toward so-called "natural law." Defoe seems to have condemned strongly the idea of enslavement (though his heroes practice it) even as he believed the black race to be un-enlightened. Natural law he viewed in the manner of Thomas Hobbes: what exists is the principal law governing human actions.

CAPTAINS COURAGEOUS

Type of work: Novel
Author: Rudyard Kipling (1865-1936)
Type of plot: Adventure romance
Time of plot: 1890's
Locale: Grand Banks of Newfoundland
First published: 1897

This novel captures the adventurous spirit of men who risked their lives to fish the Grand Banks before the days of commercial steam trawlers. One interesting aspect of the work which is often overlooked is Kipling's esteem, as a respecter of power and force, for the character of the millionaire and the tough capitalist system which he represents—a way of life as demanding of strength and talent as that of a sea captain.

Captains Courageous was written in 1896 while Rudyard Kipling was dwelling in Vermont's forests. Why did Great Britain's poet laureate—who wrote during Britain's imperial heyday when "the sun never set" on an empire stretching "from palm to pine"—have an "American period" in which he wrote a noted sea story in the North American woods? This scarcely-known phase of Kipling's career was a happy one, but has a key explanation that is curiously often overlooked today.

Kipling loved Vermont's forests, especially during the colorful autumn, but he also praised the deep, vital kinship between America and its British motherland. He equated the "Captains Courageous" of the Grand Banks, such as Disko Troop, and the pioneers who conquered the American-Canadian West (not only Daniel Boone, George Vancouver, and Kit Carson, but also railroad magnates like King Cheyne), with bold Elizabethan adventurers like Sir Francis Drake, Sir John Hawkins, Sir Martin Frobisher, Sir Walter Raleigh, and Sir Philip Sidney. The Elizabethan spirit of adventure and accomplishment was not dead, he felt, and the modern fishing captains and railroad magnates were blood-brothers of the earlier Anglo-Saxon adventurers, displaying the same spirit of freedom, free enterprise, and bravery against odds.

But it is also true that Kipling had long lived among Asian masses. Since Anglo-Saxons could not reproduce their own kind in Asia in a natural "living-space," and thus could never be more than a dissolving white drop in a colored ocean, Kipling felt a shuddering relief to plunge into Vermont's woods where his own race was prospering and having large families. Despite this typical nineteenth century racism, however, it must be conceded that a certain Kiplingesque respect for all sturdy breeds is revealed in *Captains Courageous*. In this sea novel, the Britsh poet implies that men and the civilizations that they create need challenges, not security, and must maintain healthy folk instincts while rearing each generation of their own kind in hardiness. In *Captains Courageous,* the representatives of European, expansionist, seafaring races—British, French, German, Portuguese—who have braved the Grand Banks for centuries are favorably presented. But so is the black cook; for, despite his nineteenth century belief in a White Man's Burden, Kipling sometimes praised sturdy blacks, such as the tough Sudanese.

Within the above context, the novel stresses traditional virtues like those of Horatio Alger. Harvey Cheyne learns practical skills and escapes emasculating luxury. He also learns the salutary value of hard work, sweat, and plain living, and returns to nature and healthy simplicity by recapturing his self-reliance amidst the sheer beauty of the high seas. The physical environment of sea and shore is thus a character in the story, and it has been pointed out that *Captains Courageous,* therefore, differs from most novels since it concerns the environment more than it does the protagonist. Even the theme of conversion stems from environment, but it is linked as well to individual will and hereditary character stemming from Harvey's Anglo-Saxon father, King Cheyne. The driving ambition of King Cheyne is paralleled in Kipling's eulogy of the redoubtable fishermen who brave cold storms and fogs off the Grand Banks to fish for cod in their small dories. Thus, a millionaire's son becomes a man through his hardships on a fishing boat and through sharing the lot of toiling fishermen from Massachusetts, Canada, Germany, and Portugal.

The very pith of Kipling's story can be found, therefore, in King Cheyne's conversation with the redeemed young Harvey. King Cheyne relates the story of his life—how he had had to toil for everything that he earned; how he fought Indians and border ruffians before the West was tamed; how he had many deadly struggles against odds; and how he built his railroad empire. He stresses the progress that railroads represented, enabling families to cross the immense and mountainous continent without suffering for months in covered wagons, sometimes burying their tiny children along the way, as they had had to do before Cheyne built his railroads. Infused with pride at his heritage, young Harvey returns to Gloucester, borrows money from his father, and invests it in fishing boats, hiring some of the friends that he had made on his first fishing expedition. Thus, Harvey starts his own fishing empire in the true Anglo-American tradition of creative enterprise.

Kipling's unexpected familiarity with the sea is evident. His descriptions of life on a fishing vessel, of how fish are caught and processed, and of the abrupt tragedies that sometimes overtake the "captains courageous" are not superficial. He evidently familiarized himself with the Gloucester accents and the idiom as well, for they are reproduced with the idiomatic skill for which Kipling has long been noted. Like so many Kipling works, *Captains Courageous* is easy for children to read, enjoy, and understand, but its meanings are subtle and its literary virtues considerable.

Kipling experienced personal troubles and an unfortunate lawsuit, and left Vermont. It is interesting to note that shortly after this military poet wrote one of the better novels of North Atlantic sea literature, he composed his famous *Recessional* honoring Queen Victoria's Diamond Jubilee in London in 1897. Rather than vaunting Great Britain's military might on this august occasion, however, Kipling shocked Empire enthusiasts by worrying over how England's regiments were shedding their blood over the entire earth and how Royal Navy ships were sinking on distant headland and dune. Fearing "lest we be one with Nineveh and Tyre," Kipling wrote, "Lord God of hosts, be with us yet, be with us yet," thereby shedding light on his geopolitical reasons for earlier writing *Captains Courageous*.

Rudyard Kipling died in 1936, as World War II loomed. His views on the North American land mass as being the future center of Britannic racial strength—which is the inner message of *Captains Courageous*—might well have influenced Nazi racialist geopoliticians such as Karl Haushofer and Alfred Rosenberg—not to mention Hitler himself. *Captains Courageous* meanwhile continues to be a favorite among all ages of readers in many landlocked as well as seafaring nations.

William Freitas

THE CAPTAIN'S DAUGHTER

Type of work: Novel
Author: Alexander Pushkin (1799-1837)
Type of plot: Historical romance
Time of plot: About 1774
Locale: Russia
First published: 1836

One of the first pure examples of Russian realism, The Captain's Daughter *is an exciting and concisely told narrative with a gallery of characters ranging from simple Maria to the cruel rebel Pougatcheff. The novel was written as the result of Pushkin's appointment to the office of crown historian, which gave him access to state archives and the private papers of Empress Catherine II.*

The longest of Pushkin's completed prose tales, *The Captain's Daughter* was based on true events which Pushkin wrote as history in his *The History of the Pugachev Rebellion.* The astonishing quality about *The Captain's Daughter* is the style. Although written in 1836, and the first modern Russian novel, it possesses a brisk, lean style more suggestive of twentieth century fiction than that of the early nineteenth. Pushkin wastes no words, yet his scenes are vivid, his characters fully fleshed and remarkably alive, and his tale recounted in a suspenseful and moving manner. The first person narration is realistic and adds to the verisimilitude of the story. The naïve, romantic illusions of the young protagonist are described by the narrator in a thoroughly disarming and often humorous manner. The entire story is seen through Peter's eyes, allowing the reader to share his enthusiasms, his impetuousness, and his fears, as well as his youthful ardor and romantic spirit. A sense of the vitality of youth pervades the book.

The accounts of action, such as the duel or the siege of the Bailogorsk fortress, are vivid and well-paced. Throughout the novel, Pushkin writes with extraordinary ease and vitality, bringing to life in a few strokes situations and characters. A sly humor is an integral part of the narrative. When the hero informs us that his French tutor was sent out from Moscow with the yearly supply of wine and olive oil, we know precisely where that unlucky tutor fit into the household. Many of the characters possess a humorous side to their nature. The ill-fated, henpecked Captain and his talkative but kindly tyrant of a wife are both portrayed with a light touch. Old Savelitch, Peter's servant, is the truest comic figure in the novel; devoted to his young master, as to Peter's father before, the old man would willingly sacrifice his life for Peter, but he never hesitates to talk back to Peter or even to the rebel Cossack leader if he feels that he is in the right. Even Pougatcheff, self-styled Pretender to the throne, is presented with a great deal of humor; in a sense, he is the only character in the book who does not take himself completely seriously, and this, at least in part, is due to an ironic realization of the precariousness of his existence.

Many scenes in the novel possess a double-edged humor, from the absurd, aborted and then finished duel between Peter and Shvabrin to the moment, in the midst of horror, when old Savelitch dares to present an itemized list of destroyed and stolen goods to the man who holds all of their lives in his hands. The deaths of the Captain and his wife are handled with a certain grotesque humor. As in Shakespeare's tragedies, this humor serves to heighten the horror of certain dramatic scenes, such as the fall of the fortress and the butchering of the innocent at the hands of the rebels. But, despite the terrible events portrayed in the novel, the book is not grim. It is a romantic tale of action and romance and the ending is appropriately happy. Even this conclusion, with its scenes of mistaken identity, possesses a charming humor.

At the same time, the realism of the portrayals of the duplicity of human nature, the traitorous villainy of Shvabrin, the cowardice of the garrison when they all throw down their arms in the face of the enemy, and the pettiness of many of the minor characters, is shocking. The brilliant construction of the novel, the alternating light and dark scenes, sweeps the reader along, never letting him be quite sure of where he is. Pushkin seems to delight in catching the reader off guard, of making him laugh and then gasp with horror and then hurling a piece of slapstick at him before he has recovered from the shock. The scene of the Captain's fat wife being dragged naked from her house to the gallows, screaming and shouting abuse at the Cossacks, is both funny and horrible. Shvabrin, completely despicable, is shown to be absurd as he struts and postures during his brief glory, and then, even more so, when he falls. Pushkin is extremely deft at showing both sides of human beings, the noble and the phony, the absurd and the courageous, the hateful and the loving.

The Russian land is an important part of this novel. The vast spaces almost become another character, as the hero flies across them in sleds and carriages or on horseback. Pushkin carefully builds a sense of intense patriotic fervor throughout the narrative, culminating in the scenes with the Empress. The Empress is seen as the Mother figure of all Russia, wise and warm, quick to understand and forgive and to come to the aid of her "children." Frequently, in the course of the book, words and phrases refer to the Russian people as one large family; underlings call their masters and mistresses "Father" and "Mother," and the land is referred to as the great mother of them all. The Empress and the land, of course, are inseparable. In the light of this powerful sentiment, the daring of Pougatcheff to attempt to usurp the throne becomes all the more shocking, as Pushkin intended, for to attack the throne is to attack all of Russia, and to undermine the structure of the entire country.

The Captain's Daughter exerted a tremendous influence on Russian fiction; it showed novelists the possibilities of Russian themes and Russian settings, and, above all, it illustrated the narrative capabilities of the Russian language. Never before had Russian prose been used in fiction in such a lean, vigorous, and completely unpretentious manner. The perfection of the book was awesome, but also inspiring to the writers who followed Pushkin. It can be said that the great period of Russian fiction begins with *The Captain's Daughter*. (The other great influence on Russian fiction, Gogol's *Dead Souls*, did not appear until 1842.) The great tragedy for Russian literature and the world is that the year after writing this novel, Pushkin was killed at the age of thirty-seven in a duel.

Bruce D. Reeves

THE CAPTIVES

Type of work: Drama
Author: Titus Maccius Plautus (c. 254-184 B. C.)
Type of plot: Farce
Time of plot: During war between Aetolia and Elis
Locale: Aetolia
First presented: c. 210 B. C.

One of the most innocuous of Plautus' generally racy plays, the plot of The Captives *is based on a comedy by the Greek playwright Menander and revolves around a complicated series of mistaken identities. The real source of the fun, however, is the stock character of the parasite Ergasilus, always hungry and always in search of a free meal.*

The Captives is one of the most inoffensive plays to come from the racy pen of Plautus. Largely for this reason it has been included very often in play anthologies. We also know that thirty years or so after the dramatist's death a Prologue was added to the play, indicating the harmless nature of the drama and explaining the story, a complicated series of mistaken identities.

It is highly probable that Plautus adapted this work from a comedy by the Greek playwright Menander, as were many of his plays. Here we find the favorite devices of Menander—the kidnaped child, the long sequence of co-incidences, slavery developed in a sentimental way, the recognition scenes, appealing characters. Plautus may have added the character of Ergasilus the parasite for comic relief, because this play seems unusually serious for Plautus. Whatever humor this comedy has is due to the contrast between the scrounging Ergasilus and the earnest efforts of everyone else to settle their confused affairs honorably. Even the ignominious Stalagmus has some dignity in his honesty and his Stoic acceptance of his punishment. The Roman audiences of Plautus' day would have accepted Stalagmus and jeered Ergasilus, much as our forefathers would have liked a scene of a man meeting a hard fate with determination and despised anyone accepting public welfare.

Through the maze of perplexing confusions, which are rich in dramatic irony, one important theme emerges—that of the devotion of the slave Tyndarus to his master Philocrates, a devotion which is returned in the end. Tyndarus has a noble character, while Philocrates must earn one. It is principally on the ironic play between master and slave and between father and sons that this drama derives its meaning. Like Shakespeare, Plautus was adept at revising old plays to new and alien settings. Plautus points out in *The Captives* the same thing Menander did, that a good slave is better than a weak master; but he added an idea of his own in all likelihood, that the most abject slave is better than a parasite. The Romans of the early Republic would have applauded this notion heartily.

CARMEN

Type of work: Novelette
Author: Prosper Mérimée (1803-1870)
Type of plot: Romantic tragedy
Time of plot: Early nineteenth century
Locale: Spain
First published: 1847

In this romantic tale, a beautiful but fickle young gipsy girl captures the love of a soldier whose hopes for a brilliant career are shattered when his jealousy of his rebellious and unfaithful lover leads him to murder a rival. This novelette is the basis for Bizet's opera of the same title.

Prosper Mérimée's *Carmen* is pure romance. It has all the conventions of which romance is made—a setting that is exotic and characters that are even more so, love that leads one character to surrender everything else for it, and violence in the name of love. *Carmen* is outstanding because of the believability of the characters and the plot, and because of the author's deep understanding of Spanish and gipsy folkways.

The first two chapters are narrated by an unnamed French scholar who, while studying in Andalusia, meets both Carmen and Don José by chance. The rest of the book, in which the plot comes out, takes the form of a monologue spoken by Don José to the scholar. The reader thus knows Carmen from two viewpoints. Although the story of her doomed relationship to José is told from his viewpoint, both of them can be judged objectively. To an extent, they are stereotypes: José is Navarrese and passionate; Carmen is a gipsy and fickle. Yet, the problem of deep and abiding love for one who is capable only of passing relationships is not confined to inter-ethnic love affairs. The story is realistic because there are Carmens and Josés in every culture. José's violent and tragic reaction to Carmen's fickleness might seem unreal in a person from a more law-abiding society. But it can also be explained by the slow process, carefully described by Mérimée, in which he becomes a hunted outlaw in the mistaken belief that he could thus have Carmen.

The setting, the characters' nationalities, and the touches of authenticity in Mérimée's description of them help make *Carmen* outstanding. Much of the story's beauty is in the simple rusticity of its setting, and the innocence of its characters to the industrialism and urbanness which were taking over France in 1847.

THE CASE OF SERGEANT GRISCHA

Type of work: Novel
Author: Arnold Zweig (1887-1968)
Type of plot: Social criticism
Time of plot: 1917
Locale: Russia
First published: 1927

The plot of this novel, an absorbing account of the last months of World War I, first appeared as a play in 1921. As a prisoner, Grischa is only a pawn in the struggle between the Prussian caste system and rising middle-class opportunism; at the outset there is the sense that he has little chance of escape.

The Case of Sergeant Grischa is a brilliant novel, and one of the best in any language to emerge from World War I. Zweig has a strong narrative sense, an excellent grasp of physical detail, and a fine ability to portray characters. Additionally, the novel relates the particular setting of the German Eastern Front in World War I to the historical and social forces, in the army and outside it, that brings Sergeant Grischa to his fate.

The story itself begins in a primitive setting, where Grischa is impelled by the most basic human feelings: the need for wife, child, and home. The story moves forward into progressively more richly textured social and political settings, where human emotions became more disguised and elaborate through their contact with the institutions of society and of war. But throughout this movement the story itself remains prominent. Sergeant Grischa's career remains of interest because he is so appealing as a character and because he encounters such a broadly representative spectrum of forces and circumstances in his life.

The physical details of the labor camp, forests, towns, offices, trenches, battlefields, and prisons are especially rich and provocative. Zweig is compelling in his presentations of places, using both panoramas and in-depth descriptions. This intense realism is heightened by Zweig's characterizations, which are superb. Grischa himself, despite his lowly status (or perhaps because of it), and despite his naïveté, is clearly of heroic proportions. He has courage, endurance, deep feelings, and, above all, great human potential. It is his potential that impresses those around him and that makes his final and seemingly inevitable fate all the more significant. As he grows more heroic in our estimation, especially in contrast to the corruption around him, he still never ceases to be a victim. This heroic doubleness, perhaps the central feature of European, American, and British literature of the inter-war period, marks The Case of Sergeant Grischa as an undeniably modern novel.

Unlike much literary work of this period, however, The Case of Sergeant Grischa remains firmly embedded in actual history and society. There is no Kafkaesque sliding into the abstract; everything is rooted in social and politi-

Kafkaesque sliding into the abstract; everything is rooted in social and political actuality. Real institutions and their functionaries never disappear or become merely parable; instead, they retain their particular historical features. Yet, precisely because the officials, bureaucrats, officers, and guards are so typical, and because Sergeant Grischa is himself, *The Case of Sergeant Grischa* retains its life and relevance.

CASS TIMBERLANE

Type of work: Novel
Author: Sinclair Lewis (1885-1951)
Type of plot: Social criticism
Time of plot: 1940's
Locale: Grand Republic, Minnesota
First published: 1945

Continuing in the manner of Main Street *and* Babbitt, *Lewis in* Cass Timberlane *once again attacks the smugness and cruelty of small-town life; his particular target is the hypocritical group of nouveau riche. The novel bristles with portraits of snobs who judge a person by his yearly income; "good" families one generation removed from bartenders or hod carriers; and pious gossips who condemn the easy morals of the working class while indulging freely in illicit affairs.*

Lewis' turbulent career was reaching its end by the time he attempted this "novel of husbands and wives," one of the last of his many theme novels. *Cass Timberlane* is not one of Lewis' great novels, but it is a good novel, conscientiously thought out and well crafted. Written in 1945, the novel now has the feeling of a historical novel; its period as portrayed by Lewis seems quite as removed as that of the author's earlier novels *Main Street* or *Babbitt.* Perhaps this is partly because Lewis' famous ear was not as sharp as it once had been and he used already dated slang, and satirized rather tired, well-used subjects. The novel presents a carefully thought out (although sometimes obvious) dramatic structure. It might not be fair to say that the wheels are always visible as they turn in this novel, but sometimes they creak and groan a bit.

Lewis' technique is to establish a situation and then methodically follow it through the logical unraveling of the plot with few surprises. His satire is broad, not subtle, but often effective; his style of relentless irony is softened with a genuine good humor. Lewis has a sincere fondness for the Midwest about which he is writing and a true affection for his characters. The author does not penetrate very deeply into the minds and souls of his characters, but the people he chooses to write about do not possess complicated inner lives. He deliberately limits himself to portraying certain superficial aspects of life.

Most of the people wandering through these pages are bored, but only half realize it. Lewis, in his etching of the triumphant, arrogant ignorance of many of his characters, achieves the difficult feat of writing interestingly about boredom. To be fair to Lewis, one should judge the novel against the author's intentions, and he did succeed effectively with what he set out to accomplish.

CASTE

Type of work: Drama
Author: Thomas William Robertson (1829-1871)
Type of plot: Social criticism
Time of plot: Nineteenth century
Locale: England
First presented: 1867

Reacting against the artificiality and extravagance of previous British drama, Robertson sought in his plays to introduce realism into the feeling, dialogue, and situation. If Caste, his most famous work, seems conventional by today's standards, one must remember the social and literary milieu from which the play emerged.

T. W. Robertson was one of those rare, fortunate writers who was hailed as a "revolutionary" innovator in his genre, and at the same time, achieved great popular and commercial success. He was able to realize both of these frequently contradictory goals because his theatrical approach was novel, stimulating, and in sharp contrast to prevalent dramatic styles and assumptions, while the plot substance and ideological implications of his plays were essentially conventional, conservative, and well suited to the needs and expectations of his Victorian middle-class audience. This combination of theatrical effectiveness and thematic propriety is, perhaps, best illustrated in his most famous play, *Caste.*

If the "realism" of *Caste* seems quaint, contrived, and occasionally crude today, it must be remembered that Robertson was reacting against the ornate, excessive, "stagey," theatrical style of the eighteenth and early nineteenth centuries, which was characterized by extravagant spectacle, unfettered emotionalism, overwrought acting, and pseudo-poetic speech. Robertson rightly believed that, with ascendancy of the bourgeoisie, such "aristocratic" trappings were obsolete and that the public was ready for a solid dose of realism. He was the first modern British playwright who had his characters sit in real chairs, drink out of real teacups, open and close real doors and windows —in short, Robertson more or less brought the "fourth-wall convention" to the Victorian stage, although he did so imperfectly. But even if soliloquies, asides, and many other relics of the melodramatic stage remained, the impression of contemporary reality, a sense of "environment," was new to the British theater.

This physical realism was enhanced by Robertson's attitude toward dialogue and acting. The dialogue in his best plays is quick, colloquial, witty, and intimate. The long rhetorical set pieces were out; snappy exchanges between characters became the rule. The acting style Robertson imposed, both through his scripts and his directing, was simple, natural, and relatively underplayed. The new stress was, therefore, on ensemble performance rather than individual histrionics, and this shift in emphasis has been crucial to the modern stage.

The new stress was, therefore, on ensemble performance rather than individual histrionics, and this shift in emphasis has been crucial to the modern stage.

In terms of plot and character, *Caste* seems today to be absurdly contrived. However, one of Robertson's most important contributions to English drama was his adaptation of the French "pièce bien faite"—or "well-made play" —as popularized on the Continent by Eugène Scribe and Victorien Sardou, to the middle-class Victorian environment, thus creating a distinctive genre: the British realistic well-made play.

The characterizations in *Caste* are shallow and stereotypical, but they are nicely orchestrated. The "noble" couple, George D'Alroy and Esther Eccles, is juxtaposed against the "common" one, Sam Gerridge and Polly Eccles; the haughty, aristocratic mother, Marquise de St. Maur, is opposed to the lazy, worthless father, Eccles; the honest worker, Sam, who understands his place in society, is measured against the jobless sponger, Eccles, who does not. Each character, therefore, acts as a representative of his social class and demonstrates the validity of that social arrangement. Eccles proves that he belongs at the bottom of the social heap. The Marquise is unpleasant, but her last-scene conversion to understanding, triggered by the miraculous return of her son, vindicates her character and social class. Esther, by sheer nobility of character, demonstrates herself to be the exception that proves the social rule. Sam and Polly are going up the ladder the only generally acceptable way, one rung at a time. George D'Alroy makes the play's thematic statement:

> *George*: Oh, Caste's all right. Caste is a good thing, if it's not carried
>   too far. It shuts the door on the pretentious and the vulgar;
>   but it should open the door very wide for exceptional merit.
>   Let brains break through its barriers, and what brains can
>   break through love may leap over.

Thus, T. W. Robertson discovered and fixed the form, the "well-made" play, that was to serve as the model for most "serious" English theater for the succeeding fifty years, and he wedded it to a Victorian ideology that was to permeate the British stage until the onslaught of George Bernard Shaw.

THE CASTLE

Type of work: Novel
Author: Franz Kafka (1883-1924)
Type of plot: Philosophical and religious allegory
Time of plot: Any time
Locale: Indefinite
First published: 1926

In this unfinished novel, sometimes referred to as a modern Pilgrim's Progress, *K. seeks the grace of God to fulfill his life but finds his path beset with all the confusion of the modern world. His straightforward attack on the obstacles surrounding the castle and his unrelenting singleness of purpose are finally rewarded, but only at the moment of his death.*

This fragmentary work was published posthumously, against Kafka's instructions, by his friend, Max Brod, and critics have been debating about it ever since, from the level of textual problems to that of the interpretation of the highly suggestive, symbolic structure. It is typical of Kafka's works that a final and convincing definition of his symbols is impossible; like dreams, they combine reference to the everyday world with absurd fantasies, seemingly coherent mythic structure with a discontinuity that frustrates attempts to develop a rational interpretation. The images he conjures up are compelling but they seem ultimately to stand for themselves, and not for any symbolic message. Is the castle to be equated with the divine, or is it a dominating force of evil? Have the villagers found their place in the world, or are they ignorant, superstitious pawns?

It is clear that the novel arises from autobiographical sources; K. is Kafka, and the bureaucracy of the castle must derive from his experience as a minor official in the state insurance company of Bohemia. The castle represents an authority akin to the Court in *The Trial,* or even the father figure in several works. But this authority is not an awesome power. Indeed, Kafka's vision of both the village and the castle is one of filth and degradation, with no shred of grandeur in the supposedly exalted powers of the hierarchy from which he so insistently demands recognition.

Thomas Mann defined Kafka as a religious humorist, and perhaps the ironic, satiric side of his work has been underestimated. If his meaning eludes the desire of critics to define, the experience of isolation, striving, frustration, ambivalence toward the community and toward the unknown forces that seem to dominate the individual and society are captured unforgettably in his work. The quest of his fictional alter egos to understand their world and to relate rightly to it in spite of seeming hopelessness has become for many the very embodiment of the predicament of twentieth century man.

THE CASTLE OF FRATTA

Type of work: Novel
Author: Ippolito Nievo (1831-1861)
Type of plot: Historical chronicle
Time of plot: 1775-1852
Locale: Italy and England
First published: 1867

Second only to Manzoni's The Betrothed *among nineteenth century Italian novels,* The Castle of Fratta *tells with passionate patriotic feeling the story of the half century of strife that led to the period of the Risorgimento and the liberation of Italy. Lucilio Vianello, undoubtedly modeled after Mazzini, is only one in the remarkable gallery of characterizations that make this vigorous novel come alive.*

The Castle of Fratta is a particularly striking example of those few master-pieces of fiction which encroach upon history, impress upon it their unity and values, and in so doing create our now conventional image of an era. The work is as much an epitaph as a confessional novel, for it became the means to the creation of the myth of Ippolito Nievo, a myth of patriotic self-lessness which would ultimately propagate the highest ideals of the Italian *Risorgimento.* Indeed, fictive and real authors seem almost to converge, for Carlo Altoviti, patriot and witness to his times, concludes his narrative in 1858 three years before the patriotic death of Ippolito Nievo at sea as he attempted to rejoin Garibaldi's "Thousand." Unfortunately, the posthumous success of *The Castle of Fratta* cast a retrospective pall over his two earlier novels *Angel of Goodness* (1855) and *The Shepherd Count* (1857). His *Verses* (1854), his numerous satires, short stories and even his two tragedies *Spartacus* and *The Capuans* fell prey to literary historians oblivious to their in-trinsic literary merit but intent on ransacking them for some anticipation of the later masterpiece. Nevertheless, few would deny the influence of Giusti and Parini on the early chapters of *The Castle of Fratta* or that of Heine (whom Nievo translated) on his satires. Above all, they revealed the influence of Tommaseo's emphasis on the importance of a strong, stable family to a resurgent nation. More important, however, than the simple identification of precursors or influences is the understanding of the new meaning they take on in the body of the work itself.

Although scholars such as Bozzetti, Mirmina, and others have devoted studies to Nievo's social thought, it is important to bear in mind that these studies are often derived from his fictional works and often retain their fictional qualities. One element that nevertheless remains constant to Nievo's social thought whatever its origin is his reluctance to divorce it from his understanding of the importance of his poetic vocation. The moral and national restoration he envisioned in his early *Verses* and his letters to Mathilde Ferrari could only be impeded by those eunuchoid poets who continued to rehearse their formulaic anguish in an ornate, archaic style incomprehensible to the peasants, the artisans, and the poor. Literary tradition and its misuse were simply another form of oppression aimed at excluding the experience of the poor from literature and culture. Such poetic language was little more than a social frippery intended to perpetuate class barriers by the inaccessibility which effectively travestied its true ends. Poetic language would have to be broken down, purified and polished into the shining mirror and window to truth which Dante had made of it. In his *Studies on Popular and Civil Poetry* Nievo reaffirmed his faith that Dante, the last poet capable of fusing the experience of an entire civilization, would inspire the masses to a national rebirth. Nievo's yearning for unity is apocalyptic: the union of upper and lower classes ultimately becomes in his thought the union of heart and mind. Poetry would be renewed by this mythicized people, whom it would in turn serve, once freed of its decadence and imbued with peasant spontaneity.

According to its Italian title, Nievo's novel is a confession: testimony to an apocalyptic spiritual renewal which marks the emergence of a new man from the corruption of his former self. In the case of Carlo Altoviti, however, this renewal is both political and pantheistic; it culminates in Carlo's new identity as citizen and Italian able to enjoy the calm of the "ocean of eternity." His transcendence of the oppressive ignorance and passion of his youth is the microcosm of the experience of Italy on the threshold of liberation from its political disintegration. If Italy's history will culminate in unification, Carlo's will culminate in the unity of the self, achieved through submission and adherence to the justice of nature. It is a truth he discovered as a boy one day when he wandered away from the dark, infernal kitchen of Fratta into the beautiful countryside. Carlo's realization of the contrast between the glory of nature and the bizarrely artificial world of Fratta climaxes in an overwhelmingly religious experience of natural beauty and its all-pervasive justice. The effect of this Edenic moral awakening is manifest in Carlo's refusal to break a promise not to reveal that it was the Spaccafumo who brought him home despite his punishment; this event marks the first time that pleasure and duty had ever struggled within him. Forever after, justice would demand self-sacrifice. The central theme of the novel lies in the ways in which Carlo overcomes all the internal and external impediments to his adherence to justice.

Carlo's moral education eventually teaches him to distinguish truth from appearance. He is taken in one moment by Father Pendola, only to realize in the next the duplicity of Advocate Ormenta; each is in turn the victim and perpetuator of a society inimical to justice in which capricious egoism has been petrified into system. Their venality represents a moral failure in what is ultimately a metaphysical struggle between the material and the spiritual. The heroes of the work are consequently those whose tenacity overcomes the resistance of the material to the spiritual: Clara's in maintaining her vows, Lucilio's in his unyielding fidèlity, and ultimately Pisana's in her renunciation of Carlo. Neither the claims of the body nor of personal happiness exempt them from the relentless demand of justice for integrity; thus, Pisana's apparently capricious demand that Carlo punish her by ripping out her hair prefigures her virtual martyrdom for his survival.

Carlo's ultimate identity as citizen and Italian as well as his origins are emblematic of the novel's concern with ethical and metaphysical justice and unity, since he was the child of East and West, was raised virtually as a savage at Fratta, and was destined to participate in both centuries of the struggle for Italian unification. Although Carlo must constantly contend with what he regards as the bestial in himself that seeks bodily ease and personal gain, it is his all-consuming love of Italy that purges his soul by demanding that he renounce the comforts of the Countess Migliana's household as well as the security of his inheritance. By this time, moral self-consciousness has become a continual ascetic awakening from the compromising ease of the material. Such moments are often accompanied by the reappearance of Pisana whose mere presence is an indictment of Carlo's moral lapses. Nevertheless, there is a striking reciprocity in their relationship, for although Carlo will expose her to the redemptory justice of nature, he will become in the end the beneficiary of his own earlier selflessness when she begs in the streets in order that he may eat. It is precisely this reciprocity that makes human brotherhood and indeed all community possible. Carlo must save Pisana from her capriciousness if he would save himself by becoming one with the "ocean of eternity," just as Pisana must sacrifice her happiness in order that Carlo may found the family on which civil order depends.

James Thomas Chiampi

THE CASTLE OF OTRANTO

Type of work: Novel
Author: Horace Walpole (1717-1797)
Type of plot: Gothic romance
Time of plot: Twelfth century
Locale: Italy
First published: 1764

This gothic novel, the first of the genre in English, is replete with all the stock character types, situations, and special effects associated with fiction of the haunted-castle-rattling-chain variety. The plot involves the evil Manfred's unlawful rule at Otranto and the eventual establishment, aided by numerous supernatural happenings, of the rightful heir, Theodore.

Horace Walpole's *The Castle of Otranto* is among the best-known, best-loved, and best-crafted novels of the Gothic genre in English. It is also one of the first. Gothic fiction was representative of the late eighteenth century rejection of the rational, realistic creed of Neo-Classicism, which asserted the superiority for literary purposes of things familiar and contemporary. This reaction was but a phase of the revival of interest in the recondite past, an interest which focused on medieval life and manifested itself in pseudo-scholarly antiquarianism, imitation Gothic castles, artificial ruins, balladry, and contrived narratives.

These narratives, permeated with fashionable melancholy, attempted to portray human conduct and sentiment with psychological realism while setting the action in remote and mysterious places and times. The emotional thrills of adventure thus provided the reader with an escape from humdrum existence. Hence, the villain was characteristically somber and restless. The heroine was beautiful, innocent, young, and sensitively perceptive; she waited dutifully to be rescued by a brave and courageous lover. The obligatory setting was a haunted castle, a cloister, or a ruined abbey, fortuitously furnished with underground passages, secret doors, and locked and unused rooms, and surrounded by wild and desolate landscape. The action inevitably included strange and deliberate crimes (often to the accompaniment of rattling chains and other inexplicable phenomena), incidents of physical violence, and emotional anguish orchestrated with supernatural manifestations. A strong erotic element usually underscored the plot. And any comic relief was, following Shakespeare's model, confined to servants. In a bogus historical setting, chronologically and geographically remote, novels of mystery and passionate emotion depicted the trials and misfortunes of sentimental love with an overlay of ghosts, prescience, and preternatural forces together with the titillating horror of violence and crime.

In the very forefront of this Gothic revival was *The Castle of Otranto*, whose author personally seemed ideally suited to his book (rather than the more usual obverse). Horace Walpole was a nobleman, respected for his antiquarian scholarship; he was also a fussy bachelor in precarious health, unable to join his peers in hunting, tippling, and wenching. He escaped the demands of this world by retreating into the past, psychologically as well as physically. He built himself a pseudo-Gothic retreat at Strawberry Hill where he displayed his collection of antiques and led an active fantasy life, imagining himself at one time a feudal lord and at another time a learned monk. Of an evening, he reportedly climbed his narrow Gothic staircase with his dog to his Gothic library to dream—possibly with the aid of opium—of the romantic past.

Out of such dreams *The Castle of Otranto* was spawned, illustrating two major themes in the Gothic novel. The story united a baroque view of architecture and sentiment in a repudiation of Neo-Classical ideals of proportion, balance, harmony, and ultimately narrow limitations. Thus the physical appearance of the Castle of Otranto was an exaggeration of genuine Gothic style, carrying the visual image to such excessive lengths that the structure bore hardly any resemblance to authentic examples of medieval Gothic architecture. Yet the effectiveness of the description is undeniable in the context of the novel. Likewise, the emotional overreaction of the characters—in defiance of all Neo-Classical canons of moderation—served a similar purpose: to transcend the mundane realities of common life on the wings of fancy. In the very uncommon life of this story, Walpole sought to liberate imagination and allow it to rove freely in what he characterized as "the boundless realms of invention . . . [thence] creating more interesting situations." Simultaneously (and without any sense of contradiction), Walpole claimed to strive for "naturalness" and "probability" in his character development. Yet fanciful setting and untrammeled emotion were the hallmarks of his—as well as many another—Gothic novel.

Nevertheless, Walpole employed supernatural devices—decidedly not natural or probable—to create the so-called interesting situations which he avowedly wanted to create. The totally immersed reader can, of course, become so wrapped up in the plot that inconsistencies escape notice. Thus, the plot itself is plausible even today, but the events surrounding it and somewhat precipitating it are more than a little suspect. The story opens with the ambiguous prophecy that "the castle and lordship of Otranto should pass from the present family, whenever the real owner should be grown too large to inhabit it." Intrigue thickens with Conrad's peculiar death and Manfred's frantic attempts to sire another heir. In due course, other supernatural manifestations intervene: two manservants see a strange apparition, which also appears to Bianca, Matilda's maid. Manfred's reasonable objections notwithstanding, these events very nearly unseat his reason. But even as Manfred argues with Hippolita to annul their marriage so that he can marry Isabella and produce an heir, three drops of blood fall from the nose of the statue of Alfonso, the original Prince of Otranto who won the principality through fraud and deceit. Manfred is thus given supernatural warning to desist from his wicked plan, but he is still undeterred. However, his intended new father-in-law also sees an apparition when he goes to the chapel to pray for guidance. In the end, after many such scenes of terror, violence, and bewilderment, the true heir of Otranto is unexpectedly discovered amid a thunderclap, a rattling of armor, and a disembodied pronouncement about legitimate succession.

All of these contrivances may strain the credulity of today's reader—but only in retrospect. For the chain of events is so enveloping that the act of reading suspends one's normal skepticism to such an extent that customary doubt and ordinary questions are held in abeyance. It is only after the fact that the reader begins to examine the logic and question the veracity of Walpole's highly convincing tale. And therein lies the art of the story.

Joanne G. Kashdan

CASTLE RACKRENT

Type of work: Novel
Author: Maria Edgeworth (1767-1849)
Type of plot: Social criticism
Time of plot: Eighteenth century
Locale: Ireland
First published: 1800

In this attack on the dissolute lives of absentee landlords in eighteenth century Ireland, Edgeworth depicts the gradual fall to ruin of a succession of irresponsible members of the Rackrent family. The author's use of an Irish servant as narrator imbues the story with a tone of candor and straightforwardness, enhanced by the colorful Irish wit and language.

Maria Edgeworth was famous in her day as the author of seven novels and as a writer concerned with the education of children, an interest shared with her father, Richard Lovell Edgeworth. An Irish landowner, Edgeworth settled his family in Ireland in 1782, when Maria was at the impressionable age of fifteen. He was an intellectual, a believer in social and political reform, father of a large family, and mentor to his illustrious daughter. Throughout his life, Maria Edgeworth deferred to his tastes, seeking not only his guidance, but also his collaboration in much of her writing.

Castle Rackrent is the author's first novel, written some time between 1797 and 1799, published in 1800. It is a distinguished piece of work in several ways. A successful first novel, generally regarded as her best, it is also one of the few works in which Richard Lovell Edgeworth had no part. The author herself declared that "it went to the press just as it was written."

In addition, *Castle Rackrent* holds a distinction in the history of the English novel as the first regional novel, a significance noted by Sir Walter Scott in the Preface to his first historical novel, *Waverley* (1814), when he stated his purpose of creating a Scottish milieu with the same degree of authenticity as "that which Miss Edgeworth so fortunately achieved for Ireland." In her own Preface, Miss Edgeworth takes pains to indicate the realistically Irish quality of the novel. Her first-person narrator, Thady Quirk, a character based upon her father's steward, speaks in Irish idiom because "the authenticity of his story would have been more exposed to doubt if it were not told in his own characteristic manner." Moreover, the subject is peculiarly Irish: "Those who were acquainted with the manners of a certain class of the gentry of Ireland some years ago, will want no evidence of the truth of honest Thady's narrative."

In the use of certain devices, she anticipates the historical novel later developed by Scott, for example in the historicity suggested by the subtitle: "An Hibernian Tale Taken from Facts, and from the Manners of Irish Squires, Before the Year 1782." More explicitly, Miss Edgeworth assures her readers that "these are 'tales of other times'; . . . the manners depicted . . . are not those of the present age: the race of the Rackrents has long been extinct in Ireland." Similar to the kind of documentation Scott was to employ is her anecdotal glossary of Irish "terms and idiomatic phrases." The convention of the "true story," of course, is an eighteenth century legacy; and, like many eighteenth century novels, *Castle Rackrent* purports to be an original memoir for which the author is merely the editor.

The theme of *Castle Rackrent* adumbrates Scott's characteristic theme, the conflict between a dying culture and a culture coming into being. But the resemblance stops there. Lacking historical events and personages, the Rackrent story is not too remote in time from the date of composition. Although the Rackrents indulge in gloriously absurd deeds—for example, the sham wake staged by Sir Condy in order to spy upon his own mourners— there are no heroic deeds in their bygone age. The name "Rackrent," referring to the exorbitant rents exacted by landlords from their tenants, reveals their main traits.

Thus the novel is a satire on the Irish ruling class. With the sustained irony of Thady's blind "partiality to *the family* in which he was bred and born," the author presents their reprehensible history. Except for Sir Murtagh, who wastes his fortune in lawsuits, all the Rackrents ruin themselves and their estates through extravagance and dissipation. Whether they are squires in residence or absentee landlords dealing through agents "who grind the face of the poor," they increase the misery of the common Irishman. Concealed behind Thady's comical anecdotes is the judgment that the Rackrents represent the destructive arrogance and stupidity of irresponsible landowners who answer to no one except, eventually, moneylenders such as Thady's ruthless son Jason, who finally takes possession of the Rackrent estates.

However, despite the title of the novel and Thady's unwavering focus on the Rackrents, even despite some unforgettable comic episodes of Rackrent peccadilloes, the novel is centered upon Thady himself, his voice speaking in self-importance:

> Having out of friendship for the family, upon whose estate, praised be Heaven! I and mine have lived rent free time out of mind, voluntarily undertaken to publish the Memoirs of the Rackrent Family, I think it my duty to say a few words, in the first place, concerning myself.

His self-importance is based upon his illusions of the family grandeur and the reflected glory he enjoys. If he lives by his professed loyalty, he acts upon the example of his masters. He exploits his privileges as they do, blind to the inevitable outcome. For example, throughout the novel, Thady boasts of various strategies to push forward "my son Jason," who acquires his first lease on Rackrent land because "I spoke a good word for my son, and gave out in the county that nobody need bid against us"—and, comments the opportunistic Thady, "why shouldn't he as well as another?" Yet he complains bitterly of Jason grown rich: " . . . he is a high gentleman, and never minds what poor Thady says, and having better than 1500 a-year, landed estate, looks down upon honest Thady, but I wash my hands of his doings, and as I have lived so will I die, true and loyal to the family."

Thady's praise of the Rackrents is often coupled with his appreciation of wealth. When a new heir neglects Thady, the old man is hostile. However, the first casual attention produces a characteristic response, in which money is amusingly mingled with family: "I loved him from that day to this, his voice was so like the family—and he threw me a guinea out of his waistcoat pocket." Another trait incompatible with honest devotion is Thady's evasive habit of silence at crucial moments, a silence very much at odds with his characteristic garrulity. There is a self-serving tone in the recurring motif, "I said nothing for fear of gaining myself ill will."

On the other hand, Thady's talkativeness, urged by vanity, contributes to the downfall of his favorite, Sir Condy, the last of the Rackrents. Though it is Thady's son who seizes the property, it is Thady who makes the youthful Condy his "white-headed boy," feeding his imagination with the disastrous "stories of the family and the blood from which he was sprung." He proudly takes credit for the adult Condy's unfortunate gambling instincts, boasting that "I well remember teaching him to toss up for bog berries on my knee." The ultimate irony is that his teachings indirectly bring about Sir Condy's death; for the family legend of Sir Patrick's prodigious whiskey-drinking feat, which the last Rackrent fatally duplicates, is "the story that he learned from me when a child."

Torn between his son and his master, called by his niece an "unnatural fader," he confesses, "I could not upon my conscience tell which was wrong from the right." He is unaware, even as he explains it, that Rackrent rights derive from money, even as Jason's pretensions do. Not even the designation "ancient" is appropriate for the Rackrents, the estate having come into "*the* family" in Thady's great-grandfather's time when Sir Patrick, by act of Parliament, took the surname in order to receive the property. Thady's dilemma is treated comically, but there is pathos, too, in the position in which he finds himself in the end: "I'm tired wishing for any thing in this world, after all I've seen in it—but I'll say nothing; it would be a folly to be getting myself ill will in my old age."

Thady Quirk is a masterful characterization, requiring none of the apologies which Maria Edgeworth as fictitious editor appends to his memoirs. However, the appended remarks serve the purpose, not so much of the author of fiction, but of the daughter of Richard Lovell Edgeworth, as she offers as her last word on the moral dilemma so convincingly portrayed in this short novel her thoughts concerning a political resolution: "It is a problem of difficult solution to determine whether an Union will hasten or retard the amelioration of this country." Sir Walter Scott later praised her fictional Irishmen, England's "gay and kind-hearted neighbours," as having "done more towards completing the Union" than any subsequent legislation. Fortunately, Thady Quirk lives on as a fictional character, independent of the long-standing tumultuous relations between England and Ireland.

Catherine E. Moore

CASUALS OF THE SEA

Type of work: Novel
Author: William McFee (1881-1966)
Type of plot: Domestic realism
Time of plot: Early twentieth century
Locale: England
First published: 1916

This study of a family focuses on the careers of three children as they attempt to settle on a course of living that suits their individual personalities and idiosyncrasies. Either directly or peripherally their fates are bound up with the sea, and it is in the scenes aboard ship that McFee's writing is most vivid and memorable.

William McFee's *Casuals of the Sea* is an example of one of the hundreds of novels which come out each year, receive good but not spectacular reviews, and then fall into obscurity after a year or so. The reason for the disappearance of such novels is not necessarily that they were not good pieces of literature, but that another set of novels were written to take their place on the reading tables of the general public.

Casuals of the Sea could not be considered a modern classic in the sense of *The Grapes of Wrath* or *Of Human Bondage,* in that it is not being continually read and criticized, but still it has merits which rank it as a fine novel. One of the elements which made it a success and which continues to make it pleasant reading today is its treatment of the sea scenes. McFee had spent considerable time at sea and, in fact, had written much of the novel aboard ship, although it was completed while he was living in the United States. His experience with the common seaman made his characters and their adventures at sea seem quite real to the land-locked reader. The characterizations of ordinary seamen and the English common man gave substance to a story whose plot alone might not have held the reader's interest.

An interesting sidelight of the book is McFee's treatment of the advertising world when Minnie takes to writing slogans for cough medicine. It amuses the modern reader, familiar as he is with anti-Madison Avenue literature, to find that advertising could have produced ill effects apparent enough to make the field a source of scorn in a work written in the early part of the twentieth century.

CATILINE

Type of work: Drama
Author: Ben Jonson (1573?-1637)
Type of plot: Political tragedy
Time of plot: First century B.C.
Locale: Ancient Rome
First presented: 1611

Jonson prided himself on the historical accuracy of his tragedies, and diligent research went into the writing of Catiline. *Since the action in the play involves nations rather than individuals, however, audiences have missed the personal, emotional touch and have consequently not responded to the work with the enthusiasm its workmanship deserves.* Catiline *is an intellectual drama, and foreshadows—both in its characterizations and its sculptural verse—scenes from Milton.*

To watch a dramatic work by Ben Jonson come alive on the stage, one must go to *Volpone* (1605) or *The Alchemist* (1610). Catiline's monstrous conspiracy is deftly and engagingly developed, and the ghost scene which opens the play is intensely dramatic. However, Cicero's orations were too fulsome and long-winded for Jonson's Elizabethan audience, which applauded the first two acts but jeered the third, much to Jonson's disgust. Three centuries of prospective producers have elected not to fly in the face of that lesson.

In his preface to the text, the truculent Jonson vilified the audience which had failed to appreciate the King's Player's production, a response characteristic of that feisty intellectual aristocrat when his work was criticized. Jonson considered *Catiline* his classical masterpiece. In it he had taken pains to avoid the shortcomings of his earlier and more ambitions classical tragedy, *Sejanus* (1603). *Catiline* features a Greek chorus, and observes the classical unities of time, place, and action. It is admirable for its carefully delineated characters, impressive rhetoric, and inexorable march of events. But dramatically the plot is weak. It has too many characters and too little interaction between the protagonist and antagonist. The action seems disjointed and rambling, and, typically for Jonson, none of the female characters is sympathetically drawn.

Because Catiline is too unmitigated a villain for his fall to seem truly tragic, his conspiracy becomes a social rather than an individual tragedy. The escape from condemnation of Caesar, whose complicity Jonson had emphasized, expands the social message of the play. The infamous Gunpowder Plot of 1605 had dramatized the dangers to a free society of conspiracies and of Caesars who might attempt to capitalize on them. *Catiline,* with a moral tone that assuredly recommended it to the Puritan censors, emphasizes the need for social order.

CAVALLERIA RUSTICANA

Type of work: Story
Author: Giovanni Verga (1840-1922)
Type of plot: Naturalism
Time of plot: Mid-nineteenth century
Locale: Sicily
First published: 1880

This story of swift passions, violence, and revenge reveals Verga's sympathy for the ignorant and downtrodden poor and his anger at seeing the innocent taken advantage of by those more cunning and worldly. Nevertheless, he recognizes also— and describes with relentless realism—that peasants in their greed, vulgarity, and stupidity often destroy others of their own class.

Ironically, Giovanni Verga's greatest strengths as an artist, as well as his limitations, lie in his immersion in the life and spirit of Sicily. Verga was spiritually and emotionally molded by his Sicilian upbringing; and although throughout his literary career he made repeated attempts to shift his focus and widen the range of his subject matter, he ultimately realized that his true genius lay in his capacity to explore the hearts of his Sicilian countrymen. The problem, however, was that over the course of years this single theme proved limited; after Verga had revealed every aspect of the life he knew so well in depth and with great insight and sensitivity, nothing remained but to reiterate the theme and recast the old story in superficially new ways.

Verga's story *Cavalleria Rusticana* represents the author's talent at its best. The simple story, of a basically good-hearted but rather weak-minded young man swept by jealousy into passions he cannot control or understand, is a familiar one; in Verga's hands the tale achieves heights of emotional intensity yet remains starkly simple in its powerful realism. Characters and land alike come to life through the carefully observed and meticulously recorded detail. Particularly apparent in *Cavalleria Rusticana* is the author's deep love for humanity, and especially for the poor and ignorant, the helpless and suffering.

Also representative of Verga's outlook is the feeling of powerlessness which pervades the story: behind all the events and characterizations lies a pessimistic resignation, a sense of destiny, a conviction that events in man's life are not subject to his free choice. Yet this fatalistic vision does not evince an emotional response from the author; his tone is always strictly objective and calm— sad perhaps, but unresentful. In *Cavalleria Rusticana,* as in all Verga's fiction, there is no mention of God—although the author was born and died a Catholic—and no attempt to personalize the external forces responsible for man's essentially tragic situation. Likewise, there is no concept of sin in the story; man is not to be blamed for his actions, which are inevitable, but pitied. Turiddu and the other peasants command our sympathy because they are not guilty of willful crimes so much as they are victimized by passions larger than they can comprehend.

CAWDOR

Type of work: **Poem**
Author: Robinson Jeffers (1887-1962)
Type of plot: Psychological realism
Time of plot: 1900
Locale: Carmel Coast Range, California
First published: 1928

In this poem about violence and self-inflicted suffering, Jeffers depicts charac-ters who live entirely inward lives, with no creative outlets or ability to communi-cate with and help one another. In keeping with his pessimistic and violent view of life, the author urges merely that man find the strength to exist until death brings welcome release.

Robinson Jeffers was born in 1887 in Pittsburgh, Pennsylvania, where he spent his early childhood and received his early education. He later attended various European and American preparatory schools, graduating finally from Occidental College in Los Angeles, California. Jeffers' private life was at times rather unstable, as a result of which he moved to the Big Sur area of California, where he continued to write and live in isolation until his death in 1962.

Jeffers is well known as an inhumanist poet and has also achieved recog-nition as a dramatist. His prose poem-play, *Medea,* which he freely adapted from the Greek of Euripides, won wide acclaim both from a literary and a dramatic standpoint when it was first produced with Judith Anderson in the title role.

He first received notice as a poet with the publication of early works such as *Tamar* and *Roan Stallion.* His popularity diminished, however, in 1927 with the appearance of *The Women at Point Sur,* an extremely controversial poem, the vulgarity of which revolted his readers as well as most critical reviewers. It was in reaction to this rejection that he wrote the epic-length prose poem *Cawdor.* It was an attempt to reconcile his readers by essentially playing upon the same themes which had produced *The Women at Point Sur,* but present-ing these themes in a medium more palatable to his public.

His title character, Cawdor, is a man who has turned away from society and who has made his life in a remote area of the California coast, managing to live, if not in harmony with nature, then at least with a minimum of disso-nance. In the course of the plot, Cawdor is thrown into conflict with nature, the ultimate point being reached with his murder of his son. Fera, who acts as catalyst in the story, comes to represent the inherent evil of humanity, and she brings Cawdor eventually to realize that humanity is truly inhumanity.

Jeffers uses the mountains, canyons, and sea of the Big Sur country to create a complex set of symbols. The eagle, symbol of nature's consciousness which Cawdor can neither fathom nor understand, is perhaps the best and most complete example of Jeffers poetry at its best.

Jeffers uses the plot line of *Oedipus Rex* in an inverted form, but he retains the Oedipal ending. Cawdor, like Oedipus, must punish himself, but may not kill himself because to do so would end his punishment. Jeffers fails to create a pure tragedy, but he succeeds in exploring the sense of epic tragedy, which he evokes, but is unable to resolve.

CECILIA

Type of work: Novel
Author: Fanny Burney (Madame d'Arblay, 1752-1840)
Type of plot: Sentimental novel of manners
Time of plot: Eighteenth century
Locale: England
First published: 1782

This novel, a line from which gave Austen's Pride and Prejudice *its title, is a pleasant blend of wit, sentiment, and morality. If* Cecilia *suffers from narrative weakness, it nevertheless merits our attention for its delightful caricatures and lively depictions of eighteenth century manners.*

Following the artistic achievement of *Evelina,* Fanny Burney's second novel, *Cecilia,* is in many ways a disappointment; it suffers from weaknesses of plotting, characterization, and narrative method. In spite of its flaws, however, the novel drew appreciative praise from writers such as Dr. Samuel Johnson and Edmund Burke; and even modern readers, who are distracted by Burney's sentimentality and didacticism, still find enjoyment in the amusing caricatures and the lively reproduction of eighteenth century manners.

The plot of *Cecilia* is divided into two halves, the first dealing with the heroine's financial problems during her minority, when part of her inheritance is controlled by her guardians and part is held in suspension awaiting her marriage; and the second relating the course of her romantic attachment to Mortimer Delvile. The action in both portions of the story is packed with highly improbable, unbelievable events and with sensational or melodramatic incidents. Coincidences such as Cecilia's chance meeting with Belfield's sister and mother, Mrs. Delvile's sudden stroke brought on by a broken blood vessel, and Mortimer's handy proximity when Cecilia reveals her inmost feelings to his dog, tax the reader's credulity. The plot is also replete with all the accoutrements of melodrama, including a duel, an elopement, the temporary insanity and near-fatal illness of the heroine, and the macabre suicide of her profligate guardian. In addition to its overburdened plot, *Cecilia* is cluttered with too many characters who are never explored in any detail; the major figures tend to be wooden, static, and one-dimensional, while the minor ones are often caricatures who fail to amuse because they are overdrawn or belabored.

Most of these shortcomings in *Cecilia* can be traced to Burney's decision to abandon the more limited, but highly successful, epistolary form which she had used in *Evelina,* in favor of the omniscient author technique. Her use of this point of view leads Burney into several pitfalls: she describes her characters rather than allowing them dramatically to reveal their personalities through action and dialogue; she replaces her natural sparkling prose with a more stilted and formal style; she adopts a serious, somewhat heavy tone in place of her characteristic ironic, but tolerant, comic voice; she creates in Cecilia Beverley a young woman too aloof and thoroughly virtuous to be easily identified with; and she frequently interrupts the narrative to moralize and comment in her own voice. Regardless of these flaws, however, *Cecilia* has its artistic merits. The masquerade party and the opera are excellent examples of vivid scene-painting in the best novel of manners tradition; a few of the minor characters, such as Mrs. Belfield and Honoria, are unforgettable comic portraits; and despite its improbability, the plot still has qualities of suspense and vitality.

CELESTINA

Type of work: Novel
Author: Fernando de Rojas (1475?-1538?)
Type of plot: Tragi-comedy
Time of plot: Fifteenth century
Locale: Spain, probably Toledo
First published: Burgos edition, 1499; Seville edition, 1502

The author's avowed purpose in this work, besides providing pleasant philosophy and instruction to young people, was to warn against the tricks of bawds and designing servants. In spite of its cynical realism and frank descriptions of life among prostitutes, Celestina *is essentially an idealistic and romantic love story. Along with their coarse language, even the servants cite philosophy and quote the ancients.*

Modern critics agree that *Celestina* is among the best novels in Spanish literature. The plot itself is derivative, stemming from an anonymous thirteenth century Latin poem, *Pamphilus* (the protagonist's name, which Rojas converted to Calisto), which is not readily available in English translation. The *Pamphilus* story was also incorporated as an episode in the *Libro de Buen Amor* by the "Archpriest of Hita," Juan Ruiz, in the fourteenth century. Rojas is known to have had access to both the original *Pamphilus* and the reduction in Juan Ruiz's *Libro de Buen Amor*. But Rojas greatly altered his source material.

Rojas, in effect, shifted the emphasis, wittingly or unwittingly, from a simple, tragic love story to a powerful tale of a bawdy go-between and practicing witch. The focus, therefore, is on Celestina and not on the "star-crossed lovers." This concentration upon surreptitious match-making and witchcraft is, at least in part, a reflection of the interests of the times. Rojas (a Jew converted to Christianity under the threat of immolation at the hands of the Holy Inquisition) was distinctly aware of the fate of witches and other heretics. His portrait of Celestina is thus acutely sensitive and extraordinarily vivid. And Celestina—not Calisto or Melibea—consequently becomes the protagonist of the novel.

Celestina has no religious identification; she could be Christian, Moslem, or Jew, for all three faiths co-existed in late medieval Spain. Her allegiance seems firmly rooted in the spirits of evil, judging from her imperious conjuration of the devil in Act III. Her affiliation with the occult is firmly established in the catalog of her pharmaceuticals detailed in Acts I, III, and VII, and elsewhere. From her early sympathy for Areusa's abdominal cramps to her own susceptibility to fears of death, she remains a very human and humane being. Celestina truly recognizes the limitations of her powers; and in that recognition, she becomes a vulnerable, credible human being with relevance to her times and to our own.

THE CENCI

Type of work: Dramatic poem
Author: Percy Bysshe Shelley (1792-1822)
Type of plot: Romantic tragedy
Time of plot: 1599
Locale: Rome and the Apennines
First published: 1819

This is the tale of a cruel and brutal father whose torment of his family reaches demonic proportions. When Cenci ends by raping his daughter Beatrice, the heroine, she plots his murder, for which she is at last executed. Often considered lurid sensationalism, the poem actually shares the same characteristics of tragedy found in Prometheus Unbound.

Because of its unnatural, even unseemly, themes *The Cenci* has been largely dismissed as one of the most sensational and lurid works by a young poet given to excesses in life and art. Even Shelley's admirers have tended to think of this closet drama as they do of Shelley's extravagances in living, such as his brash atheism in youth and his strange notion that his first and second wives might live in harmony together. But Shelley's idiosyncracies are deceptive. They have an inner consistency fired by his fierce idealism.

The Cenci is a "Gothic" piece in surface only. It is actually the sister work to his other famous closet drama, the epic lyric work *Prometheus Unbound.* Both works are, as his wife and editor Mary Shelley put it, "beautiful idealisms of moral excellence." Just as Prometheus rebels in his heart against the tyranny of Jupiter, Beatrice Cenci reaches the point where any further toleration of her father's tyranny becomes unthinkable. His rape of her is only the crowning act of a life devoted to Satanic evil. The difference between Beatrice and Prometheus is that the Titan conquers Jupiter through love, his love of earth and Asia, his beloved consort or, as Blake would put it, "Emanation." Beatrice has no one through whom love can release the liberating forces necessary to save her humanity. Orsino is a self-interested schemer. Left to her own devices, Beatrice's very innocence becomes the tragic instrument of her destruction. She thinks revenge enough, and experience never permits her to test that principle. Unlike Prometheus, who is chained for an eternity to the rock and suffers his way to spiritual deliverance, Beatrice is marched off to her execution.

Shelley's conception of Beatrice as a tragic heroine is absolutely sound. Not only does she meet the Aristotelian standards, but her contrast to Prometheus underscores Shelley's hope that man could move from tragedy to lyric happiness, from the contradictions of experience to the salvation of liberated hope.

CÉSAR BIROTTEAU

Type of work: Novel
Author: Honoré de Balzac (1799-1850)
Type of plot: Naturalism
Time of plot: Early nineteenth century
Locale: Paris
First published: 1837

This novel follows the career of a commercial perfumer from his beginning days as a handyman and errand boy, through his climb to a zenith of prosperity, and finally to his downfall into bankruptcy. Opinion of the relative merits of the work have differed greatly. It is an excellent portrait of honesty and diligence in a good man, but the study is dulled, for example, by monotonous digressions on the endless legal details of the bankruptcy proceedings.

Balzac's approach to novel writing was, at least in part, scientific. He was fascinated by the unfolding or the sudden explosion of some vice, passion, or mania which threatened to transform or break up a normal life. In *César Birotteau* the setting is bourgeois Paris, and the human being under the microscope is César, a self-made man who, with the aid of some Parisian scoundrels, destroys himself. The novel shows that craving for success can become a mania as much as the craving for money or power or amorous conquest.

For Balzac, environment and heredity explained both character and fate. This novel is the tale of a parvenu, an "epic of the Bourgeoisie," as Balzac called it, but the protagonist is not satirized as much as analyzed and understood. Energy, more than intelligence, is responsible for César's success, yet when he fails because of overreaching, his honesty commands respect and admiration. César learned the principle rule of city life, "each for himself," but his innate integrity was stronger than this cynical philosophy.

In Balzac's fiction, the events in the public and private lives of the characters are always linked with setting, specifically with architecture. When perfumer César, deputy-Mayor of Paris and recently appointed to the Legion of Honor, builds a ballroom and remodels his house, his fortunes begin to decline. Balzac's imaginary world in *César Birotteau* is one in which rent and bills must be paid, creditors kept at bay, marriage contracts scrutinized, and money constantly found for pleasure and business; these things determine the pattern of life for César and most of the characters. César Birotteau is perhaps the supreme example in the Human Comedy of a man caught in the financial web. The novel is brilliantly structured, with the two balls as framework for the story of César's rise and fall, and the final brief moment of triumph.

THE CHAINBEARER

Type of work: Novel
Author: James Fenimore Cooper (1789-1851)
Type of plot: Historical romance
Time of plot: About 1785
Locale: Upstate New York
First published: 1845

In The Chainbearer *Cooper combines his storytelling talents with social criticism in dealing with the relationship between landlords and renters, in which debate he sides with the former group. In spite of Cooper's usual weakness of stereotyped or wooden characters, lack of subtlety, and excessive romanticism, the novel enjoys a fast-moving, entertaining storyline.*

For his trilogy, *The Littlepage Manuscripts,* James Fenimore Cooper took his cue from a contemporary controversy which had its roots in the eighteenth century. Centered in north-central New York state, the Anti-Rent movement, as the controversy was called, stemmed from a conflict between the feudal-agrarian practices established by eighteenth century landowners and perpetuated by their heirs on the one hand, and the democratic-industrial demands of tenants on the other. The issue was joined in the early 1840's when landowners refused tenants' requests to abolish feudal rents required in perpetuity. A tenants' rebellion, the Anti-Rent War, was put down by troops, but in 1846, the new state constitution prohibited landlords from imposing perpetual dues or services when selling or leasing land.

Cooper's trilogy, published in 1845 and 1846 at the culmination of the controversy, traces three generations of a landowning family, the Littlepages, from the eighteenth century Cornelius Littlepage in *Satanstoe,* through Mordaunt Littlepage of *The Chainbearer,* to the nineteenth century Hugh Littlepage of *The Redskins.* The first of these novels focuses on the Littlepage estate at Satanstoe in Westchester County, New York, and the last, on the Littlepage confrontation with Anti-Rent agitators disguised as Indians. The second novel suggests by its title that attention will center on the Dutchman Andries Coejemans, called Chainbearer. However, the tale is cast in first-person narrative, the story being told by Mordaunt Littlepage.

The limitations of this narrative form are thus the limitations of *The Chainbearer* as a novel. In order to avoid straining the reader's credulity, Littlepage can report only what he has seen, what has been said to him, or what he has read, overheard, or found accidentally; he cannot tell about things he could or should not know, and he cannot read the minds of other characters. Consequently, the very form of the novel mandates that more be revealed about the narrator Mordaunt Littlepage than about the putative protagonist, Chainbearer. The narrator must be fully developed as a character at the expense of not developing other characters in the novel. Yet, the epic scope of the trilogy is made coherent by its concentration on the Little-page family, so *The Chainbearer* can hardly be faulted for spotlighting Mordaunt Littlepage.

The advantages of first person narrative offset many of its limitations: the eyewitness account enhances credibility, and the directness of communication creates a high degree of sympathy between narrator and reader. The result, in *The Chainbearer,* is that the reader tends to sympathize with Mordaunt Littlepage and by extension with the position of the landowners against the Anti-Renters. Still, such sympathy is a function of form rather than ideology; ideology, however, affects characterization. For the unreconstructibly romantic Cooper, characters were either noble in mind and beneficent in spirit (Mordaunt Littlepage and Chainbearer, for example) or petty in mind and mean in spirit (particularly Thousandacres), in a stark juxtaposition of good and evil. Despite so simplistic a moral viewpoint—and despite the liabilities inherent in the narrative form—Cooper has nonetheless produced an exciting adventure story worthy of more attention than it has received.

THE CHANGELING

Type of work: Drama
Authors: Thomas Middleton (1580-1627) and William Rowley (1585?-1642?)
Type of plot: Romantic tragedy
Time of plot: Early seventeenth century
Locale: Alicante, a seaport on the east coast of Spain
First presented: 1622

The greatest distinction of this drama is the brilliant characterization of the villainous protagonist De Flores, whose singleminded ambition and brutal cynicism are drawn with memorable skill. Its main plot attributable to Middleton, The Changeling *suffers from inclusion of the trivial and tasteless subplot contributed by Rowley.*

Despite its relatively late date of composition, remnants of the popular revenge play form can be found in *The Changeling,* particularly in the subplot. The use of the ghost and dumb show, irrelevant to the main plot, goes back to pre-Shakespearean drama. The actual protagonist of the play, De Flores, is clearly a Machiavellian figure. He is a villain, but is more complicated than his prototype of fifty years earlier would have been. He is captivated by Beatrice, despite himself. Beatrice, too, is a fascinating character, caught in a chain of sin. The opening of the drama finds her more amoral than truly immoral, but she becomes immoral after realizing that she is in truth damned. Gradually, she comes to love evil. The playwrights are not interested so much in what happens to these characters as in *why* it happens —in what their motivations and values are. Underneath a veneer of sensationalism, then, is a complex psychological drama.

More so than Rowley, Thomas Middleton drew men as he saw them, writing with comic gusto and searching irony. He learned to write plays by collaborating with Thomas Dekker, John Webster, and other authors for Henslowe's boy players. Later, he wrote for many theaters, including the Swan and the Globe. He wrote entertainments on commission for civic occasions and had a major success with the political satire *A Game at Chesse,* which eventually was suppressed by James I. But his masterpieces were the two tragedies *Women Beware Women* and *The Changeling,* both powerful studies of crime and its psychological effects. The willful and passionate Beatrice clears the way in *The Changeling* to marry for love by arranging a murder. However, she finds herself at the mercy of the murderer. But De Flores has no mercy: "Can you weep Fate from its determined purpose? So soon may you weep me." Beatrice is "the dead's creature." Middleton, as T. S. Eliot observed, was a "great observer of human nature, without fear, without sentiment, without prejudice."

CHARLES DEMAILLY

Type of work: Novel
Authors: Edmond (1822-1896) and Jules (1830-1870) de Goncourt
Type of plot: Naturalism
Time of plot: Mid-nineteenth century
Locale: Paris
First published: 1860

Interwoven in this story of the effects of the world on a hypersensitive young writer are frequent discussions on art and literature. In this early naturalist work, the Goncourt brothers turned their interest in the secrets behind human behavior to a dissection of the world of letters.

Charles Demailly attempts to show realistically the hardships of establishing a career as a writer, to portray the struggle against lack of recognition, the stages of the writer's progress through indifference and insults, and the sense of powerlessness that results from these frustrations. Many of the characters in the novel (Couturat, Malgras, Florissac, Bourniche) are based on people the Goncourt brothers knew. Boisroger is an affectionate portrait of their good friend Théodore de Banville. The Balzacian biographical sketch of the solicitor Nachette in the second chapter is based on Edmond's own experience in a solicitor's office.

The novel possesses none of the perfection of construction of *Sister Philomène,* nor is it as brilliantly executed as *Manette Salomon.* But confused as *Charles Demailly* is, it remains as interesting evidence of the Goncourts' inner life and mental attitudes. They borrowed copiously from their *Journal* when they wrote it. Their hatred of women and their theory that celibacy is necessary for the artist are present in this book. Charles, the victim of a former mistress, dies insane. One is not sure why the Goncourts held this grudge against women, but the theme runs through all of their novels, including the much better late novel, *Manette Salomon.*

It is difficult to analyze the brothers' method of collaboration, but it is considered that in the historical works and biographical studies of artists, Edmond's part was the more important, while in *Charles Demailly* and *Manette Salomon,* especially in regard to style, Jules dominated. An obsession which both brothers shared, which figures in most of the novels and particularly in *Charles Demailly,* is that toward illness. The hero presents an exact parallel of the Goncourts' own conditions; Jules, for example, suffered from and probably died from syphilis. They deliberately dissected their own mental and physical states while writing *Charles Demailly,* consciously sacrificing themselves for what they believed was great art.

CHARLES O'MALLEY

Type of work: Novel
Author: Charles Lever (1806-1872)
Type of plot: Picaresque romance
Time of plot: 1808-1812
Locale: Ireland and Europe
First published: 1841

The value of this light, romantic novel lies in its rich fund of anecdotes of Irish prowess and cunning. Because it painted a highly romanticized picture of the Napoleonic wars, it makes for entertaining reading. To O'Malley, war is a gaily adventurous affair much like a combination of fox hunt and banquet.

Charles O'Malley portrays a world that existed for very few people, if, indeed, it existed at all. It is a romantic and adventurous world shown in the novel, one in which honor rises above all other considerations: honor in the hunt, in battle, in politics, and in love. If necessary, duels will be fought to preserve this honor. The code can never be broken without losing caste, and, of course, the "fair sex" must be worshiped and, at all times, protected. The characters in the novel are filled out with a multitude of eccentricities of personality and behavior, but hold conventional values and are redeemed by conventional virtues. Only in such a romantic never-never-land could the protagonist's life be determined by the casual word of a girl (when Lucy remarks that any man worth noticing should be a dragoon).

The narrative is filled out by numerous anecdotes, many of which have little to do directly with the plot, but which often are amusing. Much of the humor relies on exaggerated personality quirks or on outlandish behavior, but the customs and habits of the Irish come in for a good share of humorous play, particularly the subjects of death and wakes and drinking. The accounts of Irish electioneering at the beginning of the nineteenth century are interesting and often possess a more unforced and natural humor than many of the other tales. However, Lever is not at heart a satirist. He ridicules, rather than satirizes, people and positions, as with Sir Harry Boyle, the "well-known member of the Irish House of Commons" who has so got into the "habit of making bulls that I can't write sense when I want it."

This thousand-page novel is the kind of book that once was read aloud by the fire to pass away long evenings. Today readers would be less patient with its rambling and not always witty digressions. Nevertheless, buried in the book are many nuggets of rich and genuine humor and innocent gaiety. Charles is a naïve hero, an Irish cousin of Tom Jones, in many respects, and is infectiously likable, whatever his mistakes. It is no surprise to the reader that he seems to spend a great part of his time rescuing the beautiful Lucy, or that, in the end, they are married. Anything can happen in such a romantic world, even a personal summons from Napoleon and permission to watch the battle of Waterloo from the French side.

THE CHARTERHOUSE OF PARMA

Type of work: Novel
Author: Stendhal (Marie-Henri Beyle, 1783-1842)
Type of plot: Historical romance
Time of plot: Early nineteenth century
Locale: Italy
First published: 1839

This early example of French romanticism depicts the complicated political and romantic intrigues of the Italian court of the principality of Parma. The involved plot is crowded with adventures both lighthearted and tragic; but the story also contains the elements of social comedy and underlying serious reflections on the futility of life.

The Charterhouse of Parma (La Chartreuse de Parme), the second of Stendhal's great masterpieces, was written just three years before his death. Written in is entirety over a seven-week period, the novel represented its author's return to his spiritual homeland of Italy; with its intensely beautiful landscapes and vividly detailed descriptive passages, the book is on one level a poetic hymn to the Italian spirit and land. On another level it is the complicated story of four people's search for happiness, a story rich in psychological revelations and social and historical insights. On whatever level The Charterhouse of Parma is read, however, it unfailingly impresses its readers with its unmistakably magical quality and its pervasive atmosphere of happiness fraught with gentle melancholy and romantic yearning.

The Charterhouse of Parma has often been likened to a Mozart symphony; the important section at the beginning of the novel, in which the young Fabrizio runs away to join Napoleon's army, can easily be read as a musical prelude which contains the seeds of all the themes and action to follow. When Fabrizio, after a series of mishaps and near escapes, manages to find the scene of the battle of Waterloo, it is already in progress. Instead of giving a panoramic, chronologically accurate account of the event, Stendhal fires a barrage of impressionistic detail at the reader, which leaves him at first overwhelmed and bewildered; he is as lost as Fabrizio, who in his confusion spends a whole day searching for the regiment from which he has been separated. He repeatedly stops soldiers and officers to ask them, amidst smoke and grapeshot, where the battle is. But slowly the individual, seemingly random details accumulate. Fleeing soldiers; deafening noise; a corpse trampled in the grass; the incessant cannon booming; fire, smoke, and infantry crowded so close that all sense of direction and movement is lost—all these images gradually coalesce to produce a total effect of the horror of war remarkable in its vividness and realism. At the same time, this portion of the novel serves as prelude by showing us the crucial aspects of Fabrizio's personality which are to be focal points in the narrative's later action. Against the grimness of the war backdrop, the figure of Fabrizio stands in happy contrast: he is youthful, fresh, and innocent; he has boundless enthusiasm and natural curiosity; he enjoys invincible high spirits and is filled with innate courage and grace. And although he is still very young, he will retain throughout the narrative these essential qualities, which make him the ideal protagonist to search tirelessly for happiness through a multitude of loves and adventures.

Surrounding Fabrizio are the twin heroines of *The Charterhouse of Parma,* Clelia Conti and Gina Pietranera. The two women provide an important contrast in their respective characters: Clelia is young and innocent, pure and idealistic, religious and superstitious; Gina is mature and worldly, witty and intelligent, beautiful and passionate. The fourth major character, Count Mosca, combines within his character the qualities of a supreme diplomat and an ideal knight. Among these four men and women grow up the three love relationships that are the focal point of the novel: the love of Fabrizio for Clelia, that of Gina for Fabrizio, and that of Count Mosca for Gina.

The love Fabrizio and Clelia will later feel for each other is foreshadowed very early when Fabrizio gives twelve-year-old Clelia and her father a ride in his carriage; when the hero saves Count Conti, who is traveling in disguise, from exposure to the police, the little girl does not fully understand what is happening, but suspects that the young man is somehow noble, and admires him shyly from a distance. Years later, when as adults they meet again, their love blossoms slowly as they move through phases of the process which Stendhal called "crystallization." For Fabrizio the feeling is new in its degree of intensity and joy; his love is so vehement that at one point it causes him to wish for death and refuse help in escaping rather than lose it. On Clelia's side the reaction to love is more complex. She becomes increasingly passionate and demanding, yet purer in the sense that into her love for Fabrizio she pours her entire soul, concentrating in him all her capacity for feeling. Her commitment is so total that she can feel compassion toward Gina; yet simultaneously, jealousy taints her pity, and she leans toward hatred for the older woman. Her love allows her to sleep with Fabrizio after he has become a bishop and she is married, yet superstition makes her cling to her vow to meet him only in darkness and never see his face. The lovers' depth of emotion extends to their child so strongly that when the child Sandrino dies, his mother follows him shortly afterwards, while his father retires to the Carthusian monastery that gives the novel its title.

Stendhal's portrait of Gina is a triumph of characterization. Charming, stubborn, astute, devoted, erotic, and intelligent, her richly varied personality is revealed through her relationship with Count Mosca, and most crucially, through her love for Fabrizio. What began as maternal affection for a small boy grows over the years into a love that is undefinable; Gina's feelings, which under acceptable circumstances would immediately flow into erotic channels, must be sublimated; she struggles to control her boundless energies, to guide them into outlets of devoted maternal concern, and to disguise from herself all the while what she really feels. Ironically, Fabrizio is not in actuality even related to her, since a French soldier, rather than Gina's brother, was the hero's father; but for all practical purposes, given their background and Fabrizio's attitude of boyish admiration for his aunt, any sexual relationship between the two would be psychologically incestuous.

The third love relationship in the book is that between Count Mosca and Gina. It is a one-sided affair insofar as the intensity of passion is all on the Count's side; Gina feels a great affinity for Mosca and loves him in a certain fashion, but not in the same way that he loves her. The Count is a fascinating figure—intelligent, skilled in diplomacy, and powerfully ambitious; warm, faithful, benevolent, yet capable of jealousy and anger. What draws Mosca and Gina together is their common wisdom tempered with skepticism, their basic love of humanity, and their fierce hatred of the petty tyrants who hold authority over the rest of men. In many ways, Stendhal wrote his own personality not only into Fabrizio, but into the character of the gallant Mosca; it has been said that within him Stendhal ". . . deposited, with his artist's curiosity, the residue of his knowledge and his disappointments—the supreme irony of a too ambitious ego which 'set its nets too high.' " Significantly, at the close of the novel, only Mosca is strong enough to survive the pain of loss and intense suffering.

Behind these four extraordinary figures is ranged a gallery of minor characters, the most memorable being those associated with the court in Parma. Through them, Stendhal ridicules, in a comic fashion reminiscent of Molière, all the vices and follies of mankind; people are paraded before the reader's eyes in all their vanity and pomposity to instruct the audience in the venality and pettiness of mankind. The grand duke Ranuce-Ernest IV leads this gallery of comic figures; in quick flashes Stendhal reveals a man at once cruel and terrified to indulge his cruelty; proud of his power yet ashamed that it is not greater; affectatious and overbearing, but inwardly filled with fear and indecision.

Nancy G. Ballard

A CHASTE MAID IN CHEAPSIDE

Type of work: Drama
Author: Thomas Middleton (1580-1627)
Type of plot: Farce
Time of plot: Early seventeenth century
Locale: London
First presented: 1611

Bawdy, farcical, and notable for its freedom and audacity, A Chaste Maid in Cheapside *interweaves adroitly the affairs of several households, travels through a series of wildly comic scenes, and finally reaches a satisfactory conclusion. In addition to its hilarity, the play aims barbs at such venerable folk as police informers and Puritain zealots.*

To read a comedy by Middleton—or indeed by almost any of the Elizabethan and Jacobean playwrights—is to set in relief the greatness of Shakespeare. Excellent and competent as Middleton is, he seldom reaches the lightness, the mellowness, the vivacity, or even the profundity (if we include *The Tempest*) of the great Shakespearean comedies. Nor does Middleton equal the poetry of Shakespeare at its best. But, judged on its individual merits, *A Chaste Maid in Cheapside* must be considered an artistic and dramatic success. It pretends to be nothing more than what it is: a romantic comedy, which nevertheless adds social comment to its frivolity. The plot, of course, is hardly believable: as with all good literature, we willingly suspend our disbelief, while in this case, we allow the playwright to give us a slice of the world of Cheapside.

Actually, there is little that comes cheaply in Cheapside, unless it be cuckoldry and children. Even children do not come cheaply to the Kixes. Women seem to come cheaply, at least to Sir Walter Whorehound. But Sir Walter must pay highly for his women. He has to keep the Allwits living lavishly and take on the support of each new child begotten on Mistress Allwit. Allwit, a satisfied cuckold (a "wittol"), is not really witty, but he is smart enough to know when he has a good deal going for himself. Sir Walter is, for him, the "founder" of his happiness:

> I'm like a man
> Finding a table furnished to his hand,
> As mine is still to me, prays for the founder—
> Bless the right worshipful the good founder's life!

Because of his willing cuckoldry, Allwit wants for nothing, except for dignity and self-respect. His cuckoldry comes cheaply, but at a price far too high for most men.

Sir Walter finds that, while whores are easy to come by, wives are not, at least not chaste ones. Conversely, the Yellowhammers find that rich husbands are not easily gotten. Their daughter, Moll, is the chaste maid; she is also a chased maid, chased by Sir Walter. She finds that chastity and a husband she loves are very dear indeed to keep and to possess. To keep her chastity and to possess her lover she has to resist the will of her parents, risk violence, and resort to subterfuge.

The man Moll loves and eventually marries is Touchwood, Junior. His character and that of his brother, Touchwood, Senior, fit their name. Like touchwood, which ignites easily, Touchwood, Junior, is readily incited to violence. He challenges Sir Walter to a duel, thus risking his life for Moll, who, it need hardly be said, does not come cheaply. Touchwood, Senior, on the other hand, finds that children come cheaply but money does not. The side of his nature that ignites too easily is passion.

What is most cheap in Cheapside is cant and hypocrisy, and probably the most amusing scenes in the play are those which satirize these vices in characters not part of the central plot: the promoters (or police informers) and the Puritan ladies. The promoters stop people in the street to search them for meat, which is forbidden in Lent, the time in which the events of the play take place. If the people who are stopped are carrying meat, they must hand it over to the promoters or risk exposure to the police, unless they are in league with the informers. The informers meet their match in a Country Girl, from whom they take a basket they think holds a lamb's head. Instead, they are left with an illegitimate child. The Puritan women are of course more concerned with appearances than realities; they talk more about temperance than they practice it. Middleton puts comicly ironic words into their mouths. One says, for example, that "Children are blessings, / If they be got with zeal by the brethren. . . ." The ladies are celebrating the christening of Mistress Allwit's latest baby fathered by the zealous Sir Walter Whorehound. Furthermore, the same Puritan lady who comments on children drinks so much on this occasion that she cannot stand unaided. These scenes reinforce the theme of cant and hypocrisy—of appearance versus reality—which runs through the play.

This theme is also exemplified in the Yellowhammers' son, Tim, who has come home from Cambridge a full-fledged pedant. He is perhaps too severely punished in having to marry the Welshwoman, who poses as an heiress but who is actually another of Sir Walter's mistresses. Middleton suggests, however, that marriage may change her.

Middleton's dramatic skill shows nowhere better than in his brilliant dénouement, in which an apparent funeral is turned into a marriage. Sir Walter is in prison, and his intended bride is at last married to the one she really loves. Harmony has been restored. Swinburne, that enthusiastic critic of the English Renaissance dramatists, writes that *A Chaste Maid in Cheapside* is "a play of quite exceptional freedom and audacity, and certainly one of the drollest and liveliest that ever broke the bounds of propriety or shook the sides of merriment." If it is less thoughtful than *The Merchant of Venice* or *The Taming of the Shrew*, *A Chaste Maid in Cheapside* is certainly not far removed in artistry and drama. It deserves our attention and acclaim.

Clifton M. Snider

CHÉRI

Type of work: Novel
Author: Sidonie Gabrielle Claudine Colette (1873-1954)
Type of plot: Psychological realism
Time of plot: c. 1910
Locale: Paris
First published: 1920

Expertly blending emotional truth with disciplined intellectual examination, Colette—amoral but never irresponsible—measures in Chéri *the cost of man-woman relationships. Witty and dispassionate, she explores in a language at once lyrical and precise the personality of Léa, with her shrewd vision of life and her talent for wholehearted abandonment to sensual delight. As in all her works, Colette sees to the center of the human heart through the avenue of the five senses.*

In *Chéri,* Colette deals at great length with very superficial people who place an excessive value on physical appearance. It is difficult to sympathize with Léa, who spends her time worrying about her fading beauty; Chéri, despite his relative youth, is equally vain and frivolous, always gazing into mirrors for signs of aging. The affair between Léa and Chéri is touching as it comes to its painful end, but because of who they are (and what they are not) it is not significant enough to be tragic. Yet seldom have the complexities of a love-hate relationship been so painstakingly and authentically detailed.

The rituals through which the characters move are almost as stylized as a Kabuki dance. This world of the courtesan and paid lover is a half-world, an airless place; it is a society which, because of its special ingrown nature, could not last. When World War I swept away that world, few could regret its passing.

The novel is filled with grotesques. The minor characters such as Baroness de la Berche, the aged ballerina Madame Aldonza, and the grossly fat old Lili, a bewigged, painted ex-courtesan of seventy with a boy lover, are the most obvious. Chéri himself is like a petulant child, first spurning out of contrariness what he most desires, and then destructively clutching at it, not realizing that his selfishness and heedlessness will destroy the object he loves. His immaturity is charming for awhile, but ultimately unpleasant. Despite the title of the book, the protagonist is not Chéri, but Léa. She is the most sympathetic character; she is the one finally left alone with the reality of passing time, the loser in the male-female battle.

THE CHERRY ORCHARD

Type of work: Drama
Author: Anton Chekhov (1860-1904)
Type of plot: Impressionistic realism
Time of plot: Early twentieth century
Locale: An estate in Russia
First presented: 1904

In his best-known play, Chekhov captures the frustrations, jealousies, and loves of characters who are not tragic in the traditional sense of the word because they are not capable of heroic action, but who are immediately recognizable in their real human suffering. In addition, the playwright has caught in Madame Ranevskaya's household a picture of the end of an era of semi-feudal Russian country estates.

The Cherry Orchard was published in 1904, the year Anton Chekhov died. The author's brief life had been a painful one. After an unhappy childhood he was forced, by his father's bankruptcy, to assume the responsibility of supporting his family. This he did through his writing while, at the same time, pursuing a medical degree. By the time he was graduated in 1884, his health was impaired by tuberculosis, which was to plague him the rest of his life and cut it short at forty-four. One might expect the final product of such an existence to reek of bitterness and rage; instead, like most of Chekhov's work, The Cherry Orchard exemplifies his profound humaneness and humility.

The Cherry Orchard has no heroes or heroines and, as many a hasty reader will complain, precious little action. That is precisely Chekhov's intention: his fictional world is populated by persons who do not have the perception to understand their own lives, to communicate with those around them, or to bring their dreams into fruition. Most of the characters dream; few act. Madame Ranevskaya and her friend Pischin dream that their estates will somehow be saved. Anya, the young daughter, dreams of a future without blemish; Fiers, the old valet, of the glories that used to be; Dunyasha, the maid, of becoming a fine lady; Trofimov, the student, of a magnificent new social order. Their predicament is summed up by Gaev, Madame Ranevskaya's somewhat unstable brother: "I keep thinking and racking my brains; I have many schemes, a great many, and that really means none." Only the merchant Lopakhin, the son of a serf, has the energy and will to make his dreams come true—but he does so with such single-minded purpose that we shudder to think of the ruthless manipulator he may well become.

The few characters who do not dream are perhaps more pitiable than those who do. Yephodov, nicknamed "two-and-twenty misfortunes" because of his habitual bad luck, sees failure and despair everywhere. His only triumphant moments come when he fulfills his nickname. Charlotta, the governess, performs tricks to make others laugh; herself unable to laugh, she views the future with empty eyes. Yasha, the young valet, is beyond dreams, a callous, self-centered cynic.

Only Varya, able to see her dreams for what they are, is realistic and fully human at the same time. Perhaps because she is the adopted daughter, not having inherited the thin blood of the ineffectual aristocrats, it is she who can look the future full in the face, who can see other characters—and accept them—for what they are. With the security of the estate crumbling, with prospects increasingly dim for her hoped-for marriage to Lopakhin, she finds salvation in work.

Madame Ranevskaya and her family do nothing with their plot of land, a once grand and famous estate. The cherry orchard itself has become more dream than reality. Forty years before, the cherries made famous preserves. Now Lopakhin, the pragmatic merchant, points out, "The only thing remarkable about the orchard is that it's a very large one. There's a crop of cherries every alternate year, and then there's nothing to be done with them, no one buys them." The recipe for the fabulous preserves has been forgotten. Nevertheless, to the family the orchard symbolizes their former grandeur. When Lopakhin suggests that it should be cut down and the land developed into a summer resort, Gaev protests proudly, "This orchard is mentioned in the 'Encyclopaedia.' "

The Cherry Orchard, like Chekhov's other plays, is objectively written, and different productions may vary greatly. One may play Madame Ranevskaya as a dignified if somewhat inept lady caught in the vise of changing societies —or as a silly lovesick female refusing to face any truth. Lopakhin can be portrayed sympathetically—it is certainly easy to herald his up-by-his-own-bootstraps rise from menial to master of the estate—or as a villain, seeming to warn the family while knowing full well that they are incapable of action, gloating over his triumph, heartlessly rejecting Vanya. Trofimov has been interpreted as the perpetual student, given to long intellectual rumination and little else; after the 1917 Revolution, he was frequently portrayed as the spokesman for the new social order, a partisan of the common people.

This ambiguity is consistent with Chekhov's insistence that " . . . to judge between good and bad, between successful and unsuccessful, would need the eye of God." The author himself chose not to play God but to be the eye of the camera, letting selected details speak for themselves. Madame Ranevskaya, exhorted by Trofimov to "face the truth," retorts, "What truth?" She and Chekhov are aware that there are many truths, and that reality, like beauty, is frequently in the eye of the beholder.

Chekhov's friend Maxim Gorky has commented that "No one ever understood the tragic nature of life's trifles so clearly and intuitively as Chekhov did. . . ." But if Chekhov saw tragedy, he was also capable of recognizing the comedy in man's experiments in living. "This was often the way with him," Gorky reports. "One moment he would be talking with warmth, gravity, and sincerity, and the next he would be laughing at himself and his own words."

As with himself, so with the remainder of humanity.

Chekhov saw life with double vision, the tragic and the comic almost simultaneously, so it is with accuracy that *The Cherry Orchard* is classified as tragicomedy. The comedy is evident in stretches of apparently meaningless dialogue (which makes *The Cherry Orchard* a precursor of Theatre of the Absurd, to come much later in the century), and in the superficial behavior typical of a comedy of manners. The tragedy lies in the lack of communication—much is said, but little is heard, much less understood—and in the blindness of this group of characters blundering their way through their lives, hardly ever fully aware of what is happening to them. In the final speech, Fiers, the ill, elderly valet, mutters words that echo as a coda to the entire play: "Life has slipped by as though I hadn't lived."

Sally Buckner

THE CHEVALIER OF THE MAISON ROUGE

Type of work: Novel
Author: Alexandre Dumas, *père* (1802-1870)
Type of plot: Historical romance
Time of plot: 1793
Locale: Paris
First published: 1846

In a complex plot that freely blends historical fact and fabricated circumstances, Dumas tells the story of the hero's attempt to free Marie Antoinette before she is sentenced and executed. A champion of monarchy and aristocratic virtues, Dumas imbues his heroes—republicans only for the sake of the plot—with all the qualities of sterling gentlemen of noble birth. The novel demonstrates the author's usual genius in telling a spellbinding tale.

The Chevalier of the Maison Rouge takes as its subject matter the so-called "Carnation Conspiracy" which was the attempt by the Chevalier de Rougeville to rescue Marie Antoinette from prison following the French Revolution. As a novel, it is an excellent example of Alexandre Dumas' ability to interest and enthrall his readers when the ultimate result of the action is a foregone conclusion. The title of the novel is taken from La Maison Rouge which, under the monarchy of pre-Revolutionary days, was one of the companies of the King's Household Guard, so named because of the brilliant red cloak which was part of the uniform.

The "Carnation Conspiracy" was a relatively little-known incident which occurred in September, 1793, while the French Queen Marie Antoinette was in prison awaiting execution. An officer in the Household Guard, the Chevalier de Rougeville, entered the queen's cell in disguise, escorted by a municipal officer named Michonis. De Rougeville caught the queen's attention, then dropped a carnation behind a stove in the room. The flower contained a note which detailed the plans for a conspiracy to rescue her from captivity. Unfortunately for the plotters, the action was observed by a gendarme, Gilbert, assigned to watch the queen. The incident was reported and the revolutionary government, under the impression that there was a widespread plot in Paris to rescue the queen, took severe protective measures, including the arrest and imprisonment of everyone deemed by the officials to have had a part in the conspiracy. The queen's guard was replaced by a new and more numerous force and a number of the people around her were placed in prison themselves. The harsh measures were effective and, as every student knows, the queen went to her execution as planned.

This footnote to history constituted the framework on which Dumas chose to hang his plot. The author of a historical novel is, of course, certain to be somewhat hampered in his pattern-making by the stubbornness of facts and events well known to the reader, and by the discrepancies of time and place.

Yet in *The Chevalier of the Maison Rouge,* Dumas demonstrates small care for historical accuracy and the constraints of fact. At the same time, however, he exhibits a tremendous faculty for seizing the characters and situations that best render historical atmosphere. To write a good adventure yarn, an author must have rich materials with which he is naturally, and also by education, in sympathy. That these materials have been processed by other authors and are based on fact is of little consequence because adventure, not history, is the author's prime concern. Here, history provided the skeleton that depended on Dumas for life and development.

Like Shakespeare, whom the author admired, Dumas takes the reader in this novel into the open air of the real world. His characters are active, outdoor men. Their morality is that of the camp and field. Dumas never gloats over evil and shows no curiosity regarding vice and corruption. Though his heroes, Maurice and Louis, are moved by the strongest passions, their motives are universal and, as a rule, brave and honorable. Friendship, honor, and love are the trinity which governs their movements. In many respects these two characters, like most of Dumas' protagonists, represent extensions of the author's own personality. Maurice is the romanticist and lover, an embodiment of the author, who went from mistress to mistress, frequented the society of actresses, and tended to pattern himself upon the flamboyance of the romantic author Lord Byron. Louis is the perfect gentleman and, like Dumas, the proponent of the virtues commonly found in aristocratic society.

However, Dumas' characterization represents the most serious problem in the novel. Dumas was essentially aristocratic in temperament and these qualities, when projected into the personalities of his protagonist—who ostensibly represent the post-Revolutionary common man—cause a serious contradiction in character delineation. It has been proven, however, that Dumas' readers, like the author, tend to overlook such inconsistencies, concentrating instead on the action and adventure of the narrative.

It is the action and adventure of the narrative that constitutes the strength of Dumas' style in this as in the majority of his novels. The illusion of vitality comes across strongly to the reader. The author—an exemplar of bodily prowess and animal appetite—reveled in his own physical exuberance, and reveals this very personal trait in the novel, especially in the two characters which are Dumas in disguise. In the era depicted in *The Chevalier of the Maison Rouge,* there was much material of a gruesome and painful character that could have found its way into Dumas' novel. But the author never dwells on the horrors of the torture chamber. He is all for the courage shown, not for the pain and cruelty inflicted and endured.

Accordingly, though his action scenes are not historical, he can match the greatest masters in setting a duel or battle before us. The quarrel between Maurice and Dixmer, resulting in the eventual death of Dixmer near the end of this novel, is an indication of that ability. But the gusto of the novel's action scenes is matched by the simplicity and yet the grandeur of his epic diction. For only such language is capable of portraying the enthusiasm of the protagonists, their loyalty, their courage, and the zest with which they approached a mystery or a beautiful woman.

On the other hand, *The Chevalier of the Maison Rouge* is not flawless, especially in terms of plot. The structure of the novel occasionally tends to be loose, and there are a number of inconsistencies in characterization. But such a method of evaluating the effectiveness of an adventure story is not entirely appropriate. Many authors have had wonderful plots at their disposal but have not been able to write them as effectively as Dumas. Thus, if judged in terms of the reader's reactions rather than according to codified mechanics, Dumas' novel has the kind of unity and coherence that is felt by his audience. And it is this impact that is of major importance to the author of an action novel.

Stephen Hanson

CHILDREN OF GOD

Type of work: Novel
Author: Vardis Fisher (1895-1968)
Type of plot: Historical chronicle
Time of plot: 1820-1890
Locale: New York, Illinois, Utah
First published: 1939

In Children of God, *Vardis Fisher, who calls his novel an American epic, takes the bare bones of historical fact and fleshes them out into personalities that come to life in the pages of his saga. Particularly vivid are the characterizations of Joseph Smith and Brigham Young, whose immense energies and stubbornness were responsible for founding Mormonism and transplanting it to Utah.*

It was perhaps inevitable that Vardis Fisher should attempt writing of the saga of the Mormons, for his own parents came from Mormon converts who went West with Joseph Smith. Despite much repetition, this Harper Prize novel of 1939 bursts with great vividness, especially in the mob scenes. The writing of this long novel was an enormous task, but Fisher managed to bring to the book a message of dedication rarely equalled.

Vardis Fisher's serviceable prose methodically draws a picture of the origins of the Latter Day Saints and their efforts to overcome prejudice in nineteenth century America. The scale of the narrative is grand, but Fisher does not penetrate to the depths of his characters' personalities or do more than suggest their private torments. Yet he is able through sheer energy to give the reader the feeling of a continent opening up and a people growing and affirming their newly won ambitions and dreams.

The leaders of Mormonism are revealed in their imperfections as well as greatness. The stubborn strength of Joseph Smith and Brigham Young dominates the story. Whatever the reader feels about the mission or morals of these two men, he comes away from the book with a profound respect for their power of endurance and supreme dedication. The epic of the Mormons is presented here with all of the pain and horror of history. One feels that Fisher meant this book to be more than a conventional historical romance.

Fisher tends to overexplain when he should be content to suggest, but the story itself is so interesting that the book maintains a steady pace as it follows the beginnings of Mormonism to the end of the first half-century of its existence. Perhaps the author was too concerned with appearing impartial to create a first-rate novel.

THE CHILDREN OF HERAKLES

Type of work: Drama
Author: Euripides (c. 485-c. 406 B.C.)
Type of plot: Classical tragedy
Time of plot: The age of legend
Locale: Before the temple of Zeus at Marathon
First presented: c. 430 B.C.

Presented in the early years of the Peloponnesian War, this structurally awkward play glorifies the virtues of the Athenian city-state. Its only unity lies in the fact that the play opens with Eurystheus' threat to slay the surviving relatives of Herakles, and ends with his death at the command of Herakles' mother, Alcmene.

Plays on the suppliant theme have a standard plot: the asylum, the attempted seizure, the appeal, and the struggle which ends in victory for the providers of asylum (see Aeschylus' *The Suppliants* and *Eumenides,* Sophocles' *Oedipus at Colonus,* as well as Euripides' *The Suppliants*). By setting the scene of asylum in Attica, Euripides is able to demonstrate those Athenian ideals of justice and humanity so famously praised by Pericles around the time of the production of the *Herakleidae.*

The Athenian audience was well aware that Demophon, in offering asylum despite the demands and threats of Copreus, was following the excellent example of his father Theseus who had protected Oedipus from Creon, had forced the same king to allow the burial of the Seven against Thebes, and most of all, had befriended Herakles after his homicidal fit of madness. Nevertheless, in this play it is more than right that conquers might. Euripides has infused this simple plot with divine aids. By Macaria's noble self-sacrifice to Persephone, victory over the Argives is assured—but only through the fortuitous arrival of Hyllus' army. This provides the occasion for the symbolically significant rejuvenation of Iolaus, but also ironically it distracts Alcmene from the philosophical and moral basis for Demophon's courageous decision: Athens is the world's sanctuary of just law.

Because the quick defeat and capture of Eurystheus seems to bisect the play and because this is the shortest of Euripides' tragedies (1,055 lines), one might argue that the play was hastily thrown together. This, however, is not only unprovable but unlikely; for by changing the myth to bring out Alcmene's spirited lust for total vengeance after the day has been saved, Euripides emphasizes that the struggle for justice is universal and constant and that unfortunately the Athenians will not always have the will to win. Thus the play ends in contradiction and irony: although the Athenians are spared the polluting responsibility of Eurystheus' death, they have failed their principle of justice for all; although they are assured protection from the children of Herakleidae, their fifth century descendants have recently entered into a conflict with the descendants of the Herakleidae (namely the Peloponnesian alliance), perhaps trusting more to Athenian strength than justice.

CHILDREN OF THE GHETTO

Type of work: Novel
Author: Israel Zangwill (1864-1926)
Type of plot: Ethnocentric realism
Time of plot: Nineteenth century
Locale: London
First published: 1892

This picture of the Jews of nineteenth century London has no central plot but is instead a series of loosely grouped episodes between which characters are sometimes only vaguely connected. Zangwill's gift lies in his description of the ghetto, with its seething life, racial discontent, and fierce struggles regulated only by the canons of strict orthodoxy.

Children of the Ghetto is divided into two books. The first, and more interesting, is titled "Children of the Ghetto"; the second part, "Grand-children of the Ghetto," deals mainly with the issue of assimilated Jews in England. Book I is basically a survey of the life of the ghetto; in it, a number of characters, appearing in a loosely connected narrative, struggle to survive in the hostile environment of the slum. In Book II, the central characters are Anglicized Jews who have lost the core of their beliefs. Zangwill has no sympathy at all for them and exposes their hypocrisy and fears.

The central theme of *Children of the Ghetto* is the conflict over the survival of the Jewish religion. It is possible to see, in Book I, the beginnings of the end. The younger generation is no longer willing to carry on the traditions of the past in the same manner as older generations. Social and economic pressures are moving them away from the strict observances of their ancestors.

Zangwill's manner of presentation is uneven. At times, he appears to be merely cataloging various aspects of ghetto life: he presents Jewish folklore, songs, sayings, and jokes at great length; Yiddish words abound in the text. At the same time, Zangwill attempts to portray "typical" ghetto scenes. These include dinners, religious ceremonies, a charity kitchen, and sweatshops. Along with these scenes are characters who, though sometimes touching, are often stereotyped and sentimentalized.

Nevertheless, this novel—an early work in the career of its author—is an informative, and for the most part realistic, account of the life of the ghetto. As such, it clearly falls into the tradition of European realism. What is unique is its attempt to apply the techniques of realism to the ghetto, a hidden, for-gotten community. One aspect of Zangwill's realism is a certain doubleness in approach. On the one hand, the author clearly identifies with the people of the ghetto and their life, while on the other, he often adopts an ironic and occasionally patronizing tone toward the people he depicts, in order to estab-lish the distance necessary to be objective. Later in his career, perhaps trying to resolve this contradiction, he stopped writing fiction and became a polemicist and dramatist and an early advocate of Zionism. His name is often linked to that of Theodor Herzl. It is because of his later career that Zangwill's reputation is more established in the history of thought than in the history of English literature.

CHITA

Type of work: Novel
Author: Lafcadio Hearn (1850-1904)
Type of plot: Exotic romance
Time of plot: Nineteenth century
Locale: Louisiana coastal waters
First published: 1889

In his distinctly abrupt style, Hearn weaves in Chita *a tale that is a curious blend of narrative and poetry. The romantic story of a foundling is imbued with impressionistic, almost mystical qualities by its fusion at the climax with the progress of the hurricane.*

Despite its graphic rendering of a devastating hurricane, *Chita* is not a naturalistic novel with a storm for its "hero." Although Hearn was attracted by Herbert Spencer's evolutionary philosophy and read Darwin avidly, his destiny was not to join the rising school of American naturalism descending from Crane and Norris to Dreiser. Hearn followed that other great trend in late nineteenth century literature—aestheticism. His kindred spirits were Keats, Walter Pater, and Oscar Wilde. He was a pursuer of beauty and a painter with words. Shortly after completing *Chita,* Hearn left for Japan and eventually became the most important literary interpreter of Japan's aesthetic culture to the English-speaking world.

Chita's sentimental plot—the lost child and her chance reunion with a dying father—is designed to arouse human emotions that will correspond in intensity to the turbulence of the storm. It is the dynamic impressionism of the storm itself that fascinates Hearn: after the deceptive calm of summer come the roaring breakers; the storm swirls houses and ships and creates an incredible magnitude of refuse in its wake. Endless wreckage and bodies are strewn everywhere—including the foundling, Chita.

The child is fished out of all this dying waste like a creature returned from the dead. Her rescue has all the aura of a miracle to the simple Vioscas, who see the child as sent "by the Virgin." At the end of the story, La Brierre's fevered imagination once more re-creates the chaotic horror of the storm, more impressionistic than ever because its setting is now an agonized brain. And once again a miracle is performed: the lost child is tossed up by the seething wreckage of La Brierre's tortured memories. She is there both in his mind and in actuality. The blurring of the two realities makes for the perfect impressionistic ending. The novel opens with the calm hues of a summery Renoir and closes with the brilliant frenzy of a Monet.

THE CHOUANS

Type of work: Novel
Author: Honoré de Balzac (1799-1850)
Type of plot: Historical romance
Time of plot: 1799
Locale: Brittany
First published: 1829

In this imitation of Scott's historical novels, the first of Balzac's works to gain recognition, an obscure chapter in French history comes to life. A depiction of the first struggles of the young Republic, the novel is uneven in structure and weak in characterization, but its action scenes are vividly written.

Sir Walter Scott's influence is evident in *The Chouans*. Balzac has selected a relatively minor episode in the history of the Republic and concentrated on figures of everyday life who become involved in the process of history. Their motives, military strategies, and love affairs help determine historical reality while, at the same time, taking additional significance from it. Balzac is unexcelled in his grasp of those details of life which reveal social relations to their fullest; *The Chouans* shows this talent in a way none of Balzac's earlier work does, and in a way that Scott never approached. Balzac is able to describe clothing, rooms, hair styles, furnishings, facial expressions, attitudes, and food in such a way that the reader gains a complete vision of French life of the time. It is in this distillation of a total cultural experience that Balzac shows his true talent.

The novel, nevertheless, suffers from weaknesses; although Balzac attempts to mix the elements of love and politics, he is not quite successful in analyzing and representing the passions which bring his characters to commit extreme and dramatic acts. Balzac has a sense for the malignant in *The Chouans,* which he inherited from his earlier novels, but not for the pathological, which he developed in his later work. Although instinctively a realist, Balzac had not yet overcome his romantic tendencies. Some direct personal knowledge or experience of the matters he wrote about was always necessary for Balzac, and this lack of direct military knowledge shows in the narrative, which is at times awkward and cloudy.

The book does contain the materials of a good romance; the opening skirmish, the scenes at Vivetiere, the incident of the attack on Fougères, and the finale, are exciting. Many of the characters are of more than casual interest; Hulot is one of the best of Balzac's growling and grumbling characters and Montauran is a thoroughly noble young man without being flat or false in tone. Marche-à-Terre is very nearly a masterpiece, and many of the minor characters are well handled. Mademoiselle de Verneuil is charming and Madame du Gua is well drawn; Francine surpasses her type, to become more than a mere soubrette. Unfortunately, these potentially interesting characters are often bogged down in page after page of boring conversation. Balzac had not yet learned to move the narrative by means of dialogue. The book is worth reading both for its important place in Balzac's own development as a writer and for numerous passages of fine writing and glimpses of the vivid portrayal of character which was to be Balzac's chief greatness.

A CHRISTMAS CAROL

Type of work: Novelette
Author: Charles Dickens (1812-1870)
Type of plot: Sentimental romance
Time of plot: Nineteenth century
Locale: London, England
First published: 1843

A Christmas Carol is Dickens' heartwarming story of redemption through love. As much a part of Christmas traditions as holly wreaths, mistletoe, and carols, the sentimental story relates a miser's escape from his lonely and bitter existence, and his rebirth into the comforts of generosity and fellowship.

Literally a hymn to the spirit of Christmas, this universally loved story has fascinated all ages and peoples. It appeals to a basic instinct in all of us: the need to overcome self-hate and live in benign self-esteem. We are no good to ourselves or anyone else unless we can find within our own souls the seeds of that goodness we hope to find in the world. Miser and misanthrope, Ebenezer Scrooge has given up on others; he expects nothing and gives nothing. It is ironically fitting that Dickens makes him the master of a counting house; his "ledger" is perfectly balanced: nothing has gone out and therefore nothing comes in.

Marley's ghost provides the terrifying example: this is all Scrooge has to look forward to if he continues to live without involving himself in mankind. The ghosts that follow reveal to the reader the psychological reasons for Scrooge's warped character, but they are also messengers from Scrooge's unconscious mind forcing him to confront repressed disappointments and failures of kindness; he is rewarded for standing up to the pain of confrontation with the balm of self-pity. As the various ghosts of Christmas Past, Present, and Future enable Scrooge to confront the truth about his own life, a subtle transference takes place; Scrooge shifts from self-pity to compassion and concern for others. He is reborn in Love.

He rises in the morning a man possessed with the possibilities of kindness and charity. Remade by his dream, he now awakes "to find it true," as Keats said of Milton's Adam when he awoke to find Eve at his side. It is a triumph of the moral imagination. The ecstasy of his rebirth is infectious. The Cratchits, Scrooge's nephew, and the charity collectors are not only the beneficiaries of Scrooge's largesse; they are also the heirs of his spiritual awakening. When Tiny Tim cries "God Bless Us, Every One," he is emblematic of the cripple who finds God in his own affliction, as did Scrooge in his loneliness, only to walk in the higher regions opened by the bliss of human love.

THE CID

Type of work: Drama
Author: Pierre Corneille (1606-1684)
Type of plot: Romantic tragedy
Time of plot: Eleventh century
Locale: Seville
First presented: 1636

Generally ranked as the best of Corneille's works, this tragedy is considered by many scholars to be the beginning of modern French drama. The playwright reputedly used as his source Guillén de Castro y Bellvis' treatment of the Cid legends, which form the basis of Spain's great medieval epic poem.

The neoclassical tragedies of seventeenth century France are especially in need of introductions for a modern audience; Corneille's *The Cid* only a little less than most. The Renaissance had seen, among other things, an intensification of interest in the individual and in the self. This focusing of interest (amounting almost to a vision of the nature of man) was in conflict with the medieval view which perceived of man more as a race than as an individual. The individual was perceived, to be sure, but perceived as something like a component of society, reproducing it and assuring its integrity by maintaining binding interrelationships with other individual members of society both alive and dead. In Corneille's time, the more romantic tenets of the Renaissance had been displaced by the neoclassical adoption of the life of reason and order within a cohesive community; and with this life there came, understandably, a high regard for honor.

The twentieth century does not easily understand the classical and neoclassical concern for "honor" because our age is essentially a romantic one; our concerns are primarily for the immediate future and the physically alive, concerns of the individual. Romantic love, concerning itself as it does with physically alive individuals and their immediate futures, is of extreme importance to us. But honor is based not upon immediacy or subjectivity but upon loyalty to others (particularly those to whom one is related by blood ties, marriage, or a shared set of cultural assumptions) and concern for the opinions of others. It is not merely a matter of respectfully but radically differing with one's fellows on moral questions; one's fellows are a part of oneself; to differ radically with them is to be schizophrenic. The task then, in living a life of honor, is to live it so that others approve. For if others do not approve, no man (or woman) in such an age can approve of himself.

This is the situation of *The Cid.* The Infanta's dilemma is the keynote of the play; she must choose between her romantic love for Rodrigue (to whom she is impelled by her feelings as an individual) and her honor (as demanded by her ties to her father and her attendant position in society). Love urges that she make herself available for marriage to him, but honor insists that she not marry beneath her station. She chooses honor almost instinctively, even going so far as to take direct action to decrease her own romantic love; she brings Rodrigue and Chimène together so as to make him completely unavailable to herself as a lover. In Act V she almost succumbs to love, thinking Rodrigue's newly won glories and title bring him nearly to her social station, but her lady in waiting (acting as her visible conscience on the stage) dissuades her. She goes on to aid in the final reconciliation of the principal pair.

Rodrigue and Chimène each must make the same choice, though their positions differ from the Infanta's in that theirs are seemingly impossible. While the Infanta's problem admits of the simplest (though not the easiest) of solutions, that of not declaring her love, Rodrigue cannot expect a loving response from the daughter of the man he has killed, and Chimène cannot give such a response. Both are acting in a typically honorable fashion, maintaining their fathers' reputations and foregoing their personal desires. To do less would be to make themselves less than human. Honor threatens the love affair of Chimène and Rodrigue, while love threatens the honor of the Infanta.

It will seem to some readers that love wins out in the end over honor, the honorable scruples of the principal pair having been overcome by reason and circumstances. But in fact love and honor are synthesized, neither force canceling out the other. The Infanta's moral position, being above reproach, is perfect for her role as a proponent of marriage for the pair. Had she surrendered to her own emotion, she could not have been nearly so effective a spokesman on the part of love for others. Add to this Elvira's chiding and, indeed, the king himself in the role of matchmaker, and it will be seen that Corneille is at some pains to overcome excessive preoccupation with honor, but only in such a way as to leave real honor intact and alive.

Until we reach the denouement—Chimène's admission of her love—the heroine sees herself primarily as the daughter of Don Gomès; her admission of her feelings to the king and the resolution of the play are made possible by her being persuaded to see herself primarily as a member of the Castilian community. As a result of this shift in her perception of her role, she no longer sees Rodrigue as enemy and begins to see the Moors in that capacity. As principal bulwark against the common enemy, Rodrigue both lays the groundwork for this change in Chimène and is in a unique position to enjoy the benefits of it. Thus, while upholding the concept of honor in a humanly achievable form, the play uses a typically romantic process as the underpinnings of its plot: thesis and antithesis (honor and love) are synthesized.

Critics have seen in this play certain basic similarities to Shakespeare's *Romeo and Juliet,* foremost among which is the feud between the lovers' families. But a more essential similarity lies in the use of death by both dramatists as a threat to young love. Both Romeo and Rodrigue think of death (for themselves) as a solution to their problems, and both offer the solution with such alacrity as to give rise to speculations of a death wish on both their parts. Such speculations, however, have the distinct disadvantage of focusing our attention entirely upon the character, causing us to ignore the play's overall design. Death is not initially the preoccupation of either hero. Both want simply to marry the ladies they love. Death presents itself to them as a solution only when this desire becomes both undeniable and impossible to satisfy. This renders life impossible, and when life begins to seem impossible the natural impulse is to consign it to a state of nonexistence (the natural state for any impossibility). Death is the inevitable threat. But death becomes truly inevitable only when the character is convinced that his life is indeed impossible, that there is no way out. Romeo is convinced of this on two occasions; Rodrigue repeatedly offers himself to Chimène for execution, believing there is no other solution.

Death, then, is not intrinsic to Rodrigue's character; it is a force from without, threatening the healthy love relationship with the ferocity of a tangible monster. There is a level at which most love comedies are fertility rites, celebrating and promoting the optimism and fecundity of a society. In such comedies the lovers' eventual wedding (or promise of one) affirms this social optimism. But when optimism and fertility are seriously threatened by death, as they are in this play, we revise our classification of the play and call it a "tragi-comedy." The play ends happily with the promise of a marriage, the protagonists having avoided death's many invasions into their happiness. But death's attempts were persistent, and were overcome by the slimmest of margins.

The Cid is Corneille's first major play and is today often considered his finest. His plays are often compared with those of his younger contemporary, Racine. Both authors adhered strictly to the neoclassical unities (action, time, and place), though Racine evidently worked more comfortably within those restrictions; Corneille reminds us throughout *The Cid* that the action occurs within one day, but the day is an unnaturally full one.

John J. Brugaletta

CINNA

Type of work: Drama
Author: Pierre Corneille (1606-1684)
Type of plot: Neo-classical tragedy
Time of plot: c. A.D. 10
Locale: Rome
First presented: c. 1640

Subtitled The Mercy of Augustus *and turning on the theme of royal generosity and clemency, this play was instrumental in earning Corneille the favor of his former antagonist, Richelieu. The play is chiefly remembered today for Augustus Caesar's brilliant soliloquy on the confusion of good and evil, the nature of egotism and humility, and the strength and weakness that may exist in one person.*

The concept of French neoclassicism is an outgrowth of Hellenism, and its tenets are founded on the works of Aristotle. Neoclassicism, however, went even further in its exclusivity. Corneille's heroes are elevated nobles, untouched by daily life, and uninvolved with the base concerns of everyday man. As Victor Hugo noted, no king in Corneille's plays ever asked the time of day. This isolation was thought to heighten and intensify the sense of drama in tragedy. The adherence to Aristotle forced the dramatist to focus on specific actions or events, and the resulting concentration produces occasional moments of gemlike quality, as here in *Cinna*. The reader who must rely on translations of Corneille's work should bear in mind that the declamatory style favored by this author is unusually difficult to approximate in translation, depending as it does on the literal sound of the words. The beauty and movement of his language is a controlling influence over his plays.

In *Cinna* the nobleness of the forgiving emperor is so splendid in its magnanimity and charity that the stylized actions and declamatory speeches do not seem excessively contrived. Corneille thought of his tragedies as idealisms of human behavior, exaggerated but sublimely moral revelations of man's ethical possibilities.

Augustus, in this play, is not the power-hungry "boy" emperor of Shakespeare's *Antony and Cleopatra*. Instead we have the mellowed portrait of a powerful ruler who has learned the power of humility, charity, and forgiveness. His power of goodness is so great that it averts the tragic consequences of the actions launched by the plotters. Augustus not only triumphs, but he saves his enemies from themselves.

CINQ-MARS

Type of work: Novel
Author: Alfred Victor de Vigny (1797-1863)
Type of plot: Historical romance
Time of plot: Seventeenth century
Locale: France
First published: 1826

Vigny based Cinq-Mars, *which has been called the first French historical novel, upon true incidents in the reign of Louis XIII. Relating the story of Cinq-Mars's attempt to overthrow Cardinal Richelieu, the play follows closely the actual details of the conspiracy.*

Alfred de Vigny is the Walter Scott of French narrative literature. The equation is absolute and even applies to their poetry insofar as both based their verse on historical themes: Vigny on religion, Scott on medieval Scotland. But in fiction there is no doubt that they are nearly identical, and this is largely because the young Vigny saw himself as translating Scott's historicism into a French idiom. The young Frenchman justified his nearly plagiaristic devotion by effecting, in his one novel, what he felt to be an improvement on Scott's method.

In Scott's work actual historical figures are more or less in the background. In *Quentin Durward*, for example, Louis XI, the crafty "spider king," is important to the plot, but his function in the principal story of the young Scott's adventures is primarily that of a *deus ex machina,* a powerful figure who intervenes in the lives and actions of the story's main characters. Vigny felt that Scott had made it too easy for himself. The French writer's Richelieu is actually part of the central plot; his characterization is as carefully developed as that of the dashing hero, Cinq-Mars. In order to make Richelieu part of the "fiction," Vigny was forced to overdramatize him, to make him more Machiavellian than he actually was. Since Vigny had chosen literally to fictionalize history itself, he did not hesitate to let historical figures say and do things they could not have done—such as Milton's reciting from *Paradise Lost* twenty years before he had written a line of it.

"The Idea is everything," said Vigny, and he often sacrificed the letter of history to the idea of history. Nevertheless, he did not falsify the essence of history, and many of his critics feel that his interpretation of Richelieu's historical significance is basically sound; namely, that he destroyed the balance of power between the king and the nobles and thus made the collapse of the monarchy inevitable.

In addition to its historical validity, the novel abounds in credible dialogue, exciting action, and rarely succumbs to turgidity of style. It is undoubtedly one of the greatest of the early historical novels of the nineteenth century.

THE CIRCLE OF CHALK

Type of work: Drama
Author: Unknown; sometimes attributed to Li Hsing-Tao (n. d.)
Type of plot: Romantic comedy
Time of plot: Before the thirteenth century
Locale: Nanking and Peking
First presented: Thirteenth or fourteenth century

A typical Chinese classical play of the Yuan dynasty (1259-1368), in four acts with a prologue, The Circle of Chalk *is remarkable for the beauty of its lyrical verse. Its original plot involves a case of murder and a disputed son, solved by a Solomon-like judge; the story of the love affair between a prince and a commoner was introduced by a German adapter.*

In spite of its highly stylized classical structure and its basis in Confucian ethics, *The Circle of Chalk* is a play that speaks directly to the modern Western reader. The progressively dangerous plight of the heroine, Hi-tang, coupled with her courage and sincerity; the adroit, devious, ruthless machinations of the villains, Mrs. Ma and her lover Chow; the satirical insights into society; the comedic dialogue; and the many passages of lyrical beauty all combine to provide a most impressive and universal dramatic experience.

Whether or not the changes and expansions added to the play in 1924 by its adapter, the German poet and sinologist Alfred Henschke Klabund, improved or debased the play is problematical. The love affair between Hi-tang and Prince Po adds an additional interest and poignancy to the work, and the complex subplot involving her brother Chang-ling and the White Lotus Society introduces extra intrigue and suspense. On the other hand, Klabund's emendations obscure much of the simplicity of the original, and the final revelation concerning the paternity of Hi-tang's son is a "Western style" twist that perhaps sentimentalizes the first version. The Hi-tang of the earlier version needs no extra characterizing devices to command an identification and sympathy. The final resolution of the revised play, with its happy ending and its mitigated justice shifts the focus from an emphasis on Confucian justice to that of theatrical mercy. In the original, Mrs. Ma and Chow are "cut into twenty-five pieces" and all those whom they bribed in the course of their plotting are severely beaten and exiled.

Klabund undoubtedly believed that by softening the ending and uniting the lovers he was making the play more palatable to the taste of Western viewers and, in the short run, he was probably right. But the didactic center and moral tone of the play is lost; the fascinating tension between the formal structure and the intense emotions, and between primitive seriousness and biting comedic satire are largely blunted. And these are the qualities of the play that stimulated the great German playwright Bertolt Brecht in 1945 to write his own masterful adaptation—*The Caucasian Chalk Circle.*

CLARISSA

Type of work: Novel
Author: Samuel Richardson (1689-1761)
Type of plot: Sentimental romance
Time of plot: Early eighteenth century
Locale: England
First published: 1747-1748

This epistolary novel, Richardson's masterpiece, is the longest novel in the language. The story of Clarissa Harlowe is told with subtlety and psychological depth, as we watch Robert Lovelace become obsessed with breaking down the heroine's virtue, simply because she is apparently incorruptible. He finally drugs and rapes her, causing her to flee to a secret dwelling, where she dies of grief and shame.

Few men would have seemed less likely than Samuel Richardson to be influential in the history of the novel. A successful printer, he did not publish his first work until after he was fifty. Because of a reputation as an accomplished letter writer, he was encouraged to write a book of sample letters. Even before the publication of this volume, *Familiar Letters* (1741), he turned his epistolary talent to didactic purposes in fiction with the publication of *Pamela* (1740). Predictably, *Pamela* was greeted with popular approval and critical disdain. By 1744, he had prepared a summary of his epistolary masterpiece, *Clarissa.* The massive novel was published in three installments between December, 1747, and December, 1748, and was subsequently printed in eight volumes. Richardson was aware of length (about one million words) as a serious failing in his narrative and, indeed, *Clarissa* is now rarely read except in George Sherburn's abridgement. The length was probably less an impediment for the more leisurely reading class of the mid-eighteenth century.

Richardson's main literary contribution is his mastery of the epistolary style. The use of letters as a means of narration has obvious drawbacks. Certainly the flow of the narrative is repeatedly interrupted and it takes all of the strength of one's will to suspend disbelief concerning the writing of thoughtful and informative letters by characters during periods of extraordinary stress. Conventions aside, it is difficult in this form, to sustain a continuous and progressive narrative. The method frustrated Samuel Johnson, a friend of Richardson, who concluded that one should read the work for its sentiment. Richardson himself worried that his narrative technique had let his characters do too much in too short a period of time.

Richardson did, however, capitalize on the correlative advantages of the epistolary method. The immediacy of "writing to the moment" is a prime means of developing concerned attention in the reader. In addition, Richardson's talent for dialogue transforms many of the lengthier letters into poignant scenes and the text of each letter is most decorously cast in a style appropriate to the correspondent. Moreover, there is the advantage, especially for a didactic novel, of the multiple points of view which add complexity and sympathy to the interpretation of the action. As Alan McKillop says, letters are not simply presented but "copied, sent, received, shown about, discussed, answered, even perhaps hidden, intercepted, stolen, altered or forged." The whole process of correspondence comes alive as Richardson blends theater, moral discourse, courtesy book, and romance into a compellingly tense analysis of contemporary morals and manners.

As the use of the epistolary style would suggest, action is less important to Richardson's fiction than reflection on the moral significance of actions. It may be that the author was familiar with the life of the gentry only through the theater. Nevertheless, despite an apparent ignorance of the frequent occupations of a rich country family, the focus is so much on the tenseness of the situations and the meaning of actions that little is lost by the absence of sociological verisimilitude. Although Richardson occasionally presents dramatically vivid details, he usually is less interested in setting than in what Sherburn calls, in the contemporary eighteenth century terminology, a "distress."

The main theme of the novel, as described by Richardson on the title page, is "the distresses that may attend the misconduct both of parents and children in relation to marriage." There is no doubt that the motives of the Harlowes are crassly materialistic—to improve the already comfortable family fortune by forcing Clarissa to marry the suitable, but elderly, Solmes. There is a lack of tenderness and family feeling towards Clarissa, which softens only after it is too late and she is well along in her final decline. Clarissa, for her part, is also strong-willed. As Richardson explains about his fiction, "The principal of the two young Ladies is proposed as an exemplar of her Sex. Nor is it any objection to her being so, that she is not in all respects a perfect character." This from an author especially fond of the companionship and adulation of ladies.

At first Clarissa is attracted by the roguish but fascinating Lovelace. In fact, he occasionally seems not all a bad fellow. At least he is the most vivid character in the novel. Yet his egocentrism and his attraction to intrigue, however appealing, are inconsiderate of others and are not recanted until his sentimental dying breaths. His assaults on Clarissa seem almost an agression on her sex. Still, after the deed is done, practicality seems to demand that Clarissa turn virtue into its own reward, as Pamela had done, by marrying her seducer. However, *Clarissa* is a more complex novel than *Pamela* and Clarissa and Lovelace have already shown a moral incompatibility which makes acquiescence by Clarissa impossible (despite the impassioned pleadings of Richardson's sentimental readers before the last third of the novel appeared.)

At the heart of the incompatibility is Clarissa's admirable, but rigid, idealism. Although a gentle person, she is unreserved in her commitment to virtue and, as Sherburn puts it, to decorous behavior. She is not so much a puritan as a devotee of what is morally fit, and she carries her commitment to the grave. When her friend Miss Howe suggests that she take the expedient way out by marrying the ostensibly repentant Lovelace, Clarissa cannot give in. First, she would prefer reconciliation with her intransigent family, but second, and more important, her sense of propriety would not allow such moral and personal compromise. Nevertheless, it must be admitted that she is less interesting for her idealism than for the distressing situations and dilemmas her idealism occasions.

Despite its narrative improbabilities and the moral obstinacy of its main character, *Clarissa* became a revered example not only of the epistolary novel but also of the refined novel of sentiment and, by the end of the century, it had been imitated and acclaimed both in England and on the Continent.

Edward E. Foster

CLAUDIUS THE GOD

Type of work: Novel
Author: Robert Graves (1895-   )
Type of plot: Historical chronicle
Time of plot: A.D. 41-54
Locale: Rome, Britain, the Near East
First published: 1934

A sequel to I, Claudius, *this novel again illustrates Graves's meticulous care for detail and scrupulous handling of incident and character. In his portrait of the Roman Emperor and his reign, Graves is remarkably successful in re-creating the atmosphere of a past time and place.*

In this sequel to *I, Claudius,* Robert Graves continues the development of the historical novel that he had begun in his earlier work. Before Graves, this literary form was seldom other than a romance, contemporary to whatever age in which it was written and covered over with a thin veneer reminiscent of exotic climes and distant times and places. Graves, however, uses the form of the historical novel not to disguise the present but to explore and bring to light the past. In *I, Claudius* and *Claudius the God,* Graves does successfully what Gore Vidal has done in *Julian* and more recently in *Burr.* Graves studies the original historical sources—Tacitus, Suetonius, Pliny, Varro, Josephus, and many others—and tells the story of the Emperor Claudius. It is a measure of Graves' talent and skill that he can make his evocation of the past seem real and vivid, even to those with a solid grounding in the history of the early Roman Empire.

The solid historical background of *Claudius the God* is only one of the reasons why it is worth the reader's time and effort. Another is Graves' skill with language. Readers of this book are not only educated about Roman history and enlightened by the author's interpretation of it, but are entertained.

The form Graves uses is that of a memoir; the book is supposedly written in Claudius' own words and from his point of view.

Claudius is known to most students of Roman history as a rather dull person, stupid and silly in equal measure. But Graves takes some of the historical anomalies of Claudius' life and reign and explains them from the Roman's point of view; for example, he describes Claudius' relationship with Messalina as a case of a decent and trusting man whose very decency and honesty is exploited by his wife. History seldom happened as the historians wrote it, and the great historical characters were only human beings living their everyday lives. Graves makes this point very forcefully, and his tool to do so is the poet's way with words and knowledge of motivations. Graves illustrates the fact that either poets should write more history or historians should be more poetic.

THE CLAYHANGER TRILOGY

Type of work: Novel
Author: Arnold Bennett (1867-1931)
Type of plot: Domestic realism
Time of plot: 1870-1895
Locale: England
First published: 1910, 1911, 1915

Depicting the nineteenth century middle class of England's industrial Midlands, Bennett was able to see a kind of beauty in an apparently dismal setting. The novels are largely autobiographical in their portrait of the tyrannical, puritanical father and his shy, sensitive son.

Arnold Bennett completed *Clayhanger*, the first novel of a trilogy concerning the life apprenticeship of Edwin Clayhanger, on June 23, 1910, two years after the publication of *The Old Wives' Tale*. At the height of his creative powers as well as of his critical reputation, Bennett ventured to write, in a format popular with Edwardian readers, his most nearly autobiographical novel. Compared to George Moore's *Confessions of a Young Man* (1888), Samuel Butler's *The Way of All Flesh* (1903), E. M. Forster's *The Longest Journey* (1907), and H. G. Wells's *Tono-Bungay* (1909), *Clayhanger* is a fairly typical "education novel." The representative hero of this genre is an inexperienced, often confused, but generally likeable young man who, after learning from a series of valuable adventures, develops a better understanding about himself and about life. Typically, the hero comes to terms with his weaknesses and strengths, discovers a proper vocation for his talents, and at least begins to understand the meaning and limitations of romantic love.

However, unlike the typical *Erziehungsroman* hero, whose "education" is completed at the end of the book, Edwin Clayhanger undergoes an extended apprenticeship from youth to middle age, testing the dreams and values of his young manhood against the often harsher realities of life itself. Indeed, in the novels that follow *Clayhanger, Hilda Lessways* (1911) and *These Twain* (1915), Bennett alters some of the conventions familiar to the genre. With a philosophy relentlessly deterministic, he pursues the romantic follies of Edwin and teaches him, at the last, a bitter lesson about his restricted place in the world.

It was a lesson Bennett well understood, for his own early life resembled that of his protagonist. His father Enoch Bennett—the Darius Clayhanger of the novel—was a Victorian tyrant who demanded, and usually failed to get, absolute respect from his dreamy, seemingly feckless son. One theme of the novel which appears also in later twentieth century fiction (Joyce's *Ulysses,* Wolfe's *Look Homeward, Angel,* Kafka's "The Judgment," for example) is that of the quest of a son for his spiritual father. Edwin hates Darius, longs for the old man's death. Yet he saves his father from financial ruin

when, with astonishing presence of mind, he secures a cable to hoist a collapsing printing press; and when Darius dies of natural causes (a scene as
harrowing as any deathbed drama in literature), the son is moved not to
thoughts of vengeance but of pity. Other characters and locations in the
novel are modeled after real people and places that Bennett knew intimately:
Auntie Bourne is Auntie Clara Hamps; Absolom Wood is Osmond Orgreave;
Cobridge is Bleakridge; Waterloo Road is Trafalgar Road. Probably many
characteristics of Marguerite Soulé, Bennett's French wife, appear in Hilda
Lessways. Above all, the trilogy is carefully crafted to simulate reality.
Detail upon detail, the trivia and circumstances of life are reproduced, and
the reader has a sense both of place solidly rendered and of time remorse-
lessly passing.

To be sure, time itself is a mysterious force, almost a metaphysical fate-
element in the trilogy. Like other twentieth century writers such as Proust,
Joyce, Mann, Woolf, Eliot, Bennett is deeply concerned with both the nature
and effects of time. His characters develop, change, mature to the slow
rhythm of time, and ultimately are destroyed by their silent adversary.
Whether with tantalizing deliberation, as time plays with old Mr. Shushion,
its "obscene victim"; or suddenly, with brutal finality, as time fells Darius,
it is the sole absolute, the single truth around which all life appears to revolve
as an illusion.

Counterpoised to time is the rhythm of life. In the wild sensual delight of
Florence Simcox, the "clog-dancer" of the Midlands, Edwin first perceives
the beauty of woman. At the "Dragon," where the Burseley Mutual Burial
Club holds a "free-and-easy," he responds to the vital warmth of friendship.
And with a single kiss from Hilda Lessways, a woman he both fears and
loves, he is turned for the first time, from a shy, fussy bachelor, into a man
of passion. For her part, Hilda has ignored Edwin until he utters, in a moment
of compassion and despair, "I'm ashamed of seeing my father lose his
temper." At this point, this moment of spiritual illumination, she begins to
fall in love with him. She is touched by what she believes to be his confession of weakness. Brutalized throughout her life by cruel men like George
Cannon, she senses that Edwin has the strength of his tenderness. Her judgment is flawed, however, because life has conditioned her to see Edwin not as
he is but as she wants him to be. Nor can Edwin truly understand the "real"
Hilda, who is not (as he believes) a woman of romantic mystery. Yet the illusion of the moment becomes the pattern for life. For Bennett, the small rather
than great moments of life have their deepest effects upon character. Magic is in
the rhythm of life, and beauty also; but the magic is terribly brief.

The last two novels of the trilogy, considerably less autobiographical than
Clayhanger, show a falling-off of Bennett's emotional powers but complete
his architectonic design. *Hilda Lessways* is interesting from a technical point
of view, because the novel describes the life of Hilda parallel to that of Edwin.

For each lover, the romantic partner is a projection of a dream, not the real person. Edwin and Hilda meet too late in their lives; their habits have been formed, and they are incapable of change. Indeed, the very qualities that they perceive in each other, willpower and assertiveness, are inimicable to their happiness. In *These Twain* Bennett details the inevitable results of their mismating. Hilda becomes a shrew. Edwin becomes his father—or a man very much like his father: intolerant, smug, materialistic. His decision, at the end of the trilogy, to make the best of a marriage that has lost its charm, is a triumph of practicality over romance. To Bennett, life at best is imperfect, and it is best endured without illusion.

Leslie B. Mittleman

CLIGÉS

Type of work: Poem
Author: Chrétien de Troyes (c. 1150-c. 1190)
Type of plot: Chivalric romance
Time of plot: Sixth century
Locale: England, Brittany, Germany, and Constantinople
First transcribed: Before 1164

This metrical romance combines materials from the Arthurian cycle with classical elements from Ovid, Vergil, Statius, and others. The central situation, the duping of Alis through the drinking of a potion, probably comes from a Byzantine story, but the detailed analysis of the anatomy of love is clearly medieval.

Students of medieval literature are familiar with the major characters of the Arthurian romances as they have appeared throughout the prose and poetry of the Middle Ages. Chrétien de Troyes was only one of a number of authors who incorporated the tales of the Arthurian cycle into their own works. The particular value of Chrétien's metrical romances, as represented by *Cligés,* derives from the author's ability to combine traditional stories with themes drawn from man's philosophical ideals and in so doing create a fine, multi-faceted literary work.

Beneath the surface of the exciting storyline, Chrétien was attempting to illustrate man's development from his innocent, crude stage to his highest potential as an intellectual, feeling human being. This type of theme is so basic to medieval literature that some critics have compared it to modern psychoanalytical studies in which the persons may be different but the stages of analysis are quite similar. The central character in the Arthurian romance sets out upon a particular quest such as love or glory, or in *Cligés,* knightly perfection, and throughout the journey, both real and allegorical, faces innumerable obstacles that are integral parts of the attainment of his goal.

In the course of *Cligés,* Chrétien was able to expound his own views of chivalry in the thoughts and actions of the hero. Cligés is perhaps the only hero of the medieval romance to exemplify human concern and generosity, and to provide a complete picture of the nature of chivalric love, one of the best exemplars in the entire canon of medieval literature. If one reads *Cligés* carefully, he will be rewarded not only by a delightful chivalric romance but also by an important statement concerning philosophical thought.

THE CLOISTER AND THE HEARTH

Type of work: Novel
Author: Charles Reade (1814-1884)
Type of plot: Historical romance
Time of plot: Fifteenth century
Locale: Holland, Germany, France and Italy
First published: 1861

Utilizing a variety of literary forms, including dramatic dialogue, the tale within a tale, poetry, extended letters, and picaresque romance, Reade produced a remarkably vivid, minutely detailed picture of fifteenth century life. His character-izations ring true in their vitality and humanness.

The Cloister and the Hearth is essentially a picaresque novel, rich with incident and vividly drawn characters, if not always profound or thoughtful. The accurate detail is never boring and a good-natured humor pervades the narrative. Despite its great length, the novel moves briskly, maintaining the reader's interest constantly. The scenes at the Burgundian Inn, for example, describing the gory battle between Gerard and Denys and the gang of thieves, are among the most thrilling in English fiction, and are worthy of the senior Dumas or Balzac.

The Cloister and the Hearth may have been in part an imitation of Scott's historical novels (many others, including George Eliot in *Romola,* were also copying Scott at this time), but it became much more than that. It stands by itself as a great novel. Much of the book is a quest, the story of a youth's education and pursuit of both a livelihood and a romantic goal. The pattern of the first half of the book is that of Gerard's learning process. He does not know what his destiny will be, but each step takes him closer to it. Only at the end, after his death, is the pattern finished and the meaning made clear. Gerard and his beloved Margaret are living not only for themselves, but for their son who will be.

Denys, the Burgundian bowman and "Pilgrim of Friendship," bursts with vitality and every page on which he strides and boasts is filled with life. Katherine, Gerard's mother, is another excellent characterization: lively, witty, and sensible. She begins as a type, but soon transcends type to become a sympathetic, clever, and delightfully amusing individual. One suspects that Reade was, himself, fond of her. The spinster Margaret Van Eyck emerges as a vivid personality, an intelligent, liberated female in an age when women were required to be both married and docile.

Reade kept voluminous files of clippings and notebooks in which were recorded all manner of information which interested him; in writing his novels, he made use of this material. A novel, he believed, must be based on "facts." His method brought to his books artistic truth in the handling of detail, setting, and episodes. He saturated himself in medieval history, art, and social customs and manners to write *The Cloister and the Hearth*. By absorbing himself in the literature and history of the period, Reade produced in this novel a picture of a remote era so faithfully and so finely etched, and so vividly realistic, that it never has been surpassed and rarely approached.

Charles Reade caught in *The Cloister and the Hearth* much of the tone of light and dark that dominated the end of the Middle Ages and the beginnings of the Renaissance; it was a brutal and turbulent time, stiff and heavy with death. The Dukes of Burgundy, with their ostentation, violence, and half-mad pride, were perhaps its representative rulers. At times the novel, crowded with wandering, lost individuals, becomes a *danse macabre,* a picture of rapidly growing cities, violence, wild superstition, crumbling religion, cynical realism, and ever-lusty humor. Reade's style is sometimes nervous and irritating, but it is always vigorous and compelling, and never fake or gushing like that of so many of his contemporaries. His perspective on the period of the novel is acute and perceptive, and his panorama crowded and colorful, yet never confusing.

Born in 1814 in Oxfordshire, the son of a country squire, Reade took his B.A. at Magdalen College, Oxford, and became a fellow of the college. He kept his fellowship at Magdalen all of his life, but spent the greater part of his time in London where he began his career as a dramatist. On the advice of the actress Laura Seymour, who later became his housekeeper and mistress, he transformed one of his plays into a novel. Several other novels followed in quick succession. The flaws of his fiction, a certain theatricality and occasional falseness of tone, can be attributed to the sensational theater pieces of the day and their influence upon him.

The Cloister and the Hearth was originally published serially as a long story titled "A Good Fight" in the magazine *Once a Week,* but was expanded to more than five times its length before it was published in four volumes. The novel, published (at the author's expense) on commission, provided Reade with his first real financial success. He was forty-eight.

Returning from the fifteenth century to modern English life, Reade produced another well-received novel, *Hard Cash,* in which he directed attention to the abuses of private lunatic asylums. Three other novels "with a purpose" followed, in which he grappled with trade unions, the degrading conditions of village life, and other problems. The Reade of later years, who had earned the admiration of such different artists as Dickens and Swinburne, was accused of wasting his talents in pursuit of social reforms.

Reade's greatest success as a dramatist was his last, *Drink,* an adaptation of Zola's *L'Assommoir,* produced in 1879. In that year, Laura Seymour died, and soon Reade's health failed. He died in 1884, leaving behind him a completed novel, *A Perilous Secret,* which showed no falling off in his abilities to weave a complicated plot and devise thrilling situations.

The epic theme of *The Cloister and the Hearth* is the misery caused by the vow of celibacy demanded of its priests by the Roman Church. The situation of Margaret, who loves and is beloved by Gerard, is the mother of his child, and yet is denied the privilege of being his wife because he is a priest, is described with excruciating pathos. Reade's own study of medicine led to the minor theme and indictment of the practice of bleeding patients that is so vividly presented in the novel. The growth of the arts during the first days of the Renaissance provides a continuing theme which reaches its peak of interest in the chapters in Italy.

The imaginative power of the narration is shown in many vivid scenes (for example, the frail wooden ship battling the storm off the Italian coast), yet the author's imagination seems to fail with the minor characters, who tend to be reduced to clichés of good and evil. This over-simplification of character is the one serious flaw in the novel, but it does not detract from the power and sweep of the story and the impact of the conclusion, when the reader learns that from these two troubled lives (Gerard and Margaret) will come the greatest humanist and writer of the period.

Bruce D. Reeves

THE CLOSED GARDEN

Type of work: Novel
Author: Julian Green (1900-   )
Type of plot: Psychological realism
Time of plot: 1908
Locale: France
First published: 1927

In this intense story of a woman who commits a crime of violence and goes mad after falling in love with a man to whom she has never spoken, Green probes the clash of wills and motives among members of a single household. Reputedly inspired by a Utrillo painting, the novel is somber in theme, in atmosphere melancholy and intense by turns.

Julian Green has said that his novels allow glimpses of "great dark stirrings" which he believes to be the deepest part of the soul. Quietly, but inevitably, this novel probes the deepest aspects of Adrienne Mesurat's being. Green felt from the beginning of his literary career that a novelist is "like a scout commissioned to go and see what is happening in the depth of the soul" and the writer then comes back to report what he has observed. The writer never lives on the surface, but only inhabits the darkest regions. In his diary, Green observed: "The anguish and loneliness of my characters can almost always be reduced to what I think I called a manifold dread of living in this world." Although Green's characters rarely express ideas, his books hold a view of the world, a philosophy. *The Closed Garden* stands at the head of his works, both in form and implied statement.

The characters in *The Closed Garden* try to preserve their lives as they are, but nothing can stay the same. Even passivity is a choice, an action which must have consequences; and these consequences can force one forward to the destiny waiting at the end. Monotony can lead as inevitably as more colorful events to tragedy—and perhaps more inescapably. People can tangle themselves in tragic fates without realizing until too late (if ever) what has happened. The inarticulate, Green seems to be implying in his tale, suffer as deeply as the more intelligent and sophisticated.

Adrienne Mesurat lives surrounded by quiet, but none the less deadly, selfishness. Her father thinks only of his own comfort, and her sister lives only for her illness. Adrienne is crushed beneath their wills—wretched and hardly knowing why. Green suggests that her condition is a metaphor for that of most of humanity. And what happens when she wakes up and tries to break loose from her invisible bonds? Life does not have the happy ending of the fairy tale. There can be only one ending. It is not contrived tragedy: it emerges from the characters themselves. "The author creates characters," wrote Green, "and the characters create the plot."

The style of *The Closed Garden* is typical of Green's elusive, subtle manner. His prose is quiet and unobtrusive. Gide commented about Green's books that the pencil seems never to leave the paper, the line is unbroken to the end. Green said that his intention in *The Closed Garden* and his other early works was to tell the story without ever allowing the reader to be "diverted by the style in which it was written, a sort of invisible style, good and strong, if possible, but not in any way noticeable." The complete efface-ment of the author seemed to Green one of the major requirements of literary perfection. He believed that it should be impossible for a reader to know what kind of person had written the book. He wanted the characters to speak and act for themselves, and never be interfered with by the author's person-ality.

Julian Green's conviction was that although Adrienne Mesurat appeared commonplace at first glance, she was as mysterious as any human being, and just as *alone*. She breathed and moved in an atmosphere of solitude which gradually became oppressive. Green feels that most of us never succeed in breaking down the barriers which separate us from the rest of humanity. Although we make constant contact with others, the communication is im-perfect at best. "When we are about to speak," wrote Green, "and reveal something about our inner life, who is in the mood to listen?" And if someone does hear, can he understand? This aloneness is the theme of *The Closed Garden* and of most of Green's fiction.

Julian Green was born of American parents in Paris, in 1900. While in his teens during World War I, he drove an ambulance and served in the French artillery. He studied music and art before turning to literature and achieving early recognition with his first novels. His elder sister Anne also is a novelist, although she writes in English, while the body of his work is in French. He was a close friend of Gide and was influenced by the master's style. The fall of France in World War II forced Green's return to Virginia, where he previously had attended college. During this time, he wrote his autobio-graphical *Memories of Happy Days*, his only book composed in English. In 1942, Green entered the U.S. army and worked with the office of War Information. After liberation in 1945, he returned to Paris.

A French critic has spoken of Green as a "pure" writer, explaining that he never has written a line except under absolute artistic compulsion. He lives and works under rigid self-discipline which rules out all petty distractions. In 1939, after twenty years, Green returned to the Catholic faith. This is shown strikingly in the several volumes of his *Journal*. Critics have compared his later novels favorably with those of Mauriac and Gide.

Green makes no sentimental appeal to the emotions. He creates horror in books such as *The Closed Garden* by cumulative value, not yielding to sen-sational effects. The realism of this novel is that of a nightmare. The lean style avoids decorations and seems to photograph the tragedy dispassionately. The emotion is concentrated and intense. Green maintains a firm control over the novel, avoiding the capriciousness and predictability of some of the later novels. Green's debt to the early American writers Poe and Hawthorne is evident in *The Closed Garden*. The carefully constructed prose and the moral concern that rule the story especially remind the reader of Hawthorne. At times, Green seems to suggest that sexuality is apart from the rest of life, and, because apart, evil. Certainly, Adrienne Mesurat, like so many other of his characters, cannot cope with her own sexuality and is destroyed by it as much as by anything else. Green's characters seem to feel a longing nostalgia for a peace and happiness which they have never known. But dreams and vague memories of bittersweet desires are not enough, as Green artfully demonstrates.

Julian Green received many awards and prizes during his long career, and in 1971 became the first American citizen to be elected to the French Academy.

Bruce D. Reeves

THE CLOUDS

Type of work: Drama
Author: Aristophanes (c. 448-385 B.C.)
Type of plot: Social satire
Time of plot: Fifth century B.C.
Locale: Athens
First presented: 423 B.C.

In this most popular of his plays, Aristophanes satirizes the Sophists, whom he felt were superficial in their philosophical approach. Scenes such as Socrates' logic lesson with Strepsiades, and Pheidippides' speech to his father are highly entertaining as comedy, even while their humor is so biting.

Largely because of its caricature of the philosopher Socrates, *The Clouds* is one of Aristophanes' best-known plays. This Greek master, recognized as a leading playwright in his day and still acknowledged as one of the foremost comic writers, colors this play with an air of buffoonery and raillery, sometimes savage and biting. Through Socrates, Aristophanes satirizes the entire Sophist movement in education, which he considered irreverent and demoralizing. Even though it only won third prize when it was presented in 423 B.C., a fact which vexed its author considerably, *The Clouds* must have given the Athenian audience moments of high entertainment.

Greek comedy, like our light opera, was a mixture of song and dance; and the closest examples to which one might compare Aristophanes' comedies are the satirical works of Gilbert and Sullivan, except that Aristophanes' humor is bawdier and sharper in wit. Stylistically, this art form had a conventional structure known as Old Comedy. The *prologue* set forth a problem and the comic idea by which it might be resolved. Thus, in *The Clouds,* Strepsiades has a mountain of debts incurred by his son, so he decides to send his son to learn the Sophist methods of argument. Failing that, he goes to learn from Socrates. The *parode,* or entrance song of the chorus, follows in which Socrates' new divinities, the clouds, appear singing. Later, the playwright, Aristophanes, steps out and sings a *parabasis* on a theme of public interest, which tells the audience what a fine dramatist he is and how foolish the Athenians were to let Cleon have power. Next comes the *agon,* or debate, where Right Logic and Wrong Logic, two characters, attack and defend sophistic teaching. Then a series of *episodes* follows in which we view the results of Strepsiades' original notion of sending his son to learn how to argue falsely. The *episodes* are often the funniest part of the comedy, as in this play. The *exode,* or final choral song, is unusually brief in *The Clouds* and occurs as Socrates' house is being burned.

Strepsiades can be seen as the comic version of the tragic hero, as he prospers in his scheme until, by *hubris* (overweening pride), he undergoes a fall, where he is beaten by his son. And then comes the recognition of his own error. The plot hinges on Strepsiades' attempt to evade paying his creditors; but he is not wholly to blame, since his extravagant son, Pheidippides, incurred the debts. Aristophanes burlesques the tragic theater here very inventively.

However, the brunt of the satire falls squarely on the figure of Socrates, and through him the whole Sophist movement in Athenian education. The problem is that Plato presents a very different picture of Socrates. Whereas Aristophanes' portrait shows him as completely amoral, a man who destroys traditional religion and morality and replaces these with nonsense supported by specious reasoning. A further discrepancy is that in *The Clouds* Socrates is farcically concerned with natural science, particularly astronomy and meteorology, but in Plato he is only concerned with moral questions.

Some critics explain these divergences away by saying that the comic Socrates was a composite figure of several Sophists: himself; Protagoras, the logic-twister; Anaxagoras, who was interested in natural phenomena; and Diogenes of Apollonia, who regarded air as the primal element. But this view is inaccurate. Socrates was meant to be Socrates, and there is enough agreement with Plato in this play to make the caricature ring true. Socrates did study the natural sicences as a young man. Further, there is his ugliness, his poverty, his bare feet, his unorthodox religion, his penchant for homely analogies, his dialectical reasoning in the *agon,* his poking fun at the knowledge of the old, and, above all, his tremendous influence on young aristocrats. These are all subjected to farcical representation.

But why should Aristophanes want to attack Socrates and subject him to ridicule? For one thing, Socrates was well-known as a Sophist, even though he disclaimed the name. Furthermore, Aristophanes had learned that if you intend to lambast some social ill always pick the chief exponent of it. He invariably went for the chief figures—Cleon in politics, Euripides in tragedy, and Socrates in education.

Aristophanes, after all, was a conservative in every area of life. Born of landowners, he detested the way Athens was deteriorating in the Peloponnesian War, and he felt that the new spirit of radical experimentation was ruining the city. There is some justification for his assault on Socrates, for young idlers were learning his mode of dialectical logic and using it to prove that their immoral behavior was perfectly right, and that the gods were no longer to be feared. However, it is likely that these young men would have done as they pleased regardless of whether they had arguments to support their actions. On the core of the matter, Socrates' own integrity, Aristophanes was completely wrong. It is likely that he came to realize this, because he lampooned Cleon and Euripides as long as they lived, and even after, but once he had written *The Clouds* he more or less gave up making Socrates the butt of his wit.

It is interesting that the charges brought against Socrates a quarter of a century later, in 399 B.C., were identical to those that Aristophanes harbored against him in *The Clouds*. He was accused of corrupting the youth, replacing the traditional gods with gods of his own making. Many of the jurors had seen Aristophanes' play and had been prejudiced by it. Thus when Socrates drank the hemlock after his conviction, *The Clouds* had played a part in sentencing the honorable old man to death.

James Weigel, Jr.

THE COCKTAIL PARTY

Type of work: Drama
Author: T. S. Eliot (1888-1965)
Type of plot: Social criticism
Time of plot: Mid-twentieth century
Locale: London
First presented: 1949

This verse play, with its polished style, clever comedy, and sharp social criticism, was an immediate success on Broadway. Eliot's analysis of the psychiatry fad, the dullness of the cocktail party set, and the modern standard of success exposes the peculiarities and weaknesses of contemporary civilization.

Ten years after T. S. Eliot presented *The Family Reunion* to mixed reviews, he completed another, more popular verse drama, *The Cocktail Party.* In its first draft, sketched out in June, 1948, the play was in three scenes (or acts) with a projected epilogue, and was tentatively titled *One-Eyed Riley.* According to Elliott Martin Browne, producer of all Eliot's plays except *Sweeney Agonistes,* the original draft with its revisions was based more closely than the completed work upon Euripides' *Alcestis.* The "death" of Alcestis was to correspond with Lavinia's departure from Edward, before the party begins in Scene 1. And the services performed by Heracles, who descends into Hades to restore to Admetus his sacrificing wife, were to parallel to some extent those of Sir Henry (or Harry) Harcourt-Reilly, the psychiatrist who later patches together the flawed Chamberlayne marriage. Celia Coplestone, whom Eliot later described as the major character of the play, was in the early drafts only a minor personality. And the roles of Julia Shuttlethwaite, Peter Quilpe, and Alexander MacColgie Gibbs (first called Alexander Farquhar-Gibbs) were unexpanded and mostly comic.

In the preliminary revisions of the manuscript, Alex does not appear between the party scene of the first act and the conclusion of the consulting-room scene, with its elaborate libation-ritual of the Guardians. That scene, however, was developed much more fully in the manuscripts. In the final version of *The Cocktail Party,* produced at the Edinburgh Festival, August, 1949, the scene was simplified, although its poetic values were sharpened; thus the play was offered in its present form, three acts: Act I in three fully developed scenes; Act II in one scene, Sir Harry's office; and Act III in a brief scene at the Chamberlaynes' London flat.

Because *The Cocktail Party* changed so markedly during the early stages of its writing, the parts, which separately are effective, do not perfectly cohere as a whole work of stagecraft. The play is both a comedy of manners, much like the social satires of the eighteenth century, and a theological—specifically Catholic—drama of salvation. The lighter parts, especially the entire first act and most of the last, resemble the elegant plays of Sheridan, witty, tart, urbane; or for later models, they resemble the sophisticated comedies of Wilde, Maugham, even Noel Coward. But the serious parts—also "comic" in the sense that Dante's epic may be called a *Commedia*—resemble more closely the tragic farces of the novels of Evelyn Waugh. To satisfy the requirements of both light and serious comedy, Eliot's characters play two kinds of roles. The Julia of the first act is a meddlesome, scatterbrained old gossip; but in the second act, she is a sober and indeed sanctified Guardian of spiritual destiny. And Alex in the first act is a bumbling froth, an incompetent who concocts outrageous dishes and pops in and out of the action, much to Edward's annoyance. Yet in the ritual scene at the end of Act II, he is another Guardian, perhaps more mysterious than Julia, who has connections throughout the world—"even in California."

The most difficult character to understand, because of his double function in the play, is Sir Harry, the psychiatrist. In the first act, he is described simply as the Unidentified Guest. A secretive but enlightened visitor to the Chamberlayne party, he apparently understands the nature of the quarrel between Edward and Lavinia, pulls the strings, so to speak, to arrange for her return to her husband, yet never reveals his own position. A confessor-figure, he is at the same time a drunken reveler. Before he departs, toward the end of the first scene, he sings a bawdy song (the verses in the play are quite decorous, but other stanzas are traditionally ribald). "One-Eyed Riley" may remind the audience of fertility themes in *The Waste Land*; or it may, as Eliot suggested, recall the heroic-absurd figure of Heracles from the Euripides play. Sir Harry is both savant and fool, gifted with insight but unsteady from too much gin.

The meaning of his actions is similarly ambiguous. A doctor, his professional activity becomes a parody of psychiatrists. Nobody lies on the analyst's couch but Sir Harry. He collects "information" about Lavinia and Edward, without their consent, as part of his investigation of their marital condition. And he prescribes, when necessary, a cure that may require the patient to visit a hotel or a sanatorium. The hotel, a half-way house or retreat between the sane and insane world, is Lavinia's first destination, before she is reunited with Edward. The sanatorium, still more mysterious, is intended to cure victims of illusion, unreality. Still other patients, like Celia, he urges to discover their own mental health by working out their proper salvation. No wonder Lavinia questions whether the psychiatrist is a devil or merely a practical joker. In fact, Sir Harry is called a devil several times in the play; but he more closely resembles a divine agent. Although he has no power to effect spiritual cures, he understands the maladies of human or spiritual deprivation and prescribes a course of action to remedy the problem. But the sick persons must, after all, make a decision to reject or accept the psychiatrist's advice. Gifted with prescience, Sir Harry does not control the moral choices of his patients. They have free will and, although their destinies can be predicted, they must resolve whether to follow the example of Peter Quilpe, who chooses to go to Boltwell—earthly corruption— or follow Celia, who chooses Kinkanja, martyrdom as a means of salvation.

Celia, the moral center of the play, also is a difficult person to understand. Unlike Sir Harry, she has no metaphysical function in the drama; but her character is seemingly inconsistent. In the first scene of Act I, she is a vapid young socialite, who presses Julia to finish her inane story about Lady Klootz's wedding cake. In the second scene the audience discovers that Celia has been Edward's mistress. Disappointed when her faint-hearted lover tells her that he is quite comfortable in his relationship with Lavinia and awaits his wife's return, she comes to understand that he is mediocre, unworthy of her affections. In the third scene, she is further estranged from Edward but is no longer annoyed with him. Rather she dismisses him as an amusing little boy, ludicrous but not vexing. And, like Peter, she announces her decision to go abroad. The audience is not fully prepared, then, for the change in Celia's character in Act II. She now appears to be intense, introspective, almost visionary. In her consultation with Sir Harry, the most touching and poetically effective part of the play, she reveals unexpected resources of vital strength and integrity. She is weary of herself, not because others have failed her, but because she has failed the world. Guilt-ridden for no specific cause, she confesses to sin. Her psychiatrist-metaphysician suggests a spiritual cure for her guilt. She must discover her own redemption—one that will lead to a kind of crucifixion on an ant hill, an absurd but (from Eliot's viewpoint) purposeful death.

Because Celia's death, announced by Alex in Act III, usually comes as a shock to the audience, it should be understood in the light of Eliot's theme. Although *The Cocktail Party* is superficially an elegant comedy of manners, it is beneath the surface a morality play. The theme of the play is that reality takes many disguises. All of the characters attempt to approach the real— or what is real for their needs. But most continue to play out roles of illusion. Edward, a Prufrock-like lawyer, reconciles with his practical but unimaginative wife. At the end of the play, just as at the beginning, the Chamberlaynes prepare a cocktail party to amuse other bored, lonely people like themselves. Their reconciliation to the "building of the hearth," the commonplace but necessary compromises of domesticity, is satisfactory for each partner. Edward cannot love another but at least does not have to dissemble his frailty to Lavinia. For her part, she is unlovable. Nevertheless, her vanity will not suffer any insult from a complaisant husband like Edward. So each is happy, understanding no other destiny.

Yet for the few elect souls like Celia, reality is not a casual entertainment like a cocktail party but the narrow path of Christian service. Her martyrdom (and, we assume, sainthood) is earned at the cost of terrible suffering. In Eliot's first version of the play, her death was described even more terribly:

she was a victim of devouring ants. The final version toned down most of the horror by alluding to a crucifixion "very near an ant-hill." However, Eliot's point was to affirm, through the announcement of Celia's death, the reality of divine interference in a world of the commonplace. Similarly, the transformation of comic figures like Sir Harry, Julia, and Alex into spiritual Guardians of mankind, reminds the audience that the real world itself is illusion, the unseen world real. It is significant, in this connection, to remember that the Guardian's final blessing for Edward, Lavinia, and Celia is taken from Buddha's deathbed exhortation to his followers: "Work out your salvation with diligence." That is the message of Eliot's play.

Leslie B. Mittleman

THE COLLEGIANS

Type of work: Novel
Author: Gerald Griffin (1803-1840)
Type of plot: Domestic tragedy
Time of plot: Late eighteenth century
Locale: Ireland
First published: 1828

Because he was intensely interested in Irish customs and personalities, Griffin filled the pages of his novel with items of folklore and attempted to capture the music of the peasants' language. The plot, a romantic tale of class boundaries that interfere with love, became more familiar to Americans in the drama version by Dion Boucicault.

Padraic Colum has called *The Collegians* the best of the Irish romantic novels. *The Collegians* possesses a charm and a vitality which are unique. It is definitely a young author's book, and it is no surprise to learn that Griffin was only twenty-five when it was written. A novel of love and murder, it is also a book rich with native humor and filled with delightful characterizations of the Irish folk. The book treads dangerously close to preciousness, but fortunately misses that fatal flaw.

The superstitions of the common people are used like embroidery to fill out the picture of Irish life. A wonderful example is when Lowry Looby meets the redhaired woman on his way to get his new job, turns back because it is unlucky to meet a redheaded woman on a journey, and thus loses the job. But a certain morbid quality is also discernible in many of the characters; shadings of light and dark in their personalities give them a unique vividness.

The higher an individual's station in life, the more serious and rational he or she is, it seems. The lower classes and servants tend to be filled with comic chatter and droll observations, and to perform comic routines that hold up the narrative. Eily O'Connor and her ropemaker father are the exceptions to the rule that the poor folk must be humorous, and they are soon established as living below their proper station. This is particularly true of Eily, for her beauty and learning set her apart from the other village girls; this is the beginning of her tragedy. Eily is described repeatedly as too elegant for a peasant girl, but too modest to claim the rank of gentlewoman. In this world it is necessary that no individual challenge class distinctions; lose sight of your proper place and you will have a bad end.

By the same token, Hardress should have known better than to stoop to marry a peasant; by betraying his class, he could only bring disaster to all concerned. But his arrogance is such that he believes he can get away with anything, and force people to do what he desires. Eily and Hardress upset the social balance and must pay the consequences. The world in which they live is a hard one, and allows for no escape from its rules.

COLOMBA

Type of work: Novel
Author: Prosper Mérimée (1803-1870)
Type of plot: Romantic adventure
Time of plot: Early nineteenth century
Locale: Corsica
First published: 1840

This romantic tale of vengeance between two Corsican families, one cowardly and the other honorable, centers around a girl's determined efforts to avenge her father's death. Although primitive Corsican customs are contrasted with the civilized manners of two British subjects, Mérimée depicts his Corsican heroine and her family as honorable and courageous people.

Colomba, Prosper Mérimée's second novel, is set in Corsica. When the novel was published, Corsica was part of France politically, but was, to most Frenchmen, an exotic country where life was simpler, and where the vendetta held the place that law held in the rest of France. Mérimée's talent for describing the folkways of exotic, lawless peoples is clear in *Colomba,* although not as fully developed as in his later novel, *Carmen.* But *Colomba* is not an escapist romance. Although a love story, it is also a story, told on the personal level, of the struggle between the modern state, with its laws, and the ancient Corsican family, with its vendettas.

Most of the struggle is within the soul of Orso della Rebbia, a former Corsican soldier now in the French army. Familiar with the ways of the modern state, he is goaded into the vendetta by his sister Colomba, who knows only the old ways. He is restrained, to some extent, by Lydia Nevil, the English girl whom he loves, and who has given him her Egyptian ring as a reminder that he must obey the law and disregard the vendetta. Lydia and Colomba are symbols of the modern view and the older view; their struggle for Orso symbolizes his internal torment. Ultimately, he demonstrates the victory of Lydia and her way of thinking by formally surrendering to the law to stand trial for a crime he did not commit.

Peripheral roles are played by Barricini, who cannot give up the vendetta, although he has become a lawyer and a mayor under the new system, and by the prefect, who uses both persuasion and force to do his delicate job. The struggle between law and vendetta is seen from many aspects, and brilliantly described from each of them.

THE COMEDY OF ERRORS

Type of work: Drama
Author: William Shakespeare (1564-1616)
Type of plot: Farce
Time of plot: First century B.C.
Locale: Ancient Greece
First presented: c. 1592

The Comedy of Errors *is a farce-comedy bordering at times on slapstick. The basic plot, inherently confusing, involves two sets of twins and a family, separated for years, which is reunited at last in court. For his sources in this play, Shakespeare used* The Menaechmi *of the Roman playwright Plautus, and perhaps Plautus'* Amphitryon *as well.*

Doubles are employed by Shakespeare in his comedies and, occasionally, in his tragedies. The technique, at least in the comedies, is generally introduced for the sake of exploring the nature of social identity. Indeed, for Shakespeare, one's identity could not be established outside of the social framework. To be real, to be actually one's self, consisted in becoming who one was in society. To depart from one's station, to go into exile, as the young lovers do in *A Midsummer Night's Dream* when they forsake Athens for the woods, is not only to lose one's bearings but actually to invite madness. This failure to acknowledge one's real, social identity can take on serious consequences as it does in *King Lear* when the old man refuses to concede that he is no longer king and continues to act as the monarch.

The consequences, of course, in *The Comedy of Errors* are high farce and ripping good fun, and it would be a mistake to burden the play with too heavy a significance. In this early comedy, Shakespeare plays with the idea of mistaken identity by creating two sets of twins. When they are brought together, as the two Antipholuses and the two Dromios are, the humor arises from a rather rudimentary confusion. Yet it is a humor based on the pain that each pair experiences when no one in Ephesus recognizes them for who they feel they are. In effect, by being mistaken for someone else, the four undergo a loss of identity; or to put it another way, by having two identities, they discover they really have none at all. At the conclusion everything is straightened out, normality returns, and the heroes' pains are reduced when their rightful identities have been restored. The comedy is over: they are recognizable and recognized.

COMRADES

Type of work: Drama
Author: August Strindberg (1849-1912)
Type of plot: Comic realism
Time of plot: Late nineteenth century
Locale: Paris
First presented: 1888

While his Scandinavian contemporaries, Ibsen and Bjørnson, were defending the rights of women in their plays, Strindberg was pleading the cause of male supremacy. In this relatively early and weak play, he uses comedy to illustrate the impossibility of a marriage based on equal rights and to point up the shallow meanness and viciousness of those females who aspire to masculine prerogatives.

No author has dramatized the "battle of the sexes" more starkly and brutally than August Strindberg in his plays, novels, and autobiographical writings. To Strindberg, at least in the early part of his career, the sexual conflict was primal and constant, rooted in the nature of the species, and resolved only by victory or mutually destructive stalemate. However distorted and extreme such an attitude may seem, it accounts for much of the dramatic intensity and ferocity of his most famous sexual duels, *The Father* (1887), *Miss Julie* (1888), and *The Dance of Death* (1901). *Comrades,* completed shortly before *The Father,* is his first treatment of the subject and, although it lacks the depth or impact of these others, it is the one play in which Strindberg confronts the issue of feminism in its social context.

Strindberg's message in *Comrades* is that the movement for female equality is, in fact, a strategy for primacy. A marriage, such as the one proposed for Axel and Bertha "to be as two comrades," is basically impossible, because every couple must have its dominant figure. The illusion of comradeship, however, allows Bertha to claim equality wherever Axel has the edge, but to retain her female prerogatives whenever she wants to. Axel, being naïve and taking the agreement at face value, encourages her painting, subsidizes her schooling, and pays for her model by neglecting his own work, and even enters his own painting under Bertha's name to gain recognition for her. On her side, Bertha abuses him, demeans his efforts, takes presents from Willmer, a male admirer, pockets the household money while juggling the budget books, and reacts with petulance to criticism of her work and glee at rejection of his. Her goal is not equality or independence or even superiority; it is total control of Axel. "I would like to humiliate him," she admits, "so deeply that he would come crawling to me." In short, Strindberg considers men superior intellectually, morally, and aesthetically and quite deserving of their higher social and cultural position. The female, however, because of her larger, hungrier ego, her possessiveness, her ruthlessness, and her deviousness, is more likely to win the sexual battle unless the male comes to understand his opponent and, like Axel, takes charge. Carl Starck is the only "happily married" man in the play because he has absolute domination over his wife.

However, since Strindberg considered sexual combat to be basic to the human experience, the specifically social issue of feminism probably weakens the play. Or perhaps *Comrades* is inferior because Strindberg had not yet perfected the realistic technique that characterizes his best early plays. Although he no doubt intended a naturalistic treatment, Strindberg was still strongly influenced by the contemporary French theater, and *Comrades* has many elements of the "pièce bien faite ("well made play"): the plot is contrived, the characters are superficial, and the emphasis is on long, tedious explanations. The dramatic problem is a thin one (whose picture really won the prize?) and remains largely in the background. Axel's insight into Bertha's motives actually occurs near the end of the first act when, having learned that his picture has been rejected, he becomes aware of Bertha's pleasure at his failure.

From that point on there are no real surprises left in the play. The characters discuss their feelings and ideas at great length and from all conceivable angles, but the play has little forward movement. A George Bernard Shaw might have been able to utilize such a situation, but Strindberg lacked the wit, intellectual subtlety, and sheer rhetorical power necessary for sophisticated idea comedies. Consequently, although there are some biting exchanges, *Comrades* is neither clever enough for comedy nor realistic enough for straight drama. Strindberg was a playwright of passions, not ideas, and in this play he only touches the surface of his tormented souls. Thus, *Comrades* remains a provocative preview of intense and profound dramatic struggles to come.

COMUS

Type of work: Masque
Author: John Milton (1608-1674)
Type of plot: Moral allegory
Time of plot: The age of myth
Locale: Kingdom of Neptune
First presented: 1634

Although it is in many ways closer to a pastoral drama than a conventional masque, Milton wrote Comus *in the form of a masque: a drama-spectacle popular in the sixteenth and seventeenth centuries composed of dancing, pageantry, and processions, which was presented by the nobility for special occasions in their own homes.* Comus *foreshadows Milton's later epic poetry in its verse structure, its sensuous metaphors, and its wealth of classical imagery used to further Puritan philosophy.*

The ideas debated in *Comus* were ideas which were to preoccupy Milton in much of his later poetry. The main theme, the triumph of Virtue over Vice, is dramatized by a temptation plot that Milton was to employ later in *Paradise Lost* (the temptation of Eve) and *Paradise Regained* (the temptation of Christ). In *Comus,* as in the two greater works, the intended victim is tempted to commit a mortal sin by the specious reasoning of a fiend. When the Lady rejects the apparently plausible arguments for satisfying her appetites, she demonstrates the fact that the truly virtuous and chaste person is armed against all evil, "clad in complete steel," and that "the unpolluted temple" of her mind can overrule the desires of her body. She is just the opposite of those whose judgments are ruled by their passions and appetites: those who, like Comus' men-turned-beasts, have forfeited their reason. On a less explicitly Christian level, the debate between Comus and the Lady may be seen as the conflict between an Epicurean, *carpe diem* philosophy, directed towards pleasure and the enjoyment of nature's bounty, and a Stoical philosophy, whose chief goal is temperate living and the subjugation of appetite and desire.

Milton's poetry, probably influenced by Spenser's *Faerie Queene,* is dense and lush. For instance, in the following lines of the Lady:

> They left me when the gray-hooded Even
> Like a sad votarist in palmer's weed
> Rose from the hindmost wheels of Phoebus' wain

we see in close succession such devices as extended simile, personification, classical allusion, archaic diction, and Milton's characteristic periodic construction — all used with a highly conscious intention not to imitate normal speech, but to create a heightened sense of situation and tension, along with pleasing melodic sounds. Milton takes special care in his descriptive passages, particularly those of the Spirit at the beginning and the end, and in the invocations to Sabrina. In fact, nowhere is the often noted mixture of Christian and pagan elements in *Comus* so striking as in the apparent discrepancy between the ascetic Christian doctrine that is preached, and the splendidly rich poetic texture through which it is dramatized.

CONFESSIONS OF AN ENGLISH OPIUM EATER

Type of work: Essays
Author: Thomas De Quincey (1785-1859)
Type of treatise: Confession and fantasy
Time of treatise: Early nineteenth century
Locale: England and Wales
First published: 1821

Because De Quincey was a conscious stylist who attempted to charge his prose with the imagination and emotional qualities of poetry, this work is often difficult for the modern reader to appreciate, in spite of its sensational subject matter. The essays abound in deliberate displays of erudition, protracted sentimentality, latinate diction and sentence structures, and apostrophes to inanimate objects or abstract ideas.

De Quincey's *Confessions of an English Opium Eater* remains the most arresting and, at the same time, touchingly human account we have of the widespread phenomenon of opium addiction in the early nineteenth century. Laudanam, or tincture of opium, was readily available at pharmacies in De Quincey's time, and was considered an effective cure for extreme headaches and depression. Coleridge also took laudanam for his neuralgic pains, and most readers of Romantic literature are familiar with the exotic fragment "Kubla Khan," which is purported to be the result of an interrupted attempt to capture the elusive memories of an opium dream.

In his *Confessions of an English Opium Eater,* De Quincey refrains from trying to construct art, even in fragments, from his opium reveries. Instead he is a kind of impressionistic reporter, a writer who shares with his readers the letter of his visions and their source in the common experiences of his life. The result is a curious taming of the marvelous, a domestication of the horrific. When we first encounter the gentle and simple Ann, a child prostitute, De Quincey of course knows that we shall recognize her at the end of his book in the terrifying dream of "female forms" crying "everlasting farewells." This dream, one of the "Pains of Opium" recalls the agonizing inability of De Quincey ever to find Ann again after their separation in London. The opium dream becomes a final farewell to this pathetic adolescent experience. As terrifying as it is, the dream is also cathartic and humanizing. In a sense, the dream finally "finds" Ann.

If opium dreams revivify haunting memories, they can also immortalize trivial moments. The chance visit of the Malay sailor at De Quincey's cottage in the Lakes becomes the source of a series of opium dreams on Oriental themes. These dreams become increasingly terrifying and fantastic; they reveal De Quincey's deep fears of the unknown and his subconscious racial prejudices.

It is in this sense that De Quincey's work belongs to the tradition of St.

Augustine's and Rousseau's *Confessions*. For finally we learn more about the man than we do about opium.

CONFESSIONS OF FELIX KRULL, CONFIDENCE MAN

Type of work: Novel
Author: Thomas Mann (1875-1955)
Type of plot: Social realism
Time of plot: Early twentieth century
Locale: Germany, Paris, Lisbon
First published: 1954

Like many of Mann's protagonists, Krull symbolically represents the artist, and by assigning him the profession of a confidence man, Mann dramatizes his idea of the connection between art and charlatanism. This volume, subtitled The Early Years, *was the first in a series cut short by the author's death.*

Thomas Mann is celebrated for his ironic quality, present even in his most serious works, but he seldom appears as humorist outright. *Confessions of Felix Krull, Confidence Man* is the great exception. It is in its very form a parody of the honored German traditional "Bildüngsroman" or novel of education, and has links as well going back to *Parsifal* and *Simplicissimus*. It is, furthermore, a parody of Mann's own favorite themes, and it is appreciated best by those who know Mann's other work. Felix is a variation on the theme of the artist-bourgeois conflict seen in *Buddenbrooks, Tonio Kröger,* and *Death in Venice.*

In all of these, the artist type is seen as linked to the dissolution of bourgeois standards, the collapse of families, and loss of the life force. The artist stands outside society and observes it, often with great ambivalence. He is in a sense a product of decay and even though his work achieves perfection in the aesthetic sense, this perfection undermines the solid everyday world of the bourgeois.

It was only a brief step for Mann to stretch the concept of "artist" to include a Felix Krull, consummate actor, creator of illusions, a parasite whom society welcomes because of the perfection of his role playing, for whom life itself becomes the raw material for a work of art. His family is the typical Mann artist family (in part autobiographical): once prosperous, now on the verge of ruin, tending toward refinement and art even as its prosperity gives way. Both Felix and his sister, Olympia, are "artists" but neither in the serious sense. Her career is in the dance hall, his leads him to a series of delightfully improbable adventures. That the novel was unfinished is no doubt a cause for lament—and yet it is clear that the story is open-ended, for new artistic triumphs await Felix/Armand/Marquis de Venosta wherever he turns.

THE CONFIDENCE MAN

Type of work: Novel
Author: Herman Melville (1819-1891)
Type of plot: Social satire
Time of plot: Nineteenth century
Locale: The Mississippi River
First published: 1857

Episodic in structure, this symbolic story of a con man is a quietly bitter castigation of human nature. With a pessimism to rival Mark Twain's in his darker moods, Melville relentlessly depicts man's loss of faith in his fellows and shows the facility with which most men can be duped.

The white-clad mute and Black Guinea symbolize the cosmic forces Melville dramatizes in *The Confidence Man.* While it is uncertain whether one or both these figures are manifestations of the Confidence Man, they clearly represent the Christian appeal to love and charity at one extreme, and the power of the diabolic that preys upon human weakness and gullibility at the other. Melville generalizes the *Fidele's* passengers to represent "that multi-form pilgrim species, man," so the Mississippi River setting has universal as well as particularly American implications. Finally, the barber's "No Trust" sign ironically suggests the prevailing attitude of the world in which the action takes place.

In the confrontations between the Confidence Man and his victims, the inappropriateness of the Christian values of faith, hope, and charity are explored. The Con Man, in his various guises, is actually able to elicit far more trust than the barber's sign would suggest is possible, but he does so only to victimize those with whom he succeeds. At the opposite extreme from those who trust are the misanthropes who, though immune from the devil's wiles, are in their mistrust and isolation as far from the Christian ideal as those who are gulled. The most ironic examples of the extremes of attitude are Winsome and his disciple Egbert, who make a fine theoretical case for brotherly love but offer an equally compelling pragmatic argument against helping a fellow man.

The encounter with the Bible-reading old man at the end of the novel seems to represent Melville's final commentary on the practical impossibility of a world based on Christian principles. In spite of his ostentatious display of religion, the old man is hopelessly insecure and an easy victim. As the world is plunged into darkness, we sense the final triumph of evil.

CONINGSBY

Type of work: Novel
Author: Benjamin Disraeli (1804-1881)
Type of plot: Political romance
Time of plot: 1832-1840
Locale: England and Paris
First published: 1844

Besides being a fictional history of young Harry Coningsby's fortunes, Disraeli uses this novel to trace the decline of the Whig and Tory factions in the British Parliament and the events leading to the birth of the Conservative Party. Many of the characters are readily identifiable with real personages of the time.

Reading *Coningsby,* one feels that one is in the company of a genuine Insider, who can describe from firsthand experience the workings of the government, the life at court, even the mode of existence at Eton. (Actually, Disraeli wrote with the obsessive fascination of an Outsider who had to struggle to get inside.) Life among the very rich and very powerful is meticulously detailed for the pleasure of the reader; and although this was not Disraeli's purpose in writing *Coningsby,* it made the novel popular and has contributed to its lasting interest. Disraeli's avowed intention was to give a picture of the growth of the Conservative Party and to illustrate the change facing the new generation in the 1840's. He also wanted to educate the public concerning the true history and influence of the Jews in Western Europe.

Throughout the novel, Disraeli stresses the importance of "character," that is, the moral and intellectual makeup of an individual. Some people possess weak characters, others strong, and the incidents of life reveal these characters for what they are. Some men rise to an occasion while others are incapable of coping with a situation; thus, Disraeli implies, history is made. Character reveals itself as early as in a youth's school days; Coningsby and his compatriots show at Eton the traits which cling to them throughout their lives.

The subtitle (*The New Generation*) is important because the novel immortalizes the group in the 1840's which was nicknamed "Young England." This group, which looked to Disraeli for their inspiration, was hostile to the traditional, humdrum middle-class Conservatism; they were romantic and aristocratic, and looked to a golden past where the people and the nobility were united in an alliance supporting throne and Church. In Coningsby, Disraeli's distrust of the growing industrial class is strongly evident, and lends force and direction to much of the narrative.

THE CONJURE WOMAN

Type of work: Novel
Author: Charles Waddell Chesnutt (1858-1932)
Type of plot: Regional romance
Time of plot: Post-Civil War
Locale: North Carolina
First published: 1899

Through this portrayal of an old Negro retainer, Chesnutt presents pure folktale combined with regional romance. Some of Uncle Julius' stories are fantasy at its finest, delicately and fancifully told.

Less a full-dress novel than a collection of loosely connected tales presented against a unifying background of post-bellum Southern life, *The Conjure Woman* nevertheless preserves a relatively inaccessible and easily overlooked portion of American social and literary history. Well reviewed upon publication, the book became a bestseller in Cleveland, where the author was a practicing lawyer. Interestingly, Chesnutt deemed it necessary to conceal his racial identity: at no point do the context or the stately, mannered prose indicate that the writer is a black man. Only in rendering Uncle Julius McAdoo's tales does Chesnutt have a chance to display his considerable skill with the now-defunct Gullah Afro-American dialect.

Some of these stories, in the author's words, "are quaintly humorous; others wildly extravagant, revealing the Oriental cast of the negro's imagination; while others . . . disclose many a tragic incident of the darker side of slavery." They remind us too of the Uncle Remus stories, although those tend to be more avuncular and amusing than Chesnutt's tales; both sets of tales recall the treasury of Afro-American folklore replete with bird and animal stories, tales of witches and spells, spirits and haunts, horrors, wonders, protests, and scares.

The stories in *The Conjure Woman* are valuable for their graphic and touching portrayal of plantation life in the old days, as well as for what William Dean Howells praised as, "a wild, indigenous poetry, the creation of a sincere and original imagination." The stories are, in addition, laced with a light and amusing irony. It is worth noting that Uncle Julius' white auditors are inevitably manipulated—usually successfully, sometimes not—by the devices of their simple black storyteller. Chesnutt's triumph, however, is that in the final analysis the reader is left, through these tales, with an increased appreciation of man's human stature and dignity.

A CONNECTICUT YANKEE IN KING ARTHUR'S COURT

Type of work: Novel
Author: Mark Twain (Samuel L. Clemens, 1835-1910)
Type of plot: Social satire
Time of plot: Sixth century
Locale: England
First published: 1889

In this satirical chronicle, Twain exposes the glorified days of knight errantry as childish barbarism; instead of the legendary gallantry, the Yankee finds a cruel feudalistic system under which the common people are abused and impoverished. Through the Yankee, Twain transmits his belief that a government is only good if the bulk of the people benefit from it.

A *Connecticut Yankee in King Arthur's Court* should have offered Mark Twain one of his best opportunities to attack the repressive and anti-democratic forces which he saw in post-Civil War America as well as in sixth century England. That the attack becomes in large part an exposé of the very system Twain sought to vindicate reveals as much the deep division in Twain's own nature as any problem inherent in the material itself. Ironically, though, much of the interest the work holds for contemporary readers is based upon the complications resulting from Twain's inability to set up a neat conflict between the forces of progress and those of repression. Hank Morgan's visit to King Arthur's court discovers not only the greed and superstition Twain associates with the aristocracy and the established Church, it reveals some of the weaknesses in man himself which enable these oppressive parasites to exist, and it finally comes to the realization that the industrial Utopia Hank tries to establish in old England is nothing more than a hopeless dream.

As a character, Hank Morgan is, in many respects, a worthy successor to his predecessor, Huckleberry Finn. Like Huck, Hank is representative of the common people, and, at his best, he asserts the ideal qualities Twain associates with those who escape the corruption of hereditary wealth and power and the conditioning of tradition. Unlike Huck, however, who was largely an observer powerless to change the system, Hank is given the opportunity to make his values the basis of a Utopian society. While Huck saw the threat of being "civilized" as an infringement on his individuality and freedom, Hank is, in his own way, fully "civilized" according to the standards of the world he represents. The pragmatc wit which enabled Huck Finn to survive against all odds becomes for Hank the basis of his rise in the industrial system to a position of authority and success. He fully accepts the nineteenth century doctrines of *laisséz-faire* capitalism, progress, and technology as being expressive of the best social and human principles. Hank represents Twain's vision of technological man as a new social ideal: the greatest product of the greatest society.

Twain's choice of Arthur's court as the testing ground for Hank's ideas was not accidental. Most immediately, he was offended by Matthew Arnold's attacks upon the American glorification of the common man and the Englishman's view of America as a kind of cultural desert. Thus, in attacking the golden age of chivalry, Twain simultaneously sought to expose English history, culture, and traditions of aristocratic privilege. At the same time, Twain associates the age of Arthur with the sorts of romantic attitudes he had exposed in *Huckleberry Finn* as the ruin of the American South. Making his spokesman, Hank Morgan, a product of that society Arnold deplored, Twain mounts a two-pronged attack against Arnold's Europeanism and sophistication and, in his own view, the dangerously reactionary attitudes which asserted the superiority of the "romantic" past over the present.

What begins for Hank, with his prediction of the moment of the eclipse, a simple expedient for survival, quickly becomes open war between Merlin and the Church and the Machine Age represented by the Yankee. Hank sees himself as a Promethean bringer of new knowledge and a new order to the oppressed masses of old England. Hank's humanitarian values are pitted against the selfishness and greed of the aristocracy and Church, and his reason challenges their superstition. Based upon his own and Twain's view of technological man as the apex of human development, Hank naturally assumes that he is the rightful ruler of the world. Twain as well as Hank seems to assume that because he takes up the cause of the oppressed people against their oppressors, he necessarily has, in whatever he does, a moral superiority to those he fights against. Neither Hank nor Twain seems to give consideration to the question of ends and means.

It is particularly ironic that Hank, ostensibly the bringer of light to this benighted people, should rely no less than his arch enemy Merlin upon the power of superstition to gain ascendancy over the masses. From the moment he discovers the profound effect his prediction of the eclipse has upon the audience, Hank begins to challenge Merlin to ever greater miracles. Such episodes as the destruction of Merlin's tower or the restoring of the Holy Well represent Hank's use of technology to create fear and awe like that Merlin has commanded heretofore. Thus, recognizing that man is essentially base and weak, Hank, like Merlin, maintains his power through exploitation of ignorance and gullibility.

Thus, it is man rather than technology which finally fails Hank. With the exception of the fifty-two young men who have never been exposed to the teachings of the Church, the society Hank has constructed through his technology reverts to its former state the minute his guard is relaxed. Men are, as Hank perceives them, no more than conditioned animals, and all his modern miracles cannot change that fact. In the end, Hank's technology fails him and his companions. His dream of progress has become a nightmare—a sacrifice to the very ignorance it would replace. Promethean Hank Morgan, the bringer of light and knowledge, finally only vindicates Twain's pessimistic view of human nature.

The ending of *A Connecticut Yankee in King Arthur's Court* is as bleak as anything Twain was ever to write. The scenes of Hank's Utopia destroyed by perverse human nature, the destruction unleashed by the power of technology, and, finally, the prospect of Hank's forces being overcome by the pollution of the bodies piled in their trenches are frightening to contemplate. Twain, having apparently set out to affirm the nineteenth century doctrine of progress, finally comes full circle to suggest that something permanent within human nature makes such dreams hopeless. Clearly, there is here an anticipation of the later Twain who, having lost hope in the human potential of his Huck Finn, would become a misanthropic voice crying out against the "damned human race."

William E. Grant

THE CONSCIOUS LOVERS

Type of work: Drama
Author: Sir Richard Steele (1672-1729)
Type of plot: Sentimental comedy
Time of plot: Early eighteenth century
Locale: London
First presented: 1722

This play, which began the vogue of sentimental comedy, demonstrates the virtues of a true gentleman, as contrasted to the fop or wit. Unlike earlier drama, where fathers are tyrants blocking the way to a fortune or marriage, Steele depicts the father as an object of filial devotion and affection. The playwright's use of characters who are middle-class citizens instead of nobility also marks a departure. The drama serves to further two of the author's social reform doctrines: the abolishment of marriages of convenience and the outlawing of the barbaric practice of dueling.

The opening night on November 7, 1722, at Drury Lane of the play entitled *The Conscious Lovers* by Sir Richard Steele was to be an event of importance in the development of English drama following the immensely popular Restoration comedy. The play was a success as indicated by what was then considered a long initial run—eighteen nights. During the remainder of the season it was presented eight more times. It was published by Jacob Tonson in December of the same year and took its place as the fourth and final completed play by Steele. His other completed plays were *The Funeral* (1707), *The Lying Lover* (1703), and *The Tender Husband* (1705).

Steele is probably most widely acclaimed for his journalism in *The Tatler, The Spectator, The Guardian,* and *The Theatre* and his contribution to that field of the periodical essay. His appointment to the Governorship of Drury Lane by George I enabled him, however, to maintain a close contact with theatrical affairs. When Steele in this controlling position came under attack for failing to support new plays, he undertook *The Theatre* which appeared twice weekly from January 2, 1720, to April 5, 1720. This periodical was to be closely allied to *The Conscious Lovers* which was at that time called *Sir John Edgar.*

For his spokesman in *The Theatre,* Steele chose Sir John Edgar, the title character of the unfinished play which he had been working on for approximately ten years. Sir John Edgar's son Harry, who appears in the periodical, is taken from his counterpart in the drama. Like the dramatic character, Harry has an overwhelming filial devotion and a reckless friend named Myrtle. In No. 3 of *The Theatre,* Steele again borrows from the play when he proposes a board of theatrical visitors that parallels in description several of the dramatic characters of the play—Mr. Sealand and his daughter Lucinda, Charles Myrtle, and Humphrey. The play *Sir John Edgar,* which aside from characterization contributed some thematic material to *The Theatre,* was titled *The Conscious Lovers* shortly before it was produced, and, to avoid repetition, Sir John Edgar and his son were renamed Sir John Bevil and Bevil Junior.

Steele employed *The Theatre* in yet another manner. He used several issues of that periodical as well as others to promote the upcoming production of his play. This preparation was noted bitterly by one of his critics, John Dennis, who wrote on November 14, 1722, in the *Freeholder's Journal,* "The Play of *The Conscious Lovers* had such a Reputation before it was known, that a Man of no very great Curiosity would have ventur'd to squeeze into the Crowd that went to see it the first Night."

The writing of *The Conscious Lovers* by Steele had a threefold purpose. The first purpose, probably the least significant, was to attack the common practice of dueling. That this was a subject of concern for Steele is apparent by its frequency as a topic in his periodical essays. For instance, in *The Guardian* Nos. 20, 133, and 129, he dealt with the practice of dueling. Steele wished to promote the idea that a man who refused to duel was not a coward or a knave. A scene in Act IV between Bevil and Myrtle is designed to exemplify this theory.

Steele's second purpose was to justify the merchant as worthy of a high position in social circles. After all, economic individualism was being encouraged as an important asset to England's expanding economy during the latter seventeenth and early eighteenth centuries. Despite this fact, the merchant had been much abused by Restoration dramatists. Steele was not the earliest author to make this point in dramatic form. *The Beaux Merchant,* a play "by a Clothier" identified as John Blanch, was published in 1714; and, although it was never acted, it crusades for just recognition for merchants and precedes the production of, although not the preliminary planning of, *The Conscious Lovers.* In *The Conscious Lovers,* Steele's mouthpiece for this issue is apparently Mr. Sealand who says in Act IV: "We Merchants are a Species of Gentry, that have grown into the World this last Century, and are as honourable, and almost as useful, as you landed Folks, that have thought yourselves so much above us." Indeed, the two most despicable characters of the play, Cimberton and Mrs. Sealand, suffer from the flaw Mr. Sealand points out—assumption of superiority by right of gentle birth. Despite the impact of *The Conscious Lovers* on this social problem, however, it was not until the 1830's that merchants were more favorably portrayed and more often placed in social positions of prominence.

The third purpose for writing *The Conscious Lovers* was, as Steele states in the Prologue of the play, "To chasten wit, and moralize the stage." In this endeavor Steele was taking up the cry for dramatic reform that had been precipitated by Restoration comedy. Jeremy Collier's attack on the theater in 1698 titled *A Short View of the Immorality and Profaneness of the English Stage* was joined by those of Daniel Defoe and Sir Richard Blackmore. Un-

like these contemporaries who believed that the theater was a center of un-
redeemable sin, Steele held that the stage could serve a beneficial, educational
purpose. On April 16, 1709, he wrote in *The Tatler* (No. 3), "I cannot be of
the same opinion with my friends and fellow laborers, the Reformers of
Manners, in their severity towards plays; but must allow, that a good play,
acted before a well-bred audience, must raise very proper incitements to good
behaviour, and be the most quick and most prevailing method of giving young
people a turn of sense and breeding." Four years later, in the April 30, 1713,
issue of *The Guardian,* he applauded Joseph Addison's *Cato* as "an unanswer-
able instance of how great a force the stage might be toward the improvement
of the world, were it regarded and encouraged as much as it ought." And on
November 7, 1722, he put his theory in motion with the production of *The
Conscious Lovers*. That it was thought to achieve its purpose can be seen
among other things in King George I's gift to Steele of five hundred guineas
for the play's contribution to the reform of the stage.

The reform of the stage that Steele achieved came by replacing Restoration
comedy with another type—sentimental comedy. The first attempt at this
variety of comedy was made in 1696 with Colley Cibber's *Love's Last Shift*.
The play, however, was still too tainted by bawdy Restoration dialogue and
hypocrisy to make much headway. Although Steele wrote other plays in this
vein, it was not until *The Conscious Lovers* that a positive turning point occurred and the sentimental drama seemed to find its place in the history of
English drama. This change was not welcomed by everyone, and charges
were made by critics that the Lugubrious Muse had settled in England to
perpetuate what they termed "weeping comedy."

Sentimental drama as pioneered by Steele is essentially marked by a number
of elements: (1) the idea of the innate goodness of man rather than the
depravity of man that had marked Restoration comedy, (2) an appeal to
the emotions that surpasses the appeal to the intellect, (3) the existence of an
obvious moral, (4) an attempt to place the ideal in a realistic setting which
leads to a certain amount of improbability and exaggeration, (5) a stress
upon pity and the evocation of tears, (6) a tendency to serious discussion of
ethical questions, (7) an element of mystery such as the lost-child-recovered,
and (8) romantic love scenes.

Steele, with the help of Cibber, is also credited with establishing several
character types that regularly appear in sentimental comedy: (1) a man and
maiden whose concepts of marriage are untainted by cynicism or contempt
for the institution, (2) the loyal friend, (3) the debauchee redeemed in time
for the fifth-act curtain, (4) the rejected mistress who is reunited with her
lover in marriage, and (5) the loyal wife who, though tempted, remains virtuous. In *The Conscious Lovers* we find shades, if not fully formed representations, of both the characteristics and characters of the sentimental comedy.

Four of Steele's most notable characters are Bevil Junior, Tom and Phillis, and Cimberton. Steele's model for the new dramatic hero is Bevil Junior, who exudes innate goodness by his filial devotion, romantic love, gentlemanly behavior, and lack of narcissistic tendencies. He provides quite a contrast to the Restoration comedy hero, for in the morning it is not *Pils to Purge Melancholy* or Suckling that he quotes but *The Spectator*, commenting that "such an author, consulted in a morning, sets the spirit for the vicissitudes of the day better than the glass does the man's person." The comedy of the play is provided by Tom and Phillis, whom Steele worked into a farcical subplot at Colley Cibber's suggestion. He borrowed from the June 30, 1713, edition of *The Guardian* for the window-washing scene. Tom and Phillis imitate their social betters and thus provide a satirical look at the manners and customs of the time. The further humor of the play is provided by Cimberton and has the unmistakable flavor of Restoration comedy. He boldly exhibits a self-love that blinds him to the true virtues of Lucinda and enables him only to see her as a means to his self-improvement. Thus, despite Steele's development of a new hero, he was unable to release himself completely from previous models, for Cimberton is the epitome of a Restoration character.

The importance of Steele's *The Conscious Lovers* to drama did not stop in England. When the first professional company of actors in America, the Comedians from London (who were later to be called the Hallum Company and then the American Company), decided to move to New York from Williamsburg, they confronted considerable difficulty in obtaining a license to perform because of the Puritan influence in the area. Once they obtained the license, they chose a play from their repertory that they felt would satisfy the moral ethics of the Puritan community. Steele's *The Conscious Lovers,* billed as "a moral comedy," opened on September 17, 1753, was a success, and thus contributed to the beginning of theater in New York City. *The Conscious Lovers* was also significant to American theater in another way. The first play written by an American on a native subject and produced by professional actors was Royall Tyler's *The Contrast,* produced at the John Street Theatre on April 16, 1787, by the American Company. For the context of the play, Tyler borrowed heavily from *The Conscious Lovers*.

Thus, *The Conscious Lovers* by Sir Richard Steele, despite obvious flaws, became not only noteworthy in the history of English theater but was also instrumental in beginning the history of American theater.

Phyllis E. Allran

CONSUELO

Type of work: Novel
Author: George Sand (Mme. Aurore Dudevant, 1804-1876)
Type of plot: Historical romance
Time of plot: Eighteenth century
Locale: Venice, Bohemia, Vienna
First published: 1842

In this romantic, at times even gothic, story, Sand's intimate knowledge of music and the world of musicians is revealed. If the style seems tedious, the reader is well compensated in the descriptive passages, which are moving and lyrical.

In the nineteenth century, readers demanded long, richly detailed novels, with complicated plots and exotic scenes realistically depicted. *Consuelo* fulfills these qualifications, but also offers much more. One of George Sand's best works, the book is a powerful plea for the individual rights and integrity of women. Conceived in the revolutionary atmosphere of the 1840's, the novel shows corruption on the highest levels, attacks the hypocrisy of the aristocrats, and shows the difficulties that face a woman of genius in a male-dominated world. George Sand knew the pain of independence, and she steered her heroine through the traps waiting for any woman who tried to achieve success in her own right. But Consuelo remains emotionally aloof from the men around her, thus saving herself much of the suffering that her creator endured. Consuelo subjugated her own personality to no one. Her character remains a fascinating study of female psychology and of the human need for personal integrity.

At the same time, many scenes of the novel fall into a romantic excessiveness reminiscent of the most violent of Gothic horror tales. The themes so dear to the Romantic school of fiction prominent in the first half of the nineteenth century are all in this book; George Sand devotes many of her pages, for example, to madness, both feigned and real, and to religious crises and holy ecstasies. The author plunges without warning from realistic, shrewdly observed scenes to almost surreal scenes of ludicrous passion and hatred, in which the heroine is trapped in flooding grottos or surrounded by statues coming to life in shadowy gardens. Sand wrote her novels without planning them first; her fertile imagination simply poured the tales onto her pages. *Consuelo* is a vibrant and important achievement, but it might have profited from more careful construction and pruning. Yet, perhaps some of the romantic vitality which makes the novel great would have been lost, had the author changed her method of creation.

THE COPPERHEAD

Type of work: Novel
Author: Harold Frederic (1856-1898)
Type of plot: Regional romance
Time of plot: 1860's
Locale: Four Corners, New York
First published: 1893

The Copperhead *is the story of a man in opposition to all his neighbors, as seen through the eyes of a young boy. The theme which finally emerges is the impossibility of purely judging a man's political views before one thoroughly understands his personal background and motivations. Frederic's vividly realistic descriptions and skillful use of regional dialects provide memorable local color.*

A Copperhead was a Northerner who sympathized with the South during the Civil War. The integrity of Abner Beech, the Copperhead of the title, and the pressures upon him, are the subjects of the novel. But beyond the main theme and plot is the impact of the events on the young narrator, Jimmy, and how they change him. Jimmy matures during the course of the novel, as he learns that human motivation is not as simple or obvious as it might appear. The importance of public opinion, and its power, stands over the book like a shadow. In those days of intense and bitter political convictions and violent tempers, the gossip at the general store and post office could lead to disastrous consequences. Jimmy sees all of this, and, young though he is, understands the significance of it. In a simple, unpretentious narrative, he conveys this to the reader.

Technically, the novel is an impressive achievement, a first person narration told by a character who does not participate in the main action, and yet a book with great sweep and dramatic power. The novel is perfectly designed and flows effortlessly from beginning to end, building to a dramatic climax, and then settling into a brief denouement. The tone is controlled, with no sense of hysteria or undue passion, although the book deals with irrational and hotheaded individuals. Frederic has maintained such an even tone that perhaps the narrative might even seem too dispassionate. Certainly, he leaves the conclusions of the story to the reader.

In its modest way, this short novel is as perfect as *Ethan Frome* and *The Great Gatsby*. In less than two hundred pages, it encompasses a world, and finally transcends it. Harold Frederic is writing about honor and morality in this story of the civilian side of the Civil War, about the beauty of ordinary things in a violent world, and about the need for respect for an individual's own moral code.

CORIOLANUS

Type of work: Drama
Author: William Shakespeare (1564-1616)
Type of plot: Historical tragedy
Time of plot: Third century
Locale: Rome, Corioli, and Antium
First presented: c. 1609

In this powerful study of a man's willful spirit and inability to follow much needed advice, Shakespeare achieves a faster tempo than in most of his historical plays through his terseness of line and highly compact unity of plot. Coriolanus is devoid of prolonged soliloquy and subplots. The whole action is so closely centered on the title character that the play leaves a strong single impression on the viewer or reader.

Coriolanus, often ignored in the past, is a play for our century. The protagonist, arrogant, elitist, and egomaniacal, lacks the humanizing self-doubt and uncertainty of a Hamlet, the compassionate warmth of an Othello, or the wisdom of a profound sufferer like Lear. Coriolanus is cold, proud, and disdaining, but because the play focuses our attention on the relationship between the aspiring individual and society, the play has gained an unprecedented degree of appreciation in our century.

Two broad schools of interpretation dominate the study of *Coriolanus.* One school views the play as the personal tragedy of Coriolanus: Swinburne's remarks in his preface to the *Oxford Shakespeare* set the tone for this school. The second school views the play as the tragedy of the body politic, or more broadly, as a political play. Neither of the two views, *Coriolanus* as a personal tragedy or as a political play, should be scorned; the latter is, however, the more convincing.

Coriolanus simply does not fit the mold of tragic hero cast so well by Shakespeare in his other great tragedies. Each hero is unique but shares certain characteristics Coriolanus lacks. Each, for example, learns more about himself and his world through his predicament; even if conquered and consumed by his tragic situation, the hero is wiser at the end of the play than at the beginning. Not so with Coriolanus. Hamlet discovers the universality of sin, which stains even himself; Macbeth cannot conquer his passionate ambitions, but he comes to know them well and appreciates them for what they are; Othello discovers the fool he has been; Lear discovers the profundity of his foolishness. Only Coriolanus, among Shakespeare's major tragic figures, remains unchanged from start to finish, learning nothing about himself or his world from his tragic predicament. Only Coriolanus, in this group, fails to make soliloquies, which express a character's most private thoughts and feelings truthfully. Coriolanus needs no soliloquies—he is that shallow. The play, therefore, is unsatisfying, almost ridiculous, if read as the personal tragedy of Coriolanus. As a tragedy of the body politic, however, the play makes good sense.

Coriolanus is a stiff character, infatuated with his own military successes. He disdains the plebeians, considering them no better than animals. Reputation means everything to him. When, for example, he single-handedly prevents the rout of the Roman forces before Corioli, in Act I, he refuses a hero's share of the spoils and refuses to wash the blood from his body until the general, Cominius, adds the commemorative name Coriolanus to his original name, Caius Marcius. The honor of the name is all that matters to such a proud man.

Militarily, Coriolanus has just cause to be proud. As a soldier, he is the perfect embodiment of Roman virtues. Brave, courageous, self-sacrificing, Coriolanus in battle represents the epitome of selfless Roman service to state. Unfortunately Coriolanus allows himself to be pushed to stand for the public office of consul. Required by ceremony to recite his valorous acts to the Senate and seek the approval of the plebeians, Coriolanus is constrained by pride and feelings of superiority from honoring the selection rituals. Conflict between him and the plebeians flares and Coriolanus is banished. With his cry, "I banish you!" (III.iii.123) Coriolanus reveals how alien he is to the Roman body politic. No man who knows himself to be part of society can conceive of himself as the state, able to banish all others.

As the play moves toward its conclusion, the tragic nature of the body politic becomes clearer. Coriolanus alone, in this play, seems to be a Roman of heroic stature. After his banishment, though, he forgets his Roman heritage completely, proclaiming "There is a world elsewhere." (III.iii.135) and journeys to Antium to offer his services to the Volscians. This most perfect product of Rome in the end was more loyal to himself than to the Rome that produced him. Rome's flower was Coriolanus; because he knew no loyalty higher than himself and his personal reputation, he was irreparably flawed, and so was the fatherland that produced him. Because Rome's finest citizen led the advance against Rome, the tragedy ultimately is of the body politic. Because the best Rome can produce, its foremost citizen, becomes its most dangerous enemy, Coriolanus stands as a symbol of the poison within the body politic.

In the final act, when Volumnia thwarts Coriolanus' determination to conquer Rome, the protagonist falls victim to Aufidius' assassins. He dies a most unheroic death, as befits a man who did not play the part of hero well. There are, in fact, no heroes in this play; Coriolanus lacks the moral or intellectual stature to qualify; Menenius and the two tribunes, Sicinius and Brutus are cowardly; Aufidius has little nobility and grace; Cominius and Titus Lartius are relatively minor characters. The play has no heroes, and Rome's early hero, Coriolanus, becomes its enemy. The stench of moral decay and of the decay of the body politic is strong in this play.

With *Coriolanus* Shakespeare effected a merger between two great types of plays: the history and the tragedy. With his English history plays, Shakespeare explored the political landscape of England. The constant theme was the dangers England faced in political instability, disloyalty to the monarch, and civil war. Yet even with the sad story of rebellion, civil war, and misery in these plays, there is an unwavering sense of the strength, heartiness, and indomitableness of the English body politic when unmenaced by catastrophic civil faction. In his tragedies, Shakespeare explored the nature of the human predicament through the several faces of his great and minor tragic protagonists. In *Coriolanus* Shakespeare merged the history play and tragedy to achieve a profoundly disturbing picture of a society doomed not by mere division or weak leadership but by its very nature—unchanging corruption. No English writer of Shakespeare's time could have made so direct a statement about English society, and Rome may well be England in disguise.

In this late play, Shakespeare is widening the dimensions of tragedy from the individual alone to an entire society. Ever growing as an artist, Shakespeare knew no arbitrary limitations in his art. *Coriolanus* is a play about the corruption of the body politic, presented as a tragedy. Shakespeare had the daring and skill as an artist to use the form of tragedy, in a sense a very personal form, to express ideas, attitudes, and feelings, about an entire society.

Brian L. Mark

THE CORSICAN BROTHERS

Type of work: Novel
Author: Alexandre Dumas, *père* (1802-1870)
Type of plot: Adventure romance
Time of plot: 1841
Locale: Corsica and Paris
First published: 1845

The story of Lucien and Louis, two brothers unlike in temperament and interests, yet held together by a bond that stretches even beyond the grave, is in the true romantic spirit. The novel is told with the color and robust, florid style of French romanticism, and its pace never lags.

The Corsican Brothers belongs to that most productive period in Alexander Dumas, *père's,* career, the 1840's; this period, which followed the years of playwriting, saw the publication of Dumas' best-known works, including *The Three Musketeers* (1844), *The Count of Monte-Cristo* (1844), and *Twenty Years After* (1845). Dumas, although he was much given to producing stage versions of his novels, recognized the relatively small merit of *The Corsican Brothers* and never adapted it to play form. In London, however, the story about the incredible bond between twin brothers, who were born physically attached and had to be cut apart, created a sensation; so many English melodramas based on Dumas' plot sprang up that the story soon gave rise to a rash of burlesques.

That Dumas was a playwright before he was a novelist is evident throughout his fiction; the action is always bold and dramatic, unfolding in a series of varied and vivid scenes, with scenery and costumes more than adequately recreated through the narrative description. This is especially true in *The Corsican Brothers,* where the setting is based on Dumas' observations during his travels in Corsica in 1841. The element in Dumas' fiction which continues to attract a reading audience, however, is the author's success as a historical novelist; he so skillfully blends actual history with events spawned in his own fertile imagination that often only a very trained eye can separate the two. Thus in *The Corsican Brothers* the carefully reproduced landscape and faithfully rendered pictures of the island inhabitants are merged with a plot full of the supernatural element, to create a final product that—despite the novel's many flaws—seems a vivid and realistic account of true events. Dumas' characters aid this impression of verisimilitude; they are very alive and have colorful, distinctive personalities. At the same time, they are not drawn with any psychological depth—in the sense that their subtler emotions and motivations are not delineated—and they do not grow or change appreciably throughout the story; they are clearly subordinate in importance to the plot. Nevertheless, Dumas' characters have a certain irresistible energy that captures the reader's sympathy; like their creator, they have a boundless zest for living and joy in adventure that make them perfect vehicles for romantic escapism in the audience.

Thus, *The Corsican Brothers* illustrates Dumas' usual weaknesses—his tendency to string together random and often inaccurate bits of history and geography, his unpolished style, and his shallow characterizations—as well as his distinctive strengths: a fast-moving story full of suspense and surprises and characters lovable for their passion and exuberance.

THE COSSACKS

Type of work: Novel
Author: Count Leo Tolstoy (1828-1910)
Type of plot: Psychological realism
Time of plot: Nineteenth century
Locale: The Caucasus
First published: 1863

The Cossacks, *although one of Tolstoy's lesser known novels, is one of the finest pictures of Cossack life in Russian literature. Through the story of a Russian aristocrat and a Cossack girl, the author examines the difficulty of a primitive society in accepting the domination of a higher culture, even when they are allied against a mutual foe, and shows the impossibility of happily blending two such different ways of life as Olyenin's and Maryanka's.*

Tolstoy conceived the idea of writing *The Cossacks* in 1852, although it took him ten years of intermittent work to complete the novel. The basic idea for the work was inspired by the author's long talks with an old Cossack friend, Epishka (in many ways the model for Yeroshka). Tolstoy's projected plan, first jotted down in a brief diary entry, was for a story "(a) about hunting, (b) about the old way of life of the Cossacks and (c) about his expeditions in the mountains." Tolstoy's original intention was to write a long and complex novel that would include a substantial background of Cossack history, faithful renditions of the Caucasian folk customs, and all the tales of the area told him by Epishka. As it transpired, however, Tolstoy was forced for financial reasons to finish the novel hastily for a publication deadline in 1863; the final length was approximately two hundred pages, since much of the original plan for the work had either been altered over the years or sacrificed in the hurry to complete it. *The Cossacks* is therefore a work of many peculiarities of structure and style; nevertheless it marks an important step in Tolstoy's development, being his first work to be translated into a foreign language and to capture an enthusiastic audience abroad. Above all, it remains an unsurpassed description of Cossack life and an excellent psychological study of a young man casting about for values which will fill the moral void he fears has entered his life.

The character of Olyenin, the hero of *The Cossacks,* is largely autobiographical. Like his young hero, Tolstoy left Moscow in 1852 and joined an army regiment stationed in the Caucasus, the land of the Cossacks. Throughout his four years of service—during which he fought in expeditions in the Caucasus, the Danube, and the Crimea—Tolstoy kept very careful, detailed diaries, which years later were to provide invaluable material for his fiction. In the Caucasus diaries he recorded all aspects of his life as a soldier, including not only the fighting, but the hunting and drinking, the time spent reading and writing, and the periods of idleness and boredom; it is to this minute observation and recording of firsthand experience that *The Cossacks* owes much of its verisimilitude of plot and setting, its vividness of atmosphere and impression. In addition to using his army experiences in molding the character of Olyenin, Tolstoy provided his hero with a background nearly identical to his own; both Olyenin and his creator were young noblemen who left Moscow as a result of large debts and an unsuccessful love affair, and both are concerned with discovering new values amid a different way of life from that to which they had been accustomed.

This escape from life in a teeming city, with its juxtaposition of culture and decadence, attractiveness and corruption, creativeness and stagnation, is at the thematic center of *The Cossacks*. The novel revolves around the Rousseauian concern of man's return to a more natural state from the debilitating influences of urban civilization. This idea is embodied in Olyenin's flight from the whirl of Moscow society to the Caucasus. The important question to be answered, however, is whether Tolstoy carries the "nature versus civilization" hypothesis to the same conclusion as Rousseau. Certainly, in the first chapters it would appear that the hero is headed toward an environment which will heal and renew him. But does the remaining course of the narrative prove the Caucasus to be the natural life that Olyenin is seeking? And is urban civilization as represented by Olyenin totally condemned?

The answer is that Tolstoy is able to see both strengths and shortcomings in each way of life, and condemns neither one. One illustration of his objectivity is seen in his characterization of old Yeroshka, who, if this novel were a polemic against civilization, would be the obvious candidate to represent Cossack wisdom and the superiority of their way of life. Instead, he is portrayed as a brave hunter and fighter but a fault-ridden and quite human individual; he is a lovable, if slightly lecherous old reprobate. Rather than dispensing profound insight and ancient wisdom to young Olyenin, Yeroshka simply rides, hunts, drinks, and encourages the youth to enjoy sensual pleasures without worrying about the future. Likewise, the other main Cossack figure, Lukashka, combines strength and virtue, weakness and pettiness. Yeroshka, Lukashka, and their people are admirable in their bravery, their energy, and their closeness to the land; yet at the same time they murder, steal, and lose themselves in drunkenness and debauchery.

In the same way, Tolstoy attacks all the evils of his own and his hero's class: their idleness, selfishness, shortsightedness, hypocrisy, temper, and irresponsibility. Yet even while he sees these vices in the nobility, and includes many of them in Olyenin's personality, he does not lose sight of redeeming qualities in the aristocracy. Olyenin's merit lies in his basic morality, which will not allow him to be complacent about his weakness; he is dissatisfied with his faults and his former way of life, and seeks, albeit in a rambling fashion, to find remedies and grow as a person.

Olyenin vacillates throughout the story in his opinion of what comprises happiness. In Chapter 20 he exclaims to himself, "Happiness consists in living for others," while in Chapter 33 he is convinced that "Self-renunciation is all stuff and nonsense . . . in my heart there is nothing but love for myself and the desire to love her and live her life with her." Olyenin never finds the key to happiness throughout the novel, even though he enjoys a brief period of unreflecting enjoyment with the Cossacks; but he does discover that the urban, aristocratic way of life and the Cossack culture are incompatible. He learns this lesson on the personal level when his attempt to form a relationship with Maryanka fails, and on a more general level in his inability ever to feel truly a part of Cossack culture.

In addition to the cohesiveness which Olyenin's search for happiness gives *The Cossacks*, the novel is also strongly unified through its richly evocative descriptive passages. In a powerful style marked by its clarity and simplicity, Tolstoy paints an unforgettable picture of Cossack life and of men who cultivate the land. In this early work, all of the author's love of nature, farming, and country life emerges in scenes of riding, hunting, and harvesting to create a vividness of effect that foreshadows the genius of his later novels.

Nancy G. Ballard

THE COUNT OF MONTE-CRISTO

Type of work: Novel
Author: Alexandre Dumas, *père* (1802-1870)
Type of plot: Historical romance
Time of plot: Nineteenth century
Locale: France
First published: 1844

The Count of Monte-Cristo tells the story of a young man on the threshold of a bright career and a happy marriage who is imprisoned in a dungeon for years on a false political charge. When he escapes and finds a treasure which makes him wealthy, he sets upon an implacable course of revenge against his old enemies. If the characterizations are sometimes set in conventional molds, the story is unforgettable for its suspenseful plot and the intriguing figure of the Count.

The Count of Monte-Cristo, Alexandre Dumas' best-known novel after *The Three Musketeers,* is, as improbable as it might seem, based on a true story. Dumas, who has become almost legendary for his prolific literary output of nearly 300 volumes, maintained a corps of collaborators who were engaged in searching through earlier writers of memoirs for suitably exciting plots. Through this process a volume entitled *Mèmoires tirès des archives de la Police de Paris* by Jacques Peuchet, the Keeper of the Archives at the Prefecture of Police, came to Dumas' attention.

In Peuchet's memoirs, which contained a treasure of potential plots for novels, was a record of a case of wrongful imprisonment and vengeance which strongly appealed to the French author. In 1807 there had been living in Paris a young shoemaker, François Picaud, who was engaged to marry Marguerite Vigoroux, a beautiful orphan with a fortune of one hundred thousand gold francs. Four of Picaud's friends, jealous of his good fortune, accused him of being an English agent. Picaud was spirited away in the night by the Police, who at the time were worried about certain insurrectionary movements. The unfortunate man's parents and his betrothed made inquiries, but failing to obtain any satisfaction, resigned themselves to the inevitable. In 1814, with the fall of the Empire, Picaud was released from the castle of Fenestrelle where he had all that time been imprisoned. While in captivity, he had, with great devotion, looked after an Italian prelate who had been imprisoned on a political charge and had not long to live. The dying man bequeathed to Picaud a treasure hidden in Milan. After his release, the shoemaker recovered the treasure and returned under an assumed name to the district in which he had been living. Making inquiries, he soon discovered the plot against him by his jealous friends and spent ten years of his life engaged in an elaborate plot against the perpetrators of his suffering which resulted in the eventual destruction of his former friends.

Dumas delighted in the idea of creating a character possessed of a fabulous fortune and of making that character an avenger in some great cause. This impulse was natural, for Dumas, in spite of his exuberant exterior, harbored within himself many grievances against society at large, and individual enemies in particular. His father had been persecuted; he himself was harrassed by creditors, and slandered. He shared with other major writers who had been unjustly treated, that longing for vengeance which has engendered so many masterpieces. The experiences of Picaud gave him the story for which he had been longing. But normal imagination was not responsible for the stroke of genius which produced the name, Count of Monte-Cristo, which has come to be so romantically imbedded in the memories of countless readers. The mysterious creative forces which cause the birth of great works had been enriched one day when Dumas had gone boating among the islands which lie about Elba and his guide pointed out a beautiful island named Monte-Cristo.

The Count of Monte-Cristo had a greater success than any book which Dumas published prior to *The Three Musketeers*. It, like most of Dumas' major novels, was first serialized in the daily newspaper. In this way, he kept his public excited from one day to the next by means of romantic love affairs, intrigues, imprisonments, hairbreadth escapes, and innumerable duels. Dumas had great gifts of narrative and dialogue and a creative imagination, but only a limited critical sense and an even smaller concern for historical accuracy. He did have a knack for seizing situations and characters that would render a satisfactory historical atmosphere. He wrote with a sincere gusto that action and love were the two essential things in life and thus in fiction. His writing was never complicated by analysis or psychological insights and his best works, such as *The Count of Monte-Cristo* and *The Three Musketeers,* can be read with effortless enjoyment.

Critics point to the excessive melodrama of Dumas' work quickly and rightly. They point to his lack of psychological perception and his careless style. The characters are one dimensional. They are stranded in the conventional molds the author has set for them. There is no change, no sudden insight, and no growth in the players upon Dumas' stage. But, in spite of many defects, this novel remains a great work in literature for it is a breathtaking experience, a dramatic tale filled with mystery and intrigue. For thousands of years the unhappy human race has found release in cathartic tales such as this one. The most popular characters have been the magician and the dispenser of justice. The injured and weak live with the hope, which no ill-success can weaken, of witnessing the coming of the hero who will redress all wrongs, cast down the wicked, and at long last give the good man his deserts.

At the time Dumas was writing, the magician had been confused with the rich man, with great vaults filled with jewels, whose wealth permits him to indulge his every whim and to use his treasure to provide justice for the innocent man and to punish the guilty. Dumas dreamed of becoming just such a distributor of earthly happiness, and *The Count of Monte-Cristo* gave him the framework for which he was looking. The author's hero is not a savage murderer but an implacable avenger who obtains his justice and disappears. *The Count of Monte-Cristo*, then, finds its audience among people of all ages and of all times who like a romantic adventure tale with a larger than life hero who has within his power the means to transport the reader away from the frustrations of his daily life to a new world where all things are possible and all will end well.

Patricia Ann King

THE COUNTERFEITERS

Type of work: Novel
Author: André Gide (1869-1951)
Type of plot: Psychological realism
Time of plot: Early 1920's
Locale: Paris
First published: 1925

In this finest of Gide's novels, we follow the development of a group of youths, each of whom is stimulated by his intimate contact with an older person. The author's theme is that every individual must follow his conscience and ignore convention if he is to find full happiness and self-expression.

One year after Gide published *Corydon* (1924), which provoked a literary furor, he completed *The Counterfeiters (Les faux-monnayeurs)* together with its complementary *Journal of the Counterfeiters (Le Journal des faux-monnayeurs)*. Both books had taken six years to write. The idea for the novel, however, came to the author at least as early as 1906, when he cut out from the September 16 issue of *Le Figaro* an article concerning a case of counterfeiting in which several children from respectable families had been involved. Also he had on file a report of the suicide of a certain young Nény, a student at the Lycée Blaise-Pascal. Furthermore, in 1907 news of a gang of anarchist counterfeiters was widely publicized. By 1919, Gide began a tentative draft of the novel, which he continued intermittently while he was writing his critical study *Dostoïevsky* (1923) and completing his sexual research. *The Counterfeiters*, a culmination of such long and careful thought, is generally regarded as Gide's masterpiece, although he preferred the more scandalous *Corydon*.

In a sense, *The Counterfeiters* summarizes the major ideas that Gide had presented up to that point in his career. Later he would publish other major books—*Si le grain ne meurt* (1926), *L'école des femmes* (1929), for example—but they would not break new ground. With *The Counterfeiters,* Gide's high place in European literature was assured. While its roots are in the tradition of the nineteenth century social novel and novel of ideas—for example, Flaubert's *L'éducation sentimentale* (1869), and Dostoevski's *The Possessed* (1871-1872)—its influence, both in matters of style and in philosophy, is unmistakable in such important twentieth century novels as Aldous Huxley's *Point Counter Point* (1928) and Lawrence Durrell's *The Alexandria Quartet* (1957-1960). Like these books, *The Counterfeiters* is at once a novel of ideas, of artistic development (*Künstlerroman*), and of psychological realism.

Gide's title, which is partly ironical, is the projected title of a yet unfinished —and, according to *Le journal des faux-monnayeurs,* never to be completed —novel by Edouard. Throughout the book Edouard talks about his novel, describes its theme, and at one point allows George Molinier to read a selection from it; George not only fails to understand the meaning of the passage, but he scorns the name of the protagonist. On reflection, Edouard agrees with his critic. Edouard is never satisfied with the direction that his writing takes. At first, he insists that his book has no subject, that it is a mere slice of life. Later he catches sight of its "deep-lying subject," which is "the rivalry between the real world and the representation of it which we make to ourselves." That subject is expressed in the symbolism of a counterfeit coin. In the important chapter "Edouard Explains his Theory of the Novel," he shows Bernard Profitendieu a counterfeit ten-franc piece. If Bernard were to understand that the coin is not genuine, he would naturally despise it. But if he were deluded into thinking that it is real, he would value it beyond its worth. Value, therefore, depends upon perception; but perception has nothing to do with reality. Later, the reader learns that the coin is more than a symbol of counterfeit values. George is suspected of passing counterfeit money.

Gide's trick upon the reader is characteristic of his artistic method, which is one of ironical contrast, of allowing his protagonists to play games that prove finally to be serious, or to turn their serious problems into farcical games. *The Counterfeiters* presents a wide diversity of ideas, exposes their absurdities, yet sometimes salvages their values. On one level, the book explores the risks along with the liberating energies of criminality. Bernard, who comes upon Edouard's checkroom ticket, apprehends the writer's bag, which contains money, a literary journal, and a letter from Laura Douviers. He keeps the money, at least for a while, excusing himself with the rationalization that he is not a thief; reads the confidential journal; and uses the letter as a pretext to involve himself in Laura's life as her protector. Thus he commits a "gratuitous act," outrageous in its casual, motiveless interference in the lives of others. Yet the consequences, both for Bernard and those concerned, are not as crass as the reader might expect. By exercising his total capacity for freedom, he has broken into life, enjoyed a more exciting and richer life experience than he might otherwise have known. To be sure, the ultimate consequences of his act are dangerous, and he learns that one's boldness may often cause other people unhappiness, but the lesson is not entirely cautionary. By the end of the book, more liberated than at the outset, Bernard makes his peace with his stepfather and returns, a more responsible young man, to his family.

Bernard's example, though perhaps most extraordinary, is not the only one of characters in the novel who assert their philosophies by living them. Just as Bernard's fortunes are on the rise because of his impetuosity, Vincent Molinier's decline. The seducer of Laura, whom he callously abandons, Vincent himself is destroyed by Lady Griffith. Her sensuality is greater, more destructive than his. Still other characters temporize, frozen in will, and allow the world to come to them. Gide's method is to provide brief scenes, really encounters, usually with two characters at a time. The personalities express their ideas, sometimes debate and at other times agree. Yet matched with a different partner, a different encounter, the characters change their minds, often subtly and without understanding the results of their actions. Thus the sense of reality shifts, just as the circumstances appear to turn one direction or another. Reality is not absolute. The author, who is himself a voice in the novel, is not above suspicion of error. Surely Gide's major spokesman, the writer Edouard, is at times wise, at times foolish.

More than a complex novel of ideas that explores the limitations of perceiving reality, *The Counterfeiters* is an aesthetic novel that treats the development of the artist. To be sure, there are two novelists in the book. Edouard, the more important figure, is a discreet homosexual, stoic, troubled by problems of moral ambiguity, but generous, open-natured, and like Gide, insistent that sincerity is his chief resource as an artist. His rival is the Comte Robert de Passavant, also a homosexual, more successful as a writer but more devious as a human being. The Comte, author of *The Horizontal Bar,* is also Edouard's rival for the affections of Olivier Molinier. And it becomes clear that, as Edouard develops, through constantly changing and refining, his aesthetic, his rivalry with Passavant is never far from the springs of his invention. Edouard explains his theory of art both in dialogues—or encounters—with other characters or, more fully, to himself in his journals. Like Gide's famous literary journals, Edouard's notebooks examine the philosophy and strategies of composition, relate anecdotes, puzzle over problems of structure, and attempt to analyze the writer's own motives. Both as an exploration of art and himself, the journals are filled with undigested, often contradictory, but urgent material for further investigation. It is a measure of Gide's excellence as an artist that he never exhausts but generally augments the subject that he treats.

His understanding of the craft of fiction carries over to an interest in the artist's psychology. Perhaps this concern of Gide's novel is less satisfactory for most readers, because the writer's homosexual bias allows for only a partial, inadequate view of the subject. One theme of *The Counterfeiters* is the psychosexual development of the two university friends, Bernard and Olivier. At the beginning of the novel, both prepare for their "bachot," the *baccalauréate* examinations at the Sorbonne. By the end, both pass. Similarly, they undergo a sensual education that results in a certain homosexual orientation for Olivier, a very nearly certain one for Bernard. Olivier is clearly disposed to homosexuality when he first encounters Bernard (and they share a bed); but he discovers, first through the Comte de Passavant and later through Edouard, that the relationship he prefers involves the companionship of an older patron. As for Edouard, a genteel and delicate pederast, the arrangement is ideal. Having achieved the satisfaction he has always craved from the love of Olivier, he is prepared to resume work on his novel.

Bernard's sexuality is more ambiguous, but without doubt is mainly homo-erotic. His sexual encounter with Sarah Vedel is almost farcical. Sarah, the aggressor throughout, is—incredible to say—assisted by her brother Armand, who bolts the bedroom door to make sure that the couple perform the act of love. As soon as Bernard wakes up, he runs from Sarah's chamber, never wishing to see her again. Bernard is capable only of veneration for women, as he idolizes Laura and admires Rachel, her sister, but feels for them nothing akin to desire. He is more finely attracted to Olivier. Yet, following Gide's homosexual fantasy, he bows out of the picture, so that Edouard has the youth to himself. To complete the fantasy, Gide allows Olivier's mother, Pauline, in a ludicrous scene, to bestow her blessings on the union. Curious though the scene is from the standpoint of heterosexual psychology, it is perfectly satisfactory from the context of the author's purpose in the novel. The description of the meeting, after all, is part of Edouard's journal. How much of it is imagined and how much real? Indeed, to what extent are the actions of the characters real or pretended? Gide, master of disguises, makes his characters speak their parts, cleverly or stupidly as may be, but withholds his own moral judgments.

Leslie B. Mittleman

THE COUNTESS DE CHARNY

Type of work: Novel
Author: Alexandre Dumas, *père* (1802-1870)
Type of plot: Historical romance
Time of plot: 1791
Locale: France
First published: 1853-1855

This is the concluding novel in a series dealing with events before and during the French Revolution; the other works in the group are Memoirs of a Physician. The Queen's Necklace. *and* The Taking of the Bastille. *In his typical style, Dumas captures reader interest by means of dramatic incidents and rapid plot development.*

The Countess de Charny is the sequel to *Ange Pitou* (1852) and the final work of the series *Mémoires d'un Médecin* (1848). Like its predecessor, it was originally intended to have been written in collaboration with Auguste Maquet. Although Maquet helped a little with *Ange Pitou,* financial difficulties caused a break between the two men and Dumas was left to his own resources for the authorship of both works. Much of the *Countess de Charny,* like its predecessor, is based on Dumas' boyhood memories, yet the author, inspired greatly by Michelet's *Histoire de la Révolution Française* (1847-1853), gives us more actual history than is usual in his romances. The work, however, maintains the Dumas tradition of spirited storytelling. He takes fewer liberties with fact, but he creates and revivifies the atmosphere with detail typical of romanticism and imbues it with fast-flowing action, flamboyant dialogue, and his renowned curtain lines. The story of Charny and Andrée comes to its well-rounded conclusion and leaves no need or any real wish for a sequel.

One interesting aspect of *The Countess de Charny* is the fact that Dumas prefaces it with one of his amusing "chats" in which he explains how *Ange Pitou* came to its abrupt end, an occurrence which bothered many readers. Dumas gives as his reason the fact that *Ange Pitou* was first published serially and toward the end of the series a stamp duty was imposed on papers which published stories in installments, thus the novel's conclusion was rushed to beat the tax. This did not pose a problem for *The Countess de Charny,* which was published in book form and gives no impression of hurried or sloppy writing. It has been cited by critics for its display of imagination and its excellent portrayal of action.

A COUNTRY DOCTOR

Type of work: Novel
Author: Sarah Orne Jewett (1849-1909)
Type of plot: Regional romance
Time of plot: Mid-nineteenth century
Locale: Oldfields, Maine
First published: 1884

In this successful local color novel, Jewett describes an intelligent girl's maturing process in the midst of people who consider her independence and her desire to remain single and pursue a career strange and unladylike. The customs and habits of the Oldfields community are painted with warmth and sympathy.

A Country Doctor is a novel of development rather than plot. With sensitivity and insight, Sarah Orne Jewett traces the growth and awakening of an intelligent young girl. Nan Prince has more imagination and energy than the village people are accustomed to seeing in a young girl. They like her, but don't quite approve of her; they wonder what will become of such a fanciful, harum-scarum female who doesn't act as a girl ought to act and do what is expected of her. "I don't mean to be discontented," she says, but it is clear that she has a will of her own. Nan is taught that she owes something to the world besides following her own selfish plans; duty to society is early instilled into her by the doctor, who feels that Nan is not the kind of girl who is likely to marry: she is too independent and self-reliant.

The difficulties Nan encounters because she wants to be a doctor are explored in detail. People tell Nan that a woman's place is in the home, but she insists that since any man who aspires to be a doctor is helped, so should she be. God wouldn't have given her talents equal to those of a man if she were not meant to use them, she tells her aunt. Her family tries to marry her off, but she resists, and dedicates herself entirely to her career.

Another theme mentioned in this book and elaborated in nearly all of Sarah Orne Jewett's books is that of the old people taking with them when they die their lifetime's store of local social history and tradition. Jewett saw that this valuable source should be tapped, and somehow saved for posterity. Perhaps, she suggests, the country doctors could record the memories of their old patients, rather than let them perish.

No American writer had a better ear than Jewett for the speech patterns of her people, for their selection of words and phrases, the rhythms and cadences of their conversation, and their humor. Jewett never satirizes her characters, but presents them with both affection and objectivity. She recognizes the flaws in these unsophisticated, work-hardened people, but she forgives them, and in *A Country Doctor,* she shows how a strong and intelligent person such as Nan can rise from among these people, and shine with all of the stubborn virtues of the native American tradition.

THE COUNTRY DOCTOR

Type of work: Novel
Author: Honoré de Balzac (1799-1850)
Type of plot: Naturalism
Time of plot: Early nineteenth century
Locale: Southern France
First published: 1833

The Country Doctor, which belongs to the "Scenes from Country Life" series of The Human Comedy, *is an unforgettable portrait of Dr. Benassis, who devotes all his energies to the people of his village. The characters, such as the orphan La Fosseuse and the soldier Genestas, are intriguing sketches, but are never developed in full depth.*

The Country Doctor is unlike most of Balzac's novels. One of his early books, and not added to the Human Comedy series until more than a decade after its composition, it is a lyrical, quiet novel, one more concerned with reform than revolution, with peasants rather than the ambitious bourgeoisie of Balzac's more famous books. Dr. Benassis, expounding his views on politics, airs Balzac's own attitudes. He is opposed to universal suffrage, fearing a long struggle between the bourgeoisie and the working class. He speaks of the movement of population from country to towns, and the growth of a dissatisfied, uprooted class. Dr. Benassis indicates the difference between the "destroyer" and the "builder," which are, he explains, two manifestations of human "Will." He believes in the progress of civilization; from his point of view, the welfare of people depends on the curé, the doctor, and the justice of the peace. Account must be taken of the nature of the peasants, who are neither monsters nor angels, but creatures rendered hard and narrow by the harshness of their existence. Balzac, through the mouthpiece of his doctor, states that the peasants can be uplifted if a communal spirit is fostered within them. But they can be saved only through great patience.

The almost saintlike Dr. Benassis is a man with that patience. His story is revealed gradually through a series of flashbacks and leisurely narratives. While trying to expiate the sins of his past, he proves to be the savior of this tiny valley and the wretched beings who dwell within it. As the doctor's biography is told, so are the country customs, the ways of dying and mourning, the manner of conducting business, the rituals connected with birth and marriage, and the history of the village and the valley. The novel moves slowly, without the drama of passion usual in a Balzac novel, but the tale is strangely moving, and the doctor is an impressive and memorable figure.

THE COUNTRY HOUSE

Type of work: Novel
Author: John Galsworthy (1867-1933)
Type of plot: Social criticism
Time of plot: Early twentieth century
Locale: England
First published: 1907

Before the two world wars had shaken English social institutions to the breaking point, the English country house was symbolic of the strongest traditions of the aristocracy. In this novel, Galsworthy depicts what happens when one such house is threatened by scandal and possible destruction because of the irresponsibility of one of its sons.

John Galsworthy is a novelist who grew in stature between the era of Victorian certainties and the era of post-World War I despair and doubts. Once conflicts in his personal life were resolved, he began to portray with increasing vigor in his fiction, those segments of the British upper classes which he felt were most in need of constructive criticism. In the preface to *The Country House,* Galsworthy remarks that birth into the upper class or the aristocracy is no reason for complacency. At the same time, he discounts those who mistake his attitude for that of a "revolutionary." In fact, he argues that by taking seriously the criticisms he offers, radical change can be rendered unnecessary.

The Country House is a strong novel, especially in its detailed exposure of the pettiness and narrowness of the landed English gentry. Horace Pendyce, for example, is revealed both for what he is and for what he thinks he is. The latter, of course, is the more damaging; and this satirical ingredient, more than the plot, affords the central interest of *The Country House.*

The plot itself revolves around the elements of money (and inheritance), sexual attraction, family feelings, honor, and the force of outward respectability. Galsworthy successfully maintains action and interest, particularly of a social nature. But since he is so adept at creating a social milieu, a setting of aristocratic manners and mannerisms, the plot which unfolds in that setting carries with it more external interest than internal motive. For example, the characters (including George Pendyce and Mrs. Helen Bellew) are less believable as individuals than as types, and less believable as types than as mechanical figures designed to play a role in a prearranged drama. Thus, the motivation of characters, largely external in origin, never seems entirely adequate to the weight of the action demanded of them. Hence, the more memorable characters tend to be the minor types who embody most strikingly the complacent aristocratic ethos Galsworthy wishes to expose.

In short, Galsworthy's characters as individuals lack that depth which grows from interior conflict. The real conflict occurs on the level of the social criticism itself. On this level, Galsworthy's fundamental attachment to the values of British society as a whole, and his desire to criticize and satirize, come into conflict; and the conflict is resolved in favor of the established order. Thus, the tension which might have enlivened his characters is dissipated in the reestablishment of the fictional social order; and the old world, soon to be shattered in the trenches of a barbaric war, persists.

THE COUNTRY OF THE POINTED FIRS

Type of work: Novel
Author: Sarah Orne Jewett (1849-1909)
Type of plot: Regional romance
Time of plot: Late nineteenth century
Locale: Maine seacoast
First published: 1896

Told from the point of view of a summer visitor to Dunnet Landing, Maine, this work is very slender in plot; it consists mainly of character sketches, nature descriptions, and short tales told to Mrs. Todd's boarder by local residents of the seacoast town. The book is a masterpiece of local-color writing, and is considered by most readers to be Jewett's finest work.

Willa Cather, when asked to name three American novels "deserving of a long, long life," selected *The Country of the Pointed Firs* to share this honor with *The Scarlet Letter* and *Huckleberry Finn.* One of Sarah Orne Jewett's last works, and probably her highest achievement, the novel is a moving and wise chronicle, unquestionably a genuine and great work of art. The gentle, thoughtful narrative flows with a precision of description worthy of Flaubert or Turgenev. The apparently effortless and ever graceful prose is the work of a master craftsman and a refined and gifted sensibility. The work is rich in symbols that arise naturally from the world about which the author is writing. Perhaps the dominant symbol is that of the great army of pointed firs, darkly cloaked and "standing as if they wait to embark."

The theme of balance is fundamental to the book, as much a part of it as the carefully structured narrative and perfectly poised sentences. Why, for example, does the major character, Mrs. Todd, choose to live in this tiny community? To keep the world balance true, suggests the author, to offset some other, unknown, existence. There is always a reason, if one but knows it. Hand in hand with the theme of balance moves that of solitude. Paths are trodden to the shrines of solitude the world over, writes the narrator, whether it be the island of Miss Joanna or the island of Mrs. Todd's mother, or the caves of the saints of the past. The old sea captain's story of the "Waiting Place," the strange, twilight land hovering by the North Pole, again suggests this theme. Perhaps solitude serves humanity as a kind of purgatory, a way station of the soul on its way to paradise. It can be fearful, this uncharted, inner space, but it must be encountered to achieve our full humanity. The ship that carried Captain Littlepage to this land was not accidentally named "Minerva."

The characterizations in *The Country of the Pointed Firs* are among the finest in American literature. Mrs. Todd is perhaps the glory of the book, a creation worthy of Dickens. She might belong to any age, as the narrator says, "like an idyl of Theocritus"; but with her potions and herbs, her Puritan ancestors probably would have burned her as a witch. She is an unlikely classic heroine, yet the narrator cannot resist some flattering comparisons. Mrs. Todd is likened to a grand and architectural caryatid and compared to Antigone standing alone on the Theban plain. But it is her language, her way with the Old Maine way of speaking, that breathes life into her bulky figure. One can *taste* the salty old expressions as they roll off her tongue.

The past of the whalers, so recently behind the characters, is ever present in the book. Indeed, the past is important on many levels to the characters in the novel. Mrs. Fosdick remarks: "Conversations got to have some root in the past, or else you've got to explain every remark you make. . . ." The rule might be said to apply to all civilized social intercourse. People with no respect for the past are left isolated and hopeless. In the world of Sarah Orne Jewett the present and past mutually enrich each other, and mortals wise enough to accept this are the benefactors.

The Country of the Pointed Firs is a treasure of wisdom and a lesson in the writing of pure, unaffected prose as the highest art. The individuals who stalk through its pages are loners, but they are not unhappy or unloving. Sara Orne Jewett has realized that "in the life of each of us . . . there is a place remote and islanded, and given to endless regret and secret happiness; we are each the uncompanioned hermit and recluse of an hour or a day. . . ." When she writes about her isolated New Englanders on their saltwashed islands, she is writing about all of us, about all of humanity.

THE COUNTRY WIFE

Type of work: Drama
Author: William Wycherley (1640?-1716)
Type of plot: Comedy of manners
Time of plot: Seventeenth century
Locale: London
First presented: 1673

In this delightfully racy tale of cuckoldry, a jealous husband takes his naïve country wife to Paris; where she meets Horner, a womanizer who, in order to gain easy audiences with wives of unsuspecting husbands, spreads the rumor through his quack doctor that he has become impotent. The play is memorable for its brilliant dialogue and for the whimsical characterization of Margery Pinchwife.

William Wycherley was born at Clive in Shropshire, England, in 1640. Four comedies were his contribution to English dramatic literature and in one of them, *The Country Wife,* the Restoration comedy reached its height.

Wycherley's first play *Love in a Wood* was acted in the spring of 1671 and occasioned the start of a relationship between Wycherley and the Duchess of Cleveland. Because she was mistress to the king, Wycherley was brought into the court circle and thus into the favor of the king. *The Gentleman Dancing Master,* his second play, apparently opened at Dorset Garden in the fall of 1672. It was not well received by the Restoration audience perhaps because of its simplicity and lack of vulgarity. *The Plain Dealer,* first produced in December, 1676, has the distinction of being Wycherley's last play, his most morally ambiguous, and thus the most discussed of Restoration comedies with the exception perhaps of William Congreve's *The Way of the World.* It is from a character in this play that Wycherley received his nickname of "Manly" from John Dryden.

Wycherley's third play, *The Country Wife,* is considered by most critics to be the best of the Restoration comedies. *The Country Wife* was apparently first produced by the King's Company at the Theatre Royal in Drury Lane on January 12, 1675, and was obviously well received by the audiences of the time, for it immediately became a part of the repertory at the Theatre Royal. Its popularity is still apparent in the fact that it is one of the most often revived of the comedies from this period.

The ethos of the Restoration period may have had its effect on *The Country Wife.* The theater was being promoted by a libertine, King Charles II, who surrounded himself with an equally profligate court. Many aristocrats of the period viewed man as a depraved being and affected a contempt for morality, especially in the form of Puritanism or Republicanism. It is small wonder that the bawdiness of *The Country Wife* would have suited the temper of the times.

Yet, it is the licentious nature of the play that brought to it most of the criticism during the Restoration, though perhaps it was that some people did not like their mirrored image. As Sir Richard Steele wrote of Horner in *The Tatler* of April 16, 1709, after seeing a production on April 14, he "is a good representation of the age in which that comedy was written; at which time, love and wenching were the business of life, and the gallant manner of pursuing women was the best recommendation at court." Steele also criticized Pinchwife, but again as a representative of the age, "one of those debauchees who run through the vices of the town and believe when they think fit, they can marry and settle at their ease." Steele in his criticism was contributing to the general criticism of the theater that occurred from about 1695 to 1745 and had reached a high point in 1698 with Jeremy Collier's *A Short View of the Immorility and Profaneness of the English Stage.* Collier, unlike Steele, was not generous to Wycherley or his characters, calling Horner "horridly Smutty" and accusing Mrs. Pinchwife, Horner, and Lady Fidget of a *"Rankness* and *Indecency* of their Language." Criticism of the play continued into the Victorian period where perhaps it met its strongest criticism under the pen of Lord Macaulay in an 1841 essay "The Comic Dramatists of the Restoration." He said of Wycherley's comedies: "In truth Wycherley's indecency is protected against the critic as a skunk is protected against the hunters. It is safe because it is too filthy to handle and too noisome to approach."

Despite the adverse criticism of the play, it was following, perhaps more strongly than some, the satiric method employed by Restoration comedy which was to present on the stage characterizations that were true to life— some of them to be emulated and some of them to be avoided. The use of laughter in *The Country Wife* closely follows Hobbes's observation that man laughs because he suddenly recognizes his superiority to other men. As Hobbes says, "Sudden glory is the passion which maketh those grimaces called laughter; and is caused either by some sudden act of their own that pleaseth them, or by the apprehension of some deformed thing in another, by comparison whereof they suddenly applaud themselves." The fact that Wycherley chose to follow these examples is reinforced by his epigraph to *The Gentleman Dancing Master* in which he acknowledges that a great comedy does not merely make the audience laugh; it should say something.

What Wycherley has to say in *The Country Wife* concerns the lack of deep feeling and selfish motives that permeated the sexual morality of his time. Women are not sought after as wives, or even concubines, but rather as mere strumpets. Once the man's sexual desires have been gratified, he was out looking for another encounter. To make his play instructive as well as illustrative, Wycherley conceived three intrigues in his plot—involving Pinchwife, Horner, and Harcourt—that allow the reader to make a value judgment about how well a character is able to drop his pretense and channel his natural desires into constructive results. Thus, Pinchwife exhibits the least desirably imitative character because through his selfishly motivated, zealous guarding of his wife, Margery, he is cuckolded. Horner, though admirable in

wit and clear in an understanding of himself and others, never drops the role
of eunuch and its fringe benefits and thus remains a slave to lust and what he
terms the "greatest Monster" in nature—affectation. Harcourt becomes the
most admirable as a "rake converted" who is able to translate his desires into
true love and respect for the woman Alithea and, at play's end, intends to be
a husband to her.

In his concern with the three intrigues of *The Country Wife,* Wycherley
introduces a wide variety of Restoration comedy types. There is the jealous
man whose jealousy is reproved, the hypocritical ladies of refinement who
wish to protect their "honour" yet are proved as lustful as wenches, the
trusting man whose trust is proved foolish, the rakes whose sole desire is
satiating themselves in pleasure, and the fashionable narcissistic Restoration
fop. Within this gallery, Horner is perhaps the central character despite the
fact that he does not, as previously mentioned, face a totally happy end. In
Horner's character Wycherley presents aspects to be applauded and condemned. His name suggests what he is—a cuckold maker who gains great satisfaction by awarding symbolic horns to betrayed husbands. Wycherley's idea
for Horner's trick came from *Eunuchus* by the Roman playwright Terence. In
the play, a young man pretends to be a eunuch so that he can be admitted
freely into the company of a young girl. However, unlike Terence's character,
Horner does not rape; he uses his disguise only to gain access to willing partners. In this pursuit he is a villain of sorts. Yet in his villainy—cukolding of
husbands and bedding of mistresses—he is to be commended, for he proves
that the selfish nature of the foolish men is deplorable, and that the "honour"
of the "virtuous" ladies is hypocritical. He is also to be pitied, however, because he never rises above base desire. As Horner expresses it, "Ceremony in
love is as ridiculous as in fighting; falling on briskly is all should be done on
such occasions."

In *The Country Wife* the women characters and their social behavior also
meet with varying degrees of censure and praise. With Lady Fidget, Margery
Pinchwife, and Alithea, Wycherley presents the differing levels of feminine
conduct as he saw them in the Restoration period. These levels ranged from
those lustful women who were equal to the men in their desires, to those
women of true virtue who sought a love based on more than sexual gratification. Although there are other women of "honour" in the play—Mrs. Dainty
Fidget and Mrs. Squeamish—Lady Fidget is the most verbal and active and
thus more self-incriminating. In her lustful behavior she is little different
from a strumpet except for her hypocrisy, which perhaps makes her more
damnable. For instance, at the moment she is about to give herself to Horner
her train of thought runs thus: "You must have a great care of your conduct;
for my acquaintances are so censorious . . . and detracting, that perhaps they'll
talk to the prejudice of my Honour, though you should not let them know the
dear secret." So that his dislike of such hypocrisy is made absolutely clear,

by the end of the play Wycherley has had Horner partaking of pleasure with all the ladies of virtue. Contrasting Lady Fidget is Margery Pinchwife, lustful but honest about her lust. As Horner says about the love letter she writes him, " 'Tis the first love letter that ever was without flames, darts, fates, destinies, lying and dissembling in it." She is perhaps more admirable for her honesty yet at the end of the play she is taught to lie by the "virtuous gang." The final female character of note, Alithea, is virtuous in all aspects and heading for a commendable marriage based on a true love and would seem to be, as the opposite of Lady Fidget, the character for emulation.

One of the comic devices used adeptly by Wycherley in *The Country Wife* is the *double entendre*. This was the very apparatus to which Collier took such offense in his *Short View,* saying that "when the Sentence has two Handles, the worst is generally turn'd to the Audience. The matter is so contrived that the Smut and Scum of the Thought now rises uppermost; And, like a Picture drawn to *Sight,* looks always upon the Company." Indeed, Wycherley's *double entendres* are that powerful and in Act IV, scene 3— the "china scene"—he is at his best.

The importance of *The Country Wife* lies in the fact that it signals both the height and the beginning of the fall of Restoration comedy. With its adept social satire, telling visions of selfishness and hypocrisy, and the seldom surpassed farcical "china scene," *The Country Wife* stands at the pinnacle of Restoration comedy. However, within the representation of the apparently romantic love of Alithea and Harcourt was the seed that was to grow within the comedy of that period until it destroyed it. This representation of the ideal in a realistic setting was the chief characteristic of the comedy to come— sentimental or "weeping comedy."

Phyllis E. Allran

THE COURTESAN

Type of work: Drama
Author: Pietro Aretino (1492-1556)
Type of plot: Satiric comedy
Time of plot: Early sixteenth century
Locale: Rome
First presented: 1534

In The Courtesan, *Aretino, whose biting satire earned him the title "The Scourge of Princes," settles an old score against the Papal court from which he had been forced to flee in fear of his life in 1525 as a result of intrigues against him. His portrait of the courtiers, who are all knaves, lechers, and fools, is meant to depict the court of the Medici Popes; but the play also ridicules pretentiousness in any age. This universality of theme and the unabashed ribaldry of the action make the work a perennially entertaining piece.*

By the time of Aretino, the Italian Renaissance had become overripe. It would be another half-century or more before England's attitudes and culture reached this stage of decadence, but the Italians were experiencing a decline already.

With the new concentration upon the world of mortal life, casting aside considerations for the after-life, it was inevitable that pleasure should come to be regarded as the major purpose of life. Power was important, of course, as Machiavelli attested; but, as always, the product of power was pleasure, even if only the pleasure of exerting control over one's contemporaries.

Aretino himself, though he ridicules lechery in this play, was noted for his own indulgence in excesses of sensuality. It is interesting, however, that he does not excoriate sexual liberties nearly so sharply as he does the inhumanities of court politics.

Those who are clever but lacking in wisdom and compassion have always enjoyed clambering over their fellows in their attempts to gain tactical advantage. Aretino seems to have recognized this at an early stage in his life, while discovering also the terrible efficacy of his vituperative pen. The son of a prostitute (which he was) could not rely on kindness or justice from such a world to make his life bearable. It would be difficult to believe that anyone, finding himself living the life of a servant as described by Rosso in Act V, would not seize any available means of moving to a position offering more pleasure and power (as Aretino's writings moved him). Aretino's poison pen is often amusing, sometimes distasteful, occasionally boring, but, given the circumstances, it is always understandable.

Rome, the setting of the play, is as much the butt of Aretino's jokes as courtly politics. Indeed, Rome and the life at court seem inextricably bound together in the author's mind, perhaps because he was himself nearly murdered once as a result of court intrigues surrounding the Papacy. He appears to have adopted Venice instead as his home, lavishing his praise upon that city in Act III, and, at tiresome length, upon some of its citizens. The names of those receiving his encomiums did not simply pop into Aretino's head unbidden; aside from those few, like Titian, who seem to have been his friends, he carefully praises those who can be of use to him. He is often quite forthright about this, at one point even going so far as to cause a character to mention his name and his hopes. The fact that such tactics were immensely successful reminds us that while Aretino's life may have had an offensive odor about it, so did his age.

Aretino is neither a great dramatist nor a great poet. The strengths his comedy displays arise from his ability to mingle several dialects, assigning different ones to different characters, and relishing especially those vigorous speech patterns associated with the illiterate and the poor. At times, the delight his characters show in the scatological can be entertaining.

He seems uninterested in, or incapable of, weaving circumstances of credibility into the entrances and exits, or the shifts in conversational subjects, of his characters. Often, characters simply announce that the subject will change. And in many instances the author flings personages onstage and plucks them offstage with no rationale other than the exigencies of his plot.

Only once in the play does he reach the heights of bitter wisdom scaled regularly by the Jacobeans, when Maco catechizes Andrea on life:

> *Maco*:   Tell me, how does one come into the world, Maestro?
> *Andrea*: Through a cave.
>
> .   .   .
>
> *Maco*:   But what happens when a man is through living?
> *Andrea*: He dies in a hole as spiders do.

These lines, with their gothic imagery and cynical accuracy, might easily have excited the envy of John Webster.

One recognizes in *The Courtesan* the topsy-turvy world picture painted so often by other Renaissance dramatists and moralists. Servants here, as elsewhere, are insolent and presumptuous of their masters, and their masters are lustful, foolish, and purblind. When Rosso dupes Parabolano, his deceit being exposed only in the last scene, we are reminded of the comedies of Ben Jonson, and especially of his *Volpone*. Mosca is a much more fully drawn character, wittier and more alive, but there are definite debts owed by Jonson to just such Italian comedies as this one. If there were nothing else in Aretino to attract Jonson's attention, the Italian's acidic wit would most probably impress the Englishman as emanating from a kindred spirit.

When Rosso argues that the way to advancement is through pandering to the lusts of the powerful, we hear echoes of *The Revenger's Tragedy* and *The Duchess of Malfi*. But a more revealing, if less definite, parallel lies in Andrea's tutoring of Maco in the art of being a courtier. The tutor-pupil relationship has great dramatic potential for satire on the subject taught, and Aretino makes use of this potential, as does Shakespeare in *As You Like It* when Rosalind, in disguise, instructs Orlando on the many aspects of love. Admittedly, Rosalind is much less harsh in her criticism of lovers and ladies than is Andrea on courtiers and fops, but Andrea's subject is more deserving of acrimony. In addition, Rosalind is the future beneficiary of her precepts; she is dressing a husband, while Andrea is simply plucking a chicken.

Aretino is noted for his realism, sometimes described as "unpleasant." *The Courtesan* contains many examples of realism, among which are the hawking of "histories" in Act I, the selling of lampreys, and the description of meal-taking in the servants' quarters. It is the last which exemplifies the sort of realism which has earned the adjective "unpleasant," but it is worth remembering that few realists have escaped the adjective. And Aretino, though inconsistent, is in the main a true realist.

John J. Brugaletta

THE COURTSHIP OF MILES STANDISH

Type of work: Poem
Author: Henry Wadsworth Longfellow (1807-1882)
Type of plot: Sentimental romance
Time of plot: 1621
Locale: Massachusetts
First published: 1858

This long narrative poem tells the story of a gruff captain who sends his young scholar friend to plead his case for marriage to a young girl in Plymouth settlement, not knowing that Alden already loves Priscilla himself. The sentimental tale ends romantically when Standish, after having been thought killed, appears to give his blessing to the young couple on their wedding night.

This poem is one of the lasting results of Longfellow's interest in and examination of New England history and literature. It is basically a Puritan love story which finds its factual roots in Longfellow's own remote relative, John Alden, a maternal ancestor. The obvious "pastoral" qualities are borne out in the pleasant remoteness of the scene, the physical descriptions of the land, and the simplicity of the people about whom the story is told. Moreover, the theme of innocence and youthful love ties this pastoral romance together. The love triangle is present from the beginning of the poem and the reader is immediately involved in the situation.

The landscape of the poem is definitely Puritan in its dimensions with everything seen through the eyes of the Pilgrims who looked realistically and often harshly at the Indians and the life style around them. The action of the poem takes place from the early spring to the fall, and yet the tone of the poem takes on a wintry feeling which is very much in keeping with the austerity of the Puritan outlook. For example, the ocean is pictured as

sailless, sombre and cold with the comfortless breath of the east wind.

The Scriptural imagery and language is evident, adding more to the pastoral character of the poem. There are references to the spirit of the Old Testament in event and name. Longfellow describes John Alden and Priscilla on their wedding day as

Fresh with the youth of the world, recalling Rebecca and Isaac. . . .

Despite the placid tone, there are glimpses of freshness and light as this is a poem about youth and love and new beginnings. The magnificence of the sun on the wedding day is testimony to the poet's romantic ideals for his young bride and groom.

Longfellow's use of hexameter is an appropriate means of establishing the mood of the poem. The hexameters are more loose and flexible than those used in *Evangeline*. The effect is more relaxed and far less stately, and free use of trochees provides a freshness not found in *Evangeline*.

Longfellow found it sufficient to acquaint himself very generally with the history and spirit of the times and the people about whom he was writing. A careful and scrupulous examination of the poem will find some deviations from chronology and fact, though certainly not anything that would take away from the broad popularity of this work.

COUSIN BETTE

Type of work: Novel
Author: Honoré de Balzac (1799-1850)
Type of plot: Social criticism
Time of plot: Early nineteenth century
Locale: Paris, France
First published: 1847-1848

A part of The Human Comedy *series of novels,* Cousin Bette *is a powerful character study of a bitter and frustrated old spinster who is consumed by jealousy and hate. Balzac masterfully probes the motives behind his characters' actions, both good and evil, as he unfolds the story of Lisbeth Fischer's carefully plotted destruction of the romance between her niece and a Polish refugee.*

Cousin Bette was the last masterpiece that Balzac wrote and one of the last novels of his unfinished Human Comedy series. Together with *Cousin Pons* they made up a sub-category of his complex plan titled *Les Parents Pauvres.* The book presents some of Balzac's most somber visions of human depravity, but also emphasizes loyalty and devotion. *Cousin Bette* was written during the winter of 1846-1847 under the greatest possible pressure and emotional strain to attempt to clear off Balzac's usual state of indebtedness; the labor, coming on top of many years of work no less arduous, may finally have broken Balzac's strength. It is one of Balzac's longest novels, and one of the most perfectly organized and most densely constructed. There are none of the digressions or padding that he sometimes used to lengthen stories. All of the different parts of the tale—the black "angel" Bette, the debauched Hulot, the ambitious Valérie, and her scheming husband—work togther like the pieces of a vast machine, grinding away to the inevitable, ironic conclusion.

Balzac saw society as a unit, a great drama with endless links and relationships. This theme is everywhere evident in *Cousin Bette.* All social levels are portrayed and are shown to be interwoven beneath the surface by the threads of human emotions. Hatred ties Bette to the Hulots, passion ties Baron Hulot to Valérie, ambition connects Marneffe to the Baron, love ties Hortense to Steinbock and debt ties Steinbock to Bette. The tangle is even more complicated than this, and all of it is entirely plausible. In fact, it is the very stuff of which real life is made. The amazing thing is that Balzac was able to keep not only all of the threads of this one novel in his head, but the threads for the entire series of novels, which included nearly three thousand named characters.

Balzac believed that a man's antecedents, environment, and upbringing all shaped his destiny. In this sense he was a forerunner of the realist school and of naturalists such as Zola, who relentlessly tied men and women to their pasts. Balzac saw that apparently trivial changes in events or new conditions might bring out latent possibilities in a man's character and alter his entire life. Balzac emphasized in his novels and stories the importance of the physical surroundings of his characters, the towns and streets and houses in which they lived, the rooms which seemed to trap them, the clothes and gestures which gave them away, all of the minutiae of life. In *Cousin Bette* the descriptions of Paris pinpoint the conditions of the characters, from the rundown neighborhood near the Louvre, in which Bette lives, to the shabby elegance of the Hulots' establishment. Everything is vividly detailed, explained, and placed in context. Nothing exists in isolation.

The place of women in society is reflected on many levels in *Cousin Bette*. There is Bette herself, who earns her own way with her needlework and always has; and then there is Valérie, who uses her beauty to further her unscrupulous husband's career and ends by being kept by rich men. Hortense, Bette's cousin, was bred to be a wife and must find a husband or be a burden to her family, and she knows it, but her father must provide her with a dowry; in herself she is not sufficient to win a man's name and place in society. Hortense's mother, Adeline, suffers her husband's indiscretions in silence because no socially acceptable recourse is possible. The women all must resort to intrigue and deceit to accomplish anything in the male-dominated and controlled society. Bette is the most independent of the women, and the most ruthless, but her efforts—whatever their motivation—must all be clandestine. Her success is possible only because nobody is aware of it. The other people do not suspect her because she is a woman no longer young and because she is plain, two characteristics which render her almost invisible.

In *Cousin Bette,* as in so many of Balzac's novels, the contrast between the provinces and Paris is an everpresent theme, for it is Bette's pleasant shrewdness, her lack of sophistication beside the Parisians, which gives the novel its momentum. Bette is a provincial fighting to make her way in the jungle of Paris; the reader cannot help but feel that Balzac admired her ruthless, astute maneuvering. Balzac always was fascinated by the theme of the individual in conflict with society, with the rebel or criminal personality. His villains often were more vigorous and interesting than his virtuous people, and Cousin Bette is no exception. She is one of Balzac's most intriguing and complex characters, totally unlikeable, yet hypnotic in her power. Her individuality is symbolized by the way in which she stubbornly reduces her hand-me-down garments from their modern, urban fashion to countrified, colorless rags; she makes the clothes conform to her self-image as she makes everything around her do the same. Shy and wild, vicious and hard, only her highly developed will keeps Bette from physically attacking her beautiful and resented cousin, Adeline. From the beginning, the reader knows that Bette is capable of anything. Resentment had grown within her, like a cancer, until it has possessed her, changed her into a monster. The countrywoman's pride will not stop short of complete revenge. Yet, strangely enough, she is content with a secret revenge. It does not matter to her if the Hulots never know that she was the instrument of their ruin. The silent satisfaction is enough for this peasant spinster.

The novel builds slowly, after a long and detailed preparation and exposition, establishing the characters and their setting. Then the action increases and the tension mounts to the climax, as inevitable as that of a classic tragedy. The Hulots and Valérie and Marneffe and Steinbock all pay the consequences of their sins; each of them has let his or her obsession rule his life, and finally has come to grief. Only Bette emerges triumphant; even her death is victorious, and one imagines her grinning from the grave as her victory continues its ironic ramifications after her death.

Bruce D. Reeves

COUSIN PONS

Type of work: Novel
Author: Honoré de Balzac (1799-1850)
Type of plot: Naturalism
Time of plot: The 1840's
Locale: Paris
First published: 1847

In this story of greed and inhumanity, Balzac follows the last years in the life of Sylvain Pons, an ugly and lonely old musician whose delight in good food leads him to gluttony, and whose passion for collecting works of art leaves him, unknowingly, a wealthy man at his death. In the relentlessly realistic fashion of naturalism, the author depicts the vicious scheming of those relatives who had rejected Pons in life to steal his estate upon his death.

Balzac stood at the dividing line between romanticism and realism. He was inclined toward the fantastic and supernatural and to the exaggeration of normal human types, but his desire to reproduce concrete fact and to visualize the scene or object made him a superb painter of French society in the first half of the nineteenth century. Both of these aspects of his writing are easily observed in *Cousin Pons,* part of the *Scenes from Parisian Life* segment of Balzac's *The Human Comedy.*

Balzac's own interest in the supernatural and hereafter are seen in the discussion of fortune-telling and astrology when Madame Cibot calls on the witch-like Madame Fontaine in her den. Balzac devotes several pages to an analysis of the plausibility of the seer's art and the reality of certain types of divination. Men do not understand everything that exists in the universe, he says, and should not close their eyes to some possibilities simply because they cannot be explained. This idea leads to a belief which is fundamental in Balzac's philosophy and which played an important part in his writing and in the structure of *The Human Comedy:* his belief in predestination. Balzac felt that the fates did conspire to lead human beings to their ultimate destinies. Given the circumstances of a mortal's background and the makeup of his character and the factors of his life, he has no alternative but to plunge forward to a particular fate. Balzac considered his job that of a recorder, setting down the causes and effects of the lives and destinies of his characters, and he believed that his method was scientific and objective.

In *Cousin Pons,* we see the characters of the old collector, Pons, and his beloved friend, Schmucke, and how their good and trusting natures are taken advantage of by the avaricious people around them. Given the nature of human beings, it is not surprising that the story works its way to its pathetic and painful conclusions. It would be incorrect to say that Balzac created men and women more horrible than any who lived; Balzac knew very well that people who have been taught that material values are the only important ones will stop at nothing until they have acquired everything that they can see within their grasp. The morality or lack of morality in Madame Cibot and Fraisier and Remonencq and the other characters is the result of many factors, which Balzac draws with his usual skill. None of these people stands outside of society; they all are influenced by it and in turn influence it. This is one of the fundamental themes in *The Human Comedy* which Balzac created in more than ninety volumes.

The friendship between Pons and Schmucke is portrayed with a touching humor and sensitivity. The devotion between the two old men provides a counterpoint to the grasping, almost savage natures of Madame Cibot and the others. Seldom did Balzac portray such a low level of society, but he shows both sides of the coin, the love and generosity possible between human beings as well as the cruelty and hypocrisy. If the negative powers ultimately are victorious, that is—Balzac implies—merely the fates at work. That does not mean that he believes that the negative always wins.

Cousin Pons was intended as a companion volume to *Cousin Bette*. In *Cousin Pons* we have the poor male relation, cruelly treated, but gentle of heart, and in *Cousin Bette* we have the poor female relation, also cruelly treated, but revenging herself. The symmetry pleased Balzac, and, read together, the two novels form a powerful structure, a devastating picture of human nature and its possibilities for good and evil.

The collection of old Pons is one that Balzac, himself an avid collector, would have wanted to own. Pons' passion for antiques was shared by Balzac, as was the old man's terror of other people gazing upon or possibly stealing them. Balzac was always at his best when describing a mania—think of Père Goriot and Eugénie Grandet, for example, and César Birotteau—whether the subject be greed, a passion for collecting, or obsessive parental affection. Balzac did more than sympathize with Pons' mania, he felt *with* Pons as the old man put together and attempted to guard his rooms full of bric-a-brac. The passion for the collection, also shared by the old Jew, Magus, is portrayed with so much intensity that the reader comes to feel some of the passion, as well, at least for the duration of the book.

Pons and Schmucke are two of the great characters in Balzac's vast gallery and in all of European literature. They both are extremely funny and very touching. They are "odd" yet they are never absurd. They are portrayed with a truth of observation and a subtlety of touch that renders them sympathetic despite the quirks of their personalities. Their strange habits and costumes, their odd passions for collecting, for good food, for company, or whatever, are not applied by the writer from the outside, but emerge from within their living, breathing beings. That is why their ultimate fates are so devastating to the reader; their gentle, unworldly natures soon become objects of concern, and their lives moral pictures of the most painful kind.

Cousin Pons has a reputation for being grim and brutal, but it is actually

a very gentle book. The greater part of the story is devoted to the friendship
and the devotion of Schmucke and old Pons. And Pons' loyalty for his old
friend and his effort to care for Schmucke even after his own death is touchingly shown. When the grasping natures of Madame Cibot and her allies
are held up before this picture of unselfish love, they appear doubly horrible.
A tone of quiet melancholy pervades the book, a sadness on the part of
Balzac that such a fate should await two such good men. But, as the chron-
icler of human nature in all its forms, he cannot flinch; so he draws the
Marville household in all of its pettiness and the brilliant picture of Madame
Cibot, a woman who rivals even Cousin Bette when it comes to merciless
scheming, and he lets the reader draw his own conclusions. Before Balzac few
authors had attempted such an uncompromising look at the varieties of human nature. So honest was his gaze that, even today, we find ourselves
flinching at the picture he painted.

Bruce D. Reeves

THE COXCOMB

Type of work: Drama
Authors: Francis Beaumont (1585?-1616) and John Fletcher (1579-1625)
Type of plot: Romantic comedy
Time of plot: Early seventeenth century
Locale: England and France
First presented: 1608-1610

In this comedy, one of the weakest of the Beaumont and Fletcher collaborations, all of the stock character types and comic situations of the Jacobean stage are brought into play. The various comic elements, however, are so hastily thrown together in a plot and subplot, almost unrelated, that the authors have difficulty in forcing events to a believable conclusion.

While it is true that *The Coxcomb* fails as drama, except in a few scenes, it is also true that the play is not without interest to a twentieth century audience. Antonio, the coxcomb, is really not so foolish to our eyes as he was to the eyes of the seventeenth century. A willing cuckold (a "wittol" in the seventeenth century) was indeed a fool. But Antonio's motives, while unrealistic and not clearly established, are commendable. He wants his friendship with Mercury to be as famous as the friendships of Damon and Pythias and Orestes and Pylades. He has, however, chosen the wrong friend. But in view of his willingness to offer his wife to his friend, his feeling of closeness to Mercury, with whom he has been traveling three years, must have run very deep indeed. It is comic, though, that his motivation seems to stem more from a desire for fame than to please his friend. In addition, he is also foolish not to see that his wife does not want to commit adultery, but this hardly makes him a fool.

As a romantic comedy, *The Coxcomb* is generally inferior. But the most interesting aspect of the play from a twentieth century point of view is one which may have been largely unconscious on the part of Beaumont and Fletcher. This is the relative merits of the two sexes, and it comes out in both the main plot and the subplot, but especially in the subplot. Instead of the usual slurs against the female sex, which are typical of the period, the playwrights give us Viola, who bewails the evils of the male sex. She berates herself for having trusted a man "so lightly . . . so many being false." And her attitude towards men continually hardens with experience. Even her estranged lover, Ricardo, comes to admit "how rude" men can be, and that he has been "a kind of knave." While Viola's reversal—her forgiving Ricardo so quickly—is not fully prepared for, we are ready to accept Ricardo's statement, the last word in the play before the Epilogue, "that women want but ways/To praise their deeds, but men want deeds to praise."

THE CRADLE SONG

Type of work: Drama
Author: Gregorio Martínez Sierra (1881-1947)
Type of plot: Tragi-comedy
Time of plot: Early twentieth century
Locale: Spain
First presented: 1911

The sentimental yet believable plot of The Cradle Song *revolves around the stifled mother instincts of a group of adoring nuns who bring up a girl from baby-hood in their convent. The play is divided into only two acts, separated by a poem which covers a lapse of eighteen years.*

Martínez Sierra's *The Cradle Song* is one of the most successful plays of the twentieth century Spanish theater; its production has continued both in Spain and abroad for more than sixty years with renewed critical and popular acclaim. Though only thirty when he produced the play, Martínez Sierra showed an insight into the human character which touched audiences of wide cultural and age differences. The combination of characterization, theme, and humor with a solid plot made it a success. It has been one of the few modern dramas which successfully took a sentimental story and made it powerful rather than maudlin.

One particular aspect of the play which is significant for recent critics is its characterizations of women. Martínez Sierra wrote *The Cradle Song* with his wife, the noted poetess María de la O Lajárraga. Her influence is felt quite significantly in the play in the insight which the audience obtains into the feelings of the main female characters. For a play of the early twentieth century this is highly unusual and it is a topic about which much has been written in the past few years. The analysis of the universal instinct of mother-hood and the female consciousness brings an unusual depth to the play.

The setting of *The Cradle Song* and the humor of the action add to the enjoyment which audiences have had from the play for decades and will continue to have for many years to come. As a work to read, rather than see performed, *The Cradle Song* has sufficiently good dialogue to be appreciated without benefit of stage and live actors.

CRANFORD

Type of work: Novel
Author: Mrs. Elizabeth Gaskell (1810-1865)
Type of plot: Comedy of manners
Time of plot: Early nineteenth century
Locale: England
First published: 1853

In Cranford, *Mrs. Gaskell portrays with warmth and gentleness the habits, problems, and peculiarities of poor but genteel ladies in a small English village. The humor and whimsicality of the sketches are reminiscent of Charles Lamb.*

"In the first place, Cranford is in possession of the Amazons; all the holders of houses, above a certain rent, are women." That first sentence of *Cranford* suggests an emphasis which the book as a whole does not support—that the ladies of Cranford are indeed self-sufficient. True, Cranford's society is largely made up of women alone, who often congratulate themselves that they do not have to endure the opposite sex. In times of difficulty, though—in illness or in the burglary scare or when it comes to matters of finances—the ladies admit to needing the help of a gentleman or two. The narrator, a younger participant-observer, wryly understands the inconsistencies of Miss Matty, Miss Pole, and the others, and ironically details these in her consistent tone. The epitome of the Cranford attitude is revealed when Miss Pole exclaims, "My father was a man, and I know the sex pretty well."

Cranford was already anachronistic in Mrs. Gaskell's time. She surrounds the village and the society with an aura of nostalgia: that era had gone forever, but it had had certain advantages, despite its idiosyncrasies. The motif of older childless ladies symbolically reinforces the theme of the passing of Cranford, whose traditions will not be carried on by another generation.

The novel is episodic in form, and very little of consequence happens that is not resolved in the course of one or two chapters. Like many Victorian novels, this one was published serially, in *Household Words,* a periodical edited and published by Dickens. The first two chapters appeared as a complete story in 1851, and Mrs. Gaskell had not intended to write more, but Dickens persuaded her to continue *Cranford.* This explains why two strongly defined characters, the Captain and Miss Deborah Jenkyns, who seem so important in the beginning, die in the second chapter. From there on, Mrs. Gaskell had to begin again, so to speak, and make Miss Matty the central figure.

THE CREAM OF THE JEST

Type of work: Novel
Author: James Branch Cabell (1879-1958)
Type of plot: Satiric fantasy
Time of plot: Twentieth century
Locale: Virginia
First published: 1917

The Cream of the Jest proposes fantasy and romanticism as antidotes to the harsh realities of naturalism, although reality seems to win out in the end. The novel is a combination of philosophic speculation, frequent literary allusion, and a fragile plot in which Cabell extols the virtues of chivalric love.

In 1929, James Branch Cabell collected into one eighteen-volume series all his works dealing with the fictional land of Poictesme and its legendary hero, Dom Manuel. Poictesme—the name probably derived from a combination of Angouleme and Potiers—is an imaginary province in southern France; Cabell traces its history from 1234 to 1750, and describes in detail its social customs, legal procedures, sexual mores, and legendary background. Two of the eighteen books in this Storisende Edition, however, are not set in Poictesme: these are *The Rivet in Grandfather's Neck* (1915) and *The Cream of the Jest*. Both novels are included in the series because they treat the same themes as the Dom Manuel stories; both are concerned with ideals of chivalric love and with the same values found in mythical Poictesme.

The Cream of the Jest is set in the American South, in the town of Lichfield in Virginia; its hero, Felix Kennaston, is an author who, like Cabell, has created a romantic land of fantasy in his novels. When the humdrum life of the Virginia countryside becomes too dull for his imaginative spirit, he escapes to his land of dreams, identifying with his hero, Horvendile; through the character of Horvendile he enjoys romantic adventures and feeds on the noble and beautiful ideals of chivalry in the manner of a Don Quixote. Cabell uses Kennaston's fantasies to weave an allegorical tale, charged at once with romanticism and realism, symbolism and irony. Through Kennaston's search for the perfect woman, which ends in his discovery that the elusive Ettarre is actually his boring and unimaginative wife, Cabell dramatizes his ironic and romantic comic vision of life.

Cabell's vision is that of a man who has looked deeply into life and found it wanting; he is profoundly discontented with what he has observed. As a remedy, he finds consolation in his great ambition—"to write perfectly of beautiful happenings"; he creates fantasies in exquisite language, inspired by his vision of a land of joy and love, a land untroubled by sorrow, frustration, and regret. In *The Cream of the Jest,* Felix Kennaston's career as dreamer parallels the lives of all men, who turn irresistibly to clouds, romance, and mystery to atone for the boredom or pain of their everyday lives. The gentle irony of Cabell's vision is that he not only sees the dreariness and monotony of human life and understands the saving, soothing value of dreams, but admits with objective clarity and insight that dreams are impotent and a little childish. He knows more than anyone else the necessity and beauty of romance, at the same time that he accepts the reality of life, no matter how far it falls short of his mind's imaginings.

CRIME AND PUNISHMENT

Type of work: Novel
Author: Fyodor Mikhailovich Dostoevski (1821-1881)
Type of plot: Psychological realism
Time of plot: Mid-nineteenth century
Locale: Russia
First published: 1866

Crime and Punishment *is a powerful story of sin, suffering, and redemption; Dostoevski's theme is that man inevitably pays for his crimes against his fellows by suffering, and by that suffering he may ultimately be purified. The character of Raskolnikov is a tremendous study of a sensitive intellectual driven by poverty to believe that he is exempt from moral law.*

Crime and Punishment was Fyodor Dostoevski's first popularly successful novel after his nine-year imprisonment and exile for alleged political crimes (the charges were of doubtful validity) against the czar. After his release from penal servitude, Dostoevski published novels, short stories, novelettes, and journalistic pieces, but none of these brought him the critical and popular acclaim which in 1866 greeted *Crime and Punishment*—possibly his most popular novel. This book is no simple precursor of the detective novel, no simplistic mystery story to challenge the minds of Russian counterparts to Sherlock Holmes' fans. It is a complex story of a man's turbulent inner life and his relationship to others and to society at large. The book must be considered within the matrix of Dostoevski's convictions at the time he wrote the novel, because Dostoevski's experience with czarist power made a lasting impression on his thinking. Indeed, Dostoevski himself made such an evaluation possible by keeping detailed notebooks on the development of his novels and on his problems with fleshing out plots and characters.

Chastened by his imprisonment and exile, Dostoevski shifted his position from the youthful liberalism (certainly not radicalism), which seemed to have precipitated his incarceration, to a mature conservatism which embraced many, perhaps most, of the traditional views of his time. Thus Dostoevski came to believe that legal punishment was not a deterrent to crime because he was convinced that criminals demanded to be punished; that is, they had a spiritual need to be punished. Today, we might call that compulsion masochistic. But Dostoevski, in his time, related the tendency to mystical concepts of the Eastern Orthodox Church, an Establishment institution. With a skeptical hostility toward Western religion and culture, born of several years of living abroad, Dostoevski became convinced that the Western soul was bankrupt and that salvation—one of his major preoccupations—was possible only under the influence of the Church and an ineffable love for Mother Russia, a devotion to homeland, to the native soil, which would brook neither logic nor common sense: a dedication beyond reason or analysis. Thus, expiation for sins was attained through atonement, a rite of purification.

However, the required expiation is complicated in *Crime and Punishment* by the split personality—a typically Dostoevskian ploy—of the protagonist. The schizophrenia of Raskolnikov is best illustrated by his ambivalent motives for murdering the pawnbroker. At first, Raskolnikov views his heinous crime as an altruistic act which puts the pawnbroker and her sister out of their misery while providing him the necessary financial support to further his education and mitigate his family's poverty, thus relieving unbearable pressures on him. And he intends to atone for his misdeeds by subsequently living an upright life dedicated to humanitarian enterprises. But Raskolnikov shortly becomes convinced of his own superiority. Indeed, he divides the human race into "losers" and "winners": the former, meek and submissive; the latter, Nietzschean supermen who can violate any law or principle to attain their legitimately innovative and presumably beneficial ends. And Raskolnikov allies himself with the "superman" faction. He intends to prove his superiority by committing murder and justifying it on the basis of his own superiority. This psychological configuration is common enough, but, unlike most paranoid schizophrenics, Raskolnikov carries his design through—a signal tribute to the depth of his convictions.

The results are predictably confusing. The reader is as puzzled about Raskolnikov's motives as he is. Is it justifiable to commit an atrocity in the name of improvement of the human condition? This essential question remains unanswered in *Crime and Punishment* because Raskolnikov, egocentrically impelled by pride, cannot decide whether or not he is superior, one of those supermen entitled to violate any law or any principle to serve the cause of ultimate justice, however justice might be construed. Likewise, in his notebooks, Dostoevski implied that he, too, was ambivalent about Raskolnikov's motives. Yet he added that he was not a psychologist but a novelist who plumbed the depths of men's souls; in other words, he had a religious not a secular orientation. He was thus more concerned with consequences than with causality. This carefully planned novel therefore expands upon a philosophical problem embodied in the protagonist.

The philosophical problem in *Crime and Punishment* constitutes the central theme of the novel: the lesson Raskolnikov has to learn, the precept he has to master in order to redeem himself. The protagonist finally has to concede that free will is limited. He has to discover and admit that he cannot control and direct his life solely with his reason and intellect, as he tried to do, for such a plan leads only to emptiness and to sinful intellectual pride. Abstract reason takes the place of a fully-lived life and precludes the happiness of a fully-lived life; happiness must be earned, and it can be earned only through suffering. Thus Raskolnikov has to learn that happiness is achieved through suffering—another typically Dostoevskian mystical concept. Hence, the climactic moment in the novel comes when Raskolnikov confesses his guilt at the police station, for Raskolnikov's confession is tantamount to a request for punishment for the crime and acceptance of his need to suffer. In this way, Raskolnikov demonstrates the basic message of *Crime and Punishment*: that reason does not bring happiness; happiness is earned through suffering.

The Epilogue—summarizing the fates of other characters; Raskolnikov's trial, his sentencing, and his prison term; and Sonia's devotion to Raskolnikov during his imprisonment—confirms the novel's central theme. Artistically, however, the Epilogue is somewhat less than satisfactory or satisfying. First of all, Dostoevski's notes indicate that he had considered and rejected an alternate ending in which Raskolnikov committed suicide. Such a conclusion would have been logical in an existential sense. And it would have been psychologically sound. However, the very logicality of Raskolnikov's suicide would have suggested a triumph of reason over the soul. That idea was not consonant with Dostoevski's convictions; thus, he dropped the plan. Second, the ending which Dostoevski finally wrote in the Epilogue implies that the meek and submissive side of Raskolnikov's personality emerged completely victorious over the superman. But such an ending contradicts Raskolnikov's persistent duality throughout the novel. Raskolnikov's dramatic conversion thus strains credulity, for it seems too pat a resolution of the plot. For the sophisticated reader, however, it does not greatly detract from the powerful psychological impact of the novel proper nor diminish the quality of a genuinely serious attempt to confront simultaneously a crucial social problem and a deeply profound individual, human one.

Joanne G. Kashdan

THE CRIME OF SYLVESTRE BONNARD

Type of work: Novel
Author: Anatole France (Jacques Anatole Thibault, 1844-1924)
Type of plot: Domestic romance
Time of plot: Nineteenth century
Locale: France
First published: 1881

In this best known of France's works we find the characteristic style: precise, elegant, humorous, learned, and gently ironic. The lovable characters of old Bonnard and the charming girl Jeanne are memorable portraits, but the chief pleasure in reading this novel lies in France's droll comments, quips, and asides and in his keen observations on life.

The Crime of Sylvestre Bonnard was not only an immediate popular success, but it was also recognized by the French Academy. Now, however, the novel is seldom read in English and is virtually ignored by literary critics. The reason is a fundamental one: if the novel's warm sentimentality is diverting, its failure to engage human experience in any complex way renders it superficial. Yet, *The Crime of Sylvestre Bonnard* is a work of sensitivity. It contains a level of artistry that demands a less casual dismissal than "a fairy tale for grown-ups," as one critic has defined it. The difficulty remains in identifying that artistry and assessing its merit.

The work defies successful classification. It is wholly the art of Anatole France and does not conform to any of the popular "schools" of literature; nor does it fit into any of the traditional categories. It is certainly not a novel of plot, for the plot is extremely tenuous, consisting of little more than a series of charming but loosely linked anecdotes, like bright beads threaded onto an unsubstantial chain. It is not a novel of incident or of manners. Nor is it a psychological or a sociological novel, nor even a novel of characterization, which classification it most closely approaches. Neither is it a novel that is dependent on the French schools of naturalism or realism for its form. On the contrary, it elevates beauty, extolls the nobler instincts of man, and flirts briefly with the supernatural without being romantic. It is a work of feeling, of simple truth and touching honesty, which celebrates the humanity of the protagonist.

The novel does suffer, nevertheless, from the manner of its genesis. It comprises two distinct pieces, each of which was written for the popular market. The first segment, "The Log," appeared in two issues of a popular French magazine and constitutes a short story in the tradition later made famous by de Maupassant and O. Henry. Under heavy pressure from his agent to fulfill his writing commitments, France completed the second and longer element a year later. The two pieces were then serialized in *La Nouvelle Revue*. The stitching process is all too apparent. While the two segments share a central protagonist, they have with only one exception a different cast of minor characters. Furthermore, although the "journal" format would seem to serve to extend the work effectively, it also contains the potential trap of incremental extension by anecdote—a trap into which France fell.

The critical attention devoted to *The Crime of Sylvestre Bonnard* in the last half century has been sparse. It has consisted chiefly of sporadic and curious examinations of the reasons for its survival. Some serious critics, however, have worried over the lean bone of its title and the stray scrap of the fairy incident. The consensus is that the crime referred to in the title is not, in fact, the crime of abduction of which Bonnard is guilty. But what crime the title does refer to is by no means a matter of common agreement. One critic, seduced perhaps by Bonnard's own journal entry, states with more certainty than may be warranted that Bonnard's crime is the retention of a few of his beloved books from auction, the proceeds of which he has pledged as a dowry for Jeanne. This conclusion overlooks several important factors, not the least of which is the characterization of Bonnard. It would be strange indeed for a man who held a lifelong passion for books to find himself able to part with *all* of his immense library except those few books which had been given him as souvenirs. Second, while Bonnard does feel guilt over Jeanne's dowry, there is no suggestion that any of the books he retained were of significant monetary value. Further, it seems plain that Jeanne Alexandre has been denied nothing by Bonnard's retention of them. Most important, however, this idea overlooks France's intention. Surely the fact that an act designed to save Jeanne from mistreatment and exploitation can be called a crime in an ostensibly civilized society is a poignant irony. Bonnard's "crime" is thus benevolence in a social order that is inherently malignant.

If the introduction of the fairy gives the ordinary reader more of a problem, it has provided critics with an opportunity for imaginative exegesis. One critic points out the myth behind the fairy. Certainly the curious and seemingly pointless introduction of the fairy demands explanation. Even if Bonnard were merely daydreaming, France's use of the fairy must have some logical point. If it were intended to suggest encroaching dotage, it is an incomplete suggestion, for the fairy never reenters and Bonnard suffers no further daydreams or shows other signs of deterioration of his mental faculties, except for the more subtle and effective suggestion represented by the gradually increasing vagueness and confusion of the journal dates. If the fairy incident were intended to suggest a difficulty on Bonnard's part in distinguishing between reality and illusion, it was a clumsy attempt at best and a further example of inconsistency. All these compex explanations notwithstanding, the truth seems to be painfully apparent: France needed a spokesman for his strong views on the creative process and the role of the artist. He discovered that in the character of a semi-recluse he lacked a logical choice to serve this function. Hamilcar could not talk back, and certainly Thérèse was not appropriate to the purpose. The fantastic apparition of the fairy, which could be readily related to the books—as it could have been to almost anything—was a solution. But it must be finally judged a contrived and rather unimaginative device for a writer of France's ability.

The reader is also tempted to look for a deeper meaning in Bonnard's final activity. His new source of scholarship—insects and flowers—and the publication of a short book on a study of fertilization processes in flowers is strongly suggestive. Yet to proceed any further would be to go against France's own aesthetics. He himself insisted that he wrote purely on the literal plane. More than once he expressed a strong rejection of the Symbolists and was unable to pardon them for their "profound obscurity." On the contrary, he extolled the Greek classical writers and their clarity. Believing that only the direct is beautiful, France thought he was past the age when one admires what he does not comprehend.

The chief deficiency of *The Crime of Sylvestre Bonnard,* then, is that it offers us no insight into the human condition, despite its remarkable portrait of the gentle bibliophile. The work continues to live primarily because it is a pleasant exploration of how to deal with life. It celebrates humanity with an amused tolerance of, and genial sympathy for, the pettiness to which we are all susceptible. It suggests, above all, a belief in the human heart, which can, if properly exercised, transcend that crime of which Bonnard was truly guilty—of which all of us are guilty—the crime of being human.

Terrence R. Doyle

THE CRISIS

Type of work: Novel
Author: Winston Churchill (1871-1947)
Type of plot: Historical romance
Time of plot: Civil War period
Locale: Missouri and Virginia
First published: 1901

Churchill chose St. Louis as his setting in The Crisis *because the historical personages who appear in the novel—General Sherman, General Grant, and Abraham Lincoln—all came from that city or neighboring Illinois; and because the two streams of emigration which met in St. Louis gave him the opportunity to contrast the two cultures. Churchill's natural treatment of legendary figures such as Lincoln lend an atmosphere of reality to the story.*

Judged on the basis of his later novels dealing with problems such as class relationships and divorce, Winston Churchill must be considered outmoded in his attitudes and ideas. His own conservative and wealthy background biased him in favor of genteel, romantic, or impractical solutions to tough modern questions, although his thought was often enhanced by its sincerity and moral seriousness. But as a historical novelist, his reputation is secure; his early works about events in the Revolutionary and Civil Wars are excellent examples of vivid historical fiction. One of the most popular of these novels was *The Crisis,* a novel about people whose loves, loyalties, and friendships are threatened by the divisive influences of the Civil War.

Churchill's choice of the city of St. Louis as the setting for the novel's action is crucial, since that city was a crossroads between North and South when hostilities began. St. Louis had its old established families who had emigrated both from Northern and Southern states, and after 1861 the city suffered a painful division in popular sentiment between sympathizers of the Union and the Confederate causes; at one point in the narrative, Clarence Colfax is taken prisoner by Federal troops for his involvement in the Missouri militia's attempt to seize the state. St. Louis is thus the ideal setting in which to play out characters' conflicting personal beliefs and emotions against a backdrop of factual political and social history. Families which had been friends for decades cease to speak to one another, and when Missouri is finally established on the Union side, the city becomes dangerous for its own families of Southern background who have lived there for years.

Likewise, central to the plot is the love relationship of Stephen Brice and Virginia Carvel, which is threatened by the war; Stephen becomes a Union Army lieutenant, while Virginia, whose father is a Colonel in the Confederate Army, vows that she will never marry a Yankee. The two are reconciled in a dramatic scene in Abraham Lincoln's office, where Virginia has come to beg for a pardon for her old suitor Clarence Colfax, unaware that Stephen has

already interceded with the president on his rival's behalf. The believable portraits of Lincoln, General Grant, General Sherman, and other historical
figures are feats in themselves; and the successful fusing within a single story
of personal, everyday happenings with events and characters of great historical
import makes *The Crisis* succeed where so many novels of this type have
failed.

THE CRITIC

Type of work: Drama
Author: Richard Brinsley Sheridan (1751-1816)
Type of plot: Literary satire
Time of plot: Eighteenth century
Locale: London
First presented: 1779

Using the device of a play within the play to satirize contemporary trends in drama, Sheridan ridicules the insipid quality of recent tragedies and the contrived dramatic techniques in vogue at the time. The Critic was best known in its day as being a biting satirical portrait of Sheridan's fellow playwright Richard Cumberland, who was the prototype for Sir Fretful Plagiary.

Lord Byron considered *The Critic* to be the best English farce ever written, just as he thought Sheridan's *The School for Scandal* was the best British comedy. The distinction is important, for although much of the point of *The Critic* comes from its literary satire, it does not possess the substantiality and basic seriousness of great comedy. It is a slight work, but a romp, giddy and hilarious, enjoyable even for audiences unfamiliar with the playwrights and plays Sheridan was ridiculing.

Sheridan was, like so many great comic writers for the stage, very young when he composed his comic masterpieces. *The Rivals,* his first play, was written at the age of twenty-three. *The Critic* was produced only five years later, and it marked Sheridan's retirement from activity as a dramatic author. *The Critic* followed the form of *The Rehearsal* by the Duke of Buckingham, a play which Sheridan greatly admired; but in writing his own farce, Sheridan so far bettered the Restoration playwright that *The Critic* drove *The Rehearsal* off the stage.

In *The Critic* laughable oddities of authors, actors, patrons and audiences are held up in all of their absurdity, but mocked with the lightest of touches. The fun is directed not at individuals so much as at extreme situations that naturally grow out of the world of the stage. Perhaps the slightness of intellectual substance suggests a falling off from the power which created *The School for Scandal*; and the parts in *The Critic* have no necessary connection, appearing to have been put together in an arbitrary order. But the buffoonery remains infectious.

Probably the best character in the play, although he figures in one scene only and has little to do with what plot there is, is Sir Fretful Plagiary. His name suggests very accurately his values and affectations. Humor in *The Critic* does not suffer from the fact that the modern theater no longer produces tragedies such as Mr. Puff's "masterpiece," *The Spanish Armada,* and many of the scenes involving conceited authors, and theaters with constantly late curtains, will never date.

THE CROCK OF GOLD

Type of work: Novel
Author: James Stephens (1882-1950)
Type of plot: Fantasy
Time of plot: Any time
Locale: Irish countryside
First published: 1912

This modern classic involving a tale of adventure and philosophical discussions successfully brings old Irish legends to life in a blend of seriousness and humor. The novel is a wandering tale containing many elements and telling many stories, most perfectly executed.

James Stephens was a minor member of the Irish literary renaissance which began toward the end of the nineteenth century. Like such major figures as W. B. Yeats, John Synge and Sean O'Casey, Stephens embodies the wit, imagination, and satiric vein that distinguishes the movement. Another of its identifying characteristics was its intense Irish patriotism, which discovered a focus in the rebellion against England and the campaign for home rule. This nationalism founds its way into the literature in the form of the celebration of the ordinary people—the peasants and the urban proletariat—and their history, including the myths of the ancient Irish gods.

Like all fables, Stephens' *The Crock of Gold* can be read on a number of levels. Much like *Alice's Adventures in Wonderland,* it is a delightful story in itself and can be enjoyed for Seumas' and Brigid's humorous adventures among such mythical creatures as the Leprechauns and the Greatgods, Pan and Angus Og. Yet one would be amiss if he overlooked Stephens' political and moral intention and his call for Irish unity.

At the beginning of the story the Irish people are hostile to one another. When matters are brought to a boil with the theft of the crock of gold and the arrival of Pan, the Philosopher, who is responsible for the upheaval, is unable to bring order. Representing Ireland's intellectuals, he has lost touch with his own people. Realizing his impotence, however, he seeks out Angus Og. It is in this turning toward ancient wisdom that the gold as well as harmony are restored. At the end the people are promised that Caitilin's and Angus Og's child will come to return Ireland to its rightful rulers. Following the same path, Stephens suggests, Ireland will be able to arrive at its true Renaissance and gain its freedom from English tyranny.

CROME YELLOW

Type of work: Novel
Author: Aldous Huxley (1894-1963)
Type of plot: Social satire
Time of plot: 1920's
Locale: England
First published: 1921

In this amusing satire about the ill-fated love affair of a sensitive young poet, Huxley presents a precise picture of the early 1920's in England with wit and dexterity. The author laces his discussion of the virtues, vices, and idiosyncrasies of the guests at a house party with philosophical discussions; but he retains the reader's interest with continual shifts of emphasis and point of view.

Even an early work like *Crome Yellow* shows traces of the novels which were to make Huxley into one of the major voices of his generation. Autobiographical, the novel is almost entirely taken from his early life. Written around the theme of a sensitive young poet's unsuccessful love, it is more, however, than the exegesis of his own unrequited love. Huxley uses the plot to bring together a wide variety of characters. The most interesting feature for the reader familiar with Huxley's best-known novel, *Brave New World,* is the introduction of Scrogan, whose personality undergoes a metamorphosis in the course of the book. Originally a mere house guest, though a malignant one, Scrogan gradually becomes the voice which Huxley adopts later in *Brave New World.* His function in the book is the voice of the devil, whose mad theories of the herd and the elite will blossom completely in Huxley's later social satire.

Given the idiocy and banality of those gathered at Crome, it is not difficult to imagine Scrogan's philosophy coming into existence. Like Mary Bracegirdle (a name of singular significance), all the house guests are shut off from their own feelings and obsessed by their own worlds and themselves. Like Mr. Wimbush who subjects them to his reading of the ridiculous history of Crome—to which no one listens—they all speak *at* one another, never *to* anyone. The essence of the comedy, then, arises from their failure to understand and to communicate; the pathos of the situation emerges from missed connections and, finally, from missed opportunities of love. Because Denis Stone (again an apt and telling name) fails to confront Anne, he loses her love. Only Jenny Mullion sees accurately and truly; it is an absurd world which deserves our ridicule if not our pity. And it certainly deserves Mr. Scrogan.

CROTCHET CASTLE

Type of work: Novel
Author: Thomas Love Peacock (1785-1866)
Type of plot: Comedy of manners
Time of plot: Nineteenth century
Locale: England
First published: 1831

Thomas Peacock's Crotchet Castle *provides a kindly satire on romantic themes—the central one an argument to determine the most desirable period of history—which ridicules the excesses and exaggerations in human behavior. Although the only plot is a humorous but educated discussion of various topics of curiosity, and the people are mere caricatures, the work provides a fairly accurate picture of nineteenth century English country life.*

Born and educated in the eighteenth century, Peacock carried the ideas and ideals of the Century of Reason into the nineteenth century and the age of Victoria. Although ostensibly set in the first half of the nineteenth century, the scenes of *Crotchet Castle* might more easily be from the comedies of Sheridan or Goldsmith. Artificiality reaches the point of absurdity. The scenes at the country villa might almost be out of paintings by Watteau—or even Boucher. The influence of Voltaire and the rationalists and satirists of the previous century on Peacock is well known. At one moment the exchanges of Captain Fitzchrome and Lady Clarinda are worthy of Shakespeare's Beatrice and Benedict, then the scene abruptly changes to pseudophilosophic discussions that might have been taken from *The Satyricon* of Petronius. Peacock's writing always makes the reader think of something else, because it is based on previous creations rather than upon nature and direct observation of humanity. Quotations and exclamations in Greek, Latin, French, and other languages stud the dialogue like spangles on a ballgown, glittering but at times affected and gaudy.

The word "fashion" is the be-all and end-all of the characters' existence. Only money is more important than the pursuit of the fashionable; and, in fact, often they seem to be inextricably intertwined. Even as Peacock satirizes snobbery, the reader feels that Peacock is nevertheless a genuine snob, himself; his sharpest barbs are for the *nouveau riche* Jews trying to buy their way into the gentry. Peacock looked dubiously upon the changing times, particularly upon the growth and development of science during the first half of the nineteenth century. In novels such as *Crotchet Castle,* he satirizes the coming industrial age and the newfound riches of certain classes rising on the wave of change, and glorified that leisurely age when people had the time and inclination to sit around eating and drinking and talking . . . especially talking.

THE CRUISE OF THE CACHALOT

Type of work: Pseudo-factual account
Author: Frank T. Bullen (1857-1915)
Type of plot: Adventure romance
Time of plot: Late nineteenth century
Locale: At sea
First published: 1898

The chief value of this nineteenth century adventure romance lies in its full descriptions of whale hunting. Despite the facts that the book is antiquated as a natural history source, and the author is uncritical in his acquiescence to the sailors' many needless hardships, Bullen provides a dramatic portrayal of life aboard an American whaler. Although these defects exist within the work, the harsh realities of life aboard the whaler afford the reader a historical perspective.

Frank Bullen's childhood was cruel. Like Charles Dickens, he was a home-less waif and child laborer in London who lacked schooling. He was adopted briefly by a kindly aunt and began to read Milton's *Paradise Lost* at five years of age; but the aunt, his solitary childhood friend, died when Bullen was eight, and he was cast into the street. Alone in the world, with "no-one caring a straw for me," he trusted God and was signed on an English vessel when he was twelve years old. Bullen spent the next six years at sea. He landed in New Bedford, Massachusetts, when he was eighteen and secured a berth on a sailor's nightmare, a whaler, in this case the "Cachalot," a ven-erable tub "as leaky as a basket."

The Cruise of the Cachalot is a combined autobiographical/fictional nar-ration which gives an account of a South Sea whaler from a seaman's stand-point. Bullen also described the methods employed, the dangers met, and the woes experienced by whalers, using a clear style in order not to weary the reader. He scorned padding, sought accuracy of detail, and penned a tersely thrilling story of a voyage around the world that lasted for years. Its many fascinating passages include a description of a cyclone off the remote Seychelles Islands, storms at sea, the vast face of the sea and the sky, a passage through the Sargasso Sea, labors, landings, harpoonings, beatings, and a brush with the Confederate raider "Alabama," among other adventures. All this was done while pursuing cachalots, or sperm whales, which yielded by-products such as spermaceti and ambergris, mentioned by Shakespeare and Milton. The book's minor inaccuracies are the inevitable ones produced by its fast pace and man-of-action approach.

Bullen was at first puzzled as to how to write *The Cruise of the Cachalot* but decided to write it as if he were simply spinning a yarn to a single friend. When this approach met with difficulties, he offered his rich materials to the famous Rudyard Kipling, assuming that the latter could do it literary justice. Kipling declined the material and encouraged Bullen to handle it by himself.

After reading Bullen's manuscript, Kipling wrote a Foreword to it that has since been carried in every edition of *The Cruise of the Cachalot*. Kipling's foreword describes the book as "immense" and unequaled in sea wonder and mystery. Praising the manner in which Bullen depicted whaling through fresh and realistic sea pictures, Kipling commented that Bullen must have discarded enough material to write five books.

CRY, THE BELOVED COUNTRY

Type of work: Novel
Author: Alan Paton (1903-   )
Type of plot: Social criticism
Time of plot: Mid-twentieth century
Locale: South Africa
First published: 1948

A story of personal as well as national tragedy, this book by South African minister Alan Paton recounts the life of a Zulu country parson who comes to Johannesburg to find that the racial environment has driven his sister to prostitution and his son to murder. Told in poetic and Biblical language, the novel has found permanency in twentieth century literature.

As in the novels of André Malraux, *Cry, the Beloved Country* combines a perfect blending of action, philosophy, moral indignation, and sensitive character portrayal. This is a novel which impresses its message upon the reader on many different levels. First and foremost, it is a human tragedy, a narrative which has the power to exalt the reader in the same manner as did the classic tragedies of antiquity. The Reverend Stephen Kumalo is one of the great figures of twentieth century literature. He is not rich or grand in station, although he is the spiritual leader of his people; he is a plain little man, but he possesses a great soul and magnificent courage. His story is one that could have been treated in merely political terms, but Paton saw beyond this level and penetrated to the real tragedy of the human condition.

Human values are at question in *Cry, the Beloved Country*. How can human beings treat one another in this way? How can God allow people to do such things? The events that catapult the Reverend Kumalo from his quiet village to urban Johannesburg force him to confront and question all of the basic values that he has lived by. He sees, at an advanced age, a totally different side of human existence, but he is not destroyed by what he discovers. Those whom he loves the most suffer the most, and finally are destroyed. But Stephen Kumalo comes through—stronger than ever, although never to be the same.

Mr. Jarvis, the rich white patrician, also is changed by the tide of catastrophic events which sweep along all the major characters. One feels at the end of the book that there is hope, if all human beings will learn to love one another. Through this way, each individual can save himself, and, in turn, perhaps humanity as a whole can be saved. Paton emphasizes in *Cry, the Beloved Country* that the fundamental issues which plague humanity are beyond mere political control.

CUDJO'S CAVE

Type of work: Novel
Author: John Townsend Trowbridge (1827-1916)
Type of plot: Historical romance
Time of plot: 1861
Locale: Tennessee
First published: 1863

Written originally during the Civil War to exemplify the difficulty the rural population of a border state such as Tennessee underwent when they had to decide between allegiance to North or South, Cudjo's Cave *mingles elements of propaganda with its historical setting and romantic theme. Working closely with the actual events of history, the author displays such sincerity and literary skill that he is able to transcend the now outdated political issues for which the novel was written, and to dramatize effectively the guerrilla warfare fought among the people of Tennessee and Kentucky.*

Trowbridge used a dramatic and often moving story as a vehicle to put across his antislavery message. At times, the plot comes close to melodrama, but the narrative strength and the skill of many characterizations manage to raise the action to a higher level. Although the book is not great art, it is well crafted and enjoyable. In addition, it is of genuine historical interest for the picture it draws of the emotions and attitudes of the Civil War period.

The villains in the tale are the least convincing characters; most of the time they are no more than sketches, without depth or subtlety. No doubt many men committed such vile acts, but the reader is given no insight into their deeper instincts or motivations. Another flaw in the book is the dialogue, which is at times stilted and unrealistic. In particular, Old Toby's black dialect and Carl's German accent are both unconvincing, falling perilously close to stereotypes. Cudjo's speech and actions also on occasion slip into stereotypical patterns.

Pomp, however, is a character at once noble and believable. Although on the surface he seems almost too perfect to be true, the reader comes to feel an affection for this extraordinary black man. The author penetrates Pomp's personality and creates in him one of the two best characters in the novel. Penn Hapgood, the Quaker schoolmaster, is the other character who lifts the book above the ordinary. The abolitionist Penn is shown to be an idealist of subtle feelings and courage, a man willing to risk his life for what he believes. His speeches against the system combine propaganda with genuine emotion. He shows his wisdom when he declares that "education alone makes men free," and acknowledges that many white men might be considered slaves. Pomp's testimony to the joys of freedom, however precarious, is a moving and powerful statement. Throughout the long novel, Penn and Pomp stir the reader's interest and sympathies.

CUPID AND PSYCHE

Type of work: Classical myth
Source: Unknown
Type of plot: Allegory of love
Time of plot: The Golden Age
Locale: Ancient Greece
First transcribed: Unknown

This classical myth represents Cupid in his earliest creation, a young man (as opposed to his later evolution into the familiar cherubic and mischievous little boy) who falls in love with the Greek mortal, Psyche, against the wishes of his mother, Venus. Because her love and faith triumphs over mistrust, Psyche becomes immortal. The myth is rich in classical literary devices and levels of allegory.

Although the allegorical theme of Cupid's love for Psyche (or at least a maid) was known by Hellenistic times, the one known literary source for this complete tale is the *Metamorphoses* of "Lucius" Apuleius (A.D., second century). Better known as the *Golden Ass,* this Latin "novel" deals with the transformation of Lucius into an ass, his year-long journey and checkered adventures, his ultimate restoration to human shape, and his devotion to the Egyptian goddess Isis. At the center of this eleven-book work (4.28-6.24) is couched the story of Cupid and Psyche, as told by an old crone to a beautiful girl. This "pleasant tale and old wives' story," as the old woman put it, belongs to the genre of *Märchen,* or folktale, and throughout Europe, Scandinavia, Africa, Asia, and Indonesia are known variations on this theme, which includes an enchanted lover, jealous sister, mystery, mistrust, search, tasks, and happy reunion. Apuleius' readers would have immediately recognized the character Psyche as typical of the heroines of Greek "novels" or "romances": she is, of course, lovely and in love, but she is also timid, pious, naïve, and curious. This last characteristic, her most serious fault, Apuleius uses to relate Psyche to Lucius, the central figure of the novel. Both, because of *curiositas,* were violently thrown into a life of suffering and despair; both overcame their trials and achieved true happiness by devotion to a deity.

Cupid and Psyche has through the years been recognized for its allegorical possibilities, since after all Cupid ("Desire," Eros in Greek) is one of the oldest allegorical divinities, and Psyche does mean "Soul." That Apuleius intended symbolic reflection of the larger work is hardly debatable, but that he saw the story as a vehicle of teaching *Christian* virtue is unfounded. Nevertheless, the universal charm of the story prompted Fulgentius Planciades (A.D., sixth century) to allegorize thus: the city is the world, Psyche's father is God, her mother is matter, her sisters represent flesh and the will, Venus is lust, and Cupid is "cupidity"; Fulgentius, however, is unable to perfect his allegory with satisfactory consistency. Calderón (seventeenth century) saw the three daughters as paganism, Judaism, and the Church, the last of whom was wedded to Christ. The Platonists, who no doubt recognized echoes from Plato's *Phaedrus,* saw the sisters as the tripartite soul: desire and spirit are overcome by sure reason, and the ultimate acceptance of the rational soul among the gods symbolized freedom from the Orphic cycle of death and re-birth. Jungians see Psyche as the psychic development of the feminine; Venus symbolizes fertility, and the marriage to Cupid is sexual bondage.

In this story Cupid is considerably more mature than the familiar Hellen-istic winged archer-cherub, and his beauty is emphasized; nevertheless, he is still mischievous and his mother's minion. Venus, however, is an outright burlesque; she seems to have grown more vain with age and motherhood, and her jealousy of the beautiful young virgin Psyche is painful. Still, such a characterization is necessary if Venus is to be given the role of the folktale witch who sets the apparently impossible tasks, which are also appropriate to Venus' role as mother-in-law, since the wool, grain, water, and beauty are Psyche's symbolic *Brautproben,* or dowry, representing wifely abilities and virtues.

Tasks and journeys are traditional themes in heroic tales, especially when they are punishments for some sacrilege. Psyche's crime, despite her original guilelessness, is twofold: she has offended Venus and she has violated her husband's trust. It is interesting to observe how in Apuleius' version Psyche, who was so *simplex* that she could not even lie to her sisters about her hus-band, loses her innocence as soon as she is persuaded by them to kill the "monster." Thereafter it is she, not Cupid, who lures her sisters to their deaths. Psyche, therefore, loses innocence, but she gains knowledge and a chance to regain happiness—eternally. This again is the theme of the larger work, the *Metamorphoses,* in which Lucius is initiated into the Isiac mysteries and becomes the priest of Isis, forsaking the evils of a world of asses in men's flesh.

Another addition to the synopsis above must be included. Apuleius has Cupid warn Psyche that if she keeps secret the strange nature of their mar-riage, the child she is bearing will remain divine. Apuleius ends his story with the birth of a child who is fittingly called Voluptas, or "Joy." Thus the eternal union of love and the soul does result in the soul's divine, that is, immortal, joy.

As a product of the classical age, *Cupid and Psyche* is full of familiar classical literary and mythological illusions. The "labors" motif, which has been mentioned, includes the traditional *catabasis,* or journey to the under-world (cf. Herakles, Orpheus, Odysseus, Aeneas). The deserted Psyche re-calls the despair of Ariadne, Andromeda, and of course Dido. The theme of the opened container recalls Pandora. Psyche's apotheosis, or deification, finds precedent especially in the myth of Herakles. As for the gods, their portraits become near parodies of Homeric models, in that they act with stereotypical predictability. Later versions of *Cupid and Psyche* are found in Boccaccio's *Genealogy of the Gods* and in Walter Pater's *Marius the*

Epicurean; besides Calderón, other writers who have handled the theme are Molière, Corneille, Thomas Heywood, and Joseph Beaumont.

E. N. Genovese

THE CUSTOM OF THE COUNTRY

Type of work: Novel
Author: Edith Wharton (1862-1937)
Type of plot: Social criticism
Time of plot: Late nineteenth century
Locale: New York, Paris
First published: 1913

This story of a ruthless woman's ambitious social climbing and dabbling in marriages, money, and aristocratic titles is a bitter incrimination of the society which causes the heroine to be what she is. Motivated solely by the desire for power and status, Undine Spragg uses her beauty to prove that the sole aim of society is to provide diversion and security for its women. Wharton's excellent literary style and plot construction combine to make a novel that is fine literature as well as damning social criticism.

The Custom of the Country, one of Edith Wharton's most successful novels, was published midway through her productive 1905-1920 period, which culminated in a Pulitzer Prize. The novel reflects not only her overwhelming concern with American cultural inadequacies and her contempt for the values of the newly moneyed and growing middle class, in which she resembles her contemporary, Henry James, but also her interest in the issue of woman's role in society.

By the time Wharton wrote *The Custom of the Country,* the way had been paved by writers such as Theodore Dreiser and Robert Grant for the portrayal of self-serving, cold-blooded, and unsympathetic heroines. The battle which was fought at the turn of the century between those who insisted on realistic female characters and those who still clung to traditional idealized presentations of women had, by 1913, definitely been decided in favor of the realists. Thus the public had been conditioned sufficiently to accept a heroine like Undine Spragg, who is the epitome of amoral materialism. Through her character, Wharton is able to deal with both the cultural issue and the women's issue simultaneously, since Undine has been molded into her present ugly form by the forces of the grasping, unprincipled, and uncultured new commercial class. She is vain, crude, and opportunistic; she is intellectually and aesthetically, as well as spiritually, empty.

The problem in the novel is that Wharton cannot bring herself to absolve Undine of guilt for becoming what society has made of her—in fact, the author increasingly despises her heroine. Unable to remain objective toward her creation, Wharton allows Undine to become an inhuman abstraction; in so doing, she sacrifices the chance to subordinate individual characterization to a broader indictment of social conditions, as she did so successfully in *The House of Mirth.* The novel is thus marred not only by her loss of objectivity toward the heroine, but also toward some of her minor characters;

Wharton is less harsh than she might otherwise have been in her judgment of such characters as Abner Spragg and his wife, simply because their vulgarity is never allowed to triumph as is Undine's. But the deeper reason for the author's intolerance of Undine Spragg lies in the fact that her sin of vulgarity is compounded by that of pretentiousness and lack of self-understanding—to Wharton, the worst sin of all.

THE CYCLOPS

Type of work: Drama
Author: Euripides (c. 485-c. 406 B.C.)
Type of plot: Satyr play
Time of plot: Remote antiquity
Locale: Mt. Aetna in Sicily
First presented: Fifth century B.C.

This Euripidean drama is important as the only complete satyr play preserved from ancient Greece, and as a dramatization of the story of the Cyclops, Polyphemus, whose cannibal's welcome to Odysseus and his sailors is told in Homer's Odyssey. *Euripides embroiders Homer's main theme with additional characters and a chorus, but the generally light tone of the play gives it more comic relief than classical drama.*

Since the average length of a Euripidean tragedy is about twice the 709 lines of this satyr play, we might well have expected its relatively uncomplicated plot, its straightforward, undeveloping characterization, and its reliance on the traditional trappings of such plays, namely the chorus of lustful, uncouth, undisciplined satyrs. Until the early part of this century such characteristics had to be assumed for all satyr plays, but with the discovery of considerable papyrus fragments of Sophocles' satyr play, the *Ichneutae* ("Trackers"), we may now be all but certain that so little satyric drama survived simply because it lacked variety. As comic relief it was serviceable, but as classic drama it lacked much; and it is quite likely that we have *The Cyclops* only because the ancients judged it the most worth saving.

As we might deduce from the surviving titles of other satyr plays, *The Cyclops* has several common motifs and devices: slapstick buffoonery, reversal of fortune for the hero and the villan, theft, and satyric mischief (drunkenness and lechery).

Satyr plays, like practically all Greek tragedies, were drawn from mythology, but the playwright was always free to modify the story and characters. In *The Cyclops,* Odysseus is essentially the same person as in Homer: he is brave but sensible and shrewd; he does not become the unpopular ruthless figure of Euripides' *The Trojan Women* or Sophocles' *Philoctetes.* Amid the coarse satyrs he maintains his heroic dignity and in contrast with the lawless, beastly Cyclops, he is selfless and urbane. The Cyclops, however, lacks the depth of Homer's character. The brutal punishment for his haughty violation of Zeus' law of hospitality is turned into a comic incident of the bully getting his just dessert. Euripides is able to divert our horror or pity for the monster by sublimating some of the Cyclops' disgusting personality into the more human character of Silenus; for while Silenus is himself unfit for civilized society, he is still an endearing Falstaffian rascal. Furthermore, though a thorough coward, his old age has brought him a cleverness equal to that of Odysseus.

462

CYMBELINE

Type of work: Drama
Author: William Shakespeare (1564-1616)
Type of plot: Tragi-comedy
Time of plot: First century B.C.
Locale: Britain, Italy, and Wales
First presented: 1609

One of the kings of the twelfth century history Kings of Brittain *by Geoffrey of Monmouth,* Cymbeline *is Caesar's captive, hostaged and educated in Rome. The historicity of the plot and characters is unimportant as Shakespeare presents a play of political intrigue, both domestic and international, and of personal emotional involvement. The play is typically Shakespearian in the stress placed upon personal well-being of characters rather than military and political details.*

Cymbeline, together with *The Winter's Tale* and *The Tempest,* belongs to Shakespeare's final period of writing. These last three plays are marked by their mood of calmness, of maturity, and of benevolent cheerfulness; a kind of autumnal spirit prevails. This is certainly not to say that *Cymbeline* lacks its villains, its traumatic events, or its scenes of violence—the play contains all these elements—but that the overall tone is serene in spite of them. *Cymbeline* may be classified as a tragicomedy to distinguish it from its more dazzling predecessors among Shakespeare's comedies, such as *Love's Labour's Lost* or *Twelfth Night,* with their roguish heroes and heroines, their dialogues filled with witty and sparkling repartee and their plots abounding in mischievous scheming and complications. The main characters in *Cymbeline,* by contrast, are remarkable for their virtue rather than their cleverness, wit, or capacity for mischief; Posthumus is a model of earnestness and fidelity, while Imogen is the picture of purity and wifely devotion. The text is memorable not for the brilliance and sparkle of its dialogue, but for its passages of moving poetry such as "Fear no more the heat o' th' sun." Likewise, much of the plot is composed of the trials and sufferings of the good characters brought on by the scheming of the bad ones—even though the play ends as comedy must, with the virtuous happily rewarded and the wicked duly punished.

In the plot of *Cymbeline,* Shakespeare combined two lines of action: the political-historical storyline of the British king preparing for war with Rome, and the love story of Imogen and Posthumus. For the former, Shakespeare once again used as his source Holinshed's *The Chronicles of England.* However, finding the reign of *Cymbeline,* a descendant of King Lear, too dull and uneventful to make an interesting drama, he took the liberty of assigning to that king the refusal to pay the Roman tribute, which action Holinshed attributed to Cymbeline's son Guiderius. In this way he was able to enliven the plot by introducing a war and resolving it in a peace treaty at the end. Fortunately, however, this portion of the play's action—which remains rather uninteresting despite the coloring of the accounts—is very minor in comparison to the story of Imogen, which provides the central interest in *Cymbeline*. The love story is based on a wager, between a cunning villain and a devoted husband, regarding the faithfulness of the absent wife; for this story Shakespeare was indebted to one of the tales in Boccaccio's *Decameron*. In addition to the two main storylines, *Cymbeline's* plot contains numerous instances of characters traveling in disguise and cases of mistaken identity, including the subplot (Shakespeare's invention) of Belarius' abduction and subsequent rearing of the king's infant sons in Wales. Such elements tend to make the plot of *Cymbeline* seem extravagant even to the point of parody when it is read; but when one sees the play performed, its action appears more unified, if still somewhat confusing.

Cymbeline bears many resemblances to previous plays of Shakespeare. The figure of the gullible king influenced by his wicked queen reminds one of *Macbeth,* as does the scene of supernatural intervention in the form of Zeus, the ghosts of Posthumus' family, and the tablet bearing a prophecy— although in this play the prophecy device is weak and extraneous to the plot, and believed to have been inserted by a coadjutor. Iachimo, while he does not approach Iago in malignancy, nevertheless calls to mind Othello's tormentor through his cunning strategies and his cultivation of Posthumus' capacity for jealousy. Likewise, the scenes of Imogen's travels disguised as a boy and her eventual reunion with her lost brothers are reminiscent of Viola's similar adventures in *Twelfth Night*. Perhaps most important, however, is not the affinity of *Cymbeline* to Shakespeare's earlier work, but rather its own unique merit, as well as the relation it bears to that final masterpiece which was to follow, *The Tempest*.

CYRANO DE BERGERAC

Type of work: Drama
Author: Edmond Rostand (1868-1918)
Type of plot: Tragi-comedy
Time of plot: Seventeenth century
Locale: France
First presented: 1897

In this play, based upon the life of seventeenth century French author and playwright Cyrano de Bergerac, a freethinker and soldier famed for his skill in duels as well as for his inordinately long nose, Rostand develops a character symbolizing magnanimity, unselfishness, and beauty of the soul in a seemingly bellicose and physically ugly individual. Rostand's tragicomedy ranks among the most popular plays of the modern French theater.

Edmond Rostand's family was wealthy, and he never seemed to need to be commercial. He worked at a slow and sure pace and chose his themes as they came to him. His canon includes one volume of poetry, *Les Musardises* (1890), and the dramas: *Les Romanesques* (1894), *La Princess lointaine* (1895), *La Samaritaine* (1897), *Cyrano de Bergerac* (1897), *L'Aiglon* (1900), and *Chantecler* (1910).

In keeping with his image as an individualistic writer, Rostand leaves a body of work which defies the often-held view of the late nineteenth century as an age of somber, morbid, and usually unintelligible works of art. Several parallels with Shakespeare's *Romeo and Juliet* can be traced in *Cyrano de Bergerac;* and Rostand's *Les Romanesques* is a satirical treatment of the *Romeo and Juliet* theme. Dramatic invention, the use of splendid and spectacular settings, the presence of an eloquent, witty, and adventuresome hero, the conflict of love versus honor, the recklessness and self-sacrifices of the characters, and the point of honor upon which the whole play turns—all are elements of the romance tradition and are present in *Cyrano de Bergerac.*

Motion picture and television adaptations as well as several successful stage revivals of *Cyrano de Bergerac* over the years demonstrate that Rostand's popular turn-of-the-century verse play has the earmarks of a classic. Written just before the beginning of the twentieth century, *Cyrano de Bergerac* reflects the themes and symbols of late nineteenth century romanticism, with its emphasis on the heroic individual (appropriately, one who feels he has failed), its story of ill-fated lovers and wasted lives, and its symbolic moon as mother-and-home of the hero. Considered in its historical perspective, *Cyrano de Bergerac* is the culmination of a romantic revival in French literature.

But in tone the play charts a drastically different course from the "decadent" products that filled the theaters during the same period. In creating Cyrano, Rostand reached into the seventeenth century for his character. The real Cyrano was a little-known writer who lived in France from 1619 until his death in 1655. The bearer of an unusually large nose, he wrote about it in his books—books which have come down to us as the early ancestors of the science fiction genre.

It is tempting to speculate that Rostand also found his proper tone in the seventeenth century, for *Cyrano de Bergerac* is a play based on certain Renaissance-like assumptions, such as the reality of honor and the drama it can create when confronted with a passion like love. The theme of the play —"the making of a style out of despair"—also has affinities with seventeenth century values. Men who lived three hundred years ago in Europe were still experiencing the flowering of heroic individualism: the exhilarating belief that man can, with courage, strength, and intellectual ability, will into being— create—his world as he chooses. It remained for Rostand's age to turn the two-sided coin from "man is everything" to "man is nothing." An underlying assumption of *Cyrano de Bergerac* is the presence of despair, but Rostand handles it lightly, and it is the style which a man can create within this framework of despair that interests him. Rostand's word for style becomes "panache"—literally "white plume" but a word with broad symbolic connotations in the play. The word signifies something of a swashbuckling quality. It conveys a sense of superiority, courage, pride. A man with "panache" would virtually swagger, and, like Cyrano, he is almost bound to have enemies.

In spite of its evident stage popularity, *Cyrano de Bergerac* has taken its share of critical abuse from reviewers, who have panned it as insincere, mere shallow, bustling physical activity, and a study in useless sacrifice. The extravagance of the play, in terms of setting, language, and action, and its improbabilities also clash with the expectation of critics more accustomed to realism. But Cyrano is a poet, like his author. And Rostand uses this play, as he does all of his works, as a vehicle for his own lyric voice.

This important point brings up a related problem the play offers to those who cannot read it in the original French. Those unfamiliar with French must depend upon translations, and although there are several English ones from which to choose, all suffer to some extent because of linguistic and cultural differences which accompany language barriers. Rostand uses the Alexandrine couplet, which gives the language of the play a weighty balance of rhyme and rhythm. But rhyming couplets in French are simply easier on the ear than they are in English. French has more rhyming endings and more acceptable combinations of its rhyming words than have proved possible in English. Out of five readily accessible English translations, three attempt to retain the poetic tone by using blank verse or rhymed verse. The other two avoid the restrictive nature of Rostand's perferred rhyme scheme. One is unrhymed, but a close literal translation; the other uses various rhyme schemes freely and attempts to find English or American parallels for Rostand's witty references to French life and history, providing a lengthy introduction to explain why the changes were made. Regardless of what translation is used, the high lyrical style of the play is evident. One translation focuses on the concept of "panache" by using the French term in different contexts throughout the play. It helps define this last word of Cyrano's which serves as a key to the play's meaning. For example, early in the play at the Pont Nesle battle, Cyrano declares that he came alone except for his triple-waving plume, this "proud panache." Later, in the debate with de Guiche over whether it was honorable for the latter to throw off his white scarf to escape, Cyrano argues that the white plume is a man's panache, a manifestation of his very soul, not to be bartered or squandered but to be preserved as a sign of contempt for his enemies.

Finally, at the end of the play and the end of his life, Cyrano describes the leaves as falling with a certain panache: they float down like trailing plumes of fading beauty, masking their fear of returning to the inevitable ashes and dust of Biblical prophecy; they fall gracefully, with style, as though they were flying. Truly, *Cyrano de Bergerac* is about style created out of despair.

Jean G. Marlowe

DAISY MILLER

Type of work: Novelette
Author: Henry James (1843-1916)
Type of plot: Psychological realism
Time of plot: Mid-nineteenth century
Locale: Vevey, Switzerland, and Rome
First published: 1878

This almost plotless James novelette concerns itself with a conflict between European and American customs and ideals. Daisy Miller, an unsophisticated, "strikingly, admirably pretty" girl, clashes with the conventions of Europeanized, expatriate Americans who enforce society's regulations with severity and thoughtlessness. The diversity in characterization makes Daisy Miller *an ironic study of contrasts.*

In *Daisy Miller,* James represents the conflicts between American innocence and independence and the rigid social conventions characteristic of the American colony in Rome. While Daisy deliberately flaunts convention by her unorthodox behavior, Mrs. Costello and Mrs. Walker make appearance their only basis for moral judgment. Winterbourne, troubled by the ambiguity in Daisy's character, seeks some objective basis for making a judgment.

Daisy realizes that the other Americans have no interest in her as an individual. Living in a world of moral judgments based entirely upon social conventions, they are only concerned to preserve the appearance of morality through "proper" behavior. Determined to be accepted on more meaningful grounds than these, Daisy asserts those freedoms she would be allowed in America, but which are clearly out of place in Rome. Confident in her own innocence, she refuses to conform to the restrictions her compatriots would place upon her.

Innocence and crudity are the terms characterizing Daisy, and these conflicting qualities are the source of Winterbourne's confusion about her. He, like his aunt and Mrs. Walker, has a tendency to make judgments on the basis of superficial appearances. Daisy, however, seems innocent to him in spite of her unconventional behavior, so he cannot fit her into a neat category as he would like. But discovering Daisy in a seemingly compromising position with Giovanelli in the Colosseum gives Winterbourne the evidence he needs, and with some relief he declares Daisy morally corrupt. In so doing, he places himself solidly among the other Americans who, like himself, have lived too long abroad to appreciate the real innocence which underlies Daisy's seeming moral laxity. Too late Winterbourne realizes at the graveside that his formulation of Daisy has been unjust.

DAME CARE

Type of work: Novel
Author: Hermann Sudermann (1857-1928)
Type of plot: Domestic romance
Time of plot: Nineteenth century
Locale: Germany
First published: 1887

Dame Care, an outstanding example of German romanticism, covers a wide span of years in its action yet is gracefully concise without being abrupt. Sudermann is egalitarian in his paternal sympathy for his characters and his understanding of all classes of people. The novel exhibits the romantic style colored by an atmosphere of sadness, a completely rural setting, and a sentimental tone.

Dame Care is an extraordinary study of a human being who becomes trapped by circumstances into sacrificing his life to his family. The gradual development of the conviction in Paul's mind that his life must be this way is portrayed with great subtlety and psychological penetration. Paul longs to be selfish, but never can bear to shirk responsibility. He knows that people take advantage of him, but he cannot deny help to those who need him. Sudermann poignantly describes the plight of this conscientious young man, carefully avoiding sentimentality or falseness of tone. The author perfectly captures the right sympathetic note as he writes about Paul. At all times, the style is even and restrained, allowing the events to produce the emotional reaction.

Fairy tales form a background for the story of Paul's growing up and subsequent bondage. They are the only frame of reference young Paul has, as he tries to comprehend the dark and mysterious world. It is natural that he should think of Elsbeth in the White House as a fairy princess far above him. The subtle, tender, slowly maturing relationship between Paul and Elsbeth is related by the author with a mastery of nuance and suggestion; the mutual pain that the two young people experience is never made melodramatic or false, although their situation might seem to be that of a romantic melodrama.

The power of selfishness is hauntingly dramatized in the book, as Paul's family convinces him that he must live apart from the joys of ordinary mortals. All he can do, he tells Elsbeth, is watch over the happiness of others and to make them as happy as possible. But, after the final catastrophe, he realizes that nobody has appreciated his sacrifices, nobody has noticed that he has given away his own happiness. People who take do so without concerning themselves about those who must do the giving.

Sudermann shows as much skill with scenes of action as he does with psychological analysis. The dramatic moment when Paul saves his father's life and establishes himself as master of the farm is brilliantly rendered; the two fires that destroy the farm both are described with vivid, vigorous prose.

The countryside around the farms and village is pictured clearly, with concise, yet poetic, descriptions. Sudermann is as successful at bringing to life the minor characters as he is the major ones; Paul's selfish and self-centered brothers and sisters and guilt-tormented, half-mad father are particularly well done. Frau Elsbeth, Paul's mother, might have become a cliché figure, the long-suffering wife, but she is portrayed with a sensitive and subtle understanding that makes her a genuine human being; her suffering is completely understandable and thereby pitiable. Many of the characters are unlikable, and often the story is painful to read, but it is, thanks to the author's great skill, completely engrossing from beginning to end. *Dame Care* presents a stark, but realistic, view of human nature, alleviated only by the decency of a few rare individuals.

THE DAMNATION OF THERON WARE

Type of work: Novel
Author: Harold Frederic (1856-1898)
Type of plot: Social criticism
Time of plot: The 1890's
Locale: New York State
First published: 1896

One of the first novels to deal with the problems of an American clergyman and to suggest the disintegration of religious orthodoxy, The Damnation of Theron Ware *created a sensational controversy at the time it was written. Intended to show that every individual needs a moral bulwark on which to lean in times of adversity, the work is an indictment of the hypocrisy of a particular denomination, as well as of Ware's ministerial training, which did not prepare him to meet and accept the beliefs of others while still holding to his own.*

In the nineteenth century and the early twentieth century, a great deal of religious debunking took place in American literature, both journalistic and imaginative, fueled—at least in part—by the muckraking temperament of the times. Contributions ranged from Nathaniel Hawthorne's "The Minister's Black Veil" (1836) and *The Scarlet Letter* (1850) to Sinclair Lewis' *Elmer Gantry* (1927). Harold Frederic's *The Damnation of Theron Ware* added another example to the debate. And a debate it was: clerical ethics and integrity as well as those of institutionalized religion are, in fact, still being hotly contested. Thus, Frederic's novel was meaningful in its own time and still has contemporary relevance.

From this unique position, the novel takes on a significance not usually accorded it by critical consensus, for the book has generally been viewed as a one-of-a-kind indictment of religious hypocrisy rather than as an element in the mainstream of a literary trend. Theron Ware's confusions, for example, were and are viewed in inappropriate nineteenth century terms of self-denial and sacrifice. The emotional problems of Theron Ware have thus been wrongly analyzed: the Reverend Mr. Ware, so the conventional interpretation goes, is simply trying to assert his latent creativity by attempting to write a book and expand his cultural horizons. But, this interpretation notwithstanding, Ware does not succeed, although his attempts cost him his ministry, alienate his friends, and threaten his marriage. And questions remain: "Why did Theron Ware fail? Why was Theron Ware damned?"

First of all, Ware is an extraordinarily immature person, a condition engendered largely by the narrowness of his religious upbringing and his ministerial training which left him unequipped to cope with the realities of life. Second, Ware's understanding of sexuality is, at best, adolescent, for he cannot see beyond the virgin or whore dichotomy and hence is unable to develop a mature relationship with any woman—Alice, Celia, or Mrs. Soulsby. Third,

Ware has virtually no insight into himself. He knows nothing of his capabilities, his needs, or his desires; indeed, he seems, at times, hardly to be aware of his own existence. Consequently, Theron Ware is an emotional cripple, blocked from meaningful relationships with himself, with women, and with society at large, including its cultural heritage. That religious training should prove so emotionally debilitating is a severe damnation of such training. Yet the person thus afflicted is equally damned, but in another, more profound way. For Theron Ware, even with the opportunity for a new career in real estate, shows at the end of the book no more promise of succeeding than he showed at the beginning.

THE DANCE OF DEATH

Type of work: Drama
Author: August Strindberg (1849-1912)
Type of plot: Psychological realism
Time of plot: Late nineteenth century
Locale: Sweden
First presented: 1901

One of Strindberg's most powerful works, this is a double play, the first part dealing with adults and the second with their children. Described by European critics as Strindberg's greatest dramatic achievement, The Dance of Death *is intense psychological realism in its presentation of a love-hate relationship between husband and wife. Virtually imprisoned by her tyrannical husband Edgar for twenty-five years, the play finds Edgar now gravely ill. The psychological conflict, focusing on his attempts to maintain domination and her attempts at retaliatory torture, creates characters that are shockingly real. Beneath the realism, however, there is a rich fabric of imagery symbolic of the diversity and complexity of human relationships.*

Strindberg's specialty in his plays was the stripping bare of "that yawning abyss which is called the human heart," as one of his characters calls it. Perhaps only Dostoevski in modern literature has penetrated equally to the depths of psychological torment. His characters say things that most people feel at times, but which they restrain themselves from expressing or even admitting to their consciousnesses. All of his life, Strindberg was obsessed with the dual nature of the human brain, with the contrast between inner feelings and their outer expression. The power, and horror of, *The Dance of Death* comes from this expression of the normally suppressed thoughts of the characters. This startling honesty seems to shatter moral and social conventions, and to leave both characters and audience vulnerable and exposed. "It's horrible," says one of the characters in one of Strindberg's later plays, "don't you find life horrible?" And the reply is, "Yes, horrible beyond all description." But the endurance of both Strindberg and his characters in the face of madness and violence suggests that he saw, in spite of everything, that there was no acceptable alternative.

From the first lines of *The Dance of Death,* one is struck by the intensity of the speeches. Alice and Edgar are caught in the midst of a duel, or, rather, in the last and brutally final stages of a duel. When the play opens, the conflict is only verbal, but it soon becomes more passionate and more violent. At times, the dialogue seems to be on the verge of becoming no more than an insane ranting, and yet there are moments when Strindberg rises above his fury and sums up the tragedy of life in a few sentences—and the play thus achieves greatness.

It is vital to understand the intimate relationship between Strindberg's life and work to comprehend fully his dramas, particularly *The Dance of Death*. Essentially pessimistic, August Strindberg lived a tortured existence, from a childhood of poverty and insecurity to years as both ministry and medical student, to a period as a freelance journalist. His first major play, a historical drama, was rejected by the Swedish Royal Theatre. He became famous with the publication of his first novel, *The Red Room,* but he continued writing plays. The conflict between the sexes inspired some of his most intense dramas, including *The Father* and *Miss Julie,* and, ultimately, *The Dance of Death*. Married three times, the central relationship of his life was his violent and tormented first marriage. Like D. H. Lawrence, Strindberg was obsessed with the idea of the lower-class male, himself, marrying the aristocratic lady and then bringing her down to his own level. This obsession is reflected in *Miss Julie* and in the relationship between Alice and Edgar in *The Dance of Death*. The disaster of his marriage and the loss of his four children drove him into an alcoholism which had threatened before to possess him, and, despite his growing fame as a writer, he became a lonely and unhappy man, unable to find steady employment.

In his later plays, Strindberg combined the techniques of naturalism with his unique vision of psychology. These bold dramas, with realistic dialogue, highly wrought symbols (such as the wedding ring, the fortress, the wreaths, and the piano in *The Dance of Death*), and stark settings, brought about a revolution in European drama. One of his last and greatest plays, *The Dance of Death* reflects both his first marriage and the collapse of his life afterwards. All of his work possessed extraordinary vitality, but in *The Dance of Death,* Strindberg transformed essentially autobiographical material into a drama of exceptional power; this and other late works, such as *A Dream Play* and *Ghost Sonata,* influenced modern playwrights such as Elmer Rice, Eugene O'Neill, Luigi Pirandello, and later, Edward Albee, whose drama *Who's Afraid of Virginia Woolf?* was directly influenced by *The Dance of Death*.

Strindberg has been accused of hating his female characters, and no character has prompted this statement more than Alice in *The Dance of Death*. Were Strindberg's greatest plays the product of a dangerous and intense misogyny? Is this what gives his brilliant psychological dramas their peculiarly perverse power? No doubt he did suffer from a persecution mania brought on by his intense problems, and his writing does suggest in places paranoiac tendencies. The women in the plays, such as Julie and Alice, tend to be strong and vengeful creatures, who deliberately try to lead men to destruction. But the power of *The Dance of Death* and other dramas of this late period must be due, also, to a deep introspective analysis of his sufferings, for, between his bouts of madness, Strindberg was able to examine his mental disturbance and to make use of the knowledge he gained from such examinations. From a reckless, Bohemian existence, he emerged, in his last years, into a guilt-

ridden form of Christianity, Swedenborgian mysticism, and a Schopenhauer-
ian pessimism according to which the real world exists outside human reality.
His third marriage, to the young actress, Harriet Bosse, dissolved after less
than three years and he discovered that he had inoperable cancer. Then,
suddenly, the Swedish people recognized his greatness and began speaking
of a Nobel Prize for him. "The anti-Nobel Prize is the only one I would
accept," he retorted. When his first wife died in 1912, he collapsed, although
he had not seen her for twenty years. Three weeks later, he was dead. Thirty
thousand people came to his funeral. The battle of the sexes, for him, at
least, was finished.

Some critics have said that both Edgar and Alice are monsters battling to
the death, like a pair of dinosaurs clashing in some ancient burial ground, but
the fact is that they are not monsters any more than the characters of *The
Father* or *Miss Julie* or any other of his plays. They are two trapped individuals
struggling desperately to survive, but not knowing what to do; every frantic
gesture that they make only wounds them that much more. They tear at their
own flesh, like half-mad beasts, in a terrified frenzy, but they are not evil.
They are, perhaps, two of the most pitiful human beings in modern literature.
The scenes in which Alice plays the Hungarian dance on the piano and
Edgar performs the violent jig with his jangling spurs and in which Alice hurls
her wedding ring at Edgar are excruciatingly painful, cutting beneath the
layers usually left by more conventional playwrights. Alice and Edgar are
bound together by a love-hate relationship that neither can escape, except into
death. As Strindberg himself knew, even distance and time cannot release a
man or woman from certain types of bondage. At the end of the First Part of
the play, Edgar realizes how hopelessly he and his wife are bound, and
laughs that they might as well celebrate their silver wedding anniversary.
"Let us pass on," he cries. Somehow, they endure, and that, perhaps, is the
message of the play. And Alice, when Edgar dies at the end of the Second
Part, finally understands that she loved Edgar, as well as hated him, and she
prays for peace for him. And, by implication, she prays for herself, for all
either of them ever craved was peace.

Bruce D. Reeves

DANGEROUS ACQUAINTANCES

Type of work: Novel
Author: Pierre Choderlos de Laclos (1741-1803)
Type of plot: Psychological realism
Time of plot: Mid-eighteenth century
Locale: Paris and environs
First published: 1782

This only novel of a French artillery officer-turned-writer is written in the epistolary form popularized by eighteenth century novelists such as Samuel Richardson. Dangerous Acquaintances *is a slow-paced but fascinating story in which the writer employs a theme of sexual intrigue in order to dissect the decadent society of his age and to lay bare its underlying tensions and antagonisms. Although the novel stands in sharp contrast to the contemporary erotic romances which threw an atmosphere of glamor about a subject Laclos revealed in all its starkness, it was stigmatized as pornographic upon publication. The letters are so skillfully interplayed and the characters so scrupulously presented (even with the assistance of footnotes) that readers willingly accept the letters as real and the characters as people rather than as tools for telling a story.*

Frequently, in the history of Western literature, certain works have been initially castigated as indecent, immoral, or blasphemous, only to be acknowledged later not only as artistic triumphs, but also as powerful moral analyses and statements. Such was the case with Choderlos de Laclos' *Dangerous Acquaintances.* Enormously popular, yet roundly condemned, the novel was seen as an openly scandalous book. The real hostility toward the book, however, may have stemmed, not from its immorality, but from Laclos' ruthless honesty in portraying the social, intellectual, and erotic climate of mid-eighteenth century French society, unmitigated by stylistic indirection or sentimental distortion.

But even today there is a chilling quality to the manner in which Valmont and Mme. de Merteuil manipulate and destroy the lives of others as players would move pieces around a chessboard. Although called an "erotic" novel, there is, in fact, little sexual passion and no emotional involvement in these intrigues. It is almost an entirely intellectual activity—which is Laclos' primary moral point. Valmont and Mme. de Merteuil represent the final product of eighteenth century rationalism; they have reasoned their feelings out of existence.

A closer look at the "game," however, suggests deeper and more complex motivations than the simple pleasures of manipulation and petty spite. Although Valmont and Mme. de Merteuil for the most part maintain a tone of light, elegant bantering between themselves, comparing notes as friendly rivals, their competition is in deadly earnest and their opponents are not the various victims, but each other. Cécile de Volanges, Chevalier Danceny, and Mme.

de Tourvel are merely surrogates that Valmont and Mme. de Merteuil use to get at each other. *Dangerous Acquaintances* is, finally, one of the most brilliant, elegant, and brutal "battle-of-the-sexes" works ever written.

Valmont and Mme. de Merteuil are both products and victims of their society. They have absorbed and accepted its rationalistic basis. They have subjugated their emotional impulses to it, and they are both suppressed by its social norms and rituals. Valmont is simply a soldier without a war. Predisposed by training to military command, social position, and inclination, Valmont is bored, restless, and agitated by the stagnant, aimless, ritualized society in which he finds himself, so he uses amatory combat as a weak substitute for the real thing.

Mme. de Merteuil's situation and psychology are much more complicated. As an aristocratic woman her freedom of action is severely circumscribed. Potentially passionate, she is forced into an arranged marriage with a dull old man; brilliant and resourceful, she faces a lifetime of meaningless social activity that will stultify her capacities; free spirited and experimental, she is bound by behavioral norms and a rigid double standard that threatens to ostracize her for the slightest dereliction. Mme. de Merteuil has, however, refused to accept these limitations—or, rather, she has determined to *use* them to her own advantage. "Ought you not to have concluded," she writes Valmont, "that, since I was born to avenge my sex and to dominate yours, I must have created methods unknown to anybody but myself?" Thus, although Mme. de Merteuil impresses the modern reader as a "moral monster," one has to wonder what made her that way? Given a society in which she could develop and realize her extraordinary gifts, might she not become a constructive, "moral" person? In many ways she seems to be an earlier version of Henrik Ibsen's Hedda Gabler, whose frustrated passions and abilities also turned to viciousness and eventually to self-destruction.

In a real sense Mme. de Merteuil also destroys herself. Her suppressed passion for Valmont is too strong and her need to dominate him is too great to allow the conflict to remain permanently stalemated. For his part, Valmont, too, feels he must dominate and when he puts his ultimatum to Mme. de Merteuil—"from this day on I shall be either your lover or your enemy"— she responds in kind: *"Very well—War!"*

Thus, rationalistic erotic intrigue becomes mutual self-destruction because the suppressed emotions must burst to the surface, rational self-control giving way to vindictive impulse, and love being replaced by self-defeating hate. One can hardly call a book "corrupt" in which the transgressors are so thoroughly punished for their machinations. Indeed, to the modern reader the ending seems too easy and perhaps melodramatic. Valmont's deathbed conversion is almost sentimental and Mme. de Merteuil's smallpox seems gratuitously moralistic.

DANIEL DERONDA

Type of work: Novel
Author: George Eliot (Mary Ann Evans, 1819-1880)
Type of plot: Social realism
Time of plot: Mid-nineteenth century
Locale: Rural England, London, the Continent
First published: 1876

Daniel Deronda, George Eliot's last novel, shifts from a depiction of the difficulties and romances of a small group of people to a treatment of anti-Semitism in Victorian England. Although there is heavy evidence against the evil of anti-Semitism, the novel is more important for its sharp observations of the delusions and follies of Victorian life, and for its keen sense of moral discrimination among the characters. The novel is distinguished by realistic appraisals of people at all levels of society and by Eliot's skillful propagandizing for worthy causes and varied schemes of life.

Daniel Deronda, George Eliot's last novel, is not her greatest, but it is still a powerful and in some ways inspired work. It is as fascinating in its defects as in its successess, since both reflect not only the author's established strengths as a novelist, but also her inventiveness and desire to explore new areas and strive for greater depth and breadth in her fiction. Thus *Daniel Deronda* shares with its predecessors a penetrating insight into human relationships, a sensitive portrayal of individual moral and emotional growth, an astute and critical analysis of Victorian values, and a unifying moral vision of life. At the same time, many of the novel's shortcomings result from Eliot's ambitious experimentation with new methods, issues, and emphases; *Daniel Deronda* contains several new departures. A love story like the earlier works, this novel presents a love story with entirely new angles: Gwendolen marries for power, only to be later attracted to a man (Daniel) whose loyalties are divided between her and another woman; the sexual aspect of love relationships is explored with uncommon openness; certain feelings and emotions are treated which were almost universally ignored by Eliot's contemporaries; and the typical happy ending is denied the heroine, who instead grows in emotional and moral maturity as a result of her sufferings.

The two major weaknesses in the novel lie in the presentation of the Jewish problem and in the characterization of Daniel Deronda. Eliot tends to paint too consistently glowing a picture of the Jewish characters. Mirah's father, Lapidoth, whose portrayal is splendid, is the exception, but in general, Mirah, Mordecai, Daniel and the others suffer from idealization and from their language, which is often sentimental, stylized, or oversimplified. The author's almost uniform approval of the Jewish characters is further accentuated by contrast to her portrayal of the English figures, who are without exception (although to varying degrees) treated critically or satirically. The Wessex gentry are exposed for their shallowness, hypocrisy, and greed; Grandcourt represents a particular type of English gentleman in his cruelty, oppressiveness, contemptuous superiority, and narrow-mindedness; and the numerous minor characters serve as indictments of such Victorian faults as snobbishness, dullness, pretentiousness, and complacency. The second quite noticeable flaw in the novel is in the delineation of Daniel's character. Eliot endowed him with all the qualities requisite to make an interesting and complex personality —his excessive altruism, his ambivalence toward lower-class Jews, his jealousy of Hans Meyrick—and yet he comes across as a static, somewhat wooden, and rather unengaging figure; his actions are all predictable, his personality transparent. The main reason for this problem is Eliot's failure to develop Daniel's complexity, as she does all the other characters, through varied and shifting point of view.

In spite of its weaknesses, however, *Daniel Deronda* exhibits Eliot's novelistic genius in numerous ways. The portrayal of Gwendolen Harleth is splendid; Eliot's masterful use of flashback and retrospection in the first half is highly effective; and the novel's conclusion is of rare force and realism. If Eliot's performance in *Daniel Deronda* falls short of her demanding and ambitious intent, the "experiment in life" that she has left us is nevertheless a great work of literature.

DAPHNIS AND CHLOË

Type of work: Tale
Author: Attributed to Longus (third century)
Type of plot: Pastoral romance
Time of plot: Indefinite
Locale: Island of Lesbos
First transcribed: Third century manuscript

A Greek pastoral poem generally ascribed to the third, fourth, or fifth century A.D. sophist Longus, Daphnis and Chloë *is a product of decadent Greek literature and one of the most popular of the early predecessors of the modern novel. As such it is highly romantic in both characterization and incident, alive with extravagant improbabilities, and laced with humor. The story centers about the innocent though passionate love of two children of nature, unspoiled by contact with city manners, amid idyllic scenes of natural beauty.*

The romance is the least "classical" of ancient literary genres. The name itself derives many centuries later, since the ancients apparently did not know what to call this prose that was not history, this adventure that was not epic, this love story that was neither tragedy nor comedy, this pastoral that was not bound by the verse forms of Theocritus and Vergil. Romance finds its origins perhaps in late Hellenistic times, having developed from erotic and exotic approaches to literature in Euripides, Menander, and Apollonius Rhodius, but it did not reach full bloom until the age of the Second Sophistic in the second century A.D., when rhetoricians encouraged their students to create improbable human situations rife with problems on which they might conduct debate.

Daphnis and Chloë is such an improbable theme, but the resolution of its incredible complications amid such faraway un-Roman places casts a unique charm deepened by the idealized devotion of the young lovers. The story provides an escape to a primeval state for a reader jaded by the violence and sophistication of the Roman Empire. Daphnis and Chloë personify innocent, ignorant love. They are taught by hard experience and the cruel selfishness of the real, urbane world, but they manage to survive and return to their idyllic, simple remove.

An intelligible structure is canonical in classical composition, and appropriately this work is divided into four "books" which define movements from spring to autumn, to winter and a second spring and summer, and finally to a second autumn. The blooming love of Daphnis and Chloë must be tested by the seasons, both of nature and of human life, before the matured lovers can reap the harvest. Longus uses the imagery of Philetas' and Lamon's gardens to convey the natural morality of the children's love shaped and cultivated by experience. So, too, he entrusts them to the care of Pan and Dionysus, gods of natural sexuality, and to Eros, god of irresistible love. This is further enforced by the motif of milk and wine, symbolizing innocence and passion.

THE DARK JOURNEY

Type of work: Novel
Author: Julian Green (1900-   )
Type of plot: Psychological realism
Time of plot: Early twentieth century
Locale: France
First published: 1929

Like other Julian Green works, The Dark Journey *is a bleak and somber book, impressive both in its realistic evocation of French provincial life and in its metaphysical overtones of human destiny. Shadows of disaster and doom brood in Green's characters, who have premonitions of their fates, but are powerless to help themselves. With impersonal detachment and classic gravity of style, Green tells a disturbing yet compelling story in which violence and lust are incidental to his greater effects of cumulative passion and tragic finality.*

The reader might be repelled by the content of this novel, but he cannot help being drawn into its strange dark world. The stark and intense style, the depth and sureness of the author's insight, and the inevitability of the narrative all unite to give *The Dark Journey* a unique beauty. One is reminded of the trapped, tormented souls in Hawthorne's New England and Sherwood Anderson's Midwest. Although Julian Green has a rare sense of detail, the detail does not impede his action. There is at all times a fine harmony of character and action with the background. The picture of the damned is so powerfully drawn that even the prosaic landscape seems transformed into a dream Inferno.

A bland self-centeredness seems to dominate the individuals in the story. Madame Londe is a frustrated petty tyrant, incapable of being happy, although she relishes obtaining power over other people—especially men. A deep and fundamental anger drives her to irrational acts. Desperately, she wants *to be in control*; so do all of the characters, but none of them are or can be. Paul Guéret is defined by his relations with the women in his life: his boring wife; Madame Londe, who wants only to dominate him; Madame Grosgeorge who would love him, but settles for domination; and Angèle, whom he desires so much that he destroys her. Together, these women destroy him. Only the sixty-year-old M. Grosgeorge is at all satisfied with his life; he exudes a vitality which the other characters lack. He is not profound, and his advice to Guéret can only cause the tutor more misery. Guéret's desperate craving for happiness opposes his wife's stolid acceptance of a life without joy. Life appears to Angèle as a kind of lottery, good or bad according to one's luck, but irrevocable. Green deliberately draws in the limitations of his characters, as a more romantic author might sketch in the qualities which make his characters exceptional.

The irony of the girl's name, Angèle, heightens the sense of a game master toying with these desperate lives in the drab provincial village. Angèle comes to believe that life does not give one a second chance. One should grasp what one can with eager hands. Later, she realizes that fate's treachery is prepared long in advance and only bears the appearance of chance because its workings are invisible. The message of the book is bleak, but the artistry is extraordinary and the impact strong. The image of the murderer unable to retrace his footsteps, condemned to go forward carrying the plague of his crimes, into new avenues of nightmare, is haunting and profound.

DARK LAUGHTER

Type of work: Novel
Author: Sherwood Anderson (1876-1941)
Type of plot: Psychological realism
Time of plot: 1920's
Locale: Old Harbor, Indiana
First published: 1925

Sherwood Anderson's most popular novel, Dark Laughter *deals with the escape of a Chicago newspaperman from a life he regards as oppressive and ruled by machines, and the similar escape of an employer's wife, with whom he ultimately falls in love and elopes. The "dark laughter" of this book of moods rather than plot comes from the American black who, uncorrupted by white society and morals, is the only one still capable of pure, uninhibited joy.*

Dark Laughter is an interesting, serious novel that emerged from the aftermath of World War I. Anderson's novel reflects the literary and stylistic devices pioneered in the era following that war.

World War I meant, for writers, artists, and thinkers, the end of intellectual, scientific, political, moral, and psychological certainties. Before the outbreak of war, intellectuals considered Western culture the finest flowering, the highest expression of human civilization. But the outbreak of the war, and its barbarism, and the duration and intensity of its savagery, unprecedented in human history, shattered that belief. Scientific discoveries shook hitherto unquestioned assumptions about the Newtonian universe. Marx's theories and the Russian Revolution undermined confidence in social classes and political systems. Freud, by elaborating a theory of an active unconscious, and an unconscious life, destroyed the idea that man was a given, known quantity.

All these developments form the context for "literary modernism," a movement in literature in which accepted patterns of characterization, sequence, and symbols were altered radically. It is in this context that Anderson's *Dark Laughter* can be understood best. *Dark Laughter* is a novel that tries both to formulate a criticism of the old values (made disreputable by the war), and at the same time to set forth new values by which men can live.

Given this disillusionment *and* hope, it is appropriate that Anderson establishes two dramatic poles in the novel: one embodies a natural, honest, sincere relationship to life; the other (embodying the old, prewar values) represents an artificial, mechanical, and dishonest approach.

Fred Grey and Bernice Stockton are characters leading superficial and distant lives. Grey, who imagines himself sensitive, cultured, and generous is actually a morally coarse, suspicious, and tight-fisted factory owner. He is, above all, separated from the realities of life by his economic position and his inner sterility.

Bernice Stockton, the wife that Bruce Dudley fled, is a variation of the same type. Her "specialty" is literature, but from hints of the story she is writing—a precious, unreal thing—her characters and plot only reflect her own superficial romanticism, not the actual conditions of life. She is a member of an "in group" of writers and intellectuals, and Anderson indicates that this membership is more important to her than infusing her art with truth.

Standing in opposition to these characters are Bruce Dudley, Sponge Martin and, to an extent, Aline Grey. For Anderson, these people represent the new, hopeful values which have come to life after the trauma of war. Sponge Martin (and his wife), for example, have a genuine connection to real life. Their sexual life is natural and unaffected; they have few pretensions; they are generous and simple. Dudley himself, the central character in the novel, is a writer more interested in the truth than in "word slinging." Leaving Bernice was a rejection of her literary pretensions. Falling in love with Aline, and fathering her child, meant answering the deeper, underlying currents in life.

For Aline, who vacillated between these poles, the marriage to Grey represented a confused surrender to the conventional life. Running away with Dudley meant coming to terms with life as it is—not as it exists in the decadent literary circles of postwar France, in the romantic fantasies of her adolescence, or in the expected routines of upper-middle-class-life in the United States.

It is also clear that, just as Anderson is criticizing an outworn and mechanical value system, he is also criticizing an earlier literary tradition. Does literature come to terms with the natural, primitive side of life? Does it seek out the unconscious and explore it? Does it portray the uncertainties and difficulties of life? If the answer to these questions is yes, then Anderson approves; but if literary tradition only discusses the superficial and agreeable aspects of life, then Anderson heartily disapproves. Thus, as literature, Anderson hopes *Dark Laughter* both supports and represents a new literary tradition that corresponds to the new postwar values.

Anderson himself said the literary quality of *Dark Laughter* was influenced by James Joyce, and it is true that Anderson uses a number of modernist techniques: sections of narrative broken into fragments; parts of poems scattered through the text; subjective, semi-stream-of-consciousness narration; switches in point of view. But Anderson does not have Joyce's verbal facility, depth of allusion, grammatical mastery, or density of detail.

The techniques of *Dark Laughter* probably reflect the more general literary climate of the 1920's rather than Joyce's specific influence. In a period of intellectual uncertainty, when old beliefs were brought into question, prose style itself assumed a fragmented, subjective, and somewhat disjointed character.

At the same time, *Dark Laughter* also displays certain negative features of the American literary climate of the 1920's. One of these negative qualities, perhaps the most visible, is the racist aspect of many of Anderson's passages. For example, the title of the novel, *Dark Laughter,* refers to the natural, honest pole that Anderson supports. But associated with this naturalness is the "primitive," "uncivilized," and "amoral" qualities that Anderson links to black people. In fact, *Dark Laughter* refers to the laughter of black maids in the Grey household when they learn of Aline's adultery.

Such prejudices, commonplace in the era in which *Dark Laughter* was written, need not overshadow the major intent of the book. *Dark Laughter* expresses an important opposition of ideas in modernist literary terms; the reader is asked to choose between real life and superficial life; and, in that sense, Anderson has presented the reader with a profound moral choice.

Howard Lee Hertz

DARKNESS AT NOON

Type of work: Novel
Author: Arthur Koestler (1905-   )
Type of plot: Social criticism
Time of plot: 1930's
Locale: Russia
First published: 1941

This modern novel analyzes various kinds of Communist psychology by transporting the reader into a Russian prison. The plot is an account of the moral struggles of an idealistic revolutionary falsely accused and persuaded by superiors to confess to crimes he never committed. Although highly restrained in tone, the novel is an ironic and scathing criticism of the Moscow trials, and it presents a careful analysis of Soviet principles.

Based on Koestler's own experience as a European Communist and his imprisonment in France and Spain, *Darkness at Noon* signaled his rejection of his political beliefs. Yet the novel is more profitably examined as an analysis of the totalitarian mentality that permitted such dictators as Hitler, Stalin, and Franco to control the whole of Europe at the time of the novel's publication. Koestler reveals with profound and cogent insight that the totalitarian mind, such as he dramatizes in Rubashov, is not to be understood as a manifestation of Machiavellian ethics. That is old style politics and hardly explains such historical incidents as the Moscow trials or the imprisonment of a party leader like Rubashov.

Rubashov's arrest, trial, and execution, like Ivanov's or Kieffer's, does not make good political sense seen from a pragmatic point of view. Since they are all good party men, it would seem that No. 1 would be undermining his own position by liquidating them. But No. 1 is not really interested in solidifying his political power in a conventional way, but rather in creating a mystique, more nearly a religion, which cannot be tested on rational or logical grounds. His *realpolitik,* his agents seem to suggest, is an irrational mystery that even his most faithful adherents can betray unconsciously.

A forerunner of George Orwell's Winston Smith in *Nineteen Eighty-Four,* Rubashov goes to his death actually believing he has betrayed No. 1 and yet never really understanding the nature of his treachery. With only a glimpse of the truth, he dies a good and faithful servant. As Koestler points out, such a death is only possible because Rubashov, like his comrades, agreed from the beginning to permit No. 1 to establish all truth. Having given up the freedom of their own minds, they are mere automatons in the irrational scheme of the State.

DAVID COPPERFIELD

Type of work: Novel
Author: Charles Dickens (1812-1870)
Type of plot: Sentimental romance
Time of plot: Early nineteenth century
Locale: England
First published: 1849-1850

One of the best-loved novels in the English language, David Copperfield *is a devastating exposé of the treatment of children in the nineteenth century. Admittedly autobiographical, it is a work of art which can be read and reread, chiefly for its gallery of immortalized characters. Though the novel has flaws, it enjoys a kind of freshness and spontaneity stemming from the first-person recounting of events and the sympathetic treatment of characters.*

"But, like many fond parents, I have in my heart of hearts a favorite child. And his name is David Copperfield."

This is Charles Dickens' final, affectionate judgment of the work which stands exactly in the middle of his novelistic career, with seven novels before and seven after (excluding the unfinished *The Mystery of Edwin Drood*). When he began the novel, he was in his mid-thirties, secure in continuing success that had begun with *Sketches by Boz* (1836), and *Pickwick Papers* (1836-1837). It was a good time to take stock of his life, to make use of the autobiographical manuscript he had put by earlier. Nor did he try to conceal the personal element from his public, which eagerly awaited each of the nineteen numbers of *David Copperfield*. The novel was issued serially from May, 1849, through November, 1850. Charles Dickens, writer, is readily identified with David Copperfield, writer, viewing his life through the "long Copperfieldian perspective," as Dickens called it.

Although much in the life of the first-person narrator corresponds to Dickens' own life, details are significantly altered. Unlike David, Dickens was not a genteel orphan but the eldest son of living and improvident parents; his own father served as the model for Micawber. Dickens' childhood stint in a shoeblacking factory seems to have been somewhat shorter than David's drudgery in the warehouse of Murdstone and Grinby, wine distributors, but the shame and suffering were identical. Young Charles Dickens failed in his romance with a pretty young girl, but the author Dickens permits David to win his Dora. However, Dickens inflicts upon Dora as Mrs. Copperfield the faults of his own Kate, who, unlike Dora, lived on as his wife until their separation in 1858.

However fascinating the autobiographical details, *David Copperfield* stands primarily on its merits as a novel endowed with the bustling life of Dickens' earlier works but controlled by his maturing sense of design. The novel in its entirety answers affirmatively the question posed by David himself in the opening sentence: "Whether I shall turn out to be the hero of my own life. . . . "

In addition to the compelling characterization of the protagonist, the novel abounds with memorable portrayals. The square face and black beard of Mr. Murdstone, always viewed in conjunction with that "metallic lady" Miss Murdstone, evoke the horror of dehumanized humanity. Uriah Heep's writhing body, clammy skin, and peculiarly lidless eyes suggest a subhuman form more terrifying than the revolting nature of his "umbleness." Above all the figures that crowd the lonely world of the orphan rises the bald head of Wilkins Micawber, flourishing the English language and his quizzing glass with equal impressiveness, confidently prepared in case some opportunity turns up.

Nevertheless, David Copperfield is very definitely the hero of his own story. This is a novel of initiation, organized around the two major cycles of the hero's development, first in childhood, then in early manhood. It focuses steadily upon the testing which will qualify him for full manhood. He makes his own choices, but each important stage of his moral progress is marked by the intervention of Aunt Betsey Trotwood.

To begin with, David is weak simply because he is a child, the hapless victim of adult exploitation. But he is also heir to the moral weakness of his childish mother and his dead father, who was an inept, impractical man. David's birth is, portentously, the occasion of a conflict between his mother's Copperfieldian softness and Aunt Betsey's firmness, displayed in her rigidity of figure and countenance.

From a state of childish freedom, David falls into the Murdstone world. The clanking chains of Miss Murdstone's steel purse symbolize the metaphorical prison which replaces his innocently happy home. Indeed, for David, the world becomes a prison. After his five days of solitary confinement at Blunderstone, he enters the jail-like Salem House School. After his mother's death, he is placed in the grim warehouse, apparently for life. Nor is his involvement with the Micawbers any real escape, for he is burdened with their problems and retains his place in the family even after their incarceration in the King's Bench Prison.

Although David repudiates the tyrannical firmness of which he is a victim, he does not actively rebel, except for the one occasion when he bites Mr. Murdstone. Instead, like his mother, he indulges his weakness; he submits, fearfully to the Murdstones and Creakle, worshipfully to the arrogant Steerforth. In addition, he escapes into the illusory freedom of fantasy—through books and stories and through the lives of others, which he invests with an enchantment that conceals from him whatever is potentially tragic or sordid.

Nevertheless, David's pliant nature shares something of the resolute spirit of Aunt Betsey, despite her disappearance on the night of his birth. Looking back upon his wretched boyhood, David recalls that he kept his own counsel, and did his work. From having suffered in secret, he moves to the decision to escape by his own act. The heroic flight is rewarded when Aunt Betsey relents and takes him in. Appropriately, she trusses up the small boy in adult clothes and announces her own goal of making him a "fine fellow, with a will of your own," with a "strength of character that is not to be influenced, except on good reason, by anybody, or by anything." The first cycle of testing is complete.

The conventionally happy years in Dover and Canterbury mark an interlude before the second major cycle of the novel, which commences with David's reentry into the world as a young man. Significantly, he at first resumes the docile patterns of childhood. Reunited with Steerforth, he once again takes pride in his friend's overbearing attitude. He allows himself to be bullied by various inferiors. He evades the obligation to choose his own career by entering into a profession which affects him like an opiate. In Dora's childlike charms he recaptures the girlish image of his mother. However, at this point, the firm Aunt Betsey, having cut short his childhood trials, deliberately sets into motion his adult testing with her apparent bankruptcy.

In response to his new challenges, David is forced back upon his childhood resources. At first, he unconsciously imitates Murdstone in trying to mold Dora; but he again rejects tyranny, choosing instead resignation, understanding that she can be no more than his "child-wife." He responds with full sympathy to the tragedy of Little Em'ly's affair with Steerforth, but he is finally disenchanted with the splendid willfulness which had captivated his boyish heart. Most important, he recovers the saving virtue of his childhood, his ability to suffer in secrecy, to keep his own counsel, and to do his work. As his trials pile up—poverty, overwork, disappointment in marriage, his wife's death, and the tribulations of the friends to whom his tender heart is wholly committed—he conquers his own undisciplined heart.

The mature man who emerges from his trials profits from his experiences and heritage. His capacity for secret suffering is, for him as for Aunt Betsey, a source of strength; but his, unlike hers, is joined to the tenderheartedness inherited from his parents. Her distrust of mankind has made her an eccentric. His trusting disposition, though rendering him vulnerable, binds him to mankind.

Although Aunt Betsey sets a goal of maturity before David, Agnes Wickfield is the symbol of the hard-won self-discipline which he finally achieves. She is from the beginning his "better angel." Like him, she is tenderhearted and compliant. Yet, though a passive character, she is not submissive; and she is always in control of herself in even the most difficult human relationships. Moreover, her firmness of character is never distorted by fundamental distrust of mankind. Thus hers is the only influence which David should accept, "on good reason," in his pursuit of the moral goal which Aunt Betsey sets before him.

By the time David has recognized his love for Agnes, he has also attained a strength of character like hers. The appropriate conclusion to his quest for maturity is his union with Agnes—who is from the beginning a model of the self-disciplined person in whom gentleness and strength are perfectly balanced. Furthermore, the home he builds with her is the proper journey's end for the orphaned child who has grasped at many versions of father, mother, family, and home: "Long miles of road then opened out before my mind, and toiling on, I saw a ragged way-worn boy forsaken and neglected, who should come to call even the heart now beating against him, his own." He has outgrown the child-mother, the child-wife, the childhood idols, even the childhood terrors, and he is a mature man ready to accept love "founded on a rock."

In the context of a successful completed quest, the novel ends with a glimpse of the complete man, who writes far into the night to erase the shadows of his past, but whose control of the realities is sufficient in the presence of the woman who is always, symbolically, "near me, pointing upward!"

Catherine E. Moore

DAVID HARUM

Type of work: Novel
Author: Edward Noyes Westcott (1846-1898)
Type of plot: Regional romance
Time of plot: Late nineteenth century
Locale: Upstate New York
First published: 1898

The greatest strength of this regional romance, written by an Upstate New York banker, lies in the characterization of an original and delightfully humorous horse trader, a dry, quaint, semiliterate countryman with a shrewd knowledge of human nature. Although the novel is threaded together by a love story involving Harum's banking assistant and a young heiress, the best chapters are those in which David Harum tells stories in dialect, swaps horses, and indulges in reminiscences of other days.

David Harum grew directly from Westcott's experiences both with the people and the customs of upstate New York, and with a type of small-town American banker. *David Harum* is so convincingly rooted in northeastern rural America that it stands as a good example of American "local color" fiction, fiction that developed and flourished in the United States during the last half of the nineteenth century. Although local color as a literary movement contains diverse and often contradictory elements, the main energies of its writers were devoted to sketching regional geography, customs, and dialects; it developed partly as a counter to the "American novel," or attempts to capture the whole "American" experience in one work.

What is especially interesting in *David Harum* is Harum himself. Westcott has succeeded in uncovering, with generous detail, the moral and psychological forces, and the central impulses as well as the crotchets, of a small-town banker in upstate New York. Harum's incessant horse trading, his Yankee sense, and above all his pragmatism form the central interest of the novel. On the one hand, Harum looks out for himself and so embodies that shrewd, self-interested outlook so characteristic of his type; on the other hand, Westcott has been careful to modify this selfishness with Harum's quiet charity and rough-hewn sense of economic justice. Thus David Harum stands as both a regional type and as an example of a certain economic morality. He is a banker, but he is also a good man.

The weakness in the novel is the plot concerning Lenox and his sweetheart. This plot, which takes the story too far from its central interest, both geographically and morally, seems both sentimental and contrived. Actually, the difficulty Westcott experienced in sustaining a purely regional narrative, as well as his sentimentality, are weaknesses common among the local colorists.

DEAD SOULS

Type of work: Novel
Author: Nikolai V. Gogol (1809-1852)
Type of plot: Social satire
Time of plot: Early nineteenth century
Locale: Russia
First published: 1842

Dead Souls *is unanimously considered one of the greatest novels in the Russian language for its characterizations, satiric humor, and style. The plot is not complex—a scheme to buy, from landlords, serfs who have died since the last census, in order to perpetrate the hero's own real estate deal in eastern Russia. The length of the novel is accounted for by numerous digressions adding up to a rich picture of provincial Russia. Whether Gogol's fiction is reality or fantasy, a topic much debated, he uses characterization, extravagant imagery, and hyperbolic language to color intensely his work.*

Dead Souls, one of Russia's finest works of fiction, is also one of the most unique novels in any literature. It begins in comic realism and satire, and moves through fantasy into prophecy. Like Dostoevski's *The Idiot,* its purpose was no less than the salvation of Russian society. The early chapters present us with satirical portraits of typical Russian landowners: the canny old Korobotchkina; the energetic, violent, half-crazed Nozdreff; the "bear" Sobakevitch; the miser Pliushkin, a maltreater of serfs. All these in their puzzlement and greed are willing to sell the souls of their dead serfs to Tchitchikoff, who in turn will use these dead souls in his own special confidence racket. We are presented at once with a Russia which operates crookedly. The deadest souls are the ones who perform such acts, and Tchitchikoff is chief among them; he is the most typical and nondescript—a Russian everyman. Part I of the novel details the various petty cheats of Tchitchikoff and his kind. The mood is wonderfully comic and fantastic; Gogol's moral purpose is partially obscured.

In Part II this purpose becomes clear. The character of Tentetnikoff shows us another of Russia's problems, for he has great plans for reforming his estates but paltry execution. He is cheated by his peasants and reacts harshly. Naturally, Tchitchikoff fastens to him for all he is worth. Finally, in the character of Kostanzhoglo, Tchitchikoff encounters a man who presents us with a solution to Russia's problems—a solution which makes us wonder at Gogol. This landlord is a man of action rather than theory and loose words, as with Tentetnikoff and the others of Part I. His religion of simple agriculture has more than an edge of anti-intellectualism and puritanism (he won't produce tobacco or sugar!). But his reactionary stand fails fully to convert the ceaselessly mediocre Tchitchikoff. When Tchitchikoff, having contemplated cheating Kostanzhoglo, says at the end that many are more dishonest than he, he is voicing Gogol's indictment of Russian society. Still, the finest elements of *Dead Souls* have little to do with Gogol's moralizing. The comic and fantastic elements are the novel's chief rewards.

DEAR BRUTUS

Type of work: Drama
Author: James M. Barrie (1860-1937)
Type of plot: Romantic fantasy
Time of plot: Midsummer Eve
Locale: England
First presented: 1917

In Dear Brutus, *Barrie hypothesizes through the use of a folk superstition concerning Midsummer Eve that the exigencies of human life are the fault of the individual, not of so-called fate. The plot is at once fantasy and reality. It is fantasy in that its characters are transported into the realm of the unreal, reality in the perfectly candid way in which the various relationships among the characters are set forth.*

"Men at some time are masters of their fate," Cassius tells his coconspirator in Shakespeare's *Julius Caesar* (II, ii), "the fault, dear Brutus, is not in our stars, but in ourselves that we are underlings." Beginning with this quote as a premise, James Barrie tests Cassius' notion in his play *Dear Brutus* by taking an oddly assorted group of characters and giving them that "second chance." But if the play's idea comes from *Julius Caesar,* its shape and mood are closer to that of another Shakespearean play, *A Midsummer Night's Dream*: the time of the second chance is Midsummer's Eve, the locale is an enchanted wood, and the manipulator of the action is Lob, a modernized Puck, a child-man of ancient, but indefinite age.

Matey, the butler, caught in the act of stealing the ladies' jewelry, sets up the action when he states ". . . it all depends on your taking the right or the wrong turn. . . . I would give the world to be able to begin over again." He gets his wish and proves himself to be, once again, a thief—albeit a rich one. His aristocratic antagonist Lady Caroline Laney, however, becomes his wife and thereby demonstrates that, beneath her haughty surface, she is actually servile. Jack Purdie sees himself as an exceptionally sensitive soul, trapped with an unresponsive wife, who wants only a woman who can "plumb the well of my emotions." After exchanging women and fantasies in the enchanted wood, he realizes that he is "not a deeply passionate chap at all. . . . I am just . . . a philanderer!" And it is Purdie who sums up the play's thesis:

> It's not fate, Joanna. Fate is something outside us. What really plays the
> dickens with us is something in ourselves. Something that makes us go on
> doing the same sort of things, however many chances we get.

Charming old Mr. Coade learns that he is not a potentially great scholar spoiled into amiable laziness by inherited money; he is simply a carefree, likable man without ambitions. And Alice Dearth learns that her bad marriage could have been even worse, for she might always choose the wrong man—for her.

The one exception is Will Dearth, a mediocre, alcoholic, cynical artist who meets Margaret, his "might-have-been" daughter in the woods. The Will Dearth of Act II, "ablaze in happiness and health," is quite different from the "chop-fallen, gone-to-seed sort of person" we saw in Act I and the charming, happy-sad scene between father and daughter is one of the most touching in modern theater; few curtain lines are as memorable as Margaret's fearful lament, from the darkened stage, as she fades into nothingness: "Daddy, come back; I don't want to be a 'might-have-been.' "

The question Barrie leaves us with in the final act is whether or not the magical experiences of having seen themselves fail at "second turnings" will not enable the party guests to effect real changes in their personalities. When Joanna asks Matey about this, he replies that it only happens once in a while.

The audience is left with the feeling that at least the characters now understand their own mediocrity, even if they can do little about it. And, to Barrie, even such a modest shedding of illusions is a good thing. It is also hinted that for the best of them, Will and Alice Dearth, there is some possibility of a real change and revitalization of the "rather wild love" which, Barrie states in an early stage direction, they had for each other before it went "whistling down the wind."

DEATH COMES FOR THE ARCHBISHOP

Type of work: Novel
Author: Willa Cather (1873-1947)
Type of plot: Historical chronicle
Time of plot: Last half of the nineteenth century
Locale: New Mexico and Arizona
First published: 1927

Based on the lives of two eminent nineteenth century French clerics, this novel tells of the missionary efforts of the French bishop, Jean Latour, and his vicar, Father Joseph Vaillant, to establish a diocese in the territory of New Mexico. Besides a skillful reconstruction of these dedicated lives, the novel also provides a vivid picture of a particular region and culture. Tales and legends from Spanish colonial history and from the primitive tribal traditions of the Hopi and Navajo enter the chronicle at many points, creating an effect of density and variety.

When writing of her great predecessor and teacher, Sarah Orne Jewett, Willa Cather expressed her own belief that the quality that gives a work of literature greatness is the "voice" of the author, the sincere, unadorned, and unique vision of a writer coming to grips with his material. If any one characteristic can be said to dominate the writings of Willa Cather, it is a true and moving sincerity. She never tried to twist her subject matter to suit a preconceived purpose, and she resisted the temptation to dress up her homely material. She gave herself absolutely to her chosen material, and the result was a series of books both truthful and rich with intimations of the destiny of the American continent. By digging into the roots of her material, she found the greater meanings and expressed them with a deceptive simplicity. Her vision and craftsmanship were seldom more successful than in *Death Comes for the Archbishop*. So completely did Willa Cather merge her "voice" with her material, that some critics have felt that the book is almost too polished, without the sense of struggle necessary in a truly great novel. But this, in fact, indicates the magnitude of the author's achievement and the brilliance of her technical skill. *Death Comes for the Archbishop* resonates with the unspoken beliefs of the author and the resolved conflicts that went into its construction. On the surface, it is cleanly wrought and simple, but it is a more complicated and profound book than it appears at first reading. Cather learned well from her early inspiration, Sarah Orne Jewett, the secret of artless art, of craftsmanship that disarms by its very simplicity, but which is based in a highly sophisticated intelligence.

It is true that this novel is an epic and a regional history, but, much more than either, it is a tale of personal isolation, of one man's life reduced to the painful weariness of his own sensitivities. Father Latour is a hero in the most profound sense of the word, at times almost a romantic hero, with his virtues of courage and determination, but he is also a very modern protagonist, with

his doubts and inner conflicts and his philosophical nature. His personality
is held up in startling contrast to that of his friend and vicar, Father Vaillant,
a more simple, although no less good, individual. Cather's austere style
perfectly captures the scholarly asperity and urbane religious devotion that
compose Father Latour's character. And always in this book, the reader is
aware of a sense of the dignity of human life, as exemplified in the person of
this individual. Cather was not afraid to draw a good man, a man who could
stand above others because of his deeds and because of his innate quality.
The novel must stand or fall on this character, and it stands superbly.

Although this book is based on a true sequence of events, it is not a novel
of plot. It is a chronicle and a character study, and perhaps, more specifically,
an interplay of environment and character. Throughout the book, the reader
is aware of the reaction of men to the land, and of one man to the land he has
chosen. Subtly and deeply, the author suggests that the soul of man is profoundly altered by the soul of the land, and Cather never doubts for a moment
that the land does possess a soul or that this soul can transform a human being in complex and important ways. Willa Cather was fascinated by the way
the rough landscape of the Southwest, when reduced to its essences, seemed
to take human beings and reduce them to their essences. She abandoned
traditional realism in this book, turning toward the directness of symbolism.
With stark pictures and vivid styles, she created an imaginary world rooted
in realism, but transcending realism. The rigid economy with which the book
is written forces it to stand with a unique power in the reader's mind long
after his reading. And the personality of Bishop Latour stands as the greatest
symbol, like a wind-swept crag or precipice in the vast New Mexico landscape, suggesting the nobility of the human spirit, despite the inner conflicts
against which it must struggle.

The descriptions of place set the emotional tone of the novel. The quality
of life is intimately related to the landscape, and the accounts of the journeys
and the efforts to survive despite the unfriendliness of the barren land, all
help to create an odd warmth and almost surreal passion in the narrative.
The personalities of Bishop Latour and Father Vaillant establish a definite
emotional relationship with the country, and if the other characters in the
book are less vividly realized as individuals, perhaps it is because they do
not seem to have this relationship with the land. Some of them have become
part of the land, worn down by the elements like the rocks and riverbeds,
and others have no relationship to it at all; but none of them is involved in
the intense love-hate relationship with the land with which the two main
characters struggle for so many years.

Although the chronology of the book encompasses many years, the novel
is essentially static, a series of rich images and thoughtful moments high-
lighted and captured as by a camera. This quality of the narrative is not a
fault; it is a fact of Cather's style. The frozen moments of contemplation, the

glimpses into Father Latour's inner world and spiritual loneliness, are the moments that give the book its greatness. Despite the presence of Kit Carson, the novel is not an adventure story any more than it is merely the account of a pair of churchmen attempting to establish their church in a difficult new terrain. The cathedral becomes the most important symbol in the final part of the book, representing the earthly successes of a man dedicated to nonworldly ambitions. This conflict between the earthly and the spiritual is at the heart of Bishop Latour's personality and at the heart of the book. But the reader understands, at the end, when the bell tolls for Father Latour, that the temptations were never very deep and the good man's victory was greater than he ever knew. The author does not spell out her meaning, but the emotional impact of her narrative brings it home to the reader.

Bruce D. Reeves

DEATH IN VENICE

Type of work: Novelette
Author: Thomas Mann (1875–1955)
Type of plot: Symbolic realism
Time of plot: Early twentieth century
Locale: Italy
First published: 1912

This novella of great psychological intensity and tragic power is permeated by the rich and varied symbolism of Mann's many conflicting themes—being and death, youth and age, sickness and health, beauty and decay, love and suffering, art and life, the German North and the Mediterranean South. The story of a middle-aged artist whose character deteriorates because of his hopeless passion for a young Polish boy, and whose death is the final irony of his emotional upheaval, Death in Venice *examines understandingly and critically the solitary position of the artist in modern society and uses the infatuation with the boy to dramatize symbolically the narcissism which can be one of the fatal qualities of art.*

Thomas Mann is ranked with James Joyce and Marcel Proust as one of the greatest writers of the early twentieth century. Mann was born into a wealthy German family. He was awarded the Nobel Prize for literature in 1919. In 1933 he left Germany because of his opposition to Hitler and the Nazi Party. He later came to the United States, where he taught and lectured. A scholar as well as an artist, his works show the influence of such diverse thinkers as Friedrich Nietzsche, Arthur Schopenhauer, Richard Wagner, and Sigmund Freud. The problem of the artist's role in a decadent, industrialized society is a recurring theme in many of his works such as *Buddenbrooks* (1901), *Tonio Kröger* (1903), *Death in Venice* (1912), and *The Magic Mountain* (1924).

Death in Venice, Mann's best-known novella, is a complex, beautifully wrought tale dealing with the eternal conflict of the forces of death and decay with man's attempts to achieve permanence through art. Mann portrays the final triumph of death and decay, but not before the hero, Aschenbach, has experienced an escape into the eternal beauty created by the imagination of the artist. The escape of the famous writer, Aschenbach, is accomplished, however, not by his own writings, but by the art of his creator, Thomas Mann. Form and order do finally impose themselves on the chaos of his life; corruption and death are transformed into the purity of artistic beauty. To accomplish this, Mann utilizes an elaborate technical skill in structure, characterization, and symbolism which establishes Mann among the great writers of Western literature.

The characterization of Aschenbach, the literary hero of his age, is subtle and complex. Author of prose epics, philosophical novels, novels of moral resolution, and aesthetics, Aschenbach has created the hero for his generation. He is aware that his success and talent rely on a basis of physical stamina as well as moral and mental discipline; his key word is *durchhalten* (endure). His work is a product of strain, endurance, intellectual tenacity, and spasms of will. However, he recognizes that his writing has been to some degree a "pursuit of fame" at the expense of turning his back on a full search for truth. As the novella opens, Aschenbach, exhausted, finding no more joy in his craft, and aware of approaching old age and death, is faced with the fear of not having time to finish all the works he desired to write. Restlessly walking in the naturalistic beauty of the English Garden of Munich, Aschenbach is inspired to leave his relatively rootless life on a pilgrimage for artistic renewal in Venice, the perfect symbol of man's art imposed on nature's chaos. This journey motif begins with his glimpse of a stranger, a foreigner with a skull-like face and a certain animal ruthlessness, in a cemetery.

Arriving at the port of Venice, he discovers he is being taken out to sea, rather than into the city, by his gondolier, a figure whose physical description ominously echoes that of the stranger of the cemetery. The gondola itself is specifically compared to a black coffin. The trip, then, becomes the archetypal journey of life to death and of man into the depths of himself. Aschenbach discovers Venice, the symbol of perfect art in his memory, to be dirty, infected, corrupt, permeated by the odor of the human disease and pollution spread in the natural swamp on which the artifice is built. Aschenbach's own transformation to a "foreigner," one who belongs in Venice, is accomplished at an increasingly mad tempo after the moment when, turning his back on the possibility of escaping from Venice by train, he collapses at a fountain in the heart of the city. His death becomes almost self-willed; he dies not because of the plague, not because of his love of Tadzio, but because his will to live and to create atrophy.

The exterior events of the story, which are minimal, can be properly explained only in terms of the inner conflict of the artist. To produce art, Aschenbach believes he must practice absolute self-denial, affirming the dignity and moral capacity of man in the face of a world of self-indulgence that leads to personal abasement. Yet the artist is also a man, and, as such, has drives that connect him to the chaos of the formless elements of nature. This inner conflict is objectified in the person of the boy, Tadzio, who embodies all that Aschenbach has rejected in fifty long years of dedication to Apollonian art. As his desire for Tadzio becomes obsessive, driving him to neglect the care of his body and stricture of dignity, disintegration sets in and death becomes irrevocable. Subconsciously, Aschenbach is choosing to pursue the basic sensual, Dionysian side of himself that he has always denied.

Mann utilizes dream visions to underline and clarify the subconscious conflicts of Aschenbach. Aschenbach's first hallucination of the crouching beast in the jungle is evoked by the glimpse of the stranger at the Byzantine chapel in Munich. This vision literally foreshadows the trip to Venice and meta-phorically foreshadows the inner journey where Aschenbach discovers the jungle and beast within himself. The second vision on the beach in Venice, cast in the form of a Platonic dialog, explores the interrelatedness of art, love, and beauty with the beastial in man. In a third major dream hallucina-tion, Aschenbach is initiated into the worship of the Dionysian rite and finally glimpses "the stranger god" of sensual experience, of formless, chaotic joy, and excesses of emotion. The most striking vision occurs at the end of the novella, when Aschenbach, viewing the amoral beauty of perfection of form in Tadzio silhouetted against the amoral, formless beauty of the sea, accepts the promise inherent in the sea's chaos as the equivalent of the beauty produced by order and moral discipline. The reader assumes the vision to be objective reality until he is brought sharply and suddenly into the present reality of Aschenbach's dead body. Hemingway utilized this same tech-nique later in his own novella-length study of death and art, "The Snows of Kilimanjaro."

Mann's use of natural, geographical symbols also underlines the central conflicts of the novella. Aschenbach identifies the discipline of his art with Munich, a city of northern Europe, and with the snowy mountains. These places are associated with health, energy, reason, will, and Apollonian crea-tive power. Against them, Mann juxtaposes the tropical marshes, the jungle animal and plant life, the Indian plague, the sun and the sea, which are associated with Dionysian excesses of emotion and ecstasy in art. The beast, the jungle, the plague, the chaos lie within the nature of man and art just as clearly as do the mountain, self-denial, will and reason, qualities which en-able man to construct artifice upon the chaos of nature. Great art, Nietzsche says in *The Birth of Tragedy,* is a product of the fusion rather than the sep-aration of the calm, ordered, contemplative spirit of Apollo and the savage, sensual ecstasy of Dionysus. This is what both Aschenbach and the reader discover in Mann's great work, *Death in Venice.*

Ann E. Reynolds

DEATH OF A HERO

Type of work: Novel
Author: Richard Aldington (1892-1962)
Type of plot: Social criticism
Time of plot: World War I
Locale: England
First published: 1929

Death of a Hero *expresses Aldington's bitter disillusionment with the idealistic patriotism of World War I. With cynicism that is almost morbid in its brutality, the author tells of a hero so disgusted by his society, family, and complicated love life that he invites his own death in the war. The author, in portraying the shabby childhood through which the hero lived, condemns not only that generation but also society as a whole.*

Richard Aldington records the incredible innocence and disillusionment of the first generation of the modern world—if we take that world to have begun in 1914. Like Ford Madox Ford's *Parade's End,* Robert Graves's memoir *Goodbye to All That,* and the poetry of Rupert Brooke, Charles Sorley and Siegfried Sasson, *Death of a Hero* dramatizes the impact of the "Great War" upon the children of the late Victorians. Raised in the twilight of that age to believe that their culture rested on granite, they discovered that it, as well as their own lives, had no more foundation than a bed of quicksand.

The accomplishment of Aldington's novel consists in his perception that the seeds of war lay not only in the greed and stupidity of the politicians, but also—and more importantly—in the anarchy of personal relationships. The first generation of the twentieth century was unprepared for war as well as unfit to carry on their own love lives. The repression and hypocrisy of their Victorian parents destroyed any chance that young George Winterbourne, Elizabeth and Fanny, for example, have of forming adult relationships. Their sexual lives are those of children let out of school who are unable to handle their newfound freedom; ignorance combined with license must always end in violence.

The title of the novel is of course ironic. The traditional idea of the hero —especially the military one—is of the great man who sacrifices himself for the good of society. George Winterbourne's end comes with a whimper, not a bang; his death is at last an admission that he no longer has the will to continue. Insofar as he represents his generation, his suicide suggests its inability to understand and unwillingness to deal with a world that it has not made.

DEATH OF A SALESMAN

Type of work: Drama
Author: Arthur Miller (1915-   )
Type of plot: Social criticism
Time of plot: Mid-twentieth century
Locale: New York
First presented: 1949

This work is a social criticism

Death of a Salesman *is a damning indictment of American values which blends themes of social and personal tragedy within the same dramatic framework. The traveling salesman, Willy Loman, accepts at face value the over-publicized ideals of material success and blatant optimism, but at the same time experiences a profound sense of failure as he sees his aging and lack of accomplishments. The play ends in Loman's suicide, and his personal failure is symbolic also of the failure of a way of life. Miller's ability to build the story of his hero out of the common experience of so many Americans who sustain themselves with illusions while ignoring realities makes this play one of the most significant American contributions to theater in recent years.*

Born in New York, the city that is the setting for *Death of a Salesman,* Arthur Miller in his earlier plays reacts to the social pressures and fervors of the 1930's (Depression) and 1940's (World War II). But *Death of a Salesman,* Miller's most famous and most effective play, is also his most complex, and is far more than a social document. It is, of course, a very clear attack on at least one aspect of the American success myth or dream, as that dream is defined by Willy Loman. To Willy, success, respect, affection, and authority come to those who are "well liked." Greetings given gladly, doors opened eagerly, sales made readily—these represent the good life to Willy Loman. But the dream scarcely suits everyone. It does not suit Willy, despite his great dreams and restless longings. Since, despite constant failure, Willy keeps trying, he ultimately loses sight of his own identity. Biff laments at the end that his father never learned to know himself.

The dream, to Miller, is not only destructive; it is amoral. As a boy, Biff is told that, since he is "well liked," he can get away with anything. Disillusioned with his father, Biff, after running away, discovers that he has no direction, no skill, no vocation. The dream proves just as destructive to Happy, who is a weak caricature of his father. Nevertheless, the dream's enormous power is shown again and again, particularly at the conclusion of Act I, when Willy, Happy, and Biff grow wildly enthusiastic over the prospect of Biff asking for a business loan from a former employer, an employer whom Biff scarcely knew. When all else fails, Willy can call up the image of his brother, Ben, who represents an earlier get-rich-quick version of the success myth.

The Ben fantasies also suggest another level of the play. They help define a man whose world is crumbling. His weariness, his suicide efforts, his grumbling as he thinks of the little he has made of his life, his grandiose posturing—all these are the exterior cracks in a man who is also breaking up inside, as visions and memories out of the past cross and recross the present. The final crack-up is inevitable.

The play was at the center of an interesting controversy: can a common man be a suitable subject for tragedy? Miller, of course, insisted that he could. Interesting, too, is the fact that as his own interests changed, Miller himself announced that Willy was too pathetic for genuine tragic stature. Miller's later plays—*After the Fall* and *The Price*—probe the nature not of society, but of man, asserting the individual's own responsibility for himself and his life.

THE DEATH OF IVAN ILYICH

Type of work: Novella
Author: Count Leo Tolstoy (1828-1910)
Type of plot: Psychological realism
Time of plot: 1880's
Locale: St. Petersburg and nearby provinces
First published: 1884

Coming at the end of Tolstoy's career, this work concerns the thoughts on life and death of a dying man. The theme is much related to Tolstoy's obsessive fear of death and to the conclusion that he had wasted his own life, a conclusion which culminated for him in a spiritual rebirth. The story itself is a supreme, imaginative creation presenting with frankness, simplicity, and kindness an ordinary man confronted by the irrevocable fact of death.

Written in 1886, this story is only about sixty pages long, but it is one of the greatest pieces of fiction in any language. In it Tolstoy examines the hollowness of bourgeois existence. Ivan Ilyich is a successful member of the state bureaucracy. All his life he has carefully adjusted his conduct so as to please his superiors and to arrange a life which runs smoothly and without complication. He is the perfect example of the conforming, "other-directed" man. Only at his death does he discover the horror which lies behind his seemingly successful life.

The story opens in an unusual but significant way. Rather than tell us of Ivan's early years, Tolstoy presents us with the dead Ivan stretched out at home, attended by his wife and closest friend Peter Ivanovitch. The behavior of the mourners tells us more about Ivan's life than any chronicle could. Rather than grieve over his death, they are worried about their own affairs. His wife asks Peter Ivanovitch about her pension, hoping to persuade him to help her arrange for an increase, while he frets about missing the bridge game he had planned. To make matters worse, they both pretend to feelings of grief that they do not feel. At this point the reader may well ask what in Ivan's life could bring about so little concern about his death. The rest of the story answers this question in the most powerful terms; it dramatizes the statement which opens the second section: "Ivan Ilyich's life had been most simple and most ordinary and therefore most terrible."

Ivan's progress from law school to the position of examining magistrate is marked by careful obedience to authority both in legal matters and in matters of taste and style of life. His early pangs of conscience at youthful actions are overcome when he sees people of good position doing the same thing without qualms. Still, he never becomes a rake or hell raiser; he is, rather, anxiously correct and proper. He makes a proper marriage—one that serves to advance him—and then gradually proceeds to alienate his wife and children by avoiding domestic complications in the name of his job. In this separation between his private life, with its potential for affection, and his public duties he furthers the process of fragmentation within himself. He becomes punctilious at home as well as at work. All of his life takes on an official and artificial character from which only the natural process of death can release him as it educates him. In the opening scene we are told that "his face was handsomer and above all more dignified than when he was alive." His death is a form of rescue.

His job is a game which he plays with great seriousness—like the bridge games he hurries to after work. He never abuses his power as a magistrate but instead conducts himself "by the book." Most of all, he is careful never to become personally involved in the carrying out of justice. He is a perfect arm of the state, a perfect product of its bureaucratic machinery. Naturally, he never questions the system of justice he is paid to administer. It is significant that he rises no higher than the middle rank of officialdom. Those above him have perceived that he is essentially mediocre.

Nevertheless, his life seems to flow along easily, pleasantly, and correctly. He decorates his new home, supervising much of the work closely. He imagines that the result is very special, but Tolstoy tells us that Ivan's home, characteristicaly, looks exactly like the homes of other people of his class and station. Underneath the smooth surface of this life there is something wrong which refuses to stay concealed. It manifests itself in the form of an illness, probably cancer, which gradually consumes Ivan's vitality. When he goes to the doctor he feels guilty and desperately uncertain. For the first time he learns what it is like to be the recipient of the games those in authority play —like a criminal dragged to the bar. The doctor cannot or will not tell him what is wrong (he probably doesn't know). Gradually Ivan declines until he is bedridden. His disintegrating flesh begins to give off a strange and unpleasant odor. He becomes hateful to himself and to his wife, who up to now has pursued a life of idle and superficial pleasures. Even more than physical pain, Ivan suffers from spiritual torment. His prior habits of life have given him no resources with which to face death. Moreover, he is perpetually troubled by the question of why he is suffering when he took such pains to lead a correct life. What if he has been wrong all along? In the grip of despair he searches for hope at any hand but no hope presents itself until he finds it possible to accept the kind attentions of his servant Gerasim.

Gerasim is the opposite of Ivan. A healthy, simple peasant, he has never known the artificial life of a bureaucrat and social climber. He does not fear death, and thus does not mind being in the presence of the dying Ivan. He is in tune with the natural. Ivan is able to accept him because he feels that there is no deception in Gerasim's attitude toward him, whereas he sees nothing but deception in the kind and cheerful attitudes of his wife and friends (a reaction in part, to the falseness of his former life). When Gerasim sits for hours with his master's legs propped up on his shoulders, Ivan feels unaccountable relief. Still, Gerasim's presence only modifies Ivan's agony somewhat.. Essentially he must go through the process of dying by himself. Perhaps Gerasim's naturalness does bring Ivan to the conviction of the worthlessness of his former life, but death is Ivan's best educator. It gradually and painfully strips away the artificial and the vain. It reduces Ivan to the elemental position of an organism dependent upon the natural processes of life. Interestingly, Ivan thinks most of all of his early youth at this time. He recalls when he was still an innocent, uncorrupted by the false system he slavishly aspired to enter. In a sense, he is yearning to recapture the natural instincts represented by Gerasim. Death offers him the chance. In the final hours of his interminable decline, Ivan grows still. He has a vision of light and freedom. Death becomes for him a door to a larger and purer existence.

Benjamin Nyce

THE DEATH OF THE GODS

Type of work: Novel
Author: Dmitri Merejkowski (1865-1941)
Type of plot: Historical romance
Time of plot: Fourth century
Locale: Ancient Rome
First published: 1896

One of the most successful modern Russian novelists of the old regime, Merejkowski attempted to demonstrate that European civilization was a result of the meeting of Hellenism and Christianity by using the fourth century reign of Julian the Apostate as a historical setting. The novelist's success in re-creating what is distant both in time and in place is almost unparalleled in any national literature, as vivid characterizations reflect in greater or lesser degrees the struggle between the two dominant philosophies of paganism and Christianity.

Like many authors of his generation, Dmitri Merejkowski attempted in his writings to search for solutions to the problems that plagued Tzarist Russia in the turbulent quarter of a century preceding the Bolshevik revolution. Merejkowski, one of the Russian symbolists as well as founder of the Religious and Philosophical Society of St. Petersburg, was intensely interested in identifying the philosophical underpinnings of Western civilization. This he tried to do in fictional form in his trilogy *Christ and Antichrist,* comprising *The Death of the Gods, The Gods Reborn* (1902), and *Peter and Alexis* (1905).

In *The Death of the Gods,* Merejkowski sets up the thematic structure of opposing concepts upon which the entire trilogy is built. On a general level, this structure reflects the author's perception of the dualistic nature of man, within whom the forces of flesh and spirit are constantly struggling, and his belief that all of human history has been shaped by this struggle. More specifically, he sets up two sets of values which cluster around Hellenistic and pagan beliefs on the one hand, and Christian values on the other, and counterposes them dramatically throughout the work. The author's purpose in doing this is to illustrate his theory that Western civilization grew out of and took its direction from the clash between paganism and Christianity.

The historical novel genre proved a perfect vehicle for a writer with Merejkowski's gift for recreating the past, and in *The Death of the Gods* this talent is at its best. The setting ranges from all the places visited by the young Julian during his travels in Asia Minor, to the capital of Constantinople, to the military posts along the Persian frontier which are stormed by the Roman legions. Each of these settings comes alive in the author's hands; his use of colorful and specific details infuses both time and place with uniqueness and vividness. The reader feels that he is very close to the real experience of life in the Roman empire of the fourth century.

When Herbert Trench, a fellow at All Soul's College, translated *The Death of the Gods* into English, he felt the novel to be one of the most significant works of the new generation of Russian authors and saw Merejkowski as the successor of Dostoevski. Although time has seen Trench's enthusiasm replaced by a more moderate critical appraisal, Merejkowski's novel nevertheless remains an excellent example of historical fiction inspired with crucial philosophical concerns.

THE DEATH OF THE HEART

Type of work: Novel
Author: Elizabeth Bowen (1899-1973)
Type of plot: Psychological realism
Time of plot: After World War I
Locale: London and Seale, England
First published: 1938

The Death of the Heart *is a simple story of the burdens of adolescence and its painful emergence into maturity—an evolution from innocence and idealism to an acceptance of the world as it is. It is the story of Portia, an illegitimate sixteen-year-old girl who comes to live with her half-brother when her mother dies. Portia's innocent longings and candid curiosity provide a catalyst for an upper-middle-class English household where compromise and boredom have held sway. Portia is a model for the adolescent's sense of loneliness and need for love and understanding. Although the plot is no more conclusive than life itself, the novel crystalizes some truths that are often elusive.*

Sixteen-year-old Portia Quayne may seem to be the protagonist of *The Death of the Heart,* but in fact her role is to point up the shallowness of the world of Thomas and Anna. Portia's progressive disillusionment with the "real" world of adult life is detailed in the three sections of the novel—"The World," "The Flesh," and "The Devil." Her disenchantment, sensitively portrayed by a sympathetic narrator, is in every case contrasted to Anna's passionless existence. Life at 2 Windsor Terrace, so idealized by Portia's dead father, is "the world" of the first stage of disillusionment. Eddie—with his fickle attention and passes at Daphne—constitutes the temptation and disillusionment of "the flesh." "The devil" is the novelist St. Quentin Miller, who with "no loyalty" reveals to Portia that Anna has been reading her diary and laughing with others about it. The structure of the novel is carefully worked out, so that Anna's opening revelation to St. Quentin of having read Portia's diary becomes the catalyst for the crisis of the end. The body of the novel gives the details of the contrast between Portia's romantic illusions and the Quaynes' disillusioning boredom. Significantly, the section titles of the novel refer to the baptismal rite in the Book of Common Prayer.

In the end, Portia's demand for "the right thing" forces Anna and Thomas to understand the sterility of their lives and of the "preposterous world," devoid of value. Anna finally empathizes with Portia as she muses that Portia must have a "frantic desire to be handled with feeling" as well as a wish "to be let alone." Matchett, the only adult interested in tradition or value, ends the novel with her interior monologue in the taxi. As she enters the hotel to meet Portia, the strident sounds of a piano come together in a harmonious chord. This resolution suggests, at least, a new beginning for Portia and Anna, each having learned from the other—Portia that the heart dies a little, and Anna that the heart does not completely die.

Bowen's greatest talent lies in detailing the inner life of a young person and the subtleties of the tensions between generations.

THE DEATH OF VIRGIL

Type of work: Novel
Author: Hermann Broch (1886-1951)
Type of plot: Poetic mysticism
Time of plot: 19 B.C.
Locale: Brundisium (Brindisi, Italy)
First published: 1945

This difficult yet extraordinarily beautiful novel, using as its plot the death of the Roman poet Virgil, might better be considered a poem, since both its means of presentation and its effects are wholly poetic. Using a simple plot as a basis, Broch presents a symphony in four movements, each operating on three different levels of interest: the vivid and uncanny imagery of both the real world and the fever-ridden, hallucinatory, yet visionary world of the dying Virgil; the beauty of Broch's language and rythmic sentences; and the depth of the writer's attempts to explore metaphysical truth. The mood on the whole is meditative and elegiac, and the style of each movement establishes its tempo as symbols, incidents, and phrases are re-echoed and transformed.

The Death of Virgil, which has been called a five-hundred-page lyric poem, began as an eighteen-page story, written for reading on an Austrian radio series. Broch selected the subject of Virgil's last day and his desire to burn his work as a vehicle for the discussion of a theme then intensely important to him—the role of literature at the end of a cultural epoch. He saw considerable parallels between the first century B.C. and his own time, 1936. The theme became even more personally relevant to Broch in 1938, when he was arrested by the Nazis and for a time faced his own death. The composition was finished in the years following Broch's escape to the United States, and was published simultaneously in German and English.

The term "composition" is quite accurate: Broch wished to create a new genre, and his work has a conscious relationship to symphonic form and to the lyric poem. Each of the four movements presents a new step in Virgil's development: his confrontation with the ugliness of life forms the theme of the first street scenes; his awareness that he has falsified the fullness of experience by devoting himself to the beautiful to the exclusion of the ugly leads to a decision to burn his works in the second section. In the third section, in the confrontation with Augustus, Virgil, in an abrupt change of mind, passes beyond his own selfish will and gives the manuscript to the Emperor, an act of that love which he believes necessary for healing the world. He asks, finally, that his slaves be freed. The last section depicts the return to unity as Virgil dies, passing from the conflict of opposites which opened the book to an awareness of life as a whole, and of life and death as one; the unity is symbolized by his sea voyage, and constitutes one of the most remarkable passages in modern literature.

DEBIT AND CREDIT

Type of work: Novel
Author: Gustav Freytag (1816-1895)
Type of plot: Social realism
Time of plot: Early nineteenth century
Locale: Eastern Germany and Poland
First published: 1855

Freytag's Debit and Credit *presents a German middle class—better, more honorable, and more stable than other Europeans—in whose soberness and industriousness lay the future greatness of Germany. This novel is the story of Anton Wohlfart, a model middle-class businessman, and his struggle for survival in a world of usurers and nobility, portrayed as a group possessing little talent, little common sense, and an empty sense of honor. Of all Freytag's works, this novel has received the highest praise as an example of the combination of romance and the realistic social novel, for which it is often compared to the work of Charles Dickens.*

Gustav Freytag's *Debit and Credit* was one of the most popular German novels of the nineteenth century, enjoying high sales among that class whose virtues it glorifies, the solid German bourgeoisie. Perhaps the very absence of deeper artistic qualities which have led to its later neglect was responsible for its enthusiastic reception by the audience for which it was written. It presents an idealized view of German history and society, eschewing the flights of fancy typical of Romantic literature but by no means wholly realistic in its view of German culture, which was far more complex and tension-filled than one might guess from the novel.

Anton Wohlfart is the very model of the industrious businessman, and the middle class is regarded as the representative of all that is best in German life. Freytag had been involved in the revolutionary movement of 1848, and was firmly committed to the cause of German unity under Prussian leadership, and to the exclusion of the various non-German groups which had become part of the German cultural sphere through incorporation into the Austrian Empire. This feeling of German superiority is clearly developed in the novel; Jews, Poles, and even Americans are regarded negatively, though not condemned as groups. It would be wrong to see the figure of Veitel Itzig as demonstrating anti-Semitism on Freytag's part. The slight tendency toward caricature, derived from Dickens' character portraits, reflects rather Freytag's desire to simplify and clarify the structure of his novel, especially through strong contrast.

Freytag began as a dramatist, and his novels all share something of the tight organization of a drama. His style strives for objectivity, excluding the realm of fantasy and illusion. Indeed, what he criticizes in the nobility, in the Poles, and in Itzig, is precisely the tendency toward egocentricity, illusory values, and romantic longings. Wohlfart succeeds because of his objective concentration and dispassion. He does not strive beyond his class, but steadfastly maintains his moderate and diligent way of life, representing for generations the ideal fulfillment of bourgeois values.

THE DECAMERON
(SELECTIONS)

Type of work: Tales
Author: Giovanni Boccaccio (1313-1375)
Types of plots: Romantic tragedy, farce, folk tradition
Times of plots: Graeco-Roman times and the Middle Ages
Locale: Italy
First transcribed: 1353

This collection of tales is set in 1348, the year of the Black Death. Seven ladies and three gentlemen meet in a Florentine church and decide to escape from the city and spend time in the hills of Fiesole; there they pass the time telling stories for ten days. Bocaccio broke free of past tradition and created a literature about ordinary people, and his novellas range from anecdotes and fabliaux to folk and fairy tales of ancient lineage. All are told with a wit carrying them above the range of the licentious, a term sometimes used unjustly about the tales. Their use and adaptations in literature, plays, operas, and paintings attest to their popularity throughout the ages.

Since its composition readers and critics have made much of *The Decameron's* hundred entertaining and worldly tales, comic and tragic, bawdy and courteous, satiric and serious, that compose this work. Unfortunately, much early criticism was moralistic, and Boccaccio was faulted for devoting his mature artistic skill to a collection of "immoral" stories. *The Decameron* has fared better in the latter half of this century, with more solid critical inquiries into the work's literary significance and style. Boccaccio's collection has been considered representative of the Middle Ages; it has also been viewed as a product of the Renaissance. The work is both. *The Decameron* not only encompasses literary legacies of the medieval world; it also goes far beyond Boccaccio's own time, transcending in tone and style artistic works of previous as well as later periods.

The structure with its frame characters has many analogues in medieval literature; the frame story (a group of tales within an enclosing narrative) was a device known previously, even in the Orient. Two twelfth century collections were *The Seven Sages* and the *Disciplina Clericalis*. The material for many of Boccaccio's stories was gleaned from Indian, Arabic, Byzantine, French, Hebrew, and Spanish tales.

Although *The Decameron* is not escapist literature, the idea and nature of the framework have much in common with medieval romance. There is the idealistic, pastoral quality of withdrawal into the "pleasant place" or garden, away from the ugly, harsh reality of the surrounding world. The ten young people who leave Florence—a dying, corrupt city which Boccaccio describes plainly in all its horrors—find only momentary respite from the charnel house of reality; but their existence for ten days is that of the enchanted medieval dreamworld: a paradise of flowers, ever-flowing fountains, shade trees, soft breezes, where all luxuries of food and drink abound. Furthermore, virtue reigns along with medieval *gentilesse* in its finest sense. There is no cynicism or lust in the various garden settings where the pastimes are strolling, weaving garlands, or playing chess. Even Dioneo, who tells the most salacious stories, is as chaste in his conduct as Pampinea, Filomena, Filostrato, and the others. One critic has even seen in these frame characters a progression of virtues, and their stories actually groups of *exempla* praising such qualities as wisdom, prudence, or generosity.

Against this refined and idealized medieval framework are the stories themselves, the majority marked by intense realism in a world where dreams and enchanted gardens have little place. The locale of the novella is usually that of actual geography; the Italian cities of Pisa, Siena, and especially Florence figure largely as settings. The entire Mediterranean is represented with its islands of Sicily, Corfu, Rhodes, Cyprus, Ischia. France, England, and Spain also serve as backgrounds. In one oriental story, the Seventh Tale on the Second Day, beautiful Altiel, the Sultan of Babylon's daughter, after being kidnaped, travels in the space of four years over most of the Mediterranean, the islands, Greece, Turkey, and Alexandria. Boccaccio is also concerned with restricted spatial reality, and he sketches in close detail internal settings of abbeys, bedrooms, churches, marketplaces, castles, and inns. Different social classes have their own language and clothing. Many characters like Ciappelletto, living in profanation of the world; Rinaldo abandoned in nakedness and cold by his fellow men; Peronella, the deceitful Neapolitan woolcomber cuckolding her husband; the whole convent of nuns eagerly lying with the youth Masetto—these Boccaccio describes in believable human conflicts.

Although he draws upon the entire arsenal of medieval rhetoric, the author of these one hundred novella goes beyond figures of speech and linguistic tools in his modern paradoxical style and cynical tone. Although his satire often bites deep, his comic mood generally embraces evil and holiness alike with sympathy and tolerance. His treatment of themes, situation, and character is never didactic. Like Chaucer, he is indulgent, exposing moral and social corruption but leaving guilty characters to condemn themselves.

A novella like the comic tale of Chichibio, told on the Sixth Day, is pure comic farce, moving rapidly by question and answer, playfully rollicking to a surprise ending brought about by this impusive, foolish cook. The story of Rossiglione and Guardastagno, Ninth Tale of the Fourth Day, has a tragic plot. But the narrators draw no moral in either case. The interaction of character, scene, and plot brings into relief forces that motivate the world of humanity and allow the reader to judge if he must. Again and again characters in the tales are relieved from moral responsibility by the control of

Fortune.

Throughout *The Decameron* Boccaccio concerns himself primarily with presenting a very human world as he observed and understood it. In this presentation there is no pedantry or reticence; he paints men and women in all their rascality, faithlessness, nobility, and suffering, changing his Italian prose to suit the exigency of purpose, whether that results in a serious or comic, refined or coarse, descriptive or analytical style. Boccaccio has command of many styles; in fact, his "Commedia Umana" comprehends most, and its author changes easily from one to another.

It is true that in utilizing fables and anecdotes from many medieval sources, in employing figurative and rhythmical devices from books on medieval rhetoric, in structuring his framework according to the chivalric world of valor and courtesy, his work is a product of the Middle Ages. But in its frank, open-minded treatment of flesh as flesh, its use of paradox, cynicism, and realistic handling of character, *The Decameron* transcends the medieval period and, going beyond the Renaissance, takes its place as universal art.

Muriel B. Ingham

DECLINE AND FALL

Type of work: Novel
Author: Evelyn Waugh (1903-1966)
Type of plot: Social satire
Time of plot: Twentieth century
Locale: England and Wales
First published: 1928

A bitter, satiric, farcical, and tragic novel, Decline and Fall *is a penetrating yet hilarious study of disordered English society in the period between the two world wars. The novel tells of Paul Pennyfeather, who unjustly gets expelled from Oxford, turns to teaching at an appalling boys' school where he falls in love with a student's mother but also falls into her white slave trade business unknowingly, is imprisoned, and ultimately returns to Oxford to study theology. Episodic in form, many scenes no more than a page or two in length, Waugh's distortions and exaggerations have the quality of fantasy, for in his pages the impossible and the believable exist side by side.*

Decline and Fall is the first and possibly the best work of Evelyn Waugh, a luminary of the brave company of English satirists. The novel is notable for its economy of time and space. The action extends over a year, and the protagonist's circumstances at the beginning and end are virtually identical, lending a neat roundness to the story. Another feature is the spareness of the prose, and the unlabored epigrams, as, for example, Paul Pennyfeather's quip that the English public school is a perfect conditioner for life in prison. Waugh lays low individuals and whole classes of society with a flick of a proper name: Digby-Vaine-Trumpington for a vain, trumpeting young aristocrat; Maltravers for a Secretary of Transportation; Prendergast for a clergyman aghast at his apprehension of divine indifference; Grimes for an earthy rascal; Pennyfeather for an impecunious, half-fledged scholar.

The tone is persistently cheerful. No amazement is expressed, even by the innocent and beleaguered protagonist, at anything that befalls him. Tragedies occur offstage. The death of Prendergast, for instance, is revealed in a hymn. Lord Tangent's demise is recorded as follows: in chapter eight, he is shown crying because he has been wounded in the foot by a bullet from the starter's pistol; in chapter twelve, Beste-Chetwynde reports, in an aside, that Tangent's foot is gangrened; in chapter thirteen comes the news that the foot is being amputated; and finally in chapter nineteen, it is reported in an offhand way that he has died. The list of groups and institutions which excite the author's scorn is extensive; his opprobrium falls on the aristocracy, the newly rich, the universities, the public schools, old-school penology, newfangled penology, the House of Lords, the House of Commons, the Church of England, historical landmarks, modern architecture, and the League of Nations, to name a few. But though the novel manages to be hilarious at the expense of practically everybody, it has a serious side, or rather a serious center; namely, the school-boy virtue of Pennyfeather contrasted with the cheery rascality of Grimes.

That Paul Pennyfeather is a right thinker and a square shooter is evident from the start. He owes his educational opportunities as much to his own industry, intelligence, and moderation as to the legacy left by his parents. He is earnest, diffident, and idealistic; in short, he is the very model of a middle-class English divinity student. The incredible things that happen to him seem at first reading to represent repeated assaults of a corrupt society on a gen-uinely decent character. Captain Grimes, on the other hand, shows up as a bounder of the very worst kind, a poseur who relies on public school con-nections to rescue him from his frequent immersions in "the soup." He milks the fellowship of honor and duty for all it is worth and does not hesitate to abandon ship at the first sign of bad weather—women, children, and gentlemanly behavior notwithstanding.

But for all his roguery, Grimes is not a villain. He is instead the most sympathetic character in the novel. The chief element of his personality is common sense; it is he, and not Pennyfeather, who is the author's *persona*, who embodies the impulses of sanity as opposed to the precepts of class and culture. During the war, for example, when faced with court-martial or honorable suicide, he relies on drink and old school ties to see him through alive, and they do. Trapped into marriage, he simply bolts, once into the pub-lic schools, once into the sea. Imprisoned, he makes his escape by sinking into a quicksand from which, Paul and the reader are confident, he will rise to drink his pint in new guise but with the old elemental verve. He is self-indulgent, brave, resourceful, and not to be humbugged.

Contrarily Paul, though self-disciplined, is meek, credulous, and funda-mentally passive. Everything that happens to him, good or bad, simply *happens*. His rather mild passion for Margot Beste-Chetwynde strikes him like lightning; his actual proposal of marriage is all Margot's doing. He acquiesces alike to expulsion from college and rescue from prison with the same spongy plasticity cloaked in a sort of ethical good-sportism. In fact, it may be argued that believers in this schoolboy code of ethics suffer from a profound moral laziness and invite the outrages perpetrated on them in its name by those who do not believe in it. Paul's explanation of why he does not outface Potts and take money from Trumpington is illustrative. He defines a gentleman as some-one who declines to accept benefits that are not his by right, or to profit from windfall advantage. Implicit in this stance are (a) a kind of flabby ethical neutrality disguised as self-respect, and (b) a certain pride in taking no action. Grimes' judgment is sounder, and more vigorous, for he recognizes Potts as a stinker in prosecuting Paul for a crime he committed inadvertently.

The author remarks at one stage that Paul has not the makings of a hero. No more has he the makings of a villain, for villainy requires a certain enterprise, as exemplified by Margot. It is not Paul's decline and fall which are recorded here, but the degeneration of a society in which custom and privilege combine to nurture all manner of waste and wickedness. Paul is merely part of the problem. Grimes, the voice of blackguardism and good sense, is part of the solution. Paul toasts the stability of ideals, Grimes the passing moment.

Despite Grimes, however, *Decline and Fall* ends on a rather grim note, with Peter Beste-Chetwynde a wastrel and Paul embracing a pinched orthodoxy. The underlying sense is of honorable old forms giving way to a new and nastier regime, a theme which Waugh pursued in later works. Indeed, he espoused it in his own life to the extent of rejecting the new order altogether, and as a result he was virtually a hermit at the time of his death.

Jan Kennedy Foster

DEEPHAVEN

Type of work: Tales
Author: Sarah Orne Jewett (1849-1909)
Type of plot: Regional romance
Time of plot: Nineteenth century
Locale: Maine seacoast
First published: 1877

Deephaven, a series of sketches describing an idyllic summer in an almost forgotten town on the New England coast, is filled with nature study and character portraits. Although too diffuse in its effects to be called a novel, the book is unified in background and theme. Jewett believed that a writer must know the village well before he could know the world; in Deephaven *she writes pleasantly and nostalgically of her most familiar recollections.*

The provincial characters in *Deephaven* do not yet possess the universality that they would acquire in Sarah Orne Jewett's latest stories and novels. But the author acutely observes this small fishing village, clearly defining its social gradations and representative types. Equally well detailed are the varieties of "fashion" adopted by the inhabitants of Deephaven. But it is the people themselves—their faces, their speech, and their lives—that the reader best remembers.

Life in Deephaven moves slowly, so that even the details of common existence assume importance and become leisurely and pleasant activities. The narrator details with obvious relish the housekeeping routine, and the quiet day-to-day village life. Always, a gentle humor pervades the book.

Memories constitute much of *Deephaven's* narrative. The old sailors, their widows, village spinsters, old bachelors, everyone, seems to live at least half of his or her life recollecting the past. And the "ancient mariners" of the village are the heroes, if the book has any. Sometimes, they romanticize the past, sometimes they view it clearly, but always it is present before them, as real as the ever-changing bay and the tides. The ships remembered by the old skippers assume vivid personalities. The rich history of bygone days is preserved by the people who lived it. Sarah Orne Jewett saw history as basically the story of human beings and the events of their lives. This vision dominates and shapes *Deephaven.*

The whalers and seafaring men and their families have had more contact with the world than most villagers and are not as narrow-minded as many small-town people. They possess more than folk wisdom; along with trinkets from foreign ports, they have picked up an awareness of the larger issues that face humanity. Sarah Orne Jewett especially loved and respected these people.

THE DEERSLAYER

Type of work: Novel
Author: James Fenimore Cooper (1789-1851)
Type of plot: Historical romance
Time of plot: 1740
Locale: Northern New York State
First published: 1841

Though the last of The Leatherstocking Tales *to be written,* The Deerslayer *is the novel of Natty Bumppo's youth. In it, savages and the woodsman Natty Bumppo, or Deerslayer, are depicted as having codes of honor and morality, while Tom Hutter and Hurry Harry are motivated by greed and viciousness in their efforts to obtain scalps and in their murder of an innocent Indian girl. A portion of the story deals with Judith Hutter's fruitless attempts to interest Natty romantically.*

The Deerslayer is the fifth and last published of the Leatherstocking Tales; when the entire series was republished in 1850 it became the first. Having written two books about Leatherstocking in middle age and two picturing him in his declining years, Cooper turned back to young Natty Bumppo before he had gained fame among the Indians as Hawkeye or Long Rifle. In *The Deerslayer* Natty is the idealized "natural man."

Deerslayer is initiated into warfare when he first kills a fellow man—in self-defense—and then comforts his dying foe, who confers upon him the new name, Hawkeye, which honors him as a fighter. He also learns of some of the evil in the world through his acquaintance with Thomas Hutter and Hurry Harry who kill Indians—including women and children—for profit only. Cooper's idealization of Indian character is brought out partly through what he himself writes about Indians and partly through what Natty says of them.

The common theme which ties the Leatherstocking Tales together is the protagonist. Although he is known by different names in the various novels, he is identified throughout the series by his qualities as a brave and honorable hero. As a character, he is developed from youth to old age. He is a loner and an individualist and has moral and ethical concerns about the environment. He commands a strong integrity in dealing with other human beings, treating both friends and enemies with courtesy and respect. Ultimately, he follows his own simple moral scheme and demonstrates unwavering dedication to the principle of self-reliance. *The Deerslayer* is one of two Leatherstocking Tales (the other was *The Pathfinder*) which Mark Twain chose to mock amusingly but rather unjustly in his "Fenimore Cooper's Literary Offenses." The defects of plot, characterization, and style are easily seen by modern readers, but the romance is a far better book than Twain's comments would lead one to believe. Some critics have seen it as perhaps the best of the five tales. Cooper in his 1850 Preface said *The Pathfinder* and *The Deerslayer* were "probably the two most worthy an enlightened and cultivated reader's notice."

DEIRDRE

Type of work: Novel
Author: James Stephens (1882-1950)
Type of plot: Legendary romance
Time of plot: The Heroic Age
Locale: Ireland
First published: 1923

James Stephens, brilliant Irish writer of poetry and prose, worked best in material grounded in the early literature of his own country. Thus, in his romance Deirdre *he tries to revitalize the characters and plot of early Gaelic legend. The work is filled with memorable characterizations and scenes, and although* Deirdre *is a novel of legend and fantasy, Stephens has also incorporated a core of realism at its center.*

One of the primary features of the Irish Literary Renaissance was the discovery, regeneration, and translation of ancient Irish myths into modern forms. Among the great Celtic legends, perhaps the most popular was the tragic love story of Deirdre, The Troubler, and her lover, Naoise. Probably the greatest artistic representations of this fable of fate, love, betrayal, and death are the dramatic versions by William Butler Yeats (*Deirdre,* 1907) and John Millington Synge (*Deirdre of the Sorrows,* 1910). However, although James Stephens' prose interpretation of the myth may lack the austere poetic grandeur of Yeats's play or the tragic intensity of Synge's, it has a psychological penetration and lively narrative thrust that makes it not unworthy of mention alongside those great predecessors.

In many ways Stephens' is the most modern version of the Deirdre legend. Although very different from each other, both Yeats and Synge sought to capture the atmosphere of the romantic Irish past of legend and folklore in their plays. Stephens, however, is more interested in a modern psychological analysis of the characters and their actions. At the same time he did not ignore the flavor of archaic Celtic myth; in developing his story he took great pains to present the medieval culture and background as authentically and thoroughly as he could. Thus, *Deirdre* contains that mixture of the lyrical and the realistic, the ancient and the modern, and the solemn and the irreverent that characterizes Stephens' best work in all genres.

It has been claimed—with some justice—that Stephens' emphasis on detailed psychological analysis and explanation slows down the action in the first book, and that he fails in the crucial scene—the flight of the lovers—by having it reported secondhand. But if the first book is uneven, the second is delightful and occasionally powerful. Their personalities and motivations having been carefully delineated in the first book, the characters, and their decisions and actions, are thoroughly believable in the second one. All of

Book Two is excellent, and several moments—such as the suppressed tragedy evident in the gaiety of Naoise's younger brothers, Deirdre's realization of Conachúr's treachery, and especially the finale, when Deirdre dies on the body of her freshly killed lover—approach greatness.

It was not Stephens' purpose to idolize the old Irish myths, but to make them alive and familiar for his own times. In spite of a setting eight centuries in the past, readers of *Deirdre* have little difficulty in believing in, and relating to, a gallery of vivid, passionate characters: the gentle, aristocratic King Fergus, too casual and perhaps lazy to avert tragedy; Conachúr, brave, yet insecure, whose sense of honor and duty cannot overcome his passionate nature; the sons of Uisneac, united, yet individualized, apparently carefree, yet serious and heroic; and finally, Deirdre herself, intense, intuitive, innocent yet wise, who passionately and courageously strives for a happiness that she knows from the beginning will never be granted to her.

DEIRDRE OF THE SORROWS

Type of work: Drama
Author: John Millington Synge (1871-1909)
Type of plot: Romantic tragedy
Time of plot: The legendary past
Locale: Ireland
First presented: 1910

This play deals with the legendary Irish past, dramatizing an account of the beautiful Irish heroine who preferred death with her lover to life as the wife of the king. The play contains both the rich warmth of Synge's local and distinctively Irish characterizations and the romantic quality of the legendary. Filled with romantic dedication, fully developed in Synge's rich Irish idiom, the language of the peasant is given both power and dignity as it is shaped into the tragic movement of the play. These factors coupled with touches of humane characterization provide Irish drama of endurance and worth.

In spite of his relatively small output, four full length plays and two one-acters, John M. Synge is justly considered one of the finest dramatists of the modern stage and the Abbey Theatre's most important playwright prior to Sean O'Casey. Completed shortly before his death, but never revised to the author's complete satisfaction, *Deirdre of the Sorrows* can be seen as Synge's final statement on the joys of life, the possibilities, both good and bad, of love, and the inscrutability of human destiny.

The real strength of the play, and the thing that probably sets it apart from the many other dramatic versions of this famous Irish myth, comes from the way Synge combines an austere mood of classic, almost Grecian tragedy with characterizations that are immediate, human, and sympathetic. Deirdre first impresses us as a flighty girl who chases in the woods gathering twigs and nuts with little concern for her future queenly role. Her initial reaction to King Conchubor's demand for immediate marriage is to simply beg, like a petulant child, for more time. But almost immediately her inner strength asserts itself. Faced with Conchubor's implacability, she grows into maturity almost instantly: "From this day," she tells her old nurse Lavarcham, "I will turn the men of Ireland like a wind blowing on the heath." She then dons her royal regalia, assuming the status of a queen, and, by giving herself without hesitation to Naisi, unflinchingly accepts the doom foretold for her. And yet, for all of her tragic grandeur, the "little girl" element in her character remains evident throughout.

Likewise, the other principal characters contain aspects of both the tragic and the mundane. Naisi is heroic and passionate, willing to risk exile and death for the love of Deirdre. But he is also irritable, impulsive, and occasionally inconsistent. Towards the end of the play he admits to Fergus that:

"I've had dreams of getting old and weary, and losing my delight in Deirdre."

Conchubor is also pictured as a mixture of the grand and the petty. On the one hand he establishes himself as a ferocious king, given to extremes of heroism and violence. His desire for Deirdre is intense, and his plans for her are grandiose. The strength of his feelings are evidenced by the lengths to which he is willing to go to secure her, including the destruction of his own kingdom, and by the vengeful rage that is aroused against those who stand in his way, especially Naisi and his brothers. But at the same time he is a pitiful old man desperately denying the effects of time and clinging to an image of himself as virile by taking a young and beautiful wife. "There's one sorrow has no end surely," he tells Deirdre, "that's being old and lonesome."

This powerful merging of the heroic and the human reaches its dramatic peak in the scene where the lovers separate forever. Deirdre believes that the only way they can escape inevitable disillusionment and acrimony in their passion is to give themselves up to Conchubor's vengeance, thereby avoiding the slower, but more painful ravages of time. Naisi agrees because he, too,

DELPHINE

Type of work: Novel
Author: Madame de Staël (Baronne de Staël-Holstein, 1766-1817)
Type of plot: Romantic tragedy
Time of plot: Late eighteenth century
Locale: France
First published: 1802

One of the first feminine autobiographies, Delphine *takes the epistolary form in the sentimental vein of many French and British novels of quality during the first half of the eighteenth century. The novel is an index to the temper of Madame de Staël's circle at the time and reflects ideals such as the education of women, political equality, freedom of religious conscience, anticlericism, and the devotion to reason espoused by Rousseau and other late eighteenth century thinkers.*

Delphine is a difficult novel in many ways. The manner in which it is written, the characterizations, the plot, and Madame de Staël's ideas, all make reading the novel somewhat of an ordeal. At the same time, however, beneath the narrative complexities and emotional excesses, there is a fundamental honesty and sincerity of purpose.

The use of letters offers Madame de Staël some advantages. She is able to provide a continuing psychological analysis of her characters, in some depth, and sustain a rather complicated plot. Still, letters as a narrative medium can be severely limiting, and even confining. There are logistical problems to solve—who will write to whom?—but there are also matters of tone. One problem in *Delphine* is that the letters, though differing in content and in intellectual point of view, sound rather as if they have all been written in the same voice. This difficulty tends to blur character and motives. A second problem has to do with Madame de Staël's idealization of her main characters. Though the Vernons, Madame d'Ervin, and her lover appear lifelike enough, Delphine herself and Léonce are not as believable; passions, in the worst romantic tradition, appear stronger than characters, and motives are purer than real life generally allows.

Delphine is more important, perhaps, as a document in literary and intellectual history than as a work of fiction. Madame de Staël used *Delphine* especially to explore the role of women in society and in the cultural, religious, political, and intellectual life of the nation. Although the subtitle of the novel is "A man must be able to brave opinion, a woman to submit to it," Madame de Staël does not advocate the submission of women; on the contrary, taking an advanced position for her day, she argues that women have been placed in an especially precarious social role, and that they must be strong enough in their own feelings to be independent of the narrow and limiting prescriptions of social convention.

The idea that people must be free to follow their deepest passions echoes the sentiments of the most important romantic novels of the nineteenth century. It is in that tradition, as well as in the tradition of the novel of ideas, that *Delphine* should be placed.

DELTA WEDDING

Type of work: Novel
Author: Eudora Welty (1909-   )
Type of plot: Regional realism
Time of plot: Early 1920's
Locale: Mississippi
First published: 1946

Delta Wedding *is the chronicle of a remarkable family living during the 1920's in Mississippi. Although the plot centers around the preparations for a wedding of one of the daughters to a man considered inferior, the main theme is both the portrayal of the Fairchild family and of the Southern way of life. Eudora Welty superbly demonstrates that life on the Delta is a thing apart from that of any other region of the United States.*

Eudora Welty has created in Shellmound, the home of the Fairchild family in *Delta Wedding,* a world set apart from the rest of Southern plantation society of the 1920's. Shellmound is a haven, isolated from the mainstream of Southern life and unaffected by extremes of grief and suffering: there is no racial tension; no poverty; no war or natural catastrophe; none of the sense of alienation and instability generated by contact with modern urban society; and none of the severe moral deficiencies in the characters that would preclude natural human happiness. The Fairchild estate is thus the perfect stage upon which to play out a drama about the growth of every type of love, from romantic to filial to platonic.

The main focus of the book, therefore, is on the nature of the numerous members of the Fairchild clan and on their relationships; Welty shows how the men are different from the women, how the "insiders" are different from those who have married into the family, how each person relates to the others, and how each person grows individually and privately. In order to explore these various aspects, the author utilizes different narrative voices, thus enabling the reader to view the characters from different perspectives. Aunt Tempe, for example, provides the older generation's point of view; she believes that Delta women have inherited traits that cannot be learned by outsiders, traits which enable them subtly to control their men and the plantations. At the young end of the spectrum is nine-year-old Laura, who comes to live at Shellmound temporarily after her mother's death; she provides the child's viewpoint of events during the hectic wedding preparations. The most objective, wise, and clear-sighted outlook, however, is provided by Aunt Ellen. As an "outsider" (she married Battle Fairchild), she not only sees more accurately than her more involved and subjective relatives, but brings to her judgment insights from the world beyond the plantation.

What distinguishes the Fairchilds most of all is their simultaneous independence from and reliance upon one another; each person is at once intensely caught up in family concerns and fiercely private and separate. The only member who transcends the insular closeness of the circle to achieve a more universal outlook on life is Uncle George; able to feel and see beyond the limitations of life at Shellmound, he is nevertheless tied to the Fairchilds in his heart. Through the family's constant attempts to study and understand George, and through George's emotional involvement in events at the estate, Welty reveals a group of people at once selfishly exclusive and warmly affectionate, tender, loving, and devoted.

DESIRE UNDER THE ELMS

Type of work: Drama
Author: Eugene O'Neill (1888-1953)
Type of plot: Romantic tragedy
Time of plot: 1850
Locale: The Cabot farmhouse in New England
First presented: 1924

Desire Under the Elms *was the last of O'Neill's naturalistic plays and one of his best, exemplifying interest in Freudian psychology and in the conflicts between repressive Calvinism and Dionysian surrender. Set in New England, the play deals with Ephraim Cabot and his new young wife Abbie, who seduces Ephraim's youngest son, Eben, in order to have a child which she can claim is Ephraim's. O'Neill's daring reduction to the simple impulses of love, hate, lust, and greed gives an impression of human nature as convincing and complete as in his more complex plays.*

One of O'Neill's most admired and frequently performed plays, *Desire Under the Elms* provoked enormous controversy during its first stagings. Some audiences were scandalized by what one critic called "distresses" which "range from unholy lust to infanticide, and include drinking, cursing, vengeance, and something approaching incest." In Los Angeles, the cast was arrested for having presented a lewd, obscene, and immoral play. A bizarre trial followed—at one point the entire court witnessed a special private performance. The jury was finally dismissed, having deadlocked with eight members voting for conviction and four for acquittal. However, it gradually became apparent that O'Neill was aiming at something more than a shocking revelation of unconscious drives and primordial fears. These elements were clearly subordinated to his larger purpose of reintroducing authentic tragic vision to American theater. And O'Neill's supporters could point out that the Greek and Biblical sources which inspired the play are replete with the very "immoralities" he depicted.

Euripides' *Hippolytus* and Racine's *Phèdre* served as O'Neill's principal models. These works both draw on the archetypal plot in which a father returns from a journey with a wife who falls in love with her new stepson. This attachment, at first resisted or concealed, results in a struggle between father and son. The father achieves a Pyrrhic victory which costs him both son and spouse. The situation is tragic in that all participants are forced to make conscious choices of evil for the sake of a higher good. It is Fate which so structures events as to necessitate the downfall of these essentially noble characters. O'Neill complicates the classic plot by introducing Old Testament motifs: the "hardness" and vengeance of God; the superiority of justice over mercy; and the battle among sons for birthrights and fatherly favor. He also relies on Freudian psychology in treating all sexual relationships.

Does O'Neill finally succeed in giving true tragic stature to his characters? There can be no doubt that the drama possesses genuinely tragic aspects; this much has been confirmed by two generations of criticism. But that the whole deserves the term "tragedy" is doubtful. Three considerations sustain this judgment. First, Eben's basic motivation remains unclear throughout the play as does the central matter of whether he is the rightful heir to the farm. Second, both Abbie and Eben are far too preoccupied with struggles for possession and revenge; they lack that nobility of purpose which we associate with tragic characters like Oedipus, Antigone, or Hippolytus. Third, Eben is made to seem so totally a victim of psychological drives that his choices are not freely arrived at. Especially this latter element makes *pathos,* not tragedy, the dominant quality in *Desire Under the Elms.*

Edgar F. Racey, Jr., has persuasively argued that O'Neill designed his play around a single moral fact: Ephraim Cabot ruined the life of Eben's mother —"murdered her with his hardness," as Eben says—and this sin now cries out for retribution. O'Neill's opening stage directions indicate his intention. The two enormous elms which bend over the farm house are to be expression-istically rendered; they should suggest suffering women and dominate the entire scene with "a sinister maternity." From the beginning, Eben proclaims his monomaniacal desire to take "her vengeance on him—so's she kin rest quiet in her grave." When Abbie enters the parlor, her scheming and erotic tendencies are momentarily subdued by the felt presence of the dead woman's spirit. Eben does not allow himself to be seduced until he is assured that he is doing his mother's will.

The structure of the action reinforces this central theme. In Part One, Eben solidifies his claim to the farm by inducing his half brothers to leave. He uses his mother's money in the process, thus depriving Ephraim of both the fortune and the assistance of his older sons. In Part Two, Eben takes Ephraim's wife from him, begets a son, and sets in motion the process where-by Ephraim is humiliated in the eyes of the community. In Part Three, Abbie's killing of the child prevents Ephraim from naming a new heir. Further, the departure of Abbie and Eben dooms Ephraim to that condition of isolation which he has always feared above all. He becomes in effect an exile, living on a farm which now is a curse to him. The pattern of crime and justified punishment has been completed.

Tragic in outline, *Desire Under the Elms* is, however, less than tragic in substance. Quite inexplicably, O'Neill lets the basic issue of Ephraim's perse-cution of Eben's mother become clouded. Since we learn of her suffering only from Eben himself, some skepticism about his truthfulness is engendered. This skepticism grows when two additional factors come into view: Eben's overwhelming Oedipus complex and his deep desire to inherit the farm. That

Eben stands to benefit economically by his revenge-taking tends to tarnish his character and further undermine his credibility. O'Neill intensifies this economic theme both by showing how deeply Peter and Simeon covet the farm, and by casting doubt on Eben's claim that he has a clear legal right of ownership. Ephraim discounts this claim completely, and we are inclined to believe that his long work of reclamation gives him at least some moral right to the property.

More importantly, O'Neill does not seem to realize that the addition of certain Freudian motifs is not compatible with his purpose. For Freud, fathers and sons are natural rivals; despite the outward show of paternal and filial love, they both unconsciously desire to monopolize the love and sexual favor of "their" woman. This tendency operates even if the father treats the mother with perfect love and respect. This Ephraim most certainly did not do. But how much of Eben's motive is Oedipal and how much is filial devotion? The very fact that such a question can arise demonstrates O'Neill's failure to produce a convincingly tragic work. Had Eben's duty to avenge his mother's suffering run directly counter to his psychological and economic needs, he might have assumed tragic stature. In this respect the case for *Mourning Becomes Electra* as tragedy is much stronger.

Ironically, the fact that *Desire Under the Elms* is not fully realized tragedy probably accounts partially for its appeal, as does O'Neill's choice of a pastoral, precivilized setting which helps convey the workings of unconscious forces with astonishing power.

Despite the fact that the outraged protests responsible for such odd and sensational events as the Los Angeles court case came from irate middle-class viewers, such viewers were only a small minority; actually it was the literate American middle class which formed O'Neill's most avid audience. O'Neill was an iconoclast whose attacks, likened in one of his early poems to torpedoes fired from the submarine of his soul, were directed against middle-class complacency. Much to its credit, however, the audience whose values were under fire responded to plays such as *Desire Under the Elms* with that respect and enthusiasm which springs from recognition of the truth, however disconcerting or uncomfortable that truth may be.

Leslie E. Gerber

DESTINY BAY

Type of work: Short stories
Author: Donn Byrne (Brian Oswald Donn-Byrne, 1889-1928)
Type of plot: Regional romance
Time of plot: Early twentieth century
Locale: Ireland
First published: 1928

Destiny Bay is a series of nine stories, differing greatly in length, which are told by Kerry McFarlane, heir to Destiny Bay, a house and district in the northern part of Ireland. Both the region and the characters are wonderfully colorful and powerful. The setting is a region of high hills, wild ocean, sun, and heather, inhabited by courtly individuals whose stories are full of courage and humor.

In the preface to one of his works, Donn Byrne made the rather immodest claim that he was the last of the great Irish storytellers. Certainly the statement was an exaggeration, but it nevertheless accurately identified the author's two main appeals: his gift for engaging the reader's imagination through romantic and effectively told tales; and his ability to capture in his prose the spirit of the Irish people and the beauty of the land where he grew up. All of Byrne's fiction, whether novels or short stories, reflects these two concerns, and reveals the author's preoccupation with Irish themes and love of his childhood home.

Destiny Bay was the first of a series of Byrne's works which were published posthumously. In form it is a collection of nine short stories which are unified by their common narrator, Kerry MacFarlane, who will inherit his uncle's estate in Destiny Bay. The point of view of Kerry—a thinly disguised version of the author as a young man—gives consistency to the tales, as does Byrne's use of the same cast of characters throughout the book, with a different character coming into prominence in each new story. The characterizations in *Destiny Bay* are not deep, but they are colorful and memorable in their lovable eccentricities. Leading the cast is the protective, patriarchal figure of Uncle Valentine, with his red beard so huge that it covers his chest like a breastplate, and his blind sister Jenepher, who whistles bird calls and "sees," with her wisdom and kindliness, much more clearly than anyone around her. The minor characters are equally romantic and eccentric: Uncle Cosimo, driven to alcohol over love of a Chinese girl he has seen but never met; his faithful gipsy friend Anselo, who travels six years to find Cosimo a replacement for the "Fair Maid of Wu"; James Carabine the prizefighter, who is taken in by a scheming New York singer and left heartbroken; the Spanish duke's shy and elusive "grandson," who turns out to be Ann-Dolly; and her eventual husband, the courtly and sensitive dreamer Jenico.

The incidents which form the plots of Byrne's stories are as romantically improbable as his characters. Stories such as that of Ann-Dolly's disguise as

Don Anthony, Cosimo's deliverance from drink and subsequent missionary work in London, and Uncle Valentine's twelve-year correspondence with Aunt Jenepher under the name of her dead lover Digory, abound in *Destiny Bay*. But what ties such scattered events as these together is the ever-present Irish background. The nostalgic mood and vivid setting is established early in the first tale, and remains, as tangible a presence almost as the characters themselves, throughout the book. Although Destiny Bay is not on any map of Ireland, Byrne's stories make it a real place, with its thirty square miles of territory on the North Sea, unvisited by any trade save that of the gipsies; with its sometimes gentle, sometimes ruthless coast, and its brown bogland studded with flowers and inhabited only by snipes and moor hens; with its tall mountains purple with heather and its tiny, ten-house village of Ballyfale.

When Donn Byrne died in 1928 in an automobile accident, he was only thirty-nine years old. When one reads his lyrical descriptions, rich with Gaelic imagery and vivid scenes of natural beauty, one feels that if his talent falls far short of excellence, he nevertheless died with a great deal of his potential yet unrealized.

THE DEVIL'S ELIXIR

Type of work: Novel
Author: Ernst Theodor Amadeus Hoffmann (1776-1822)
Type of plot: Psychological fantasy
Time of plot: Eighteenth century
Locale: Germany and Italy
First published: 1815-1816

This psychological fantasy deals with an innocent who sins and is then confronted by all the devices of the powers of darkness. Customary to his style, E.T.A. Hoffmann presents the bizarre as an ironic facet of the natural in this work. He takes pleasure in creating odd situations and weaving out of them a confusing and fantastic web of associations, intimations, and recapitulations, all made grotesque, of what had gone before. Throughout, as soon as a reasonable pattern begins to emerge from the course of events, a new mystery rises to destroy it.

From a plot summary, this novel seems like the purest madness, barely comprehensible, a series of nightmarish adventures woven into an incredible framework of family relationships. While it is true that Hoffmann's talent leaned more to the short story form, this work, his only completed novel, does reveal beneath all the fantastic elements, a coherent structure and a conscious plan. There is a polarity between the convent world, where the novel begins and ends, and the world of sin and chaos, represented in the central section of the work. The life of Medardus follows the traditional pattern of a redemption myth. One is reminded inevitably of Parzival, or of a saint's life. The elixir, in fact, is a relic of Saint Anthony, given to him as a temptation, which he resisted. Medardus, lacking the strength of that hero of asceticism, succumbs, falls from grace, and sinks into crime, sin, and guilt. This life of crime is also one of madness, from which he is released only as he comes to expiation and reconciliation with the world of faith. Many of the trappings of the fantastic adventures are simply borrowed from popular literary tastes of the day: the family curse, the hidden relationships, fatal dangers, and the like. But Hoffmann himself had a deep fascination with the dark side of the human psyche. He was acquainted with the director of an insane asylum, and he feared at times for his own sanity. The device of the *Doppelganger,* or Double, expresses this potential for madness hidden within every sane man. This madness seems rampant in the world of chaos Hoffmann depicts; here as in several works, the convent appears as a symbol for the refuge which he could never obtain, a world ordered by Christian faith, where the Divine still intervenes in human life.

THE DEVOTION OF THE CROSS

Type of work: Drama
Author: Pedro Calderón de la Barca (1600-1681)
Type of plot: Religious tragedy
Time of plot: Seventeenth century
Locale: Siena, Italy
First presented: c. 1633

The most popular Spanish playwright after the death of Lope de Vega in 1635, Calderón de la Barca wrote both secular and religious dramas until he took holy orders in 1651. Althouth The Devotion of the Cross *appears in many versions, all that is definite is that the author claimed it under its present title in his* Primera Parte *of 1636. It is representative of the deeply religious feelings and ideas of seventeenth century Spain.*

For Calderón's contemporaries, *The Devotion of the Cross* was little more than a religious thriller, a lesson in heavenly clemency steeped in blood and spiced with incest. Some modern readers, however, have been annoyed by the play's apparent hypocrisy, its religious propaganda, and its perverse morality, a code that pardons the devout, but is unsympathetic to the criminal. But only when the play is read allegorically does it become intelligible despite its strange morality.

To the allegorical, the world is a permanent battleground for the conflict between body and soul. Calderón's *The Devotion of the Cross* presents just such a struggle. The soul (Eusebio) and the body (Julia) seek to be reunited but are frustrated. Yet Calderón's allegory goes deeper. Through Eusebio, its chief character, the play represents the figurative fall and redemption of mankind. Eusebio gradually becomes transformed from the human agent of his crimes into a symbolic force voicing the redemptive hope of all mankind. In this manner, he defeats the exactions of earthly penalties, and also overcomes the harsh, tyrannical laws of honor represented by Curcio, the father who survives his wife and all his children.

As a figure for the fallen Adam, Eusebio is redeemed by the Cross ("tree divine") which bears him heavenward, thus fulfilling his "secret cause." Julia, Eusebio's twin, may be said to be Eve and shares a common destiny with Eusebio, part of which is to be restored through grace by the cross, the tree of eternal life. The concept of incest in this play represents original sin and frustrates the reunion of body and soul in the figures of Eusebio and Julia.

Calderón, whose favorite theme of honor is eclipsed in the play by the incest situation, is not as comfortable in these surroundings as he is within the confines of the themes of his other plays. There is a blurring of dramatic action and an impression of structural imbalance which weakens the drama. Yet these weaknesses are somewhat overcome by the play's resonant tone of outrage and the depths of implication at its center.

LE DIABLE BOITEUX

Type of work: Novel
Author: Alain René Le Sage (1668-1747)
Type of plot: Picaresque romance
Time of plot: Early eighteenth century
Locale: Madrid
First published: 1707

Although known today for his long picaresque novel Gil Blas, *Le Sage's earlier publication of* Le Diable boiteux *created far more excitement in his own day. An interesting example of an early realistic novel of manners, the work contains a wealth of anecdotes and reminiscences, portraits and sketches of some of the most prominent Parisian personages. His satire, trenchant and ironic, is best focused on persons of quality and society. Like most picaresque fiction, the novel is loosely plotted; within a central narrative concerning the fortunes of Don Cleophas, a young Spanish cavalier, Le Sage introduces scores of other tales, ranging from brief summaries of a few sentences to short stories running pages or chapters.*

Although a satire on human nature, *Le Diable boiteux* is an amiable, almost lighthearted work; the author attacks his victims with wit and grace, his high spirits and good humor balancing the grotesqueness inherent in the story. Asmodeus, the lame devil, helps Don Cleophas to see through the false fronts, both physical and moral, assumed by most people. The devil and his young rescuer thereby provide a framework for the stories that compose most of the narrative; Asmodeus shows Don Cleophas a man or woman and then exposes the person, telling his or her story with merciless truth. If there is any consistent message in *Le Diable boiteux,* it is always to doubt first impressions and to seek to penetrate beneath the façades that individuals hold up to the world.

Asmodeus is a unique character, a grotesque vision comparable to Caliban or Milton's fallen angels. Without possessing the dark powers of the greater demons, he presides over the vices and follies of mankind, rather than the crimes. He is malicious, but not cruel, and likes to tease and ridicule humanity, rather than to torture it. He possesses so much wit and playful malice and is so vividly portrayed that he almost walks away with the book, making the reader forget that he is not intended to be anything more than a momentarily friendly fiend.

Don Cleophas, the fiery young Spaniard, is the perfect foil for Asmodeus. He is lacking enough in discretion to be glad of the opportunity to peek behind closed doors and barred windows and discover the shocking truths about apparently respectable people. The other characters, who come and go in the secondary tales, are described with precision and amazing dexterity; few authors can summarize human nature, in its many shades and phases, in so few words. Le Sage's satire is never heavy-handed and his humor is never blunted by anticipation. In many respects, *Le Diable boiteux* is surer of touch and wittier than the author's more famous *Gil Blas;* certainly, the skill of the drawing of the scenes and the richness of the characterizations are reason enough for the book to be at least as well known. And, at times, the author reaches heights in this book that he never does in *Gil Blas,* such as in his personification of Death. Even here, his humor breaks through to add still another dimension to his vision, when, having described one of the terrific phantom's wings painted with war, pestilence, famine, and shipwreck, he adorns the other with the picture of young physicians taking their degrees. The narratives that make up the book are of differing lengths and of varying interest, but all of them are entertaining and executed with wit and style.

DIANA OF THE CROSSWAYS

Type of work: Novel
Author: George Meredith (1828-1909)
Type of plot: Psychological realism
Time of plot: Nineteenth century
Locale: England
First published: 1885

Diana, beautiful, witty, and skeptical of social convention and moral expediency, is the embodiment of George Meredith's philosophy and art. As such, she is a character far above most heroines of nineteenth century English novels. She offers the charm of femininity, perplexed by convention and yet aware of its force. Her career compels a belief that life will not let go its harvest of errors until they are thoroughly winnowed in a human drama of deepest interest, for life extracts the wisdom experience can offer.

Diana of the Crossways is the most emphatically "feminist" of Meredith's novels, but the woman too intelligent and spirited to accept willingly her "place," as defined by Victorian society, figures prominently in virtually all of his fiction. Some, such as Diana's friend Emma Dunstane or Lady Blandish of *The Ordeal of Richard Feverel,* manage to confine their protest to witty commentary while playing their assigned roles; others, like Diana, are forced by circumstances into active rebellion.

It is generally agreed that Meredith's chief model for his beautiful, brilliant, and hard-beset heroines was his own first wife. In the fine poem sequence *Modern Love,* he traces in thin disguise the course of their marriage, from its happy and passionate beginnings, through the conflicts that led to his wife's running off with an artist, to her early death. Although bitter at first, Meredith learned much from the failure of his first love and came to accept major responsibility for it. His novels repeatedly depict a loving and loyal woman virtually driven into the arms of another man by the blind egotism of her husband or lover. Asked by Robert Louis Stevenson whether the protagonist of *The Egoist* was not a portrait of him, Meredith replied that his fatuous hero was drawn "from all of us but principally from myself."

Meredith saw his society as dominated by egotism, chiefly male, and both fearful and suspicious of the bright and beautiful because of the threat they posed to complacency. He shared the Victorian belief in progress, but he defined progress in terms of intelligence and sensibility. Choosing the comedy of wit as his preferred mode, he attacked the dull and smug, and called for "brain, more brain." He recognized the tragedy of life but ascribed it to human failure. As he wrote in *Modern Love,* "no villain need be. We are betrayed by what is false within." The falseness may spring from self-deception or from unquestioning acceptance of what "the world" proclaims. What can save us is the ability to be honest with ourselves and see the world as it is, and the courage to act on our perceptions even in defiance of social norms.

Many of Meredith's contemporaries shared his belief in a continuing evolution of man's spiritual and intellectual capacities, but few besides Browning were as ardent in affirming also "the value and significance of flesh." For Meredith, the goal of life was to realize one's full potentialities in a vital balance: "The spirit must brand the flesh that it may live."

Meredith's Diana fully exemplifies his philosophy of life. The central metaphor of the novel is the "dog-world" in hot pursuit of its quarry, a beautiful woman too intelligent and sensitive to play the roles society demands of her, either "parasite" or "chalice." Yet Diana is no spotless, perfect victim of malign persecutors. In precept and practice, Meredith scorned sentimental melodrama. Young and inexperienced, Diana brings much of her trouble on herself. She marries for protection and position, a prudent move by worldly standards, but disastrous in its consequences. Achieving a measure of independence, she soon endangers it by her extravagance, and she is finally almost destroyed by an impulsive act of desperation. Although elements of the "dog-world" are moved by envy and malice, most of Diana's adversaries act "honorably" in their own eyes; it is the conventions of honor, respectability, and— most importantly—of woman's place in Victorian society that nearly overpowers her.

The resolution of the plot would seem a compromise if the novel were the feminist tract it has been called: Diana does not finally triumph as a fully independent person, accepted by society on her own terms and admired for her wit and nerve. Only rescued from despair by her friend Emma, she does prove herself capable of standing alone but chooses instead to marry again. As Meredith presents her choice, however, it is not compromise but fulfillment. Her marriage to Redworth, who truly understands and values her, represents the ideal wedding of flesh and spirit, achieved not by good luck but by striving, blundering, learning from mistakes, and finally seeing and accepting life as it is.

Diana of the Crossways was an immediate success upon publication, probably because its theme had been taken from a recent scandal involving a brilliant and beautiful Irishwoman, Mrs. Caroline Norton, who had been accused (as it proved, falsely) of selling an important government secret. However, the novel has not maintained its popularity, despite its wit, its vitality, and its vivid characterizations. Critics generally rate it high among Meredith's works, often second only to his masterpiece *The Egoist,* and its themes are of perhaps even broader interest today than they were in 1885, yet it is apparently little read. The difficulty is probably with Meredith's famous style, the joy and the despair of his admirers.

From his first work of fiction, *The Shaving of Shagpat,* to his last, the prose of this admirable poet became progressively more poetic in its richness, its precision, its compactness, and its indirection. In the earlier novels, it is a beautiful addition to plot and characterization; in the later, it may detract from or even obscure them. Oscar Wilde may not have been entirely right in saying that as a novelist Meredith could do everything but tell a story; but in *Diana of the Crossways* and other later novels, he often seems fastidiously averse to saying anything directly. The texture of his prose places demands upon his readers that not all are willing to meet. The attentive reader is richly rewarded in beauty, wit, and subtlety of thought and expression. Let his attention waver, though, and he may find that he has missed a significant turn in the plot.

The very dazzle and density of Meredith's style, embodying as it does his vigorous and invigorating vision of life, will certainly continue to delight those willing to submit to it; among less strenuous readers, however, he may continue to be as he has been for decades, more honored than read.

Katharine Bail Hoskins

THE DIARY OF A COUNTRY PRIEST

Type of work: Novel
Author: Georges Bernanos (1888-1948)
Type of plot: Psychological realism
Time of plot: The 1920's
Locale: France
First published: 1937

This novel, meager of plot because Bernanos is more concerned with showing a man's thoughts and basic principles than with picturing human behavior, describes the struggles of a young priest, uncertain as to whether his interventions into the Count's family is service to God, and wrestling with his diseased body and ineffective parish projects. A realistic and philosophical treatment of life in a small French parish, the novel is characterized by compassion and tenderness.

A Catholic novelist in the manner of Julian Green and François Mauriac, Georges Bernanos was a visionary for whom the forces of good and evil were genuine presences. He shows a fierce integrity in his writing, although sometimes his views are oversimplified or inconsistent. His characters, while representing extremes of human behavior from saintliness to depravity, are battlegrounds for good and evil, and their souls the prize. These people are powerfully imagined and realistically drawn, particularly the priests and other individuals who devote their lives to God.

One of the themes of *The Diary of a Country Priest* is that of the conflict between individual religious ecstasy and the day to day "housekeeping" of the Church. The young priest's aspirations, at once naïve and noble, are very touching, but his failure to live up to them causes him increasing unhappiness. Above all, he wants to be of use to God and to his parishioners, but he feels thwarted at every step and is not sure why. The picture of the hard, narrow villagers, with their materialistic and shallow ways, their stubbornness and malice, is vivid and complete; the reader soon understands the pain of the youthful priest's frustration at his inability to elevate them spiritually.

Boredom, Bernanos suggests, is the beginning of evil, or at least the ground in which it grows. The young priest sees that life for his parishioners is nothing but boredom. The nature of injustice worries him as does the nature of true poverty. Everyone constantly gives him advice, warning him of intolerance, excessive dedication, or pride, but none of them can see into his heart and mind and understand what really troubles him. The naïve and unworldly qualities of the young priest give him an innocent charm, despite his almost frightening intensity.

Despite his inexperience, the priest knows that "each creature is alone in his distress." His growing wisdom is a growing realization of the loneliness of each individual. From the beginning, he is beset by ailments and becomes obsessed by them; soon, illness dominates his physical existence. But his spiritual life grows richer and more intense.

At the end, the priest has learned that true humility does not lie in self-hatred, but rather that the supreme grace is to "love oneself in all simplicity." His death is revealed in a moving letter from his friend to his superior, expressing his ultimate sense of peace.

DIGBY GRAND

Type of work: Novel
Author: George J. Whyte-Melville (1821-1878)
Type of plot: Picaresque romance
Time of plot: Early nineteenth century
Locale: England
First published: 1853

Digby Grand *was Whyte-Melville's first novel, termed by the author an autobiography of his own early career as an officer in a Highland regiment. Because Whyte-Melville wrote particularly for the sporting world and has been catalogued as a sporting-fiction writer, his place in English literature has never rightfully been claimed. His writings possess an air of liveliness, a note of authenticity, and a unique freshness.*

The values and traditions of Eton play a significant part in this rambling tale of "old boys." The horseman and huntsman (the two aspects of the "gentleman" considered most important, aside from perfect grooming and decorum) are the models that the motherless hero aspires to emulate. His interests are as narrow as those of the people around him; lacking intellectual drive, he is content with a physically active but superficial existence. The military is considered the only "acceptable" career for a gentleman or sportsman such as he early considers himself. Cigars, sherry, and horses are the main interests of the men in the book, except for brief encounters with a tepid form of romance.

The preparations for a career in the Guards are detailed with humor and enthusiasm, and the six-week voyage of the young soldier across the Atlantic is exhaustively presented. The author tends to overwhelm the reader with unselective details, but the enthusiasm of the telling carries the reader over the dull spots, and the unusual facts and novelty of some of the events are often interesting in themselves, although they contribute to no pattern or plot in the book. The novel, like a genuine "autobiography" (as the book is subtitled) simply recounts one event after another. The life of the Guards, on duty in Canada, is described with as much indefatigable detail as everything else in the narrative. The narrator-protagonist devotes much space to describing the scenery he encounters in his travels, from Niagara and Lake Erie to the northwoods sites of hunting parties to the fields and streams of England. In England, America, or wherever the hero is, horses, horse-racing, and hunting play the major part in both his thoughts and actions.

The book is not subtle in either its humor or its efforts for effect. The names of most of the characters suggest caricatures rather than efforts to create fully-developed personalities: for example, the reader encounters Admiral Portfire, Mr. Stubble, Arabella Ramrod, Lawyer Sheepskin, and Mrs. Mantrap. The heroines are all conventional, pale maidens, with little per-

546   *Digby Grand*/WHYTE-MELVILLE

sonality of their own; they are merely mannequins of ethereal beauty upon which the hero can shine his admiration and devotion.

The strengths of the novel lie in the density of the narrative and the variety and vividness of the boldly sketched characterizations. Some of the characters are overdrawn, but others are humorous and colorful, and often entertaining. The accounts of the activities of the class portrayed (gambling, hunting, racing) are described with authenticity. As a record of the attitudes and occupations of these people and their age, the mid-Victorian period, the book presents an interesting, if limited, portrait. By the highest, most objective standards, the book is greatly flawed, but it has a place in literary history as an example of a type of popular novel and in social history as a document of a bygone era.

THE DISCIPLE

Type of work: Novel
Author: Paul Bourget (1852-1935)
Type of plot: Psychological realism
Time of plot: Late nineteenth century
Locale: Paris and Riom
First published: 1889

Paul Bourget represents a transition in French letters from naturalistic material-ism to the more traditional religious and moral disciplines. The Disciple, an impeccable novel combining solid psychological analysis with a sensational murder story, marks the midpoint in Bourget's career. The work is a psychological study of the moral bases in abstract learning.

Paul Bourget defines the moralist as a writer who not only portrays life exactly as it is, but deals with its profound lessons of secret atonement. In the Preface of *The Disciple,* he proclaims that it is a writer's duty to point out the cure for the evils of his time. With an almost Jansenistic rigor, Bourget in this novel, denounces perversities and disorders of human nature and attempts to find the remedy for them. Inspired by the environmental theory, he attacks belief in the power of science and certain types of progress that stem from scientific systems. *The Disciple* caused Bourget to be widely acclaimed as the founder of the Catholic psychological novel, due in part to his proposed solutions to social problems. His ideas in *The Disciple* are reactions against the positivism and skepticism that dominated the novels of some of his contemporaries in the French literary world, notably Anatole France.

Although Bourget vigorously criticizes society in *The Disciple,* he was able to see a solution to its problems. He found it not in socialism as did Zola and France, for example, but in a return to Christianity. This marked a change in the author's point of view from detached psychologist to a con-vinced moralist. Further, it marked the arrival of a new epoch in the French novel. The book caused a sensation, and certain intellectual battles raged over it. Anatole France, as might be expected, expressed a strong negative reaction to it, but others, notably the critic Ferdinand Brunstiere, himself a moralist, hotly defended it. It was admitted by all factions, however, that *The Disciple* marked an important date in the intellectual and moral history of France. Modern critics have found Bourget's moralistic attitude and Roman Catholic sympathies disproportionately evident in this book and the ones following it, but the novel is still widely read for its superb psychological studies and for its influence on the modern psychosociological novel.

THE DIVINE COMEDY

Type of work: Poem
Author: Dante Alighieri (1265-1321)
Type of plot: Christian allegory
Time of plot: The Friday before Easter, 1300
Locale: Hell, Purgatory, Paradise
First transcribed: c.1320

Dante's greatest work, an epic poem in one hundred cantos, is divided equally after an introductory canto into sections, each thirty-three cantos in length, which see Dante and a guide respectively through Hell, Purgatory, and Paradise. The cosmology, angelology, and theology of the poem are based on St. Thomas Aquinas. Dante's literal journey is also an allegory of the progress of the human soul toward God and the progress of political and social mankind toward peace on earth. Characterization is drawn from ancient Roman history and from Dante's contemporary Italy, making the work a realistic picture and an intensely involved analysis of human affairs and life, even though in structure it appears to be a description of the beyond. It is, in essence, a compassionate, moral evaluation of human nature and a mystic vision of the Absolute toward which mankind strives, and it endures more through the universality of the drama and the lyric quality of the poetry than through specific doctrinal content.

Dante was born into an aristocratic Florentine family. Unusually well educated even for his time and place, he was knowledgeable in science and philosophy and was an active man of letters as well as an artist. He lived in politically tumultuous times and was active in politics and government. All of his knowledge, his experience, and his skill were brought to bear in his writings. During an absence from Florence in 1302, he was sentenced to exile for opposing the government then in power. For a time, he engaged in revolutionary activities, but even later he was never allowed to return to his beloved Florence upon pain of being burned. In exile, Dante wrote *The Divine Comedy*. He died in Ravenna.

This masterpiece was originally written in Italian, but Dante also wrote in Latin, the language of scholarship at that time. His Latin treatise *De Vulgari Eloquentia* (On the Vulgar Tongue)—a compelling defense of the use of the written vernacular, instead of Latin—argued in conventional Latin the superiority of unconventional written Italian as a medium of expression. His other major Latin treatise was *De Monarchia* (About Monarchy), a political essay. He also used Latin for some very important letters and for a few poems. But Dante's choice was his native Italian. His earliest major work—*La Vita Nuova* (The New Life), a mystical-spiritual autobiography, combining prose and poetry—was written in Italian. So, too, was *Il Convivio* (The Banquet), a scholarly and philosophical treatise. And he wrote a number of lyric poems in Italian, as well. But standing above all as a tribute to the eloquence of written Italian is *The Divine Comedy*.

La Commedia—as it was first titled; *Divina* was added later—is an incredibly complex work. It is divided into three sections, or canticles, the *Inferno* (Hell), the *Purgatorio* (Purgatory), and the *Paradiso* (Heaven). The entire work is composed of 100 cantos, apportioned into segments of 34 *(Inferno)*, 33 *(Purgatorio)*, and 33 *(Paradiso)*. The rhyme scheme is called *terza rima*—aba bab cbc dcd—resulting in each rhyme occurring three times to create an interlocking scheme which produces a very closely knit poem. This structure is neither arbitrary nor a mere intellectual exercise.

Number symbolism plays an important part in *The Divine Comedy*. As an essentially Christian poem, it relies heavily on mystical associations with numbers. Inasmuch as the poem deals with Christian religious concepts, it is not difficult to discern the relationship between one poem in three canticles and one God in Three Persons. So, too, *terza rima* becomes significant. But then more complex intricacies come into play. The unity or oneness of God is diffused on a metric basis: one is divided into one hundred cantos, for example. And two becomes the duality of nature: corporeal and spiritual, active and contemplative, Church and State, Old Testament and New, and so on. Three signifies Father, Son, Holy Ghost; Power, Wisdom, Love; Faith, Hope, Charity; and other combinations. Four—as in seasons, elements, humors, directions, cardinal virtues—combines with three to make a mystical seven: days of creation, days of the week (length of Dante's journey), seven virtues and seven vices (cf. seven levels of Purgatory), planets and many more. Moreover, multiples of three—three times three equals nine—create further permutations: choirs of angels, circles of Hell, and the like. And adding the mystical unity of one to the product nine makes ten, the metric permutation of one discussed above.

These complex relationships of number symbolism were deliberately contrived by Dante and other medieval writers. Dante himself explained, in *Il Convivio,* his view of the four levels of interpretation of a literary work and by doing so legitimized such explanations of number symbolism. He proposed that a text be read (1) literally, (2) allegorically, (3) morally, and (4) anagogically. The literal reading was, of course, the story itself. The allegorical reading uncovered hidden meanings in the story. The moral reading related to matters of human behavior. And the anagogical reading, accessible to only the most sophisticated, pertained to the absolute and universal truths contained in a work. Hence, *The Divine Comedy* has something of each of these four levels of interpretation.

As a literal story, it has the fascination of autobiographical elements as well as the features of high adventure. The protagonist Dante, led by Vergil, undertakes a journey to learn about himself, the world, and the relations between the two. In the course of his journey, he explores other worlds in order to place his own world in proper perspective. As his journey progresses, he learns.

As an allegorical story, *The Divine Comedy* traces the spiritual enlightenment of Dante's soul. It also delineates social, political, cultural, and scientific
parables. By integrating all of these aspects into an intricately interwoven pattern, the poem becomes an allegory for the real and spiritual world order.

As a moral story, the work has perhaps its greatest impact as a cautionary
tale to warn the reader about the consequences of various categories of
behavior. In the process, it helps the reader to understand sin (Hell), penance
(Purgatory), and salvation (Heaven). Thus, *The Divine Comedy* becomes
a vehicle for teaching moral behavior.

As an anagogical story, the poem offers a mystical vision of God's grand
design for the entire universe. The complex interdependency of all things—
including the web of interrelationships stemming from number symbolism—
is, in this view, all part of the Divine Plan, which humankind can grasp only
partially and dimly. For God remains ineffable to the finite capacities of
human beings, and His will can never be fully apprehended by humans, whose
vision has been impaired by sin. The anagogical aspects of *The Divine
Comedy* are thus but aids for the most spiritually enlightened to approach
Eternal Truth.

To be sure, no brief explanation can do justice to the majesty of this
monumental achievement in the history of Western poetry. The very encyclo-
pedic nature of its scope makes *The Divine Comedy* a key to the study of
medieval civilization. As such, it cannot be easily or properly fragmented into
neat categories for discussion, and the reader must advance on tiptoe, as it
were. Background in history and theology are strongly recommended. But,
above all, the reader must recognize that no sweeping generalization will adequately account for the complexity of ideas or the intricacy of structure in
The Divine Comedy.

Joanne G. Kashdan

THE DIVINE FIRE

Type of work: Novel
Author: May Sinclair (1870?-1946)
Type of plot: Psychological romance
Time of plot: The 1890's
Locale: England
First published: 1904

This modern twentieth century psychological romance is the chronicle of a gifted but unknown poet of genius whose artistry is wasted in a struggle to survive an enormous self-imposed financial burden. His story is one of conflict between genius and the man, with first one then the other being uppermost but with the two never being reconciled. Through the help of an inspiring woman he is at last able to find himself. In this work, May Sinclair is attuned to the important psychological assumptions becoming prominent in the early twentieth century.

The Divine Fire, one of May Sinclair's numerous and varied novels, deals with the frustrations of a young poet of exceptional talent whose valuable energies are wasted in the struggle to make a living and to fulfill an enormous self-imposed financial obligation. Despite the wide variety in her work, Sinclair uses techniques in *The Divine Fire* which are characteristic of her general style; the novel also contains many of the same attitudes and psychological concerns frequently found in her fiction.

Stylistically, May Sinclair is somewhat of a naturalist. Although *The Divine Fire* is relatively long and leisurely paced compared to her other works, it shares with them an acute attention to detail and an objectivity of observation. Through her skillful and unobtrusive selection of which details are to be presented, Sinclair creates a powerful impression of realism that carries its own meaning without need of comment by the author. Thematically, this novel—like her others—reveals a strain of naturalism. Influenced by H. G. Wells, Sinclair was interested in exposing the mediocrity of middle-class values and their deadening effect on the spirit, and in dramatizing how an individual life—whether an unusual one like Keith Rickman's or a quite ordinary one such as Harriet Frean's—is molded by external forces. Thus, Keith Rickman's career illustrates to some extent the dictum found in an earlier novel, *Audrey Craven* (1897): "In our modern mythology, Custom, Circumstance, and Heredity are the three Fates that weave the web of human life." Nevertheless, Sinclair does not approach the pessimisim of Hardy or Dreiser, and she is often unwilling to accept the naturalist solution; Rickman, after all his suffering, is finally recognized as a genius and united with Lucia.

Although May Sinclair was not a Freudian, she was certainly aware of the important psychological assumptions beginning to be made in her generation, and of their implications. We find in all of her work that same sensitivity and insight into emotions and motivations that inspires *The Divine*

Fire. She is particularly aware of the various kinds of oppression that produce frustration; one type that appears frequently—and reminds us of Sinclair's similarities to Henry James—is the oppressiveness of parents toward their children. Also reminiscent of James are her portraits of seemingly nice people who are in reality self-serving and unscrupulous—portraits which reflect not only her interest in the discrepancy between appearances and reality, but her desire to expose hypocrisy and false values.

DOCTOR FAUSTUS

Type of work: Novel
Author: Thomas Mann (1875–1955)
Type of plot: Philosophical chronicle
Time of plot: 1885-1945
Locale: Germany
First published: 1947

Mann's Doctor Faustus, rather than treating directly the Faust legend, uses it as a parallel to the fall of his own hero, Adrian Leverkühn. The work has many levels of understanding. It is a biographical story of a strange and fascinating genius; a story of the destruction of a human soul in the demon-haunted world of the imagination; and a study of the problem of the artist in contemporary society. Leverkühn, who trades his soul to the devil for twenty years of creative genius, symbolizes the German breakthrough to world power; the rise and collapse of the Nazi dream runs parallel to Leverkühn's tragic story. The novel is intricately constructed, profoundly serious, and beautifully written with meanings which extend beyond the purely national and temporal.

This immensely complex work, written in America during the years of Mann's emigration, is both a continuation of his investigation of the relationship between the artist and society begun in his first novel, *Buddenbrooks* (1901), and a symbolic representation of the fate of Germany in this century, intertwining three levels of time in a fabric that is in itself akin to the highly structured, mathematical compositions of the protagonist, Adrian Leverkühn, who may be seen as a projection of Mann, as well as of Germany as a whole. The Faust figure is a creation of the German sixteenth century, a troubled time of religious and political unrest leading up to the catastrophic Thirty Years' War, a time when it seemed to many that the Devil was literally loose upon the earth. The identification of Faust with the German soul is more due to Goethe's *Faust,* however, and the precarious mingling of the demonic with the controlled creativity of art was the subject of Mann's previous novel, *Lotte in Weimar.*

With the historical time level constantly in mind, the actual life of Leverkühn is recounted by his friend, Serenus Zeitblom, who works during the rise and fall of the Nazi regime. If Leverkühn, who, like Faustus, obtains to the highest levels of human knowledge and abstract intellect, falls prey to an inner demon which fructifies his art but at the cost of his capacity to love, so Germany, the "land of poets and philosophers," gives birth to an inner demon who brings about the destruction of the whole society. Nazism is likened to an infection, which is at the same time a pact with the Devil.

Mann constantly shifts from the subject of the novel, Leverkühn, to develop the character of the narrator, Zeitblom, and in the counterpoint between the ironic, isolated, infected artist and the unextraordinary, sometimes bewildered, indeed slightly philistine recorder, Mann creates a texture of interrelationships that demands the utmost concentration from the reader, but which repays him with one of the most profound meditations upon the malaise of our century.

DOCTOR FAUSTUS

Type of work: Drama
Author: Christopher Marlowe (1564-1593)
Type of plot: Romantic tragedy
Time of plot: Sixteenth century
Locale: Germany
First presented: c. 1588

This drama should be regarded as only the skeletal structure of the original play written by Marlowe, since the surviving manuscripts are so interspersed with comic scenes and lines revised at the whim of actors that one must sort and sift to discover Marlowe's original poetry. In addition to the adulterated poetry, there is the problem of altered symbolisms and reinterpreted characterizations; in places, Mephostopilis falls into a caricature, while the exploits of Faustus are frequently rendered pure low comedy. When the hand of Marlowe is discernible, however, the play enjoys considerable artistry, although it is never comparable in depth or scope to the treatment of the same theme in Goethe's Faust.

Marlowe's *Doctor Faustus* is a problematic play, and scholars are strongly divided as to its interpretation. Its dating is uncertain, and its text highly controversial. Yet it is regarded by many as Marlowe's masterpiece, and many scholars argue that even the comic scenes are part of an overall artistic intention, and contribute to, rather than detract from, the serious aspects of the play.

The work is based upon the *Doctor Faustus* published in Germany by Johann Spiess in 1587, in which the characters and almost all the episodes of Marlowe's version appear. But Marlowe concentrated the plot, arranged the episodes in a significant way, and developed the characters of Faustus and Mephostopilis. In Marlowe's hands, Faustus becomes a representative of Renaissance man, intoxicated with the rapid expansion of knowledge, and filled with pride in the power of the human mind. This humanistic pride, however, is countered by the doctrines of the Christian faith, in which man's knowledge is regarded as irrelevant in comparison to God's, and grace, rather than knowledge, is the supreme good.

Faustus in his willful pride rejects God's grace for knowledge and power, though these are offered him by Mephostopilis, a fallen angel damned for his own pride in trying to usurp God's position. Marlowe stresses the irony of Faustus' blindness repeatedly, but Faustus, who is as much poet as scholar, loses himself in grandiose visions and ignores the reality of his situation. Faustus, in fact, gives his soul for trifles—a fact pointed up by the interspersed comic scenes where Faustus' servants imitate his conjuring, expressing their own petty desires. Faustus himself sinks to the level of petty tricks, and finally consoles himself by conjuring up Helen of Troy—who is really only another demon in disguise. At the end, his pride turns to despair, the unforgivable sin, and he wastes his time in irresolution. His life and death are a warning, but more, perhaps, the tragic expression of a man caught between two worlds: Renaissance will and Christian faith.

THE DOCTOR IN SPITE OF HIMSELF

Type of work: Drama
Author: Molière (Jean Baptiste Poquelin, 1622-1673)
Type of plot: Farce
Time of plot: Seventeenth century
Locale: Paris
First presented: 1666

Although this drama is considered one of Molière's less important works, it demonstrates well his ability to ridicule the fads of his day, such as the habit of showing obsequious deference to men of science no matter what their real qualifications may be. Doctors become Molière's prime satiric target in this immediately successful and constantly popular play which exposes the fact that ignorance often hides behind a smattering of superficial learning.

Molière was France's greatest writer of comic drama, and his forte was farce. *The Doctor in Spite of Himself (Le Médecin malgré lui)* is one of his best pure farces. In this play, he takes to task two issues with special contemporary relevance: medical venality and the medical mystique. It was as much a fact of life in Molière's time as it is now that doctors are more concerned about money than about the welfare of patients. Thus, when Sganarelle accedes to the role forced upon him, he does so out of greed, rather than for any other motive. Furthermore, he is able to pull off the charade because of the general cultural attitude toward physicians—a religious respect for the doctor's presumably arcane knowledge. Hence, Sganarelle can indulge his most outrageously eccentric fantasies in the course of deceiving—and bilking —Géronte while pretending (as an authentic doctor would) to cure Lucinde, all the while abetting the latter to elope with the mate of her choice.

In the course of these wildly hectic machinations, Molière manages to assail not only the medical profession but also its gullible clients, as well as social climbers, materialists, impractical lovers, faithless servants, and many other social types endemic to his times and persistent in ours. Such, after all, is the impetus and goal of satire, whether it be couched in Molière's farce, in irony, or in some other comedic form. The point of this kind of drama is to expose human folly and social foibles—a feat which Molière accomplishes with considerable finesse. He makes Sganarelle out to be as foolish as Géronte, and Leandre hardly lags far behind. Lucinde at first appears to have some reasoned craft behind her actions, but finally she is revealed to be as vulnerable, and as crafty, as the rest.

The Doctor in Spite of Himself is not usually included among Molière's masterpieces—*Tartuffe* (1664), *The Misanthrope* (1666), and *The Miser* (1668); however, *The Doctor in Spite of Himself* shares many of the qualities of the presumably greater works. It is superbly crafted as drama; it demonstrates keen insight into character; it portrays universal character types;

and it maintains an unflagging sense of the comic. Although Molière wrote some of his plays—*Tartuffe,* for example—in verse, *The Doctor in Spite of Himself* is written in prose, but without detriment to the play or its pointed barbs. All in all, the play has retained its acerbic wit over the years remarkably well, and Molière's reputation is in no way diminished by its continuing popularity.

DR. JEKYLL AND MR. HYDE

Type of work: Novelette
Author: Robert Louis Stevenson (1850-1894)
Type of plot: Fantasy
Time of plot: Nineteenth century
Locale: London
First published: 1886

This classic romantic adventure and fantasy has steadily maintained its popularity ever since it was first published in 1886. Based upon the dual personalities of a single man representing beauty and beast, Stevenson's understanding of human nature and his mastery of English prose provide the story with subtle values as an illustration of man's dual nature.

The gothic Novel in England enjoyed its heyday in the eighteenth century. In this sense, Robert Louis Stevenson's *Dr. Jekyll and Mr. Hyde* is but a late appendage to a popular trend. In terms of content and style, however, it is in the mainstream of that highly popular genre. The novel has predilections for the far and remote, the marvelous and abnormal. It is an escape from reality, emphasizing intuition over reason and impulse over rationality. Like most romantic novels, it values impulsive, childlike, savage, or peasant behavior as uncorrupted by civilized ways. It is transcendental, grotesque, and bizarre while maintaining a sensitive approach to nature, beauty, and women. It is anti-intellectual and Rousseauistic in philosophy, but it is notable for being remote, simple, and democratic while focusing on the supernatural.

The central feature of *Dr. Jekyll and Mr. Hyde* is its theme of duality. Two personalities—opposite and antagonistic—mesh within one body, a psychological insight which, in its time, was remarkably prescient. Dr. Jekyll, an essentially good man, was fascinated by the idea of evil. As a research scientist, he pursued the idea to the point of developing a drug which would alter his conscious state from an intrinsically good person to a fundamentally bad one. Taking the drug, he developed a dual personality, combining the extremes of good and evil. The evil self emerged as the violent Mr. Hyde. This schizophrenia persisted until the "bad" Mr. Hyde overcame "good" Dr. Jekyll to become the dominant personality of the two—at which time it became apparent that Mr. Hyde would have to be annihilated—by then a solution both inevitable and desirable.

The process of transformation was alchemic, tainted with witchcraft. This touch of the occult—a distinct Gothic feature—rescued the novel from the banal, and elevated it to the realm of genuine Gothic horror. Alchemy, witchcraft, and the occult were to earlier ages what technology—especially the computer—is to the present day: a threat to the status quo and comfortable assumptions. The occult and technology are usually treated in like manner: with awe and apprehension. *Dr. Jekyll and Mr. Hyde* continues to

fascinate readers—as well as motion picture audiences—for just those qualities of verisimilitude, fear, and hostility. The novel ultimately succeeds by
terrifying us, for who among us does not contain the potential for developing
that split personality of good and evil which the protagonist so vividly portrays. It is Stevenson's almost mystical capacity in language and characterization to evoke reader identification with his protagonist which accounts for
the powerful impact of his novel.

DOCTOR PASCAL

Type of work: Novel
Author: Emile Zola (1840-1902)
Type of plot: Naturalism
Time of plot: Late nineteenth century
Locale: The south of France
First published: 1893

This is the last volume of twenty in the Rougon-Macquart series, in which Zola intended to apply the methods of experimental science to the social novel. Using Dr. Pascal, a Rougon, as a researcher in heredity who chooses his own family for investigation, the novel allows Zola the opportunity to conclude the whole series with flashbacks to the former volumes and to expose his own conceptions of reality through Pascal's exposition of his theories.

Doctor Pascal, the twentieth and final novel in Zola's Rougon-Macquart series, is significant both as a reflection of Zola's personal life and as the culmination of his vast, ambitious "history of the Second Empire." If *Doctor Pascal* does not possess the literary energy of some of the other novels in the Rougon-Macquart series, it does reveal many of Zola's characteristic interests and obsessions.

Doctor Pascal centers on the love between an older doctor and a young woman, his niece. This relationship mirrors Zola's love for Jeanne Rozerot, a seamstress that Zola's wife had hired. Jeanne was a beautiful, modest girl twenty years old. Zola made her his mistress in 1888 (he was near fifty at the time) and promptly went on two crash diets to lose weight. Apparently, he loved her very much and eventually had two children by her (although he had none by his wife, Alexandrine). He was not willing to divorce his wife, however, despite the fact that he scorned extramarital affairs. Alexandrine had stuck by him in very hard times, and no matter how much he loved Jeanne, he was not willing to walk away from his wife. Alexandrine was furious when she heard about the affair. But after Zola died, she acted most humanely, met the children, treated them kindly, and even made it legally possible for them to bear their father's name.

In any case, it is clear that *Doctor Pascal* is a very personal novel in terms· of the life of the novelist. But it is also personal in the sense that Doctor Pascal, as much as any other character in Zola's fiction, directly reflects the intellectual interest and commitments of the author. Doctor Pascal the scientist is devoted to curing nervous disorders and to keeping a record of his family. First, Zola often viewed himself and his work as "scientific." In opposition to what he considered to be the unreality of the romantics, Zola was determined to place his work on a firm scientific basis; and, in fact, he often saw his own fiction as a form of "experimentation." Second, Doctor Pascal's record of the Rougon-Macquart family permits Zola to review the chronicle of the figures and incidents in this "history" and, at the same time, to express his views on the significance of heredity in the affairs of men and families. Doctor Pascal and, by inference, Zola take the genetic material of the Rougon-Macquarts with extreme seriousness. Although the laws of heredity may not be completely understood, and although Dr. Pascal's injections are not medically successful, Doctor Pascal's belief in the power and explanatory force of science remains unshaken.

In fact, Doctor Pascal's belief in science—and the opposition to that belief —form the chief intellectual concern of the novel. There are two objections to the doctor's scientific approach, religious and social. The former, though virulent, is ultimately less threatening to Zola than the latter. Doctor Pascal's treasured servant, Martine, is opposed to Pascal's "tampering" with God's plan. But she only takes action to help destroy the doctor's valued historical files when she is incited by Madame Rougon, Doctor Pascal's mother.

Madame Rougon's motives are entirely selfish. She does not want the honor of the family stained by an exposure of defects. Her only pride is her family, and she cannot tolerate the prospect of the family's being shamed in years to come when Pascal's files are opened. Taking advantage of Martine's simplicity, she finally succeeds in destroying all of Pascal's meticulously recorded chronicle. In a sense, this destruction of the family records is a logical conclusion of the degeneration of the Rougon-Macquarts. The family —a few branches still growing, others degenerated and collapsed—is self-destructive.

But an interesting question, if the parallel between Pascal and Zola holds, is whether Zola's literary work is also metaphorically destroyed as the Rougon-Macquart series comes to an end. Perhaps Zola believed that life would take its revenge on literature, that the truth he sought to express could not be borne. The forces of reaction, both social and religious, would stifle and burn his work.

That fate was not in store for Zola's literary work, though it was, in a sense, in store for Zola himself. Shortly after the publication of *Doctor Pascal,* Zola intervened in the notorious Dreyfus affair. Dreyfus, a Jewish officer, was convicted of treason by the French authorities. The conviction was, incredibly, upheld despite the fact that another officer actually confessed to the crime and fled the country. Clearly, the issue was racism (anti-Semitism), not treason, and Zola could not resist attacking the authorities for their cover-ups, hypocrisy, lying, and racism. As a result, Zola was forced to go into temporary exile in England.

Zola's courageous action in behalf of Dreyfus, and his opposition to anti-Semitism, are especially important in evaluating Zola's naturalist theory, a theory that occupies such a central role in *Doctor Pascal.* Because of Zola's emphasis on genetic determinism, his work might be open to accusations of racialism. Because of the stress he places on forces that mold men's lives, over which they have no control, he also may be accused of fatalism. As a result, the critic Georg Lukacs, for example, refuses even to include Zola in the literary tradition of progressive realism. But the fact is that, in his literature as well as in his life, Zola affirmed his confidence in the forces of science, progress, and, above all, life. Despite the destruction of the doctor's files, the reader is left with the impression, at the end of the novel, that Doctor Pascal's work will continue after him. It is the love between the doctor and his niece which is responsible for this impression.

The emotional interest of the narrative, the center of gravity of the fiction, lies in the love of an older man for a young woman. Zola explores their feelings with extreme delicacy and insight; and the child resulting from their love is meant to signify the rebirth of hope and humanity. The child more than compensates for the destruction of the files. If that destruction is seen as revenge against scholarship, science, and art, then the birth of the child signals the victory of the positive forces of life over the forces of despair and negativism.

The literary qualities of the novel are, however, uneven. The style is some times lyrical and moving (as in physical descriptions of the countryside and of Clotilde's and Pascal's lovemaking), but at other times it is slow moving and even ponderous. Further, though Pascal, Martine, Madame Rougon, and Clotilde are well conceived and portrayed, there is an absence of those numerous, strong secondary characters which lend so much life to other novels in the Rougon-Macquart series.

Although there is significant intellectual content in the novel and although the novel is highly relevant to Zola's life and career, one feels a certain weariness in Zola's telling. But Zola had already written an enormous number of pages in his vast chronicle. Further, like Doctor Pascal, Zola was no longer a young man. If the narrative lacks the intensity of his earlier works, it nevertheless glows with compassion and loving faith; and these qualities, so rarely associated with the name of Zola or his works, certainly deserve to be recognized.

Howard Lee Hertz

DOCTOR THORNE

Type of work: Novel
Author: Anthony Trollope (1815-1882)
Type of plot: Domestic realism
Time of plot: Mid-nineteenth century
Locale: "Barsetshire," England
First published: 1858

   This third novel in the Barchester Series continues the mixture of sentiment, humor, romance, and fidelity to human nature and experience of Trollope's chronicle of clerical and country life. The usual Trollopian theme of making money and a successful marriage is portrayed against the background of an English country estate and the life connected with it. Trollope's chief value lies in his authentic depiction of middle-class country life in nineteenth century England, which reproduces better than that of any other writer of his time the manners and morals of the Victorian period.

   The third novel in Trollope's Barsetshire series, *Doctor Thorne,* like its two predecessors, *The Warden* and *Barchester Towers,* describes with psychological insight the social realities of his mythical county. Unlike the first two works, which were concerned with the insular ecclesiastical world of a cathedral town, Trollope turns his attention in this novel to the landed wealth of Barsetshire. The gentry, represented by the Greshams, are in decline because of the political imprudence of the squire who early in his married life aligned himself with his wife's family, the De Courcys, notoriously aristocratic and notoriously Whig. Having lost his Tory constituency and his money, Squire Gresham attempts to retrench to save the estate for his son.
   It is at this point that Doctor Thorne, one of Trollope's ideal gentlemen, enters the story. The squire's only confidant, he serves not only as the family physician, but also as its moral and spiritual counselor. Rigorous in his ethics, proud of his social station and in no way awed by the upper classes, Doctor Thorne joins the squire in an attempt to restore the estate to its former vigor. An enemy of the snobbish and pretentious aristocrats like the De Courcys, who have no loyalty to the life of the land, he seeks by advising various economies and by suggesting judicious loans to help his friend.
   If the moral strength which saves Greshamsbury Park comes from the doctor, it is the money of Sir Roger Scatcherd, however, which enables Gresham to recoup and permits young Frank and Mary to wed. Scatcherd, part of the new industrial wealth, unwittingly saves the agriculture of the area from the moneylenders of London. It is in this alignment that Trollope reveals his political sympathies with the English upper-middle class and his antagonism to the aristocracy and their morality.

DODSWORTH

Type of work: Novel
Author: Sinclair Lewis (1885-1951)
Type of plot: Social criticism
Time of plot: The 1920's
Locale: United States and Europe
First published: 1929

This novel by Sinclair Lewis is titled after Samuel Dodsworth, a rich automobile manufacturer who retires and goes to Europe with his frivolous wife Fran. The plot describes convincingly the degeneration and unmasking of the shallow, snobbish Fran and the disillusion and final rebellion of her idealistic husband. One of the last novels in the tradition of comparisons between American materialism and European civilization, the book contains brilliant insights into the relationships of the two cultures and is successful in spite of its sprawling and rambling style.

Sinclair Lewis was born a member of the American middle class, and his novels suggest that he both loved and detested his own kind, a crucial fact in understanding the unevenness of his satirical portraits. Alfred Kazin (*On Native Grounds*) views Lewis with Sherwood Anderson as New Realists—post World War I reporters freed by the war into a struggle for "freedom of conduct" in middle America. Both writers, liberating forces in American literature of the 1920's, made "transcriptions of average experience," sometimes reproducing it and sometimes parodying it, but always participating in the native culture if primarily to reveal its shortcomings. Thus a typical Lewis novel, domestic satire, affords a mixture of scorn and compassion for its characters. To read his work in its own time was to see oneself or one's neighbor and to marvel at the likeness. He became immensely popular with such readers, an irony when one realizes that his ostensible intention was to expose the provincial, materialistic, bigoted, go-getters whom Mencken tagged the "booboisie."

Although Lewis published more than twenty novels, a play, short stories and sketches between 1914 and his death in 1951, his reputation as an artist now rests on four novels of the 1920's: *Main Street* (1920), *Babbitt* (1922), *Arrowsmith* (1925), and *Dodsworth* (1929). The protagonists of the "big four" continue to generate interest and empathy because Lewis' feeling for the characters as human beings overrode his abiding skepticism. These characters are memorable, living individuals whose natures and problems transcend Dickensian caricature and the topical.

Dodsworth, whose working title was *Exile,* was written in Europe, where Lewis had journeyed in the aftermath of his ruined marriage. There he found or imagined that he found a culture superior to that of America's half-educated, anti-intellectual boosters. Lewis' strong if troubled vision of middle-America appears to have come from a deep sense of his own inferiority (a chronic state documented in Vincent Sheean's *Dorothy and Red,* an account of the courtship and marriage of Lewis and Dorothy Thompson). Although he was the first American to receive the Nobel Prize for Literature, he later remarked that it ruined him; he could not "live up to it." This sense of native inferiority and resulting attempts to gain self-respect and love are duplicated in Sam Dodsworth's experiences in Europe. Lewis blends autobiography with fiction in a well-controlled third-person narrative technique in *Dodsworth,* focusing primarily on the protagonist, creating a fully realistic account of Sam's travels by simultaneously documenting the journeys and the reassertion of Dodsworth's value as a human being.

Lewis sees Dodsworth idealistically for the most part, but so skillfully that the romantic and nostalgic are veiled by the realistic surface of events. Sam is the Post-Victorian embodiment of American virtue. He is essentially honest, doggedly willing to remain open to new experience, boyish in his sincere if awed appreciation of femininity and womanliness but reluctant to be henpecked forever. His almost monkish physical courtship of Edith Cortright entails only kissing her hands. He is reserved, well-mannered, admirably dignified for an American even while clutching his Baedeker. By contrast, most other American male characters are inferior if not nefarious. Arnold Israel engages in questionable financial pursuits, is sensual, and is more European than the Europeans. Tub Pearson is the perennial adolescent whose idea of humor is to address French waiters as "Goosepeppy" and to ask for fricassee of birds' nests. Brent, the Dodsworths' son, decides to live by selling bonds, hoping to reach the "hundred and fifty thousand a year class."

Most significant in the characterization of Dodsworth, however, is his devotion to a work ethic of substance which proves to be his salvation. Sam slowly but persistently weighs his values against those of older cultures: England, France, Italy, Spain, and Germany. Europeans know wine, history, women, politics, and are not afraid of things theoretical, even socialism. Therefore, they can just "be"; that is, they can rest in the self-confidence inherent in their familial and cultural heritage. But Americans, Sam dimly realizes, are born apostles and practitioners of technology. They must "do." Forces beyond their knowledge and control harness their dreams and energies. Their destiny is to build more and better autos, plumbing, and electrical appliances. Sam and Edith decide to return to Zenith to work, but not on what Sam calls "kitchy banalities."

Lewis uses architecture as the symbol of Dodsworth's new life and work. In Europe, Sam, becoming absorbed in architecture, observes and sketches bridges, towers, doorways. He is impressed by their lines, their strength, their beauty, but he recognizes that they are European. So rather than return to Zenith to build a phony pastiche of villas and chalets in the San Souci development, Sam and Edith talk of building homes for Americans, native to the soil and spirit. Optimistically Edith cries that the American skyscraper is the only new thing in architecture since the Gothic cathedral. Working together, their future promises a sharp contrast to that of the pitiful Fran, to whom all culture was interesting as "social adornment."

Occasionally Lewis abandons the detached third-person narrative technique to speak directly to the reader, to regale with satirical comments about travelers in general, or with a series of descriptions of American tourists complete with names in the comedy of humours tradition. Evident also are some forced metaphors, a few poorly integrated references to "morality hounds" in America or to the absurdities of Prohibition. Yet Lewis endows the novel with great power, basically by making Sam Dodsworth a sympathetic, authentic American whose life matters after all, to him and to the reader.

Mary H. Hayden

A DOLL'S HOUSE

Type of work: Drama
Author: Henrik Ibsen (1828-1906)
Type of plot: Social criticism
Time of plot: Nineteenth century
Locale: Norway
First presented: 1879

Nora Helmer, the central character of this play, realizing that after eight years of marriage her husband has never viewed her as anything more than a sheltered, petted doll, leaves him in order to learn to become a person in her own right. One of Ibsen's best-known and most popular works, A Doll's House *has become a classic expression of the theme of women's rights.*

Although Henrik Ibsen was already a respected playwright in Scandinavia, it was *A Doll's House (Et Dukkehjem)* that catapulted him to international fame. This drama, the earliest of Ibsen's social problem plays, must be read in its historical context in order to understand its impact not only on modern dramaturgy but also on society at large.

Most contemporary theater up to the time, including Ibsen's earlier work, fell into two general categories. One was the historical romance; the other was the so-called well-made (or "thesis") play, a contrived comedy of manners revolving around an intricate plot and subplots but ultimately suffocated by the trivia of its theme and dialogue as well as by its shallow characterization. An occasional poetic drama—such as Ibsen's own *Brand* and *Peer Gynt* —would also appear, but poetic form was often the only distinction between these plays and historical romances, since the content tended to be similar.

Into this dramaturgical milieu, *A Doll's House* injected natural dialogue and situations, abstinence from such artificial conventions as the soliloquy, the "aside," or observance of the "unities" of time and place, and insistence upon the strict logical necessity of the outcome without wrenching events into a happy ending. These theatrical innovations—now so familiar that twentieth century audiences hardly notice them—constitute Ibsen's fundamental contribution to the form of realistic drama.

Realism in the theater emphasizes believability; the guiding question is, "Could this event actually have happened in the lives of real people?" There is no attempt to achieve the comprehensiveness of, say, photographic reality; rather, realism is selective, striving for representative examples in recognizable human experience. And through selectivity, realism implicitly assumes a critical stance. Thus, the Helmers' domestic crisis had, and still has, a there-but-for-the-grace-of-God-go-I impact on theater audiences. Since *A Doll's House* was first produced, drama has not been the same. And it is for that reason that Ibsen is called the father of modern drama.

However, Ibsen's influence on modern drama was twofold, for he combined both technique and content in the realism of his *A Doll's House.* Specifically, Ibsen elevated playmaking to a level above mere entertainment by validating the respectability of plays about serious social issues. And one of the most volatile issues of his day was the position of women, for at that time women throughout virtually all of Western civilization were considered by law and by custom chattel of fathers and husbands. Women were denied participation in public life; their access to education was limited; their social lives were narrowly circumscribed; they could not legally transact business, own property, or inherit. In the mid-nineteenth century, chafing under such restrictions, women began to demand autonomy. They pushed for the right to vote and the opportunity for higher education and entry into the professions. By the last two decades of the nineteenth century, open defiance developed as women began engaging in such traditionally men's sports as bicycling, hunting, and golf. Their demands and their behavior predictably evoked cries of outrage from men.

Against this turbulent background, Ibsen presented *A Doll's House.* The response was electric. On the strength of the play, suffragists construed Ibsen as a partisan supporter, while their opposition accused the playwright of propagandizing and being an *agent provocateur.* Yet Ibsen was neither a feminist nor a social reformer in the more general sense. (Indeed, Ibsen personally deplored the kind of emancipation and self-development which brought women out of the domestic sphere into the larger world; he saw women's proper role as motherhood, and motherhood only.) His apparent feminist sympathies were but a facet of his realism. His own responsibility extended no further than describing the problems as he saw them; he did not attempt to solve them. Nevertheless, he had a sharp eye and many sharp words for injustice, and it was the injustice of Torvald's demeaning treatment of Nora— a deplorably common occurrence in real life, Ibsen conceded—that provided the impetus for the play.

In the raging debate over the morality of Nora's behavior, however, it is altogether too easy to neglect Torvald and his dramatic function in the play. For this smug lawyer-bank manager is meant to represent the social structure at large, the same social structure that decreed an inferior position for women. Torvald is, in effect, a symbol for society: male-dominated and authoritarian. Thus, he establishes "rules" for Nora—the petty prohibition against macaroons, for one; requires her to act like an imbecile; and insists upon the rightness, empirical as well as ethical, of his view in all matters. (In fact, Ibsen remarks in his "Notes" for the play that men make the laws and judge a woman's conduct from a man's point of view, "as though she were not a woman but a man.") His righteous refusal to borrow money is a particularly ironic example. And his contemptuous attitude toward Nora's intelligence and sense of responsibility—he calls her *his* "little lark," *his* "little squirrel," *his* "little featherbrain," *his* "little spendthrift," and so on—actually reflects the prevailing view of men toward women: that they are owned property, play-things, dolls to be housed in toy mansions and be indulged, but only sparingly.

In this Neanderthal context, it is difficult not to view Torvald as a thorough-going villain. But like society, Torvald is not completely devoid of redeeming grace—else why would Nora have married him to begin with; why would she commit forgery at great personal risk and use her utmost ingenuity to save his life and to protect him from shame; why would she continue to sacrifice for him, if he possessed not a shred of virtue to elicit from her a feeling of genuine love? For Nora is both sensible and sensitive, despite Torvald's disparaging insinuations, and her awareness of her own worth is gradually awakened as the play unfolds—and with it her sense of individual responsibility. When at last she insists on her right to individual self-development, the spoiled girl-doll becomes a full-fledged woman. She slams the door of the doll house in a gesture symbolic of a Biblical putting away of childish things and takes her rightful place in the adult world. Needless to say, that slam shook the very rafters of the social-domestic establishment, and the reverberations continue to the present time. So powerful an echo makes a powerful drama.

Joanne G. Kashdan

DOMBEY AND SON

Type of work: Novel
Author: Charles Dickens (1812-1870)
Type of plot: Sentimental romance
Time of plot: Early nineteenth century
Locale: England
First published: 1846-1848

Dombey and Son *was Dickens' effort to regain the popularity he had lost with the publication of* Martin Chuzzlewit, *which had heavily satirized America and Americans. The novel is noted for its complex structure and was a milestone in Dickens' work in that he placed the story at a higher social level than he had done in his previous novels. The novel is a very serious one, involving the downfall of a dignified, pompous merchant and his learning of the power of love over money. For the first time, Dickens indicates an interest in and a sympathy for the upper middle classes and the aristocracy, but continues to include a whole catalogue of characters to provide a humorous background.*

In *Dombey and Son,* Dickens for the first time attempted to portray the full panorama of English society, from beggar to magnate, from baronet to housemaid. Although less successful than *Bleak House* in expressing the connection of each level of society to every other level, the novel is nonetheless prodigious in scope.

The theme of the work is the relationship between parents and children, chiefly Mr. Dombey's with Paul and Florence, and subordinately those of various parents and their offspring, ranging in social station from Mrs. Skewton and Edith down to Mrs. Brown and her Alice. Each family situation is thrown into relief by contrast with another, similar in social class yet utterly different in kind. Thus in opposition to Edith Granger, schooled almost from infancy to be "artful, designing, mercenary, laying snares for men," there is the son of Sir Barnet Skettles, whose parents willingly interrupt his studies at Dr. Blimber's academy in order to enjoy his company during their sojourn abroad. Mr. Dombey's crude attempt to mold his fragile son to a shape that does his father honor in the world's eyes contrasts with the honest and unpretentious course that Solomon Gills recommends to his nephew Walter: "Be diligent, try to like it, my dear boy, work for a steady independence, and be happy!" And the miserable devices of greed which Mrs. Brown urges on her daughter as the only recourse of the poor is given the lie by the love and warmth shown by Polly Toodle toward her erring son Rob.

The sad ends of Edith, little Paul, and Alice Marwood all result from two things, or perhaps two facets of one thing: the corruption of childhood by adult concerns, and that disregard of individuality in children which sees them as *things,* as counters in a game, or as a hedge against destitution or mortality. Mr. Dombey, for example, views Paul as an object, a little mirror of his own greatness. He expects his son to reflect himself, that is, to love him as he loves himself. When Paul in his stubborn individuality perceives the merit of Florence and turns to her, Mr. Dombey is amazed and outraged; because he sees Paul as an extension of himself, he cannot conceive of the little boy's having a private opinion. A mirror, after all, cannot have a point of view. Thus in Mr. Dombey's own mind, no blame accrues to himself; Florence, he decides, must be the cause of the "distortion" of Paul's feelings. In this way she too falls victim to her father's self-love, and becomes the object of his hatred, almost a scapegoat for his fiercely repressed feelings of guilt about Paul's death; for in his view she had spoiled Paul as a tool for advancing his father's self-approbation, the function for which his elaborate education was to prepare him.

In the same way, Edith Granger was formed in her youth to fulfill her mother's nasty ambitions. And the shining ideal that both Mrs. Skewton and Mr. Dombey urge on their children is a glossy standing in the eyes of the world, a value which is essentially an adult concern. In contrast, Walter's mentor in his own invincible childishness (he rebukes himself for being "old-fashioned") guides his charge in the path of honesty, the natural behavior of childhood. Young Paul is the chief exemplar of this virtue in the novel, and his resistance to corruption is likewise referrable to that curious quality of being "old-fashioned." Paul was "born old"; he possesses that wisdom of extreme age which constitutes a return to the innocence of childhood. He is fey and resists classification. His obdurate honesty shows itself in his concern for first principles. For example, he inquires of his father what money can do, and when his father proudly replies that money can do anything, suggests two things that it cannot do: bring back his mother or give him health. Then he asks the question again, still more pointedly: "What's money, *afterall?*" as if to direct his father's attention to the extreme paltriness of those things which money *can do,* to that vain show which nurtures his father's pride. But his father takes no notice; it is not for him to be lessoned by a child. Florence, despised and neglected, not thought fit to prepare for any great purpose, has her brother's memory for a master, and educates herself to his truth rather than to her father's ambition.

Dombey and Son is unique among Dickens' novels in its profusion of strongly drawn female characters. Indeed, the author seems intent on ringing the changes on female nature from best to worst. For the most part these figures though vivid have but one dimension, but two evidence a greater depth of understanding than the author had heretofore achieved in his representation of women. One is the character of Florence, whose states of mind illustrate a classic psychological progression. Rejected by a loved parent, she reasons thus: "I am unloved, therefore unlovable." Her early conviction of unworthiness dictates not only her subsequent actions, but indeed shapes the main plot of the novel.

Dickens marks Florence with the token of ideal womanhood, a little display of housewifery in Solomon Gills's parlor; where she learned it though is a mystery. Still, she is truly good without being saccharine, a major advance in Dickens' treatment of women characters. Miss Tox is even more an unusual creation; for heretofore Dickens had not produced a female character at once such an object of satire and so generally sympathetic. She comes in for her share of ridicule for her delusions about Mr. Dombey's intentions and for her genteel pretentions in general, but the author allows her the virtue of her consistency: " . . . poor excommunicated Miss Tox, who, if she were a fawner and a toad-eater, was at least an honest and a constant one. . . ." She is as unlikely a vessel of kindness and simple wisdom as the dandy Toots, or Cousin Feenix the exhausted aristocrat; yet Dickens puts wisdom into their mouths, as if to show that though corruption might seem to reign supreme everywhere, truth remains, and though hidden, can flourish and even prevail.

Jan Kennedy Foster

DOMINIQUE

Type of work: Novel
Author: Eugène Fromentin (1820-1876)
Type of plot: Psychological romance
Time of plot: Nineteenth century
Locale: France
First published: 1862

Although primarily a painter, Fromentin was a man of great sensitivity who translated his abilities into many genres. Dominique *is a psychological romance on the old theme of an individual, like a moth, being drawn to the flame despite morality, orthodoxy, or common sense. The psychology of personality is deftly explored in a polished prose style as the hero is torn in a choice between the rigors of excellence and the pleasures of mediocrity. Drawing on experiences from his own youth, Fromentin exhibits the powerful and permanent hold that the French countryside and seacoast exerted on his mind.*

Dominique is part of the great romantic tradition of European literature that began with Rousseau and Goethe and swept into the nineteenth century with the fiction of George Sand. But the sentimental attitude of the Romantic school is almost overcome in this book by Fromentin's extraordinary sense of style and technical control. An evenness of tone and mood unusual for novels of the period is maintained throughout the book. An underlying realism gives the book a resonance that overcomes any excessiveness of sentimentality. The scene of the pressing of the grapes and the accompanying festivities near the beginning of the novel establish a tone of poetic realism which is carried through the work.

This novel explores the nature of friendship and the power of love. These themes, worked into an almost elegiac vision of time remembered, are treated in a surprisingly modern manner. The external plot is slight, and the incidents are used for the purpose of revelation of character; there is no melodrama in *Dominique* to attempt to maintain reader interest. Only four characters occupy the foreground of the novel: Dominique and Madeleine, the protagonists, with Olivier and the ill-fated Julie as foils. Their stories are bound up in a quest for happiness, and the reality that human beings must settle for, when the ultimate dream proves unattainable.

The unique vision of Fromentin lies in his approach to memory as the greatest reality. The significance of the present, in the novel, lies in the past. In *Dominique,* the beauty of the landscape is enhanced both by the experiences of childhood and the poignancy of the young love for which it was the background. The tranquil recollection of a life's joys and pains provides the subtle and fascinating center to this unusual novel. The prose is vivid and poetic, but restrained, and the descriptions of place are handled with the artistry and perceptive skill of a master painter. The framework of the narrator gradually discovering the truth about the past adds to the impression that the reader, during the course of the book, has had a glimpse into a bygone, pastoral age.

DON CARLOS

Type of work: Drama
Author: Johann Christoph Friedrich von Schiller (1759-1805)
Type of plot: Historical tragedy
Time of plot: Sixteenth century
Locale: Spain
First presented: 1787

This play is based upon the life of the son of the Spanish king Philip II, and upon a historical novel of the same title, published by the Abbe de Saint-Réal at Paris in 1672. Written in blank verse rather than his usual prose, this exceedingly long play finds Schiller's own ideas of humanity and liberty expressed in words spoken by Don Carlos and the Marquis de Posa. The most advanced drama by Schiller, it was also his last before turning to the writing of aesthetics, ethics, and literary criticism.

Don Carlos, though it was written over a period of only four years, shows strong signs of Schiller's change of conception. It was begun in prose and reworked in blank verse, printed first in individual installments through the third act, and then issued in a completed version of over six thousand lines, which was reduced later to about five thousand lines. During this process, Schiller's conception of the characters changed, as did the emphasis of the play, and most critics admit that the resultant complexities of motivation are sometimes baffling. Yet the play contains some of Schiller's greatest work, and many of its themes and speeches are among the classics of the German stage.

During the writing, Schiller's sympathy shifted from Carlos, the youthful, impetuous prince guided by pure emotion, to Posa, who himself begins as an idealist of noble sentiments, but who reveals the flaw in his nature by forgetting his love for individual men in his passion for humanity. In fact, the initially sentimental Carlos does gain in stature by his loyalty, even after the death of Posa. The truly tragic character of the drama is King Philip, initially conceived as a tyrant, the villain in the domestic tragedy of Carlos and Elizabeth. As the play progresses, Philip gains the sympathy of Schiller, and is revealed as a lonely man isolated by his kingship, unloved by his wife, hated by his son, needing a friend, and losing the hoped-for friendship of Posa. Ultimately, he is deprived even of the consolation of religion in the scene with the Grand Inquisitor, who represents the Church in a form that is authoritarian even above kings, and totally inhumane in its loyalty to a faith that has become an end in itself.

THE DON FLOWS HOME TO THE SEA

Type of work: Novel
Author: Mikhail Sholokhov (1905-)
Type of plot: Historical chronicle
Time of plot: 1918-1920
Locale: Russia
First published: 1933, 1938

Written as a sequel to And Quiet Flows the Don, *this work portrays the fortunes of the Cossacks after the peace with the Central Powers in 1917 up to the dominance of the Communists in 1920. Although written under the Soviet regime, the insurgent Cossacks are sympathetically portrayed. The scope of this work is vast, and Soviet autocratic ruthlessness is portrayed as base and inhuman but inevitable. It is one of the best Soviet productions.*

Mikhail Sholokhov's work, *The Don Flows Home to the Sea,* is actually the last half of an immense historical work which follows a Don Cossack, Gregor Melekhov, from peacetime Czarist Russia through the German-Russian Civil War and Revolution. Although the focal point of the novel is war, the cultural life of Cossack Russia—its love for the land, and the roles of men and women in the agrarian family—is equally well portrayed. The length of the work enables a unique panorama of history to unfold.

Sholokhov intensely loves the Don, the steppe, and the cycles of the seasons and his poetic language beautifully captures the bond of the Cossacks with their land. Theirs is a peasant's life. They are in tune with the wind, the coming of rain, the swelling and cracking of the frozen Don. Numerous scenes begin with landscape paintings, subtle but insistent reminders that it is from the land that life comes. Death, undisguised, is omnipresent. Gory and detailed descriptions of the dying and of the dead become commonplace in the scourge of war, but the Don and the steppe survive all tragedies. Sholokhov evokes the sights, sounds, and smells of that earthy existence so vividly that the pain of Cossack uprootedness is totally convincing. Young soldiers who have fought valiantly near the Don are ineffectual, lifeless, on foreign soil; refugees wander meaninglessly when forced to flee their Don home.

The Melekhov family and the other townspeople of Tatarsk are typical of agrarian society and culture. Roles are assumed within family units unquestioningly, although not always obediently. The head of the Melekhov household, old Pantaleimon Prokoffivich, Gregor's father, is responsible for all who live under his roof: his wife, his sons and their wives and children, and his daughter until she marries. He is the patriarchal authority. Pantaleimon orders the marriage of Gregor and Natalia when he learns of Gregor's affair with Aksinia; Gregor complies. Old Pantaleimon becomes confused about his authority over his sons, however, when their military ranks surpass his.

Pantaleimon expects and demands to be served and respected by women who are his subordinates. In Cossack society, females are less valued than males and are treated as possessions by husbands. When Stepan Astakhov first learns of the affair between his wife, Aksinia, and Gregor, he returns home to beat, then stomp on Aksinia as if he were doing a Cossack dance. He is within his rights to thus punish her transgression.

The matriarch of the Melekhov family is Ilinichna, Pantaleimon's wife, who is not only the female head of the household (wife, mother, and grandmother), but also the mother to her sons' wives. The relationship between the mother-in-law and the daughters-in-law is an interesting one. Ilinichna gives orders to Daria, Pyotr's wife, and Natalia, as a mistress would to servants. The young married women have no rights except as granted by their husbands and mother-in-law.

Children are reared in an extended family and parental authority is often less than that of the grandparent. The middle generation—sons and daughters-in-law—are treated as overgrown children by the older generation. A major role for the young men (Cossacks) is to serve in the military. Service is seen as an honor, a duty that is fulfilled unquestioningly. The process of maturation for young men seems to occur in the military. When Gregor and his friends return home from war, the townspeople comment on how broad-shouldered they have become.

A strain of violence permeates Cossack life. Even during peacetime there is an air of exaggerated rivalry in which anger is expressed overtly. When old Pantaleimon proudly races through the village with his hero son, Gregor, he becomes infuriated with an old woman who scolds him for nearly running over her livestock. His anger could easily lead him to using his whip on her. Wartime violence is seen both on the battlefront and within the civilian population. There is an irony in the reverence a soldier holds for his own mother when he mistreats another's mother; an irony when he who has shared another soldier's wife returns home enraged to find that his wife has been similarly unfaithful.

The length of the novel gives the feeling of the flow of history, not in generalized sweeping trends or wartime strategies, but in a long series of specific circumstances that enables the reader to become involved with numerous major characters and to care about their lives and deaths as much as about the life of the one centralizing figure, Gregor Melekhov. A dead soldier by the side of the road becomes a vital loss, as the reader learns in retrospect from a small diary of the soldier's life and love. The relationship which grows between Podtielkov and Anna Pogodko is another mini-novel that is given life and death within the confines of Sholokhov's world. The deaths which affect Gregor most deeply are those of his and Aksinia's daughter, Piotra on the battlefield, Piotra's wife by suicide, Natalia by an unsuccessful abortion, Pantaleimon of typhus as a refugee, and, finally, Akinsia. The reader participates in Gregor's suffering because Sholokhov has fully developed all these characters.

This long-range focus on history through specific tragedies gives the indelible impression of the war-weariness, resignation, and readiness for death that Gregor feels when he finally returns home for the last time.

This work and the first part of the narrative, *And Quiet Flows the Don,* have been published together under the title of *The Silent Don.*

Mary Peace Finley

DON JUAN

Type of work: Poem
Author: George Gordon, Lord Byron (1788-1824)
Type of plot: Social satire
Time of plot: Late eighteenth century
Locale: Spain, Turkey, Russia, England
First published: By Cantos, 1819-1824

This unfinished epic satire is written in ottava rima *and contains 16,000 lines in its sixteen cantos. Rather than following the epic tradition, the poem becomes a vehicle for digression on any subject; Byron, through his hero, gives his views on wealth, power, society, chastity, poets, diplomats, and England. For this reason the poem holds a high place among literary satires.*

George Gordon Byron, who became the sixth Lord Byron by inheriting the title from his uncle, William, was born on January 22, 1788. Because his father, the notorious "Mad Jack" Byron, deserted the family, young Byron was brought up in his mother's native Scotland, where he was exposed to Presbyterian concepts of predestination which distorted his religious views throughout his life. In 1801 he entered Harrow, a public school near London; in 1808 he received the Master of Arts degree from Cambridge; in 1809 he took his seat in the House of Lords. From June 1809 to July 1811, Byron traveled in Europe in the company of his friend Hobhouse. In 1812 he met Lady Caroline Lamb, who later became his mistress; in 1813 he spent several months with his half-sister, Augusta Leigh, who later bore a daughter who may have been Byron's. Byron married Annabella Milbanke in 1815; she bore him a daughter, Ada, a year later and left him shortly thereafter. In 1816 Byron left England, never to return. That year found him in Switzerland with the Shelleys, where in 1817 Clare Clairmont bore his illegitimate daughter Allegra. After 1819 Countess Teresa Guicciola, who sacrificed her marriage and social position for Byron, became his lover and comforter. Byron died on April 19, 1824, in Missolonghi, where he had hoped to help Greece gain independence from Turkey. His most famous works are *Childe Harold's Pilgrimage, Manfred, Cain, The Vision of Judgment,* and *Don Juan,* his masterpiece.

Don Juan, an "epic" poem written in *ottava rima,* is permeated throughout with Byronic philosophy. Its episodic plot, narrated in first person by its author, tells the story of young Juan, who, victimized by a narrow-minded and hypocritical mother, an illogical educational system, and his own fallible humanity, loses his innocence and faith and becomes disillusioned with man and his institutions. The poem's rambling style allows for Byron's numerous digressions, in which he satirizes many aspects of English life: English government and its officials, religion and its confusions and hypocracies, society and its foibles, war and its irrationality, woman and her treachery, man and his inhumanity to his fellows. Even English poets feel the fire of Byron's wrath. Thus Byron has been accused of a completely negative view in *Don Juan*—anti-everything and pro-nothing. And though it is true that to Byron all is relative because there can be no absolutes in a world without reason, sanity, or justice and where the precepts of Christianity are so contradictory that they offer no panacea for life's problems, the philosophy of *Don Juan* is not wholly pessimistic. Admittedly, the undertone, especially in the digressions, is often sardonic; yet the overtone, created by a flippant refusal to take Juan's story (or life) too seriously and by extensive use of exaggerated feminine rhyme, such as "intellectual" and "hen-peck'd you all," is essentially comic. Thus the zest and the laughter in *Don Juan* belie the idea of total despair and lend an affirmation of life despite its ironies; the lapses into lyricism reveal a heart that sings despite the poet's attempt to stifle emotion with sophistication.

In *Don Juan,* Byron's philosophical confusion seems to be caused by his natural affinity for a Platonic, idealistic view, which has been crushed under the weight of a realism he is too honest and too perceptive to ignore. Though he denies that he discusses metaphysics, he comments that nothing is stable or permanent; all is mutable and subject to violent destruction. Yet Byron, in calling the world a "glorious blunder," is not totally blind to its temporary beauties. During the Juan-Haidée romance, the lovers live in an Edenic world of beautiful sunsets and warm, protective caves. Still, Juan's foreboding and Haidée's dream are reminders that nature's dangers always lurk behind its façade of beauty. And even Haidée, "Nature's bride," pursued pleasure and passion only to be reminded that "the wages of sin is death."

Byron's view of the nature of man is closely akin to his complex view of natural objects. Man has his moments of glory, integrity, and unselfishness. For example, Juan, the novice, does not flee from the horror of battle; he shuns cannibalism even though he is starving; he refuses to be forced to love the sultana; he risks his life to save young Leila. Often Byron emphasizes man's freedom of mind and spirit. Yet he believes that man's self-deceit is the chief factor in his decadence; his false ideas of glory lead to bloodshed. Ironically, Surrow lectures his soldiers on "the noble art of killing"; man kills because "it brings self-approbation." In fact, Byron suggests that man is more destructive than nature or God. Still, he does not condemn man; some taint at the heart of nature and of man turns "simple instinct and passion" to guilt; besides, society's corruption in turn corrupts man. Lord Henry as the elder sophisticate is perhaps the best example of man's inability to retain his innocence; caught in the trap of his own greed and hypocrisy and of society's political game, Lord Henry finds that he cannot turn back, even though "the fatigue was greater than the profit." Byron also strikes out against political corruption. He had strong hopes for England's budding liberalism: a "king in constitutional procession" had offered great promise in leading the world to political freedom and morality. Yet Byron boldly declares England's failure to fulfill this promise.

Byron does, however, offer positive values in *Don Juan*. He believes that momentary happiness and glory and love *are* worth living for. Although "A day of gold from out an age of iron/ Is all that life allows the luckiest sinner," it is better than nothing. Man must fight, though he knows that he can never redeem the world and that defeat and death are certain. Since hypocrisy is one of the worst sins, man should be sincere. To Byron, the creative act is especially important, for it is man's only chance to transcend his mortality.

Throughout *Don Juan,* then, one follows man through his hapless struggle with life. Born in a fallen state, educated to hypocrisy and impracticality, cast out into a world of false values and boredom, man follows the downward path to total disillusionment. He learns, however, to protect himself from pain by insulating himself with the charred shell of burned-out passion and crushed ideals. Blindly, he stumbles toward that unknown and unknowable end— death. Yet he goes not humbly but defiantly, not grimly but with gusto.

Therefore, Byron's philosophy, despite its harshness, is one which embraces life, seeking to intensify and electrify each fleeting, irrevocable moment. It is a philosophy of tangibles, though they are inadequate; of action, though it will not cure man's ills; of honesty, though it must recognize man in his fallen state. And, though death is inevitable and no afterlife is promised, Byron maintains his comic perspective: "Carpe diem, Juan, . . . play out the play."

Janet Wester

DON JUAN

Type of work: Drama
Author: Molière (Jean Baptiste Poquelin, 1622-1673)
Type of plot: Social satire
Time of plot: Seventeenth century
Locale: Sicily
First presented: 1665

Written to fatten the lean exchequer of his company's theater because of the enforced closing of Tartuffe, *as well as to please his fellow actors,* Don Juan *is an excellent example of the skill and speed with which Molière could write a play. Also departing from his usual technique in making use of the melodramatic and supernatural elements which characterized the original Spanish drama from which it was adapted, he nevertheless holds to his genius as a revealer of the hypocrisies and manners of his day. The play brought down on itself the harsh criticism of those who had been shocked by the boldness of* Tartuffe, *but it delighted the spectacle-loving Parisians of his day.*

Molière's *Don Juan* is one of the great examples of a work of literature or drama that was ahead of its time. The play scandalized and confused Molière's contemporaries, and only in modern times has it achieved a worthy appreciation. It was the complexity of Don Juan's behavior that made him a puzzle to the French and a fascinating figure to later audiences. The spectators of the classical age were bewildered by a play, really a tragicomedy, in which the unities were neglected, and which contained magic, fantasy, and buffoonery. Yet today we are intrigued by the impossible task of analyzing the haughtiness and arrogance of Don Juan, of trying to understand the depths of his hypocrisy, villainy, and despair. Molière took the Spanish hero and made him not merely a heedless libertine and unbeliever, but, by strengthening the atheism suggested by his predecessors until it dominated the play, gave his hero the deep and bitter philosophy of the man who cannot help himself, who must deny even if it destroys him.

The play lays bare the hero's soul, yet the plot is surprisingly weak. It is structured in loose sequences of scenes, the main characters providing the only strong link; the great speeches, the rhetorical rhythm, are what carry the drama forward. Don Juan thought himself free from all obligations, believing neither in God nor hell nor doctors, nor in the sacredness of promises, yet as an aristocrat he assumed that others would keep their obligations to him. His servant, Sganarelle, was his opposite in every way, earthy where Don Juan was lofty, meek where the Don was scornful, superstitious where his master was skeptical. They were the perfect French counterpart to Don Quixote and Sancho.

Molière improved upon both the comic and retributive elements of the original story, and elected to make Don Juan's climactic act of self-damnation his decision to play the hypocrite, hypocrisy being the vice most loathesome to Molière. When Don Juan begins a speech by stating that he is entirely sincere, it is a sign to the audience that he is being quite the opposite. Don Juan combined in his personality the romantic qualities of the lover and the supreme egoism of the tragic hero. He gloried in his own exaggerated image of himself, even comparing himself to Alexander. Don Juan, like all tragic heroes, caused his own doom, by violating, through his hubris, the basic moral laws.

DON JUAN TENORIO

Type of work: Drama
Author: José Zorrilla y Moral (1817-1893)
Type of plot: Fantastic-religious comedy
Time of plot: c. 1545
Locale: Seville, Spain
First presented: 1844

Though Zorrilla himself deprecated his work, this is one of Spain's most popular plays, regularly performed during the first week of November for All Saints' Day. Written in twenty days for a theater owner threatened with bankruptcy, the play is based on a well-loved Spanish legend, spiritedly written in seven acts and in excellent and varied poetry. Audiences see the story not only as a play about a rollicking adventurer, but also as a story with deeper meaning. The implication of the drama seems to be that since God's love is infinite, a man can sin as much as he likes provided that he wins the love of a pure woman. The play presents a combination of the romantic with the mystic which has perennial appeal to the Latin temperament.

José Zorilla fortunately missed the notorious years of repression under King Ferdinand VII that most Spanish Romanticists endured, but he was forced to flee his own authoritarian father and spend several years hiding in Bohemian poverty. One of Spain's few Romanticist poets destined to live a long life, Zorrilla was shy and evasive: his life resembled his escapist poetry, which shunned reality for the unreal. Zorrilla considered himself a troubadour. He loved to versify, and wrote poetry as easily as he conversed. At twenty, he became famous overnight by pushing forward suddenly at the funeral of the noted poet, José de Larra, and passionately reading poetry dedicated to the deceased.

Zorilla is best remembered for *Don Juan Tenorio,* which became a Spanish national institution and still delights the average Spaniard today. Zorrilla scorned his own play and sold it for a trifling sum, since it was based on the original Don Juan created by Fray Tirso de Molina, a great Golden Century dramatist. Zorrilla's Don Juan is nevertheless a more human, flexible, and generous personality. He is also universal enough to belong to all cultures, not only displaying his romantic airs convincingly, but also using bewichment to attain his evil ends. The marrow of Don Juanism is the mysterious power of bewitchment through love; hence Zorrilla's Don Juan conquers through this element as well as through mere lying. Doña Ines dies of love for him, in a near-hypnotic state. Seduction is thus drawn by Zorrilla in its original sense of bewitchment, while Don Juan's dual hallucinatory-realism, along with his diabolic acumen, are exalted also. Don Juan was nonetheless perplexed before the hair-raising prospect of boiling in Hell's lake of fire, which floats in a fog before his rolling eyes. The play thus salutarily terrifies sinners, then soothes them with the theme of Don Juan's romantic redemption.

The First Act (*Libertinage and Scandal*) is almost architecturally exact. The stage represents a magnificent cemetery with Doña Ines' tomb in the foreground, while in the background are flowers and cypresses tapering upwards toward Heaven. Act IV (*The Devil at Heaven's Door*) is filled with love, vengeance, and the tension created by Don Juan's looming, last-minute intent of repentance. The latter element is the key to the action of *Don Juan Tenorio,* and helps compensate for its flaws and even the "improvising hastiness" with which Zorrilla claimed to have written it. Some critics see a superficial knowledge of theology in the work, but there is also an influence from Ferreira's Portuguese classic, *Inês de Castro,* which also has a theme of love beyond the grave. *Don Juan Tenorio* also has more original touches than even Zorrilla seems to have realized, along with vigor, freshness, color, and feeling that captivates audiences. Although several contemporaries of Zorrilla branded him as a hasty and wordy writer and a shallow thinker, Zorrilla was crowned poet laureate of Spain in his old age.

DON QUIXOTE DE LA MANCHA

Type of work: Novel
Author: Miguel de Cervantes Saavedra (1547-1616)
Type of plot: Picaresque romance
Time of plot: Late sixteenth century
Locale: Spain
First published: Part I, 1605; Part II, 1615

One of the best-loved novels of all time, Don Quixote *was intended to be a satire on the exaggerated chivalric romances of Cervantes' time. However, the author soars above this purpose in his wealth of fancy and in his irrepressible high spirit as he pokes fun at social and literary conventions of his day. The novel offers a good cross-section of Spanish life, thought, and feeling at the end of the chivalric age as it parades a variegated assortment of minor characters—shepherds, innkeepers, students, priests, and nobles—through its pages. Contrasting characterizations of Don Quixote, the visionary idealist, and Sancho Panza, the practical realist, symbolize the duality of the Spanish character in this essentially humane novel.*

"For my absolute faith in the details of their histories and my knowledge of their deeds and their characters enable me by sound philosophy to deduce their features, their complexions and their statures," says Don Quixote (II:i), declaring his expertise in knight errantry. This declaration affords a key to understanding Miguel de Cervantes' *Don Quixote de la Mancha,* for it demonstrates both the literal and the symbolic levels of the novel—and the distinction between those levels is crucial to grasping the full import of the story. The literal level, of course, is superficial; it reveals the obvious. The symbolic level, however, probes much deeper; it reveals the significance. In fact, the symbolic level deals, as all good literature must, with values. Thus Don Quixote's declaration must be considered on both levels, and when set in context, it will lend insight into the novel as a whole.

On the literal level, Don Quixote is eminently qualified by his extensive reading to assert familiarity with the history, the deeds, and the character of virtually every knight whose existence was recorded. Indeed, his penchant for reading books of chivalry is established on the first page of the first chapter of the book. Even his niece and his housekeeper refer frequently to his reading habits. Moreover, the inventory of the don's library, made just before the books were burned, reveals the extent of his collection, and earlier mention of his omnivorous reading leads to the assumption that he had read all of them. Further evidence of Don Quixote's erudition is his ready knowledge of the rules of knight errantry and his recalling the legend of Mambrino's helmet in connection with his oath of knighthood as well as elsewhere in the novel. Later, after an encounter with Yanguesan herdsmen, there is evidence, in a very lucid and pragmatic statement for a presumably insane old man, of Don Quixote's having read Machiavelli, followed by the don's citation of the misfortunes which befell his hero, Amadis of Gaul.

Other adventures provide internal evidence of Quixote's knowledge about the history of chivalry. A thrashing by muleteers jogs the don's memory to analogies between his plight and similar outrages visited upon the Marquis of Mantua, Baldwin, Abindarraez, and Don Roderigo de Narvaez. After his lance is broken by a windmill, Don Quixote remembers the makeshift tree-limb weapon used by Diego Perez de Vargas when the latter's weapon was broken in battle. At another time, he explains and defends the code of knight errantry to fellow travelers, citing Arthurian legend, the ever-present Amadis of Gaul, the stricter-than-monastic rules of knight errantry, and the noble families of Italy and Spain who contributed to the tradition. In fact, incredible as it may seem, just before the don attacks the herd of sheep, he attributes to each sheep a title and an estate culled from his reservoir of reading—or from his overactive imagination. In addition, to rationalize his own designation as the Knight of the Sorry Aspect, he recalls the sobriquets of other knights errant. In an attempt to inculcate Sancho Panza with the proper respect for his master, Don Quixote even relates biographical incidents from the lives of the squires of Amadis of Gaul and Sir Galaor. Significantly, almost craftily, he mentions that Gandalin, Amadis's squire, was also Count of the Firm Isle—a blatant inducement for Sancho to remain in the don's service. Yet, all in all, on the literal level, Don Quixote's mastery of chivalric lore seems to serve only as a rationalization for his ill luck.

On the symbolic level, more questions are raised than are answered. Quixote claims to have reached a "sound philosophy." But is reliance on reading alone—as he has done—a valid basis for "sound philosophy," or has the don become so absorbed in his books that he is unable to formulate or express the applicability of his reading? Can, for example, literature serve as a basis for understanding reality as Don Quixote avers? In lieu of a clear-cut answer, Cervantes offers a paradox. Early on, Don Quixote learns from Sancho that the Squire has never read any histories because he is illiterate; but later, trying to divert the don's attention with a story, Sancho, under questioning, admits that although he had not seen the person in question, ". . . the man who told me this story said it was so true and authentic . . . I could swear on my oath that I had seen it all" (I:xx). The issues of verisimilitude and credibility are not really resolved in this novel. Consequently, these issues generate further questions about distinctions between reality and fantasy. Sancho represents empirical, commonsensical reality; the don stands for whimsy and unfettered imagination. Whose view of the world is more accurate? Cervantes is ambiguous, at best, about the answer. However, the question persists, as Luigi Pirandello's *Henry IV* vividly testifies. We are thus left to ponder this paradox which Emily Dickinson has so succinctly described: "Much madness is divinest sense. . . ."

Another issue raised on the symbolic level involves the possible immorality of reading "too many" books. Books, in this sense, are a symbol of education, and this facet of *Don Quixote* may be a veiled protest against the *Index Librorum Prohibitorum*. The literal lesson emphasizes the corruptive power of books (and, therefore, education); however, the symbolic implication—given Cervantes' sympathetic treatment of Don Quixote—is that books and education are liberating influences on the human psyche. Thus the symbolic purport of *Don Quixote* may be a parody of the Church's monopoly of literacy in the Middle Ages, with the uninhibited don a counterfoil to the insensitive, book-burning priest.

To be sure, Don Quixote became a tragic figure toward the end of the novel, but not for failure of his philosophy; rather, it is society's failure to accommodate a deviation from the norm. And herein lies another symbolic level of the novel: society's intolerance of deviance. For Cervantes certainly did not make the don contemptible, nor did he treat him with contempt. Such treatment would have been repellent after the tender tolerance of the first part of the story. Despite the satirical thrust of the novel on the symbolic level, the don himself is a sympathetic character throughout he story. Although he strives to push time back, his efforts are depicted as noble, though nonetheless futile. The sympathy he evokes is that popular sympathy for the underdog who defies all odds and is broken in the attempt in contrast to the protagonist who has everything in his favor and succumbs to a surfeit of success.

Cervantes' novel is a complex web of tangled skeins, subject to many more interpretations than those suggested here. Suffice it to say that *Don Quixote* is unequivocally judged the finest Spanish novel ever written and one of the greatest works in world literature.

Joanne G. Kashdan

DON SEGUNDO SOMBRA

Type of work: Novel
Author: Ricardo Güiraldes (1882-1927)
Type of plot: Regional romance
Time of plot: Late nineteenth century
Locale: Argentina
First published: 1926

Considered the outstanding fictional example of Gaucho literature, Don Segundo Sombra *captured the essence of the gaucho myth in its scenes of life on the pampas and in the idealization of Don Segundo. The novel reflects a pastoral form of life that has all but disappeared in Argentina and presents a vivid and varied documentation of details about the people, the customs, and the countryside.*

This novel is considered the classic novel of the gaucho. It has the clean lines of Hemingway's "The Old Man and the Sea," for Don Segundo Sombra, the patriarchal old gaucho, and Fabio, the boy, are thrown into relief as they ride across the billowing pampa. Don Segundo is introduced into the novel dramatically for, when first seen by the boy, he looms enormously, a giant and almost overwhelming horseman. And when Don Segundo rides off at the novel's end, we see only him, the pampa, and the sky as he disappears, shadowlike, into the distance.

A touch of the American movie "Shane" is present, in the friendship between the boy and the mature man, and the hero worship of the former for the latter. It is almost a fantastic example of youth forming an image of the ideal that it wishes to reach, and at the same time finding an example of this ideal upon which it can concentrate its attention and imitation.

Another theme is the passing of a breed, as represented by Don Segundo himself, the last of the true gauchos. Freedom is still another theme—the wild wandering of the duo across the pampa; the freedom, now disappearing, once enjoyed by the dying gaucho; the gradual smothering of such freedom by civilization. *Don Segundo Sombra* is simultaneously set late in the day of the gaucho's traditional frontier enemy, the wild Indian tribes, who have already been pushed up against the setting sun, into the Andean foothills. Thus, while entertaining, the novel has various social and historical messages.

Güiraldes made unusual use of water imagery. The pampa itself is almost presented as an ocean of land, the reflecting sky overhead being an overhead ocean. Ponds and streams add other touches of water imagery, while Don Segundo and Fabio even reach the Atlantic Ocean itself once and stare raptly at it. Life itself is symbolized by water, for life flows like water, as does the novel's action.

Adventure and travel give another element, in this case Quixotesque. The two riders wander at will, like Don Quixote and Sancho Panza, satiating the human yen to travel and see what lies over the horizon. The appeal to wanderlust is so intense that it has a strong mystic touch. The novel is realistic and true to life, but it can almost be classified as a romance of chivalry since it exalts the virtues of Don Segundo and his adventures with Fabio in the field of struggle of a gaucho's daily labor, and in battle against the inclemencies of weather and nature.

The vocabulary has many Argentinisms, some of colonial vintage brought down centuries before from Jesuit mission lands in Paraguay, but is never difficult. The plot develops serenely to a logical climax; the novel's style is good but not distinctive; the few characters are well done, or deliberately shaded out so as not to distract from the protagonist, Don Segundo, and his young companion, Fabio. The reader thus identifies easily with both.

Güilraldes' use of nature is not equal in some respects to that of, say, Louis L'Amour, but is blended so well into the narration that one can almost hear the rustle of leaves in the trees, the murmuring of the streams, and even the sound of the wind. There is some use of colors and tints—the green ombú trees, the colors of the steers and horses, while gaucho lore is presented extensively and authentically without any touch of "drug-store gauchoism." In general, relatively little of the milk of human kindness or warmth is presented, for Fabio is very much alone in a cold world until he meets Don Segundo.

As genres, the gaucho novel and poetry are extensive. They are important not only because of their intrinsic worth as genuine, regional products of the American hemisphere, but also because they have tinged other aspects of Argentine literature, even the theater and essay. This is true in Argentina itself—where the core, pampa heartland insinuates itself into other geographical regions of the country—and in "The Purple Land" of Uruguay and the undulating pampa of Southern Brazil. In the latter area an additional, entire gaucho literature exists in Portuguese, forming a natural component to the unique gaucho genre, produced in the River Plate world and its collateral systems, such as the Uruguay, Paraná, and Paraguay. To this day one even finds a certain impregnation of gaucho culture in southernmost Paraguay, a little-known and historically isolated area that for long was almost a semi-tropical Tibet.

Although moving even further from the classic gaucho age in time, and despite paved roads and mechanization, Argentina, Uruguay, Southern Brazil, and Paraguay's southernmost tip still have gaucho flavor in dress and speech. In Brazil, for example, as one travels southwards in a bus from gigantic, modernistic São Paulo the first individuals of gaucho dress may board the bus in the mountains of the Brazilian-Germanic state of Santa Catarina. Novels in the tradition of *Don Segundo Sombra* are still being published from Santa Catarina southward, while a faint gaucho tinge has even spread northward into Brazil's immense "wild west" of Minas Gerais, Goiás, and Mato Grosso. Gaucho novels are still a favorite of the urban Argentine reader in such centers of the true gaucho core-land as Buenos Aires, Rosario, and Bahia Blanca, or in Montevideo, Porto Alegra, Córdoba, and Santa Fe.

The modern gaucho uses barbed wire and rides a jeep, but the average *estancia* still has gauchos in whose hearts beat the spirit of Don Segundo and Martin Fíerro.

William Freitas

DOÑA BÁRBARA

Type of work: Novel
Author: Rómulo Gallegos (1884-1969)
Type of plot: Regional romance
Time of plot: Early twentieth century
Locale: The Arauca Valley of Venezuela
First published: 1929

One of Venezuela's democratic leaders and president of the country until overthrown by a military dictatorship, Gallegos and his party stood for a liberal, social-minded government which would improve living conditions for the masses. This novel, though little-known in the United States, has a high reputation with readers in South America. Rich in vocabulary, symbolism, and universal themes, Doña Bárbara *remains one of the most potent novels of social reform in all of Latin America.*

Doña Bárbara is *the* novel of the *llanos.* In it is painted the llanos, or tropical grassland bordering the Orinoco River, in the center of Venezuela, a republic almost as large as America's Southwest. Next to the llanos itself, the ranch-woman Doña Bárbara is the most clearly-etched character, symbolizing barbarism, for she is a wild, dreadful, beautiful half-breed from beyond the remotest tributaries of the Orinoco. Her very name reeks of barbarism. Opposed to her is Santos Luzardo, who symbolizes the civilizing energy that is trying to penetrate the llanos' savagery and tame it.

Gallegos uses symbols for barbarism, such as the great *tolvaneras,* or whirlwinds, that periodically flay the llanos. There are also rampaging herds of horses and steers; the power of flowing rivers and currents; a midnight-black stallion as savage as Satan, but tamed by Santos Luzardo; a fire that scorches the plains, leaving blackened embers in its hellish path; and, evoking the violent spirit of the llanos, are the llanero horsemen who almost destroy the tendrils of civilization that come within reach. Gallegos does bring in beauty such as flowers, sunset tints, breezes, white clouds, rains, the pink herons, and other delicacies, but, ever lurking wraith-like in the background is the malaria that had earlier nearly depopulated the llanos, causing its historical decline (the llanos had once supplied the cavalry that had filled General Simón Bolívar's revolutionary army's ranks, giving it victory over Spain's Royalist armies during Venezuela's War of Independence from Spain).

Gallegos uses symbols for barbarism, such as the great *tolvaneras,* or but not overdone—we see the llanero, or cowboy; the boatmen of the Arauca River; a stock military official; ranch owners; and the itinerant Syrian peddlers, both rascally and otherwise. Some of Gallegos' sociological types are presented as clearly as if they inhabited an animated museum. Possibly his only near-caricature is Mister Danger, a one-dimensional villain who over-represents the alleged Yankee rascality that is the compulsive whipping-boy of so many Spanish-American novelists.

Gallegos' plot is logically developed. Coupled with worthy subject matter, and knowledge of his fellow Venezuelans, it produces a near-masterpiece. Human cruelty is not overdrawn, realism is almost never lacking, and there are few distortions, but—as a city-dweller and intellectual, belonging to a professional class not noted for dirtying its hands with physical toil—Gallegos did not give an in-depth study of the llanos' lowest social types. The novel is thus limited at times by an unconscious social prejudice, and the author's perception of the llaneros' religious views, or psychology, or superstitions, is superficial. Human suffering is not presented feelingly, introspection is generally lacking. But most of the characters do live, and are not likely to be forgotten by the reader, for they develop and change subtly but gradually. The reader thus lives with them through the pages of *Doña Bárbara,* and with their llanos grasslands.

The basic themes of *Doña Bárbara* are universal ones. Civilization against barbarism is about as dominant a theme as in Domingo Sarmiento's *Facundo* (the noted masterpiece of Argentine literature). Also present are such themes as man against nature, female against male, cruelty against kindness, justice against oppression, and freedom against bureaucratic government. Nowhere in *Doña Bárbara,* however, is it suggested that hard work and thrift such as practiced not only by Horatio Alger, but by, say, Japanese, Germans, Jews, Mormons, or even Venezuela's Syrian peddlers, could alleviate the llanos' poverty.

Doña Bárbara is rich in Venezuelan expressions, idioms, and flavor of speech, but its vocabulary is not difficult. Gallegos' style moves effortlessly along and reader interest is not sacrificed by excess words or structural disorganization. The plot also moves briskly and is never clouded by deviant subplots or excessive complexity, yet even discerning readers cannot anticipate events, including the climax with its curiously passive finale for Doña Bárbara, the violent woman of the barbaric Venezuelan plains. From the first page, violence hangs over the story like a Sword of Damocles or a nightmare. It either lurks in the background, like a boa constrictor coiled in the llanos grass, or it erupts like a llanos fire.

Doña Bárbara, like various other Venezuelan novels, exposed and spotlighted national ills. Realistic reform could have come earlier to Venezuela, aided by such revelatory writings, but it was slow even when Gallegos himself became president. Gallegos was apparently not strong enough, or perhaps lacked enough political horse sense to accomplish what was accomplished in the nineteenth century by Argentina's two literary presidents, Bartolomé Mitre and Domingo Sarmiento, who were men of action as well as of the pen. As a genre, the novel remains, nevertheless, the most important literary tool not only in Venezuela but in all Latin America. Being the broadest and least restricted literary form, and mirroring social ills, it is a supple tool in the hands of would-be reformers such as Rómulo Gallegos, who are brave enough to risk political persecution for their writings.

William Freitas

DOÑA PERFECTA

Type of work: Novel
Author: Benito Pérez Galdós (1843-1920)
Type of plot: Tragedy of religious bigotry
Time of plot: Late nineteenth century
Locale: Órbajosa, Spain
First published: 1876

Doña Perfecta is one of three Pérez Galdós novels dealing with different aspects of religion; it tells the story of a town dominated by the clergy. The author describes the clash of modern ideas against the wall of bigotry and prejudice in a small Andalusian town removed from the main current of life. The result is a suspense novel that has shown such popularity that it has been translated into eight languages.

Jesus Christ warned almost two thousand years ago that his church was like a fisherman's net, containing both good fish and rotten fish. In *Doña Perfecta,* the Spanish novelist Pérez Galdós portrays religious intolerance in a cathedral town of interior Spain; in so doing, he attacks religious hypocrisy and emphasizes Christ's warning. *Doña Perfecta* was the first of four novels that Pérez Galdós wrote in the late 1870's picturing current Spanish life. It graphically presents what Gerald Brennan labeled "the stagnant, stupid, fanatical Spain of the country districts."

The shadow of intolerant Doña Perfecta herself lowers darkly over Órbajosa, just as the cathedral looms over plaza and town. The human beings within the cathedral make it a somber place, rather than the mellow, beautiful, hope-inspiring temple of God that it should have been. Pérez Galdós does not attack religion itself, however, for his purpose in writing *Doña Perfecta* is to reform religion. He thus criticizes Catholicism for its faults, but indirectly acknowledges that it had once given strength to robust, rural Spain. Pérez Galdós also champions the cause of progress, while condemning the abuses of traditionalism, even though aware that traditionalism should be a life-giving flame rather than dead ashes.

The novel's characterization is skimpier than that of the author's later works. Father Inocencio clearly symbolizes one of the many types of rural priests of his time, but other characters are not depicted with finesse. Character motivations are also vague; gorgon-like Doña Perfecta herself is one of Pérez Galdós' weaker female characterizations. Individuals are not strongly etched because Pérez Galdós viewed them as representatives of their class or profession. Atmosphere and setting *are* stressed for the same reason. Gloomy scenes and stock social types thus loom in the reader's memory more than do specific individuals themselves.

An interesting element in *Doña Perfecta* is Pepe's hope that man can be led upward by education, a view which reflects the influence on the author of nineteenth century Spanish intellectuals who held that education can reform man. Pepe Rey also exemplifies accurately the type of impractical idealist always to be found in Spain; hence he is more realistically drawn than many critics have implied.

Perhaps the most genuine praise that can be given to *Doña Perfecta* is that its satire has helped to modernize religious institutions in Spain. The Spanish Church today is not entirely lacking in social consciousness, while it has sometimes been observed that religious old ladies in Spain strive visibly to avoid being branded as Doña Perfectas.

THE DOUBLE-DEALER

Type of work: Drama
Author: William Congreve (1670-1729)
Type of plot: Tragi-comedy
Time of plot: Seventeenth century
Locale: London
First presented: 1694

Because Congreve departed from the established tradition of Restoration comedy, this play failed at the time of its presentation in spite of its firm construction and witty dialogue. Yet the plot, characters, and light dialogue make it one of the best comedies of the period, and the themes reflect the interests of its time: the attack on Puritans and Puritanism, dissolute dandies, devastatingly witty maidens, faithless young wives of old men, rascally servants, and devious intrigue.

After the great success of his first comedy, *The Old Bachelor,* Congreve was disappointed at the poor reception of *The Double-Dealer,* which he considered a better play on a more serious theme. Serious it was; like other contemporary comedies, it satirizes the follies and vices of the time, but here the emphasis is on the vices rather than the follies. An unusual combination of Restoration comedy and Jacobean melodrama, its action is largely devoted to the intrigues of the "villain" Maskwell. Audiences were no doubt uncomfortable at being forced to take such a long hard look at Machiavellian treachery and romantic knavery at work. As Dryden pointed out, "The women think he has exposed their bitchery too much and the gentlemen are offended with him, for the discovery of their follies, and the way of their intrigues, under the notion of friendship to their ladies' husbands." Maskwell, in the depth of his resourceful villainy, reminds us of Iago; Lady Touchwood compares him to a devil.

Lady Touchwood, of course, is herself a villain, but, as one of the victims of Maskwell's double-dealing, a lesser one. As she reminds Maskwell, her excuse is "fire in my temper, passion in my soul, apt to every provocation, oppressed at once with love, and with despair. But a sedate, a thinking villain, whose black blood runs temperately bad, what excuse can clear?" In any case, the ability of burning love to turn into burning hatred has seldom been shown so powerfully in a work professing to be a comedy. Lady Touchwood, indeed, has struck some critics as an almost tragic figure (she attempts to stab Mellefont and then Maskwell, at different points in the play, after her passion has been thwarted). Other indications of the playwright's striving for tragic effect are the unusual number of soliloquies, and the play's ending with a piece of moralizing, rather than (as was customary for Restoration comedy) a dance.

Congreve's focus of attention being Maskwell, his hero and heroine are given relatively short shrift. Mellefont and Cynthia are an agreeable pair of lovers, but no more than that. Cynthia is shown to be sensible and sincere, but she has none of the sparkling wit that was to make his Millamant so admirable. Nor is there any of the almost obligatory battles of wit between hero and heroine. Indeed, the passive Mellefont appears much of the time to be a dupe and a fool, so much so, that Congreve felt obliged to defend his hero from such charges in the play's dedication.

The plot is original; and Congreve was proud that "the mechanical part of [the play] is perfect." Consciously trying to incorporate the three unities into a classical form, he succeeded at least in molding a work that has unity of time (the action is continuous, over a three-hour period) and place (it all takes place in one "gallery"). As for unity of action, the plot is unusually tight, but there are subplots in the form of the cuckolding of Sir Paul Plyant by Careless, and of Lord Froth by Brisk. Indeed, what levity and wit the play has to offer is largely contained in these subplots. The various affectations of the minor characters, the romantic intrigues between the ladies and their gallants, and such brilliantly actable passages as the dialogue between Brisk, Lord Froth, and Careless on whether or not one should laugh at comedies, are ample evidence that Congreve had not forgotten that his prime task as a comic playwright was not to moralize—at least, not overtly—but to entertain.

THE DOWNFALL

Type of work: Novel
Author: Émile Zola (1840-1902)
Type of plot: Social criticism
Time of plot: 1870-1871
Locale: France
First published: 1892

The theme of this Zola novel is retribution; specifically, France's punishment for seventy years of indulgence, by her wretched defeat at the hands of Bismarck and Von Moltke. Each character becomes a symbol of an economic or social group. Zola expertly utilizes historical reality and accuracy in such matters as his account of Sedan, of the events leading up to Sedan, and of the insurrection in Paris, to provide a plot which even more dramatically fleshes out the historical facts.

The Downfall is a part of Zola's compendious social ledger chronicling the fortunes of the Rougon-Macquart family in France during Napoleon the Third's Second Empire (1852-1870). This work, like others of Zola, is an excellent historical-social document; it documents in a way that only literature can the social and intellectual proclivities of one articulate Frenchman.

In *The Downfall,* Zola angrily indicted the pompous and decadent posturings of French society, particularly the imperial court and the upper officer corps. He described an army top-heavy with sallow, aging, and porcine officers who suffered the collective delusion that the French military was as powerfully energetic and capable as it had been throughout the nineteenth century. The Franco-Prussian War (1870-1871) quickly shattered that myth. Zola made an incisive comparison between the two armies when he described the wizened appearance of the French Emperor and that of the young Prussian faces marching toward Paris.

Zola was militantly nonmilitant. When he wrote this book he saw a revival of the same kind of militarism which led to the Franco-Prussian war. By 1890, military circles in France, particularly the dashing General Georges Ernest Jean Marie Boulanger, had gained a zealous following devoted to his program of revenge against Germany and the reclamation of Alsace-Lorraine, provinces taken from the French by the Germans in 1870. In Zola's mind, such sentiments were folly. The key problems begging the attention of the French nation lay within French boundaries, not outside them.

As Balzac hoped to show in his novels, France had to marshall its forces to remedy the many social ills of the Third French Republic. France needed effective social legislation aimed at easing the plight of the urban working classes. *The Downfall,* like Zola's other novels, expressed Zola's sincere concern for the plight of France's social outcasts.

DRACULA

Type of work: Novel
Author: Bram Stoker (1847-1912)
Type of plot: Horror romance
Time of plot: Nineteenth century
Locale: Transylvania and England
First published: 1897

This work is a classic of the gothic novel genre, and its principal character, Count Dracula, the vampire, continues to live on in contemporary entertainment media. Utilizing the rhetorical device of letters and diaries, and staging scenes full of gothic horror such as mysterious gloomy castles and open graves at midnight, the overall effect of the novel is one of excitement, realism, and horror.

Legend is inextricably twined with Bram Stoker's novel *Dracula,* for the novel is based on the legend. It is impossible to separate the two: the reader will inevitably supply legendary associations between the lines of the novel. But more often than not, everyone tends to forget that both legend and novel were based on reality. This is not to say, of course, that vampires do or did roam Transylvania or elsewhere. However, the prototype for the Dracula legend was a verifiable historical figure, Prince Vlad Tepes, ruler of Transylvania and Walachia (now Rumania) in the mid-fifteenth century. Tepes— nicknamed "The Impaler"— earned a bloody reputation by spearing his victims (some 100,000 of them in a six to ten-year reign, so it is reported) on wooden sticks, a tactic which served to deter domestic criminals and potential outside invaders alike. He assumed the name Dracula—variously interpreted as "son of the dragon" and "son of the devil"—as a further reminder of his vicious tendencies. But the subjects of his small kingdom were convinced that such blood lust could be found only in a human vampire. Hence, Vlad Tepes, self-proclaimed Dracula, was the basis for the legend which Stoker captured so well.

Vampirism has been traced by historians, studied by scholars, embellished by artists and writers, and feared by the superstitious. And although vampirism has, in Western culture, been associated mainly with the Transylvania region of Eastern Europe, the vampire phenomenon in one form or another is attested in all parts of the world from ancient times onward. Outside of Europe, the vampire has appeared in the ancient cultures of the Middle East and the Mediterranean, in China as well as throughout Asia, in several African cultures, and in Aztec civilization and later in Mexico. Some references are in allegedly official reports and in religious works on demonology; others occur in folklore and in literature, drama, painting, and sculpture. Clearly, the vampire was no nineteenth century European invention, but the Romantic obsession with Gothic horror certainly stimulated a spate of vampiric literature, among its other supernatural preoccupations. A short story, "The

602 *Dracula*/STOKER

Vampyre," by John Polidori, was published in 1819. The melodrama *Les Vampires,* by Charles Nodier and Carmouche, was first produced in Paris in 1820. *Varney the Vampire, or The Feast of Blood* (authorship is disputed; either John Malcolm Rymer or Thomas Peckett Prest), a long novel, appeared in 1847. And Joseph Sheridan Le Fanu's redoubtable "Carmilla" first saw print in 1871. But it was Stoker's *Dracula,* published in 1897, that surpassed them all and remains the paragon of vampire stories even today.

Drawing primarily upon European sources, Stoker produced a terrifyingly credible tale by eliminating the inconsistencies and the contradictions common to legendary matter. Wisely avoiding some of the more outlandish explanations of vampirism, for example, Stoker portrayed the trait as transmitted from vampire to victim, who in turn became a vampire, and so on. But to evade straining credulity, Stoker required prolonged contact between vampire and victim before the victim was irrevocably enlisted in the ranks. Thus, Jonathan Harker, whose sustenance of Count Dracula was brief, recovered with no lasting ill effects. But Lucy Westenra was literally drained and consequently became a vampire herself. As a result—and given the perilous circumstances—Van Helsing was compelled to restrain forcibly Lucy's erstwhile fiancé Arthur from giving her a deathbed kiss on her frothing fanged mouth. Stoker also conceded the vampire's power to exercise a species of demonic possession, without physical contact, as the affliction of Mina Murray Harker illustrates.

In like manner, Stoker employed only the most conventional techniques for repelling vampires: garlic and the crucifix. And the requirements for vampire survival were equally simplified from the vast complexity of alternatives which accumulated in the legend. Stoker limited his vampires to nocturnal acvtivity; mandated, of course, the periodic sucking of blood (allowing for moderate stretches of hibernation or abstinence); insisted upon daylight repose in a coffin filled with Transylvania soil; and claimed vampiric invulnerability to ordinary human weapons.

Finally, Stoker's methods for the total annihilation of vampires were similarly conventional, without resort to esoteric impedimenta. He stipulated that a wooden stake be driven through the vampire's heart (although Dracula himself was dispatched with a bowie knife); that the vampire's head be cut off; and the vampire's mouth be stuffed with garlic flowers. Again the inconsistency of these remedies accounts for much of the impact of Stoker's horror story.

In fact, Stoker's recounting of the vampire legend has become the "standard version" in Western culture. Short stories and novels have spun off from the Stoker novel—all distinctly imitative and inferior; attempted sequels have been likewise unsatisfactory, never rising above the level of cheap journalism. A number of theatrical and film adaptations have been mounted. But the classic stage and screen performances of Bela Lugosi, based upon Stoker's

Dracula, have never been equaled. Lugosi's 1932 portrayal of Dracula still spellbinds motion-picture audiences as no other production has been able to do. And in this atmosphere of at least semi-credulity, reported sightings of vampiric activity—much like reported sightings of flying saucers or unidentified flying objects—continue to the present.

In the meanwhile, Vlad Tepes's castles in Walachia and the Carpathians have been refurbished by the Rumanian government as tourist attractions, and the historical Dracula is being hailed as a national hero who strove to upgrade the moral fiber of his subjects. Thus, in many ways, Stoker's Dracula lives on to influence the present as powerfully—albeit in a different manner— as he influenced the past.

Joanne G. Kashdan

DRAGON SEED

Type of work: Novel
Author: Pearl S. Buck (1892-1973)
Type of plot: Social chronicle
Time of plot: World War II
Locale: China
First published: 1942

As a social chronicle this novel is accurate and convincing until the appearance of the missionary Mayli, at which point the emphasis shifts to the rather improbable love affair between Mayli and Lao San. The colorful details which Buck weaves into the narrative leave the reader with a vivid impression of the Chinese culture and what World War II meant to the peasantry.

Pearl S. Buck's novel *Dragon Seed* was written during the early part of World War II, which partially accounts for its views on the Sino-Japanese conflict of the late 1930's. Miss Buck, the daughter of American missionaries, was raised in China, although she was born in the United States. Many of her works are about China, and she came to have a great affinity for these people. *The Good Earth,* her greatest novel, was written in 1936 about China, and became the major factor in leading her to the Nobel Prize for literature in 1938. *Dragon Seed,* though similar in scope, never demonstrated the power of that great first work. It provides a colorful background to the Chinese people during the Japanese occupation of China prior to World War II, but the story is not a profound one.

The basic plot involves the common people's struggle against the oppression of a tyrannical regime. This is a typical war-oriented story line and one which can only rise above the commonplace if it has good characterization and excellent writing. Pearl Buck's characters are real, which is the saving grace of the book, and her writing style is lucid; thus, readers accepted *Dragon Seed* with fervor, and it was a nationwide bestseller. However, the book is seriously limited by its polemical topicality, which borders on the propagandistic. It has not survived the test of time as has her earlier work, *The Good Earth.*

Much of *Dragon Seed*, particularly near the end when great hopes are raised after the announcement that the United States has entered the war on the side of China, is an expression of wartime patriotism, and as such limits the lasting value of the book. One excellent aspect of the book, however, is the characterization of Ling Sao, the female protagonist. Her strong will was atypical for a woman from China, at least in popular fiction. Traditionally Chinese women have been portrayed as silent, subservient creatures. This is not the case in the books of Pearl Buck, however, where females are usually the stronger and therefore deeper characters.

DREAM OF THE RED CHAMBER

Type of work: Novel
Author: Tsao Hsueh chin (c. 1715-1763), with a continuation by Kao Ou
Type of plot: Domestic chronicle
Time of plot: c. 1729-1737
Locale: Peking
First published: 1792

First published anonymously, this greatest of Chinese novels is now ascribed to Tsao Hsueh-chin, who wrote the first eighty chapters, and Kao Ou, who expanded the work with forty additional chapters based on notes left by Tsao Hsueh-chin at his death in 1763. The portrait of Pao-yu, the petted, spoiled younger son of a powerful aristocratic family already in financial decline at the time of his birth, is probably largely autobiographical. The long and complicated plot, containing over four hundred characters, is at once a family history, a lively comedy of manners, and a moral fable.

A pattern of downfall dominates *The Dream of the Red Chamber,* a book which is a realistic novel of manners as well as a metaphysical allegory.

On the metaphysical level, the stone and the flower, originally located in the Ethereal, suffer a fall when they enter earthly reality in the Red Dust. Here the novel may be read as an allegory endorsing a Taoist-Buddhist system of otherworldly values (represented by the mysteriously recurring priest and monk) and rejecting the this-worldly view of Confucianism (represented by Chia Cheng). Interestingly enough, this novel's critique of feudalist and Confucian China has won praise from Marxist readers.

The Ethereal stone's fortunes translate into a novel of manners when the stone falls into earthly existence as the protagonist, Chia Pao-yu. In this mode, the novel becomes, through its portrayal of the Chia family, a brilliantly realistic document of upper-class life during the Ching dynasty. It encompasses financial affairs and sexual aberrations, fraternal jealousies and tragic suicides. The Chia fortunes reach their apogee when Cardinal Spring becomes the Emperor's concubine. The Takuanyuan Garden, built to honor Cardinal Spring, symbolizes these halcyon days; it becomes the domain of the younger Chia generation led by Pao-yu. Here their way of life is carefree, innocent, almost Edenic. But, just as Pao-yu must grow into adulthood, so evil invades this Eden. The fall begins when an indecent purse is found. A general search ensues, scandals surface, a tragic death results. Analogous disasters overtake the family. Their financial dealings incur the Emperor's displeasure; Imperial Guards ransack the Chia compound. Then bandits raid the garden itself.

Finally, Pao-yu chooses to deny the folly of this world and join the Buddhist priest and the Taoist monk journeying presumably to the Ethereal.

To Western readers, this novel will seem episodic; Chinese novels, however, did not aim to tell a particular story but to weave a rich tapestry of life. This latter purpose Tsao achieves brilliantly, and his novel remains widely appreciated for its skillful interweaving of philosophical allegory with unblinking realism.

DRINK

Type of work: Novel
Author: Émile Zola (1840-1902)
Type of plot: Naturalism
Time of plot: Second half of the nineteenth century
Locale: Paris
First published: 1877

Drink *belongs to the Rougon-Macquart series in which Zola attempted to apply the methods of science to the writing of social criticism as fiction; it describes with devastating clarity and objectivity the effects of alcoholism on the working class. The atmosphere evoked is one of fatalism and hopelessness; but Zola imparts to the social group he describes an intensity and humanity that make the bleakness of the narrative more bearable.*

Even if Zola had never written *Drink,* his stature among the pantheon of French writers would have been secure. Only Balzac could rival Zola for sheer literary fecundity. Balzac's epic Human Comedy is continued in spirit in Zola's meticulous, multivolume chronicle of the trials and tribulations of the Rougon-Macquart family. Zola's fame was guaranteed not only by the volume of works produced but also by the subject matter of the French working classes.

In *Drink,* the author again directed his scalpel-like pen to the most bruised spot on the French social body, the impoverished urban working class. Zola's surgical gaze left no part of the wound unexamined. Indeed, *Drink* is perhaps Zola's most severe and hopeless diagnosis of French society. Trapped by a mean environment as well as by genetic proclivities toward alcohol, the heroine of the story proves no match for the degrading life Zola made her lead.

Zola's bleak depiction of French society stemmed from two scientific influences, one methodological, the other ideological. Zola, like many European intellectuals, was convinced that science held the key to social improvement. If one only remained objective and observed reality, he could establish the truth of a given situation. Zola pressed this scientific method into his literary service. He likened all literature to a scientific experiment, and like the most dogged and objective chemist, Zola recorded all of the seamiest "data" he could observe.

The second expression of Zola's literary tryst with science came from Darwin. The vogue of Darwin's theories reached a climax in the 1870's when Zola was at work on *Drink.* Darwin emphasized the biological nature of man, the influence of environment, and to a lesser degree genetic inheritance on his character. Thus, when Zola described the downfall of a Gervaise, he could claim to be describing a condition for which science had an answer.

Naturally, Zola wrote *Drink* for reasons other than to demonstrate his knowledge of contemporary scientific methods and theories. He was genuinely concerned with the plight of the French working class and wished to bring their baleful state to the attention of his fellow Frenchmen. And with good reason, for throughout the nineteenth century, French social legislation remained the most backward in all of Europe.

DRUMS

Type of work: Novel
Author: James Boyd (1888-1944)
Type of plot: Historical romance
Time of plot: American Revolution
Locale: North Carolina and London
First published: 1925

In this pleasing mixture of history and adventure, Boyd attempts to reproduce the thoughts and ways of life of various classes of Americans during the Revolution. His scenes at the race track and on the sea are particularly vivid in their descriptive power.

At a time when major American novelists like Hemingway and Fitzgerald were involved in expatriate experience for its test of character and enlargement of their social and artistic consciousness, James Boyd sought similar enrichment closer to home. *Drums* was hailed as one of the finest novels yet written about the American Revolution when it appeared in 1925; it launched Boyd, who had been a moderately successful short story writer, on a major career as a historical novelist. *Marching On* (1927), another war novel (this time about the Civil War in the South), was followed by *The Long Hunt* (1930), *Roll River* (1935), and *Bitter Creek* (1939). The later novels continued to explore the evolving American character.

In many ways *Drums* is a conventional historical romance: a morally sound young hero weathers the temptation of superficial but charming aristocrats, lovers, and friends, and discovers his democratic soul in the heat of battle. His bravery in the battle between the *Bonhomme Richard* and the *Serapis* recalls the fictional treatment of the same fight in Melville's *Israel Potter,* and is the kind of ordeal by fire that American youths have endured from Crane to Hemingway.

Boyd was trying to do more than simply write a traditional historical novel with the usual trappings of adventure and romance. He wanted to suggest some of the things that went into the making of the American Revolution itself. John Fraser's assuming of the American cause is the psychological and moral equivalent of the emergence of what Boyd felt was the American identity. The indifference of the English aristocrats to the dying vagabond, and Sir Nat's coming to the defense of American honor despite his basic social detachment, are the kind of examples that gradually educate John Fraser to the strong emotional response to the democratic army that marches across the horizon at the end of the novel.

DRUMS ALONG THE MOHAWK

Type of work: Novel
Author: Walter D. Edmonds (1903-   )
Type of plot: Historical chronicle
Time of plot: 1775-1783
Locale: The Mohawk Valley
First published: 1936

Set during the years of the Revolutionary War in the Mohawk Valley of Upstate New York, Drums Along the Mohawk *presents a focused rather than a sweeping view of the war years. Edmonds achieves an air of authenticity through his descriptions and his characterizations, many of which are based upon real people.*

During the 1930's the historical novel became extremely popular. Most of them followed the same pattern: they were long, had many characters, were full of action and realistic detail, and usually ended happily. *Drums Along the Mohawk* has all of these qualities, but it is one of the best of the genre. In 1936 it was on the best-seller list. Edmonds in his author's note defends the genre, noting that the life presented is not a bygone picture, for the parallel is too close to our own. The valley people faced repercussions of poverty and starvation and were plagued by unfulfilled promises and the inevitable redtape of a central government which could not understand local problems. Thus, the valley farmers, in the typically American tradition, learned to fight for themselves and for the land they had worked so hard to wrench from the wilderness and could not abandon.

Contrary to the patriotic myth, for all American soldiers the war was not a glorious fight for freedom. Many fought only because it was necessary to protect their families. They never thought of the American troops in the South and East; that was too remote, while the ever-present threat of instant disaster was too near. When Captain Demooth says to Gil, "Who gives a damn for the Stamp Tax?" Gil admits that it had not bothered him and asks the key question of most of the farmers: "Why do we have to go and fight the British at all?" The attitude of many of the men conscripted for the militia is "Damn the militia! I need to roof my barn." Yet, as the attacks upon the small settlements begin, they realize that they must band together and fight.

At times the western settlers wonder which side is the enemy. Denied food, munitions, and the protection of regular troops by the government at Albany, their seed grain commandeered, and their fences burned for firewood, the settlers of German Flats become extremely bitter at the indifferent treatment they receive. When the widowed Mrs. Reall with her many children tries to collect her husband's back pay, she is denied because he is not marked dead on the paymaster's list. Even though Colonel Bellinger swears he saw Reall killed and scalped, the money is withheld. The only alternative she is given is to file a claim before the auditor-general which must then be passed by an act of Congress. In the meantime the family must starve or rely on the charity of others who cannot really afford to help. They find that the Continental currency is practically worthless, but the climax of the colonists' disillusionment with the Congress comes when the residents receive huge tax bills for land which has been abandoned, buildings that have burned, and stock that has been killed. The incredulous settlers realize that the tax list is the one formerly used by the king.

The bestiality of what war does to men dominates the book. As the Indian raids become more ghastly, the Continentals grow more brutal. Scalps are taken by both Indian and white, and the atrocities and mutilations committed by both sides become increasingly barbarous.

Yet, in spite of the ever-present atmosphere of horror, fear, and death, Edmonds also presents the forces of life. There is fierce energy in the characters in spite of their hardships. This is seen most clearly in the character of Lana, who, though weakened by starvation, work, and fear, manages to bear and care for her two boys. There is a mystery about her as she nurses and cares for her babies. Although she deeply loves Gil, with the birth of the first child she becomes mother first. Even the rough scout Joe Boleo senses the maternal mystery she exudes. There is also beauty in life itself as seen in the human body and in reproduction. The pregnant Nancy becomes more beautiful as she carries her illegitimate child, and the marriage of young John Weaver to Mary Reall begins another generation when Mary becomes pregnant.

Edmonds' style is free flowing, and he has an excellent ear for natural folk speech. As omniscient narrator, he goes deeply into the minds of the main characters and captures their reactions to the many things going on about them. All of the main characters have individuality and the gift of life.

The praise that is often given the novel is for the realism which Edmonds achieves by minute detail; however, this is also a weakness. His accounts of the many battles and raids become repetitious, for in the interest of historical truth, he does not want to eliminate anything. Thus, the action becomes blurred because there are so many similar accounts.

Structurally the book is well handled with the exception of the last chapter, "Lana," which occurs three years after the preceeding one. It appears to have been tacked on simply to tie up a few loose ends and to give the story a happy ending. In a book which has proceeded slowly season by season for five years, the three year interval startles the reader.

The theme of the novel is the strength of the men who will endure anything to achieve the American dream. Through their own efforts they hope to earn their land, houses, animals, and the material things necessary to make life easier and more beautiful for themselves and particularly for their children. Lana and Gil begin their marriage with a cow, a few pieces of furniture, and Lana's most valued possession—a peacock feather which, with its mysterious beauty, symbolizes the beauty of the dream. All of this is lost in the war, but in the last chapter Gil realizes his ambitions. He is farming his own land, he has built a new house, and he owns a yoke of oxen. Lana has her two boys, a baby daughter, security, and even the now battered but still gorgeous peacock feather which the Indian Blue Back returns to her. She is supremely content and secure as she tells herself, "We've got this place. . . . We've got the children. We've got each other. Nobody can take those things away. Not any more."

Vina Nickels Oldach

THE DUCHESS OF MALFI

Type of work: Drama
Author: John Webster (?—Before 1635)
Type of plot: Romantic tragedy
Time of plot: Sixteenth century
Locale: Amalfi and Milan, Italy
First presented: (?-Before 1635)

Although this play is typical of the "blood tragedies" which flourished during the reign of James I, its melodrama is not so overpowering as to detract from a general dignity which comes across in the lines. Webster's plotting is peculiar in this drama in that one year elapses between Act I and Act II, and another two years between Act II and Act III; the lapses are indicated to the audience by the birth of children to the Duchess.

Little is known of John Webster's life, although the title page of his pageant, *Monuments of Honor* (1624), calls him a "merchant-tailor." In the custom of Jacobean playwrights, he often collaborated, probably with Dekker, a practice supported by Philip Henslowe, whose *Diary* gives much information about the theater of the period. Webster's reputation rests almost entirely upon *The White Devil* (c. 1612), and *The Duchess of Malfi* (c. 1613). Both are studies of illicit love, revenge and murder, and intrigues worthy of the Machiavellians so appealing to Elizabethan and Jacobean audiences.

The Duchess of Malfi is a finer play than *The White Devil,* in part due to the noble character of the Duchess herself. Her story has the reputation of being the best poetic tragedy written after Shakespeare. It reveals Webster's powers, often compared to Shakespeare's, to present themes of great moral seriousness in magnificent language while also creating flesh-and-blood characters. Webster and Shakespeare mastered thinking in images so well that the images develop themes and meaning as fully as does plot.

Not all critics find Webster's work excellent, however, partly due to distaste for the violence of revenge and blood tragedies which may obscure finer qualities of the plays. Bernard Shaw referred to Webster as "a Tussaud-laureate." Few critics underestimate Webster's brilliance as a psychologist despite the melodramatic or surrealistic qualities of his work. One can appreciate the psychological insights and also the fact that the dramas reflect their origins: many descended from Kyd's *The Spanish Tragedy,* Senecan tragedy, the medieval morality play with its preoccupation with death. They also reflect the tempestuous Renaissance history. Many of the dramas are set in Italy, the epitome of evil locales to Renaissance Englishmen, a view which history supports.

The Duchess of Malfi was an actual Italian duchess, but Webster's immediate source was Painter's *Palace of Pleasure* (1567), a collection of tediously moral stories. Painter's work was in turn based on twenty-five novellas of

Matteo Bandello which provided themes for several plays by Shakespeare and his contemporaries. Painter concentrates on two major "sins" or weaknesses: the Duchess' sensuality and Antonio's excessive ambition. Bosola is referred to only once in Painter's story. Webster does not alter Painter's version so much as he enlarges it by surrounding the limited Romantic-Tragic world of the lovers with other worlds: the corrupt court of Amalfi and the religious state of Rome, thus exposing a universal corruption that expands concentrically beyond the lovers' chambered world. Moving beyond the lovers into other worlds, he enlarges and magnifies the role of the villain Bosola, using him to bind the various worlds together. A "revenge tragedy" results which treats the question of personal honor (still tied to feudal values), the political and moral problems of lawlessness, and the supreme question—human vengeance and Divine or Providential vengeance.

Webster creates this fallen world through the actions of the Duchess, Ferdinand, the Cardinal, Antonio, and Bosola, particularizing the questions mentioned above. First, what does passionate and true love do in the presence of family pride and social taboos; second, how can man rise in an evil, power-dominated world without corrupting himself; and finally, does not man create his own heaven or hell? Free will is implicit and explicit throughout the play: man is responsible for his choices. Webster forces the smaller worlds into collision in the working out of the themes, and tragic destruction ensues. Providence asserts its influence finally through the hope vested in the Duchess' and Antonio's innocent son.

The Duchess of the play is a headstrong but noble woman who says to her executioners: "Pull, and pull strongly, for your able strength/Must pull down heaven upon me. . . ." Nobility notwithstanding, her "passion is out of place," for Antonio is but head steward of her household. She denies the chain of being on its social level in wooing Antonio. Even at the moment when she and Antonio confess their love, they are therefore threatened. She tries to ease his fears:

> Ant.:   But for your brothers?
> Duch.: Do not think of them:
>   All discord without this circumference
>   Is only to be pitied, not fear'd:
>   Yet, should they know it, time will easily
>   Scatter the tempest.   (I.111.176-181)

Her optimism is that of the pure soul; she misjudges the power of those outside "this circumference." Her willfulness and passion are lust in the eyes of brothers, Church, and society at large. Webster communicates the sweetness of the romance, however, so thoroughly that the lovers are totally sympathetic throughout.

Second to the Duchess in importance is Bosola, a symbol of Webster's disgust with an era which admired ambition excessively, but provided little opportunity for its honest realization. This melancholy scholar perverts his intelligence to "serve" Ferdinand and the Cardinal, representatives of political and ecclesiastical corruption. Bosola's evil actions continue after the Duchess' murder so that Webster can complete the theme of corruption. This accounts for the extended action of Acts IV and V sometimes found objectionable. Ultimately, of course, Bosola recognizes his misplaced devotion and his responsibility for the horrors, a recognition too sudden for some readers. But outside Shakespeare's works, dramatic characters of the period seldom changed gradually, a vestige of the parent morality plays.

Even Ferdinand (who may hide incestuous feelings for his sister) accepts his guilt, saying:

> Whether we fall by ambition, blood, or lust,
> Like diamonds, we are cut with our own dust. (V.v.75-76)

Ferdinand's marvelous image is characteristic of the powerful figurative language of the play. The image refers to all the characters, identifying them as the most precious of jewels, yet paradoxically made of dust. Man's place as a little below the angels, Webster tells us, is secure only so long as he acts in accordance with the moral laws established by Providence. He may rise or fall by his own acts. Delio's words close the play in Webster's imagistic way of a final comment upon the fallen of Amalfi:

> These wretched eminent things
> Leave no more fame behind 'em, than should one
> Fall in a frost, and leave his print in snow:
> (V.v.117-119)

Mary H. Hayden

THE DYNASTS

Type of work: Verse drama
Author: Thomas Hardy (1840-1928)
Type of plot: Historical epic
Time of plot: 1806-1815
Locale: Europe
First published: 1903-1908

Written in a variety of verse forms as well as poetic prose, The Dynasts *is a vast, panoramic drama of the years of Napoleon's domination of Europe. Hardy's intention is to depict mankind as powerless against the forces of Destiny. Both the drastic switching of points of view and settings—from extraterrestrial space to emperors' courts to cottagers' firesides—and the array of allegorical spectators who comment on the events of the drama, make the alarms and skirmishes of man seem trivial.*

The Dynasts represents Hardy's most ambitious attempt to portray his philosophic fatalism. An epic-drama written for "mental performance," it combines the skills of Hardy, the novelist with those of Hardy, the poet. Hardy's ability to tell a story is nowhere more apparent than here, and his drama, with its scenes of battle, court life, and common life, anticipates the great motion picture spectacles of such directors as D. W. Griffith. At the same time there are powerful lines and much extremely competent verse which make the stuff of poetry.

Unlike the great Victorian long poems, Hardy's poetic drama deals with recent events. As in his novels, Hardy is concerned with the plight of the common man in an indifferent world. But, unlike in his novels, he is concerned also with potentates, whose will often seems to control the lives of common men and women. This, however, is an illusion, for even the great are moved by the Immanent Will, an impassive, unmotivated force, which at one point is described as having "films or brain-tissue" which "pervade all things." In his final defeat, Napoleon himself comes to acknowledge that he has always "passively obeyed" this Will. His gradual physical deterioration symbolizes his spiritual decay.

The Dynasts is also implicitly antiwar in its vivid portrayal of the carnage that always accompanies war. It is a democratic drama, holding up parliamentary government as preferable to rule by monarchical fiat. And it is a very English work, portraying even the typical English xenophobia. In spite of the gloom that pervades *The Dynasts,* there are moments of humor, and Hardy permits the Chorus of the Spirit of Pities to have the last, semi-hopeful word.

EARTH

Type of work: Novel
Author: Émile Zola (1840-1902)
Type of plot: Social realism
Time of plot: 1860's
Locale: La Beauce, France
First published: 1887

Earth, *the fifteenth volume of the Rougon-Macquart series, is Zola's horrifying vision of the French peasantry before the Franco-Prussian War. The earth itself dominates the novel, its beauty and indifference contrasting dramatically with the peasants' absorption in possessing the land and the crimes they commit to obtain it. Zola's introduction in the novel of a Rabelaisian brand of humor in the figure of Jésus-Christ was an innovation in literary realism.*

Zola began as a literary romantic and an idealist. In his youth, he wrote fairy tales and dreamt of perfect beauty and perfect love. But the poverty he experienced early in life and the general Europan literary climate brought him to try to picture an imperfect but real "corner of nature."

Earth, a magnificent example of Zola's groping for the authentic details in life, can be best understood when placed in the literary context of realism and naturalism. Literary realism developed in the nineteenth century partly as a response to the conditions of modern society. It stressed fidelity to the facts of everyday existence. Scenes, characters, motives, conflicts were presumably drawn from experiences in life rather than from dreams of other worlds or of the supernatural. Within the realist tradition are distinct and coherent groupings. Naturalism is one of them. But it is easier to place a work such as *Earth* in the naturalist tradition than it is to define literary naturalism. In general, however, for the purposes of examining *Earth,* we can establish two basic points: first, naturalism attempts to portray the actual and significant details of life and especially (though not exclusively) the life of poor and working people; second, naturalism most often attempts to uncover those forces, in the environment and in the genetic make up of the individual, that determine the course of life.

Earth tries to give an accurate picture of French rural life in the 1860's; and this picture is not merely a general account, but a brilliantly detailed canvas that conveys the humanity and density of rural life.

The basis of the action of the novel is the division of his land by an old man. Much of the novel, therefore, describes the unending, vicious, implacable hatreds and the unyielding tensions that emerge within the farmer's family. Domestic life appears in the conversations, the cooking and cleaning utensils, the jealous glances, the dirt, the cobwebs, and the small, damp rooms of the peasant households. The smells of the fields, the manure, the sweat, the musky odors of water and age saturate everything.

The life of the countryside is further explored in relation to the fields, skies, and attention to the weather. The division of these fields, the occasional run-down cottage, the seeding and fertilization of the fields are communicated in the most meticulous detail. Pages are devoted to storms of various kinds, including a hailstorm. But unlike the romantics, for whom the excesses of the weather are often merely spectacular, these storms are viewed as destructive and, toward the end of *Earth,* in the tradition of *King Lear*, as brutalizing and humbling.

Main events in the harvest are not omitted. A grape harvest, for example, is sketched by Zola. The workers pick these grapes, stuff themselves, and get sick. In fact, sickness, drunkenness, perversity, and violence—all inherent in the life of these times—are examined with special intensity. Fevers, passions, obsessions, jealousies, and the mutual destruction inseparable from the conditions of the life of the peasants are not spared. The reader feels that Zola leaves out nothing, including the sexual aspect. From the beginning of the novel, wherein Zola describes a young man and woman helping a bull and cow to mate, without embarrassment, the sexual theme is established. Rape and incest are not excluded.

Zola's accumulation of detail from real experience becomes more and more powerful as the novel advances. These details—linked through action, character, and theme—become, for the reader, the tightly woven, actual fabric of life. Reading *Earth* is, in fact, to be submerged in this life; and this feeling of submersion accounts, no doubt, for the powerful influence the novel continues to exert. At the same time, the accumulation of these details naturally raises the question of selection. Can Zola be accused of presenting only the sordid side of life, of emphasizing the nasty aspects of life unnecessarily? Has he only selected those details which demonstrate the obscene or degraded features of country life? *Earth* was sharply attacked when it was first published precisely for these reasons. The novel was even thought to be deliberately pornographic. Although a modern reader may tell himself that such an accusation is outdated or humorously quaint, it must be said that the brutality and often unexpected violence and sex remain, to this day, quite literally shocking. But a good argument can be made that these scenes are included not for their shock value but for more serious reasons. These reasons are, strangely enough, connected to Zola's understanding of science.

The second important feature of literary naturalism, its attempt to portray the underlying forces that shape human destiny, is especially evident in the work of Zola. These forces were understood by Zola in a scientific context. They were describable, measurable, and inevitable. In his view, in fact, by understanding the genetic and environmental forces working on his characters, and by altering these forces, he could explain his characters scientifically and, at the same time, actually experiment on them and test them in his fiction. Zola did not carry out this experimental procedure vigorously in his novels.

In *Earth,* the forces that are most evident are those associated with the land. The greed for the land, which is manifest in Buteau, one of the central characters, overcomes all obstacles. Buteau will have the land or destroy it, himself, and his competitors and family. Also connected to the earth is the power of sex. The opening scene of the novel deals with the fertilization of the land. A sexual life "close to the earth" is also described. Sexual activity takes place in the fields as well as in the home.

Finally, there is the genetic composition of the characters. Their strengths and weaknesses, determined by the strengths and weaknesses of their ancestors, provide a spectrum of responses to the conditions of rural France. The family thus helps place *Earth* in its proper position in the massive architecture of Zola's Rougon-Macquart series.

Although Zola may have seen his characters as more or less determined by forces outside their control, *Earth* leaves the impression that men and women can, within limits, choose their course in life. It should be said that some other practitioners of naturalist fiction—such as Frank Norris in the United States—took a much more mechanical approach to the "scientific" forces that shape human life. In Norris' work, the reader is left with the impression that human freedom is simply low farce. But Zola, in the novel *Earth,* does not communicate this sense of a claustrophobic fate. No matter how awful Fouan's end may be, Zola never shifts the responsibility away from Fouan to the abstraction of heredity.

Earth, in the last analysis, certainly demonstrates the limits and the narrowness of the life of the peasant in nineteenth century France. But within those limits Zola shows that freedom survives, and with freedom the refreshing possibilities of birth.

Howard Lee Hertz

EAST OF EDEN

Type of work: Novel
Author: John Steinbeck (1902-1968)
Type of plot: Regional chronicle
Time of plot: 1865-1918
Locale: California
First published: 1952

East of Eden is an ambitious but not altogether successful attempt to present three stories simultaneously: a panoramic history of the Salinas Valley (symbolic of America as a whole); a melodramatic chronicle of two families in the valley; and a symbolic re-creation of the Cain and Abel story. In each story the theme is the same: good and evil are always in conflict, but man's freedom and glory lie in his ability to choose the good to direct his own life.

Compared to other novels by John Steinbeck, *East of Eden* has received relatively little attention, and most of it has been adverse. The primary reason for relegating *East of Eden* to the status of an inferior novel seems to be that it is atypical of Steinbeck's corpus. After all, in most of his other works Steinbeck was concerned with social issues from a realistic or a naturalistic point of view, portraying human travail with relentless accuracy through an intensive examination of a short time span. But in *East of Eden,* Steinbeck departs from his customary literary style to write an epic portrait which ranges less intensively over a much broader time span of about seventy years. Although depictions of characters and events are really no less vivid than in his other novels, Steinbeck's *East of Eden* is certainly less structured, a looser novel than his dedicated readers had come to expect. Thus, despite some quite explicit sex scenes, disappointed reader expectation accounts in large measure for the failure of *East of Eden* to win popular or critical acclaim. It simply was not what people had come to expect of Steinbeck.

But the novel is at least respectable if not brilliant. In fact, it is, in many ways, a historical romance in its panoramic sweep of significant history overlaid with specific human problems. The story ranges from the Civil War to World War I, from the East Coast to the West Coast, over several generations of two families. It displays all of the conventional elements of historical romance. Genuinely historical events and people providing the backdrop, even the shaping forces which mold the fictional characters' lives and determine their destiny. These characters thus appear to have only partial control over their lives, at best; and external factors consequently determine to a large extent what they must cope with in order to survive. They appear to be buffeted mercilessly by fate.

However, Steinbeck's philosophical commitment to free will aborts the naturalistically logical conclusion. As a result, both Charles and Adam Trask appear to select freely their own paths in life, the former indulging fantasies of evil and the latter choosing to disregard everyone's evil inclinations, including his own. So, too, is Cathy made to seem capable of choice and responsible for it. Likewise, the other major characters are depicted as having the capacity for moral choice and for living with the consequences. Yet it is just this aspect of *East of Eden* which flies in the face of the reader's expectations of "typical" Steinbeck and flies in the face of both logic and reality. Finally it is Steinbeck's own ambivalence about free will and determinism which constitutes the major weakness in *East of Eden*. For whatever we or Steinbeck believe about a historical-Biblical Garden of Eden, neither we nor Steinbeck believe that a Garden of Eden exists now—east or west—even in the Salinas Valley.

EASTWARD HO!

Type of work: Drama
Authors: George Chapman (c. 1559-1634) with Ben Jonson (1573?-1637) and John Marston (1576-1634)
Type of plot: Realistic comedy
Time of plot: About 1605
Locale: London
First presented: 1605

The result of the unlikely collaboration of such different personalities as Chapman, Jonson, and Marston is a comedy that is smooth, unified, fast-moving, and entertaining. The plot encompasses both the heartwarming theme of the Prodigal Son and satiric thrusts at contemporary society. Even the victims of the satire, however, are treated without the cutting bitterness that the authors' other works might lead the reader to expect.

A product of collaboration by three successful playwrights in their own right, *Eastward Ho!* is one of a genre of Jacobean plays called city comedies. As such, the play deals heavily with the domestic imbroglios of merchants and their apprentices and seems designed to appeal to just such individuals in the audience. Those to whom the play would most readily appeal would be those who accepted the conventional morality of the day. It is this morality —a solid aggregate of thrift, hard work, and humility—which forms the foundation on which the play's didactic message is based.

The plot builds upon the timeless and popular exemplum of the Prodigal Son. In this case, the son has been split into an artificial son, the apprentice Quicksilver, and a natural daughter, Gertrude. They are balanced by their virtuous counterparts, the good apprentice, Golding, and the good daughter, Mildred. Quicksilver and Gertrude (with Sir Petronel Flash thrown in for interest) are wasteful, lazy, and proud; Golding is thrifty, hardworking, and humble, as is Mildred. Touchstone, as his name indicates, provides the play with a judgmental intellect, one who tests the various characters and pronounces them false, or good as gold.

But the play transcends its precursor, the medieval morality play, in presenting characters who are more than merely their types. Quicksilver, who had previously been a stealer of unconsidered lines from other plays, becomes something of a didactic poet and is saved through his repentance. Touchstone, embodiment of morality though he is, shows his weakness in willfully denying his own impulses to mercy. Finally, from a position of power gained by his life of virtue, Golding rises above all as the dispenser of impartial justice and selfless mercy.

Eastward Ho! was written to compete with a play of similar title, *Westward Ho!,* produced by a rival company. It is famous in part for a passage (III, iii, 42-47) insulting to Scots, which offended James I, causing Chapman and Jonson to be imprisoned.

THE ECCLESIAZUSAE

Type of work: Drama
Author: Aristophanes (c. 448-c. 385 B.C.)
Type of plot: Utopian comedy
Time of plot: Early fourth century B.C.
Locale: Athens
First presented: 392 B.C.

Not one of the playwright's best works, The Ecclesiazusae *lacks the wit and ingenuity of* Lysistrata, *which it most resembles. The scatological humor seems gratuitous, but the satire on the communistic Utopia enforced by the women of Athens is effective. The action is swift, especially since Aristophanes has reduced the role of the chorus to the barest minimum.*

The Greek title of this play means "Assembly women"—a contradiction to the male-oriented society and politics of ancient Greece. Yet, like the *Lysistrata,* this play must not be seen as a vehicle of feminine protest. In both plays Aristophanes is criticizing the mismanagement of affairs of state and is turning toward women not as the proper alternative but as the last desperation. Both situations and solutions are intolerable, but in the course of each drama the playwright exposes the vanity of power and its consequences.

As Aristophanes' penultimate play, *The Ecclesiazusae* tends away from personal invective and reliance on the chorus. The play contains no *parabasis,* a device essential to Old Comedy, whereby frequently the chorus would address the audience with the playwright's indignation over contemporary or current social or political outrages. This, then, marks the beginning of Middle Comedy, the fourth century transition to New Comedy. In *The Ecclesiazusae* we see the stock types so popular in later comedy—such as the shrewish wife, the hellish hag, the amorous young man, and the lecherous old one. Yet, unlike New Comedy, plays of this period still rely heavily on misrepresentation of philosophic schools. The communism of goods and sex proposed by Praxagora was not Plato's, since in *The Republic* the philosopher aimed at removing from the guardians of the state any temptations to selfish interests; in Aristophanes the motive for shared property is basely selfish. While Socrates wants to manage the breeding of the best class, Praxagora wants sex to be widely available to those who have the least chance for it.

There is little doubt that Aristophanes is cynically warning his fellow Athenians against yearning for Utopia; simplistic solutions bring abominable consequences. Praxagora ("Mrs. Forum-Business") does away with prostitution but dissolves marriage, thereby turning wives into loose women and their husbands into free men. She provides a free dinner for everyone, but only at the expense of one's entire property.

EDMUND CAMPION

Type of work: Novelized biography
Author: Evelyn Waugh (1903-1966)
Type of plot: Historical chronicle
Time of plot: Sixteenth century
Locale: Oxford, London, Douai, Rome, Prague
First published: 1935

In this intelligent and sober fictionalized biography of the English Catholic martyr, Waugh warns against intolerance as an evil which has yet to be banished from human affairs. The author implies that a modern age of persecution is not by any means an impossibility.

Evelyn Waugh was awarded the Hawthornden Prize for *Edmund Campion* as a work of marked distinction by an author under forty. Some critics have found Waugh's descriptions of Campion's last Mass and sermon at Lyford, his subsequent hiding with two other priests, and their final discovery and arrest among the most descriptive and dramatic passages in all his writings. Others have pointed out that the story is related with bias, and without any attempt to create a true historical atmosphere. In any case, the short novel is told simply and does relate the tragedy of a martyr in the service of Catholicism.

It is interesting to note that the novel was written shortly after Waugh's own conversion to Catholicism and reflects his search for inner peace and joy which he ultimately found in the martyred Englishman. Waugh reveals in Campion's life what the Catholic faith meant to him personally, and his book is full of reverence and complete affirmation of the Church. He held a nostalgia for the past and his romantic sense of history comes out in this novel. At the time Waugh undertook to write the novel, the Jesuits were rebuilding Campion Hall on a new site at Oxford. Waugh pledged all the royalties he received from the book to the building fund for Campion Hall.

Reviewers of the book, including most of those who were unsympathetic to the general thesis it contained, praised its style and overlooked some of the inaccurate historical details. Throughout *Edmund Campion* there is a sense of historical continuity. The opening pages picture Elizabeth on her deathbed and reflect upon the profits and losses of her reign. Waugh glances forward many years beyond Elizabeth and then returns to the queen's encounter with the scholar, hero, and martyr, Campion. Everything is seen in the light of the "Catholic" perspective. In the last pages, the author looks historically beyond Campion, thirteen years later, and describes another martyr for the Catholic minority in England, Henry Walpole. At times, *Edmund Campion* seems to reach beyond the boundaries of a short novelized biography, and attempt to make a larger statement about Catholicism and its struggle for survival during different periods in various places. Such a task is a large one and Waugh's efforts seem rewarded by a generally well-accepted and respected religious biography.

THE EDUCATION OF HENRY ADAMS

Type of work: Novelized autobiography
Author: Henry Adams (1838-1918)
Type of plot: Intellectual and social history
Time of plot: 1838-1905
Locale: America, England, France
First published: 1907

The theme of this autobiography is the process of technological growth and the multiplication of mechanical forces which led, during the author's own lifetime, to a degeneration of moral relationships between men and to the lapsing of their pursuits into money-seeking or complete lassitude. The book is a masterpiece of intellectual writing, tracing intimately the author's thought processes and his moral and emotional maturation.

As a work of literature, *The Education of Henry Adams* may be read in at least three ways: first, as a conventional autobiography; second, as a work in the mainstream of the European *Bildüngsroman* tradition, a personal narrative of one person's intellectual and emotional coming of age; and third, as a critical treatise on Western civilization and culture. In this latter sense, Adams anticipated the twentieth century preoccupation with the relationship between technological science and humanistic cultural assumptions.

No matter how Adams' work is read, however, the key chapter is "The Dynamo and the Virgin." Here he uses the two symbols of the "Dynamo" and the "Virgin" to spell out his analysis of the shaping forces of civilization, a synthesis of ideas reflecting his entire education, first broached in *Mont-Saint-Michel and Chartres.* This excursion into historiography places Adams in the front rank of nineteenth century historical philosophers, for it is at this point that he posits the thesis that "belief" is the guiding force of socio-political and cultural phenomena.

Just as religious beliefs, the "Virgin," created the great works of the Middle Ages, he says, so also the modern belief in science and technology, the "Dynamo," will shape the major creations of the modern age. At last, though, he views that latter age with trepidation and anxiety, for he realizes that in some ways the humanistic education he received from his forefathers did not suit him for the Age of the Dynamo. Indeed, he sees that moral values of great worth, values which underlie the significant achievements of his grandfather, John Quincy Adams, and his father, are being destroyed by the machine. At last, then, Henry Adams defines for us the major conflict of twentieth century American civilizations, a drama whose denouement still remains undecided.

EDWARD THE SECOND

Type of work: Drama
Author: Christopher Marlowe (1564-1593)
Type of plot: Historical chronicle
Time of plot: Fourteenth century
Locale: England and France
First presented: c. 1590

This historical drama was the last play written by Marlowe shortly before his untimely death. Unlike his earlier works, The Troublesome Reign and Lamentable Death of Edward the Second *is polished in form, sustained in theme, and consistent in characterization.*

Marlowe's last drama—the dating of Marlowe's dramas is, of course, conjectural—is regarded by many as his finest work, showing tighter structure and greater clarity and unity than his earlier works. Since it was published almost immediately after his death, the text escaped the corruption which his other works suffered, and there are relatively few problems with establishing an accurate text. We also possess the source material for the work, Holinshed's *Chronicles of England,* in the edition of 1577 or 1587. By comparing this play with others of its genre and with its source, it is possible to arrive at an appreciation of Marlowe's achievement.

Holinshed's account of the reign of Edward II (1307-1327) is relatively unstructured and, though providing much material, does not establish clear relationships or a connected series of events. Marlowe, who worked closely enough with Holinshed's text to incorporate actual phrases from the chronicle, nevertheless set about to structure the story and bring out salient features, developing relationships and characterizations, and compressing the events of over twenty years—from Gaveston's return in 1307 to the execution of Mortimer in 1330—into what seems on stage to be a relatively short span. While this creates some problems in terms of improbably swift shifting of loyalties and changes of policy, it gives the drama a tightness of structure and a forward movement that underscores the alienation of all Edward's associates—his wife, the loyal Kent, and the well-meaning, but outraged barons.

It is this surging wave of hostility that is the central event of the play, which begins with the return of the king's beloved Gaveston from exile. Marlowe makes it quite clear that the two men are lovers, but it is not the homosexual relationship that disturbs the barons—in fact, at one point the Elder Mortimer explains "the mightiest kings have had their minions," and lists famous pairs of male lovers in history. Rather it is the fact that Edward ignores his role as king for the sake of Gaveston that enrages the nobles. Gaveston is lowborn, but Edward elevates him to share the throne, and in his infatuation, he forgets his duties to his realm. He is following his personal will, and shows this weakness in his inability to give up his personal pleasure for the good of his kingdom. He is childlike both in his willfulness and in his stubbornness, and he remains blind to the fact of his own misrule and the justice of the nobles' grievances.

Yet the Tudor world saw rebellion against an annointed king as the most grievous breach of natural law, and the play documents the slow evolution of rebellion. At first it is solely against Gaveston that the hostility is directed. Only gradually does this hostility spread to the king, the more especially after the death of Gaveston, however, when Edward fastens his affections upon new flatterers, primarily Spencer. Whereas the loyalty of Gaveston and Edward, for all its folly, had a touch of nobility about it, Spencer is merely a sycophant, and the king, in listening to him, reveals his irredeemable weakness of character. His early frivolousness turns to vengeance when the barons move to open revolt, and even his loving queen and the loyal Kent slowly turn against him. It is perhaps a weakness of the play that neither party in the conflict can arouse our admiration; there is no moral framework here, no good and evil, or even wisdom to oppose the folly. The misrule of the king is overthrown by a Machiavellian villain, the hypocritical Mortimer. Whereas Shakespeare tended to glorify those who put an end to misrule, as Bolingbroke in *Richard the Second,* which bears many similarities to *Edward the Second,* Marlowe paints a picture of unrelieved gloom, as the rebels, led by the unfaithful queen and the power-grabbing Mortimer, depose the weak and yet bloody king. It is only at the very end, as Edward III comes to the throne, executing Mortimer and imprisoning the queen, that rightful rule is restored. Edward III specifically seeks the counsel of his nobles before he acts and in so doing restores the reciprocity upon which the well-being of the realm rests.

Beyond the concept of divine right, there remains the concept that the king must rule not by whim, but with concern for the welfare of his land, and in concert with his nobles, who, like him, are born to their station. Though the play has strong political overtones, the absence of any developed conflict between right and wrong robs it of the sort of symbolic value that is possessed by Shakespeare's finest history plays. Indeed, the absence of a figure with whom the audience can identify may be in part responsible for the unpopularity of the play, which perhaps because of its historicity lacks the fascination of the powerfully imaginative *The Tragedy of Doctor Faustus* or *Tamburlaine.*

Marlowe's genius was at its best when expressing powerful emotions and characters with extravagant poetic imaginations. In *Edward the Second* there is less opportunity for such luxuriant language, and for many, the play does not really come alive until the downfall of the king, when in spite of his unsympathetic character, the pathos of his situation commands the involvement of the audience. To be sure, Gaveston is also very much a Marlowe character, perhaps much like Marlowe himself—impulsive, poetic, a lover of pleasure and beauty, both irresponsible and passionate—for Marlowe was repeatedly involved in dueling and was killed in a tavern. But it is Edward who sticks in the mind. Though aside from his touching and loyal love for Gaveston he has no redeeming qualities, the extremity of his suffering gives him a nobility that is not destroyed even by his anguish. Even at the end he can still exclaim "I am still king!" Marlowe has constructed one of the most harrowing death scenes to be found in Elizabethan drama—though he actually softened the even more horrible historical fact—and the pathos of Edward's intense emotional suffering elevates the play beyond the level of historical chronicle and assures its place among the world's great dramas.

Steven C. Schaber

EFFI BRIEST

Type of work: Novel
Author: Theodor Fontane (1819-1898)
Type of plot: Domestic tragedy
Time of plot: Second half of the nineteenth century
Locale: Germany, Prussia
First published: 1895

Sixty years old when he wrote his first novel and seventy-five when he wrote Effi Briest, *Fontane introduced the modern realistic and psychologically oriented novel in Germany. The subject of* Effi Briest *is how a human being can become entangled in the net of rigid rules and unshakable principles that govern a forcibly "stabilized" society.*

Theodor Fontane's *Effi Briest* is a novel without passion, in spite of its tale of adultery, dueling, and death. It is, however, precisely in its depiction of basically pleasant, uncomplicated characters, living their lives according to a strict code of behavior, that the work achieved its strength and remarkable subtlety. The novel is generally regarded as Fontane's best, and its classical form is a model of construction and narrative technique. It moves in equal divisions from the Briest estate, through the events at Kessin, in Berlin, and finally back to the family home. Throughout the novel, Fontane describes the psychological state of the characters, revealing their inner life through their gestures and words. He does not take sides, nor moralize, letting both the characters and their society speak for themselves.

The story itself is unremarkable, one of a number of adultery stories popular at the time. But the import of the novel lies beyond the story line. Fontane depicts a class of people—the Prussian Junkers, or old nobility, whose lives have settled into a meaningless prescribed form. Effi's parents married without love, and never question their lives; Effi may break with the code, but not because she questions or rejects. She is merely bored and frivolous.

Her husband, basically a good man, is unable to act otherwise than social convention dictates, and when, after some years, he discovers the adultery, he takes the consequences—duel and divorce—with some vague regret, but no real anger or hurt. Powerful emotion, grief, anger, or happiness seems beyond these people, and father Briest's refusal to go into the matter—"that is too wide a field,"—is typical. The characters are incapable of taking distance from their situation, of seeing the degree to which their lives are impoverished by their adherence to a class code. Fontane, too, does not examine an alternative, but leaves it to the reader to draw his own conclusions.

EGMONT

Type of work: Drama
Author: Johann Wolfgang von Goethe (1749-1832)
Type of plot: Romantic tragedy
Time of plot: Sixteenth century
Locale: Brussels
First presented: 1788

Taking its plot from an episode in the struggle of The Netherlands to throw off Spanish rule, this drama is the tragic account of the martyrdom of Count Egmont. In developing the theme of man's unconquerable desire for freedom, Goethe depicts Egmont as a warm, generous, and brave man, but the other characters are less well delineated.

Of Goethe's dramatic works, two are singled out as his "history" plays. One is *Egmont*; the other is *Götz von Berlichingen* (1774). These plays, like many others of the time, not only in Germany but throughout Europe, reflect the growing interest in democratic principles which found its strongest expression in the American Revolution of 1776 and the French Revolution of 1789. The drama was a powerful vehicle for generating revolutionary spirit, and during this period many plays with nationalistic themes were written to encourage patriotic feelings in the fight for liberty from oppression, both internal and external. Goethe's plays certainly fall in the mainstream of this trend, but they share more than historical content.

As literature, *Egmont* and *Götz von Berlichingen* are often discussed in tandem as examples of Shakespeare's influence on Goethe; however, the plays have intrinsic similarities with or without Shakespeare's influence. Looseness of structure typifies both plays, allowing *Egmont,* like *Götz von Berlichingen,* to emphasize character over action. But the character Egmont, unlike the character Götz, tends to balance action with reflection. To be sure, Egmont led an active life, disregarding danger and never fearing the untried. He was also adept at the practical and worldly skills required of a man in his position. He was a competent marksman, firm and equitable in financial matters, familiar with the temperament of the commoners in his provinces, and he knew how to govern them; he could maneuver around devious feminine logic (Margaret) even while he appreciated feminine wiles (Clärchen); and he was both wise and just in the administration of governmental affairs. These combined qualities bespeak a man more temperate than the often impetuous Götz.

Indeed, the hallmark of Egmont's character was dedication to the principle that justice should be tempered with mercy. Toward that end, Egmont sought to obtain justice for The Netherlands and his people from their Spanish rulers. Like Goethe himself, Egmont felt driven by an inner spirit over whom he had no control (Goethe called it his *"Daimon."*) Edmont's consequent bold route of action, however, ran afoul of the Duke of Alva's abuse of power. Yet, in his death cell, Egmont was consoled by a vision in which "Freedom" (closely resembling Clärchen) told him that his death would spark a revolution which would ultimately free his people. Reassured, Egmont accepted his fate as the means to attain his goal.

Egmont's personality thus emerges in the course of the play to contrast with Götz's, as a balance between active and contemplative components: judicious action preceded by thought and impulsive action followed by thought. That balance, in turn, lends untity to the protagonist's personality: Egmont's character is far less melodramatically one-sided than that of Götz. As a result, just as Egmont is a more unified character than Götz, so *Egmont* is a more unified play than *Götz von Berlichingen*. Still, it is the demon-driven character of Egmont who dominates the play, insuring for Egmont and the play a special place in Goethe's own demon-driven affections throughout his long life and prolific career.

THE EGOIST

Type of work: Novel
Author: George Meredith (1828-1909)
Type of plot: Social satire
Time of plot: Nineteenth century
Locale: England
First published: 1879

In this unique comedy, Meredith satirizes with droll, intellectual humor the various virtues and vices of his characters. The focal point of the satire and the basis for numerous digressions on the author's theory of comedy is the egoist, Sir Willoughby, a wealthy, handsome, self-satisfied country gentleman whose lack of humility and any sense of humor leads to his desertion by two successive fiancées.

George Meredith expressed what he thought were the essential social conditions for successful comedy in his famous essay "On the Idea of Comedy and of the Uses of the Comic Spirit," first delivered as a lecture two years before the publication of *The Egoist.* In the essay Meredith argues that the comic poet cannot function without the stimulus of a clever society, a society sensitive to ideas and witty in its perceptions. A merely fad-conscious period, giddy and emotional, is too primitive to inspire true comedy. Of major importance is at least some intellectual activity and a tolerance of women in society; that is to say, feminine wit is essential to a healthy social climate, one that will permit a society to laugh at itself.

Meredith's curious anti-hero, Willoughby, is devoid of any ideas, totally wrapped up in a giddy love affair with himself, and singularly incapable of any objective perceptions. Clara tells him to his face that he is boring her to death. Immersed in his own ardor, he is so oblivious to insult that he calls her a "sleeping beauty" immediately after she has intimated that he is putting her to sleep. In other words, Willoughby is the incarnation of everything that makes the Comic Spirit impossible. And yet, the irony of the novel is that he is at the same time the ideal subject for Comedy's ridiculing power.

Willoughby's selfishness and egotism are nowhere more clearly revealed than in his insistence on the servility of women to men. This is his primary violation of Meredith's "Social Law" of Comedy, and it is what finally brings about his comic punishment. Laetitia treats him as an object, by agreeing to marry him without love, and caps his downfall by condemning him to the same treatment he extended to others: "I was once a foolish romantic girl; now I am a sickly woman, all illusions vanished. Privation has made me what an abounding fortune usually makes of others—I am an Egoist."

ELECTIVE AFFINITIES

Type of work: Novel
Author: Johann Wolfgang von Goethe (1749-1832)
Type of plot: Philosophical romance
Time of plot: Eighteenth century
Locale: Germany
First published: 1808

Written late in the author's career, Elective Affinities *displays Goethe's romantic qualities as well as his philosophical tendencies. The emotionalism of Edward, the quasi-scientific theme, and the poetically fitting but entirely unrealistic deaths reflect the romantic elements, while the probing of human relationships, the discussions of education and teaching techniques, and the comments found in Ottilie's diary all contribute to the meditative, philosophical effect.*

Goethe's middle years as a classicist were bracketed by early and late years dominated by romantic characteristics. *Elective Affinities* is a product of that late romanticism. As he aged, however, Goethe was less adamant than he was in his younger days about his own adherence to any set of aesthetic principles. As a consequence, *Elective Affinities* contains elements of both classicism—primarily in form—and romanticism—mainly in content. The novel has a classic symmetry of form which complements the symmetrical arrangement of the four protagonists, dividing the married couple, Edward and Charlotte, between their two guests, Ottilie and The Captain. The classic harmonious structure of *Elective Affinities* is created by its cool, formal, generally unemotional style—particularly evident in the distancing between narrator and action evoked by Goethe's use of a third-person narrator. These classical qualities lead to the expectation that the issues with which the novel deals will be rigorously pursued to the necessary logical conclusion.

Such, however, is not the case, because Goethe treats content from a predominantly romantic perspective. In *Elective Affinities,* the absolute moral imperative of the classical social order collides with the irresistible force of romantic natural law. The classical view would mandate that society emerge the victor. Indeed, classic orthodoxy would reject the simultaneous existence of two immutable but antithetical laws in its organically unified universe. Rather than affirm a clear-cut endorsement of either law, however, Goethe concludes the novel ambiguously: although death is the fate of the lovers who defied the moral code of society, those disciples of natural law ironically carry off a moral victory of sorts by wringing sympathetic comments from the narrator, who thinks about the existence of some higher plane where there is no conflict between social order and natural law. The implication—a thoroughly romantic one—is that the two lovers, buried side by side, may yet reach that plane.

In addition to the fusion of classic and romantic elements typical of

Goethe's works, *Elective Affinities* also illustrates another of the author's life-long preoccupations: the nature of the learning process. From *The Sorrows of Young Werther* (1774) to *Faust II* (1832), Goethe was concerned with epistemology and its relation to education, although that concern is most obvious in the two *Wilhelm Meister* novels. The *Bildüngsroman,* as these novels were called, is a tale of character development and the shaping of one's innate endowments. As such, the term applies equally well to *Elective Affinities,* since this novel subtly delineates the evolving mental and emotional qualities of the four protagonists as each one's elective affinity—in chemistry, the irresistible mutual attraction between two elements—changes over the course of the story. To be sure, *Elective Affinities* is much more than a novel about the philosophy of learning or a study in classic versus romantic, but a delicately woven intense psychological drama.

ELECTRA

Type of work: Drama
Author: Euripides (480-406 B.C.)
Type of plot: Classical tragedy
Time of plot: After the fall of Troy
Locale: Argos
First presented: c. 413 B.C.

Euripides' Electra *is a psychological study of a woman's all-consuming hatred for her mother and stepfather on the one hand, and her love for her murdered father and exiled brother on the other. The plot revolves around the attempts of Electra—who has been forced to marry a farmer so that she will have no power—to spur her brother Orestes on to murder her enemies.*

Electra is a compelling example of Euripides' dramaturgy. But it also affords us a means of comparing his purpose and techniques with those of Aeschylus and Sophocles, for each of them used the same legend and presented roughly the same action. Aeschylus in *The Libation-Bearers* (part of *The House of Atreus* trilogy), Sophocles in *Electra,* and Euripides in his *Electra* all treat Orestes' return to Argos, his presentation of himself to his sister Electra, their planning of the revenge against Aegisthus and Clytemnestra, and the execution of that revenge. But each treatment is individual and unique, showing the distinct temper of mind of these three tragedians.

With Aeschylus the twin murders of Aegisthus and Clytemnestra are the culminating crimes in a family polluted by generations of kin slayings. Regicide and matricide are evils instigated by Apollo to punish and purge the earlier murder of Agamemnon. Orestes alone takes on the burden of these crimes. A minor character, Electra offers him encouragement to the deeds, but her gentle nature shrinks from being an actual accomplice. Aeschylus shows us Orestes' revenge as an act of divine justice, a crime that will in time earn an acquittal.

Sophocles takes a different view of the matter. The regicide and matricide are justifiable for him in human terms mainly, as the proper retribution for Agamemnon's killing. Electra is portrayed as a hard, bitter, determined young woman who aids her brother as a rightful duty. This perspective is similar to that in Homer's *Odyssey*.

Euripides, however, calls both points of view into question. He sees the murders of Aegisthus and Clytemnestra as wholly unmitigated evils that are neither humanly nor divinely justifiable. Euripides says in effect that no killing is permissible for any reason. And he carries this logic to its ultimate conclusion—that killers have as much right to live as anyone else no matter how twisted their psyche or how questionable their motives. This is a radical stand, but it is based on Euripides' firm conviction in the value of every human life. This belief shines through the whole of *Electra* and makes the idea of just retribution a mockery. One has the impression that Euripides would have liked to abolish all courts and prisons, turning justice into a matter of individual conscience. What is interesting is the way he works out these ideas dramatically.

Whereas Aeschylus and Sophocles concentrate on royalty and heroes, Euripides does not hesitate to depict an honorable peasant or to show ignoble blue bloods. In fact, the entire action of *Electra* takes place in front of a peasant's hut. To Euripides each life had worth, but the index to that worth was strength of character. Position, wealth, power, beauty, and physique were nothing to him. He is chiefly interested in an accurate, realistic psychology— a direct consequence of his beliefs.

Each of the main characters is shown as a clearly defined personality in relation to a specific environment. Euripides tends to concentrate on the sordid aspects in *Electra* as the legend would seem to demand, yet it is here that his faith in human dignity reveals its power. We find it easy to love good people, but to love people as warped by circumstances as Electra, Orestes, or Clytemnestra requires moral courage. Euripides had it, and he portrayed their pain as though it were his own.

Electra has fallen from lavish prosperity to squalor in a forced, loveless marriage to a peasant, which is nonetheless chaste and compassionate. She is slovenly and full of self-pity and spite. Further, she envies her mother, Clytemnestra, who lives in luxury and power, and she hates Aegisthus. Her single passion is to kill them both, and when she discovers Orestes, she uses him to obtain revenge. Orestes himself is a neurotic vagabond of no status, with authorization from Apollo to kill his mother and her lover, yet he declaims pompously about nobility of character.

Clytemnestra seems like a housewife in queen's clothing, operating by a retaliatory logic. She takes a lover because her husband had a mistress, and she kills Agamemnon because he killed their daughter Iphigenia. But none of this has made her happy. And when she visits Electra out of motherly concern, she is hacked to death by her two children. Even Aegisthus appears to be decent. It is precisely their ordinariness that makes the realistic descriptions of their murders so hideously sickening. We feel with Euripides that they deserve to live.

Once their passion for revenge is spent, Orestes and Electra are filled with self-revulsion, having arrived at the depths of a nightmarish degradation. Then Euripides brings two gods on stage, Castor and Polydeuces, to settle the matter. This *deus ex machina* ending puts the action in a new light. Apollo is directly responsible for the murders, just as Zeus is responsible for the Trojan War. These are not wise or just gods by human standards, and an individual person has infinitely more worth than their abominable edicts. Euripides is supremely confident in his position, and he does not shrink from judging gods by it.

Consistent with his faith in man's value, he allows Orestes and Electra a good measure of compassion in the end. These two share in the blood guilt and will be exiled. Orestes will even be driven mad by the Furies, which only he can see. But they deserve to live too, Euripides says in essence, and in time they will win forgiveness. The belief in human dignity has rarely had such a steadfast champion as Euripides.

James Weigel, Jr.

THE EMIGRANTS

Type of work: Novel
Author: Johan Bojer (1872-1959)
Type of plot: Regional romance
Time of plot: Late nineteenth century
Locale: Norway and the American West
First published: 1925

This American story written in Norwegian is a saga about the Norwegians who settled the wheatlands of the Dakotas in the late 1800's. Bojer achieves depth in his characterizations by first showing the emigrants' way of life in Norway and their reasons for leaving home, and then by depicting the various hardships of pioneer living and pressures toward cultural assimilation in America.

The moving story of the difficulties of transplanted national loyalties forms the basis of Johan Bojer's *The Emigrants*. The novel is carefully constructed, carrying the principal characters through their lives, from beginnings in Norway to old age in America. Along the way, the characters grow and change as the new land they have adopted is equally transformed and developed. The author begins with a precise delineation of the social structure of nineteenth century Norway, illustrating the many varying reasons that the people have for emigrating. Some want to escape local scandals, others hope to overcome poverty, some are possessed by ambition, many desire to escape what they consider unfair class distinctions.

The subtle psychological transformations among the settlers are sensitively portrayed. From the beginning of the new life, a growing sense of community binds the emigrants together. The relationships among them change; people who had had nothing to do with each other in the old country become friends, and social distinctions dissolve. The new land affects the settlers in different ways; to some the flatness of the land is depressing after the mountains of Norway; others find the work to build a settlement and a new life more difficult than they anticipated. Karen Skaret could adjust only after becoming convinced that a Norwegian brownie had emigrated with them.

The trials of the life on the prairie are dramatically portrayed; the breathless account of the prairie fire that nearly destroys the settlement is a masterpiece of narrative writing. But through the many disasters and years of labor, the settlers cling to their visions of the future. The construction of the first church becomes a touching symbol of their success. Yet they never forget the old country; they seem to possess two souls, as Morten Kvidal says, one Norwegian and the other American. This double vision gives a rich poetry to the book, and a subtle poignancy combined with the joy of the settlers' triumph.

THE EMIGRANTS OF AHADARRA

Type of work: Novel
Author: William Carleton (1794-1869)
Type of plot: Local color romance
Time of plot: 1840's
Locale: Ireland
First published: 1848

An outstanding local color writer, Carleton describes Irish peasant life in the mid-nineteenth century with warmth and realism. The speech of the people, their homes and farm routines, landlord-renter relations, and whiskey smuggling activities are all described in colorful and specific detail. Highlights of the novel include chapters on a "Kemp," or spinning contest, a country funeral, an election, and the illegal process of whiskey distillation.

By the time that he wrote *The Emigrants of Ahadarra* in 1848, Carleton was considered the truest novelist of Ireland's "awfullest hours," and Yeats was to concede that the Irish novel began with him. *The Emigrants of Ahadarra* was avowedly written not to amuse, but to reform and inform. Published while the Potato Famine was raging, it is informative and readable. Folkloric value is enhanced by Carleton's exuberance and hyperbole, which are similar to the imaginative flights that created the ancient Celtic wonder tales. The novel loftily defends virtue. Kathleen's simple dignity and virtue are not cloying but almost Biblical, and contrast with the paler virtues of other characters. Bridget M'Mahon is also convincingly admirable, and uniquely graces the story, which expounds human ideals. Landlords are near-ogres, members of secret societies, and Orangemen (although to a less prominent degree than in other of Carleton's works), but many individuals are tenderly etched. The novel is realistic, and in the Spain of the same day would have been classified as *costumbrista,* owing to its museum-like pictures of customs.

Modern critics sometimes flay *The Emigrants of Ahadarra* for allegedly sloppy construction, mushy sentiment, and—curiously enough—vagueness of purpose. Carleton is also accused of inserting excessive scenery and folklore for their own sake rather than to augment the novel's dramatic effect. Carleton did lack the benefit of proofreading by his publishers, but the novel accomplished its obvious objective of dramatizing the life of the Irish of over a hundred years ago. Even its supposedly overdone rhetoric does not bore the reader.

Herbert Kenney maintains that we have a true picture of the famine-ravaged Irish peasants from Carleton alone. Carleton was an enigmatic novelist who hated landlordism and the Penal Laws, and who was a convert to Protestantism in a very Catholic land. But he scarcely owed loyalty only to his own pen, as has been accused, and some critics concede that they did not really know Irish life until they read *The Emigrants of Ahadarra.*

EMILIA GALOTTI

Type of work: Drama
Author: Gotthold Ephraim Lessing (1729-1781)
Type of plot: Romantic tragedy
Time of plot: Early eighteenth century
Locale: Guastalla and Sabionetta, two mythical principalities in Italy
First presented: 1771

Emilia Galotti was one of the first tragedies to break from strict adherence to the French neoclassical unities. Based on a classical theme, the plot tells the story of an innocent maiden murdered by her father to prevent her loss of chastity. A drama of middle-class life, the work is also a problem play dealing with the topic of revolt from aristocratic tyranny.

Lessing was the first major German dramatist of the eighteenth century and his work provided the foundation on which Goethe and Schiller built. While he strongly advocated rejection of the French classical style in favor of a more Shakespearean approach, his work retains much of the formal balance and classical unity of the French tradition. Each scene is calculated as an indispensable advancement of the plot; the motivation of the characters is made almost painfully explicit. Each character is sharply defined even to the use of individual styles of speech. Later writers of the Romantic school thought the play was admirable for its craft, but excessively rationalistic and cerebral. "A good piece of theatrical algebra," said Friedrich Schlegel.

But the play was also an important development for the German stage. It is a strongly political drama, which places the tragedy in a bourgeois milieu —an innovation in the eighteenth century—and develops the tragedy out of class conflicts. The depiction of the corrupt world of the absolute monarch was the first sounding of a theme that would return in the 1770's and 1780's as a main theme of German drama. Lessing goes beyond the political, however, to search the mysteries of the human personality. The death of Emilia is necessary because she herself recognizes the weakness of her will. It is not force she fears but seduction, and in acknowledging the potential for nonrational behavior, Lessing anticipates those Romantics who would rebel against the one-sidedly rationalistic view of man held by the eighteenth century Enlightenment. This vulnerability is accentuated by the elaborateness of the plot contrived by the scheming Marinelli. Emilia is enmeshed in a net from which there is no escape except death. Though her father actually kills her, she wills her own death and this moral suicide has something of old Roman virtue. Her will triumphs over her weakness and elevates her above all those who are, like the prince, the prey of their own emotions.

EMMA

Type of work: Novel
Author: Jane Austen (1775-1817)
Type of plot: Social comedy
Time of plot: Early nineteenth century
Locale: Surrey, England
First published: 1816

In this novel about a headstrong, snobbish, intellectually proud young woman, Austen's genius for ironic comedy is displayed at its peak. The plot involves finding the proper husband for the heroine, but behind the deceptively simple and everyday events lies the author's moral vision of a world in which social responsibility and familial obligation are key virtues, and compromise a necessary response to the irreconcilable opposites encountered in life.

Jane Austen had passed her fortieth year when her fourth published novel, *Emma,* appeared in 1816, the year before her death. Although *Pride and Prejudice* has always been her most popular novel, *Emma* is generally regarded as her greatest. In this work of her maturity, she deals once more with the milieu she preferred: "3 or 4 Families in a Country Village is the very thing to work on." Having grown to womanhood in her native Hampshire village of Steventon, the seventh of the eight children of the learned village rector, and having spent the remainder of her life, except for brief intervals in Bath and Southampton, in another Hampshire village, Chawton, she was thoroughly familiar with the world she depicted.

The action of *Emma* cannot be properly considered apart from the setting of Highbury, the populous village only sixteen miles from London, its physical attributes presented in such circumstantial detail that it becomes a real entity. London seems far away, not because of the difficulty of travel, but because of the community's limited views. It is a village where a light drizzle keeps its citizens at home, where Frank Churchill's trip to London for the alleged purpose of getting a haircut is foppery and foolishness, where the "inconsiderable Crown Inn" and Ford's "woollen-draper, linen-draper, and haberdasher's shop united" dominate the main street. Emma's view of the busiest part of town, surveyed from the doorway of Ford's, sums up the life of the village:

> Mr. Perry walking hastily by, Mr. William Cox letting himself in at the office door, Mr. Cole's carriage horses returning from exercise . . . a stray letter boy on an obstinate mule . . . the butcher with his tray, a tidy old woman . . . two curs quarrelling over a dirty bone, and a string of dawdling children round the baker's little bow-window. . . .

The novel concerns the interrelationship between such an inconsequential place and Emma Woodhouse, a pretty and clever young lady almost twenty-one who is rich and has few problems to vex her. Ironically, however, her world is no bigger than the village of Highbury and a few surrounding estates, including her father's Hartfield; nevertheless, in that small world, the Woodhouse family is the most important. Therefore, states the author, the real dangers for Emma are "the power of having rather too much her own way, and a disposition to think a little too well of herself."

Moreover, these dangers are unperceived by Emma. Thus, in the blind exercise of her power over Highbury, she involves herself in a series of ridiculous errors, mistakenly judging that Mr. Elton cares for Harriet rather than for herself; Frank Churchill for herself rather than for Jane Fairfax; Harriet for Frank rather than for Mr. Knightley; and Mr. Knightley for Harriet rather than for herself. It is the triumph of Jane Austen's art that however absurd or obvious Emma's miscalculations, they are convincingly a part of Emma's charming egotism. The reader finally agrees with Mr. Knightley that there is always "an anxiety, a curiosity in what one feels for Emma."

Emma's vulnerability to error can in part be attributed to inexperience, her life circumscribed by the boundaries of Highbury and its environs. No mention is made of visits to London, though Emma's only sister lives there. She has never been to the seacoast, nor even to a famous scenic attraction nearby, Box Hill. She is further restricted by her valetudinarian father's gentle selfishness, which resists any kind of change and permits a social life limited to his own small circle, exclusive to the degree of admitting only four people as his closest acquaintances and only three to the second group.

Nonetheless, Emma's own snobbery binds her to the conclusion that she has no equals in Highbury. Mr. Knightley well understands the underlying assumption of superiority in Emma's friendship for Harriet Smith: "How can Emma imagine she has anything to learn herself, while Harriet is presenting such a delightful inferiority?" Emma fears superiority in others as a threat. Of the capable farmer Robert Martin, Harriet's wooer, she observes: "But a farmer can need none of my help, and is therefore in one sense as much above my notice as in every other way he is below it." Her resolution to like Jane Fairfax is repeatedly shattered by the praise everybody else gives Jane's superior attractions.

While Emma behaves in accordance with her theory that social rank is too important to be ignored, she fails to perceive that she is nearly alone in her exclusiveness. Indeed, the Eltons openly assume airs of superiority, and Jane Fairfax snubs Emma. Emma's increasing isolation from Highbury is epitomized in her resistance to the Cole family, good people of low rank who have nevertheless come to be regarded socially as second only to the Woodhouse family. Snobbishly sure that the Coles will not dare to invite the best families to an affair, she finds only herself uninvited. Thus, ironically, she imagines her power in Highbury to be flourishing even as it is already severely diminished.

Emma's task is to become undeceived and to break free of the limitations imposed by her pride, by her father's flattering tyranny, and by the limited views of Highbury. She must accomplish all this without abandoning her self-esteem and intelligence, her father, or society. The author prepares for the possibilty of a resolution from the beginning, especially by establishing Mr. Knightley as the person who represents the standard of maturity which Emma must assume. Emma is always half aware of his significance, often putting her folly to the test of his judgment. There are brief, important occasions when the two, united by instinctive understanding, work together to create or restore social harmony. However, it is not until Harriet presumes to think of herself as worthy of his love that Emma is shocked into recognition that Mr. Knightley is superior to herself as well as to Harriet.

Highbury itself, which seems so confined, also serves to enlarge Emma's views simply by proving to be less fixed than it appears. As John Knightley observes: "Your neighbourhood is increasing, and you mix more with it." Without losing her desire for social success, Emma increasingly suffers from it. She is basically deficient in human sympathy, categorizing people as second or third rank in Highbury or analyzing them to display her own wit. Yet, as she experiences her own humiliations, she begins to develop in sensitivity. Thus, while still disliking Jane, she is capable of "entering into her feelings" and granting a moment of privacy. Her rudeness to Miss Bates is regretted, not only because Mr. Knightley is displeased but also because she perceives that she has been brutal, even cruel to Miss Bates.

Despite her love of small schemes, Emma shares an important trait with Mr. Knightley, one which he considers requisite for his wife—an "open temper," the one quality lacking in the admirable Jane. Emma's disposition is open, her responsiveness to life counteracting the conditions in herself and her circumstances which tend to be constricting. Her reaction to news of Harriet's engagement to Robert Martin is characteristic: she is "in dancing, singing, exclaiming spirits; and till she had moved about, and talked to herself, and laughed and reflected, she could be fit for nothing rational." Too ready to laugh at others, she can as readily laugh at herself. Impulsive in her follies, she is quick to make amends. She represents herself truthfully as she says, in farewell to Jane, "Oh! if you knew how much I love every thing that is decided and open!"

A fully realized character who develops during the course of the action, Emma is never forced by the author to be other than herself, despite her new awareness. Once Harriet is safely bestowed upon Robert Martin, she complacently allows their friendship to diminish. The conniving to keep her father reasonably contented is a way of life. Mr. Knightley, if he wishes to marry her, is required to move into Hartfield. Serious reflection upon her past follies is inevitably lightened by her ability to laugh at them—and herself. The novel is complete in every sense, yet Emma is so dynamic a characterization that one shares Mr. Knightley's pleasure in speculation: "I wonder what will become of her!"

Catherine E. Moore

THE EMPEROR JONES

Type of work: Drama
Author: Eugene O'Neill (1888-1953)
Type of plot: Expressionistic melodrama
Time of plot: Early twentieth century
Locale: West Indies
First presented: 1920

In this departure from traditional dramatic form, O'Neill deals expressionistically with the question of what forces make a man what he is. The play moves in time backward and forward simultaneously. In the present, Brutus Jones, a black, is swept from emperorship to his death from fear; at the same time, by means of short, interspersed dramatic episodes which symbolize Jones's and his race's history, the action regresses to a point in time several hundred years ago in the Congo jungle.

By the time Eugene O'Neill wrote *The Emperor Jones*, he had joined the current of experimental playwrights who were reacting against realism. *The Emperor Jones* employs a technique popularized in Germany called expressionism, a form that employs exaggerated sets and stylized action. It seeks to project feelings and mental states directly, without the intervention of character development and without much concern for the externals of realistic sets, action, and motivation. While a number of such plays were written and produced, few have survived; among the few are *The Emperor Jones* and O'Neill's other completely expressionist play, *The Hairy Ape*. Like Joseph Conrad's *Heart of Darkness,* among other works, *The Emperor Jones* suggests that beneath the surface of civilized existence there is, in each of us, a savagery that marks our true identities. Public masks versus private realities, identity conflicts, and divisions—these are among O'Neill's central concerns. Further, since Jones moves into and is held and controlled by his past, the play suggests another of O'Neill's major themes: that one cannot escape his past.

Jones's physical journey through the jungle becomes a symbol of his mental journey into his past, even an entering into his own subconscious. The first three jungle scenes contain Jones' private past; the last three take us into his racial past. With each step into the jungle, Jones loses bits and pieces of clothing, his cherished bullets, and his composure—all external marks, not only of the stripping away of his civilized self, but of his mental and spiritual reduction. Toward the last—on the auction block, in the slave ship, on his knees before the witch doctor—Jones becomes increasingly passive, merging with the scene, and thus losing his sense of individual being.

There is very little dialogue in the play. But the throbbing of the tom-toms, the shooting of the gun, and the playing of the lights and shadows of the jungle, take the place, quite effectively, of conventional dialogue and action. The play is, in many ways, an exercise in pure theater.

ENDYMION

Type of work: Drama
Author: John Lyly (c. 1554-1606)
Type of plot: Romantic comedy
Time of plot: Remote antiquity
Locale: Ancient Greece
First presented: 1588

Endymion; or, The Man in the Moon *is an effete, even trivial play: the plot is inconsequential and artificial, the characters unreal, and the dialogue pedantic. These reasons, however, illustrate the historical significance of the play, for Lyly was responsible for attempting to make the drama a conscious art. Writing for the court rather than the populace, he therefore replaced the earthiness and crudity of earlier plays with refinement and polish, and in so doing set new standards which later dramatists, including Shakespeare, were to emulate.*

Most famous for his novel *Euphues, the Anatomy of Wit,* John Lyly was also a prolific playwright. He was the most fashionable English writer in the 1580's, praised as the creator of a "new English." Certainly *Endymion* made possible such later plays as Shakespeare's *A Midsummer Night's Dream* and *As You Like It.* Lyly's comedies were a great advance over those of his predecessors. He possessed a unique skill in taking the Italian pastoral and Latin comedy of intrigue and adapting them to the English style by combining them with fanciful plot and mythological characters as well as characters from the lower levels of English life. The grace and charm of his witty dialogue and his analysis of love were not surpassed until Shakespeare's later comedies.

Lyly was chief dramatist for the company of boy players attached to St. Paul's Cathedral, the favorite entertainers of Queen Elizabeth's court. The structure and style of *Endymion* would have been appreciated by their educated audience. The play is filled with references and allusions directed especially to this audience. The division of *Endymion* into acts and scenes is molded on Latin precedent, and the stage directions are of the classical pattern also employed by Ben Jonson: at the head of each scene are listed the characters who take part in it. The stage setting, however, is romantic; places separated by vast distances (the lunary bank, castle in the desert, and fountain) were represented by sections of the same platform stage, and the journey visualized by stepping across the stage. The treatment of time in the play was that of a fairy tale.

The story of Cynthia, the moon goddess, and Endymion was probably borrowed from the Roman poet Lucian. Sir Tophas derived his name and mock-epic exploits from Chaucer's *Tale of Sir Tophas*; in his constant hunger and boastfulness, Tophas was a blend of Latin parasite and braggart soldier. To the Elizabethan court, the main interest in the play lay in its reference to contemporary personalities. Cynthia was the Queen, and Tellus—in her jealousy, captivity in a desert castle, and her wiles—must have recalled Mary, Queen of Scots, who was beheaded in 1586. Endymion must have suggested the Earl of Leicester, and Eumenides, the worthy counselor, Lyly's patron, Burghley. Although today we find the play precious, it nevertheless possesses great charm and wit, much beauty and humor, and probably has been unjustly neglected in the centuries since Lyly's death.

AN ENEMY OF THE PEOPLE

Type of work: Drama
Author: Henrik Ibsen (1828-1906)
Type of plot: Social criticism
Time of plot: Late nineteenth century
Locale: Southern Norway
First presented: 1883

In An Enemy of the People *Ibsen relates the story of a doctor who is rejected by society for upsetting the* status quo *and the financial security of a Norwegian coastal town when he exposes the health hazards of the local Baths, a lucrative tourist attraction. Ibsen uses Dr. Stockmann to dramatize the problem of an individual faced with personal disaster if he speaks out against majority opinion.*

Following the anger and hostility of the public's reaction to *A Doll's House* and *Ghosts,* two realistic and powerful indictments of social convention, Henrik Ibsen wrote *An Enemy of the People,* a play that may be read as a reply to the fiery public response directed at the two earlier dramas. On a deeper level, this drama about the blindness, selfishness, and greed that motivates majority opinion in society reflects those same themes which concerned Ibsen throughout his career.

The most obvious interpretation of *An Enemy of the People* sees Dr. Stockmann as parallel to Ibsen, and the author's mouthpiece. Both author and protagonist have been rebuked by the populace for publicizing the truth which they have discovered; Ibsen has been censured for exposing the falsity of social values through his dramas, while Stockmann is ostracized by his community for campaigning against the pollution of the baths. Through the doctor and his actions, *An Enemy of the People* dramatizes the problem of the idealist: when the entire opinion of the people is against him, even after facts have been made public, should he bow to the will of the majority, or fight for the truth which only he recognizes? Ibsen's answer is clear: the honest man has no choice but to defend the truth, regardless of the personal expense to himself.

The play illustrates the result of this kind of commitment in the course that Dr. Stockmann's affairs take after his stand against the spa's supporters; he is rejected socially and driven out of his medical practice. The play's message is that the idealist must always be an outcast, but his very isolation is a source of strength; as Dr. Stockmann says, "The strongest man in the world is he who stands most alone." Related to this central message is the theme of democracy: *An Enemy of the People* dramatizes the author's belief that in a democratic society, truth and justice are inevitably overruled, since wise men are always in a small minority.

A more in-depth interpretation of the play, however, reveals subtler themes and more complex questions. The foremost of these is the problem Ibsen

raises concerning the advisability of many of Stockmann's actions as an idealist. Why is it that society consistently rejects or ignores what the idealist has
to say? Why are even the most ardent forms of idealism usually powerless
to change the *status quo*? Ibsen poses these questions in the play, and suggests
that the reason might be the idealist's impracticality and tendency to remain
oblivious of the nature of his foe. Dr. Stockmann's uncompromising behavior
not only leads him and his family to ruin, but fails to effect any change in
society. Ibsen suggests that the methods of idealism are naïve, and that they
would benefit greatly from a less lofty, headstrong attitude and a more
common-sense, realistic approach.

ENOCH ARDEN

Type of work: Poem
Author: Alfred, Lord Tennyson (1809-1892)
Type of plot: Sentimental romance
Time of plot: Late eighteenth century
Locale: England
First published: 1864

Enoch Arden *tells the sentimental story of a shipwrecked sailor who returns home, after ten years spent on a desert island, to find his wife prosperous and happily married to another man. Rather than shatter her newfound happiness, Enoch slips quietly away and dies soon afterwards, but not before sending his landlady to give his blessings to the pair from his deathbed.*

In *Enoch Arden,* Tennyson relies on heavily adorned treatment of rather simple subjects. The plot as well is relatively straightforward: the problem of money or the lack of it accounts for much of the action. Enoch fears that his family will be reduced to a miserable existence because of their financial situation and Annie comes to know the misery of his fears when she has to face poverty alone when he goes to sea. Tennyson reaches the height of his power to evoke pathos and sentiment, however, in two scenes that balance each other. The first is at the beginning of the poem when Annie rejects the suit of Philip, the rich boy, for that of Enoch, the poor but noble fisherman. The second, which reverses the situations, comes near the conclusion: Enoch experiences Philip's earlier deprivation after he returns from the sea to discover that he has lost his family and his wife. In both scenes, Tennyson is at his best; they are realistic, restrained, and lacking the sentimentality that characterizes the majority of the poem.

It was precisely this sentimentality, however, that Tennyson's Victorian audience clamored for. Living in an age of emotional repression in which sentiment and feelings were to be masked by dedication and earnestness, the middle class looked in their literature for unabashed emotionalism. Sharing their need, Tennyson, along with Dickens, for example, supplied it unashamedly. *Enoch Arden* possesses all the ingredients to supply the feelings his readers were seeking: the vivid contrast of rich and poor; the pain of unrequited love; the stoical man, Philip, unable to express his love; and, of course, the sufferings of children. But with all their demand for vicarious pain, the Victorians also needed to be reassured, and Tennyson, therefore, offered his bittersweet conclusion: the happiness of the new family is blessed by the dying husband.

THE ENORMOUS ROOM

Type of work: Novel
Author: E. E. Cummings (1894-1962)
Type of plot: Autobiographical fiction
Time of plot: 1917
Locale: France
First published: 1922

The Enormous Room *is Cummings' account of the three months he spent in a French government prison during World War I; it describes the outrage and fear suffered by men imprisoned on vague or unspecified charges who have no idea when they will be released. More than merely an indictment of the rigidity and overreaction of wartime governments, however, the work is also a study and vindication of people, with all their faults and weaknesses.*

The Enormous Room reveals the disillusionment and cynicism character-istic of the writers who emerged after World War I, and Cummings' particu-lar hatred of systems which threaten individualism and freedom. The human capacity to keep feeling alive in a dehumanizing world is Cummings' basic theme. As in his poetry, he seeks to present his characters through their own particular idioms. Though showing the influence of Fielding, Dickens, and (especially) Bunyan, Cummings' highly autobiographical novel is new both in content and technique.

Chapters entitled "I Begin a Pilgrimage," "A Pilgrim's Progress," "Apolly-on," and "An Approach to the Delectable Mountains" make clear parallels between the journey of Bunyan's Pilgrim to salvation and Cummings' own metaphorical journey. From the moment of his arrest, Cummings finds himself in the power of an insecure authority administered by a mindless bureau-cracy. Intolerant of the smallest deviation from its norms, the French govern-ment—ironically representative of the "democracy" the war was fought to preserve—imprisons all nonconformists, derelicts, and misfits who come to its attention. Ironically, the enormous room holds no real traitors, spies, or enemies of the state.

Supreme among the inmates of the prison are those characters Cummings calls the "Delectable Mountains." Though they are widely diverse types, Cummings seems to find in them a wonderful capacity for feeling which sets them apart from their peers. Thus, these "delectable mountains" in particular come to symbolize for Cummings the beauty and honesty of human emotion in contrast to the unfeeling, mindless and cruel institution. Through his pil-grimage, Cummings comes to believe in the indomitable ability of men to preserve the best of their humanity even in the face of dehumanizing oppres-sion. The novel ends with a bright ray of sunshine, symbolizing Cummings' hope for a future founded upon man's best rather than his worst qualities.